PENGUIN BOOKS

HOUSE OF CARDS

'A riveting, blow-by-blow account' *Economist*

'In this exciting, action-packed and engaging read, the ten days prior
to takeover are described in minute-by-minute detail . . . provides an
accurate, real-time history. In this book, William Cohan has lifted
the veil on the corporate world and provided his readers with a
ringside seat to this fascinating corporate theatre' Niamh Brennan,
Irish Times

'The flabbergasting story of how the great Bear fell'
John Gapper, *Financial Times*

'A chilling, minute-by-minute account of the ten, vertigo-inducing
days that revealed Bear Stearns to be a flimsy house of cards in a
perfect storm . . . Cohan writes with an insider's knowledge of the
workings of Wall Street' Michio Kakutani, *The New York Times*

'The story of Bear Stearns is one of obscene wealth, testosterone and
high-stakes gambling' Howard Davies, *The Times*

'Compelling and timely . . . the definitive work . . . vividly documents
the mix of arrogance, greed, recklessness and pettiness that took
down the 86-year-old brokerage house and then the entire economy'
Roben Farzad, *Business Week*

'There are plenty of complex technical reasons for the crunch, but if
anyone is still in doubt that a prime cause was uninhibited,
foul-mouthed, money-driven machismo, they should look no further
. . . Cohan has laid bare the venality, greed, profanity, coarseness and
irresponsibility of the men who brought down Bear Stearns . . .
Cohan has had fantastic access to the key characters'
Ruth Sunderland, *Observer*

William Cohan is an award-winning journalist and veteran of Wall Street. His previous book, *The Last Tycoons*, won the 2007 *Financial Times*/Goldman Sachs Business Book of the Year Award and was a *New York Times* bestseller. A regular on the pages of the *Financial Times* and *Fortune*, the deal for this book was big news in the *Wall Street Journal*.

House
of
Cards

House of Cards

OF

Cards

How Wall Street's Gamblers Broke Capitalism

William

D.

Cohan

PENGUIN BOOKS

PENGUIN BOOKS

Published by the Penguin Group
Penguin Books Ltd, 80 Strand, London WC2R ORL, England
Penguin Group (USA), Inc., 375 Hudson Street, New York, New York 10014, USA
Penguin Group (Canada), 90 Eglinton Avenue East, Suite 700, Toronto, Ontario, Canada M4P 2Y3
(a division of Pearson Penguin Canada Inc.)
Penguin Ireland, 25 St Stephen's Green, Dublin 2, Ireland
(a division of Penguin Books Ltd)
Penguin Group (Australia), 250 Camberwell Road, Camberwell, Victoria 3124, Australia
(a division of Pearson Australia Group Pty Ltd)
Penguin Books India Pvt Ltd, 11 Community Centre, Panchsheel Park, New Delhi – 110 017, India
Penguin Group (NZ), 67 Apollo Drive, Rosedale, North Shore 0632, New Zealand
(a division of Pearson New Zealand Ltd)
Penguin Books (South Africa) (Pty) Ltd, 24 Sturdee Avenue, Rosebank, Johannesburg 2196, South Africa

Penguin Books Ltd, Registered Offices: 80 Strand, London WC2R ORL, England

www.penguin.com

First published in the United States of America by Doubleday, a division of Random House, Inc., 2009
First published in Great Britain by Allen Lane 2009
Published in Penguin Books 2010

2

Printed in Great Britain by Clays Ltd, St Ives plc

A CIP catalogue record for this book is available from the British Library

978-0-141-03959-6

www.greenpenguin.co.uk

Penguin Books is committed to a sustainable future
for our business, our readers and our planet.
The book in your hands is made from paper
certified by the Forest Stewardship Council.

TO TEDDY, QUENTIN, AND DEB

"A soothsayer bids you beware the Ides of March."

—Brutus to Julius Caesar, Act I, *Julius Caesar*,
William Shakespeare, circa 1600

CONTENTS

HOUSE
OF
CARDS

PART I

How It Happened:
Ten Days in March

CHAPTER 1

THE ULTIMATE ROACH MOTEL

The first murmurings of impending doom for the financial world originated about 1,100 miles from Wall Street in an unassuming office suite just north of Orlando, Florida. There, hard by the train tracks, Bennet Sedacca announced to the world at 10:15 on the morning of March 5, 2008, that venerable Bear Stearns & Co., the nation's fifth-largest investment bank, was in trouble, big trouble. "Yep," Sedacca wrote on the Minyanville Web site, which is dedicated to helping investors comprehend the financial world. "The great credit unwind is upon us. Credit default swaps on all brokers, particularly Lehman and Bear Stearns, are blowing out, big time."

Sedacca, the forty-eight-year-old president of Atlantic Advisors, a $3.5 billion investment management company and hedge fund, had been watching his Bloomberg screens on a daily basis as the cost of insuring the short-term obligations—known in Wall Street argot as "credit default swaps"—of both Lehman and Bear Stearns had increased steadily since the summer of 2007 and then more rapidly in February 2008. Now he was calling the end of the credit party that had been raging on Wall Street for six years. "I've been talking about it for years," Sedacca said later. "But I started to notice it that fall. Because if you think about it, if you have all this nuclear waste on your balance sheet, what are you supposed to do? You're supposed to cut your dividends, you're supposed to raise equity, and you're supposed to shrink your balance sheet. And they did just the opposite. They took on more leverage. Lehman went from twenty-five to thirty-five times leveraged in one year. And then they announce a big stock buyback at $65 a share and they sell stock at $38 a share. I mean, they don't know what they're doing. And yet they get rewarded for doing that. It makes me sick."

Sedacca had witnessed firsthand a few blowups in his day. He worked at the investment bank Drexel Burnham Lambert—the for-

mer home of junk-bond king Michael Milken—when it was liquidated in 1990 and lost virtually overnight the stock he had in the
firm as it plunged from $110 per share to zero (Drexel was a private
company but the stock had been valued for internal purposes). "It
was enough that it stunned," he explained. "It was more than a
twenty-nine-year-old would want to lose." Many of his Drexel colleagues had taken out loans from Citibank to buy the Drexel stock
and were left with their bank loans and worthless stock. "I know
people with millions and millions of dollars of debt and the stock
was at zero," he said. They either paid off the loans or declared personal bankruptcy. "That's what happens when everyone turns off
your funding," he added.

He then moved on to Kidder Peabody and watched that 130-
year-old firm disintegrate, too. As a result of these experiences and
those at other Wall Street firms, he had developed a healthy skepticism of both debt and the ways of Wall Street. Starting in the summer of 2007, he began to feel certain that the mountain of debt
building across many sectors of the American economy would not
come to a good end. He started betting against credit. "I've watched
enough screens long enough to know something was wrong," he
said.

The problem at Bear Stearns and Lehman Brothers, Sedacca informed his clients and Minyanville readers, was that both firms had
huge inventories on their balance sheets of securities backed by
home mortgages. The rate of default on these mortgages, while still
small, was growing at the same time that the value of the underlying collateral for the mortgage—people's homes—was falling rapidly. Sedacca could not help noticing that the effects of this double
whammy were beginning to show up in other, smaller companies involved in the mortgage industry. He could watch the noose tighten
in the credit markets. "Look at what is happening to Thornburg
Mortgage," he wrote, referring to the publicly traded home mortgage lender, which specialized in making what were known as
"Alt-A" mortgages, those greater than $417,000, to wealthy borrow-
ers. Thornburg had been "overwhelmed" by margin calls from its
lenders. "It supposedly only has a 0.44% default rate on its [$24.7
billion] mortgage portfolio that it services but the bonds it owns are

getting pounded. Result? Margin call. The worst part is that the company went to sell some bonds to settle the margin calls but couldn't. The ultimate Roach Motel."

That Thornburg, based in Santa Fe, New Mexico, appeared to be hitting the wall was somewhat surprising considering its customers' low default rate and high credit quality. The problem at Thornburg was not that its customers could no longer pay the interest and principal on their mortgages; the problem was that the company could no longer fund its business on a day-to-day basis. Thornburg had a liquidity problem because its lenders no longer liked the collateral—those jumbo mortgages—Thornburg used to obtain financing.

Unlike a bank, which is able to use the cash from its depositors to fund most of its operations, financial institutions such as Thornburg as well as pure investment banks such as Lehman Brothers and Bear Stearns had no depositors' money to use. Instead they funded their operations in a few ways: either by occasionally issuing long-term securities, such as debt or preferred stock, or most often by obtaining short-term, often overnight, borrowings in the unsecured commercial paper market or in the overnight "repo" market, where the borrowings are secured by the various securities and other assets on their balance sheets. These fairly routine borrowings have been repeated day after day for some thirty years and worked splendidly—until there was perceived to be a problem with either the securities or the institutions backing them up, and then the funding evaporated like rain in the Sahara. The dirty little secret of what used to be known as Wall Street securities firms—Goldman Sachs, Morgan Stanley, Merrill Lynch, Lehman Brothers, and Bear Stearns—was that every one of them funded their business in this way to varying degress, and every one of them was always just twenty-four hours away from a funding crisis. The key to day-to-day survival was the skill with which Wall Street executives managed their firms' ongoing reputation in the marketplace.

Thornburg financed its operations very similarly to the way investment banks did. But in mid-February 2008, Thornburg was having a very difficult time managing its perception in the marketplace because its short-term borrowings were backed by the mortgages it held on its balance sheet. Some of these mortgages were prime mortgages—money lent to the lowest-risk borrowers, and some were those Alt-A mortgages, which were marginally riskier than prime mortgages and offered investors higher yields. At Thornburg, 99.56 percent of these mortgages were performing just fine.

But that did not matter. What mattered was that the *perception* of these mortgage-related assets in the market was deteriorating rapidly. That perception spelled potential doom for firms such as Thornburg, Bear Stearns, and Lehman Brothers, which financed their businesses in the overnight repo market using mortgage-related assets as collateral.

For Thornburg the trouble began on February 14, halfway around the world, when UBS, the largest Swiss bank, reported a fourth-quarter 2007 loss of $11.3 billion after writing off $13.7 billion of investments in U.S. mortgages. Amid this huge write-off, UBS said it had lost $2 billion on Alt-A mortgages and, worse, that it had an additional exposure of $26.6 billion to them. In a letter to shareholders before he lost his job on April 1, Marcel Ospel, UBS's longtime chairman, wrote that the year 2007 had been "one of the most difficult in our history" because of "the sudden and serious deterioration in the U.S. housing market."

UBS's sneeze meant that Thornburg, among others, caught a major cold. By writing down the value of its Alt-A mortgages, UBS forced other players in the market to begin to revalue the Alt-A mortgages on *their* books. Since these were the very assets that Thornburg (and Bear Stearns) used as collateral for its short-term borrowings, soon after February 14 the company's creditors made margin calls "in excess of $300 million" on its short-term borrowings. At first, Thornburg used what cash it had to meet the margin calls. But that did not stop the worries of its creditors. "After meeting all of its margin calls as of February 27, 2008, Thornburg Mortgage saw further continued deterioration in the market prices of its high quality, primarily AAA-rated mortgage securities," the company wrote in a March 3 filing with the SEC. This new deterioration of the value of its prime mortgages resulted in new margin calls of $270 million—among them $49 million from Morgan Stanley, $28 million from JPMorgan on February 28, and $54 million from Goldman Sachs.

This time, though, Thornburg was "left with limited available liquidity" to meet the new margin calls or any future margin calls. From December 31, 2007, to March 3, 2008, Thornburg received margin calls totaling $1.777 billion and was able to satisfy only $1.167 billion of them, or about 65 percent—a dismal performance. The balance of $610 million "significantly exceeded its available liquidity," the company announced on March 7. "These events have raised substantial doubt about the Company's ability to continue as a going concern without significant restructuring and the addition of new capital." The company's stock, which had traded for more than $28 per share in May 2007, closed at $4.32 on March 3, 2008, down 51 percent on the day. "The turmoil in the mortgage financing market that began last summer continues to be exacerbated by the mark-to-market accounting rules which are forcing companies to take unrealized write-downs on assets they have no intention of selling," explained Larry Goldstone, Thornburg's CEO. By March 10, Thornburg's stock was trading at 69¢ per share.

Goldstone's explanation of what was happening at his company was merely a heavily lawyered version of what Sedacca referred to as the "ultimate Roach Motel." A vicious cycle of downward pressure on the value of mortgage securities, which had begun at least a year earlier, was reaching a crescendo and affecting the entire asset class, not just the most junior and riskiest mortgages—so-called subprime mortgages—but also the more secure, performing mortgages. The very word "mortgage" was now a synonym for "toxic waste," or, as one wag wrote, "Financial Ebola."

To be sure, other firms were having serious mortgage-related problems, too. "I realized the market in general was far worse than I had imagined," Goldstone told the *Washington Post* in December 2008. "If UBS had that much, what about Goldman? What about Citi? What about everyone else?" For instance, there was Peloton Partners, a high-flying $1.8 billion hedge fund started in June 2005 by Ron Beller, a Goldman Sachs alumnus. Beller had become well known in financial circles a few years earlier when his secretary at Goldman Sachs stole £4.3 million from him and his partner, Scott Mead, without them realizing it. Before the secretary was convicted, Beller told the jury that he suspected something was amiss when he noticed his bank account was "one or two million light." In

2007, Peloton's asset-backed securities fund returned 87 percent to investors and was named the best fixed-income fund of the year by *EuroHedge* magazine. But the fund closed in February 2008 after its investments in Alt-A mortgages fell precipitously in the wake of the UBS announcement about its write-downs on February 14—the same announcement that caused Thornburg's problems. Like Thornburg, Peloton faced repeated margin calls from its Wall Street lenders, but unlike Thornburg, Peloton ran out of cash to meet those calls before a rescue plan could be implemented. Beller lost $60 million personally.

Beller's problems had a viral effect on Wall Street. His fund's collapse had the misfortune of occurring on Leap Day, February 29. In another year, the fund would have collapsed on March 1, the beginning of the second quarter. Instead, the collapse came at the end of the first quarter. The new valuation in the market of the securities Peloton owned meant that Wall Street firms such as Bear Stearns had to take into consideration these new marks for their own like securities and reflect those marks in their first-quarter numbers. Since Bear was hoping to show the market that it would have a profit during the first quarter of 2008, the Peloton collapse caused the firm to reevaluate just how profitable it was.

"February 29 was the day Peloton blew up," explained Paul Friedman, a Bear senior managing director and the chief operating officer of the fixed-income division, "and so you had a huge liquidation, us and others, of really high-quality stuff that went at really distressed prices. There were a lot of rumors of that being on dealers' balance sheets, that they couldn't sell it, and we were for once the first out and we got rid of all of it. So you've now got a really serious amount of high-quality paper, and reasonably high-quality counterparties—the whole Peloton thing. This was fund of the year in 2007. Ten weeks later, you're out of business. You've now got a data point. Everybody, at least at our firm and I think at the other firms, is looking on February 29, 'Okay, where are we going to mark our stuff?' because this is now a liquidation. You mark to where you blew out Peloton, which is going to be huge losses, where you couldn't even blow them out the following week. It was sort of the beginning of the end."

Born in Schenectady, New York, Friedman graduated from Colgate University in 1977 with a degree in economics. He then headed off to one of the Big Eight accounting firms, as they were then known, and ended up auditing Drexel Burnham, the last major Wall Street firm to blow up before Bear Stearns. He figured he knew something about Wall Street as a result and applied for the wrong job—something to do with mortgage-backed securities, which he knew nothing about—at Bear Stearns in March 1981. By serendipity, as he was leaving his botched interview, he heard about another job in the operations department and accepted it on the spot. He did that for a while but disliked being in the back office. One day he told his boss that he hated his job. "About an hour later, I was interviewing for a job on the trading desk," he said, "and then moved to being a trading assistant, and then ultimately to a trader on the mortgage desk in the very early days of mortgage-backed securities. Did that for a couple of years, and was a highly, highly mediocre trader." Soon he was the assistant to the guy running the fixed-income department, a job he held for the next twenty years even as the person who ran the department changed often during that time period.

Another clear sign of trouble, along with the margin-call messes at Thornburg and at Peloton, were margin calls being made in Amsterdam against a seven-month-old publicly traded $22 billion hedge fund controlled by the Carlyle Group, the Washington-based investment firm with $81 billion under management run by David Rubinstein. Carlyle has been the home from time to time of many very well-connected politicos, including George H. W. Bush, James Baker, and Olivier Sarkozy, the half-brother of the French president. Rubinstein had very carefully managed the firm's reputation for years with considerable success. Despite its obvious political ties, Carlyle had become one of the most admired private equity firms on Wall Street. "Our mission is to be the premier global private equity firm, leveraging the insight of Carlyle's team of investment professionals to generate extraordinary returns across a range of investment choices, while maintaining our good name and the good name of our investors," the firm proclaimed. On March 5, the global credit crisis began to consume a piece of Carlyle's "good name" when a fund known as the Carlyle Capital Corporation, listed on the Amsterdam exchange and 15 percent owned by the Carlyle Group, ran into serious trouble because it was heavily invested in residential mortgage-backed securities that were increasingly difficult to value.

In the week between February 28 and March 5, the hedge fund had received margin calls from lenders requiring the fund to post an additional $60 million of collateral. The fund met these margin calls. But on March 5, seven of its thirteen funding counterparties demanded another $37 million of collateral. Carlyle Capital met the demands of three of the seven counterparties but not those of the other four, which led one to send a default notice.

Also, on March 6, Tim Geithner, the ninth president and CEO of the Federal Reserve Bank of New York, gave a speech at the Council on Foreign Relations, on Park Avenue, about the unfolding financial crisis. Geithner had served three presidents and five Treasury secretaries, culminating in his appointment as undersecretary for international affairs for Treasury secretaries Lawrence Summers and Robert Rubin. In front of this distinguished audience, Geithner expounded on the origins of the immediate financial crisis in particularly clear language. He explained how a number of unusual factors had come together to undermine the country's economic foundation: the irresponsible availability of credit to the less-than-creditworthy, allowing them to buy homes, cars, and other goods and services they could not afford but thought they needed; a historic and ongoing increase in real-estate values; a "rapid innovation" on Wall Street that made credit risk easier to manufacture, to trade, and, in theory, to hedge. He said these insurance policies—the dreaded credit default swaps—gave investors the appearance of having hedged their bets. "These instruments allowed investors to buy insurance or protection against a broader range of individual credit risks, such as the default by a homeowner or a company," he said. But "as underwriting standards deteriorated over this period, this exposure grew." Investors did not fully appreciate that their risks were not hedged because they continued to predict forward into the future a market awash in liquidity and relative stability. "That confidence in a more stable future led to greater leverage and a larger exposure to the risk of a less benign world," Geithner said. "The interaction of these forces made the financial system as a whole more vulnerable to a range of different weaknesses."

He said everyone became blinded to the risks being created. "As is often the case during periods of rapid change, more significant concentrations of risk were present than was apparent at the time," he said. "Banks and investment banks sold insurance"—the credit default swaps—"against what seemed like low probability events, but did so at what even at the time seemed like low prices. And on the assets they retained, these same institutions purchased insurance from financial guarantors and other firms that were exposed to the same risks. The crisis exposed a range of weaknesses in risk management practices within financial institutions in the United States and throughout the world." After he finished his talk, Geithner took a few mundane questions from the audience. Then he bolted. "I've got to go," he told the guests, to an outbreak of laughter.

The next day, it became obvious why Geithner had had to leave. Before the market opened, he and his fellow Federal Reserve Board governors announced two unusual steps designed to pump additional capital into the markets "to address heightened liquidity pressures" in short-term funding. The effect of the Fed's actions was to inject $200 billion into the banking system by offering banks and securities firms (there were actually two separate loan programs of $100 billion each, one for banks, one for securities firms) one-month loans at low rates and allowing them to pledge mortgage-backed securities and other, riskier loans as collateral. A few hours later, the Labor Department announced that some sixty-three thousand jobs had been lost in February, far more than had been expected. "Godot has arrived," wrote Edward Yardeni, an economist and Pulitzer Prize–winning author who had been one of Wall Street's most relentlessly upbeat forecasters. "I've been rooting for the muddling through scenario. However, the credit crisis continues to worsen and has become a full-blown credit crunch, which is depressing the real economy."

By March 7, the Carlyle hedge fund was hitting the wall, as more margin calls were pouring in and the fund could not meet them despite having a $150 million line of credit from the Carlyle Group in Washington. The fund's publicly traded shares were suspended. "Although the Company believed last week that it had sufficient liquidity, it was informed by its lenders this week that additional margin calls and increased collateral requirements would be significant and well in excess of the margin calls it received Wednesday," John Stomber, the CEO, said in a statement. "The Company believes these additional margin calls and increased collateral requirements could quickly deplete its liquidity and impair its capital. Management is closely monitoring the situation and considering all available options for the Company." Nine days later the fund was forced into compulsory liquidation and eventually dissolved.

FOR ANYONE WILLING to listen to Sedacca in early March, the price of the credit default swaps for both Bear Stearns and Lehman Brothers was broadcasting a potentially catastrophic liquidity problem similar to that faced by Thornburg, Peloton, and Carlyle: Bear and Lehman had, respectively, approximately $6 billion and $15 billion of unsalable Alt-A mortgages on their balance sheets. Others, such as John Sprow, a bond fund manager at Smith Breeden Associates in Boulder, Colorado, had noticed that the Bear Stearns swaps "were off in a world of their own," and by January were twice the cost of similar protection that could be bought against the debt of Morgan Stanley and four times that of insuring the debt of Deutsche Bank.

"Enter Lehman and Bear Stearns," Sedacca continued in his March column. "Lehman reportedly has two times [its] capital in CMBS"—commercial mortgage-backed securities—"and nearly five times [its] capital in 'hard-to-price' securities. Hard-to-price in my book equates to hard to sell. . . . Bear Stearns is actually in worse shape. It has irritated so many clients that its business model is broken. What would happen if you told it to sell its 'hard-to-price bonds'? The company couldn't. No one has the balance sheet to absorb it. So you can see the vicious cycle developing."

Sedacca explained how the cost of insuring the obligations of Lehman and Bear Stearns—the credit default swaps—had increased dramatically in a month. Insurance for the Bear Stearns obligations cost more than those for Lehman, meaning the market thought the risk of default for Bear was higher. The insurance premium for the Bear debt, which had been $50,000 per $10 million of debt for the first half of 2007 and then crept up slowly, had spiked up to $350,000 per $10 million of debt by March 5. "In my book, they are insolvent," he concluded. "I feel bad for all my friends that work there, but I did the Drexel Burnham stint and I saw my stock go to zero. Yes, it can happen. Quickly." Sedacca seemed unconvinced by Bear's announcement the day before, on March 4, that it would release its first-quarter 2008 financial results on March 20, which would show the firm had "available liquidity" of $17.3 billion and had made a profit for the quarter of $115 million, a turnaround of sorts from the first quarterly loss in its history, $857 million. (In the previous year's first quarter, the firm had earned $554 million.) Nothing *seemed* amiss at Bear. But some inside the firm were very scared indeed.

CHAPTER 2

THE CONFIDENCE GAME

While Sedacca proselytized from a Florida office building, Tommy Marano, Bear Stearns's top mortgage trader, then forty-five years old, had a feeling of impending doom. Marano was at the center of the engine that had powered the firm's success during the previous twenty-five years, generating upward of $2 billion of the firm's $9 billion in revenue in recent years. He was sitting in the sixth-floor trading room at Bear Stearns's sleek new $1.5 billion corporate headquarters at 383 Madison Avenue, in Manhattan, in the left ventricle of metaphorical Wall Street, which had long before moved to various Manhattan locations—mostly in midtown—away from the real Wall Street.

Not wanting to telegraph his concern about Bear Stearns into the market but anxious to determine whether his concern was well founded, at eleven in the morning on March 6 Marano placed a phone call to Roddy Boyd, then a writer at *Fortune*. Marano had been a source of Boyd's for years, when the journalist was covering Wall Street at the *New York Post*, and had freely offered commentary about his competitors and the markets generally. Boyd had been a trader for eight years before switching careers to journalism, and the two men spoke the same language. "I know the mortgage product dead cold," Boyd said. Their relationship was a well-defined *pas de deux*. "It was unusually well defined," he explained. "We knew exactly what we were saying. I could have a very long conversation in two minutes. I protected him always. I never BS'd with him. I never got him in hot water. The corollary was he never BS'd with me, and he would give me good stuff."

This time, Marano called Boyd to talk about Bear Stearns, and specifically about his concern that the firms he had traded with for years were suddenly asking him whether Bear had enough cash on hand to execute his trades. "He called me at 11:00 A.M. that day and we talked about one or two things," Boyd continued. "It was weird. He knew it was weird. We did small talk in under ten seconds. I said to him, 'What's up?' He said, 'What are you hearing about Bear?' I said, 'You know what I'm hearing and you know what I'm seeing.' He said, 'I know what you're hearing and you're seeing. It's just baffling.' Now here I'm playing him a little because I'm hearing things and I'm seeing some things, but he's not saying much more than I am, so I let him walk and talk. He said to me, 'Roddy, our guys, our senior guys here, are hearing a really strange thing from custies.' That's customers. He said, 'We were not prepared to hear stuff like this. This is baffling. People are quite literally questioning our solvency, questioning our ability to go on. The shorts are having a lot of fun with us today.'"

Since Wall Street is a confidence game as much as anything, for counterparties on routine trades to start asking pointed questions about things as fundamental as cash and liquidity is not likely to be good for business. "What he meant," Boyd continued, "is that the shorts are putting out rumors about Bear Stearns, and eventually their bigger customers are saying, 'If I sell this big block of securities or derivatives to you, can you clear it or is this coming back at me in three days in distress?'" These kinds of questions are serious for traders and their firms, because if a firm you are trading with has financial problems and those financial problems cause it to need to raise cash quickly, the trader may have no choice but to sell into the market the securities just purchased at a lower price, forcing other firms holding a similar security to adjust the value of that security to the lower price. This is called "mark-to-market," a source of great consternation on Wall Street throughout the financial crisis.

"Do you understand the reason that would be so horrific for a customer?" Boyd continued. "Because if you sell something at 95—say, half of your position—and you sell it to a guy who's in trouble economically and he has to puke it back out in five days at 81, the second half of your position, or securities like that, have to be legally marked starting around 81. That's your new value conversation. Traders who do that stuff just as a course of business are despised. . . . That's what customers are saying to Marano, and Marano said, 'I cannot imagine.' This is like me questioning your mental health.

"He's thinking two things," Boyd continued. "One, he's got to stop this whole line of inquiry right here, right now, because if you have to ask the question, oh my God. Second, he's thinking about the trajectory of rumor and supposition, and that thesis of smoke versus fire. He's thinking that people are going to have a lot more hesitancy to trade mortgage-backed securities. Volumes are already drying up. Trading flows are already slowing down sharply. It's already hard enough to get your average trade done. With a question of their ability to act as a counterparty on the table, that's unimaginable. I mean, this is Bear Stearns. This is a company that was regularly making $6.00, $7.50, $8.00 a share in profits, and then these guys are making $25 million to $30 million [annually in salary and bonuses]. Now they're being questioned from the standpoint of fundamental liquidity. He said that he believed that these short sellers had been speculating in the credit default swap market and telling counterparties at other firms that they had concerns about Bear Stearns's liquidity and solvency, and that was driving the cost of spreads wider. What that was doing was making their overnight funding more expensive. That was cutting into their profit margin, and in turn was also starting a sort of a cottage industry of rumors about Bear Stearns."

Although the two men spoke for about fifteen minutes, the import of the call was clear immediately. "'There's no need to explain anything between us,' he said. I said, 'Are you sure you're seeing this?' He said, 'Look at [the credit default] swaps.' So I looked them up and then I see the hockey sticks"—a sharp spike up in their cost, as Sedacca wrote. "He said, 'It's unbelievable. It's all bullshit.' At that point—he's very much a corporate guy—but he had left me [with a clear message]. I'm not stupid. Hedge funds and prime brokerage accounts are unusually skittish about questions of financial health, financial solvency, and he said, 'I'm hearing there's questions about our financial health.' At that point, Marano is telling me he knew he was done, because once that question of credibility goes out there, and serious people say it to you enough, you're done. It's all that there is to it. It's all that there is to it. Where do you go to get your reputation back?"

Concern was spreading beyond the granite walls of 383 Madison Avenue, too. On Bear Stearns's Yahoo message board, someone using the name "rutlando" wrote of these fears on the afternoon of March 6: "Funding costs surging. Way overleveraged—33 to 1. There was no shrinkage in the balance sheet between the last two quarters. . . . Bear has $320 billion in debt. BSC is insolvent!!!" By 2008, the Yahoo message boards related to individual publicly traded companies had become a popular venue for anonymous venting. Their wisdom is best taken with a healthy dose of skepticism, as biases or the depth of research upon which conclusions are reached is rarely disclosed. Still, the running commentary does provide a real-time oral history of sorts. "The mighty Bear Stearns is finished," wrote "bwhal40er" after the market closed on March 6. "The SEC will be relieved." That night on *Mad Money*, his manic CNBC show about investing, the hedge fund manager Jim Cramer said of Bear Stearns: "The brokers have been killing us. At $69 [a share], I'm not giving up. I think it's a good franchise, but it's going to be a rocky ride."

❀

FOR YEARS BEAR Stearns had been among the leading underwriters of mortgage-backed securities, even going so far as buying firms that originated mortgages to the less-than-creditworthy so that it would have a ready source of mortgages to package up and sell in bulk to the market. Bear also was a big holder of the Alt-A mortgages (theoretically of better credit quality than subprime mortgages) that UBS's February 14 decision had made less valuable for everyone. Bear Stearns had also been a lender to Carlyle's hedge fund, Peloton, and Thornburg. Bear's net exposure was minimal, although that may have been of little consequence. Then there were the rumors in the marketplace that Marano and Boyd had been discussing. "It really didn't impact us," explained one Bear Stearns executive. "But people probably assume that between the lending we had to them and the fact that we owned other assets similar to what they owned and what the impact must be on their mark-to-market value, we were going to have another wave of issues, which may have been true. I don't know. [With] those three firms all going bust in a short period of time, the next week started to trigger the customer flight."

The Fed's capital injections and the rapid and high-profile meltdown of the Carlyle hedge fund did little to stem the growing concern about Bear Stearns and may even have fueled additional liquidity issues. On Yahoo, "elrrambu" announced on the afternoon of March 7 that he had bought Bear Stearns "puts," an option to sell the stock at a certain price before a certain time and a reflection of increasingly negative sentiment. "Even Fed action this morning could [not] stop this pig from dying," he wrote. A few minutes later, another observer agreed. "Bear is ready to rip," he wrote, "just watch. Yeah, just wait till March 20 earnings announcement day. Only it should be called losses announcement day. It will rip all right. Like in r.i.p.—rest in peace. Bear has no business happening these days. They might just as well close the shop." Added another bear on Bear: "It is SO f#@king over for BSC!!" That same Friday night, a "major bank" denied the firm's request to provide $2 billion in short-term financing. "Being denied such a loan is the Wall Street equivalent of having your buddy refuse to front you $5 the day before payday," *Fortune*'s Boyd wrote later. "Bear executives scrambled and raised the money elsewhere. But the sign was unmistakable: Credit was drying up."

Boyd worked hard that night and over the weekend trying to figure out which bank—said to be European—had decided it would no longer be a counterparty to Bear Stearns in the overnight financing markets. Obviously, this would be a huge negative development for the firm and sad confirmation of what Marano feared. It would also be a big story for Boyd. "At that point, I'm pulling my fucking hair out—pardon my language—calling everybody," he said. "I'm calling Deutsche Bank, I'm calling UBS, and I'm very aggressive. 'Get your senior guys on the phone. Get your financing desk on the phone.' I don't want to talk to some stupid flack. I spent eight years on a desk. I'm smarter than all those flacks. They're all Kool-Aid drinkers. They don't honestly know a derivative from a bond from a stock. None of them are going to be able to ask their financing desk. They don't even know enough to call the repo guys on the financing desk. I told them, 'Get your financing guys or get your credit guys on the phone with me, or you're going in *Fortune*.' Here's the *New York Post* coming out of me. I said, 'There's two ways this is going to work: bad or good. This hand is good; this hand is bad. I shake your hand or I punch you. Let me know.'"

He talked to the traders on the repo desks at both UBS and Deutsche Bank, with a special focus on Deutsche because it had displayed an increasing ability to act like an American firm in its willingness to trade for its own account. "I'm talking to the guys in New York, and they're saying, 'We swear to Christ we are not the ones to have done that.' If Deutsche Bank had done it, I'm thinking, 'Okay, that's the story right there.' The minute a repo line gets pulled, you die, okay? They die a terrible death." But Boyd could never nail down which European bank had pulled Bear's line of credit.

A cover story in *Barron's* that appeared on Saturday, "Is Fannie Mae the Next Government Bailout?" served as a coda for all the growing speculation about just how bad things were looking in the housing market. "It's perhaps the cruelest of ironies that in the U.S. housing market's greatest hour of need, the major entity created during the Depression to bring liquidity to housing, Fannie Mae, may itself soon be in need of bailout," Jonathan Laing wrote. He offered a cogent and prescient argument about the extent of Fannie's potential troubles given its increasing cost of borrowing, the rising cost of its credit default swaps, and the huge amount of subprime and Alt-A mortgages it had on its books. Nowhere did Laing mention the words "Bear Stearns," but there was no question in the minds of many savvy readers—including some Bear Stearns senior executives—that if Fannie Mae was in trouble, Bear Stearns could be in trouble for the very same reasons. "I can't remember if [the *Barron's* article] contained a specific reference to Bear," recalled one senior managing director, "but the ensuing belief that a Fannie Mae insolvency was coming and that it would be devastating to Bear was one of the things that started that horrible week of speculation."

If any of this speculation about Bear Stearns's future—either real or perceived—bothered Alan D. Schwartz, the firm's fifty-seven-year-old CEO, he did not give even the slightest hint of it. After thirty-three years at Bear Stearns, Schwartz, a well-regarded media banker and Bear's longtime head of investment banking, had reluctantly taken the reins of the firm from the legendary Jimmy Cayne on January 8 after Bear's board accepted Cayne's resignation in the wake of the firm's first quarterly loss in its eighty-five-year history. When Schwartz announced Cayne's resignation at a breakfast meeting with the top leaders of the firm, he not only spoke about Cayne's contributions to the firm over the years—"Jimmy's legacy will be this wonderful building that we're all in," Schwartz said finally, leaving some attendees scratching their heads—but also urged everyone to keep focused on doing business and not on the ongoing chatter about the firm. "'You have to stop,'" Paul Friedman remembered Schwartz saying at that meeting. "'You can't be influenced by stock price. You can't be influenced by our credit default spreads. Those are determined by people on the outside. They don't know what's really going on here. They don't know that we have a vibrant franchise. You can't have your mental state be governed by what they say. You need to put your head down and work and go about your day, and ignore the stock price as best you can.' Which is easy to say unless you have your entire net worth wrapped up in it. I mean, it's the right line for the CEO to say. It makes sense conceptually. What could he say—'Hey, I know we're all going bankrupt here'? There was nothing more he could do other than that."

On Thursday, March 6, Schwartz flew down to Palm Beach a few days in advance of the firm's twenty-first annual four-day media conference, which was to begin at the luxurious Breakers Hotel on March 9. The night he arrived, he spoke to the board of Verizon Communications, the giant telecommunications company, about the state of the telecommunications industry. He spent much of the next two days playing golf on the sumptuous Ocean Course that surrounds the hotel. Very few of Bear's rank-and-file had any idea Schwartz was in Florida.

The turnout at the media conference was always stellar, with the likes of Sumner Redstone, chairman of the board of both Viacom and CBS; Robert Iger, chairman and CEO of Disney; and Jeffrey Zucker, the president and CEO of NBC Universal. The year before, Schwartz had made a point of telling the audience that Bear's media conference was the only one he participated in, which made sense given the other demands on his time and the chance it afforded him to hobnob in a relaxed and luxurious setting with his media clients.

During the 2008 conference, Schwartz and Redstone got to talking about how Redstone had stayed so physically and professionally active at nearly eighty-five years old. Redstone mentioned how he exercises seventy minutes a day and eats and drinks "every antioxidant known to man." Schwartz then asked Redstone what advice he could give about developing and maintaining a long and active professional career. "I don't think you begin by thinking about your career," Redstone said. "You take each step at a time, recognizing that opportunity never knocks. You have to go look for it, and I've looked for it all my life. I enjoy my life because I love what I do. I have a passion to win, as you know. You don't always win, but you need to have that passion and, most important, you have to be able to look ahead."

While Schwartz was roaming around the Breakers and waxing philosophical with his clients, back in New York the concerns about Bear Stearns's liquidity were intensifying. The firm's stock fell 11 percent on Monday morning, March 10, to its lowest level in five years, after Moody's, one of the three independent ratings agencies, downgraded portions of fifteen mortgage bonds underwritten by the firm, including the Alt-A securities, and suggested that further ratings cuts in these mortgage securities would be likely. Moody's said the downgrades were based on "higher-than-anticipated rates of delinquency" and "foreclosure . . . in the underlying collateral relative to credit enhancement levels." The Rabobank Group, a Dutch bank, told the firm before noon that it would not roll over a $500 million loan coming due later in the week and it was unlikely to renew a $2 billion line of credit coming due the following week. "Though Bear Stearns's overall financing from other banks totaled $119 billion, the Rabobank decision signaled that lenders were getting antsy," the *Wall Street Journal* reported.

With Schwartz down in Palm Beach and Cayne "retired"— though still chairman of the board of directors—and playing bridge at the North American championships in Detroit, it fell to Alan "Ace" Greenberg, the eighty-one-year-old former Bear chairman and CEO (and still chairman of the executive committee), to try to calm the roiling markets. He told CNBC at around lunchtime that the liquidity concerns about the company were absurd. "It's ridiculous, totally ridiculous," he said in a brief telephone interview from his desk with Michelle Caruso-Cabrera at CNBC, who called him out of the blue. Greenberg prided himself on answering his own phone without screening and on saying what was on his mind. This time his partners cringed. "Just another Ace-ism," one of the more sympathetic executives called it. The firm then put out a statement denying "market rumors regarding the firm's liquidity" and adding that "there is absolutely no truth to the rumors of liquidity problems that circulated today in the market." The release included a quotation from Schwartz: "Bear Stearns' balance sheet, liquidity and capital remain strong."

CNBC Wall Street reporter David Faber described these public statements of denial as wholly "atypical" for Wall Street executives. "No firm is going to say it's having trouble with liquidity, and in fact you've either got liquidity or you don't," he said on air at around two o'clock in the afternoon. "So if you don't have it, you're done. But these are the kinds of concerns in this market—concerns of confidence that people need to be aware of, because we are in a very difficult market where credit continues to be the driving concern and you can have a crisis of confidence, causing a meltdown."

Wall Street operates on trust, and in a world of instant communication that trust can be eroded instantly. The old saw "It takes a lifetime to build a reputation—and a moment to destroy it" is as true as ever in financial markets. Sometimes even the truth cannot act as a tourniquet to stanch the bleeding. "We are now pretending our entire economic system is sound," wrote Michael Shedlock, a blogger and an investment advisor at Sitka Pacific Capital Management, in Edmonds, Washington, on March 10. "Clearly it's not."

Next came the massive jolt the rumor mill received on Monday as word began seeping into the market that a federal regulator—believed to be the Office of the Comptroller of the Currency, a relatively obscure federal agency responsible for chartering and supervising all national banks—began making pointed calls to the banks it supervises asking them directly and specifically about their exposure to Bear Stearns. The calls were not about their exposure to a group of banks, Bear Stearns among them, but rather solely about Bear Stearns. There was no question that by the beginning of March, John C. Dugan, the comptroller of the currency, was plenty worried about the financial condition of the banks he regulated. "In general, due to a long period of strong economic growth, exceptionally low credit losses, and strong capital ratios, the national banking system has been healthy and vibrant," he testified before the Senate Committee on Banking, Housing, and Urban Affairs on March 4. "Now, however, the system is being tested. Two powerful and related forces are exerting real stress on banks of all sizes and in many different parts of the country. One is the large and unprecedented series of credit market disruptions, still unfolding, that was precipitated by declining house prices and severe problems with subprime mortgages. The other is the slowdown in the economy, which has begun to generate a noticeable decline in credit quality in a number of asset classes. The combination of these forces has strained the resources of many of the national banks we regulate." Whether Dugan's office made these calls or not—and a spokesman from the comptroller's office, Dean DeBuck, had "no comment" but did not expressly deny that the calls had been made—the tempest that raged as a result of the presumption that they were made was of historic proportions. There were indications on March 10 that Bear Stearns might no longer be able to control its own fate. The firm's public statements that day had the counterintuitive effect of fueling the market rumors rather than removing the oxygen from them.

The number of put options sold on Monday—short-term bets made by investors that Bear's stock would decline quickly—rose to 158,599, some seven times the twenty-day average, with the bets that the stock would fall outnumbering by 2.6 times those that it would rise.

More startling, though, was what bets investors were actually making. The most active contract sold on March 10 gave investors the right but not the obligation to sell Bear Stearns stock for $30 a share anytime before the options expired on March 21, in eight trading days. In other words, for the buyers of these puts to make money, Bear's stock, which closed at $62.30 on Monday, would have to fall a stunning 52 percent in eight sessions.

Equally as startling as these bets was the fact that some investors wanted to make even more of them. On and around March 10, requests poured into the Chicago Board of Options to open up additional put opportunities for Bear Stearns. The CBOE, where options are traded, has guidelines to determine when to open up a series of options and usually avoids doing so if the strike price is either way in or way out of the money. But in this case, investors demanded that the CBOE make available a new March series of puts with an exercise price of $25 per share—a bet that the price of Bear's stock would fall below $25 in seven trading sessions—and a new April series with strike prices of $20 and $22.50. The CBOE agreed to accommodate the demand and opened up the new options for trading the next day, but will not say who asked that the new series be opened. These were major negative bets on Bear's short- and immediate-term prospects. Where were these large and seemingly highly improbable bets coming from? Nobody seemed to know for sure.

Logic suggested that major hedge funds who used Bear Stearns as a prime broker, keeping billions of dollars of their investors' money with the firm and clearing their trades through it, could have been buying the puts, for the simple reason that a bet that Bear's stock would fall rapidly was perhaps the only way these funds could actually hedge their exposure to the firm aside from taking out their cash balances (as many were doing). If there really was a problem at Bear Stearns and the firm was vulnerable to the proverbial run on the bank, putting access to their accounts at risk, then the only logical way to protect against this terrible outcome would be to bet against the firm in a major way. So if the money in the accounts was blocked by a disaster at the firm, at least the hedge fund would make a ton of money in the interim by betting the firm would fail. This thinking was perfectly logical, and not without a recent precedent in the form of the 2005 failure and liquidation of Refco, a broker of commodities and futures contracts. When Refco filed for bankruptcy protection, hedge funds that were Refco customers could not get immediate access to their money. The memory of Refco was still fresh in the minds of many hedge funds, and they were in no mood to get caught in that situation again. Any inkling of trouble at Bear Stearns led them to consider seriously taking their money out of the firm first and asking questions later.

The calls from the Office of the Comptroller of the Currency provided the perfect cover to perform this delicate hedging operation. "On Monday, before the Thursday run, one of the heads of a small bank told me that he got a call, his CEO or president got a call, from the regulators, asking what their exposure was to Bear Stearns," explained an incredulous Bear Stearns banker. "Not 'What's your exposure to Bear, JPMorgan, Morgan Stanley, Lehman, UBS?' Just 'What's your exposure to Bear?' He said his president walked into his office and said to him, 'Hey, I just got this call. We've never gotten a call like this before.'"

The bank—Emigrant Savings—that received this call from the regulator was not a large bank. "They must have gone down the list," this Bear Stearns banker recalled. "If they'd got to this guy, they'd called everybody else. The rumors were there, but now you're getting, 'Well, look, the regulators called me.' What kind of a rumor is that? That's a self-fulfilling rumor. He said to me, 'What did you think I was going to do? I got out of everything.'" Around this very moment, the Bear banker happened to be on the phone with a senior person at one of Bear Stearns's investment banking competitors and mentioned the conversation about the phone call from the regulator. During that second conversation, the Bear banker reported, the competitor said, "'We got the same call, and they basically said to us, "Don't tell your traders and don't get out of any counterparty agreements that you have. But what's your exposure to Bear Stearns?"' He says, 'What do you think I'm going to do? Of course I told my traders. I bought puts, sold short, and got out of everything I could possibly could get out of.' I was so blown away when the second guy told me about getting a call. This guy [is] just an incredibly well-respected risk manager on the Street, [so] I knew that this wasn't made up. Now the rumors were even there, okay. But imagine you're getting calls. I mean, what fucking institution with any sense in their head calls up and asks what's your exposure to one thing and then says 'Oh, but don't do anything about it'?"

The outbreak of these significant rumors led to the huge increase in the purchase of the Bear puts—and also in their price. It also was not surprising that the cost of insuring Bear's obligations skyrocketed on March 10 to around $700,000 to protect against $10 million of debt for five years, an increase of fourteen times over the previous week and yet another sure sign that the vultures were circling with increased velocity. Rival firms were starting to prey on Bear Stearns with increasing intensity. "On Monday, we started hearing a lot of rumors," explained one Bear senior managing director, "that Joe Lewis"—Bear's second-largest shareholder, who had invested more than $1 billion in the stock of the firm in the previous six months—"was starting to get margin calls, which were not true, to guys who aren't taking the other side of trades. And I think it was Monday when our credit default swaps spreads started to really, really spike. I think a lot of people attributed that to the rumors around Goldman. Goldman was not willing to stand on the other side of the trade. Goldman [was] saying that we had DK'd"—essentially failed to make good—"on a trade, which was—the rumor might have been a real rumor, but the fact that we DK'd on a trade was not true. And so that clearly started, at least in my mind, what happened so quickly that week. It became very apparent—not what was going to happen, but what was happening as our credit default swaps started to just gap out huge. We couldn't do anything anymore. We couldn't do business. It was too expensive. We were completely paralyzed."

Some senior executives inside the firm were pushing Sam Molinaro, the CFO, to release Bear's first-quarter earnings early. Molinaro, from Binghamton, New York, joined Bear Stearns in 1986 after six years at Price Waterhouse in Syracuse. He was the first significant hire into the firm's accounting department after the company went public. He rose through the ranks, becoming CFO ten years later and adding the chief operating officer title in August 2007. The firm had been profitable in the first quarter of 2008, even after the new marks forced by the Peloton liquidation, and the argument went that this news could calm the jittery throngs. "There was a lot of begging: 'Can we release earnings early? Can we do something?'" remembered Paul Friedman. "Those of us who were doing conference calls with lenders and with customers were totally hamstrung. You couldn't talk about earnings. Theoretically, you weren't even supposed to talk about balance sheet or liquidity or risk or anything else until the earnings call. You'd have lenders and customers wanting to know what's going on and you'd go, 'It's okay. Trust me.' I got in the mode [where] I would say to them, 'Listen, we're in a blackout period. I can't talk about earnings, but let me preface this by saying we're trying to move up the date at which we announce earnings. I'll let you draw your own conclusions as to why somebody would do that.' That was the best I could do. So we danced. We all did it differently, but there were a bunch of us doing it. We gave a general picture of how our liquidity worked, how our funding worked, why we had this $18 billion funding reserve, and nobody needed to worry about a run on the bank or running out of cash. We would describe it as, 'Here's where we were at the last quarter. I don't expect this quarter to be materially different.' You'd have to sort of dance around it. They wanted to hear about liquidity and they wanted to hear about earnings, and you really couldn't talk about either one."

Meanwhile, Schwartz remained in Palm Beach. He discovered quickly that the 2008 media conference would not be all fun and games. While he and Robert Iger, the Disney CEO, were preparing for Schwartz's late-afternoon interview of Iger, Schwartz was interrupted repeatedly by calls from the office in New York seeking guidance about how to respond to the growing list of rumors about the firm's liquidity. He felt he could not betray any concern in front of his powerful and important clients. Schwartz kept his cool and continued the preparation for the Iger interview.

That evening, Schwartz announced that the guests at the media conference could demo Rock Band—a full-blown band simulation game that combines guitar, bass, drum, and singing—"compliments of Viacom," and enjoy cocktails and hors d'oeuvres "compliments of Martha Stewart."

THE NEXT MORNING, ING Group NV, another large Dutch bank, followed Rabobank's lead and pulled its $500 million in short-term financing for Bear Stearns. ING professionals told Bear that the bank's management "wanted to keep their distance until the dust settled." Also, before the market opened Tuesday morning, the Federal Reserve did something that it had not done since the Great Depression. Through a new Term Securities Lending Facility, the Fed agreed to make $200 billion in Treasury securities available, starting March 27, to securities firms for a period of twenty-eight days, to be secured by pledges of other securities, including federal agency debt, residential mortgage-backed securities issued by federal agencies such as Fannie Mae or Freddie Mac, or highly rated non-federal-agency residential mortgage-backed securities. Previously, the Fed had made Treasury securities available to securities firms only on an overnight basis. Now the additional liquidity would be available through auctions for nearly a month and was designed to supplement the cash the Fed had made available the previous Friday. The new program was "intended to promote liquidity in the financing markets for Treasury and other collateral and thus to foster the functioning of financial markets more generally," the Fed explained. In other words, the Fed was offering to swap Wall Street's toxic mortgage securities for easy-to-value Treasury securities that could be used as safe collateral.

While the import of the Fed's decision was substantial and Wall Street was initially elated, its near-term effect on the liquidity of Bear Stearns or Lehman Brothers was nearly meaningless, since the funds were not going to be made available until March 27 at the earliest. Indeed, the Fed had been discussing the creation of the new facility with Wall Street for months before it became a reality and very much would have liked to have made it available earlier than March 27. But it was such a radical departure for the central bank that the logistics required to implement the new system took time to coordinate. So while the intent was to permit securities firms to swap some of their illiquid mortgage securities for highly liquid Treasury securities, the real effect was to further spook the market into wondering why the Fed would take such a radical step.

Some observers saw the Fed's decision positively. Certainly the market took a liking to the Fed's decision, as the Dow rose 417 points on the news. This was "a Fed-induced rally," CNBC's Jim Cramer explained that night. "It's a coiled-spring rally." He believed the market would likely go higher for the rest of the week, and called the jump "a respite from the gloom." Even Christopher Cox, the commissioner of the Securities and Exchange Commission— the regulator of securities firms such as Goldman Sachs, Morgan Stanley, Merrill Lynch, Lehman Brothers, and Bear Stearns—added his imprimatur to the adequacy of Bear Stearns's capital, which he said was monitored on a "constant" basis, especially during the credit crisis. Asked March 11 by reporters about the firm's financial condition, he said: "We have a good deal of comfort about the capital cushions at these firms at the moment."

Others were far more pessimistic about the Fed's move. "I don't see how this helps," commented "DK" on the *Wall Street Journal's* "Real Time Economics" blog. "It will temporarily allow these banks to use crappy [mortgage-backed securities] as temporary collateral, but eventually these will have to be written down. I think this is just an attempt to cause markets to go down gradually, versus a huge crash." And then "Clear Skys Ahead" wrote with an acid pen, "Now that the Fed is lending to primary dealers and accepting unimpeachable items, such as mortgage debt, as collateral things can get back to normal. Now what exactly do we do when the collateral turns out to be worth less than the loan? Thank goodness everyone woke up and realized that unless the taxpayers were the ones ultimately stuck with the bill, Wall Street couldn't rally! Let the party resume at least until sanity takes hold."

Richard X. Bove, a research analyst at Punk Ziegel (now part of

Ladenburg Thalmann), told his clients that he thought the Fed's historic move "may have been strongly influenced by Bear Stearns' problem." (The president of the New York Fed, Tim Geithner, denied that the Fed's move had been motivated by the problems at Bear Stearns. "This was designed to cool the fever a little bit, to give people a little more confidence that they could finance stuff with us," he explained. "But it was more for the market as a whole than it was going to be about an individual institution.") Bove also wrote that Bear's business model was "broken" because it had relied too heavily in recent years on the origination and sale of mortgage-backed securities. Now that the market for those products had closed, Bear Stearns had not figured out a way to replace the lost revenue. "Bear did not get out of the way fast enough," he wrote. "Consequently, its balance sheet, its business operations, and its reputation were all hurt badly. One key result of this is that the firm's borrowing costs rose sharply according to reports." The sale of the company was likely the only solution, Bove asserted.

The ever-provocative CNBC picked up on Bove's report on Tuesday around midday and stirred up a frenzy of negative implications. On-air Wall Street reporter Charlie Gasparino explained that "the market was saying" that Bove's claim about the Fed's action was correct, although he was quick to point out that he had not confirmed independently what the analyst had written. "This is trader talk we are engaging in here," he said. Bob Pisani, the network's reporter on the floor of the NYSE, cautioned that he heard rumors all the time and discarded most of them. But not this time. "Here your radar is really high," Pisani said, "because volume is titanic in the last couple of days and the trading range is titanic and more importantly the options trading is titanic. There is huge put volume in the $30 range for this stock, and that's telling you that people are making some bets here that something may be wrong." He made no mention of the fact that buying the puts may have been a perfectly logical hedge against a run on the bank at Bear Stearns. Nor did he mention—he probably was not aware—that someone (who is still unknown to this day) had just made a $1.7 million bet that Bear Stearns stock would fall dramatically within nine days, first by buying 57,000 puts at $30 and then by buying 1,649 puts at $25. "Even if I were the most bearish man on earth, I can't imagine buying puts 50 percent below the price with just over a week to expiration," Thomas Haugh, a general partner of Chicago-based options trading firm PTI Securities & Futures, told Bloomberg. "It's not even on the page of rational behavior, unless you know something." Added Michael McCarty, chief options and equity strategist at New York–based brokerage Meridian Equity Partners: "That trade amounted to buying a lottery ticket. Would you buy $1.7 million worth of lottery tickets just because you could? No. Neither would a hedge fund manager." Gasparino added to Pisani's comment, summing up the growing consensus: "Bear is the whipping boy right now because there is no confidence in that firm or its management. . . . The rumors might cause a run on the bank even though they deny it."

AT ABOUT THE moment when CNBC was reporting on the Bear Stearns rumors, Geithner and Ben Bernanke, chairman of the Federal Reserve Board of Governors, were hosting a long-scheduled luncheon in the windowless Washington Room on the thirteenth floor of the New York Federal Reserve Bank, at 33 Liberty Street in lower Manhattan, for the CEOs or senior executives of nearly every important Wall Street firm. It was an august gathering of Wall Street's most powerful men. In attendance were Lloyd Blankfein, CEO of Goldman Sachs; Richard Fuld, CEO of Lehman Brothers; Jamie Dimon, CEO of JPMorgan Chase; and Robert Rubin, the former Goldman CEO and U.S. Treasury secretary who was then chairman of the executive committee at Citigroup. Also in attendance were, among others, Steve Schwarzman, CEO of the Blackstone Group; Kenneth Griffin, CEO of Citadel Investment Group; and Stanley Druckenmiller, CEO of Duquesne Capital Management. Alan Schwartz, Bear Stearns's CEO, was not there. Nor was he invited. He remained in Palm Beach, at the Breakers, hosting the firm's annual media conference.

One would think such a meeting would be the perfect opportunity to share frank concerns about the credit crisis then engulfing the financial markets. Some of that did occur. But there were "no surprises," according to one participant, even though there was a spirited discussion of the increasingly worrying events, including the causes of the crisis, what else could possibly go wrong, and who or what was to blame. But a room full of alpha males apparently was not the setting in which to bare one's soul. "These guys don't complain," said one of the attendees. "They would never in that context express weakness or concern about themselves. You can imagine you're sitting around the table with a bunch of predators and you'd never do that. But I would say people were very, very nervous about the world. So there was a lot of talk about what the system was vulnerable to." No notes are kept of such meetings, and the general rule is never to speak about what happens there or who said what to whom.

A few hours later the indefatigable Gasparino reported on his conversation with Sam Molinaro, the longtime chief financial officer of Bear Stearns who had recently been promoted to be the firm's chief operating officer. Molinaro was at a total loss to explain what was going on. "The rumors about Bear's inability to make margin calls and its illiquidity are completely false," Gasparino said Molinaro told him. "Why is this happening? I don't know how to characterize it. If I knew why it was happening, I would do something to address it. I've spent all day trying to track down the source of these rumors, but they are false. There is no liquidity crisis. No margin calls. It's all nonsense."

Once again, the denial of liquidity problems by a Bear Stearns senior executive did nothing to quell the concerns, especially since competitors knew full well that cash was draining out of the firm, as it had to make good on its hedge fund clients' legitimate request to get back their free-cash balances. The cost of Bear's credit default swaps moved up again. And the option volume that Pisani alluded to was in fact skyrocketing. Starting March 11 there were 79,000 March $25 put contracts traded, 20,000 April $20 puts traded, 3,700 April $22.50 puts, and 8,000 April $25 puts. Not surprisingly, very few call options—the right to buy Bear stock—traded at these prices.

Steven Smith, a columnist for TheStreet.com, focused on the fact that on Tuesday, with Bear Stearns stock trading at around $65 per share, more than 55,000 put contracts betting that the stock would fall to $30 a share by March 20 were bought and sold. "So that left only ten days for some event to occur that would cause these puts to go into the money and have some value," Smith wrote. "So it appears that as rumors began swirling early in the week that Bear was having liquidity problems and might possibly be bordering on insolvent, someone took that to heart and bought the puts as disaster insurance."

Whether Molinaro knew it or not—and he certainly should have known—Bear Stearns's trading partners across Wall Street, the firm's counterparties on trades and overnight funding, began to seriously question the wisdom of continuing to trade with Bear or to accept its collateral as security for overnight funds. At 5:06 on the afternoon of March 11, Stuart Smith, a trader at Hayman Capital, a Dallas, Texas, hedge fund, sent an e-mail to Goldman Sachs's credit derivatives desk in New York asking Goldman to "please novate"— or take over Hayman's position on—a February 2007 $5 million derivatives trade between Hayman's Subprime Credit Strategies Fund and Bear Stearns. In other words, Hayman wanted out and asked Goldman to take its place on the trade with Bear Stearns as the counterparty. About forty minutes later, the Goldman desk wrote back, "GS does not consent to this trade."

The message this left with Hayman Capital was a profound one. No less than the mighty Goldman Sachs had told one of its hedge fund clients that it would no longer act as a stand-in for it on trades with Bear Stearns. During the previous weeks, Goldman had been willing to provide this service—at a price—as its clients became increasingly nervous about Bear's ability to honor its obligations. Late in the afternoon of March 11, Goldman apparently no longer believed the risks equaled the reward. And the firm told that to at least two of its hedge fund clients. "I was astounded when I got the [Goldman] e-mail," Kyle Bass, of Hayman Capital, told Boyd at *Fortune*. Bass, a former Bear Stearns salesman, checked with a friend at Goldman to see if the e-mail had been sent out in error. "It wasn't," Bass said. "Goldman told Wall Street that they were done with Bear, that there was too much risk. That was the end for them." As the manager or co-manager of hedge funds in Dallas with $4 billion that had bet—correctly—that residential mortgage–backed securities would lose value, he had testified before Congress in

September 2007 about the growing credit crisis: "It is becoming increasingly clear as each month passes, subprime credit has become the mad cow disease of structured finance. Nobody knows who consumed the infected product." Bass was a heavyweight in the market and made a killing when the mortgage market crashed. "When that got out, that's when the unbridled selling started," *Fortune*'s Boyd explained.

Maybe so, but Goldman's decision at that moment not to take over Hayman's position was only half the story. While certainly Goldman's decision not to immediately novate Hayman's trade sent a message that Hayman interpreted as concern—and, given the rest of the swirling rumors and bets being made against Bear Stearns, it is not hard to understand why he did—inside Goldman, Hayman's request was unusual enough and the rumors about Bear Stearns's liquidity position were credible enough that Goldman decided to "escalate" the decision, bringing it to the attention of Gary Cohn, the co-president of the firm, and his partner, David Viniar, the Goldman CFO. Cohn's concern was actually the opposite of Hayman's reaction, since he was worried that if Goldman took over the Hayman trade with Bear Stearns, the market would get the message that a large hedge fund did not want to wait around and see if Bear Stearns made good on the money it owed Hayman on this particular trade. "The reason we didn't take novations is because we had conversations with the senior leadership of Bear Stearns and said, 'If we start taking novations, people pull their business, they pull their collateral, you're out of business,'" Cohn said. Indeed, Goldman's view was that the best way to keep these firms in business was to force clients to do business with them and force them to keep trading. For that reason, Cohn said, he had considered not novating the Hayman trade.

The argument may seem counterintuitive, but not to Cohn. "Look, I need these guys to survive," he said of his competitors. "I just said to someone, 'We all live in the same neighborhood. Right now, I'm the only guy that's got a nice house. My gutters are attached. My windows aren't broken. My shutters are on. But the house to the right and the house to the left, broken windows, shutters. So it doesn't matter how nice my house is. It's worth less than if those houses are nice. So I need to help them, and it's better for my industry to make sure their houses at least look good from the outside.' The last week of Bear Stearns's existence, we were working on it to try and help them and buy assets from their balance sheet. We were there to be helpful. We weren't looking to take advantage. We were looking to be helpful."

Cohn asked Schwartz that night if Bear wanted Goldman to take over the Hayman trade. In other words, Goldman would assume the risk that Bear Stearns would pay the money owed. "Now, no one ever wants to tell you to novate a trade," Cohn said, "because basically, when you novate a trade, the person that asks for the novation, when it's a credit novation, has basically said, 'I don't want to do business with you anymore.' So if we don't novate the trade, the client's only other alternative is to go back to you and trade with you." In this case, Schwartz told Cohn that Bear was actually looking to settle the trade and said it was fine to novate the trade.

The next morning, just after nine, Goldman sent Smith at Hayman a new e-mail: "GS would like to consent to the trade" with "details to follow." And then Goldman sent Smith one more e-mail a few hours later. "GS consents to the novation. Please see trade details below." Just like that, Goldman had taken Hayman's place in the trade with Bear.

But that seemed like a lifetime of waiting to Hayman, which had wanted immediate service and did not get it. "All he knew was we couldn't do it instantaneously," Cohn said of Hayman. "All he knew is he picked up the phone to his sales guy, and his sales guy, every time he talks to him, says, 'Anything I can do for you today? How can I help you?' He calls up and says, 'Here's how you help me today. I want you to novate this trade.' The sales guy goes, 'Okay, let me see if I can get that done.' Hangs up the phone. The sales guy goes running. 'Hey, I need to novate this trade.' Everyone's like, 'Whoa, hold on a minute. It's a Bear Stearns novation. Let's elevate.' And eventually it ends up in my office. It takes us twelve or fourteen hours to make a decision and have the conversations whether we want to do that or not. Meanwhile, Hayman Capital is going—every hour that goes by—he's going, 'Oh, my God. Am I not going to get paid? Am I not getting paid? If they won't novate this, things must be worse than I even think. I want out quicker.' It's just an avalanche of brain waves that go off that allow people to panic."

Cohn said Goldman was doing "nothing different than everyone else out there" but that whatever he did in that particular circumstance became "a double-edged sword." "I've got my client franchise over here that I'm trying to protect and do what they want," he explained. "I've got my equity shareholder base over here that I've got a fiduciary responsibility to protect at all costs. We are trying to do what's best for both sides of this equation all the time. Clearly, novating everything instantaneously was best for my client base, because they were going to love me. Right? They could call instantaneously and know they could get rid of 100 percent of their credit risk. My shareholders over here would have said, 'You're fucking crazy. Why are you guys taking credit risk without making money?' See, when I take credit risk from a normal client, they're paying me a bid/offer spread. When you're novating, you're stepping into someone else's shoes. You get paid no money to do that. So that's why you usually do it when it just nets you down and offsets, because you've made your money on the other side of the trade. So my shareholders on this side and my employees would be going, 'Why are we taking all this credit risk?' So you balance the client needs versus the firm's needs and the shareholders' needs. And that's never, never a simple equation."

(Soon after Boyd's *Fortune* article appeared on March 28 with the news of Goldman's e-mail to Bass, a Goldman Sachs spokesman disputed the implication that Goldman had stopped acting as counterparty for Bear Stearns and therefore had helped fuel the firm's liquidity problems. "We received a request to novate the trade [from Bass] late in the day on Tuesday, March 11, escalated it for a decision consistent with our normal procedures when an increase in credit exposure is requested, and agreed to the novation the next morning," Goldman said. The firm further criticized Boyd for telling only half the story—that Goldman had refused the trade—and not that Goldman had accepted it the next morning, albeit at a higher cost of execution.)

The rumor quickly spread in the hedge fund community that Goldman Sachs was finished with Bear Stearns. The damage to

Bear in the marketplace was substantial. "That was just one of many e-mails," said Paul Friedman. "There were internal memos at Goldman. There were internal memos at Credit Suisse. There were internal memos at JPMorgan. Various flavors of how to deal or not to deal with give-ups generally, assignments generally, or Bear generally. Everybody was trying to figure out, in fairness, what to do with the assignments that they were getting. . . . By Tuesday afternoon, they were starting to increase. In fairness, the credit default swaps assignment process is extremely manual. It's extremely cumbersome. Firms didn't really have a handle on what their risk was to us, let alone what to do with new assignments of trades coming in over the transom. For a firm to put the brakes on dealing with us—if I were the credit guys, was it done for the right reason? I don't know, but it doesn't surprise me. We were putting out fires every day, all day every day, for firms that wouldn't take assignments, or wouldn't take our name in the foreign exchange markets, or wherever, either localized within departments or at the corporate level. I'd have done the same thing."

At least two major hedge funds began pulling their cash from the firm. "The prime brokerage withdrawals began in earnest that Tuesday night," Boyd explained. "I think the two big funds that kicked it all off were Renaissance Technologies—Jim Simons's $30 billion fund. I had two or three people tell me that he pulled, and I think he had $20 billion [at Bear]—and I think Highbridge did, too." (Since September 2004, JPMorgan Chase has controlled Highbridge Capital Management, a hedge fund with around $35 billion in capital.) To be sure, the cash was theirs and they were entitled to it at any moment, and this cash was not to be confused with Bear's own corporate cash, which was in a separate, segregated account.

"The thing about prime brokerage withdrawals," Boyd explained, "is if I put in my withdrawal request at 9:00 A.M., that cash is back to me, wherever I want it, by 4:00 P.M. the latest. Wired, okay? It's not like there's a lot of room for negotiation. If a guy's got a $10 billion account with you, you've got to get him $10 billion in assets. Whether it's his five-year position, or his IBM stock, or his cash account, or whatever, it's got to get to him. Now, obviously, what Bear Stearns had done, and every Wall Street firm has done—they don't like you to know it too much—is the securities that were on account there that are held in margin accounts, the hedge fund accounts, they rehypothecated those, so they used those to borrow more money." To meet the requests of its hedge fund clients for their money, Bear had the stark choice of liquidating some of the assets it had bought with their cash or using some of the firm's own cash. This was very troubling indeed. "I remember Tuesday morning, we were in management committee, and Bruce Lisman got a call, and when he finished he told the committee that Renaissance moved out all the rest of their remaining prime brokerage business," recalled Steve Begleiter, the head of corporate strategy, a forty-six-year-old Haverford College graduate and, since 2002, a member of the firm's management and compensation committee. "That was a particularly chilling moment because they had been such a long-standing, loyal and significant client. For me, that really crystallized the seriousness of the client flight we were experiencing."

On one side of the ledger, Bear clients were withdrawing cash as fast as they could. But something equally catastrophic was happening on the other side of the ledger.

CHAPTER 3

"BEAR STEARNS IS NOT IN TROUBLE!"

One of the other ways Wall Street funds itself on a daily basis is in the so-called repurchase agreement (repo) financing market, where a firm's securities are pledged as collateral for funding. At Bear, the mortgage repo desk arrived at work around six-thirty in the morning. "They dial for dollars," Friedman said. "Our guys would borrow maybe $75 billion a day, something in that neighborhood, most of it daily. It's not like you're dialing strangers. You're calling up the guy who loaned you the money yesterday and going, 'You okay with it today? What's the rate today? Okay, great. Thanks.' You tweak it up and down as people need money, and you tweak it up and down as you buy or sell collateral. Basically, the vast majority of it just rolls in the normal course. It's of course insane. In the normal world it would be insane, and in this world it's really insane. But that was the only choice. By the way, it wasn't just us. I guarantee you, if you went to Lehman or Goldman or Morgan Stanley right now, they're doing most of their funding overnight. It's just what they're doing."

The daily funding drama, such as it is, is usually resolved around eight-thirty each morning. And it is usually an inconsequential discussion, until the moment it's not—and then it can be life-threatening. It would be as simple as being able to breathe one second and not being able to breathe the next. "Most lenders, even Monday and Tuesday, continued to roll," Friedman continued. "They'd tell you Monday morning, 'Okay, we're rolling for today. Talk to you tomorrow.' Some of them would say, 'Listen, I'll roll but I need more margin,' or 'I used to lend to you and I'd take whole-loan collateral. Now I'll only take agencies,' or 'I need a higher rate. I need a higher something,' or some of them just said, 'Hey, I've got extra cash. Do you need it?'"

On Monday and Tuesday, the net effect of these ongoing discussions with the overnight lenders was that the twenty largest firms became increasingly conservative about how they valued the collateral Bear Stearns had been offering them and were demanding more collateral to provide the same amount of financing. "You saw this widening disparity between what we thought we owed them for collateral and what they thought we owed them," said Robert Upton, Bear Stearns's treasurer. To a certain degree, disputes among dealers about the value of collateral are normal, but by Tuesday the debate had ratcheted up to a new level. The upshot of the disagreement was that the top twenty dealers believed that Bear Stearns owed them about $1.5 billion more collateral. But the firm disagreed with the market's conclusions and decided not to make the payments. "We didn't make a lot of those margin calls," Upton said. "So if you think about it, what did that do? That just exacerbated counterparties' concerns."

During the afternoons at the repo desk—which was just outside of Friedman's office on the seventh floor—a form of the morning discussion would continue when the desk would touch base with the lenders to see whether it looked like the next day's funding would be available. Recalled Friedman: "I'd say, 'How are we doing?' They'd say, 'It's okay. Here's what we've seen, but it's okay.' What you'd then find is in the afternoon, a handful of firms would call you and say, 'Listen, just came out of a credit meeting,' or 'I just talked to my boss. I'm not going to be there tomorrow for you.' This is Monday afternoon a little bit, Tuesday afternoon more, Wednesday afternoon in a huge way. It grew every day. Every morning, we'd come in and we'd know that there were lenders from the previous day who weren't going to be there. You'd hold your breath, and it would be, 'Okay. We lost a couple of guys.' We came in with a lot of excess money because we were overborrowing in the anticipation of losing money. We go, 'Okay, we ate through a little bit of our cushion, but it's okay.' Then, about three o'clock, the repo guys would come in and they'd have this spreadsheet that was a bunch of names—'These are the people who won't be lending to us tomorrow.'" For instance, Fidelity Investments, the mutual fund giant based in Boston, had been lending Bear Stearns $6 billion a day, every day. But that week, Fidelity pulled its overnight funding. Federated Investors, another large mutual fund company, based in Pittsburgh, provided Bear with $4.5 billion in overnight funding on Monday, and then nothing the rest of the week.

Nerves were starting to fray all around at 383 Madison Avenue, especially among the traders, who were the first to hear the rumors as they spread. Bruce Lisman, the sixty-one-year-old co-head of global equities, tried to calm people down. "Let's stay focused," he yelled to the traders from atop a desk near his fourth-floor office. "Keep working hard. Bear Stearns has been here a long time, and we're staying here. If there's any news, I'll let you know, if and when I know it." Ace Greenberg performed magic tricks in an effort to keep people amused.

At the same time, Drake Management announced it would likely close its $3 billion Global Opportunities Fund after a series of bad bets forced the fund to put a hold on redemptions in December 2007. "It would seem more probable that the market disruptions we have experienced will not abate in the short term, but will instead continue for some time," Drake wrote its investors. In all, "at least a dozen hedge funds have closed, sold assets or sought fresh capital in the past month as banks and securities firms tightened lending standards," Bloomberg reported on March 12. "The industry is reeling from its worst crisis because bankers—staggered by almost $190 billion of asset writedowns and credit losses caused by the collapse of the subprime-mortgage market—are raising borrowing rates and demanding extra collateral for loans."

Still, on the edition of *Mad Money* following the market's 417-point rally on March 11, host Jim Cramer responded to a viewer who asked, "Should I be worried about Bear Stearns in terms of liquidity and get my money out of there?" with a patented Cramer tirade: "No! No! No! Bear Stearns is fine. Do not take your money out! If there is one takeaway other than the plus 400, Bear Stearns is not in trouble! If anything, it is more likely to be taken over. Don't move your money from Bear. That's just being silly! Don't be silly!"

If Cramer had the last word of the night about Bear Stearns, the first word the next morning belonged—finally—to Alan Schwartz, Bear's CEO. Schwartz had emerged from the shadows of the emerging crisis in a live news feed from the Breakers Hotel in Palm Beach. The decision that Schwartz would appear had been made late the prior afternoon in the wake of ongoing speculation about the firm's liquidity position. Prior to his CNBC appearance, Schwartz had just finished interviewing Sumner Redstone, the Viacom emperor, in the hotel's Ponce de Leon IV Room about the wonders of consuming antioxidants and living a long and prosperous life.

Schwartz appeared live on CNBC just after nine o'clock on the morning of March 12. He looked tired and pale but spiffy in his blue-and-white-striped spread-collar shirt and Hermès tie. In his lead-in to the interview—a scoop, to be sure—CNBC's David Faber reminded viewers that it had been a "hard week" for Bear's stock since the firm had been "buffeted by constant rumors of a looming liquidity problem." Faber's first question to Schwartz was about rumors that Wall Street firms no longer wanted to take counterparty risks with Bear Stearns. Was this true?

"No, it's not true," Schwartz answered calmly. "There has been a lot of volatility in the market, a lot of disruption in the market, and that's causing some problems administratively on getting some trades settled out, and we're working hard on getting that done. We're in a constant dialogue with all the major dealers and the counterparties on the Street and we are not being made aware of anybody who is not taking our credit as a counterparty."

Without naming Kyle Bass at Hayman Capital, Faber then asked Schwartz about the novation that Bass had tried to execute the day before with Goldman Sachs. (Goldman completed the novation on the morning of March 12, around the time of Schwartz's CNBC appearance.) "I'm not aware of a specific trade from one counterparty to another and where we're a third party," he said. "We have direct dealings with all of these institutions and we have active markets going with each one and our counterparty risk has not been a problem." Schwartz's answer was counter to the explanation offered by Gary Cohn, Goldman Sachs's co-president, that he had spoken with Schwartz about Bass's novation request.

Where then, Faber asked, had all these rumors originated, especially if they weren't true? "Well, you know, it's very hard to say," Schwartz replied. "Why do rumors start? If I had to speculate, I would say that last week was a difficult time in the mortgage business. There was talk about problems at GSEs"—government-sponsored entities, such as Fannie Mae and Freddie Mac. "There were certainly some problems with some funds that were invested in very high-quality instruments but on a lot of leverage, and there were some problems there, and some people speculate that Bear Stearns could have some problems in those since we're a significant player in the mortgage business. None of those speculations are true. It's a market that's concerned about things"—and here CNBC anchor Erin Burnett broke into the interview with the news that New York Governor Eliot Spitzer would resign later in the day after revelations about his involvement with high-priced prostitutes.

"So I don't know where the rumors started," Schwartz continued after the news flash. "Maybe I can just say this: I think that part of the problem is that when speculation starts in a market with a lot of emotion in it and people are concerned about the volatility, then people will sell first and ask questions later, and that creates its own momentum. We put out a statement—I did—that our liquidity and balance sheet are strong, and maybe I should expand on that a little." Schwartz's comments bring to mind the truism first penned by the financial writer Walter Bagehot, a former editor of the *Economist,* in 1873: "Every banker knows that if he has to prove that he is worthy of credit, however good may be his arguments, in fact his credit is gone."

Faber encouraged Schwartz to try to prove to the world his firm was still worthy of credit, and reminded him of their conversation two months before when he'd become CEO of Bear and "you were fairly positive about Bear having taken the marks"—marking securities to market—"that you thought were necessary, having treated its balance sheet conservatively." How had things changed in two months?

"Well, the markets have certainly gotten worse," Schwartz answered. "But our liquidity position has not changed at all. Our balance sheet has not weakened at all. So let me just talk about that for a few seconds. What I did say to you a few months ago is that we had spent last year moving away from any reliance on the unsecured markets into secured facilities, using our collateral to borrow against, and we finished the year and we reported that we had $17 billion in cash sitting at the parent company as a liquidity cushion. As the year has gone on, since year-end, that liquidity cushion has virtually been unchanged. So we still have many, many billions— $17 billion or so—in excess cash sitting on the balance sheet of the holding company as a liquidity cushion. That's in addition to billions of dollars of cash and unpledged collateral that are at our subsidiaries. So we don't see any pressure on our liquidity, let alone a liquidity crisis." Schwartz made no mention of the fact that Bear's hedge fund clients had started to ask for their free-cash balances back and that fulfilling that obligation had begun to drain Bear's cash reserves.

The two men then had a conversation about the outlook for Bear Stearns's first-quarter 2008 performance—the earnings announcement that had been scheduled for March 20—and Faber asked Schwartz if he thought the Fed's action the day before would relieve the crisis. "I think there is still going to be a bunch of volatility," he said. "I think the Fed's moves—as opposed to any one of them making the situation that much better—I think it shows that they are really on top of the situation. They understand that it's not just the level of interest rates but the technicals of the market that have been very difficult, and I think they're looking at a variety of ways to make sure that liquidity is available to all of us as dealers to be able to finance appropriately our customer activities. I think we'll continue to do that and I think the situation with time will stabilize." Certainly that is what the Bear Stearns executives hoped would happen. "I think everybody hoped that things would subside" after Schwartz appeared on CNBC, explained Robert Upton.

But Schwartz's comments did not calm anyone down. "Mr. Schwartz's delivery made some experts wince," *Wall Street Journal* columnist George Anders wrote. "He gazed upward before speaking. He pinched his lips tightly after several answers." Anders then quoted a communications coach who said, "Such grimaces made Mr. Schwartz look uncomfortable."

His own partners noticed, too. "Everybody on the trading floor, we must have had ten TV screens, they were all turned on," Friedman recalled. "Business came to a grinding halt while everybody watched it. . . . Then Alan finished and there was this 'Oh. Back to work.' The hope was he was going to announce the earnings. He didn't. He gave that lame 'It's well within the range of estimates,' or whatever it was. That didn't help. It was a nothing. It was terrible. It certainly didn't stop phone calls [from] people wanting to take cash out."

Added a senior investment banker at the firm: "Alan is usually a very effective guy, but how bad was he on Wednesday morning? He was awful on TV. He looked like he was warmed-over death on Wednesday morning. That didn't provide any comfort to anyone. . . . The fact that he was where he was and that he wasn't here, that was bad enough. But he showed just terribly."

What Schwartz may not have realized—or more likely was in no position to admit publicly—was that there were powerful forces aligned against Bear Stearns at that very moment, ones that stood to benefit from the firm's failure to "stabilize": short sellers, buyers of put options and credit default swaps, and competitors who hoped to scoop up some of the $9.2 billion in net revenue Bear took in during 2006. By March 12, billions of dollars had been invested on this dour bet. Others—such as journalists and research analysts—also stood to benefit from enhanced reputations if they could cut through the rumor and innuendo and be able to quickly and definitively predict for their readers or clients that Bear's demise was imminent.

Roddy Boyd, at *Fortune,* knew in his gut that the firm was in serious trouble but was also acutely aware of his responsibility as a journalist not to fan the flames with his reporting. His March 6 call with Marano left him infinitely more curious but seriously worried. "I was thinking, 'I'm going to poke around in this more,'" he said, "but then I was thinking, 'This is strange.' This is like a situation where you can abuse your position as a reporter. When you're at *Fortune,* you have to do stuff right. When you're at the *New York Post,* you have to be there first and fastest. At *Fortune,* you write the first draft of history, and you have to get it right and you have to be consistently right. I'm thinking, 'I don't really want to screw with this company'—I don't want to spread rumors. I don't want to become part of the story. I don't want to hurt people unnecessarily. I'm an aggressive guy and I'll pick fights with anyone or anything, but there's a right way of doing my job and there's a wrong way. I weighed my duty as an employee here versus the right thing to do."

He decided to lie a bit low and went off on a long-delayed vacation. "One of the media's major problems in this is that you lose track of forests and woods, and if the swap spread is doing this"—widening out—"that means what exactly? Just because X exists does not logically mandate Y occurring, let alone Z. So I said to myself, 'Okay, I am going to'—and discretion here is going to be the better part of valor for me—'I'm going to sit back and watch this,' and a couple things [could] happen. One is that nothing is going to happen. Yeah, whatever. He's just hearing some BS. It all works out, and in the morning it's all good. Life is okay. The second situation, which is more gripping, is there's going to be trouble in the repurchase market for them. So I did my best to quietly monitor that. I had some sources there, and they had heard roughly similar stuff. But they weren't being told by their credit officers, nor were they themselves demanding more money or more collateral from Bear

Stearns to put on repurchase agreements. But everybody's hearing the same stuff. That's sort of more confirmation bias to me—and this is a problem for reporters—that you hear the same thing from five or six people you respect at the same time, so you know something's happening but you can't prove a damn thing. You can't prove it's happening. You're just aware of a current of thought. I called up repurchase desks and they're like, 'Yeah, look what's going on. Bear Stearns, the swaps are getting killed. The stock is getting killed. We're hearing the same stuff. I have a billion with them right now, overnight. And it's clearing. We're not asking for anything special. We've had the same trade on.' Same old, same old."

Like Boyd, Meredith Whitney, a well-respected thirty-eight-year-old research analyst at Oppenheimer who covered a number of Wall Street brokerages and banks, was also trying to comprehend what she was hearing about Bear Stearns that week. Whitney had become very well known around Wall Street during the fall of 2007 when she alone predicted that problems at Citigroup were worse than everyone thought, and she was right. On Saturday, March 8, Whitney was getting her hair colored at the fashionable Pierre Michel Salon on East 57th Street when she received a phone call telling her that Marcel Ospel, of UBS, was in New York trying to sell PaineWebber for around $9 billion to JPMorgan as a way to raise badly needed capital. Since Whitney knew that Ospel rarely left Zurich, hearing that he was in New York on a mission—which proved impossible—sent her scurrying on Monday morning to the investor relations department at JPMorgan. She concluded quickly that while JPMorgan would have liked to own PaineWebber and was one of the few banks around that appeared to be weathering the financial storm and thus would have been a serious potential buyer, even JPMorgan could not afford to pay the $9 billion all-cash purchase price that Ospel wanted.

When she finished speaking with JPMorgan, Whitney headed from her office on 42nd and Madison to have sushi for lunch at Nobu 57, on West 57th. On the way, she began hearing rumors about Bear Stearns's and Lehman's solvency. She called people she knew at several of their competitors and discovered that these traders were very worried about having Bear Stearns as a counterparty on their trades. That night, she flew to London. By the time New York opened for business she had already had a meeting with an institutional client and had heard the news about the Fed making available its unprecedented lending facility to investment banks. Although she was a little concerned about the lack of specifics in the Fed's announcement, "My first reaction was, 'Oh, this is going to be completely fine.'"

But as the details emerged, she learned that the funds would not be available until March 27. She also learned that the supposed beneficiaries of the Fed's largesse were basically indifferent to it because access to the funds was weeks off. Whitney thought, "What the fuck is going on? This doesn't make any real sense. By Wednesday, I'm seeing accounts all day and a client calls me and I was like, 'This is an orderly unwind, I just feel it. I just absolutely feel it.'" She worried that, given the increasing lack of liquidity in the overall financial system, "if the counterparties are an issue, meaning 'I don't trust you and you don't trust me,' and there's no liquidity in the system and we're already careening towards a pretty significant recession, if this happens, then we go into a depression."

She called back the traders she'd spoken to on Monday—the ones who'd voiced serious concern that day about having Bear Stearns as a counterparty—but now they clammed up and acted as though there was no problem at all. "When the brokers were saying, 'Yeah, of course, we're still trading,' I'm like, 'Fucking liars.' When people outright lie to you that you deal with all the time, then you know there's serious panic there." She fired off an e-mail. "Bear's the next Drexel, isn't it?" she wrote to one of her sources. She concluded: "It's possible. Unfathomable. But possible."

Whitney is perhaps one of Wall Street's most pessimistic research analysts, and she began to look at what was happening to Bear Stearns through that lens. She knew that many of Bear Stearns's businesses were contracting, and she knew that Goldman Sachs, Morgan Stanley, and Lehman Brothers had been telling her they had been taking market share from Bear Stearns's prime brokerage business as hedge funds withdrew their cash. "This is it—Bear's out," she thought. "Because all of Bear's businesses are in runoff. So if people start pulling assets, they can't cover their debt service. Then they have debt covenant violations. And then it's over . . . it was so outside of the realm of possibility because it was too simple." Like Boyd, she knew what was happening, but after the firestorm she'd started with her Citigroup research the previous fall, she did not publish a report at that moment.

"By Thursday I knew it clear as day," she said. "This has happened to me several times in the last year where I know things in my gut. But I can't believe I'm the only person who is putting it together." She called a friend of hers, a Wall Street historian, and said, "This is insolvency, I know it. I know it. I know it clearly." But he dismissed her concerns, which gave her pause. "You're paranoid that you're going to do something that's going to jeopardize your investors' money," she said. "And that's what you're paid for. That's your responsibility." Given what had happened with her call on Citi, she decided not to publish her report. "It was a conscious choice not to write anything," she explained. "Because I thought it was such a tenuous situation that I was going to get in serious trouble. . . . I thought Bear failing was such a massive deal and the orderly unwind was more important than a disorderly" unwind that a published report from her might have caused.

⁂

AT BEAR STEARNS, meantime, the senior management of the firm had failed to explain to its workforce internally at any point during the week what precisely was going on or what they should say to their customers and clients. Ace Greenberg's comments to CNBC on Monday that the liquidity concerns were "ridiculous" had left people baffled. "Why is he speaking for the firm, for starters?" asked one banker. Then came Molinaro's comments to Charlie Gasparino on Tuesday and Schwartz's on Wednesday. All were flat-out denials of a problem. But there was no internal communication. "Alan, or whomever, just sort of sitting down with the rest of the guys and saying, 'Okay, these rumors are out there, these are true, these aren't true, and here's what we're doing' would have been nice," said one senior Bear banker. "You've got a multi-hundred-person sales force out there getting phone calls saying, 'I've heard this is happening and this is happening,' and then you're guessing or not knowing how to respond. Because they didn't. I had guys at Blackstone calling me saying, 'I heard you guys DK'd on a trade, is it true?' And you either lie and say no, though that was true, or 'I don't know,' which is a horrific answer, right? No communication. None. And the communication that was provided externally was poor at best. It was really amateur hour in a big way. It was really sad in hindsight."

While Schwartz was flying back to New York from Palm Beach on Wednesday afternoon after the end of the media conference, Molinaro and Upton, respectively Bear's CFO and treasurer, were meeting for several hours with representatives of Moody's, the credit rating agency, to give them an update on the firm's prospects. "We're talking about our commercial mortgage book," Upton said, "what it looks like for the quarter, what we think the P&L's going to be, and the status of funding and liquidity. Nothing formally prepared, just brief discussions around equity repo, fixed-income repo, commercial paper, bank funding, some of the things that were still hanging in."

Rumors were now rife about how other Wall Street firms' clients had asked them to act as a counterparty to Bear, taking the clients out of the transaction, and that some of these competitors had refused to face off against Bear Stearns for their clients. Then there was that same persistent rumor about Goldman Sachs telling its hedge fund clients it would not act as a counterparty to Bear. Some traders of credit default swaps and other derivative securities at Deutsche Bank were charging higher prices when Bear was the counterparty and were also charging bigger fees to their hedge fund clients who wanted the bank to take their positions as a counterparty to Bear. Margin calls to the firm were also increasing. On Wednesday afternoon, Bear's repo desk had already heard that $20 billion of the daily $75 billion needed to finance the business was not going to be there for it on Thursday morning. "By Wednesday, the cushion was basically gone," Friedman said. "We were back to 'Hope is our strategy. Let's hope it doesn't get any worse.'" Friedman began talking with Upton about using some of Bear's $18 billion in cash to make up for the lack of funding in the repo market. "How much money can you lend us if we need it?" Friedman asked Upton that afternoon. "Because Alan's speech didn't help. The Wednesday afternoon list for Thursday was really horrible."

Bear Stearns then found that it could not replace an untapped $4 billion credit facility with a group of banks that was set to expire in April; it turned out the line had actually expired in February and had been replaced by one for $2.8 billion. Bear was waiting until the release of its quarterly earnings on March 20 to make this information public. "It was a line that we never really believed could ever be used," Friedman said. "The joke was that it was appropriately named a 'revolver,' because the only way it would ever get used is if you'd take it and put it as a gun to the heads of the banks and say, 'Listen, lend me more on a secured basis, or I'm drawing down this $4 billion on an unsecured basis.' The theory was—there were so many theories that seemed good at the time—the theory was if you could give them enough collateral, the banks would lend you almost unlimited amounts of money to keep you from drawing down the revolver." Bear had been paying fees on the revolver for ten years without ever using it. The idea was to restructure it to make it more likely it could be used if needed. "We were going to structure it that we were going to draw it down from time to time," Friedman continued, "and not have the signaling risk we were always afraid of, that everybody knows if you draw down your revolver you're dead. So yeah, the revolver was going to be smaller. It didn't seem like a big deal."

Five minutes after Molinaro and Upton's meeting with Moody's ended, Molinaro called Upton and told him to "get Paul" and together come and see him immediately in his office. "I talked to Paul Friedman," Upton said, "and Friedman said, 'It's a fucking bloodbath at the repo desk. Everyone's calling and stepping away.' It felt like more free credit money had gone out that day, too." They decided there needed to be an all-hands-on-deck meeting around 5:15 that afternoon, including Schwartz, who had just returned from Palm Beach. "We went through what the cash flow was," Upton said. "What had happened was we had gone from $18 billion-ish down to where we were at that time, to substantially south of $18 billion." Upton pulled out a sheet of paper that had a list of about $15 billion worth of securities that Bear Stearns owned on its balance sheet that could be sold relatively quickly to generate some much-needed cash. For the previous nine months he had been unsuccessfully "pounding the table" that the firm should sell these assets, shrink the balance sheet, and generate cash. "Okay, the mortgages weren't going to be liquid, fine," he recalled saying about his list. "But let's sell the assets that were liquid and start raising cash and shrinking our balance sheet and putting ourselves in a more fortress-like position to weather the coming storm. There was a whole list of $15 billion worth of assets that we had put together at different times over the course of the previous three quarters that we thought we could sell. We thought we should sell some mortgages, do what we can to sell some. Don't just hold on to them and try to hedge them and hope that they come back. Just sell them and take your losses and live to play another day."

After Friedman finished with the crushing report on the repo financing, Upton followed with one about the cash fleeing from the prime brokerage accounts and about how tenuous the overall cash position of the firm was. Then he suggested selling assets, fast. After some debate, Upton recalled, "finally Schwartz, who now has the big testicles, says, 'Well, I don't think we can do that. It's signaling risk. We can't signal the market, we can't just start selling assets wholesale, it's too much signaling.' Signaling was not an issue, should not have been an issue. Anyone who wasn't aware that there was the possibility that we had a problem was living in a cave and wasn't lending us money anyway."

Although Upton was overruled on the idea of selling assets to raise cash, the group did agree that afternoon to resolve Bear's disputes with its repo dealers over putting up more margin by agreeing to send them $1.5 billion in cash. "But the more pressing issues," Upton said, "about selling assets, raising cash, raising liquidity, and any other constructive action we could take, was indicative of the previous nine months' paralysis. We got nothing. . . . I mean, everybody would have their own little fucking reason that was very silo-centric but didn't look at the good of the bigger firm."

By Wednesday night, the Bear executives were increasingly concerned about their predicament. "During the course of that day," the firm later admitted in an SEC filing in May 2008, ". . . an increased volume of customers expressed a desire to withdraw funds from, and certain counterparties expressed increased concern regarding their ordinary course exposure to, Bear Stearns, causing senior management of Bear Stearns to become concerned that if these circumstances accelerated Bear Stearns' liquidity could be negatively affected." In other words, all the rumors were true. Now, on Wednesday night, the firm's management was worried about what effect they could have on the firm's business. As the repo desk confirmed through the course of Wednesday afternoon that the funding the next morning would be light, calls started going out to both the SEC and the New York Federal Reserve Bank to give them a sense of the deteriorating situation. Recalled Friedman: "The message was, 'We're still alive. We're getting a little close to the edge, but we're still okay.' I didn't think so, but that was the speech we gave the SEC, that was the speech we gave the Fed. . . . I thought it was already pretty much over." Repo money was disappearing and customers were sending their equity positions elsewhere, "which created some funding problems because you had longs and shorts of customers. Firm positions funded each other and you have pieces going away, and we're running out of cash."

In late 2007, Bear Stearns had hired Gary Parr, the highly regarded Lazard financial institutions banker, to help the firm explore potential joint ventures or other strategic combinations. Parr had had a small role in helping Bear Stearns's management evaluate the possible merger of Bear with Fortress Investment Group, a ten-year-old Manhattan-based hedge fund and private equity management company with $34 billion in assets. Wesley Edens, Fortress's CEO, was close to many Bear executives. The potential merger, which would have given Bear's shareholders two-thirds of the combined company's ownership, had been discussed in earnest from September to December 2007. Ultimately, Schwartz vetoed the deal after he became CEO in January 2008. Nothing came of the Fortress idea or any of Parr's other efforts, although not from a lack of trying.

After the hair-raising discussion about the firm's cash position in Molinaro's conference room late Wednesday afternoon, Schwartz and Molinaro discussed the firm's predicament with Parr and H. Rodgin "Rog" Cohen, the senior partner of the Wall Street law firm Sullivan & Cromwell and an expert in deals involving financial firms. Cohen was at his home in Irvington, New York, on the Hudson River north of Manhattan. Parr had been in Brooklyn watching Patrick Stewart in *Macbeth* at the Brooklyn Academy of Music—he has a passion for Shakespeare—but he hailed a cab for Manhattan at the play's intermission. Schwartz told his advisors he was concerned that hedge funds would continue to withdraw their money from the firm. They batted around different ideas about what could be done to help Bear Stearns, including considering whether private equity firms or commercial banks might be able to put together a solution quickly. But soon enough they concluded there was just one answer. "The only people who can do anything about this are the Fed," Cohen recalled saying to Schwartz and Molinaro. "So that's when I did call Tim Geithner about it very late at night." Cohen urged the president of the New York Federal Reserve Bank to speed up the timing of the loan program announced the day before, rather than waiting until March 27. He also urged the Fed president to consider opening the so-called Fed discount window so that the Fed could lend money to investment banks directly, as it did already for commercial banks, which of course are more closely regulated as a result. "I think I've been around long enough to sense a very serious problem, and this seems like one," Cohen told him. Geithner's response was, "If it's this serious, Alan should pick up the phone and call me first thing in the morning."

As instructed, Schwartz called Geithner the next morning. Schwartz was focused and calm, but also very worried about the firm's future. The *Wall Street Journal* had reported that morning that Bear's counterparties were increasingly cautious about dealing with the firm. The two men talked through Bear's options and specifically who could be found quickly to either finance the firm with longer-term capital or buy it outright. On Schwartz's behalf, Parr began making calls Thursday morning to see if he could determine who might be interested and able to help Bear Stearns grapple with its emergency. Among those Parr contacted on Thursday morning were JPMorgan and Barclays. Barclays did not really show much interest; JPMorgan's reaction was that they'd think about it, but they didn't really engage over the course of the day, either.

Ironically, on the same morning that the crisis inside Bear Stearns was intensifying, Henry M. Paulson, Jr., the U.S. Treasury secretary and the former CEO of Goldman Sachs, issued the findings of the President's Working Group on Financial Markets on the "developing financial market turmoil," as Paulson called it. As the depth of the credit crisis began revealing itself during the previous summer, President George W. Bush had asked Paulson and the working group to review the underlying causes of the problem and to recommend remedies. In many ways, the report echoed many of the points Geithner made in his March 6 speech at the Council on Foreign Relations. "Our objectives—which we believe these recommendations will achieve—are improved transparency and disclosure, better risk awareness and management, and stronger oversight," Paulson wrote in his cover letter to Bush. "Collectively, these recommendations will mitigate systemic risk, help restore investor confidence, and facilitate economic growth." He also added presciently, "Obviously, market turmoil is still playing out, and all market participants and policy makers are deeply engaged in addressing the current situation. We must implement these recommendations with an eye toward not creating a burden that exacerbates today's market stresses."

At the start of the day on March 13, Bear Stearns had about $18 billion of unencumbered cash—"liquidity resources," as another Bear insider described it—on its balance sheet, roughly the same amount that it had had at the end of its first quarter of the fiscal year. Bear's repo desk was worried about whether its traditional group of overnight lenders would show up, and Schwartz hoped that $18 billion would be enough of a cushion should the firm's hedge fund clients continue their demands to get their cash out of the firm.

Like the skilled mergers-and-acquisitions (M&A) banker he was, Schwartz was careful not to let most of the Bear Stearns executives know how concerned he had become. Only a very few were aware that Cohen had called Geithner the night before or that Schwartz had called Geithner that morning. This came as a shock to even the firm's most senior executives when they learned of it, especially since in public Schwartz was making every effort to play down his concerns and reassure the troops. At noon on Thursday, Schwartz presided over a lunch of grilled chicken and sandwiches for the firm's President's Advisory Council (PAC), a group of Bear's top fifty or so professionals. (The group kept growing in size because, in typical Bear fashion, people would be added over time but nobody would be told they were no longer important enough to be part of it.) "At that lunch, Alan said everything was fine," recalled one PAC member who was there. "Is he going to lie to us and say that he couldn't conceive of a scenario where it wouldn't be fine? No. But you know, he wanted us to get back to our business with our clients."

Another senior managing director at the PAC lunch had received an e-mail from a colleague in Saudi Arabia that morning with the news that the Saudis were willing to invest immediately in Bear Stearns. The gist of the e-mail was, "They want to give us a significant amount. We can set it up. They want to do it now. They can act quickly." The banker sent the message on to Schwartz but got no real response other than being told to speak to Steve Begleiter, the head of corporate strategy. Begleiter was understandably preoccupied and did little to advance the Saudi idea when it was presented that morning. "Then I decided to physically go up to Alan" at the PAC luncheon, the banker remembered, "and after the lunch, where he says, 'Everything's fine. Don't worry,' I said, 'Alan, I just want you to know, the Saudis want to give us money.' He said, 'We don't need capital.'" The banker believed it would have been a good move to announce that afternoon that the Saudis were willing to put money into Bear. "But there was just this feeling of we didn't need to do it."

Although Schwartz did his best to reassure his elite troops, the lunch ended in a bit of a chaotic fashion, with Schwartz receiving increasingly alarming e-mail messages on his BlackBerry, as did the firm's other top executives. "Everybody went back to their work," Fares Noujaim, a Bear vice chairman, recalled. "At the end of that meeting, Mike Minikes, who ran the clearance business, was getting e-mail messages saying there were issues. So when we disbanded, we weren't sure what those issues were. He was clearly getting messages that there were accounts that were beginning to withdraw their money, and then the meeting disbanded."

Another banker at the meeting remembered seeing Minikes afterward, too. "Minikes was going crazy because he's looking at his BlackBerry, seeing the clearing accounts, just like pull, pull, pull, pull, pull. He said, 'Alan, we've got to do something.'" Word spread quickly that hedge fund giant D. E. Shaw & Co. had pulled $5 billion of its cash and that Renaissance Technologies, the giant hedge fund run by James Simons, was following suit. In the previous two months, S3 Partners, headed by Robert Sloan, had moved $25 billion out of Bear's prime brokerage. The $18 billion in cash was leaving the building, and fast. "You had Mike Minikes interrupt Schwartz and say, 'Do you have any idea what's going on? We're watching our entire franchise walk out the door. All our customers are pulling their money,'" recalled Friedman. "I've known Mike since the day I joined the firm, and he is one of my favorite people there—the greatest rah-rah company guy you'll ever meet. Terrific with customers. Always, sometimes painfully, upbeat and optimistic about things. For him to crack—and there was a crack in his voice and he was the color of that napkin—was really startling to me and to a lot of people, [who thought], 'Well, if Mike thinks it's game over, we've really got issues.' The meeting sort of dribbled to a close not long after that. I think that was the first [moment] that people really started to get the sense that it was over. That anybody was then surprised that we ran out of cash that night is still a mystery to me."

As the lunch was winding down, around a quarter after one, David Schoenthal, the head of the foreign exchange desk, e-mailed Friedman with a comment about what they'd just heard: "Not a great voice of confidence."

Friedman replied a few minutes later: "Nope. Not that much to say." After Minikes's comments about clients pulling cash from the firm, Friedman e-mailed David Rawlings, the head of client relationship management: "Wow, that was a startling thing to say in a room full of people."

Rawlings answered, "He's right."

"One of the things we were trying to do," Schwartz explained later, "was get facts out that discounted the rumors that were out there. The minute we got a fact out, more rumors started that were a different set of rumors. So you could never get facts out as fast as the rumors. I would just say that, as an observer of the markets, it looked like more than just fear. It looked like there were people that wanted to induce a panic." But a longtime major client of Bear Stearns said he found it appalling that Schwartz chose not to deliver the truth to his most senior partners. "If this is your top thirty or so guys and there is a fucking crisis going on, you can't lie to your own people! It's fucking surreal."

CHAPTER 4

THE RUN ON THE BANK

Neither Sam Molinaro nor Robert Upton went to the PAC lunch on Thursday. They were too busy trying to figure out whether the firm's repo lenders would roll the next day. They also had a scheduled meeting with senior executives from the Bank of New York, which was a lender to Bear Stearns, to discuss the overall relationship between the two firms. After that meeting, which ended around three o'clock, Upton went back with Molinaro to Molinaro's office. When they got there, Molinaro found a message from David Solomon, the co-head of investment banking at Goldman Sachs and a former senior managing director at Bear Stearns, wanting to know if there was anything he or Goldman could do to help. If Goldman was calling to be "helpful," Molinaro and Upton thought, that meant everyone on Wall Street knew that Bear Stearns was in serious trouble. "So that's taps," Upton said. "That's the trumpet playing because all that means is they want to come in and see our positions so they can trade against us and make money. Sam said, 'Bob, we're tapioca'—meaning we're done. He and I had been working like fucking crazy for nine months [to prevent just that sort of crisis]. . . . I believed right up until then. Everyone was squeezing our nuts, we were running out of cash, and customer money was flying out the door."

Solomon had called Molinaro at the request of David Viniar, the Goldman CFO, because Viniar thought that Solomon, as the most senior Goldman banker who had also worked at Bear Stearns, could get through to Molinaro. Solomon had also placed a call to Alan Schwartz, but only Molinaro phoned him back. "I said, 'I'm really sorry that you're going through this,'" Solomon recalled telling Molinaro. "'I'm calling on behalf of the firm. David Viniar didn't know you, so he wanted me to call. If there's anything we can do, if there are any positions you want us to look at, if there's anything we can do to help, we want to be as helpful and supportive as possible. That is a message from the senior leadership of the firm.' Sam said, 'Thank you, I really appreciate it. We're working through it.'"

From Upton's perspective as the treasurer of the firm, from that moment on everything else was "wholly irrelevant." He grabbed a cigar and went outside and had a smoke. "I was fucking mortified," he said. Upton, who described himself as "a dirt farmer from New Mexico," had had the single ambition of becoming the treasurer of a major Wall Street firm. He had achieved that goal in April 2006 after years of working for a variety of firms, including Fidelity Investments, the huge money manager, and Fitch, one of the second tier of ratings firms. Now, on Thursday afternoon, his dream lay before him in tatters. "When this thing was over, I was just shell-shocked," he said. "It just crushed me. . . . I tried to pull my shit together, but it just didn't feel the same. I called Martha"—his wife—"and I said, 'It's done,' and I closed my door and I cried." At one point, Begleiter came into his office and asked if he was all right. He yelled at Begleiter, "'Well, no, I'm not fucking all right, you asshole! What kind of stupid question is that?' I was just livid because I had been fighting so hard all the silo mentality and the inability to spend money to get systems right and to clean up the shit show that had been built over the years that I always felt was a contributing factor to our downfall. But at the end of the day, it was a crisis of confidence."

A Bear senior managing director went to see Schwartz that afternoon and told him he had started getting calls from his hedge fund clients who were telling him that both Goldman Sachs and Deutsche Bank had stopped accepting Bear Stearns as a counterparty on trades. "I had two hedge funds call me and say, 'The run on the bank is happening. We think that there is collusion,'" he said. "They said, 'Ever since the beginning of the week, Goldman and

Deutsche have been relentlessly calling us. Goldman has been telling us they're going to stop accepting Bear as a counterparty credit.' Well, once that happens, it's game, set, match." He believed that Lloyd Blankfein, Goldman's CEO, was "playing" Alan Schwartz. "I think Schwartz is convinced Lloyd wasn't involved in anything," he said. "I'm amazed, and I think the SEC is going to continue to investigate this. For a major securities firm to start calling people and saying, 'We're about to dust another major securities firm's position as a counterparty,' when it's Goldman, I mean, you're basically precipitating a run on the bank. How are you not? What hedge fund prime brokerage client in the world is going to take a chance when it costs nothing to remove their cash balances?" (For his part, Cohn, at Goldman Sachs, said that Goldman tried everything it could to help Bear Stearns improve the look of its house. "I don't even know how to react," he said of the conspiracy suggestion, "any other way but to say it's preposterous and laughable to say that we're involved in a conspiracy theory with certain select groups of clients to try and take down a firm on Wall Street that we actively did business with every day of the week, that we had huge exposures to every day of the week, that we were simultaneously, we thought, trying to be very supportive of in Congress, at Treasury, at the Fed, where we're having active conversations with the company itself, trying to be helpful.")

To drive home his growing concern, the senior managing director put Schwartz on the phone with James Chanos, the legendary short seller and founder of Kynikos Associates. Schwartz asked Chanos, a longtime Bear client who was then short Bear Stearns stock, if he would agree to appear on CNBC and explain that the firm was fine. "Is it?" Chanos asked Schwartz. Schwartz responded that the firm was poised to announce positive first-quarter earnings. But Chanos declined Schwartz's request. "They were the ones trafficking in false information," Chanos told the *Times* four months later.

Tom Flexner, another vice chairman of the firm and a longtime real estate investment banker, said his boss remained calm throughout the afternoon. "I think he was a little numb," he said. "He just seemed a little bit shell-shocked. You could see that he had a huge amount on his mind. He was dealing with some very difficult issues, and you could just see that. But he does not become emotive."

After the call with Chanos, Schwartz went off to a series of internal meetings in order to monitor the rapidly depleting funds and to analyze the firm's options. "Over the course of the day," the firm later explained in a May 2008 SEC filing, "and at an increasing rate in the afternoon, an unusual number of customers withdrew funds from Bear Stearns and a significant number of counterparties and lenders were unwilling to make secured funding available to Bear Stearns on customary terms, which resulted in a sharp deterioration in Bear Stearns' liquidity position."

Also at 4 P.M., the SEC, which had been monitoring the firm during the course of the day, had a conference call with Tim Geithner, at the New York Fed. "We had a bunch of conversations with the SEC over the course of the day," Geithner explained. "They were trying to catch up and figure out if things were as bad as they seemed, and Thursday afternoon we had our one call and they said, 'We need to wait till the end-of-the-day numbers and see what our numbers are. We'll call you after the numbers.'" Geithner went home for the day. "I don't want to say we passed the point of no return" that afternoon, he said, "but things were bleeding at such a rate that their options were very limited."

Various constituencies that interacted with Bear Stearns during the normal course of business—hedge funds that would normally have been happy to leave their free credit balances at the firm; counterparties that would normally have been willing to have Bear Stearns on the other side of a trade or a derivative; providers of the firm's overnight financing, either in the repo market or in the commercial paper market; brokerage customers who rarely worried about a thing and were pleased to be clients of Bear Stearns—all more or less simultaneously lost confidence in the firm. A Bear Stearns senior executive described what happened that afternoon as "akin to trying to force an apple through a straw. The straw is not getting any bigger and the apple is not getting any smaller. It was as if someone yelled 'Fire' in a crowded theater and then noticed that there was only one exit door and it was only eight feet wide." All of them wanted their money back and all of them wanted it at the same time.

"I had spent the first part of the week—Monday, Tuesday, [up until] Wednesday noon, almost every waking minute—talking to customers and lenders," Paul Friedman explained. "I had the speech down pretty good. I could take them through our whole liquidity profile. Do the dance around the earnings thing. Take questions. In and out in an hour. Through Wednesday morning, I still felt pretty good that I could conclude with, 'We've still got $18 billion in cash, and yes, we've lost some lenders, but we picked up some new ones. Yes, some customers have taken their money out, but it's not a big deal. Yes, we've got some people who won't take our name in the credit default swaps markets, but it's not a big deal.' By Wednesday, I couldn't do it with a straight face and feel I wasn't breaking the law, and so I had a series of conference calls set up for Wednesday afternoon [and] I just canceled them all. I just said to the salespeople who had set them up, 'I'm really busy. I can't do it,' because I couldn't come up with anything to say. I couldn't tell them the truth, and I couldn't lie to them. It seemed easier just not to deal with that. I spent a lot of time at the repo desk. I spent a lot of time with Bob Upton and Treasury trying to figure out, 'Where do we stand?' I had a lot of meetings to figure out, 'What's our plan?' We're into Plan C at this point. . . . I was not in any of the meetings with JPMorgan or Barclays or whoever else it was that we talked to about trying to do something strategic." Was his role something like keeping a finger in the dike? "Yes, but I was running out of fingers. It was an eerie thing. I gave a presentation to the sales force Tuesday night, basically the same speech. Took them through our balance sheet in liquidity and where we stood, and Tuesday night felt really good that hundreds of people at the firm are listening and I'm telling them the truth—I'm not making this stuff up, I'm not just trying to make them feel better. Twenty-four to thirty-six hours later, I was unable to speak. In terms of how quickly did it happen, and could it possibly happen that quickly, it really did. It really went from Wednesday morning to Thursday afternoon, twenty-four hours from solvent to dead. It seems inconceivable."

Around six on Thursday night the senior Bear Stearns executives gathered in Sam Molinaro's sixth-floor office. In attendance were, among others, Schwartz, Molinaro, Friedman, Begleiter, Upton, and

John Stacconi, the treasurer of the securities company. "We go through the cash position, and there's a lot of questions as to how accurate is it," Friedman explained. "It's hand-scribbled on a piece of legal pad. The firm was not really set up—most firms are not—to do real-time cash accounting. You come in in the morning and you reconcile your bank accounts and you see where you stand, and try to put this all together. To try to do it on the fly in the evening was like scribbles. But the bottom line is $2.5 billion of cash. Over here, I've got this spreadsheet that I got from the repo desk of money they already know that they're losing tomorrow, and that's $14 billion. They know they're going to need at least $1 billion or so that they're going to have to borrow out of the cash reserve. Basically, if nobody else pulls any money, we're down to zero when we open the day. Not a good place to begin. We go round and round, challenging the numbers, but they're pretty accurate. Then we're like, 'Okay, what now?'"

Remembered Begleiter: "We still had cash, but we had items we had to repay in the morning"—for instance, a multibillion-dollar cash repayment to Citigroup. "When the team finished going through everything related to our cash situation, I remember saying, 'Guys, we need advice; it is not clear that we should repay Citi. At some point our responsibilities shift from working for the stockholders to working for the debt holders. It's essentially all the money we have left and we'd have to send it out to just one party first thing in the morning.' Everybody knew this. I was just the first one who said it. Whether we repaid Citi or not, given the other likely cash requests on Friday, it was clear to me that this was the end. We were gone as an independent, viable firm. If you're talking about seminal meetings, that meeting on Thursday at 6 P.M. in Sam's conference room, that's when I realized we were done."

"What are my options?" Molinaro asked Upton. Since the previous Friday, Upton reported to Molinaro, the firm's cash had declined to $5.9 billion, from $18.3 billion, and Bear still owed Citigroup $2.4 billion. "Mr. Molinaro buried his head in his hands, Mr. Schwartz looked ashen and left abruptly," the *Wall Street Journal* reported.

Regulators from both the SEC and the New York Fed began arriving on the sixth floor. They were put in separate conference rooms and told to cool their heels. Molinaro called Vincent Tese, the lead independent director on the Bear Stearns board. He was in Jupiter, Florida, just north of his Palm Beach home, having dinner at Buonasera Ristorante with his fellow director Fred Salerno, a former CFO of Verizon, and their wives. Coincidentally, at the next table was Rocco Marano, an old colleague of Salerno's from New York Telephone who ran Bellcore and was the father of Tommy Marano, the head of Bear Stearns's mortgage desk. "We're sitting next to each other and I introduce Rock to Vince," Salerno recalled, "and we had just finished saying to Rock, Vince had, what a great guy Tommy was, you should be so proud of him and everything. Then boom, boom, boom, and his phone goes off. And we get the bad news." Molinaro told Tese how desperate the situation was. "Nobody expected this to hit the fan that quickly, so we all ran back to our houses and we got on the [board] phone call later that night," Salerno said. "The next day we're on the plane going back."

At 7:30 P.M., Geithner had a conference call with the SEC to talk about how Bear Stearns's predicament had worsened during the course of the day. The SEC had been monitoring Bear Stearns's cash balances through the afternoon, and their early-evening report was not the least bit encouraging. According to the federal agency, Bear's $18 billion cash balance at the start of the day had dwindled to $2 billion at the end of the day (in the vicinity of where Upton had told Molinaro and Schwartz the firm's cash balances were) as hedge fund customers stampeded for the exits. The firm had to use its own cash to make good on their demands since it had—perfectly legally—used its customers' free cash balances to buy assets that were now difficult to sell quickly. The firm had effectively run out of cash on Thursday afternoon. Absent a major shot of capital, there would be no way for the firm to keep up with cash withdrawal demands during the next business day. Bear Stearns's fellow Wall Street firms would no longer take Bear's Treasury securities as collateral for the overnight loans essential to the smooth running of the global capital markets. The confluence of the two events—either one of which on its own likely would have been fatal—proved devastating.

According to Geithner, the seven-thirty call changed the dynamic completely. Without additional financing in the repo markets, Bear Stearns would have to repay billions of dollars in repo borrowings beginning twelve hours later. If the firm could not repay, the lenders could then seize the pledged collateral and begin selling that to get their money back. The repercussions of such an action—which had never happened before—could have plunged the interconnected global economy into uncharted waters, as Bear Stearns had trading positions with some five thousand other firms worldwide. "The SEC gets on the call," Geithner explained, "and says, 'We've looked at the numbers, the end-of-day numbers. Our sense is that [Bear] doesn't have enough resources relative to what's maturing. They believe they have no option but to file for bankruptcy. That's our view too.' . . . We talked for forty-five minutes or so. Then I got everybody back here. We tried to think through what we could do to protect the rest of the system because we didn't really think there was a viable option."

After the SEC call, Schwartz called Geithner. Recalled Geithner: "At that point, I said, 'Alan, you told me in the morning you were talking to a bunch of other people about funding. Where are those conversations?' He said, 'Well, so-and-so said they were interested but haven't gotten back to me.' I said, 'Why don't you call them? Now might be a good time.'"

CHAPTER 5

THE ARMIES OF THE NIGHT

While Geithner headed back into his office to grapple with the emergency, Gary Parr called the cell phone of Jamie Dimon, the chairman and CEO of JPMorgan Chase, to ask if he had a moment to speak with Alan Schwartz. Dimon was having dinner at Avra, a Greek restaurant on East 48th Street, just down the street from his midtown Manhattan office. Dimon was celebrating his fifty-second birthday with his parents and one of his three children. He was in no mood to be disturbed, but he reluctantly agreed, and stepped out on the sidewalk in front of the restaurant. Schwartz told Dimon that Bear Stearns "might not have enough cash to meet obligations coming due the next day," Dimon said later, "and that it needed emergency help." How much money did Schwartz need? "What I remember is something like $30 billion," Dimon said, "to which I said, 'No, we cannot do that.'" Within ten minutes, Dimon had called Paulson, Geithner, and Ben Bernanke. "The real question was what would happen if Bear Stearns went bankrupt," he said.

Dimon quickly realized that the bankruptcy of a securities firm such as Bear Stearns would be a disaster. "Unlike bankruptcy of something like a factory, where you continue to produce and the courts figure out how to split up the debt and equity and who gets what," he said, "[here] you would have had an implosion. People the next day would have grabbed on to hundreds of billions of dollars of collateral that would have been sold on the Street. People would be quitting. Bear Stearns would have no revenues. It would have been an implosion of a financial company, not even like a commercial bank." Dimon, the Fed, and the Treasury all agreed that the best outcome for Bear Stearns was to figure out a way to get the firm to the weekend, when there would be slightly more time to sort things out.

There were at least four principal reasons Schwartz reached out to Dimon that Thursday night. First, Dimon had expressed interest in buying Bear Stearns before. At least once between March 2000, when Dimon became the CEO of Bank One, then the nation's fifth-largest bank, and mid-2004, when he agreed to merge Bank One with JPMorgan Chase (and become its CEO in short order), he had approached Cayne about buying Bear Stearns. At the time, Cayne said, both he and Dimon realized quickly that such a deal would never get done; his concern was that such a deal would have been dilutive to Bank One shareholders and the market would have reacted negatively, all but erasing any premium Bank One would have paid for Bear Stearns shares.

The second reason for the call was that JPMorgan Chase had a number of existing commercial relationships with Bear, including being a counterparty on derivatives contracts, being part of the group of banks that lent money to the firm, and, most important, acting as Bear Stearns's "collateral clearing agent," meaning that JPMorgan had a regular and ongoing sense of the value of the collateral that Bear Stearns used on a daily basis as security for its overnight repo financing. Therefore, Schwartz's thinking went, JPMorgan would know exactly what it was getting as security for a quick loan to Bear or, alternatively, if JPMorgan chose to acquire Bear in its entirety, what it was buying on a granular level.

Third, as the Oppenheimer analyst Meredith Whitney knew all too well when she heard the rumor that UBS was looking to unload PaineWebber and she thought immediately of JPMorgan as the buyer, JPMorgan was the only bank (as opposed to an investment bank) that still had the financial wherewithal and the management credibility this late into the credit crisis of 2007 and 2008 to potentially pull off a deal of this magnitude in the required time frame. The financial industry had become so paralyzed by self-inflicted wounds by March 2008 that the only serious private-market solution to Bear's mounting problems was to fashion some sort of rescue through JPMorgan—and everyone knew it, from the Fed on down. If Dimon, for whatever reason, balked at making the deal, the federal government would have only two choices: let Bear face liquidation and brace for the consequences reverberating across the global financial system, or take full control of the firm itself, much as the British government had done a month earlier when it nationalized Northern Rock, the large British mortgage lender. Neither was a palatable option.

Finally, one of the more compelling reasons for Schwartz's call to Dimon was sheer proximity. JPMorgan's headquarters was literally across 47th Street from Bear Stearns. Even if others had the slightest interest—for instance, Wells Fargo or Bank of America—their corporate brain trusts were in San Francisco and Charlotte, respectively. "We thought Bear Stearns would be talking to other people and the government would be thinking of other solutions," Dimon recalled. "But we said we would do everything we could. One of the reasons we could do it was we had the balance sheet and the capital. But that is not the important thing. The really important thing, and people forget, [is] the human side—you know, this kind of almost brings tears to my eyes. I called up Steve Black and Bill Winters [JPMorgan's co-heads of investment banking], who then called up audit, tax, traders, derivative traders, options, lawyers, real estate people from around the world, called them up, got them out of bed, and they drove back to work. Hundreds of people by Thursday night, through the night. I don't even know the number."

"We called JPMorgan because we knew we needed a large bank to provide us a liquidity line," Molinaro said. "We knew we had a lot of collateral. We felt that we had plenty of equity. We felt the company was sound financially, and we were dealing with a liquidity run on the bank, and we needed somebody to provide liquidity. . . . We thought Jamie was tough and shrewd. We thought that he was entrepreneurial enough and had the capacity to do this, if it made sense." While it was true that Bear Stearns had around $6 billion of untapped credit facilities globally, Molinaro believed they would be insufficient and, if drawn down, likely to cause concern among the bank group. "We felt that to do that in the condition that we were in was going to be to take on a battle with the banks, and we weren't looking to fight with the banks," he said. "We were looking to get them in to work with us. And the decision to go to JPMorgan— given the speed at which [the situation] deteriorated, we didn't have time to go try to put a syndicate together."

Within hours the various armies of the night began descending on 383 Madison Avenue. Lawyers from Cadwalader, Wickersham, & Taft, one of Bear's principal outside law firms, took over much of the sixth floor of the Bear Stearns building, the floor where both Cayne and Molinaro had their offices. Other lawyers from Skadden, Arps and Sullivan & Cromwell also arrived at the firm. One set of lawyers worked on drafting documents for a potential financial rescue involving new third-party investors, assuming any could be found; the other group of lawyers worked on drafting the papers for the bankruptcy of Bear Stearns, both Chapter 11 for the Bear Stearns holding company and those that would lead to the liquidation of Bear Stearns's broker-dealer in accordance with the Securities Investors Protection Act of 1970. "It took about fifteen minutes to decide that a Chapter 11 bankruptcy was not a viable option [for the broker-dealer]," explained Greg Milmoe, a bankruptcy lawyer at Skadden,

Arps. "I was amused at the speculation in the press about how viable the [Chapter 11] bankruptcy option would have been. It was so obvious that the only way you would consider it is if you had no other choice and you wanted to close the doors and turn the lights out." Since the chances of finding a viable third-party financing option looked grim, the bankruptcy options for Bear Stearns quickly started to seem like Bear's only choices. At 8:35 P.M., Bruce Geismar, the firm's head of operations, asked Paul Friedman, "How bad is it?" To which Friedman replied, "Very. End-of-the-world bad." Geismar also wanted to know if the repo lines for the next day had been pulled. Friedman told him that, at the moment, "repo isn't the problem; free credits, CP"—commercial paper—"and bank lines are."

After the calls with the SEC, the Fed, and Jamie Dimon, Molinaro and Schwartz wandered back to Molinaro's sixth-floor conference room to give an update to the non-executive-committee senior management that had been waiting around, wondering what was going on. "Sam had wandered off and Alan had wandered off, and the rest of us are just sitting there going, 'What are we doing?'" Friedman recalled. "A couple hours go by. There was some food somewhere. We had some food. I can't remember if Alan came back, or Sam came back and said, 'Okay, JPMorgan was coming in,' which seemed like good news at long last." Friedman recalled, "Our view was, 'Somebody needs to lend us a lot of money really fast. JPMorgan is coming over. Perfect. JPMorgan is going to lend us a bunch of money.'" But for hours nobody from JPMorgan came into the sixth-floor conference room to discuss the situation. This led Tim Greene, the co-head of the repo desk, to begin strategizing about possible solutions to the growing funding crisis. Just after 9 P.M. he sent an e-mail to Friedman: "Do you guys think it is worth calling the Fed in the morning and see if they will lend to us against whole loans"—large securitized mortgages. "The other alternative may be to ask a bank to go to the [Fed's discount] window with them. That will free up the cash against master note money which Treasury will need tomorrow. I know I'm reaching but I cannot think of another way to free up the unsecured money." Friedman gave Greene a quick update: "Sam [Molinaro] and Alan [Schwartz] just finished an hour with the Fed. They don't plan to lend to us.

We're still strategizing." Greene replied a few minutes later, "Is there a bank we are comfortable asking to go to the window? I can ask Citi in the morning, but I know there was an end-of-the-day problem. We would free up billions of cash if we can get to the window."

At one point, a few people from JPMorgan's treasury department—one from an office in southern New Jersey and another from an office "way out" on Long Island—came around to the conference room, but Friedman began to wonder if any decision makers were intending to show up. Tim Greene, from Bear's repo desk, remained optimistic, though. At 11:17 P.M., he wrote Friedman, "We'll fund as usual tomorrow. Plan on doing more until 6/30 unless market fades on us." A few minutes later, Friedman sounded a note of caution. "Maybe," he wrote. "Discussions with Board and SEC include whether we need to make a statement in the morning." As the hour got later, the intensity of the situation ratcheted up exponentially. "That's why that night became such a crazy night—with JPMorgan there, the discussions with the Fed and the SEC—because we were going to have real problems in the morning," said one senior executive.

Finally, around midnight, Matt Zames, the co-head of global rates and currency trading at JPMorgan, arrived in the conference room. The brusque Zames had been a trader at Long-Term Capital Management when it blew up ten years earlier. The Bear Stearns executives started to run through the situation for Zames. "About ten minutes into it he goes, 'Where's the Fed?'" Friedman said. "We said, 'They're in one of the other conference rooms.' He goes, 'Well, we can't talk about anything until we talk to the Fed. We've got Reg W issues'"—referring to a complicated regulation that limits the transactions between a bank and its affiliates. "Some number of weeks later, he actually apologized to me for being rude at that meeting. I said, 'No, we'd been sitting there for hours. You're the only one who made any sense.' For the group of us to sit in this little conference room all by ourselves made no sense at all, so that was the catalyst for getting serious with the Fed. They had issues of lending to us the amount of money that we needed and that was going to trigger capital issues for them." All the JPMorgan executives left to go find the Fed representatives. "My assumption was that they'd get their head around whether or not they could lend us money against the collateral, and what the haircut would need to be, and that they would go to the Fed to get the financing for that," Molinaro said.

❀

FROM MOLINARO'S SIXTH-FLOOR office conference room, at around 8 P.M., Schwartz convened a telephonic board meeting to provide directors with an update. As it was late, most board members phoned in from home. Molinaro reached Ace Greenberg, to tell him about the impending board meeting, at a restaurant in Manhattan. "'We're going to have a board call at whatever time and we got a problem,'" Molinaro recalled telling him. "He said, 'What's the problem?' I told him what the problem was. I said, 'We're going to have a board call. We've got JPMorgan coming in. You might want to either come here or be on the call.'"

Jimmy Cayne, the board's chairman and the firm's former CEO, phoned into the call late from a Detroit hotel, where he had been playing championship-level bridge at the North American Bridge Championships, just as he did three weeks of every year. Cayne's team—composed of Cayne, longtime partner Michael Seamon, and four professional Italian players, whose services Cayne hires for around $500,000 annually—was out of the major event of the tournament by Wednesday, March 12, but he stuck around Detroit anyway to play in the minor events with Alfredo Versace, his sometime teammate and one of the world's best bridge players. Although incredulous that Cayne did not fly back to New York after losing on Wednesday, one of his former partners did allow that the chance to play with Versace made his absence at least plausible. "It would be like playing the pro-am tournament with Tiger Woods," he said. "I can understand that."

The call to join the board meeting on Thursday night was the first time, Cayne said, that he knew just how difficult things were for the firm of which he had been CEO for fifteen years and remained the chairman of the board of directors. "Thursday night I got a call from Schwartz," he said, "saying it's over. I knew what he was talking about. He said he tried hard as he could. It happened with rumor and innuendo. He also mentioned how and what happened. As far as I'm concerned, I knew the cash position was what it was. I knew that we were highly dependent on overnight repo, except there was no flag. There was no 'We're worried about Dreyfus. We're worrying about Fidelity. We're worrying about people rolling in the overnight repo.' Because this wasn't term repo, it was overnight. This was good collateral, and all of a sudden, poof! You're vulnerable to it being over at any time when you're leveraged. You didn't have a chance. So, that same lesson that we learned today, Long-Term Capital Management had back then [in 1998] and the tulip people had it back in the 1400s." Although he had watched Schwartz on Wednesday morning on CNBC, until Thursday night Cayne, who had spent his last forty years at the company and built it into the fifth-largest securities firm on Wall Street, had no idea what had been transpiring. Nor, for that matter, did any of the board members. Salerno and Tese dialed into the call from their homes in Palm Beach after their aborted dinner. "Everybody was in shock," Salerno said. Schwartz told the board that he and the other senior executives were speaking with the Fed, the Treasury, and JPMorgan to try to fashion an overnight solution to the liquidity crisis.

Schwartz and Molinaro walked the board through Bear Stearns's liquidity position, "including the possibility that Bear Stearns would not be able to meet its liquidity needs the next day" without new funding. The Bear board reluctantly authorized the bankruptcy filing if it proved necessary to go that route and agreed to reconvene in a few hours to get a further update. "Everybody was stunned," Molinaro remembered. But Schwartz held out hope—increasingly slim—that third-party financing could be found.

At one point, after going round and round with the board about the various options, a question arose that Cayne was best able to answer. "They needed Jimmy's opinion on something," Paul Friedman remembered being told by someone there. "They said, 'Jimmy, are you there?' and there was dead silence. They sent someone out to call Pat, his wife, who said, 'No, Jimmy left the call. He's playing bridge.' They sent Pat to go get him, and they dragged him out of the bridge tournament to come vote on, I'm told, whether or not we were declaring bankruptcy Thursday night."

To an outsider, the Bear Stearns board's lack of involvement to this point in the firm's financial meltdown could be interpreted as a near-complete abdication of its fiduciary responsibility to shareholders. There are more than a few financial heavyweights who have just that view. "The Bear Stearns debacle was a corporate governance error of the most profound kind," said Steve Schwarzman, the co-founder of the Blackstone Group. But at the quirky and insular Bear, which continued to operate as a small partnership despite having been a public company since November 1985, the lack of involvement by the board or its chairman, Jimmy Cayne, was not particularly disturbing or unusual for the rank and file. "Jimmy who?" asked Paul Friedman rhetorically. "I guess because I've never worked at a real firm. We used the phrase all the time: 'If only we were a real firm . . .' I guess because I'd never worked at a firm with a real board, it never dawned on me that at some point somebody would have or should have gotten the board involved in all of this, because we didn't have a board. We had this group of cronies and Jimmy. I guess if you had a real board that had real outsiders with real expertise, you would actually get them involved and they might have some role to play, but not here. What would they do? What would the board do? We were living it and we couldn't figure out what to do. What the hell are they going to do? But I can see in the real world that's an odd thing." On the other hand, there was no question that once the board was informed of the dire straits the company found itself in, it sprang into action and did everything it could—however narrowed the choices quickly became—to bring the crisis to the most satisfactory conclusion.

Meanwhile, downtown at 33 Liberty Street, the home of the New York Federal Reserve Bank, Geithner and his team were frantically trying to fashion a solution to Bear's immediate problem and what he feared might lead to a cataclysmic disaster in the financial system. He commandeered a bunch of conference rooms near his office and invited his legal, liquidity, infrastructure, and markets supervision experts to begin thinking through possible solutions.

In Washington, a group of government leaders including no less than Fed Chairman Ben Bernanke, Fed Vice Chairman Donald Kohn, Treasury Secretary Hank Paulson, Treasury Undersecretary

Robert Steel, and SEC Chairman Christopher Cox were all working hard to see if liquidity could be found for Bear Stearns. This financial brain trust knew well that despite the revolutionary steps taken by the Fed earlier in the week to help investment banks trade their illiquid assets for more easily salable Treasury securities, this financing option would not be available for another ten days or so. Commercial banks, of course, could borrow from the Fed's discount window, a privilege of long standing that came with the cost of giving the Fed direct oversight over them and their capital requirements (which were generally quite high as compared to pure investment banks). The SEC, not the Fed, regulated investment banks. As a result, investment banks could not borrow from the Fed's discount window and were permitted much higher levels of leverage on their balance sheets. For instance, the ratio of assets to equity capital in investment banks—one measure of leverage— often approached 50:1 during the middle of a quarter. (Before the ratio was published at the end of each quarter, investment banks would take the necessary steps to sell enough of the assets to get the leverage down to a more "acceptable" 35:1 ratio.) Commercial banks, by contrast, had leverage ratios of around 10:1.

There remained the possibility—and Bernanke, Geithner, and Paulson had been lobbied about it relentlessly—that the Fed could open its discount window to investment banks for the first time since the Great Depression, when a 1932 amendment to the Federal Reserve Act allowed access to the discount window for "individuals, partnerships and corporations in emergency situations." (From 1932 to 1936, twelve banks accessed the "window" for 123 loans totaling $1.5 million. The largest single loan was for $300,000.) Alan Schwartz, for one, had been an outspoken proponent of allowing investment banks access to the discount window. One of the first things he did when he took over from Cayne as CEO in January was to meet with Senator Christopher Dodd, Democrat of Connecticut and the chairman of the Senate Committee on Banking, Housing, and Urban Affairs, and push for access to the window. Dodd had gone so far as to ask Bernanke to extend the privilege to investment banks, but the Fed rebuffed Dodd's request. "It was widely rejected out of hand as something that would just be inadvisable," Dodd said he was told.

Schwartz remained concerned that since the repeal of the Glass-Steagall Act in 1999, allowing commercial banks to once again compete with investment banks without limitations, universal banks such as Citigroup and JPMorgan would have a competitive advantage over firms like Bear Stearns and Lehman Brothers because, with ready access to the Fed's discount window, they knew they always had a lender of last resort to finance their collateral, a luxury investment banks did not have. Schwartz believed this advantage "created a situation that I thought was precarious for the whole financial system." Although Schwartz's concern ignored the benefits that Bear Stearns and other investment banks received gladly from the arrangement—among them much less rigorous regulatory oversight and the ability to leverage their balance sheets with steroid-like effects—his worry was more theoretical than genuine. "I never dreamed it would be as rapid as things happened here, but I always had a concern that the lack of a known liquidity facility for your collateral is something that can cause a problem with the lenders against that collateral," he explained. "All of us, as investment banks, lend against high-quality collateral, and we turn around and use that collateral. We never believed we could rely on unsecured financing. We always felt like we needed a collateral pool. I did worry that there was an environment that could happen if the market couldn't see that we had someplace to go and borrow against that collateral, then the fears could start. I just never, frankly, understood or dreamed that it could happen as rapidly as it did."

Tom Flexner, the Bear vice chairman, was very friendly with Senator Dodd and on several occasions introduced Schwartz to him. Flexner got it in his head in February, about a month before the crisis hit his firm, that the Fed should open the discount window to investment banks and other nonregulated financial entities. He penned a short essay, "Liquidity," and sent it around. "The time has come for the Federal Reserve to take more decisive remedial steps to reverse the seizure in the credit markets and facilitate the flow of liquidity into those market sectors where it will be productively and immediately deployed," Flexner wrote. "Utilizing the emergency lending provisions" under the Federal Reserve Act of 1932 "to extend credit to this wider universe of financial intermediaries—in a manner which does not contemplate a real transfer of the risk of loss to the Fed—will have an immediate restorative impact on the credit markets. It is not a bailout. Bad loans will not be eligible for discounting. Lenders will be stuck with their own losses. But the lubricant that ultimately creates both capacity and confidence— liquidity on commercially reasonable terms—will facilitate the first necessary step in getting the markets to function properly again."

Flexner's plea, while prescient, was met with silence, too. But on the long evening of March 13, the Fed governors and the leaders of the Treasury confronted a situation dire enough for them to consider changing the rules of engagement in a hurry. Geithner prepared for a sleepless night by reserving a room at a nearby hotel. He would eventually enjoy only ninety minutes or so of rest. Others would be less fortunate.

❁

AS OFTEN HAPPENS when the hour gets late enough and people who would normally be asleep find themselves awake and dealing with a situation that requires serious attention, the Bear executives trying to fashion a solution to their firm's crisis began losing focus and entering a netherworld where caffeine no longer has the desired effect. They knew that various parties—JPMorgan, the Fed, the Treasury, and the SEC—were working on something; they just did not know what it was. After Matt Zames, the co-head of global rates and currency at JPMorgan, left the sixth-floor conference room at midnight, they never saw him again. They just sat around, looked at each other, and wondered what they were going to do. Recalling his occasional late-night friendly poker games where the later it got the more poorly he played, Friedman looked at his watch. "It's midnight," he said. "I know what happens at midnight. I lose track of what I'm rooting for. I guess we're waiting. We're going to see what happens. Nobody's going home. None of us could come up with the strategy that worked. Nobody believed JPMorgan was going to lend us $50 billion, or whatever we needed. Nobody knew what the number was, and it wouldn't make any difference."

The bankruptcy lawyers were running around trying to figure out which of Bear's 350 subsidiaries could be part of a holding company Chapter 11 bankruptcy proceeding and which ones needed to be liquidated immediately, depending on the applicable statute. Then they were trying to put together balance sheets so that a proper court filing could be made in the morning. "We were trying to figure out, 'Okay, if we don't come up with a solution, what do we do, and what does it even mean?'" Friedman said. "There were really three choices, none of which seemed remotely possible: One is some magical JPMorgan thing. One was we walk in and we declare bankruptcy, but how? In which entities, in which jurisdictions worldwide, how? Then there was my favorite, which was actually, to coin a phrase from [Bear senior executive] Jeff Mayer, what we were going to call 'pencils down.' The theory was if we could get to the weekend—this was Thursday night—if we can get to the weekend, we've got a lot of time to figure things out. We'll have everybody come in Friday, and just won't let anybody do anything. So traders won't trade because it was a big issue—if you know you're bankrupt, and you go out and you enter into transactions, are you committing fraud? We didn't want to commit fraud. We didn't want our people to commit fraud. Therefore, if we opened for business, no one could be allowed to trade. We would take requests to send out money, but we wouldn't actually do anything. Pencils down. Everybody comes in. Nobody does anything. We were heading towards the place where that was going to be the only solution because there were no other plans. What do we tell people? Do we tell them, 'Don't come in'? What do we tell them when they do come in? How do we communicate, 'We're not bankrupt, but you're not allowed to do any trading'?"

Jeff Mayer, since August 2007 a member of the firm's powerful executive committee and the co-head of the fixed-income division, e-mailed at two in the morning to urge Friedman to call him at home in New Jersey when "you know the outcome." Friedman replied he would but added, "We're a long way from getting anything done." At three in the morning, several other senior Bear executives joined the party, including Elizabeth Ventura, head of media relations; Mike Solender, general counsel; and Ken Kopelman, general counsel of the fixed-income division. There was "lots of talk with lots of lawyers," Friedman said, "but to take this firm and have a rational bankruptcy plan in six hours was insane. On the other hand,

I guess you had to do something." Friedman and the others knew the Bear Stearns board had met but had no idea what it had authorized, if anything. They knew the Fed was meeting with JPMorgan but had no idea what they were considering.

Molinaro and Schwartz had been kept abreast of events periodically through the course of the early-morning hours through the occasional calls from Rodgin Cohen, the Sullivan & Cromwell lawyer. "The Fed, Treasury, everybody was engaged and they were working on it," Molinaro said. "So we thought—and we were being led to believe—something was going to happen." At 2:00 A.M. Geithner called Don Kohn, the vice chairman of the Federal Reserve, and told him he "wasn't confident that the fallout from the bankruptcy of Bear Stearns could be contained." Two hours later, Geithner called Bernanke, "who agreed the Fed should intervene."

At a few minutes before four, Friedman e-mailed his wife. "It's almost 4:00 A.M. and we're still here," he wrote. "There is an outside chance that JPMorgan Chase will bail us out. They have about 3 more hours to decide and I make it less than 50/50 that they will. If they do, we get to announce to the world that they've agreed to backstop us and we live to the weekend, at which point we probably give the firm away to them. Followed by their firing 10,000 people or so. If they say no, we're declaring bankruptcy and I really can't believe we came to this. And that will be worse. But, as you said, we'll be fine. Life will certainly be different but we'll be fine." At 4:24, Friedman sent a note to Jeff Mayer: "It's 4:00 A.M. and no decision. The JP folks took off an hour or so ago and we're sitting here waiting to see. Absolute torture." A few minutes later, Marc Feuer, in Bear's treasury department, wrote Friedman: "Oh, to be back in kindergarten." Friedman replied, "Don't I know it."

AT 5 A.M., FRESH from a short period of sleep, Geithner arranged for a conference call with Bernanke and Paulson to discuss what the consequences would be of the Fed not stepping in to help Bear Stearns in some fashion. Their concern was that the financial system had become increasingly fragile since the previous summer, and Bear Stearns's failure might cause tsunami-like damage if it was not contained. They tried to remain calm. "The Central Bank exists to deal with these things," Geithner explained. "So the people who are good at this and do this stuff here generally, I think if they're good, they get calmer during these things, not any more excitable. But there's no rulebook for these things. By their nature, they're always different. They occur in areas where nobody's got some terrific plan for dealing with them." After about an hour of discussion, and knowing that Bear Stearns had until about eight in the morning to refresh its repo funding for the day, Geithner called the question. "What's it going to be?" he asked. The most powerful men in American finance agreed to provide an unprecedented interim financing solution to JPMorgan, which in turn could provide the financing to Bear Stearns. "The further we got into it, the more we said, 'Oh, my God! We really need to address this problem,'" a Fed official told *The New Yorker*. "People use the term 'too interconnected to fail.' That's not totally accurate but it's close enough." He worried the failure of Bear Stearns "would have caused a run on the entire market. That, in turn, would have made it impossible for other investment banks to fund themselves."

The time had come to let Bear Stearns's management know that a federal rescue was in the offing. "I think somewhere in the early morning, before this thing went official," Molinaro said, "Alan got a call from Paulson. Paulson asked him if he was sure that he wanted to do this. He implied to him that you realize that once you do this, a lot of these decisions are out of your hands. We viewed that to mean once we're borrowing money through JPMorgan [from] the Fed, we know that they're going to be in our shorts. . . . from the standpoint of selling assets, doing whatever we needed to do to raise liquidity, they'd be involved. That's what our expectation was. We didn't think that it meant that they could pull the plug on us Friday night and say enough."

At around 5:30 A.M., on his first all-nighter since college, Friedman walked across Park Avenue to 277 Park, the home of JPMorgan's investment banking division. Friedman's health club was in the building, and he decided to go there and take a shower. He used to belong to the small health club in the Bear Stearns building, but he'd given that up: "It involved spending too much quality time naked with people I worked with." At the health club at 277 Park he ran into a friend who had shown up to get some exercise before work. The friend had, of course, no idea what Friedman was going through. "We had this really weird conversation, because my head was not particularly well held together at that point," he said. He put on a clean pair of underwear and a different necktie, and then all of the same clothes he had been wearing. At 5:53, he e-mailed Greene that he was "still waiting to hear from JPM." He got back to the sixth-floor conference room at 6:15 to find that Ventura had arranged for some Dunkin' Donuts coffee and donuts to be sent up. "We were tanking up to face the new day," Friedman said. He still had not heard anything from anyone at JPMorgan since Zames left the conference room more than six hours earlier.

By the time Friedman returned to the office, the board had already been in another conference call for fifteen minutes. Salerno was surprised to have awakened to the news that nothing had yet been agreed on. "We [said], 'Holy shit, we've got problems, because we're open already in Asia.'" Nobody had any idea what to do, although Schwartz and Molinaro were aware the Fed was meeting and discussing various possibilities. Time was running out, and everyone knew it.

Finally, at 6:56 A.M., Michael Solender, Bear's general counsel, announced that he had just received a BlackBerry message from Stephen Cutler, JPMorgan Chase's general counsel and a former director of enforcement at the SEC, with a copy of a draft press release about the loan facility that JPMorgan, with the Fed's help, had agreed to make available. "Today, JPMorgan Chase & Co. announced that, in conjunction with the Federal Reserve Bank of New York, it has agreed to provide secured funding to Bear Stearns, as necessary, for an initial period of up to 28 days," the draft read. "Through its Discount Window, the FRBNY will provide back-to-back financing to JPMC and has agreed to bear the counterparty, credit and price risk associated with the transaction. Accordingly, JPMC does not believe this transaction exposes its shareholders to any material risk. The Fed has agreed to waive all Section 23A requirements"—restrictions on transactions with affiliates—"otherwise applicable to JPMC in connection with this funding. JPMC is currently exploring with Bear Stearns the possibility of providing more permanent financing or purchasing the company."

After a long, delirious, sleepless night for Schwartz and his top executives, with little or no idea about whether their firm would need to file for bankruptcy or to somehow be able to squeak through another day, Cutler's e-mail message seemed like manna from heaven. The Bear executives were euphoric. "It basically announces what we thought of as the Hail Mary to end all Hail Marys," Friedman recalled. "JPMorgan and the Fed are going to lend us all this money, this up-to-twenty-eight-day thing, and it sounds like this is great. We've got JPMorgan—we've skipped the part about where JPMorgan went from lending to us to where they're now just a conduit and the Fed is lending to us, but it's okay. We're going to get all the money we need. We've got a month to figure out what we want to do next. This was absolutely impossible to dream of. It was the greatest thing that could ever happen. We did high-fives." Added Molinaro: "When we got it, I think the view was very, very excited. We felt that we had accomplished what we set out to accomplish, which was to get a liquidity facility in place so we could weather the storm." Molinaro didn't give a whole lot of thought at that moment to the "up to 28 days" language in the release, figuring that was standard Fed language for most of their facilities. "My assumption was that it was basically a twenty-eight-day repo facility, and that at the end of the twenty-eight days, we'd either better have a deal done or we'd better be in negotiation with them to roll it," he said. "They'd want to see credible progress in either reducing the positions, increasing the liquidity, or getting the company sold in that twenty-eight-day period, and we'd have to deal with them in a very involved way, meaning JPMorgan and the Fed. But we clearly felt that this was a big win." A little after seven-thirty, Friedman e-mailed his wife: "We're alive!"

A few hours later, JPMorgan released the final version of the statement: "Today, JPMorgan Chase & Co. announced that, in conjunction with the Federal Reserve Bank of New York, it has agreed to provide secured funding to Bear Stearns, as necessary, for an initial period of up to 28 days. Through its Discount Window, the Fed will provide non-recourse, back-to-back financing to JPMorgan Chase. Accordingly, JPMorgan Chase does not believe this transaction exposes its shareholders to any material risk. JPMorgan Chase is working closely with Bear Stearns on securing permanent financing or other alternatives for the company." Gone were the explicitly stated ideas that JPMorgan had "agreed to bear the counterparty, credit and price risk associated with the transaction," that the Fed had waived JPMorgan's Section 23A requirements, and that JP-Morgan was considering buying the company. Although Schwartz, a longtime M&A banker, had hoped the language about JPMorgan buying Bear Stearns would be in the final version of the press release, since it would put more pressure on that firm to do a deal for Bear, Schwartz could appreciate JPMorgan's reasoning in taking it out. Why commit yourself to deal publicly if you don't have to?

CHAPTER 6

FEEDING FRENZY

JPMorgan's final publicly released statement was a bit of a Rorschach test, allowing different people to see in it different things. For the Bear executives, the emergency facility looked like an unlimited line of credit from the Fed that would allow them to fund their business for the next four weeks by using the collateral that others in the marketplace were beginning to shun. True, it meant that business as usual would likely be over, but they could use the month to try to fashion a long-term solution: They could now definitively raise badly needed capital, sell a division, or sell the company. They could once again exhale.

At JPMorgan, the facility was an accommodation to the Fed, but since there was no documentation at that early stage about how the loan would work, the devil was in the details. "For JPMorgan it was two things," Dimon explained. "One is that we thought—and I actually spoke to my board about this extensively—about what obligation did we have to do the best we can to help the United States of America. To a person, they thought we had an obligation, that it wasn't simply 'Walk away.' It would have been very easy, by the way, to take that phone call, finish my drink and forget it, okay? Because it was a backbreaking thing to take on. But it also had to make sense for shareholders. So kind of go as far as you can, but it had to make sense for shareholders." After the initial pressure was removed from the situation, it became clear that the terms on which JPMorgan would lend Bear Stearns money would be onerous indeed.

For the Fed, the emergency facility was nothing short of brilliant, allowing the central bank to walk the tightrope it had so carefully constructed during the previous months. The Fed had deliberately not opened its discount window to Bear Stearns or other investment banks—as they had repeatedly hoped—but it did in effect speed up the delivery of the Term Securities Lending Facility it had announced all of three days before. By lending the money to JPMorgan, which in turn could lend it to Bear, the Fed had done something it had not done since the 1930s, signaling the seriousness of the situation generally and at Bear specifically. But the New York Fed made no announcement about the rescue financing itself, adding a measure of ambiguity to the deal that would become apparent to the market almost immediately. (On June 27, the Fed released the minutes of its March 14 deliberations on Bear Stearns's "funding difficulties" and "the likely effects of its bankruptcy on financial markets." The four board members present—the fifth was flying home from Helsinki—agreed unanimously that "given the fragile condition of the financial markets at the time, the prominent position of Bear Stearns in those markets, and the expected contagion that would result from the immediate failure of Bear Stearns, the best alternative was to provide temporary emergency financing" to Bear Stearns through JPMorgan. "Such a loan would facilitate efforts to effect a resolution of the Bear Stearns situation that would be consistent with preserving financial stability." The minutes also make clear that the financing was to be "secured" to the "satisfaction of the New York Fed" for a period not to exceed twenty-eight days and was limited in amount by the collateral that Bear Stearns was willing to post to secure the funding.)

Naturally, the Fed's rescue of Bear Stearns early Friday morning was historic news. The *New York Times* led with the story and highlighted both its rarity and its potentially devastating effects on the firm: "The Fed's intervention highlights the problems regulators face as they contemplate the prospect that investment banks, saddled with toxic securities tied to subprime mortgages, are losing the trust of their lenders and clients—the kiss of death on Wall Street, where confidence has always been the most precious asset of all." The paper then quoted Samuel Hayes, a professor of investment banking at Harvard Business School. "The public has never fully understood how leveraged these institutions are," he said. "But the market makers understand the inherent risk. This is a run on the bank, just like Long-Term Capital Management, Kidder and Drexel Burnham."

On Friday morning, Bear Stearns put out its own announcement that followed the JPMorgan script precisely, though Schwartz added his own clarifications. "Bear Stearns has been the subject of a multitude of market rumors regarding our liquidity," Schwartz explained. "We have tried to confront and dispel these rumors and parse fact from fiction. Nevertheless, amidst this market chatter, our liquidity position in the last 24 hours had significantly deteriorated. We took this important step to restore confidence in us in the marketplace, strengthen our liquidity and allow us to continue normal operations." Or so he hoped. The firm's press release ended with the required but ominous caveat, "The company can make no assurance that any strategic alternatives will be successfully completed."

Whether the ambiguity was by design or occurred simply because time ran out before more precision could be provided, the lack of precision became problematic almost immediately. As the initial euphoria subsided, Friedman went up a floor to the repo desk to tell what seemed to him like good news to his colleagues at the epicenter of the firm's funding mechanics. "Interestingly, not having spent the night with me, they had what turned out to be the right response," he said. "They were horrified. I said, 'Look at this. It's terrific. We've got all the money we need from JPMorgan and the Fed for as long as we need it. It's terrific.' They went, 'Oh, my God. We're out of business.' I said, 'No, this is great! Let me roll back to how the night went, and let me take you all through it and you'll understand. This is great.' They're going, 'No, this is horrible.'" The guys on the repo desk were convinced that the market would take these events to mean that Bear was in worse shape than people had thought. Still, just after 8:00, Tim Greene e-mailed his boss, Paul

Friedman, "We funded 12 of the 14 billion so far" on the repo desk. "You the man!" Friedman responded.

David Faber's reporting on CNBC at 9:15 A.M. about the new financing reflected the confusion. "JPMorgan is basically saying to Bear Stearns, 'We're there for you for twenty-eight days,' and the Fed is saying to JPMorgan, 'We're there for you,'" he said in trying to explain what the possible outcome of the announcement would be. But he wasn't sure, since, understandably, he had not had the chance to speak to anyone about it. "It begs a lot of questions," he continued. "I'm reading the release here for you, so I haven't had an opportunity, as you might expect, to make a lot of phone calls to try to understand this more fully in the sense of what exactly it is that Bear Stearns needed. Is this simply to infuse confidence into the market to essentially say to everyone out there, 'Hey, there is no way we're letting Bear Stearns fail and that nobody should be concerned about doing business with Bear Stearns'? Or was there something in terms of a potential loss? Again, I've got to make calls here."

Dick Bove, the outspoken research analyst at Punk Ziegel and CNBC favorite, phoned in his view to the cable network that the Fed's action was nothing short of "a bailout of Bear Stearns." He opined that the move was "absolutely necessary because Bear Stearns has a balance sheet that is about $400 billion in size and it has about $176 billion worth of securities plus it has $42 billion in loans outstanding to others who own securities. If Bear Stearns had gone under, virtually all of these securities would become available for sale and be pushed into the market"—at prices that would have forced all securities firms to mark their own assets down in what surely might have led to the financial equivalent of mutually assured destruction—"and the result would have been a fairly significant financial collapse. So the Fed had no choice but to bail out Bear Stearns. This is a too-big-to-fail situation."

Inside Bear, the news about the Fed facility was announced around the firm. "We went out and we announced it to the trading floor," Friedman said. "I got high-fives. Oh, man, we were doing a victory lap. One of the salespeople made the comment, 'We're now a sovereign credit. All those people who wouldn't deal with us, we're now a sovereign credit.' That was the line. Oh, man. We thought this was great. Somebody put out on their Bloomberg message, 'We've got money to lend at Libor less 50,' because we got access to all the cheapest money in the world. All we need."

Initially, Bear Stearns stock rallied on the news by about 10 percent, to around $64 a share, but about a half hour later, while everyone was still scrambling to figure out the repercussions of the Fed's move, the stock started to fall. "Initial reaction seemed to be very positive," Molinaro said. "Why it went south I don't know. I can tell you I had analysts calling me on Friday morning. They couldn't figure out why the stock was getting pummeled this way, because they were saying, 'I don't get it. It seems like a good thing. Why is the market reacting like this? It seems like a good thing.'" Friedman added, "You couldn't answer the phone fast enough of people wanting their money out."

Even though there were virtually no details of how the JPMorgan loan would work, the market was quickly forming the view that the very fact that the Fed had had to step in and arrange for this facility meant that the situation at Bear Stearns was tenuous at best. By 10:15, Bear Stearns stock had erased all of its earlier gains and was now trading at around $30 per share, down close to 50 percent. The Federal Reserve Board then put out a statement, which was a paragon of banality: "The Federal Reserve is monitoring market developments closely and will continue to provide liquidity as necessary to promote the orderly functioning of the financial system. The Board voted unanimously to approve the arrangement announced by JPMorgan Chase and Bear Stearns this morning."

A friend of Friedman's from Barclays Capital, Peter Glinert, wrote and asked him how he was holding up. "I was here all night working on this JPM thing," Friedman responded. "Running on fumes right now. Didn't expect this horrible reaction."

His friend wrote back that the "perception is [JPMorgan] are going to cherry pick a few divisions, and let the rest of [Bear Stearns] go under. It seems to me wrong, but [the] market is killing it."

Responded Friedman: "Killing it is an understatement."

"Why JP?" Glinert asked. "Seems to me they are tapping the window for you."

"Had no time," Friedman responded. "Needed someone in NY with lots of money and without their own problems. Pretty much ruled out Citi. Also, JPM had the most exposure to us and the most to lose. Didn't expect them to strongarm the Fed into taking the risk and making it a bailout."

"Someone has to stabilize the stock now or [those actions] will be irrelevant," Glinert observed.

"Agreed," Friedman wrote. "Didn't expect this insane response to it but I guess I should have. But when they write the book on this one I can say, 'I was there.'"

Fifteen minutes later, Schwartz broadcast a video message to the firm's employees telling them he was disappointed in the events of recent days and urging them not to lose faith. Asked by a reporter how he felt, Ace Greenberg said, "I feel fine," but declined to answer more questions.

Coincidentally, at 11:20 A.M., President Bush appeared before the Economic Club of New York to speak about the economy. To laughter, President Bush opened his remarks with the observation, "It seems like I showed up in an interesting moment during an interesting time." His speech focused on whether a recession was looming and the steps the government had taken in trying to avert an economic crisis. He spoke briefly about the efforts by the Federal Reserve during the course of the week to pump additional liquidity into the financial system. "This week the Fed also announced a major move to ease stress in the credit markets by adding liquidity," he said. "It was strong action by the Fed."

The president's speech, while upbeat and not without its touches of humor, did little to assuage the market's concerns about Bear Stearns. That responsibility, as it should, fell to the top Bear executives, Alan Schwartz, the CEO, and Sam Molinaro, the CFO and chief operating officer. A conference call, hastily arranged for 12:30 P.M., was designed "to address speculation in the marketplace." Neither Schwartz nor Molinaro had left the firm's office in the last twenty-four hours.

There is no question that both Schwartz and Molinaro believed that the situation, while still dire, was no longer as cataclysmic as it had seemed just twelve hours earlier. Molinaro began by stating that the firm had decided to push up to Monday the announcement of its first-quarter financial results. Clearly this was an effort to calm the market down and to convey that, as Schwartz had said on Wednesday, he remained "comfortable" with the range of analysts' estimates about the company's performance, all of which projected that the firm would be profitable again.

Schwartz then spoke about Bear's financial hurricane. "As we said in our release, Bear Stearns has been subject to a significant amount of rumor and innuendo over the past week. We attempted to try to provide some facts to the situation, but in the market environment we are in, the rumors intensified, and given the nervousness in the market, a lot of people, it seemed, wanted to act to protect themselves from the possibility of rumors being true and could wait later to see the facts." He noted that while Bear's capital ratios remained in good shape, and the company had started the week with good liquidity, "the concerns on the part of counterparties, on the part of our customers and lenders, got to the point where a lot of people wanted to get cash out. We were responsibly trying to deal with those needs, and we were meeting those needs in every case, but they accelerated yesterday, especially late in the day. As we got through today, we recognized that, at the pace things were going, there could be continued liquidity demands that would outstrip our liquidity resources. In light of that, we felt like we needed to move quickly to allow us time to conduct normal operations and calm things down and allow us time to get some more facts out into the marketplace and have people get a chance to assess them."

The question lingered in the air about whether the firm was simply in the eye of the storm. Schwartz explained that Bear had been working with Lazard to arrange the facility with JPMorgan, which he hoped "will allow us to achieve the objective of calming down the marketplace and giving us the chance to get some facts out into the marketplace." Schwartz said Bear would continue working with Lazard on "alternatives"—often banker code for pursuing a sale of the company—"with a focus on ensuring that we can handle and protect our customers well and at the same time maximize shareholder value." Schwartz then opened up the call to questions and said he looked forward to speaking with everyone again on Monday for the earnings release.

Guy Moszkowski, Merrill Lynch's Wall Street research analyst, asked the executives to explain, if they could, what had led to the liquidity crunch. Was it the failure of overnight lenders in the repo market to offer financing, the withdrawal by hedge funds of the free cash balances from their accounts, or both? Molinaro responded: "I would say that it's really a combination thereof."

There was also the not unexpected question, asked by Nick Elfner, at Wellington Management, about whether Schwartz could share more information about the new credit facility and how it would work. Without getting into the details—probably because he did not know himself—Schwartz tried to provide assurance that the new financing would allow the firm to continue to operate as close to normally as possible. "The facility that we have basically is lending against a lot of collateral that we have, and essentially provides all of the liquidity we're going to need to maintain a regular course of business," he answered. "We just want to make this point: The reason—one of the reasons, amongst others—that we went to JP-Morgan, after thinking about our alternatives, was that JPMorgan is a clearing agent for our collateral. Therefore, it was easy for them to see the kind and quality of the collateral that we had available and therefore could move very, very quickly." Molinaro elaborated briefly that the new financing would allow Bear Stearns to pledge its collateral and borrow against it. "That is what was really causing the difficulty," he said.

Before the call ended, Schwartz said he was confident the credit facility would calm down the marketplace and allow Bear Stearns to fashion a more permanent solution. "I think [with] the terms and size, we will be able to convince customers and counterparties that we have the ability to fund ourselves every day, to do business as usual," he concluded. "But I think, frankly, what this is, is a bridge to a more permanent solution."

Even before Schwartz could finish the conference call, the pundits over at CNBC were questioning whether the firm would survive until Monday. Bob Pisani repeatedly called the firm a "house of mirrors." Dave Faber spoke about the Fed facility being a "short-term fix that doesn't deal with long-term confidence" and said the Fed had been trying to "forestall a massive run on the bank." He added, ominously, that "typically a run on the bank becomes a self-fulfilling prophecy." Steve Liesman blamed Bear Stearns for not doing "enough to plan for the worst-case scenario" during the nine months since the credit crisis had first taken hold. In his daily afternoon commentary, Faber continued his trenchant analysis: "Bear Stearns finds itself in a difficult position, having failed to stem the crisis of confidence that engulfed the firm this week." He predicted that a "sale of the company" as "soon as Monday" seems "most likely," with JPMorgan being the "leading" candidate. He closed with the tantalizing thought from "one of my sources" that with Bear's tangible book value at around $75 per share and the stock then trading around $30 a share, a deal for the firm "will be the greatest financial services deal for the buyer ever done." The *Financial Times* called the Fed's rescue of Bear nothing less than "the final humiliation in a nine-month fall from grace that has humbled one of Wall Street's toughest fighters," Jimmy Cayne. "The rescue is galling for the cigar-smoking 74 year old, who personified Bear Stearns' reputation as Wall Street's scrappy underdog whose continued survival as an independent defied persistent predictions of its demise."

Along with the ruminations going on over at CNBC and the *Financial Times* about Bear Stearns, there were two other public blows about to descend on the firm. First, just after Schwartz's conference call was ending, Meredith Whitney, the Oppenheimer research analyst, decided she could hold back no longer and downgraded Bear Stearns's stock to "underperform," her firm's sell rating. She had just landed in London and had missed the conference call, but her associate told her about the Fed's action, which she considered to be of little significance, especially since details about the JPMorgan facility were still sparse. "The problem that Bear Stearns and other financials face is a great unwind of leverage," she wrote. "A company is only as solvent as the perception of its solvency. When a company that is leveraged over 30-to-1"—and here she was being kind, since Bear's leverage was often as high as 50:1 during a given quarter—"faces a crisis of liquidity and confidence of creditworthiness, that company will be unable to leverage its collateral and its leverage will be forced down to 1-to-1. [Bear Stearns's] equity could become worthless as forced sales create asset deflation, which could cause cannibalization of remaining capital. We are in a tenuous market environment and experiencing a true crisis of confidence. The Fed's action in providing JPMorgan access to funding essentially buys time for Bear's counter-parties to unwind their position and deliver. The great unwind of leverage that will occur will further depress the stock prices of financials."

Given all that was occurring that afternoon, Whitney's down-grade received little attention, even though she said the stock, which ended the day around $30 a share, was now worthless. "That's a bigger call than any call I made," she said, "and it didn't re-ally get much note. But the [key] quote was, 'You're only as solvent as people believe you to be solvent.'"

One of the reasons Whitney's call went unheralded was that her note came out around the same time that the ratings agencies de-cided to downgrade Bear Stearns, too. Whitney's downgrade was made on behalf of equity investors, who had already taken a drub-bing in the past year on Bear's stock. The ratings agencies' revisions, however, were made for the holders of the firm's debt and went to the heart of Bear Stearns's ability to survive. It was as if the Fed's de-cision to step in and help the firm had done nothing whatsoever to calm creditors. Standard & Poor's cut its long-term credit rating on Bear Stearns by *three* levels, to BBB, and suggested further down-grades were possible. "Although we view the liquidity support to Bear as positive, we consider it a short-term solution to a longer term issue that does not entirely affect Bear's confidence crisis," Whitney wrote. "We also remain concerned about Bear's ability to generate sustainable revenues in an ongoing volatile market envi-ronment."

Moody's and Fitch also cut their ratings on Bear Stearns's debt. "What their rating is now is irrelevant," Andrew Harding, chief fixed-income investment officer at Allegiant Asset Management, in Cleveland, told Bloomberg. "Whether it's BB, AAA or A, I just think it's a response to the emergency funding today." Not surprisingly, after the ratings agencies cut their outlook for Bear Stearns, the firm's cost of credit insurance—those credit default swaps—increased considerably, to as high as 810 basis points, up from 675 basis points the day before. In an interview with Bloomberg, Standard & Poor analyst Diane Hinton, a ten-year veteran, said, "In a normal market environment, we would not see this kind of movement, but we are not in a normal environment. One rumor gets started and people get more nervous than they already are and it becomes a feeding frenzy."

EVEN BEFORE THE downgrades that afternoon, Friedman knew he had completely misjudged the situation. The repo desk was right. The Fed's supposed lifeline proved to be nothing more than a poorly tied tourniquet on a severely hemorrhaging wound. Nobody wanted to do business with the firm. Bear Stearns had become like the proverbial frog placed in warm water that gradually becomes acclimated as the temperature is raised until it becomes cooked. "By the end of the day—we'd been downgraded by then, but even before that—every single lender had pulled their money, with three exceptions," Friedman said. "It was all gone. The overnight lenders were all gone. Even some of the ones that were not overnight. Fidelity, for instance. We got in a huge fight with them. They had a $1 billion term trade on that they wanted to terminate. They kept arguing that this is not what they signed up for. It was after we had been downgraded, but they still argued, 'You represented to us that you would remain an investment-grade firm. We're not willing to keep this outstanding. We want our money back.' They had actually done a trade first thing Friday morning to lend us money overnight, and they wanted that back, too. They wanted all their money back." Added another Bear Stearns executive about the dangers of relying on repo financing: "When Bear's liquidity crisis developed, their repo book had expanded dramatically over the past year to the tune of two times the previous year. During the same period Lehman's repo book had declined by roughly 25 percent. Bear got a taste of [its] own medicine by virtue of committing the cardinal sin of overreliance on short-term funding. For repo lenders, perception in many instances is reality. The last man standing gains nothing; the first out gets his money back."

By early afternoon, Bear Stearns could see that the Fed's rescue plan was not going to work. "By midday, the money is gone," Friedman explained. "The customers are gone. The customer credits are to the point where the wire room shut down. They couldn't process them fast enough. We had a lot of customers who had put money in money funds through us, and we were taking the money back from the money funds to wire out to the customers and couldn't do it fast enough. We actually ended Friday night with $8 or $9 billion of cash simply because we had to shut the room down because we couldn't get the money out."

Shortly after Schwartz's conference call ended, Dave Schoenthal, the head of the firm's foreign exchange desk, told Friedman that counterparties no longer would do business with the firm and that Friedman had to do something. "I'm just physically and emotionally a mess," Friedman recalled, "and I start to tell him, 'Dave, I can't help you. There's nothing we can do.' I actually find myself sitting at my desk sobbing, with my head down on the desk. Literally. The tears are coming out. The combination of the whole thing, plus not having slept in two days, I've lost it, and David goes, 'Oh,' and he was graceful enough to wander out of my office."

What Friedman had discovered through the course of the day on Friday was that even though the Fed's back-to-back facility with JPMorgan appeared to be genuine, nobody knew how it was supposed to work—and of course there was no documentation for it. There was only the press release, which was hardly a blueprint for how to design and build a multibillion-dollar lending facility. "The JPMorgan facility is real, but they spend the entire day torturing us on it," Friedman said. "They were insisting on 20 points margin on everything. Everything we do, they'll lend us 80 cents on the dollar on market value. So you give them something worth 100, even though they're not taking any risk, even though this is not how the facility was supposed to work. My repo guys are fighting with JPMorgan and grabbing our treasury guys to fight with JPMorgan. We're trying to get money. We're actually not getting any money. We have customer money going out, we have lender money going out, and JP is going, 'We'll get to you.' In fairness to them, they didn't really understand it—maybe. Certainly their operational and treasury people were making it up as they went along. They're giving us an argument that they will only take collateral eligible at the discount window, which is a pretty limited list of things in terms of what you could get. By midafternoon, we had only squeezed a couple of billion dollars out of them, and it's chaos."

Chaos seemed to be the theme of the day. "We never really had time to figure out the line of credit," Molinaro said. "It happened so quick. And the market reacted so badly. We had a very substantial run on the bank on Friday. Not only was the stock under pressure, but customers were trying to pull their money out at increasing levels. Prime brokerage clients, they didn't want to do business with us. Stock lenders didn't want to lend us securities. It was chaos. I think the tipping point of that day was the downgrade by the rating agencies. I think that tipped us over the edge. That was the end. Because when they downgraded us, there are money funds that can't own the paper, that can't do repo with you. I mean, people were just bailing. We were going to have very little repo capacity left away from the Fed, the way that this was going."

A problem developed on Friday afternoon when State Street Bank, in Boston, and other large custodial institutions that provided back-office-type services to Wall Street refused to lend Bear Stearns securities overnight to cover their short positions or those of their customers. This seemed odd to Schwartz, since the firm supposedly had the backing of the Fed through its new lending facility with JP-Morgan. But, as he well knew, the market was not responding with any confidence to Bear Stearns. Schwartz called Geithner and explained to him that the State Streets of the world were not behaving in a constructive way. Geithner called the bank and reminded it that Bear Stearns had the backing of the Fed, but State Street still was not willing to lend the securities overnight. "So we went, 'Oh, shit,'" a Bear Stearns executive said of Schwartz's reaction. "He knew we had a big problem then." By the end of Friday, Bear Stearns estimated that its available liquidity had dropped to $4.8 billion, from $18.3 billion on Monday, and that its funding requirements on March 17 would be between "$60 billion and $100 billion assuming counterparties to secured repo facilities were unwilling to renew these facilities."

In retrospect, Molinaro wondered if the firm should have anticipated the downgrades by the rating agencies. "I think the downgrade really killed us. Really made it almost impossible to operate.

The downgrade triggered so many bad things. . . . There were money funds and other institutions that are lending you money through the repo lines that can't do business with you if you're not rated at least single-A. If we had not been downgraded, my guess is we wouldn't have had as big a run on the bank. We would have needed to borrow less money from the Fed, and we probably would have got through that day in reasonable order."

Begleiter also suspected the JPMorgan facility wouldn't do Bear Stearns any favors. "We were able with this—whatever you want to call it—arrangement that came out in the wee hours of Friday morning, to work our way through Friday, but I didn't know how we were going to get through Monday if something didn't happen over the weekend," he recalled. "Without the Fed facility, we were probably going to file bankruptcy shortly afterwards unless we sold the company or got a major investment over the weekend. The liquidity we started the week with had eroded. Now, some of it was due to be replenished because of the timing of flows, but if you fail, you fail. You don't get a chance to say, 'Hey, we'll pay you in two days, as soon as we get the money we are owed from others.' Everything conspired to work against us. For example, other firms were demanding margin from us but not sending us margin they owed us. We had customer money that needed to go out, which we had in segregated deposits, but there's a process to get it released and that takes a couple of days even though the customer wants his money right away. There were many other items that contributed to the cash drain. It all happened very quickly."

Tom Flexner, the Bear Stearns vice chairman, had been out visiting clients on Friday for most of the day. But when he returned to the office Friday afternoon, he knew that the JPMorgan facility was not working the way everyone at the firm had hoped it would. "From what I was told by our treasury department . . . we were posting collateral to JP and it was haircutting at 20 percent, and then taking the same stuff to the Fed and getting 98 cents on the dollar for it," he said. "This was a liquidity facility that was putting us out of business, and JP was making money off of it. Sam Molinaro told me at one point that we had to post $25 billion of collateral to get $15 billion in liquidity. That's game, set, match."

With his firm looking on Friday afternoon increasingly like St. Sebastian—and feeling especially rattled that Geithner's call to State Street had not worked—Schwartz decided he had better speak with his contacts at the Federal Reserve and the Treasury to give them an update. He placed a call to his friends Robert Steel, a fellow Duke alumnus and undersecretary of the Treasury, and Kevin Warsh, a thirty-eight-year-old former Morgan Stanley M&A banker turned Fed governor. Even though Schwartz believed he had up to twenty-eight days to fashion a solution, he worried that the events of Friday afternoon had made the government extremely nervous about the potential repercussions for the whole financial system. "I understand completely that you guys are in a situation that all you can worry about is what's going to happen in the market and the U.S. economy," Schwartz told them. "I'm not calling you as a favor for Bear Stearns; I get it. It just so happens, in my opinion, if we can keep this alive and I can get this thing sold at 40 bucks a share or 50 bucks a share, it's a heavy discount from book so there's got to be people that want to do it. That's a much better outcome for the market than waking up and finding out that over a two-day period Bear Stearns was toast. So we really need to work together to figure out what's not working here and get it done." Both Steel and Warsh told Schwartz, "We hear you."

CHAPTER 7

TOTAL PANIC

The exhausted Bear Stearns management team started heading home at the end of the day on Friday knowing that while things were looking grim, at least they could take comfort that they still had another twenty-seven days to try to find a more permanent solution to the funding crisis. While it was true that the JPMorgan facility was not working particularly smoothly, at least it would allow the firm to continue operating. Schwartz felt that Steel and Warsh understood the predicament. "We left Friday night thinking that we'd be at it through the weekend, negotiating with JPMorgan over the sale of the company," Molinaro said. "That was kind of our plan. We thought we'd be talking to them through the weekend over a possible sale and begin the process." Indeed, that afternoon that process had already begun, with Jeffrey Woods, the chief operating officer of JPMorgan's investment banking business in North America, contacting Steve Begleiter and suggesting that "tomorrow would be much more productive" if JPMorgan's bankers "can get access to available content tonight." The Bear team agreed Friday afternoon to get JPMorgan "up and running as soon as we receive a signed" confidentiality agreement regarding the nonpublic information to be shared.

At around six o'clock Friday evening, in a stupor that was equal parts exhaustion and gloom, Friedman wrote a friend, "27 years at this place and it only has days left to live. Hundreds of people I care about and thousands [of] others will be out on the street. I've been at this long enough that it won't kill Susie"—his wife—"and me but I'm surrounded by people who will have their lives ruined."

Meanwhile, the Fed and the Treasury were closely examining Bear's liquidity at the end of Friday and were not happy. Treasury Secretary Hank Paulson, the former CEO of Goldman Sachs, decided there was no way Bear would be able to open for business on Monday morning. Paulson and Geithner called Schwartz, who was then in the backseat of a car taking him home to Greenwich, Connecticut. "You have got to understand that we're not having this thing [be unresolved] on Monday morning," Paulson told Schwartz. "This thing has got to be done over the weekend." Schwartz made his pitch for more time, which would allow for a more orderly process and, he hoped, a higher sales price for shareholders. But Paulson would have none of it. "I hear ya," he said. "But this thing's got to be done. You need to have a deal by Sunday night." Paulson later told the *Wall Street Journal*: "It was just clear that this franchise was going to unravel if the deal wasn't done by the end of the weekend." Recalled Geithner: "That evening Paulson and I together told him that it was going to have to be Sunday night because we didn't see an option that would buy more time. The run accelerated over the course of the day Friday, and I wasn't going to lend into the run.

We didn't have any authority to guarantee their whole liabilities or buy them, no ability to do that. So given [that,] the only options really were to maximize the chance that they were going to get bought and guaranteed before Asia opened. Paulson and I were very clear to him, crystal clear to him Friday night. He understood it, didn't like it. Kept hoping Saturday morning that there would be a way to give him a longer period of time—understandably, because it's very hard to run an open process to get people to do due diligence. On the other hand, it wasn't impossible. It was earth-shattering but not impossible. We didn't know what was possible. We were doing two tracks."

After hearing the shocking news from Paulson and Geithner "that a stabilizing transaction needed to be accomplished by the end of the weekend," Schwartz called the equally exhausted Molinaro, who had stopped for a cup of coffee at a Mobil station on the Merritt Parkway on his way home to New Canaan, Connecticut, with the news that Bear Stearns had to somehow find a buyer by Sunday night or face liquidation. Paulson had reminded him, Schwartz told Molinaro, that Bear had known it would have no control once it accepted the financing deal. "You've got to be kidding me," Molinaro said. "I thought we had twenty-eight days."

"So did I," Schwartz answered. "Now we've got to get a deal done this weekend."

"He was clearly upset," Molinaro recalled. "And I was dumbfounded, candidly, when I heard it. I couldn't believe it."

This was not even remotely the news the exhausted Bear Stearns management wanted to hear on this particular Friday night. "To be honest," Molinaro said, "I was so exhausted at that point, I just wanted to go home and go to bed, and to get back in here and see what we had to do the next day," he said. "I guess in hindsight, I think that the conclusion was reached because this was unprecedented, what had happened. And the markets were in chaos. And I think there was concern that there would be other investment banks that might be right behind us, and that was not going to be a good outcome obviously. Lehman Brothers was [also] under significant duress."

Other Bear executives, who had not been part of the previous night's vigil, freaked out as Paulson's dictum began to circulate. "Everybody went into a panic," one disillusioned senior managing director explained. "The general feeling was, 'You've got to be fucking kidding me. We can't get anything done in forty-eight hours. Nobody here has slept in three days and you're giving us two days to find a long-term solution? There is no long-term solution here.' It was a total panic."

At that moment, given how radically the dynamic had shifted in the wake of Paulson's call to Schwartz, Vincent Tese, the multimillionaire wireless entrepreneur and the lead independent director on the Bear Stearns board of directors, thought that it might be useful for the independent directors of the board to retain their own counsel. Tese called Rodgin Cohen, of Sullivan & Cromwell, on his cell phone. Cohen, who had not been involved in the evolving situation since his call to Geithner late Wednesday night, had just landed back at LaGuardia Airport from Washington. "We really could use your help at the board level," Tese told Cohen. Tese then told Cohen about how, instead of having twenty-eight days, they'd been told they needed to have a deal by Sunday night. Cohen decided to call Geithner to see if the Fed had any flexibility at all. "I was told it was done," Cohen said. "There was no extension beyond Sunday night. . . . The gun was absolutely to their head at that point."

By the end of Friday, Paul Friedman was exhausted, emotionally and physically. He took the train to his house in Scarsdale, at the end of a cul-de-sac. He collapsed in bed with the help of an Ambien and hoped to get some sleep. It was around 7:30 at night. His head was spinning with the calamitous events of the previous forty-eight hours. "At 9:15, I'm asleep," Friedman said, "and I hear knocking. [My wife] Susie comes upstairs and says, 'Timmy Greene is on the phone for you.' Timmy is one of the co-heads of the repo desk. I said, 'He's on the phone for me now? What day is it?' She said, 'He needs to talk to you right now. He's still at the office.' I pick up the phone. I'm lying in bed like this, I've got the phone, and I'm staring at the ceiling barely coherent. I go, 'Yeah?' Timmy goes, 'JPMorgan has sent over an agreement. It's only good until Monday.' I said, 'What do you mean it's only good until Monday?' He said, 'The agreement that they sent says this loan facility terminates Sunday .

night.' I said, 'Okay, get the lawyers involved.' He said, 'I did. I called Mike Solender,' who had also gone home and taken a sleeping pill. 'We were in the middle of the conversation and he fell asleep.' I go, 'Okay,' and I'm not a whole lot better. I said, 'We need to get the Fed involved.' Timmy said, 'We just spoke to the general counsel, the guy who works for Geithner, and he says this is a private transaction and you should work out the details with JPMorgan.' I said, 'Okay, what does JPMorgan say?' He said, 'They're saying it runs out Sunday night.' It's a one-day facility. The 'up to twenty-eight days' came out as, 'It's a one-day facility. We'll decide later on whether we want to renew it for more days, up to twenty-eight.' I said, 'Okay. You've gotta get Alan on the phone.'"

Greene then set up a conference call between himself, Friedman, still half asleep, and Alan Schwartz, who was not much better. "We take Alan through it," Friedman said. "Timmy is saying, 'JPMorgan is saying unless we sign the document tonight, they won't lend us the money tonight that we need to not run out of cash tonight.' There was a whole lot of technical repo stuff that I've forgotten how exactly he described it. Alan goes, 'Sign the document.' Timmy goes, 'It says the loan expires Sunday night,' or Monday morning. I forget which. Alan goes, 'It doesn't make any difference. We're out of business. Just sign the damn document.' I said to Timmy, 'Okay, you got your orders.'"

By then, Schwartz had also received his orders from on high. Paulson and Geithner had reviewed the events of Friday and told Schwartz he needed to "find a solution" for the firm before the markets opened Monday morning in Asia—also known as Sunday night in New York. Recalled Schwartz: "We believed at the time that the loan and the corresponding backstop from the New York Fed would be available for twenty-eight days. We hoped this period would be sufficient to bring order to the chaos and allow us to secure more permanent funding or an orderly disposition of assets to raise cash, if that became necessary. However, despite the announcement of the JPMorgan facility, market forces continued to drive and accelerate our precipitous liquidity decline. Also, that Friday afternoon, all three major rating agencies lowered Bear Stearns's long-term and short-term credit ratings. Finally, on Friday night, we learned that the JPMorgan credit facility would not be available beyond Sunday night. The choices we faced that Friday night were stark: Find a party willing to acquire Bear Stearns by Sunday night, or face what my advisors were telling me could be a bankruptcy filing on Monday morning, which could likely wipe out our shareholders and cause losses for certain of our creditors and all of our employees."

Geithner is not sure why there ended up being such confusion about the proposed JPMorgan facility. "I don't understand actually what happened," he said. "All I know is the following: The only thing in the public domain about terms [of the facility] was what JP-Morgan put out. They said 'up to twenty-eight days.' Alan saw that. All we said was the board had voted to approve the arrangement announced by JPMorgan. We didn't say anything else. I told Alan that morning when it was announced that he was going to have to find some solution for his company. That evening Paulson and I together told him that it was going to have to be Sunday night because we didn't see an option that would buy more time."

Molinaro believes that the Fed and the Treasury had a strategy—relatively early on—of pushing Bear Stearns into the arms of JPMorgan for the good of the financial system. "I think that was the plan," he said. "Force us to merge into JPMorgan that weekend. From what I know from talking to the JPMorgan people, they were getting leaned on by the Fed to do this. So the Fed [was] pushing them to do the deal, pushing us into their arms, trying to make sure that the shareholders didn't get any money out of this. It would be effectively a liquidation of the company, a bankruptcy, if you will. The bondholders all get bailed out and get paid off. That was just a by-product of the whole thing. JPMorgan is the beneficiary of that, for stepping in and being there."

AS A HIGHLY regarded M&A banker, Alan Schwartz knew something about selling a business. A former fastball pitcher who played in high school and college and almost made it to the Cincinnati Reds before an elbow injury sidelined him, Schwartz also knew a little something about pressure situations. After getting the news from Paulson and Geithner that Bear Stearns needed to consummate a deal for the company by Sunday night or file for bankruptcy Monday morning, Schwartz knew he had lost nearly all of his leverage in negotiating a deal. With such stark choices, so little time, and so much negative publicity about the firm's trouble already part of the zeitgeist, how could Schwartz hope to pull off something "earth-shattering," as Geithner described it, in thirty-six hours? The odds were long and seriously daunting. Geithner had made a difficult situation even more difficult by insisting that Schwartz run a "competitive" process, making sure that as many parties as possible had access to the potential deal. "We told Alan that he had to run an open process," Geithner said. "I told Jamie that he couldn't—whether he was interested or not—he couldn't have any exclusive thing. But [Bear Stearns] had a huge interest in talking to everybody they could. They talked to a bunch of people. I think a bunch of people were polite and said, 'Yeah, we're really interested.' But only two people seemed really focused and engaged."

Schwartz went into deal mode. At least two of his advisors, Gary Parr, at Lazard, and Rog Cohen, at Sullivan & Cromwell, believed that Schwartz's background as a dealmaker made it possible for something to get done in such a short period of time. "The fact that he'd done complex deals, where there were lots of pressures, lots of different moving pieces, [where it was important] to be able to keep your wits about you and withstand the pressures and sort of circle everything together and make sense out of it, probably being an M&A banker helped," Cohen said. While much of the previous day had been consumed with the Fed's action and the market's unhelpful reaction to it, after making calls around the world, Lazard had managed to gin up at least one other party besides JPMorgan that was interested in thinking seriously about some sort of deal for Bear Stearns. Starting late on Friday afternoon, private equity firm J. C. Flowers & Co., led by the former Goldman Sachs partner Chris Flowers, began conducting due diligence on Bear Stearns—studying its financial records—in the offices at 383 Madison. Flowers, then forty-nine, had been a financial institutions banker at Goldman until he founded his eponymous firm in 1998. With $7 billion in his second fund, Flowers was best known for his 2000 purchase, along with former Lazard banker Tim Collins, of Japan's Long Term Credit Bank, which he turned around, cashing out with a personal profit of around $1 billion. Flowers became known as

"Bidder A." The only other bidder interested in pursuing a deal for Bear Stearns was, of course, JPMorgan.

To accommodate the full-blown due diligence efforts of both Flowers and JPMorgan, Schwartz and Molinaro met back at 383 Madison at around seven-thirty Saturday morning to map out a plan for the day, which included immediately reassembling his weary bankers and traders with various expertise about the firm—its cash balances, its trading book, its real estate holdings, its securities holdings—and setting them all up in various conference rooms at 383 Madison. JPMorgan's due diligence efforts were confined to the firm's conference center on the twelfth and thirteenth floors. Flowers's sessions were in and around Cayne's office on the sixth floor. "Those of us running business units were each assigned to a spot," Friedman explained. "We'd go in, and the JPMorgan people, who matched up with us, would come in and start to do the transfer of knowledge, which went most of Saturday. I spent time with Matt Zames and with the treasury people and with the repo people. I was sort of flitting from group to group because we don't line up that well with them from a funding standpoint and from a business standpoint. At the same time, the lawyers are swirling around, the bankruptcy lawyers are back, and they have a whole bunch of offices and they're working on what happens" if no deal can be agreed on by Sunday night.

Flowers went through Bear's books thoroughly and came away impressed. "Your books are in a lot better shape than I thought they would be," he told Schwartz and others, and recounted some "horror stories" about what he had found at other firms where he had been asked to consider an investment. He added: "I've never been through a process where we could get answers from people who knew what they were talking about." On the other hand, he said, he felt as if he were in the "middle of a hurricane" and wished the process could have been less pressured. Still, he pledged to work hard and to try to cobble together a group of banks to provide billions in financing. He also hoped that he could somehow convince the Fed to open the discount window to Bear Stearns as part of any deal he might do. Schwartz knew well the long odds Flowers faced. But he also needed Flowers to be a serious competitor to keep JPMorgan honest.

There also had been some belief that Deutsche Bank and Barclays—the giant German and British banks, respectively—or maybe even Goldman Sachs, the Blackstone Group, or Warburg Pincus might be interested in making a run at Bear Stearns, but when it came to crunch time, none of those other institutions decided it made sense. Deutsche's partner on its potential bid was to be the publicly traded Fortress Investment Group, a global hedge fund and private equity firm. From August 2007 until around the time that Schwartz took over as CEO from Cayne, in January 2008, Fortress had been taking a serious look at merging with Bear Stearns. Even though Fortress was the smaller firm by some two-thirds at that time, Fortress's well-regarded CEO, Wesley Edens, was to have been the CEO of the combined firm, which may have been enough of an obstacle for Schwartz to kill the deal two months earlier. With Deutsche deciding against a bid for Bear Stearns, Tom Flexner, the Bear vice chairman, invited Edens, his client and longtime friend, to join him at 383 Madison to witness the historic events then unfolding, and to help Schwartz and Molinaro if asked. Flexner had planned to be out of town that weekend, but after Friday's extraordinary events, he changed his plans. "There was no way I was going to miss the front-row seat," Flexner said. "Just so I could tell my grandkids someday."

The due diligence centered around two key but difficult-to-discern facts: the assets that Bear Stearns actually owned and their value, and the firm's "funding vulnerabilities"—in other words, how much money the firm needed to continue operating come Monday morning. That shortfall was, more than likely, the amount of federal funds that would have to be made available if a deal was to happen. In rough numbers, if Bear Stearns's balance sheet had $400 billion of assets and $100 billion in long-term capital, that left some $300 billion that needed to be financed to support those assets. Of that $300 billion, about $150 billion consisted of Treasury securities and another $100 billion consisted of "agency" securities, Freddie Mac and Fannie Mae—all of which could be used as collateral for repos or for a margin loan, assuming markets had normalized somewhat. By this logic, Bear Stearns's funding gap that weekend was around $50 billion, but this was just a rough guess. On Saturday, Flexner recalled, they were trying to determine the size of the problem. "Because if the problem is $3 billion, you can get it solved. Fortress will write the check. If it's $30 billion or $40 billion, it takes a major bank, probably with Fed backing. Remember, this was all happening in an unprecedented and condensed time frame to do a merger, to get one of the largest deals in the history of the financial services industry done in two days. It was wild."

While the due diligence was being done at 383 Madison on Saturday morning, the full Bear Stearns board of directors met by telephone for the first time since Paulson had rendered his sobering decision. Some of the board members had heard the news the night before, but not all of them. "That was a very down meeting," Rog Cohen remembered, "because that's when everybody on the board was informed that the twenty-eight days was two and a half at that point." After that board meeting, Cohen "rushed" into Bear Stearns, arriving around 1 P.M., and then spent the next twelve hours negotiating with JPMorgan, the Flowers Group, and the federal government about what, if anything, could be done.

❧

WHILE ALL THE parties were getting their minds around the magnitude of the funding need, Flowers made a preliminary proposal whereby his funds would invest $3 billion into the firm in exchange for a 90 percent fully diluted stake in Bear Stearns. The Flowers deal valued Bear's equity at around $2.80 per share, well below where it had ended the day on Friday afternoon. But his deal had two major contingencies. First, Flowers would need to assemble a consortium of banks willing to provide Bear Stearns with the $20 billion of financing he thought Bear needed to continue operating. And in case that was not enough money to keep the firm fully financed, Flowers also required a commitment from the Federal Reserve that Bear would have guaranteed access to its discount window to obtain additional loans, if needed, for one year. Given that no investment banks had access to the Fed's discount window at that moment, Flowers's second condition made sense theoretically but was inordinately impractical, especially under the tense circumstances. "I think what the Fed basically told Flowers," Cohen said, "was, 'Look, we're not saying no, but we're certainly not saying yes unless you've got the funding.'" But the Fed encouraged Flowers to keep working on a proposal, as far-fetched as it was. "Not for our benefit," Molinaro said, "just for theirs."

"We were past Plan B and up to Plan C or D and possibly beyond," Friedman said. "This was the most absurdly impossible thing to ever imagine that they were going to do—that they were going to put in a couple of billion dollars and they were going to arrange some loans for us, and the whole thing was going to be predicated on the Fed allowing us to go to the discount window, and Flowers was going to arrange that, well, it was like, '*Okay.* . . .'"

Despite the problems with Flowers's proposal, Gary Parr, at Lazard, took it seriously enough—or seriously enough as a useful stalking horse—that he reviewed the details of the proposal with Bear's senior management, which then authorized Flowers to make the calls necessary to see if the $20 billion of financing could be raised. But this remained a long shot, "because without access to the Fed window, a $3 billion injection or a $6 billion injection, it doesn't matter," said one senior Bear banker. "We've lost $20 billion in 24 hours, so what was $6 billion going to do for us? The game was over. Flowers continued to do its work and they were coming up with more money. They had five or six financial institutions, which all ended up bailing on them anyway. There was just nothing to do. It was a disaster. That was the end right there." Added Cohen: "I think within that extraordinary pressure cooker, although Flowers is an extraordinarily smart guy and he has smart people around him, I think they did a lot of due diligence just around the $20 billion or so, but it was not in the cards."

There was no question in anyone's mind, from the Fed and the Treasury on down, that if a deal was to be consummated by Sunday evening, JPMorgan would have to be the buyer, for all the very same reasons that the firm had been the best candidate to provide rescue financing twenty-four hours earlier. At around five in the afternoon on Saturday, Bloomberg reported that Royal Bank of Scotland was interested in buying Bear. But that was an error; it was the Royal Bank of *Canada,* not Scotland, that "likes us a lot," Friedman reported, but there were too many issues and not enough time for that bank to get serious. "Everything else was noise over the weekend," a senior Bear banker said. "Flowers being there became noise. Goldman being there was noise, Blackstone and Warburg at a minimum I know had made phone calls on Thursday and Friday saying, 'We'd like to come in and help.' But it was too late. They could never have done what they needed to do. Nobody had an A-plus balance sheet to back anything up. So all of that was noise. It was all bankruptcy or JPMorgan."

❀

MORE THAN TWO hundred of JPMorgan's top managers were conducting due diligence with their Bear Stearns counterparts. In addition to the group working at the Bear Stearns offices, JPMorgan had set up a war room on the eighth floor of the big bank's 270 Park headquarters, in and around the office of CEO Jamie Dimon. On Saturday evening, with some considerable misgivings and a feeling that not enough work had been done, JPMorgan's bankers met with Parr, from Lazard, and Schwartz and Molinaro, from Bear Stearns. According to one of the participants in the meeting, "Jamie said, 'Look, you're not going to like this, blah, blah, blah, but if we have to do it over the weekend it's going to be $8 to $12.' Then Schwartz said, 'Yeah, I'm not going to like it, but all I got is the weekend.'" In that meeting, based on its preliminary due diligence, JPMorgan said it was willing to consider an all-stock deal for Bear Stearns that valued the company between $8 and $12 per share, which in Wall Street talk meant that JPMorgan was thinking about offering $10 per share. At that valuation, which was two-thirds below the Friday closing price but obviously higher than what Flowers was thinking about or the goose egg that shareholders would receive in liquidation, JPMorgan also wanted a few other goodies: an option to purchase 19.9 percent of Bear Stearns stock (as a way to help ensure that shareholders would vote for the deal) as well as options to purchase the two assets the bank most coveted—the seven-year-old Skidmore, Owings & Merrill–designed headquarters building at 383 Madison, which it could use to house its dispersed investment banking operations, and the prime brokerage business that cleared trades and managed accounts for hedge funds. The JPMorgan representatives made clear that their "thinking" was "still preliminary" because they were awaiting further reports from their due diligence teams and that the ultimate price "could be lower than $8 per share." There was by no means a uniform view at JPMorgan that the deal made sense. One senior banker in the firm's asset management division who had been reviewing the similar business at Bear reported, "This is insane. Why would you ever want to take on this piece of shit, other than out of some sort of patriotic sense of obligation?"

At 9:15 Saturday evening, Friedman sent a "confidential" e-mail to Craig Overlander and Jeff Mayer, the two heads of fixed income, with the news that "Alan and Sam are with JPM. They showed us a bid of 8–12/share. I'm with Flowers but I think they have no shot, if only because their plan assumes we can get to the [Fed] window directly."

Dimon then called Schwartz. "Okay, things are looking pretty good, we'll talk tomorrow," Dimon said. "But I don't want to go through all this if your board is going to turn it down. So I need to know you're prepared to do something in this range."

Schwartz responded: "Well, I have to know that you're prepared to do it, too. I know you can't get board approval without a board meeting, but I have my board sitting here and you've talked to your directors. So where are you guys?"

Dimon replied, "Well, let's just say I'd be very surprised if they turned it down."

Schwartz said, "Okay, talk to you in the morning."

With time and choices dwindling rapidly, Bear's board of directors met on Saturday night to hear from Parr about the current state of the proposals from Flowers and JPMorgan. "I think the board was obviously very disappointed," Cohen said about the JPMorgan offer, "but Alan made it clear the Flowers deal remained both more problematic and of no greater value. There was a discussion about could there be others and there was no time to do that. Again, the company had zero negotiating leverage. So we did advise the board that in addition to price we had to have absolute certainty of closing. We went back and the board accepted it. Again, it's a board where there were realists. Schwartz was a realist, Tese was a realist, Fred Salerno was a realist. And I think Ace was a realist. I'm talking about people who spoke up and said something."

Molinaro agreed. "The board's reaction to it is that everybody was surprised by the number, because it was low," he recalled. "There was some feeling of helplessness. [Still, it was] better than zero. Could have been zero. At least it was a number. We were really not in a very good negotiating position." Jimmy Cayne, who had arrived in New York at around 6 P.M. on Saturday on a private jet from Detroit, heard the news about the value of the proposed deal and started doing the math. "I'm saying to myself [I've got] six million shares, I just got my ass kicked," he recalled. "But I was almost dispassionate, because to me, $8 and $12 were the same. It was not $170, and it wasn't $100. And it wasn't $40. The only people [who] are going to suffer are my heirs, not me. Because when you have a billion six and you lose a billion, you're not exactly like crippled, right?"

The board then agreed to continue to pursue both transactions. What choice was there? Paulson and Geithner had made clear that the financing that had been arranged through JPMorgan the day before would be disappearing. While there can be no question that Bear's management and board bore near-absolute responsibility for the sorry state the firm was in, there is also little doubt that by pulling the "up-to-twenty-eight-day" financing, the federal government had forced the firm into an utterly untenable Hobson's Choice: either find a buyer in less than twenty-four hours or file for bankruptcy protection, which, given the existing laws, would have led to the liquidation of the firm and very little, if anything, for shareholders, debt holders, and employees. "We really needed to keep Flowers engaged, and the board was trying to make sure that there continued to be some level of negotiation going on, and that we were continuing to reach out to anybody who could potentially be a bidder, and also that we were keeping very plugged in to what was going on with the Fed," Molinaro said. "The board was trying to make sure that we were doing all the things that we needed to do to properly safeguard the shareholders' interests here, and at the same time trying to get a deal done."

There was, however, brewing inside the boardroom a slight variant to the liquidation option, which became known as the "nuclear card." The idea was to reject the lowball offers to buy the company and threaten to blow the company up by filing for bankruptcy. With the company would go the global financial system, to which Bear Stearns was so deeply connected. The thinking was that nobody—not the federal government, not JPMorgan, not other banks and investment banks—would want to experience the consequences of such mutually assured destruction and that, accordingly, the threat of such an option would be sufficient to award Bear more time—for instance, a *real* twenty-eight days—to fashion an orderly sale process or to be offered a price for the firm that would allow everyone to save face. It was just a germ of an idea, but one that was largely in keeping with the firm's image of being a bunch of rough-and-tumble iconoclasts. Jimmy Cayne was the loudest advocate for playing this hand. "I knew that there was very strong probability that if Bear Stearns went down, there might be systemic failure," he explained. "I knew I had a nuclear card. But you can't play it. . . . If anybody on earth would have played it, it would have been me."

Throughout the night, the Flowers and JPMorgan teams continued their respective due diligence efforts and occasionally reported in to Parr and the Bear executive team. Flowers was finding it increasingly difficult to line up the necessary $20 billion in financing and so informed Lazard. There was a discussion about the importance, given the dire circumstances, for both Bear Stearns and JPMorgan to have a high degree of certainty that any deal would, in fact, close. This led to the decision to make sure the lawyers did not gum up any merger agreement with all sorts of typical closing conditions and legal caveats. According to Molinaro, the plan for Sunday was to "try to push it"—the $10 per share deal with JPMorgan—"to the conclusion. Get it done." He said that while everyone was "taken aback" by the $10 deal, there was also a feeling of resignation: "It is what it is. Let's go get this done. Let's go do what we have to do to get done here." People started trickling home after midnight on Saturday, somewhat confident that a deal with JPMorgan would coalesce the next day before the deadline.

CHAPTER 8

THE PRICE OF MORAL HAZARD? $2

On Sunday morning at around eight-thirty, Bear's team of fifty professionals reassembled in the thirteenth-floor conference center. Schwartz kicked off the day by telling everyone how it "was going to unfold," explained one participant, "but people were not in a good mood." Bear's lawyers had received a draft of a proposed merger agreement from Wachtell, Lipton, JPMorgan's lawyers, as well as a draft of an option agreement that would allow JPMorgan to buy a large chunk of Bear Stearns's stock. The draft merger agreement, as would be typical, did not have a price included. Schwartz knew that the Flowers bid was not coming together and that the JP-Morgan deal, if it happened, would be in the $10 range. "We have a deal," he told his team, "but you're not going to like it."

Vince Tese showed up at Bear Stearns early that morning. "When I got in at seven o'clock, the merger agreement was in pretty good shape," the lead director said. "The lawyers had read it. There were a couple of issues, but nothing earth-shaking." After Schwartz and Molinaro spoke, Tese's driver took him to Cayne's apartment, at 510 Park Avenue, and together the two men headed up to the Jackson Hole restaurant, at 91st and Madison. Tese wanted to talk sense to Cayne about the wisdom of continuing to think about the nuclear card. It was best, Tese told him, to accept reality and push to get the deal on the table done. They had a hearty breakfast and a frank chat. "I picked Jimmy up, and we went and had a couple of eggs," Tese said. "I told Jimmy at the time that . . . bankruptcy's not an option. 'Yeah, but,' he kept on saying, 'they won't let us go bankrupt. We can get more money out of them.' And I said, 'We've been doing that for two days. They know we don't have a hand. That'll get you nowhere. You can't go to the eleventh hour, because you got to start declaring bankruptcy between four and five [in the afternoon]. I don't mind playing the game a little bit. But you got to realize at the end of the day, it ain't an option.'" Tese said Cayne understood what he was saying. "I told him, 'This is in your interest, just like it's in everybody else's interest.'" And he reminded Cayne that if the deal fell apart because Cayne convinced the board to press the nuclear button, it was Cayne they'd go after. The former CEO took that message to heart.

While Cayne and Tese were at breakfast, though, events took a curious turn, one of many that would make for a long and nerve-wracking day. The two co-heads of investment banking at JPMorgan, Steve Black and Bill Winters—the two men Schwartz and

Molinaro were talking to regularly—had agreed to resume the negotiations on Sunday morning at 383 Madison, but they didn't show.
"We were all sitting around for hours waiting for the JPMorgan guys
to show up and nobody did," Paul Friedman remembered. Schwartz
attempted to get in touch with Black—his fraternity brother at
Duke—and discovered he was in a meeting with Jamie Dimon. The
word was that JPMorgan's executives were meeting with their board
to decide whether this shotgun marriage made any sense whatsoever. "We assumed that they were doing what they got to do, to figure out where they're standing," Molinaro said. Under the extreme
circumstances, a delay to consider carefully the wisdom of such a
deal seemed prudent from both a fiduciary point of view and a tactical point of view. After all, if you are the only serious bidder in a
situation where time is limited and the deadline is clear, why rush
into anything?

"The first thing I get in, in the morning," Schwartz told his colleagues, "I get Steve Black calling me saying, 'We're 50/50 at best.'
Schwartz said, 'What the fuck happened?' He said, 'We ran it
overnight. We threw all this stuff through our models and you may
be $6 billion overmarked in your mortgage portfolios.' Schwartz re-
sponded, 'Steve, that's not fucking possible. I've had Wes Edens
through here, one of the mortgage experts, and Chris Flowers
through here, another one of the mortgage experts. I'm not saying
we're marked perfectly, but these guys can't walk away saying they're
very comfortable with our portfolio and you have it off by $6 billion.
There's some mismatch here. So let's get on that.' Black said, 'Well,
you just need to be aware we're 50/50 at best. You've got to be thinking about that.' Great." Just before ten Sunday morning, with some
sarcasm, Friedman e-mailed his guys about the sudden disengage-
ment of JPMorgan: "I guess it's a long walk over here." Then
Schwartz called Rog Cohen. "Look, we've got a much bigger problem," Cohen recalled Schwartz telling him. "I just got a call from
Black saying they ran their models all night and they're not sure
they're going to do the deal."

❋

THE JPMORGAN TEAM had spent the night studying Bear's "book" of
securities and became increasingly uncomfortable with what it saw.

At first, JPMorgan thought that of Bear's $300 billion of assets, $120 billion might be worth less than they were marked on the books for and might continue to deteriorate in value. By the end of the night, the firm's analysis concluded that more like $220 billion of the assets might be toxic. "We kind of slept on it," according to a JPMorgan banker, "or not slept on it, kind of closed our eyes for a half hour, and we realized that if you take a step back and remove yourself from the enormity of it, what we were being asked to take over, from a risk factor [point of view], was gargantuan." Also weighing on the JPMorgan executives was that morning's Gretchen Morgenson column in the Sunday *New York Times,* which openly questioned the Fed's decision on Friday to provide the rescue financing for a firm that "has often operated in the gray areas of Wall Street and with an aggressive, brass-knuckles approach." Morgenson then ran through the litany of Bear Stearns's missteps over the years, from being the only member of the Wall Street fraternity not to participate in the billion-dollar, Fed-orchestrated 1998 bailout of the hedge fund Long-Term Capital Management to the firm's willingness to "provide its balance sheet and imprimatur to bucket-shop brokerages like Stratton Oakmont and A. R. Baron"—for which the firm was fined $38 million in 1996 and its head of clearing fired—and for being one of the engines of the mortgage securities business and the originator of subprime mortgages. She also mentioned the collapse of two Bear Stearns hedge funds the previous summer that had cost investors $1.6 billion in losses. Morgenson could have gone on to mention Bear's roles in both the mutual-fund scandal and the scandal involving the exchange of favorable research coverage for investment banking business, but she did not, as her point was already well made. "And so, Bear Stearns, a firm that some say is this decade's version of Drexel Burnham Lambert, the anything-goes, 1980s junk-bond shop dominated by Michael Milken, is rescued," she wrote. "Almost two decades ago, Drexel was left to die. Bear Stearns and Drexel have a lot in common. And yet their differing outcomes offer proof that we are in a very different and scarier place than in the late 1980s."

Black insisted that the JPMorgan teams camped out on the firm's eighth floor read Morgenson's column. "That article certainly had an impact on my thinking," one anonymous JPMorgan banker recalled for *Vanity Fair*. "Just the reputational aspects of it, getting into bed with these people." Added another JPMorgan banker about the prospects for the deal as the executives discussed it over and over Sunday morning: "Things didn't firm up, they got more shaky." Black called Schwartz and told him JPMorgan was out. "Whatever other things you are working on, you should actively pursue them," Black said. At the time, Schwartz didn't think this was a negotiating tactic. He pointed out that if you asked any bunch of traders in that kind of pressured atmosphere where they would mark these illiquid and toxic securities if they had to be sold immediately, of course they would say, "Sorry, that's down fifteen points because there's no buyers."

Jamie Dimon then called Geithner downtown and told him the news. Given the unknowable interconnectedness of the various firms and their counterparties worldwide, Geithner decided he could not—the world could not—afford to risk the liquidation of Bear Stearns. "For the first time in history, the entire world was looking at the failure of a major financial institution that could lead to a run on the entire world financial system," a Fed official recalled. "It was clear we couldn't let that happen." Geithner called Dimon back and urged him to keep working on the deal. That call initiated several hours of back-and-forth discussion between JPMorgan and the Fed about how a deal might be cobbled together—with the Fed's considerable help—before the markets opened in Asia at 7 P.M. New York time on Sunday evening.

Word started trickling out at 383 Madison that JPMorgan had passed on the deal, although the parties had agreed to continue negotiating and marking up the contracts, assuming a deal could be somehow orchestrated with the Fed. "We went to bed on Saturday thinking we might have had a deal with JPMorgan, at $8 to $12," Bear board member Fred Salerno recalled. "Get up Sunday, JPMorgan's out. Whether they were trying to position for a better deal or really had concern for itself, I had no idea, but clearly it is what it is. If I were Jamie Dimon, I would have had some concerns myself because you never do a deal as big as that on one day's due diligence. What's the upside versus the downside? So I give him that benefit of the doubt. I would have had a hard time with it, although at eight to twelve bucks it sounded like a great deal economically, but I would have had a hard time. Give him credit that this is really an issue that he was uncomfortable with. But it was very disappointing to us because we thought we had a deal."

Everyone at Bear Stearns just sat around and waited. For his part, Molinaro too did not think JPMorgan was pulling a fast one on Sunday morning. "I think that they were nervous about—everybody was nervous about—us going into bankruptcy," he said. "That was going to be a bad outcome because they were a huge financial markets player. They have enormous credit derivatives exposures, mortgages, they've got all the same stuff we do. They have counterparty exposures to worry about. Systemic failure problems could exist. I think they were very nervous that if you take a major player and it just implodes in the market, it's uncharted waters. Nobody knows what's going to happen. Whatever it is, it's not going to be good. I heard that they had assessed their exposure in the billions to our going out of business." In fairness, Molinaro believed JPMorgan had a tremendous amount to analyze in a short amount of time. "They had to get their arms around the mortgage book," he said. "They had to try to figure out if there were any other landmines that might be out there that weren't apparent. Litigation had to be understood. And our liquidity picture needed to be understood."

Naturally, the delay was discouraging to the rank and file. "We decided to send everyone home," Friedman said, "and then we went back to huddling with the bankruptcy lawyers. We were back to figuring out how we declare bankruptcy." Richie Metrick, a longtime consigliere to Alan Schwartz, urged caution. "Don't worry, we'll have a deal by seven o'clock," he told people, referring to when Bear Stearns had to open for business in Asia on Monday morning.

When Tese and Cayne returned to 383 Madison, they learned that the JPMorgan deal was off. "Everybody felt there was brinksmanship going on," Tese said. "Chase [didn't] have to do this." On the other hand, "that portfolio was what it was. [Chase] didn't have a chance to scrub it the normal way you would scrub it. They really didn't know what the bottom was in this market. So even if the portfolio was everything [Bear] thought it would be, there was still a lot of exposure on that portfolio, because of the way the market is."

Throughout the day on Sunday, the Flowers team continued to work on crafting a proposal, but it was increasingly looking futile. Parr and Flowers explored the idea of selling pieces of Bear's businesses. Flowers told Parr he was hoping to find buyers for Bear Stearns's prime brokerage and derivatives businesses and then—assuming the elusive financing could be found—make an offer to buy the rest of the company. But, given the short time frame, none of the deals Flowers was contemplating came together. "It's not unlike any M&A process," Parr said. "We try to run things in parallel and keep optionality. When I go to core beliefs about investment banking, one is to always have options. Don't ever get narrowed down to one thing until you're done. Always have options. So in trying to run parallel, I continued to make phone calls to people. There were still some that were 'maybes' or 'might have an interest in a business.' There was a point of time where I had conversations with Lehman about doing something in the mortgage area. Then there was a time when I had conversations with John Mack, at Morgan Stanley. We had conversations with Goldman about the prime brokerage business." One idea was for Goldman to invest in the parent company of Bear Stearns and have that investment convertible into an ownership position in the prime brokerage business. But all of these ideas—while interesting and creative—required the luxury of time, which simply was not available.

The only real hope remained JPMorgan. But the firm had stopped its due diligence process at 383 Madison. The Bear faithful were despairing of finding a savior. Cohen went out to lunch with one of his colleagues and lamented, "I've worked on so many of these rescues and it's the first time I've felt quite this helpless." He said the five hours on Sunday after hearing JPMorgan would not proceed with the deal were torturous. People were "just shell-shocked," Cohen remembered.

Marc Feuer e-mailed Paul Friedman around one o'clock with another false report. "I heard that we're done, news release @ 3."

"Not even close," Friedman replied. "JP is bailing out."

"Truth?" Feuer shot back.

"Yup," said Friedman. "Financial chaos."

"Financial chaos if the proposed deal goes thru?" Feuer wondered.

"No, if it doesn't," Friedman corrected his colleague. "And right now I don't think it will. We go toes up."

Friedman saw Richie Metrick around four in the afternoon. "Richie, any word?" Friedman asked.

"Is it 7 P.M. yet?" Metrick responded. "No? So, why would you expect anything?"

At 4:40 on Sunday afternoon an exasperated Friedman wrote Feuer about the silence: "The (optimistic) view is that this was JP's plan all along: bid, pull the bid, string it out to the last minute to force the Fed to take all the risk and then steal us cheap AND risk free. The pessimistic view is that we're wrong, JP truly has no interest and the world's financial system ceases to exist tomorrow."

Although not apparent to those wandering the halls of Bear Stearns, JPMorgan was busy explaining to Geithner and Paulson that in order to consider seriously a deal for Bear Stearns, the bank needed an unprecedented amount of financial support from the Fed. Dimon, who had concluded that the toughest problem was the extra $30 billion of Bear Stearns's mortgage-backed securities and leveraged loans, asked the Fed directly for that support. "The New York Fed indicated that it would be willing to consider the possibility of an arrangement that would result in the New York Fed assuming some of the risk associated with the Bear Stearns balance sheet," the firm blandly reported later. "As a result of these discussions, it was agreed that as a part of a transaction, the New York Fed would provide $30 billion of non-recourse funding secured by a pool of collateral consisting of mortgage-related securities and other mortgage-related assets and related hedges."

The import of this massive direct intervention to save a securities firm from failing was historic. Yet there was little choice, the key participants felt at the time. "People were saying, 'You have to save them, you're JPMorgan!'" Dimon remembered. "It was a wise thing to do. . . . JPMorgan should not stand in the way of doing something good because we're being selfish or parochial." He later clarified his thinking. "My perspective, from the start," Dimon explained, "was that we could not do anything that would jeopardize the health of JPMorgan. That would not be good for our shareholders and it would not be good for the financial system. But I also felt that, to the extent it was consistent with the best interests of shareholders, we'd do everything we reasonably could to try to prevent the systematic damage that the Bear Stearns failure would cause. We and the whole board—we, the management team, and the whole board of the company—viewed that as an obligation of JPMorgan as a responsible corporate citizen. By Sunday morning, we had concluded the risks were too great for us to buy the company entirely on our own. We informed the New York Fed, the Treasury, and Bear Stearns of our conclusion. This wasn't a negotiating posture. It was the plain truth. The New York Fed encouraged us to consider what kind of assistance would allow us to do a transaction. That is what we did."

By this time Geithner and Bernanke had also concluded there was no other way to save Bear Stearns—and potentially other firms, such as Lehman Brothers or Merrill Lynch, which were similarly at risk—if the Fed did not act, and with authority. Even the leading Senate Democrats on the Senate Banking Committee, Charles Schumer, of New York, and Christopher Dodd, of Connecticut, said they supported the decisions made over the weekend by Paulson, Bernanke, and Geithner. "When you're staring into the abyss, you don't quibble about details," Schumer said. Added Dodd: "I believe this is the right action that was taken over the weekend. To allow this to go into bankruptcy, I think, would have [created] some systemic problems that would have been massive."

But on Sunday morning, when Paulson appeared on ABC's *This Week,* he gave no indication how high the stakes had been increased since the Fed stepped in on Friday morning. He dutifully defended that decision when asked about it by George Stephanopoulos. "The right decision here, I am convinced, was the decision the Fed made, which was to do things, work with market participants, to minimize the disruptions." He said he was "very aware of moral hazard. But our primary concern right now—my primary concern—is the stability of our financial system." When Stephanopoulos asked Paulson if the Fed's back-to-back loan to Bear Stearns had solved the problem, Paulson used evasive tactics, even though he knew full well that the situation was then at its most flammable. "I'm not going to speculate about what the outcome of this situation is going to be," he said. "We're working our way through this right now. We have a lot of conversations going on." When Stephanopoulos asked Paulson about a comment by William Fleckenstein, president of Fleckenstein Capital, that Gretchen Morgenson had featured in her column that morning—"Why not set an example of Bear Stearns, the guys who have this record of dog-eat-dog, we're brass knuckles, we're tough? This is the perfect time to set an example, but they are not interested in setting an example. We are Bailout Nation"—Paulson demurred and said that "every situation is different" and "we have to respond to the circumstances we're facing."

There were certainly voices—including Fleckenstein's and even some within Bear Stearns itself—that the free market should be the one to render judgment on the firm's years of strategic and tactical choices, among them the decisions to finance itself with short-term borrowings, to pack its balance sheet with hard-to-sell and hard-to-value mortgage-backed securities, and not to diversify its revenue either geographically or by product. "My personal view is that [Bear Stearns] should have been made more of a victim," said one Bear senior managing director. "I don't think it should have been saved. I don't buy the argument that the whole system would have unraveled and collapsed. I really don't. I think it's a terrible precedent. I don't think the Fed should be in the business of assuming this kind of risk. I think it would have been a much better wake-up call for everybody had things followed their course."

However, this was not a risk that Paulson, Bernanke, or Geithner was willing to take. "On March 13, we learned from the SEC that Bear Stearns was facing imminent bankruptcy, and this presented us with some extraordinarily difficult policy judgments," Geithner explained. "Bear Stearns occupies—occupied—a central position in the very complex and intricate relationships that characterize our financial system. And, as important, it reached the brink of insolvency at an exceptionally fragile time in global financial markets. In our judgments, an abrupt and disorderly unwinding of Bear Stearns would have posed systemic risks to the financial system and magnified the downside risk to economic growth in the United States. A failure to act would have added to the risk that Americans would face lower incomes, lower home values, higher buying costs for housing, education, other living expenses, lower retirement savings and rising unemployment. We acted to avert that risk in the classic tradition of lenders of last resort with the authority provided by the Congress. We chose the best option available in the unique circumstances that prevailed at that time."

Bernanke said he, too, became concerned by Bear Stearns's deteriorating liquidity position during the week and then especially by the market's counterintuitive reaction to the back-to-back financing facility that the Fed had made available on Friday morning. "This news raised difficult questions of public policy," he said. "Normally, the market sorts out which companies survive and which fail, and that is as it should be. However, the issues raised here extended well beyond the fate of one company. Our financial system is extremely complex and interconnected, and Bear Stearns participated extensively in a range of critical markets. The sudden failure of Bear Stearns likely would have led to a chaotic unwinding of positions in those markets and could have severely shaken confidence. The company's failure could also have cast doubt on the financial positions of some of Bear Stearns's thousands of counterparties and perhaps of companies with similar businesses. Given the exceptional pressures on the global economy and financial system, the damage caused by a default by Bear Stearns could have been severe and extremely difficult to contain. Moreover, and very importantly, the adverse impact of a default would not have been confined to the financial system but would have been felt broadly in the real economy through its effects on asset values and credit availability."

Dimon obviously agreed with Bernanke, Geithner, and Paulson that allowing Bear Stearns to fail was too risky a proposition. "We don't know what would have happened," he said. "But I always look at what are the possibilities. And I think that [a meltdown of the whole system] had a very good possibility of happening. . . . So my attitude was we can't take that chance. We should fix it in the good old American way. You should feel good that a lot of people were up all night trying to get this thing fixed. And then go backwards and say, 'What went wrong and how should we fix that?'" He made an analogy to someone who had been drinking and then went swimming and began to drown. It would be the wrong thing to do, Dimon argued, to say, " 'Well, moral hazard, they are drowning, let them die, that will teach them.' Bad idea."

At 3:45 on Sunday afternoon, with the stakes growing exponentially and time running out, the five members of the Federal Reserve Board met in Washington to consider two historic decisions. First was whether to make a massive, $30 billion secured loan to a new company—eventually named Maiden Lane LLC, after the narrow street in downtown Manhattan that runs parallel to Liberty Street, the home of the New York Federal Reserve Bank—that would then buy $30 billion worth of Bear Stearns's most toxic assets and help to facilitate JPMorgan's acquisition. Second, as many Wall Street executives had been lobbying, was whether to open the discount window to securities firms, as opposed to commercial banks, for the first time since the depths of the Great Depression. The Fed's actions were meant to promote "orderly market functioning."

In approving the $30 billion loan, the Fed cited the "unusual and exigent circumstances" and observed, in slightly less than its usual cryptic way, that "the evidence available to the Board indicated that Bear Stearns would have difficulty meeting its repayment obligations the next business day" and that "significant support, such as an acquisition of Bear Stearns or an immediate guarantee of its payment obligations, was necessary to avoid serious disruptions to financial markets." The Fed noted that although "many potential investors" had been given the opportunity to make a deal for Bear Stearns, Bear "determined" that JPMorgan "was the most suitable bidder." To make the deal possible, JPMorgan "had requested assistance in financing a specific pool of assets that Bear Stearns had difficulty financing in the market and that [JPMorgan] believed added significant uncertainty to the level of risk it would assume at the same time it was acquiring the remainder of Bear Stearns." The Fed also approved two 18-month exemptions from its own rules that would allow JPMorgan, or its affiliates, to extend fully secured credit or guarantees to Bear Stearns and that would also allow JPMorgan to exclude the "assets and exposures" of Bear Stearns from the calculation of its tier 1 leverage capital ratio, effectively allowing JPMorgan to avoid raising new capital if the Bear Stearns assets ended up being worth less than originally thought. "It is fair to characterize both exemptions as unusual and significant," explained Andrew Williams, a spokesman for the New York Fed. "There was some precedent for the 23A exemption"—transactions with affiliates—"but there was really no precedent for the regulatory capital exemption. We felt that the exemptions were an appropriate risk to take in light of the whole package deal. The 23A exemption was defensible because of its short-term nature, limited amount (50 percent of bank's capital), the full collateralization, daily mark-to-market, and indemnity from JPMC. We also felt the short-term nature of the capital exemption was quite important—along with the fact that we did not provide exemption from capital rules at the bank level."

With the Fed's $30 billion in hand, the only remaining open question appeared to be how much JPMorgan would offer to pay for the equity of Bear Stearns—and who would make that decision. The Fed's willingness to participate in the rescue in such a major way, to the tune of $30 billion of the American people's money, put the government in the unusual position of caring about an entirely different issue, that of the potential for creating a "moral hazard" if by rescuing Bear Stearns's debt holders and creditors, the government also provided financial comfort to the firm's shareholders. What kind of message would the market hear if the government rescued both the creditors and the shareholders of a bankrupt firm? Clearly, the Bear shareholders were going to have to suffer if the Fed was to be involved. Parr, in Lazard's requisite fairness opinion, noted that since the choice for Bear's shareholders was grim indeed absent a deal with JPMorgan, any price greater than a penny could be justified. So the overriding question quickly became, how low is low?

With this turn of events, the idea of the $10-per-share offer that JPMorgan had made on Saturday seemed preposterous. At 5:36, Noel Kimmel, who worked in Bear's prime brokerage business, wrote Paul Friedman looking for an update. Kimmel reported that the prime brokerage executives seemed "to be negotiating a contingency plan" with Goldman Sachs and Morgan Stanley "to be able to move client positions, then [Bruce] Lisman came out and thought a deal might be close. They want people around to call clients."

Fifty minutes later, Friedman responded, "Latest rumor is that there will be an announcement of a sale to JPM at 7:00. Price is even lower than expected, as if that matters now."

At 6:37, Kimmel responded, "Hearing $2 for the whole enchilada . . . what a steal."

Replied Friedman: "You got it."

In fact, Friedman missed the penultimate step, which was easy to do given how briefly it was available. "Chase came back and said $4," Tese recalled. Having agreed to take $30 billion of Bear Stearns's riskiest assets onto the Fed's balance sheet, Paulson and Geithner phoned Dimon, who put the two senior regulators on speakerphone and told them he was thinking of offering $4 to $5 per share for the Bear. "That sounds high to me," Paulson reportedly said to Dimon. "I think this should be done at a very low price." At the same time as Dimon and the Feds were chatting, the Bear board of directors was ruminating about how $10 a share had become $4 a share. Nobody in that room was very happy. Then Parr got an urgent message on his BlackBerry asking him to call Doug Braunstein, the JPMorgan M&A banker on the deal. "The time frame was relatively quick," Parr remembered. "We barely had time to say the number was $4. There was enough time to begin discussing what that meant and for people to express their anger or disappointment." He stepped out and called Braunstein. "He was apologetic," Parr said. "He said, 'I'm sorry to have to do this, but I do have to convey the number is $2.' To which I said, 'You can't really mean that. Are you serious? You really don't want me to go back into the board and tell them this.' It was my way of partly trying to say to him, 'Don't do this. Whoever you need to talk to there, [tell them] this is a bad idea. . . . The tone is bad enough. [The difference between $4 and $2 is] no money of consequence. It's not an amount of money . . . that's material in the scheme of things, so who do you need to talk to? You shouldn't do this.'"

But Braunstein had his orders. Explained Dimon later: "I tell people, buying a house and buying a house on fire are two different things. So it wasn't really the value. The people at Bear Stearns built a great company. A lot of them had nothing to do with doing this. It was how much risk can we bear? A lot of people are in the situation where you may have a great bargain but you don't have the money, or a great bargain but you can't get it home. That was all we could bear. So we needed what I call that margin of error [and] a lot of it has been used up [already]. Remember that day, when we signed that piece of paper, we bought someone else's $350 billion of assets.

Honestly, that was all we could do. There was nothing else we could do. We wouldn't have done it. The issue wasn't the price at two or ten dollars. In any event, that was a very low price. The issue is, was there enough margin for error such that I can go to my shareholders a week later and a year later" and essentially defend his actions? "We just needed the margin for error. And without that, we simply couldn't do it."

Parr hung up the phone and dutifully reported the news to the board. Bear directors were stunned by the new, lowball offer. "We didn't even get a chance to say, 'How did you get $4?' when they came back and said $2," Tese said.

"We just couldn't believe it," Molinaro said. "There was already some sense at the board at $10 that it was an unfair deal, and we should just push the button and let's take our chances in bankruptcy."

For his part, Cayne was livid. At breakfast with Tese earlier that day, he had come to realize that blowing up the firm wouldn't do anyone any good. But now, upon hearing that the JPMorgan deal was at $2 per share—meaning that his six million or so shares, which at their height had been worth more than $1 billion, would now be worth around $12 million—he was incensed. His finger moved back over the red button. He wondered if the firm's bondholders, who together held $70 billion of debt and who in a merger with JPMorgan would be made whole but in bankruptcy would be severely impaired, should be asked to make a contribution to the shrinking pie for shareholders. The question was unorthodox for sure but in keeping with Cayne's proven ability to think through all the angles of a situation and land upon one that might improve his position. As Cayne knew, the bondholders had by far the most to gain from a deal with JPMorgan. Whereas all through the week, the cost of insuring against a default in Bear Stearns debt had been increasing rapidly—the so-called credit default swaps—a deal with JPMorgan would transfer these obligations to JPMorgan's balance sheet and immediately make them worth 100 cents on the dollar. In bankruptcy, these obligations would be worth pennies. "I brought up the fact maybe they should throw something into the pot because these guys are going to be made whole," he said. "They got

$70 billion of debt that's going in the tubes." There was a clear recognition at the board level that there was a bailout under way for the holders of Bear's debt. "It was really important to Paulson, whether the number was $4 or $2 or whatever," that it not appear to be a bailout, one person involved said. "He went on television: 'This is not a bailout.' But it was a bailout to the creditors, the $70 billion." The lawyers told Cayne that getting a contribution from creditors was unlikely to happen, especially in such a short time frame.

Recalled Cayne: "I then say, 'Okay, well, so, let me get this straight. We take $2 as opposed to bankruptcy.' Right? Right. I said, 'Okay, stop the meeting.' I want to talk to Dennis Block and Tony Novelly." Block was the lead Cadwalader attorney advising the company and a longtime Bear Stearns legal advisor; Novelly, the CEO of Apex Oil Company and a Bear Stearns board member, had had direct experience with bankruptcy when the St. Louis–based Apex filed for Chapter 11 protection. According to the *Washington Post*, in the middle of negotiating with his creditors prior to the bankruptcy filing, Novelly "jumped up, according to various accounts, and made an obscene hand gesture at his bankers, called them stupid and walked out." Novelly was also an outspoken advocate on the Bear board for pursuing the bankruptcy option.

Cayne left the meeting with Block and Novelly. "What does bankruptcy mean for a securities firm?" he wanted to know. "What happens in bankruptcy? How bad is it if Bear Stearns goes into bankruptcy? In the back of my mind I know I've got a board that ain't gonna vote for bankruptcy regardless of how I feel. But on the other hand, I want to know. What are the actions? You just can't tell me $2 a share [or] goodbye, unless I've explored it and I agree that it's $2 a share or goodbye. Actually, as it turned out, 20¢ a share was okay, as long as we didn't go into bankruptcy, because in bankruptcy the fourteen thousand employees suffer dramatically. Dramatically. What's my responsibility? My responsibility was to the employees. My responsibility was shareholders, but I was a shareholder. My responsibility was to the bondholders, but they're big boys. They're buying at 300 over or 200 over, and they'll sell it at 100 over. I mean, there's no family there. But the fourteen thousand people, that's family."

"The board meeting was very tense," a board member recalled. "I think on Saturday night Jimmy was in the camp of 'Fuck them, why don't we just take this thing under.' . . . I love Jimmy, but this card-player-that's-going-to-take-the-system-to-its-knees routine . . . isn't going to work. We had no idea what the alternatives are. We think we got this great hand to play . . . 'You want to do that to us, then fuck you, we'll take the whole system down.' We have no idea what kind of emergency legislation they have in their back pocket to say, 'They just took us down, here's the emergency relief to step in to keep the system from melting down.' They could have done all the same things that happened where we were actually being bought, only saying, 'But you're not being bought. You're going into bankruptcy. You got no bankruptcy protection. You got no board. Your employees are out the door tomorrow. You got no indemnity. By the way, the U.S. attorney is going to be in and investigate you guys until the cows come.' But the most important thing is you have fourteen thousand people on the streets the next day. If you understand bankruptcy law, if you go into Chapter 7, there's a sign on the door, you don't show up. The phone's gone, the computer's gone, there's no severance, there's no nothing. We'd have had fourteen thousand people out on the streets because we don't need their lousy $2? So it was never something a thoughtful person could do, and I'm not saying that to diminish Jimmy. I mean, I know the emotion of the times. You think you've got a powerful hand here, but we're like a fucking kid in the schoolyard surrounded by bullies. In prison let's not show how tough we are. We're way over our heads here. That's why even on Saturday night, when we were doing the $10 deal, I told Sam, 'Look, $10 should be $20 should be $30 should be $40, whatever. You've got to understand what we're facing in the alternative. This isn't the worst thing in the world.' By the time the $2 deal came around, all of a sudden the $10 deal looked good."

Way back on Thursday night, the board's independent directors had realized quickly that their interests might well diverge from the interests of Cayne and Greenberg, the two officer-directors (although technically, since he had retired as CEO three months earlier, Cayne was no longer an officer of the firm), and so they decided to hire their own legal counsel. Their choice was Rodgin Cohen, the head of Sullivan & Cromwell, who had made the call to Geithner on Wednesday night at home, on behalf of Schwartz and Molinaro, to tell him Bear Stearns was in trouble. Now he was back in a new role representing the independent directors. For a brief moment, while Cayne was contemplating voting against the $2 deal—which, he claimed, Paulson had actually wanted to be a $1-per-share deal—the independent directors, led by Tese, began to meet separately with Cohen to discuss their fiduciary responsibilities in this complicated situation. As for bankruptcy, Tese said, "I knew it wasn't a viable alternative. Rog knew it wasn't a viable alternative. Jimmy wasn't so sure. A lot of the bankers and the other people, they weren't so sure. But we were sure. Jimmy's a very smart guy. You explain things to Jimmy, he gets it. But he also said, 'Well, why don't we tell them to go screw themselves?' And '$2 is like zero dollars.' And I said, 'The independents outweigh everybody else.' So the independents met independently. There was a brief time there where the independents would have voted for a deal . . . because it was explained to us that anything is better than nothing. And there's $70 billion worth of bondholders that you have to consider. Therefore, if Jimmy doesn't want to vote for it, that's too bad."

This was the crucial moment for Cayne. "I don't have a degree in law," he said. "Basically, I don't have a degree in anything, but it seemed to me that that was off the table, bankruptcy. After my meeting I came back in and I said, 'Okay, the fourteen thousand people.' Which way do I go? . . . I agree $2 a share, saying in my mind that this guy would have paid $20, now it's $2. Now I'm thinking, it's over. It's like you got a bad grade on your test. That's it. No appeal. This thing that you spent forty years building, it's over."

Tese explained just how difficult a decision this was for Cayne. "I said to Jimmy, 'You believe in doing the right thing. This is the right thing to do, even though in your case, it's very painful.' . . . Here's a guy that saw something that he worked for, for forty years, implode." But Cayne got with the program. "Jimmy, after he got to understand how the bankruptcy system would work, he voted for it," Tese said.

Still, there was a fair amount of incredulity among the board members about the $2 per share offer. "I think they were unhappy," Molinaro said. "I think Jimmy expressed his unhappiness with the price, the ridiculous price that we were getting. But I think the other board members basically were of the view that we don't have any hand. Once the conclusion was reached that we were not going to go down that path, now it's simply just trying to get the best terms and conditions that we can get for them, and make sure the file's properly prepared."

Further efforts were made by Parr to see if JPMorgan would increase the consideration being offered by adding some form of contingent value right, or CVR. CVRs were popular once upon a time on Wall Street as a way to cleverly bridge the valuation gap between buyers and sellers or to offer more value to sellers if certain hurdles were met, most famously in Viacom's 1993 $10 billion acquisition of Paramount Communications. But CVRs have been used infrequently since then. In proposing the use of a CVR-like security, Parr told Braunstein, the JPMorgan M&A banker, "You're fundamentally telling us you don't believe our book value. We do believe our book value, so that this should be easy to give. You don't believe it. We believe it, so we'll take a CVR. If you're right and there's nothing there, well, fine."

But JPMorgan wouldn't go for it. When Parr came back into the room to explain that Braunstein told him the offer would be $2 period, Cohen asked him if he knew why. "He said, 'The government is insisting on it,'" Cohen recalled. "I said, 'Is that what you were told?' He said, 'Yes.' I said, 'I'd like to talk to the government.'" Cohen stepped out of the room and called Geithner and Paulson. He told them the board had been informed by JPMorgan that the government had insisted on the low price and that fact would be written just that way in the proxy statement seeking the shareholder vote for the merger. "They said, 'You'll have to do what you'll have to do,'" Cohen remembered. (The proxy subsequently stated that following "discussion with government officials," JPMorgan refused to increase its offer beyond $2 per share.) But the government's Sunday afternoon hard line was a new posture. Previously, a participant recalled, "There was a whole round of, 'No, no, we don't set prices. We don't negotiate deals. That's for other people to do.'" Not anymore. Now, with the markets in Asia and in Australia getting closer to opening, what little flexibility that seemed to exist evaporated quickly. "When Dimon got the backing of the Fed, what I was very upset about was it came down to two bucks," Bear director Fred Salerno said. "It was clearly this moral hazard issue. Somebody gave him the signal—I don't know who, I could guess. I'm very upset we're now down to $2. . . . [W]e had no choice but to take the $2 because we lived for another day and the bondholders are okay. When you get that close to bankruptcy, right, you had to represent the bondholders—it was punitive. The *building* was worth $10 a share. It was punitive. To me, it was something done for political reasons. The Democrats were yelling on Friday, 'How could you bail out Bear Stearns and you couldn't help the homeowners?' All right? And Lord knows why it came all the way down to $2. It didn't have to be."

CHAPTER 9

THE FED COMES TO THE RESCUE
(AFTER THE BATTLE IS OVER)

As had happened many times during the previous seventy-two hours, the Bear Stearns executives found themselves in the uncomfortable position of having accepted their horrible fate but still not being entirely sure if they even had a deal. JPMorgan had gone silent again, presumably because it was awaiting the outcome of the Fed's meeting. Without the Fed's agreement on the $30 billion emergency loan, there was no deal. Over at Bear, nerves were once again getting frayed. "There was some concern," Parr said. "There were gaps of time when our board would be sitting in the room saying, 'Where's the other side? They asked us to make a decision. We review it. We go through all the discussions and we're ready to make a decision. Now where are they?' . . . It became a very tense time because truly you felt like you were sitting on a bomb and the clock was ticking. And there we sat for whatever period of time wondering, 'What's going to happen? Have we got a deal? What's it going to look like, and are they going to sign or aren't they?' And we're running into Japan and Australia time." Finally, the call came from JPMorgan that its board had approved the $2 deal. But time had indeed run out. "We were given like forty-five seconds to sign," Cayne recalled. Cohen remembered being told: "There is no negotiating room. It's either this or nothing."

The moment had come to seal the fate of Bear Stearns, the fifth-largest Wall Street securities firm. The lawyers walked the board through its fiduciary duties under Delaware law, which required them to consider their duty to creditors if they turned down the JPMorgan deal and opted for bankruptcy. Given that the choice was between nominal consideration for shareholders and 100 cents on the dollar for creditors or nothing for shareholders and pennies for creditors, Sullivan & Cromwell's advice for the board was that its fiduciary duties had shifted from shareholders to all the other stake-holders of Bear Stearns, among them creditors, employees, and retirees. Dennis Block, at Cadwalader, walked the board through the material terms of the merger agreement, including that stunning $2 per share in stock, as well as the option JPMorgan would get on 383 Madison Avenue—an agreement, regardless of whether the deal closed, for Bear Stearns to sell the building to its rival for $1.1 billion, some $400 million below its market value—and the option to buy 19.9 percent of Bear's stock. (As part of the deal, JPMorgan was to take over some two million square feet of office space around the world, including sixty-five acres and five buildings with 673,000 square feet in Whippany, New Jersey.) The lawyers also explained that the merger agreement called for JPMorgan to "guaranty Bear Stearns' trading and certain other obligations" and that the New York Federal Reserve Bank would provide "up to $30 billion" of "supplemental funding" secured by a "pool of collateral" consisting primarily of Bear Stearns's "mortgage-related securities and other mortgage-related assets and related hedges."

Parr then reviewed for the board the process he had undertaken since Wednesday night—a mere five days earlier—to scour the world for potential buyers for all of Bear Stearns or its salable pieces. He reported to the board that, aside from JPMorgan's modest offer, Lazard could find no buyers for the firm or its assets in such a seriously constricted time period. Parr told the board that Lazard was prepared to issue a "fairness opinion" (for which it would receive a $20 million fee at closing) to the effect that the "exchange ratio"—the ratio of the $2 being offered to the Friday closing price of $36.78 for JPMorgan's stock—of 0.05437 was "fair, from a financial point of view, to holders of Bear Stearns common stock." Given that the choice was between about $290 million for the 145.4 million Bear shares outstanding and nothing, Lazard's fairness opinion was not a hard one to give, nor was it particularly meaningful—which does not mean that Parr and his team did not work hard but does raise the question of why corporate boards agree to pay so much money for a couple of pieces of paper that are of so little value.

Then the discussion turned to the all-important indemnity by JPMorgan of Bear's officers and directors. According to the terms of the merger agreement, JPMorgan agreed to "indemnify and hold harmless" each current and former Bear director and officer "from liability for matters arising at or prior to the completion of the merger" as well as keeping in place Bear Stearns's existing indemnification agreements "for six years following completion of the merger." The indemnification agreement was a hugely important deal point for Bear's officers and directors, who knew by the evening of March 16 that they were already the target of numerous lawsuits—with more to come—questioning the individual and collective decisions and judgments that had allowed the situation to reach the edge of the abyss. The board also agreed to amend the company's bylaws to allow Bear Stearns to pay the legal and other expenses of any indemnified person "promptly upon demand by such person."

Corporate governance experts—along with the justice system—will likely debate for years to come whether the Bear Stearns board properly exercised its fiduciary duty during this crisis, or in the years leading up to this crisis, but Parr is confident the board did all it could. "They asked lots of questions," he said. "They asked that every option be pursued and considered, so it wasn't as though they said, 'This is the right answer' or 'That's the right answer.' They didn't have prejudice—indeed, to the contrary. In many respects, they didn't like the way things were going, so they wanted to make sure other options were considered, other things were pursued."

Parr was especially impressed by the way Greenberg and Schwartz conducted themselves during the deliberations. "Ace did a good job as a board member," Parr said. "He didn't like where things were. It was clear he hated this outcome. But he was very measured and very good about focusing on the right thing to do. It was really quite helpful in just setting a tone." Schwartz's long experience as an M&A banker—his ability to herd the cats—was essential. "He was really the right guy to be the CEO," Parr said. "Many CEOs have never dealt with something as complex as an M&A transaction, so it takes time. . . . Alan, thankfully, having been through it so many times, knew how to take in information and then cut through it and say, 'This is what needs to be done.' It was extremely helpful."

Finally, the time had come for Schwartz to lead his fellow directors into purgatory. "Two dollars is better than nothing," he said. For the next thirty minutes, he spoke. According to the *Wall Street Journal,* "A price of $2 and the right for shareholders to vote, [Schwartz] explained, was better than a price of zero and a bankruptcy filing. He also pointed out the untold consequences a bankruptcy filing would have on world markets—a scenario Bear Stearns directors didn't want to be held responsible for." At another point, Schwartz reportedly looked at the directors and said, "What can I say? It's better than nothing." Then he called for the vote. "Do I have anyone who's opposed?" he asked. No one said anything. At around 6:30 P.M., with markets just opening in Asia, the board voted unanimously to approve the JPMorgan deal. Parr and Cohen then informed JPMorgan of the Bear board's approval.

A press release announcing the deal soon hit the wires. "Effective immediately, JPMorgan Chase is guaranteeing the trading obligations of Bear Stearns and its subsidiaries and is providing management oversight for its operations," it read. "Other than shareholder approval, the closing is not subject to any material conditions." Dimon added, "JPMorgan Chase stands behind Bear Stearns. Bear Stearns' clients and counterparties should feel secure that JPMorgan is guaranteeing Bear Stearns' counterparty risk. We welcome their clients, counterparties and employees to our firm, and we are glad to be their partner." Schwartz, the man who presided over Bear Stearns's demise, chimed in: "The past week has been an incredibly difficult time for Bear Stearns. This transaction represents the best outcome for all of our constituencies based upon the current circumstances. I am incredibly proud of our employees and believe they will continue to add tremendous value to the new enterprise." In delicious corporate fashion, both Black and Winters, the co-heads of investment banking at JPMorgan, offered some inspiring words in the press release as well: "This transaction helps us fill out some of the gaps in our franchise with manageable overlap," Black said. "We know the Bear Stearns leadership team well and look forward to working with them to bring our two companies together." Added Winters: "Acquiring Bear Stearns enables us to obtain an attractive set of businesses. After conducting due diligence, we're comfortable with the quality of Bear Stearns' business, and are pleased to have them as part of our firm." JPMorgan scheduled an investor conference call for eight o'clock that night.

THE OTHER ACTION the Fed took at its 3:45 Sunday afternoon meeting—but which did not get disseminated until 7:19 that night, about fifteen minutes after the JPMorgan deal for Bear Stearns was announced—was the equally momentous and historic decision to open the Fed's discount window to Wall Street securities firms directly for the first time since the 1930s, because of "the unusual and exigent circumstances." Ironically, this was exactly the decisive step Bear Stearns executives had been seeking for months, and now it had happened—but too late to help the firm. Once the Fed had "evidence" that "adequate credit accommodations" were not available elsewhere, the overnight loans could be made as long as they were secured by a "broad range of investment-grade debt securities" and had recourse to the individual Wall Street firm borrowing the money. In making this historic decision, the Fed claimed "there had been impairment of a broad range of financial markers in which primary dealers"—many Wall Street firms—"finance themselves" and that "the dealers might have difficulty obtaining necessary financing for their operations from alternative sources." Beginning March 17, the window would be open to Wall Street for an initial six-month period. The Fed also lowered the interest rate charged at the discount window to 3.25 percent, from 3.50 percent. "These steps will provide financial institutions with greater assurance of access to funds," Bernanke said in a press release about the new initiatives. Geithner said, "This is designed to help get liquidity to where it can help play an appropriate role in helping address the range of challenges." Paulson added, "I appreciate the additional actions taken this evening by the Federal Reserve to enhance the stability, liquidity and orderliness of our markets."

During congressional hearings on April 3 that followed the events of March, just as certainly as little boys on sleds follow a winter snowfall, Bernanke and Geithner further explained their thinking at this crucial moment in the history of American capitalism. "We made the decision to [open the discount window] on Sunday," Bernanke said. "At the time we did it, we didn't know whether the Bear Stearns deal would be consummated or not, and we wanted to be prepared in case it wasn't consummated, that we would need to have this facility in order to protect what we imagined would be pressure on the other dealers subsequently to that. Whether opening up earlier would have helped or not is very difficult to say. Perhaps President Geithner can add to this. But Bear Stearns was losing customers and counterparties very quickly. They were downgraded on Friday. And we did lend them money, of course, to keep them [going] into the weekend, but it's not at all obvious to me that it would have been sufficient to prevent their bankruptcy."

Like Bernanke, Geithner also defended the decision to open the discount window on Sunday evening based upon the events that occurred at Bear Stearns on Friday. "Friday morning we took the exceptional step, with extreme reluctance, with support of the Board of Governors and the Treasury, to structure a way to get them to the weekend, so that we could buy some time to explore whether there was a possible solution that would have them acquired and guaranteed," he said, noting that "the scale of the loss of confidence" in Bear Stearns was extraordinary. "The number of customers and counterparties that sought to withdraw funds" and the "actions by rating agencies" to downgrade Bear's credit "accelerated that dynamic, despite the access to liquidity and despite the hope that that might buy some time." Geithner also defended the Fed's decision not to open the discount window until Sunday night, after Bear could have benefited from it. "The way the Federal Reserve Act is designed, and the way we think about the discount window for banks, is we only allow sound institutions to borrow against collateral in that context," he said. "I can only speak personally for this, but I would have been very uncomfortable lending to Bear, given what we knew at that time." He said that both the opening of the Fed window and the earlier creation of the facility "were exceptionally consequential acts, taken with extreme reluctance and care, because of the substantial consequences it would have for moral hazard in the financial system going forward. And I do not believe it would have been appropriate for us to take that act Sunday night if we had not been faced with the dynamics that were precipitated by, accelerated by, the looming prospect of a Bear default."

In a separate interview a few months later, Geithner again defended his decision not to open the discount window to Bear Stearns. He said he would not have taken that extraordinary step three months earlier, as Schwartz, Dodd, and others had been hoping. "People had been pushing us to do it for a long time," he said. "We consciously chose not to do it, and I think rightly so, because it is a consequential act. You don't want to do it unless you think there's no other option available to mitigate the risks of the system." He reiterated the fact that Bear Stearns was no longer creditworthy on Sunday night. "We don't lend to banks if we're not pretty comfortable with their financial position and how prudent they are," he said. "These facilities were not giving the dealers the same protections banks have. My own personal view is it would not have mitigated significantly the risk that Bear faced because they were in a position where they were uniquely vulnerable to the same kind of loss of confidence they faced and we would not have been lending freely to them no matter what. Who knows, you can't wind back the clock. But I don't have any regrets about not opening the window earlier. In fact, I think it's kind of unfortunate in some ways we did do it. We're trying in some ways to let the air out of this thing gradually and mitigate the risk [of] too much damage to the economy. We're not trying to put a floor under stuff artificially. We can't protect people from the risks they took in the boom. We just want to protect the economy to some extent from the damage that can come if the air gets let out too traumatically. It's not our job to come keep the air in there and let people operate at a level of leverage and risk that was true before this thing. So there were a huge number of people that were pushing us from the beginning to put a bigger safety net under everything and we chose consciously not to do that, and I think for good reasons. We want the system to be stronger coming out of this, not weaker. It will be weaker if all we do is give people a whole bunch of comfort that we protect them on the other side. Very hard line to draw, though. This is a pretty wrenching thing."

Geithner said he knew he and Paulson would be criticized no matter what the regulatory decision. "We're going to get two types of criticism," he continued. "Some people will say, 'Oh, my God, you guys way overdid it. That wasn't necessary. You should have let all this damage happen. You gave too much away to the priority of the adverse outcome.' And a bunch of other people say, 'If only you had been more aggressive earlier, it would have been terrific.' But frankly, we've been way aggressive on monetary policy and on a bunch of other fronts, and even before this we had a bunch of people saying to us we had overdone it. We're operating in difficult judgments, fog of war, and so we're going to be second-guessed by a bunch of people." One early critic was Paul Volcker, the former chairman of the Federal Reserve, who told the Economic Club of New York on April 8, "Sweeping powers have been exercised in a manner that is neither natural nor comfortable for a central bank."

Wall Street executives immediately appreciated the import of the Fed's decision. "This is a five-vodka event," one said. "Liquidity is no longer an issue." But, by and large, the Bear Stearns executives were furious. They had been lobbying the Fed for months to take this very action. Just fifteen minutes after the firm had been dispatched, for a pittance, into the waiting arms of JPMorgan, the Fed moved at last. Only the most diplomatic among them, such as Alan Schwartz, were able to convey a professional understanding of how their competitors would benefit at Bear Stearns's expense, and claim to be okay with it. "One part of me was thrilled they were opening the window," one executive said. "I didn't want Lehman to be next. The other part was . . . it feels a little raw to say, 'It's really complicated, it's really complicated, oh, okay, done, stroke of the pen.' But you're so strung out by then you don't know how you feel."

The others were simply appalled and were willing to say so. Fred Salerno heard about it from a friend who called him in the airport after the Bear board had signed the deal. "What upset me the most was . . . they opened the window a half hour after they told us we had to sign," Salerno said with some anger. "No excuse for that. . . . I'll never forget about that. I found out about that in the airport. I almost went ballistic. How could they hang out all those people? Now, maybe it wouldn't have made a difference, maybe we're so far gone that when we really looked at the numbers we had to take the deal anyhow, but they should have told us. I was sick. . . . Not because of me, but because of the fourteen thousand people that got disadvantaged by some political play, in my mind. I'll never forget that. No excuse. You talk about transparency. You talk about disclosure. You can't play a game like that, not with people's lives."

Asked about Geithner's comments and his decision regarding opening the discount window to Wall Street after Bear had been sold for $2 a share and not earlier, Jimmy Cayne became spitting angry. "The audacity of that prick in front of the American people announcing he was deciding whether or not a firm of this stature and this whatever was good enough to get a loan," he said. "Like he was the determining factor, and it's like a flea on his back, floating down underneath the Golden Gate Bridge, getting a hard-on, saying, 'Raise the bridge.' This guy thinks he's got a big dick. He's got nothing, except maybe a boyfriend. I'm not a good enemy. I'm a very bad enemy. But certain things really—that bothered me plenty. It's just that for some clerk to make a decision based on what, your own personal feeling about whether or not they're a good credit? Who the fuck asked you? You're not an elected officer. You're a clerk. Believe me, you're a clerk. I want to open up on this fucker, that's all I can tell you."

CHAPTER 10

MOONING AT THE WAKE

Bear Stearns slipped out a press release on Sunday night stating that it would not be announcing its first-quarter results on March 17, as previously scheduled. By this time, Paul Friedman had wandered back to the trading floor. There were about seventy-five other traders hanging around, too, "most of them sitting with their feet up on the trading desk, trying to figure out what to do," Friedman remembered. He heard from Steve Begleiter and Sam Molinaro that the board had approved the $2 deal. Then Jeff Mayer, one of the two heads of the fixed-income division, called everyone together. "Mayer got up on the trading desk and called everybody over and told them about it," Friedman said. "He said, 'You can go home, and we'll come back tomorrow and start to deal with this, and figure out what do we do now.' I then went back into my office with a handful of other people, and we sat and commiserated and started drinking." Out came a bottle of Glenlivet scotch and a couple of bottles of wine. "We're now holding our wake," Friedman said. "We're crying and drinking and working on getting pretty drunk." They were also mooning the JPMorgan traders who were just opposite them on the north side of 47th Street. "There are five stages of grief," he said, "and I had seen a lot of those stages on Sunday night. I mean, I was the closest of anyone to what happened and it still blew my mind." Friedman and his wife kept telling each other that they would "still be okay if something happens," but, like many others, he lost one-third of his net worth that day.

"Once the thing was announced, people were unhappy, upset, angry, depressed," Molinaro recalled. "All those feelings. People were crying. People were angry. I was feeling depressed and sad. I couldn't believe it. But I knew that we didn't really have any choice. We were fucked. We didn't have any choice. We did the best we could do with what we had. I couldn't say I was as angry. I wasn't that angry, because I had lived through what had happened, and I knew how we got to where we had gotten to." Fred Salerno held out some hope—a prayer, really—that when the inevitable shareholder lawsuits were filed in the Delaware courts questioning whether the board had done all it could have and whether the deal lockups that JPMorgan had demanded were fair to shareholders, the courts would throw out the deal. "The more lockups there are, the worse it is," he said. "They'll throw the whole damn thing out. So we always had, when we left that night, the hope that the Delaware court would look at this and say $2 is not the right number for the shareholder. But what we didn't know is they"—JPMorgan—"screwed up."

At about 7 P.M., the *Wall Street Journal* broke the news online that JPMorgan would buy Bear Stearns for $2 per share. The reactions were immediate and shocking. "This is like waking up in the summer with snow on the ground," said Ron Geffner, a former SEC enforcement lawyer. "The price is indicative that there were bigger problems at Bear than the clients and the public realized." The price must be a typo, the consensus seemed to be, since surely a company that fourteen months earlier had been trading at $172.69 per share could not now be worth so little. Steve Schwarzman, the head of The Blackstone Group, had been vacationing with his wife in St. Barts, the exclusive Caribbean island. He had spoken to Schwartz on Friday for about thirty minutes to see if Schwartz needed Blackstone's help and was told, "We're fine. We're good. We don't need any help." That Sunday evening, he had just sat down for dinner with fellow Philadelphia billionaire Ron Perelman on Perelman's 188-foot yacht, the *Ultima III,* when the news paraded across his BlackBerry that Bear Stearns had been sold for $2 a share. "It must be $20," Schwarzman and Perelman said to each other. "It can't be $2." John Mack, the CEO of Morgan Stanley, had a similar reaction. But there was no typo. "I've got to think we can get more in a liquidation," a midlevel Bear executive told the *Wall Street Journal.* "I'm not selling my shares, this price is dramatically less than the book value Alan Schwartz told us the building is worth. The building is worth $8 a share."

At 7:11, Friedman e-mailed John Shrewsbury, at Wells Fargo

Bank in San Francisco, one of Bear Stearns's large lenders. "We have been acquired by JPM," he wrote, and then, paraphrasing the REM song, added, "It's the end of life as we know it but all will ultimately be fine."

Friedman then heard from his friend Glinert again, wondering how he was doing. He answered: "Angry, sad, depressed. Sitting in the office drinking scotch." Glinert wanted to call, but Friedman suggested, "Not till I have lots more scotch. Got a room full of angry people and we need the venting."

Thirty minutes later, Friedman wrote Glinert again. "Still drinking," he allowed. "Getting less coherent but no less angry. Death of a family member. Loss of friends. Wouldn't work at JPM on a bet— which is good since they wouldn't want me."

Glinert urged some restraint. "One day at a time—ok?" he wrote. "You still gotta get back in tomorrow."

Replied Friedman: "Maybe. If I come in I come in. If not . . . who gives a damn."

Starting at eight that night, while Friedman and his colleagues were busy getting drunk, JPMorgan convened a conference call to discuss the deal. "It's been a long weekend," JPMorgan's chief financial officer, Mike Cavanagh, conceded with some understatement. Cavanagh walked the listeners through a hastily assembled six-page "investor presentation" that highlighted the acquisition's benefits, including the view that "when fully integrated" the deal would add about $1 billion annually to JPMorgan's earnings. The bank seemed especially excited to be buying Bear Stearns's prime brokerage and clearing businesses, its energy-trading business (which had attempted to raise money for the firm on Friday by liquidating its physical stores of natural gas), and its four hundred brokers (both Dimon's father and grandfather were brokers, and Dimon has always liked that business, which JPMorgan did not have). Cavanagh also announced that JPMorgan would provide "management oversight" and "guarantee the trading obligations" of Bear Stearns immediately and that, in addition to the $290 million purchase price for the equity, JPMorgan also estimated that it would cost another $6 billion, pretax, to cover other related costs: Bear Stearns's litigation; consolidating people (including paying severance), technology, and facilities; selling off large chunks of the $350 billion of assets just acquired; and conforming the accounting systems. "I want to hit right off the bat that this is a good economic transaction for JPMorgan Chase shareholders," he said. "Obviously the price that's being paid here . . . gives us the flexibility and margin for error that was appropriate given the speed at which the transaction came together."

Cavanagh pointed out that the merger agreement did not contain a typical material adverse change (MAC) clause, in part to demonstrate to the market the likelihood that the deal would close. Without such a clause in the contract, JPMorgan would have very little legal recourse if Bear Stearns's business materially deteriorated further; this decision exposed JPMorgan to some additional risk but also was meant to send a strong signal to the market. "This is a deal we all want to see close and will close," he explained. Cavanagh also made clear that all the counterparties that had worried about doing business with Bear Stearns during the previous week need be concerned no longer. "We're also, effective immediately, providing a JPMorgan guarantee to all trading obligations of Bear Stearns," he said. "So all counterparties facing off against Bear Stearns should understand that they're dealing with JPMorgan Chase on that basis." JPMorgan's agreement to guarantee immediately, before the deal closed, Bear's trading obligations—its daily operating activities, as opposed to the firm's long-term holdings of company debt—was a hugely important signal to the market that Bear remained sufficiently open for business until the merger could close, estimated by Cavanagh at ninety days. "Having taken Bear Stearns out of the problem category, and the strong action by the Federal Reserve, we would anticipate the market will behave quite differently on Monday than it was on Thursday or Friday," Cavanagh said on the call. Parr said this was an essential deal point, recognized by both sides. "Otherwise they'd be buying a rapidly melting ice cube," he said.

But such an interim-period guarantee by one firm of another firm's obligations was another place in this historic deal where new ground was broken, and right away this led to confusion in the marketplace. The very first question on the conference call was about whether Bear Stearns would be open for business. "Bear Stearns is absolutely open for business," Bill Winters answered. "That's the purpose of the guarantee that we've put in place. That should absolutely give everybody in the market complete comfort that when dealing with Bear Stearns you're backed by the full facing credit of JPMorgan. So Bear is open for business today, with all the credit backing that we can provide. And it obviously intends to remain completely active in the market up to and through the date we complete the acquisition."

The next caller picked up on Winters's answer and wanted to know what would happen to the guarantee if Bear's shareholders voted down the deal. "First of all, the guarantee applies to all transactions on the books today and any transactions that are entered into while that guarantee is in place," Winters said. "We have every expectation that Bear Stearns shareholders will approve this deal. I think we're offering the best alternative that they've got at this point and . . . we'd be surprised if a better alternative came along. If in the future the shareholders do fail to approve the transaction, then our guarantee would no longer apply prospectively. But of course everything that was on the books up to and to that point would be covered by the guarantee."

At this point Steve Black added a rather confusing comment: "And that shareholder vote is an ongoing process. It takes place—if it does fail—over the course of a continuing vote brought back again throughout the period of twelve months." He seemed to be suggesting that even if the Bear shareholders voted down the deal, the guarantee would still apply for a period of twelve months.

To clarify, analyst Brandon Seward asked, "How long is that guarantee good for if shareholders do fail to approve this transaction?"

Black tried again. "The guarantee is good for the period of time that the shareholders have to approve the transaction for everything that is on the books now or will be put on the books over that time frame. If the shareholders were to choose not to approve the transaction, they have to continuously take it back to a vote over the course of a twelve-month period."

"Okay, so the guarantee is good for twelve months because that's how long the vote has to stay outstanding?" Seward asked again.

"No," Black replied. "Let's be clear. We all firmly believe that the shareholders at Bear Stearns will approve the transaction. So we think that it will be a moot point. But the fact is if they were to choose not to approve it, then the guarantee would eventually go away when that process has run its course, which is over the course of twelve months."

"Okay," Seward pursued, "so the guarantee is the lesser of approval or twelve months?"

Cavanagh jumped in this time. "So just to be clear, we have a guarantee on all trades on the books as of today, all trades that get put on the books up to any date where our deal could ever fall away, which we don't think would happen. Only prospectively from that point forward would the JPMorgan guarantee not exist."

Still confused, Seward tried one more time. "But as part of the process, they have to continue to go back and seek shareholders' approval over a twelve-month period?"

"No," Winters replied. "We would expect that shareholders would approve this transaction on the first pass. But of course that's up to the shareholders to decide."

It seemed evident that Cavanagh, Black, and Winters either did not understand fully how the guarantee would work or did but had failed to make clear what would happen to the guarantee if the Bear Stearns shareholders voted down the JPMorgan deal. A three-page Guarantee Agreement had been executed on March 16 and signed by Dimon along with the Merger Agreement itself, but these documents were not particularly clear about how this very important aspect of the deal would work. Indeed, it would not take long for that confusion to manifest in the marketplace, for Dimon to lash out publicly at his high-priced lawyers for failing to anticipate the issue, and for the resulting dispute to almost derail the deal consummated just hours before.

First, though, the government wanted to make sure the markets saw the events as a positive and would react calmly. "Last Friday, I said that market participants are addressing challenges and I am pleased with recent developments," Treasury Secretary Paulson said in a statement. "I appreciate the additional actions taken this evening by the Federal Reserve to enhance the stability, liquidity and orderliness of our markets." The New York Fed also wanted to explain to the Wall Street mafia what had just happened. In a conference call late Sunday night, at about the same time of the JP-Morgan call with investors, Geithner explained how the opening of the discount window to investment banks would work, including what collateral would be accepted by the bank. According to the *Wall Street Journal,* "Geithner and Dimon led off with some brief remarks, noting that J. P. Morgan would be guaranteeing Bear Stearns's debts and that if the pact hadn't come together, the market impact may have been catastrophic. During the question-and-answer session, Citigroup Inc.'s new CEO, Vikram Pandit, spoke up. Mr. Pandit—who did not initially identify himself—asked a shrewd but technical question" about whether JPMorgan would be guaranteeing trades with Bear Stearns until the deal closed. "How would the deal affect the risk to Bear Stearns's trading partners on certain long-term contracts? The query irked Mr. Dimon. 'Who is this?' he snapped. Mr. Pandit identified himself as 'Vikram.' Offended that Mr. Pandit was taking up time with what he considered granular inquiries, Mr. Dimon shot back, 'Stop being such a jerk.' He added that Citigroup 'should thank us' for staving off further mayhem on Wall Street.' " Schwartz was listening on the call but found he was having "an out of body experience."

Just after midnight, as the few remaining Bear Stearns stalwarts were trickling out of 383 Madison, James Egan, head of Global Fixed-Income Sales, sent an e-mail to his bosses, Craig Overlander and Jeff Mayer, and a few others, including Tom Marano. "I had always heard about a job described as a '$2.00 Broker,'" he wrote. "I was never really sure what that was but now I do—it's us!"

By the time the Bear employees arrived at work the next day, some wag had already taped a $2 bill above the Bear Stearns logo on one of the revolving doors leading into 383 Madison Avenue. That image quickly became an apt metaphor for the brutal decline and fall of a once-proud firm, a firm that had survived every other crisis of the twentieth century, from the Depression to World War II to the market crash of 1987, without a single losing quarter but could not make it through the global credit crunch of 2007 and beyond. "Once you have a run on the bank, you are in a death spiral and your assets become worthless," observed David Trone, a brokerage industry analyst at Fox-Pitt, Kelton. "Banks and brokerages are a house of cards built on the confidence of clients, creditors and counterparties. If you take chunks out of that confidence, things can go awry pretty quickly."

On Monday morning, as "firefighters in kilts and St. Patrick's Day revelers on their way to the parade streamed by Bear employees smoking cigarettes in front of the firm's headquarters," the *Wall Street Journal* reported, the Bear brethren had to start picking up the shattered glass of their firm. "Basically we're all wondering first if we'll keep our jobs, second, if we'll get severance if we don't," one anonymous investment banker told the *Times*. "And then we're hoping that Lehman won't go under because then there will be way too many bankers looking for jobs." Carol Guenther, thirty-eight, who had been an administrative assistant at the firm for thirteen years, said, "I am very, very upset—heartbroken, actually. I figure I will probably be laid off. I love the people I work with. And Bear is very good to employees. So, we have a great sense of teamwork. Now, we are all in a daze."

Not surprisingly, Bear Stearns's eleventh-hour capitulation to JPMorgan was gargantuan news around the world, making for banner headlines in newspapers in the major money centers of New York, London, and Hong Kong and on television screens the world over. The general reaction was no different from that of Steve Schwarzman, Ron Perelman, John Mack, or the 14,153 Bear Stearns employees—utter and complete disbelief. "The hard capitalist truth is that Bear's most senior managers have mainly themselves to blame," the *Wall Street Journal* editorialized. "They bought their second and third homes with fabulous bonuses during the good times, and they must now endure the losses from Bear's errant investment bets. Bear took particular pride in its risk management, but it let its standards slide in the hunt for higher returns during the mortgage mania earlier this decade. There's no joy in seeing a venerable firm expire, but it has to happen if financial markets are going to have any discipline going forward." Added Andrew Ross Sorkin in the *New York Times*, "Make no mistake: this was one of the greatest corporate euthanizations of all time. And Wall Street played its own gleeful role in it." And Paul Krugman, the *Times*'s economics columnist, picking up on his colleague Gretchen Morgenson's criticisms of Bear Stearns from the morning before, opined: "Bear, in other words, deserved to be allowed to fail—both on the merits and to teach Wall Street not to expect someone else to clean up its messes. But the Fed rose to Bear's rescue anyway, fearing that the collapse of a major investment bank would cause panic in the markets and wreak havoc with the wider economy. Fed officials knew that they were doing a bad thing, but believed the alternative would be even worse. As Bear goes, so will go the rest of the financial system."

Alan Greenspan, the former chairman of the Federal Reserve Board whom many blamed for lowering interest rates too far too fast after September 11 and thus inflating the credit bubble that burst in the conflagration that consumed Bear Stearns, weighed in with his own thoughts on the financial crisis in an opinion piece in the *Financial Times*. He made no mention of Bear Stearns, its liquidity crisis, or its sale to JPMorgan (probably because the deadline for the piece preceded the events of the previous week), but in his opaque way he did capture the zeitgeist of the unprecedented events. "We will never be able to anticipate all discontinuities in financial markets," he wrote. "Discontinuities are, of necessity, a surprise. Anticipated events are arbitraged away. But if, as I strongly suspect, periods of euphoria are very difficult to suppress as they build, they will not collapse until the speculative fever breaks on its own. Paradoxically, to the extent risk management succeeds in identifying such episodes, it can prolong and enlarge the period of euphoria. But risk management can never reach perfection. It will eventually fail and a disturbing reality will be laid bare, prompting an unexpected and sharp discontinuous response."

※

BUT IN THE face of *this* "unexpected and sharp discontinuous response," there was not a lot of time for reflection and Monday-morning quarterbacking. In accordance with the contract, JPMorgan started moving into Bear Stearns's offices almost immediately. Black and Winters, the co-heads of investment banking, reminded their colleagues to be gentle. "As we now begin the important work of integrating the two firms, we are counting on you to embrace our new partners at Bear Stearns in a first-class way and ensure they feel welcome at our firm," they wrote in an e-mail. So warned, the JPMorgan army tried to be understanding. "My office looked out across the street over at their window and their trading floor," Friedman said. "They actually put a sign up that we couldn't quite read, but which we think was actually well-intentioned, as some sort of 'Welcome to the JP Morgan family' or something, trying to be good guys. I stood at the window and they waved. They may have been making some nasty, sarcastic aside. They may have been thumbing their noses at us. It felt like they were trying to be *mensches* about the thing. They then started to come over, and by and large, they were extremely sympathetic. They treated it with great sensitivity. They were very clear that this was a tragedy. That they thought this was unfair, what had happened to us, and so let's get through this the best that we can. Considering that they had no interest in having to go through all of this, they were remarkably grown-up."

Given the guarantee, JPMorgan was very focused on getting as much information as quickly as possible about Bear Stearns's trading positions. "They were trying very early on to take control of the risk, because as of that moment, they were effectively guaranteeing everything that we did," Friedman said. "They were immediately interested in all the positions, all of the customer exposure— everything that we had that could cause losses to them, they took command of almost instantly." JPMorgan immediately got a computer feed on all of Bear Stearns's long and short trading positions. "It's great to have 180,000 people, I guess," he continued. "You just keep putting people to work. They ran it through their models. They sat with our traders. They came back with marks, with hedges. They were obviously most focused on the mortgage positions. I spent hours and hours and hours with them, going through the credit risk that we had and what was our customer exposure. They didn't particularly care for our list of customers that we were dealing with. The orders came very quickly. Any material transaction—and the definition of material kept getting smaller and smaller—had to be approved by JPMorgan."

On Monday morning, just hours after he had reluctantly agreed to approve the merger with JPMorgan, an agreement that perfected for him a loss of more than $1 billion on the Bear Stearns stock he had accumulated since joining the firm in 1969, Cayne walked into his ebony-paneled sixth-floor office at 383 Madison and found Bruce Sherman waiting for him. Sherman, the CEO of Private Capital Management and a Naples, Florida, activist money manager, owned some 5.5 million Bear Stearns shares at the beginning of 2008. Sherman had lost around $475 million, based on the stock price at the beginning of 2008 (and more than double that amount if the stock's peak value in January 2007 is the measurement stick), by the time he showed up on Cayne's doorstep. "I walk into the office and he's sitting in the anteroom," Cayne recalled. "I don't have a date with him or anything. He said, 'We got mugged.' I said, 'I agree.' He says, 'Can I spend a few minutes?' I said, 'Sure.' Comes in with this guy; 'I don't want to be alone,' he says. I get Vincent [Tese]—that's our lead director—because I want a witness. I have no fucking idea what he's going to do. He may be carrying a wire, I don't have any idea."

Cayne had known Sherman for years. "I've had many, many conversations with him," he said, "and never once, not once, did he say, 'Jimmy, you're not doing the right thing' or 'I'm not happy with what you've done.' Not one. Forget irate, not one upset call." Indeed, in 2006, when Bear stock was approaching its all-time high, Sherman said, "They're a wealth-creation machine. Jimmy's leadership over the past decade has been central to that." But by January 2008, Sherman had turned on Cayne and played a crucial role in convincing the board that Cayne had to go.

"Sherman starts talking about the absurdity of the $2 per share JPMorgan deal," Cayne said. "He's sitting there and he's talking about shareholders' actions and campaigns. I said, 'Bruce, let me get this really straight with you. I agree there was a mugging. I agree that the Fed did something. We had Jamie. We had Flowers in here. He wasn't given the Fed backing or whatever. So it was just a good old-fashioned fucking.' He says, 'Well, what about the vote?' I said, 'I want to make it very clear. I'm not discussing the vote. You vote the way you want to vote for $2 a share. And I vote the way I want to vote.' He says, 'Well, how can they possibly win the vote?' And I said, 'I'm not saying they will.' He said, 'Jimmy, they have no chance of winning the vote because you've got five guys that own 40 percent of the company. They're all going to vote it down.' I said, 'That's a conversation I'm not having. I vote the way I want to vote.'" Sherman left Cayne's office after about ninety minutes. (Sherman did not respond to requests for comment.)

By then, Bear Stearns stock had opened for the day and was trading at around $3.50 per share, 75 percent higher than JPMorgan's offer (the stock traded as high as $5.50 that day and closed at $4.81), a clear signal that the market believed that the deal was not going to happen at the original price. This could have been just a hopeful bet by merger arbitrageurs wanting more or a clever analysis of the deal's dynamics—as Sherman had pointed out, five shareholders controlled 40 percent of the company's stock (and the employees as a group, including Cayne, controlled 30 percent). With the stock at $2 a share, after having traded as high as $172.69 little more than a year before, investors had little to lose and everything to gain by voting no—especially since JPMorgan's guarantee apparently would stay in place for a year if shareholders continued to vote down the deal, although it's unlikely that anyone had yet figured out that subtle wrinkle.

Meanwhile, JPMorgan and Dimon were receiving near-universal plaudits for their deal savvy and their opportunism. There was an avalanche of glowing publicity. JPMorgan's stock was up nearly 10 percent, to around $40 per share. The *Wall Street Journal* referred to him as "Wall Street's banker of last resort." To the *New York Times*, Dimon had "suddenly become the most talked about—and arguably the most powerful—banker in the world today." *Bloomberg Markets* wrote, "In a Wall Street convulsed by crisis, it's Dimon, grandson of a Greek immigrant and son of a stockbroker, who has emerged as the closest thing modern finance has to a statesman." On Monday at around noon, Andrew Bary, at *Barron's,* provided some analysis. "Jamie Dimon appears to have pulled off the coup of his career," he wrote. "The best analogy for the Bear Stearns deal could be the government-orchestrated takeovers of savings and loans in the late 1980s that turned out to be windfalls for well-connected buyers, including financier Ron Perelman and the Bass brothers of Texas."

Just how sweet a deal was it for Dimon? "JPMorgan is paying a tiny fraction of Bear's previously stated book value of $84 a share," Bary continued. "It is also getting the company's valuable clearing business, which generated $566 million in pretax earnings last year, and Bear's headquarters building on Madison Avenue in Manhattan, which could be worth $1.5 billion." Bary also noted that JPMorgan predicted it would generate $1 billion in annual after-tax earnings from the Bear Stearns deal. Brad Hintz, a former CFO of Lehman Brothers and a research analyst at Sanford C. Bernstein & Co., told his clients that Bear Stearns's "good businesses" were worth $7.7 billion, or $60 per share. The discrepancy—between $60 and $2— came as a result of assuming the estimated $6 billion in transaction-related expenses—litigation, severance payments, and absorbing the losses of the sale of big chunks of Bear Stearns's $395 billion of assets. (On May 14, JPMorgan upped its reserve for the deal by 50 percent, to $9 billion, as the cost of liquidating the assets climbed along with the cost of running Bear between signing and closing; it wound up costing another $1 billion.)

Dimon tried to take the coronation in stride. He praised Black, Winters, Paulson, and Geithner. "Same with the team at Bear Stearns," he said. "God knows what pressure they had to be under." He added, "You are on an emotional roller coaster on any deal, but much more so on this one. For all the drama today, it could have been much worse." He hoped to get some sleep now that it was over. "There are two types of not getting sleep," he said. "There is not getting sleep because there is a lot of work. The other is because you can't sleep. I had a little of both."

※

BUT, IN ITS coolly efficient way, the market was already in the process of rendering its judgment on the idea that JPMorgan stood behind Bear Stearns's obligations. On Monday, "Bear Stearns' customers continued to withdraw funds, counterparties remained unwilling to make secured funding available to Bear Stearns on customary terms, and funding"—other than from JPMorgan and the Fed—"was not available," according to the proxy statement about the deal. It became increasingly clear that the market would no longer fund Bear Stearns, despite all the public statements of support from the Fed and JPMorgan. That meant the burden would fall solely on JPMorgan and the Fed. There were now serious doubts about whether the deal, struck at $2 per share less than twenty-four hours earlier, could ever be completed at that price, and so the long-term viability of the guarantee was also suspect. "What happened that week was that despite the guarantee, the market, of course, was shocked by the price," Molinaro said. "Nobody believes the deal's going to get consummated at that price. We're never going to be able to get the shareholder approval. Customers were therefore spooked by that. I would say the arb community clearly doesn't think the deal's happening at that price because the stock's trading well above the offer price. And as a result, customers were not showing a willingness to do business with us, even though we had a guarantee from JPMorgan, and that was becoming a particular problem in the stock borrow world, because the State Streets and big securities lenders weren't prepared to lend us securities for fear that the guarantee wouldn't be there."

Customers and counterparties quickly reverted to the same strategy they had employed the previous Thursday and Friday: curtailing their trading and pulling their money out. "Over the course of the day our phone lines stopped ringing and no trades were being done," a Bear executive said. Even Dimon realized the trouble wasn't over for Bear Stearns just because JPMorgan had guaranteed its trades. "Even after we bought it, even after we guaranteed globally some of the trading obligations, there was still a run on the bank," he said. "We still had to put out billions of dollars on an unsecured basis to them." Added Molinaro: "It's like the market didn't believe the merger." In Washington, the White House team behind the deal was all smiles. President Bush invited Paulson, Bernanke, and Cox, among others of his economic brain trust, to a meeting in the Roosevelt Room. Bush praised Paulson particularly for showing "the country and the world that the United States is on top of the situation" and added, "I want to thank you, Mr. Secretary, for working over the weekend." Bush added that his administration was committed to taking other steps, as needed, to reduce the financial crisis. "We obviously will continue to monitor the situation and when need be, will act decisively, in a way that continues to bring order to the financial markets," he said. Outside the White House, after the meetings, Paulson defended the decision to bail out the Bear Stearns debt holders and to sanction the $2 for shareholders. "This was an easy decision," he said. "This is the right outcome. And again, in terms of moral hazard, look at what happened to the Bear Stearns shareholders."

At some point on Monday, the lawyers on the deal began to realize there was a "serious wrinkle," in Parr's words, about how the guarantee had been structured. "The problem was if our shareholders kept voting down the deal all the way for a year," Parr explained, "at the end of a year we could get out of the deal and whatever guarantees were in place at that point in time remained in place. That was the critical issue." Bear's shareholders began to figure out something that Cavanagh, Black, and Winters had not understood during the previous night's conference call. The poorly drafted guarantee—in fairness, the time allotted to draft it was extremely circumscribed and the concept was somewhat novel—gave Bear's shareholders a free, one-year option to run the firm using JPMorgan's balance sheet. All they had to do was continuously vote down the deal for the next year. What's more, not only had JPMorgan agreed to guarantee all the trading and counterparty obligations, but it also had agreed to assume all of Bear's long-term debt at the time the deal closed. This got some clever people on Bear's side thinking that as long as shareholders voted down the deal and the firm continued to operate based on JPMorgan's credit, Bear Stearns could systematically replace its short-term financing with longer-term debt. In effect, the logic went, JPMorgan could be forced to finance Bear Stearns for a good long time whether the deal closed or not. "Jamie was really upset when he found out that he was locked up in the same jail he locked us up in for a year," Salerno said.

There were at least two other counterintuitive aspects to the deal as well. Normally, in a newly announced merger, arbitrageurs rush in to buy the stock of the target company (while shorting the stock of the acquirer) and then begin to hope, lobby, or both that they can finagle a higher price. Usually, the deal dynamic is such that a small percentage increase in price—say, a move to $70 a share from $65 a share, to cite the case of InBev's 2008 acquisition of Anheuser-Busch—combined with a relatively quick resolution will yield a desirable annualized return. Everyone's happy and the deal gets done. In this case, a very different dynamic quickly became apparent. Since Bear Stearns's book value was $84 per share and the offer price was $2 a share, there was a sense in the market that the potential upside on pushing to recut the deal was huge, even if the book value was discounted aggressively. The *Barron's* analysis helped to fuel this thinking among investors. Even if an arb bought the Bear stock at, say, $4 per share on Monday, if the deal were renegotiated to $6, the nominal return would be a whopping 50 percent and the annualized return would be even higher. On the other hand, the downside risk was minimal. If you were an existing stockholder and the stock went from $2 to zero, so what? The vast majority of the money had already been lost as the stock went from $172.69 to $2. The incentive was clear: there was far more to be gained for shareholders by voting down the deal each and every time for the next year knowing that JPMorgan remained on the hook for operating Bear's business. This was that rare instance where the arbs believed the magnitude of the potential upside more than offset the prospect of having "dead money"—money locked up in a deal earning no return. "Here it's easy to think you might get another 100 percent," Parr said, "and for that matter, what do you have to lose between two and zero? Next to nothing. So the mind-set is different. The shareholder vote is entirely different under the Bear Stearns facts. The fact pattern is shareholders have all kinds of reasons to vote no. The year's time is not that big a deal when you're talking about the possibility, however remote it might be, of a double or a triple." One arb told the *Wall Street Journal:* "If you're a shareholder, why not make some noise and see if JPMorgan raises its offer or roll the dice and take your risk in bankruptcy? They're stealing the company. What do you have to lose?"

Counterbalancing the impulse to vote down the deal was the equally unusual dynamic where the holders of Bear's $70 billion of debt—who stood to be bailed out at 100¢ on the dollar when the deal closed—were desperate for shareholders to approve the deal. The debt holders started buying the stock in droves, pushing its price up, to ensure they would be able to vote for the deal. For the debt holders, who had far more to lose than shareholders, a busted deal would be devastating.

The traditional M&A dynamic had been turned on its head. But the lawyers at Wachtell, Lipton—no doubt with the approval of their client, JPMorgan—had drafted the contracts anticipating a more typical response. "You come back to the shareholders," Parr said. "If they understood all this dynamic, and even if they didn't understand the dynamic, they could say, 'Wow, upside/downside. I go from two to zero or I could go from two to ten.' That dynamic is a no vote. The company's protected and there are these guarantees. So there are a lot of reasons to vote no, and that was the flaw. Fairly quickly at JPMorgan they realized, 'Oh, it's not two versus zero. It's optionality to the upside by voting no.'"

This was a major mistake, for sure, but one that appeared to leave no fingerprints. The JPMorgan executives on the Sunday night conference call gave no indication—publicly, at least—that there was any misunderstanding about how the guarantee was to work. They described it exactly as it was drafted. Regardless, once JPMorgan became aware of the drafting flaw, Dimon was quick to blame Wachtell. "They are a superb firm," explained Rog Cohen, at Sullivan & Cromwell. "They had their best lawyers on it. Maybe if there's any criticism—and I'm not sure there is—they should have been more skeptical with what their client agreed to do. I think the real problem is people looked at this as a straight M&A deal, but they didn't think through perhaps everything that was relevant. People didn't really consider what would happen if you didn't get the vote, that that was a low likelihood, and how that interacted with the guarantee. Who knows? Victory has a thousand fathers and defeat is an orphan. But whatever was the cause, it was a real mistake, there's no question about it." (Ed Herlihy, the lead partner on the deal at Wachtell, Lipton, did not return a phone call seeking a comment on how this happened.)

In retrospect, even though Dimon thought his law firm had screwed up, Schwartz wasn't so sure. He said that the offending language came about because Wachtell was trying to prevent a situation in which another bidder swooped onto the scene after the deal was announced, benefiting from the market-stabilizing risks JP-

Morgan had agreed to take. The worst thing, he said, would have been if JPMorgan suddenly found itself in a bidding war against, say, Bank of America, after JPMorgan's merger agreement had steadied the ship. That's why Wachtell wanted there to be a year where nothing could happen without JPMorgan's approval. What nobody had counted on was that the JPMorgan guarantee would not provide confidence to the market to keep doing business with Bear Stearns. "If B of A came along and thought it was worth $80," explained someone familiar with Schwartz's thinking, "JPMorgan would be in a situation, unless they paid $81, that they were going to not get it. So let's say B of A is willing to go to $50, JPMorgan would have had to pay $51. So they took all the risk to get into an even-handed bidding contest. That's a disaster."

Regardless of the debate, while the lawyers toiled away trying to repair the deal, the rank-and-file Bear Stearns employees no longer had a whole lot to do, and didn't even know if they would have jobs under the new regime. Paul Friedman wrote to David Rawlings, another senior managing director at the firm, on Monday night that the day had been "surreal." "I came in and canceled everything on my calendar since none of the items were relevant any longer. None of what I do—business building, problem solving, customer interaction or any other part of a normal day—exists any more. The transition planning—such as it will be in Fixed Income—hasn't started. So I wandered around all day. Probably more of the same tomorrow. Let's def catch up, if only to relieve my boredom." Later that night, Friedman wrote his sister, trying to describe to her his emotional state. "To say the least, it has been a surreal week," he wrote. "As recently as last Wednesday, I was eagerly approaching my 27th anniversary of being happily employed at the Bear and all was reasonably right in the world. Even if the financial world is a mess, we were doing great and were about to announce to the world how good our first quarter earnings were. By the end of Thursday night, after being a victim of a series of incredibly inaccurate but self-fulfilling rumors about our having a liquidity problem, there had been a run on the bank and we were bankrupt (although we managed to postpone the actual collapse until Friday). We ended up working all night Thursday (my first all-nighter since Colgate) and all weekend trying to save the place, only to have it end with our being mugged by JPMorgan on Sunday. They are the absolute worst merger partner for us since there is enormous overlap between the two firms and, as a result, probably 12,000 of our 15,000 employees will ultimately be fired. And an 85-year-old firm disappears in a blink of an eye. In many ways, it's been like watching a family member die in front of your eyes—except maybe 15,000 times worse. Moreover, since the press doesn't quite understand what happened, half of them keep saying we somehow deserved this, something that is truly saddening.

"A truly distressing statistic," he continued, "is that between Thursday and today, the employees of Bear Stearns—who own 40% of the company's stock—lost a combined $4 billion of personal net worth. Many of my friends there thought that the way to truly achieve wealth was to keep every share ever awarded and use that as their retirement planning (did they never hear of Enron? Drexel Burnham?) and now they are wiped out. Fortunately for Susie and me, I never believed in combining job risk and net worth risk in the same company so, while my deferred compensation evaporated over the weekend, I've always sold any freely available Bear Stearns stock the instant I received it. So I have the luxury of not having to worry about money problems and we live to fight another day. Not so for many of my friends, particularly those in their 30's and 40's who were just starting to earn real money and got overextended."

CHAPTER 11

NEW DEVELOPMENTS FROM HELL

On Tuesday morning, the reclusive Joe Lewis, Bear's second-largest shareholder, showed up in Jimmy Cayne's office. Lewis, who made his $3 billion fortune trading currencies, was the 368th wealthiest man in the world. (Some estimated his fortune at $5 billion.) Lewis had been buying Bear Stearns shares since the late summer of 2007. Cayne first met Lewis, a longtime brokerage client of the firm, in 2000 when he flew down to visit him at his massive Orlando, Florida, estate. They hit it off and spent five hours together, bonding over a shared love of gin rummy. Cayne said he never spoke with Lewis about making an investment in Bear Stearns. In September 2007, Lewis announced, in a filing with the SEC, that he had made the first of several purchases of Bear stock, spending $864 million for a 7 percent stake. He kept on buying right up until the end—including making a $31.4 million purchase on March 13, when the stock was trading at $55.13—until he had invested more than $1.26 billion in the stock. The day before he came to see Cayne, he gave a rare public statement to CNBC, saying of the JPMorgan deal for Bear Stearns: "I think it is a derisory offer and I don't think they'll get it."

He was no more in favor of it when he showed up in Cayne's office wanting to talk about a PR campaign against the deal. "I said, 'Joe, look, whatever plan you have as far as moving forward or PR issues or whatever, I'm not part of it. I signed the piece of paper saying I was in support of the $2 thing. How I vote is my business. I can only tell you that your idea of what you might settle for is far different than me because if the price is dramatically different than $2, which doesn't have to be $30, but different than $2, I'd go along with that on one hand. On the other hand, I'm not really talking about it.' He said, 'I understand.'"

By the time Lewis and Cayne said their goodbyes on Tuesday morning, Bear's stock was trading near $8 per share, more than four times the JPMorgan offer price. While the Bear Stearns executives appreciated the implications of this kind of trading—the likelihood the deal would get voted down was increasing exponentially—they were even more focused on what to do if that actually *did* happen. "There was a decent chance there was going to be turmoil in the business of Bear Stearns while shareholders said, 'We're not voting in favor,'" Parr said. "So then there wouldn't be a deal, but the business of Bear Stearns would continue to deteriorate." Upton was worried about that, too, and had started to try to raise money almost immediately that week. "The fucking sad thing is Monday morning I came in and started trying to raise money in our own name again," he said. "I started talking to rating agencies, I started talking to lenders. I said, 'We effectively are now an AA bank, right? We got a guarantee.' I wanted to get talking points on the guarantee, what's covered, let's get that out, let's start funding ourselves in our own name again." But as he carefully read the guarantee document and then tried to refinance some of Bear's debt, he discovered relatively quickly that "there was a lot of very senior-level tension going on, on both sides of 47th Street," regarding "the guarantee and what's covered and what's not and can we fund ourselves and can we not, and under what conditions can they walk away. Quickly what became clear was Jamie was unhappy because he'd given himself some open-ended exposure. As it was constructed, we were really not going to be able to successfully fund ourselves in our own name because they would walk away and we would just be declaring bankruptcy again."

There was also a lot of chatter in the market on Tuesday, as the stock continued to trade at nearly four times the offer price, that in addition to bondholders buying up the stock to make sure the vote for the deal was positive, there were rumors that "angry Bear employees were teaming up with outside investors to buy Bear stock to force JPMorgan to increase its $236 [sic] million offer or to lure a higher bid from a rival bank," the *New York Times* reported. One blogger, Ami de Chapeaurouge, a U.S.-educated German lawyer, wrote, "It's about time for a good, old-fashioned management buyout by . . . those hardworking senior managing directors who have gotten short shrift, and may be in the best position to rescue Bear, realign the interests of employees and outside shareholders by offering a meatier purchase price and redirect strategy away from credit enhancement and repackaging folly to a sounder product mix." The idea, however far-fetched, was a clear indication of the depth of the dismay in the market with JPMorgan's offer.

At one o'clock, Dimon convened a conference call with Bear's four hundred or so brokers. Dimon was anxious to keep as many of them as possible, since JPMorgan had no brokers and the ones at Bear were among the top revenue producers in the industry. Then there was his own DNA. "I have broker's blood in my veins," Dimon told the brokers on the call.

In the meantime, the lawyers were trying to tie up any loose ends in the various agreements that had been so hastily drafted the previous weekend. "It was understandable that there was some cleanup to do," Parr said. "It is not unreasonable that there might be some things where somebody would say, 'Hey, you know, we need to change this' or 'We didn't mean that' or 'We need to flesh this out.'" But at some point late in the day on Tuesday, JPMorgan had figured out the flaw that meant it could get stuck with the guarantee for a year even if the Bear Stearns shareholders voted down the deal. The JPMorgan lawyers asked the Bear Stearns lawyers to make a change. But this request was more than a simple matter of "cleanup"; this was beyond the lawyers' ability to resolve on their own. "When they said, 'We want to change this'—meaning the guarantees going beyond the year—that was clearly a substantive point, and there was no way we could give a substantive point without getting something," one of the participants recalled.

On Wednesday, with the lawyers unable to resolve the matter, Dimon called over to Bear Stearns. Dimon's message: "You know this wasn't what anyone intended, this guarantee. This wasn't what any of us meant to have happen. You know that we want to get this deal done. You know you need our guarantee. But this has to change." Dimon's tone, according to one person, was "pretty tense. He wasn't yelling. But this is a big issue. It's a business issue and it needs to be fixed. He was quite irritated with [Wachtell], but that wasn't aimed at us. He just wanted it fixed." Later that day, Dimon called Schwartz. "Don't you understand that we have a problem?" he said. "Shareholders may vote this down!" Schwartz, the seasoned M&A practitioner, would have none of it. "What do you mean, *we* have a problem?" he told Dimon. Remembered Fred Salerno: "Jamie's a very bright guy, but it sort of was a little bit too arrogant of a position to take. So I told Alan, 'We're not going to change anything. My vote is we're not going to change anything.'"

For the first time since the world had started collapsing on them sometime around March 7, the Bear Stearns executives felt they had some serious leverage, and they were anxious to use it. JPMorgan needed relief, whether from some poor legal drafting or from a poorly conceived business concept (where the blame truly lies has never been made clear), and Bear Stearns intended to use that fact to try to regain a shred of its dignity. Even though JPMorgan had signed a contract without a material adverse change provision, the firm left the distinct impression in the minds of the Bear executives that JPMorgan "would do what it had to do to protect itself," according to one participant. This meant, unmistakably, that if an agreement could not be reached to revise the guarantee provision, JPMorgan would walk from the deal, and if that led to a lawsuit with Bear Stearns, so be it. The clear message for JPMorgan, if the Bear Stearns board didn't agree to changing the agreement, was "We will find ways to hurt you," this person recalled. "We will find ways to protect our interests." Rog Cohen, for one, thought that a lawsuit between the two merger partners would result in, at best, a pyrrhic victory for Bear Stearns, since JPMorgan was the only firm still providing overnight financing to Bear, and should it walk away, the firm would soon thereafter be liquidated. "That lawsuit was not one that we thought had a lot of merit, and even if it won five years down the road, the company is totally kaput," Cohen said. "All the heartache and destruction would have occurred."

Parr, too, urged caution. "We had some leverage because everyone needed to find a solution," he said. "But let's set aside the arrogance. Everyone realized we have to find a way to increase the likelihood of a yes vote. There's this problem, and we want something for changing the error." But some members of the Bear board, particularly Cayne and Tese, were not so anxious to make the change Dimon wanted without some meaningful compensation. If the mistake was material, their thinking went, then the cost to fix it was going to be material, too. "Sometime during the week I find out Chase wants to make a change in the deal," Cayne said. "Oh, really? Why? Well, it seems that they fucked up. Wachtell Lipton. Chase had an obligation to fund Bear Stearns for a year if they lost the vote. Whoever heard of anything like that?"

When the Bear Stearns board heard that Dimon wanted the provision changed, it agreed there would be no change made unless the price went up dramatically. Tese and Salerno, who had come up to New York from their homes in Palm Beach for the drama of the previous week or so, flew back to Palm Beach on Wednesday to be there for the Easter weekend. "The negotiations continued day after day with us saying, 'We're not going to give on this without getting something,'" Parr said. He couldn't believe that he was going through this debacle a second time; it was déjà vu all over again. "On Sunday night when we had finished the first deal and we were rolling it out, I could not have imagined we'd be negotiating within three days again to restructure the deal," he said.

Also that day, the billionaire shareholder Joe Lewis filed a document with the SEC showing that he owned 12.2 million Bear shares, or 8.35 percent of the total outstanding, and that he intended "to take whatever action that [he] deem[ed] necessary and appropriate to protect the value of [his] investment," including communicating with Bear Stearns or "other shareholders or third parties regarding their concerns about the actions taken by" Bear Stearns and encouraging Bear "and third parties to consider other strategic transactions or alternatives." In other words, Lewis was not going to go down without a fight. He had let Dimon know that he was angry about the deal. For his part, Dimon had been calling the CEOs of other Wall Street firms "pleading with them" not to poach Bear's employees. He was also telling his colleagues at JPMorgan that he was prepared to "send Bear back into bankruptcy" if the deal did not get approved by shareholders.

AT THIS MOMENT, with the deal's prospects looking increasingly bleak on nearly every front, Dimon walked across 47th Street, with a steady rain falling, to meet with about four hundred of Bear's most senior executives at 383 Madison. According to the *New York Times,* the Bear employees were "seething, fearful and to their dismay, far poorer than they were a week ago." The hostility in the room was palpable. "I don't think Bear did anything to deserve this," Dimon said to them from a podium where he was flanked by both Black and Winters. "Our hearts go out to you. . . . No one on Wall Street could have anticipated this. I feel terrible sometimes when people think we took advantage. I don't think we could possibly know what you are feeling but I hope that you give JPMorgan a chance." He told the group that there would be job cuts but that JPMorgan intended to retain the best people whether they worked at JPMorgan or Bear Stearns. Since JPMorgan especially coveted Bear's prime brokerage business, its retail brokerage business, and its energy-trading business, chances were high that most of the people who gathered to hear Dimon were going to lose their jobs. One of the most angry among them, Ed Wolfe, a ten-year Bear veteran and a highly respected research analyst in the transportation sector, spoke up after Dimon had finished making his pitch. "In this room are people who have built this firm and lost a lot, our fortunes," Wolfe said. "What will you do to make us whole?" The room broke out in applause.

"You're acting like it's our fault, and it's not," Dimon responded. "If you stay, we will make you happy."

But Wolfe was not mollified. "I think it's galling you come into our house and you call this a 'merger,'" he continued. Dimon, "ruddy-faced and sharply dressed in a light blue tie and white shirt," according to the *Times,* said nothing in response. One of Wolfe's colleagues noted that Dimon could not even look at Wolfe after the latter asked his question. Wolfe was highly pissed off and, his colleagues say, resigned twice during that first week. "His bosses didn't know if he had gone completely around the bend," a Bear research analyst said. "I asked Ed if he resigned and he said, 'Well, I can't talk about that but I'm never going to work for those fucking assholes.'" (Wolfe declined to comment further about this incident.) At the meeting, Dimon went on to say that those employees who stayed until the deal closed would receive a one-time cash payment and those who were hired—and stayed—would receive at least 25 percent of their previous year's Bear stock awards in the form of JP-Morgan stock. At one point, Dimon explained that Bear Stearns's "shotgun marriage" to JPMorgan "is not the sort of thing we set out to do." Ed Moldaver, a forty-year-old broker, stood up and blasted Dimon. "I've heard some people refer to this as a shotgun wedding," Moldaver said. "I wouldn't use that term. I'd call this a shotgun wedding *to a rapist*. Yeah, yeah, the girl was lying there naked on the ground when you found her, that's true, *but you did it anyway*."

According to Clive Dobbs, who was in the room, Moldaver "went on to attempt to exhort the audience to meet him down on Madison Avenue en masse 'and get the cameras back here,' and generally seemed to expect his colleagues to get all 'Battle of Seattle' with him. This did not transpire." Dimon said nothing after Moldaver finished.

Gary Parr, the Lazard banker, had some sympathy for the tough position Dimon, his occasional client, found himself in. "The people were so unhappy," he said. "I just don't think it would have mattered who walked into that room or how genuine they were or how good they intended to be, and I'm sympathetic. It wasn't Jamie's doing. I'd say, they could blame the markets generally; they could blame the government; they could blame themselves. I could make the case that for those that kept their jobs, Jamie was the best thing that could have happened to them."

Paul Friedman decided to skip the Wednesday afternoon show. "It was childish and petty, and it was my personal revolt over the whole thing," he said. "I didn't want to hear Jamie come and tell us, 'It's all going to be okay, and everything's going to be great, and we love you. There's jobs for everybody, and it's going to be a meritocracy, and it's going to be a matter of who's the best.' I could write the script for him: 'Whoever's the best person is going to get the job, whether it's a JPMorgan person or a Bear person.' It's nonsense. It was never going to happen. I didn't want to hear it." Upton stayed around just long enough to hear Dimon explain what the benefit would be if a Bear employee was offered a full-time job and chose to accept it and stay. "Once that was over, I just left," he said, "because I was really pissed at everyone in the room because those were the guys who fucking filibustered and didn't allow me to save the firm. So they could bitch and whine and moan, but this is where we are, and at the end of the day I'm not sure the bitching and whining and moaning was going to get anything done. I was very narrowly focused and I just left, went back upstairs, and tried to do some more work."

❧

ON THURSDAY NIGHT, Schwartz, Molinaro, Salerno, and Cohen called Tese. Recalled Tese: "Rog says, 'They want to change the deal or they're going to pull out.' So I said, 'That's great. If they want to pay us $10 [a share], we'll change the deal.' Rog said, 'Well, that's the idea.' I said, 'But how can they pull out?' 'Well,' he goes, 'it gets into this contract. The contract had a guarantee. But it was silent as to the duty to fund, because we didn't have enough time to write it.' It was just assumed that the guarantee came with the funding, that they would get to write that part of it later. It never got written. They were funding us through that Wednesday. They were going to cut off the funding. Then we'd be back in the same box, but we had a lawsuit." Although no one relished the thought of JPMorgan cutting off the funding or of Bear launching a lawsuit against it, when Molinaro left the office on Thursday night he thought the matter would get resolved satisfactorily. Indeed, he was sufficiently confident that he flew to the Ritz-Carlton in Jamaica.

On Good Friday, Schwartz called Jamie Dimon. "Jamie was very agitated over the guarantee," Molinaro recalled, "because I think his worst fear was that he's now on the hook for twelve months, while we can go shop the company and even vote it down, in fact, and he's still on the hook. . . . They wanted to shrink the time period if there was a failed vote, and they wanted to make the deal much more certain of being completed." Schwartz asked Tese and Salerno to fly back to New York from Palm Beach. They were the only two outside directors involved at that point. "I was upset it all was perpetrated over the holiday weekend," said Salerno, who is a religious Catholic. "All my family's down there. Everybody's down in Florida, my kids and my grandkids, but who cares? Fourteen thousand people are depending on me, so who cares about that?"

Suddenly, bankruptcy lawyers reassembled at 383 Madison in case the two sides could not reach a new agreement and JPMorgan pulled out of the deal. On the other hand, Schwartz realized that for the first time he had some leverage. "I think Alan recognized that in order to make the deal more certain, we had to get a higher price," Molinaro said. I think he told Jamie that without a higher price, the board's not going to be able to recommend it. . . . It was really the first opportunity we had to try to get more out of them." The Bear executives—Cayne, Greenberg, Schwartz, and Molinaro, joining in by phone from Jamaica before flying back on Saturday night—plus Tese and Salerno reassembled at Sullivan & Cromwell's midtown office, at 250 Park Avenue, to see if they could reach a new agreement with Dimon. "We went through everything," Salerno said, "and the fact of the matter is JPMorgan's share price had gone up

$12 billion [since the deal had been announced]. So we figured that . . . Jamie has some egg on his face if this deal goes belly up. But we also know that if it goes belly up that we have a problem because we represent the bondholders and we had a deal. So we're on the horns of a dilemma."

The market's reaction to the deal in the previous four days showed that nearly everyone was very reluctant to do business with Bear Stearns. As a result, JPMorgan had become Bear's sole overnight repo lender. Now JPMorgan was threatening to walk away from that essential role. "If they walked away, it was over," Salerno said. "We'd just close the doors." Suddenly, everyone on the Bear Stearns side of the table was thinking about filing a lawsuit against JPMorgan if they chose to walk away from funding Bear Stearns.

Upon hearing what was going on, Paul Friedman wrote a friend around seven-thirty on Friday night of the "new developments from hell." "As of this moment, the world has shifted again," he wrote. "It had suddenly dawned on JPM that if the [Bear] shareholders vote down the deal—and they will—that they will have to leave their guarantee in place for a year without having control. In addition, the Fed, which had previously agreed to buy $30 billion of our stuff, now says that what they really meant was that they'd buy it after the deal closed. As a result, JP has informed us that unless we grant them sufficient stock to guarantee that the deal is approved, they're telling the world on Monday that they're pulling their guarantee. They will also stop lending to us (currently around $10 billion) and demand repayment. Whether they can do that legally is another question but they're doing it anyway, damn the consequences. Meanwhile, our Board has said that we can't give away something that the shareholders currently have without getting something in exchange. So we're deadlocked and we're back to thinking about going b/k [bankrupt]. You can't make this stuff up."

With a scrap of leverage for the first time, with Bear Stearns stock having closed on Thursday at just under $6 per share (Good Friday was a stock market holiday), and with Schwartz leading the charge, the strategy quickly gelled at the board level. "Alan was terrific, 100 percent great," Salerno said. "There wasn't anybody I respected in that room more than Alan Schwartz and what Alan

Schwartz did. His interests were 100 percent aligned with the four-teen thousand people. He was more upset about that than losing $200 million himself. I have enormous respect for that man. I will always, always remember how he behaved during these very trou-bled times. He stepped up to the plate and he did the right thing every time. Not what was best for him, but he did the right thing throughout this whole weekend."

On Saturday morning, Schwartz and Cohen, at Sullivan & Cromwell, called Dimon. "We said, 'We want to go back to $10 to $12, and do not come back at $9.99,'" Cohen said. "'We need two numbers.'" Dimon told them he would consider offering a revised exchange ratio for Bear shareholders that would get the Bear share-holders $10 a share but wanted the guarantee revised and near cer-tainty that the shareholder vote would be an affirmative one. To that end, Dimon asked that JPMorgan be able to buy a block of Bear stock that would equal 53 percent of the fully diluted shares out-standing. He also asked for a lockup on the shares of the officers and directors of the company. The 53 percent number was well be-yond New York Stock Exchange rules (which required a shareholder vote in order to issue more than 20 percent of the shares of a com-pany, unless the circumstances were desperate—a waiver was sought and issued) and also, the lawyers feared, could be easily challenged in court. There was a lot of back-and-forth on Saturday night but no agreement. "Nothing happened Saturday night, no movement," Salerno said. "Still at $2." Dimon's position remained that he wanted the guarantee changed but refused to change the price. "We said no," Salerno said.

On Easter Sunday, the group reconvened at Sullivan & Cromwell. After having slept on their decision, they decided to hold firm with it. "'Get ahold of the Fed, let them know we're going to file.' That's what we say to Alan," Salerno recalled. "Vince said it. I said it." Tese and Salerno then left the law firm and headed up to St. Jean-Baptiste, a Catholic church at the corner of Lexington and 76th Street, for Easter mass. When they came out, the phone rang. It was Alan Schwartz. "They changed their mind; they're going to give us $10 per share. So if you're a spiritual person, it happened not *because* we were there but *when* we were there."

For Schwartz, in the end, Dimon's calculus was simple. "The excess alpha"—Wall Street jargon for profit—"was $12 billion or $14 billion that went to JPMorgan's stock price the day they did the [first] deal in a down market," he told his partners. "That hasn't come back out of them relative to the market. They got a $12 or $14 billion windfall. So . . . maybe they paid three billion for it instead of two. But that's a lot better than taking all the risk and then letting somebody else take it away. A lot better."

After they got Schwartz's phone call, they quickly returned to Sullivan & Cromwell. "Now it's easy," Salerno continued. "Now just get it done. . . . I think the board stepped up to the plate. Now $10 is a rotten number anyhow, but it's five times what they would have gotten had they blinked. It's as simple as that, and it was right that these people should have gotten more. People will say it's a bailout and all this other stuff, [but] there would have been havoc in the marketplace had they not done it."

❋

LATE ON SUNDAY afternoon, after the revised deal had been agreed upon—as a result of the brief shifting of leverage, divine intervention, or both—and while all the various documents that accompany a merger of this magnitude and import were being drafted or amended, someone on the JPMorgan side of the deal leaked the story to Andrew Ross Sorkin at the *New York Times*. Very late Sunday night, Sorkin reported on the *Times* Web site that JPMorgan and Bear were in talks to raise the price of the Bear deal to $10 a share in stock. By the next morning, Sorkin was reporting that a new exchange ratio of .21753 shares of JPMorgan stock would be used for each Bear Stearns share. The exchange ratio was 3.97 times greater than the original exchange ratio agreed upon the week before, but because JPMorgan's stock had increased to around $46 since the first deal was announced, the new deal equaled $10 a share, a quintupling of the original offer. JPMorgan agreed to pay $1.45 billion for Bear's equity, up from $290 million seven days earlier. Sorkin also reported that JPMorgan—for which certainty of closing had become a paramount issue—had negotiated an agreement with Bear Stearns to buy 95 million new shares, representing 39.5 percent of Bear's fully diluted shares outstanding. During the week, Dimon had been convinced that his initial demand for a 53 percent voting bloc would have violated Delaware corporate law in addition to NYSE rules, and he decided that 39.5 percent was a safer number. Dimon also won from Bear's board members a tacit agreement to vote their shares—representing another 5 percent of the stock—for the amended merger, with the one caveat that they would do so assuming they still owned the shares at the time of the "record date" for the shareholder vote, which was to be sometime after April 8, when JPMorgan expected to purchase the 95 million Bear Stearns shares. This ambiguous provision about the board's "intention" to vote its shares for the deal was done to accommodate Jimmy Cayne, who had no desire whatsoever to do so.

Sorkin further reported that JPMorgan and the Fed had renegotiated *their* deal, so that now JPMorgan would absorb the first $1 billion of loss—should there be such a thing—on the $30 billion asset portfolio the Fed would purchase from Bear Stearns. The Fed would finance the remaining $29 billion on a nonrecourse basis. Sorkin also wrote about the poorly worded clause that required JPMorgan to continue to guarantee Bear Stearns's trades for a year, even if shareholders voted down the deal. More startling was the fact that Sorkin reported that Dimon had been "apoplectic" when he discovered the mistake and went out of his way to blame his high-priced lawyers at Wachtell, Lipton. "Finger pointing over the mistakes in the contracts began as bankers blamed the lawyers and vice versa," Sorkin wrote. In the clubby but highly competitive world of big-deal M&A, for Wachtell, Lipton to be blamed so publicly and in such a high-profile way was yet another piece of raw meat for the Street to chew on.

Later Monday morning, both JPMorgan and Bear Stearns announced the revised deal exactly as Sorkin had described it. The public announcement even contained the precise canned quotations from Dimon and Schwartz that had appeared in Sorkin's article. "We believe the amended terms are fair to all sides and reflect the value and risks of the Bear Stearns franchise," Dimon said, "and bring more certainty for our respective shareholders, clients and the marketplace. We look forward to a prompt closing and being able to operate as one company." The issuance of the 95 million shares to JPMorgan—the 39.5 percent block—was plenty controversial since it violated the New York Stock Exchange rules that required a shareholder vote on the issuance of more than 20 percent of the outstanding shares of a listed company. Of course, this was yet another rule meant to be broken. The NYSE policies "provide an exception" in situations "where the delay involved in securing shareholder approval for the issuance would seriously jeopardize the financial viability" of the company in question.

In the mounds of paper produced as part of the public announcement, there was no mention of the supposed legal error that caused the whole deal to be renegotiated. "It was $8 a share on six million shares," Cayne explained. "That's what I made out of that mistake."

There would be no further mistakes. The revised deal was now exceptionally well vetted by legions of lawyers. This time there was no late-night conference call for investors to badger the JPMorgan executives about the details of the deal. In its place was a three-page Q&A document that spelled out the details of how the revised Guarantee Agreement would work. If Bear Stearns's shareholders voted down the deal, the merger agreement would end four months later unless extended by JPMorgan. JPMorgan would also be on the hook for all of Bear Stearns's agreed-upon obligations until the termination of the agreement but none thereafter. The guarantee could be enforced directly against JPMorgan by Bear's customers.

The reaction from the market was equally predictable. There were the cynics, who remained incredulous that Bear Stearns had not been allowed to fail. "So everybody wins in this deal but the taxpayers (surprise)," wrote one observer on the *New York Times* blog. "The BS shareholders, many of whom are the same executives who drove the firm into the ground, are not wiped out after all. JPMorgan gets a bargain on the remaining worthwhile parts of the business. The rest of us get to bail out the creditors, to the tune of $29 billion in public funds. Why not just skip all the window-dressing and open up a Fed booth on the sidewalk in lower Manhattan to hand out public cash to finance types who happen by? They could add one in Connecticut to make sure all the hedge fund folks get theirs as well (too big to fail, you know)." But the new agreement seemed to solve many of the problems found in the first deal. There was a slow but steady increase in the number of customers and counterparties willing to do business with Bear Stearns because there was no longer nearly as much confusion about how the guarantee would work. And the Bear Stearns stock traded up immediately, although some people buying the stock in the following days—driving the price up to as high as $13.85 per share on March 24—remained foolishly optimistic that a higher bid from either JPMorgan or another buyer would materialize.

JPMorgan had no intention of allowing anything remotely like another bidder to materialize. In the days following March 24, the firm steadily added to its 39.5 percent stock ownership by buying more shares in the open market. For instance, on the day the revised deal was announced, JPMorgan bought 11.5 million shares at a price of $12.24 per share, for a total of $140.7 million. That purchase brought the bank's total share ownership up to just under 13 million Bear shares. In the end, JPMorgan amassed 49.73 percent of the total number of Bear Stearns shares outstanding, all in an effort to ensure that the vote would go its way.

CHAPTER 12

"WE'RE THE BAD GUYS"

Whether any of the shares JPMorgan bought following the announcement of the revised deal included the 5.66 million shares Jimmy Cayne and his wife, Patricia, sold on March 25—for a total of $61.34 million—is not clear since buyers and sellers rarely know each other in the marketplace. Cayne's sale not only cemented his loss of more than $1 billion on the Bear Stearns stock but also saved him from having to vote at all on the JPMorgan deal, either for or against. His sale not only signaled to the market that it was highly unlikely that a better deal from any quarter was in the offing but also gave the general public a rare glimpse into the longrunning, behind-the-scenes feud that existed between Cayne and Alan "Ace" Greenberg, Cayne's onetime mentor at Bear Stearns and the CEO of the firm for fifteen years until 1993, when Cayne deposed him. It turned out that when Cayne sold his shares on March 25, Greenberg—who remained a trader at the firm and was on the executive committee even though he was eighty years old—charged Cayne the non-employee commission of $77,000. (Cayne had retired some two months earlier but remained non-executive chairman of the board.) The commission for an employee selling such a large block of stock would have been a maximum of $2,500. Despite the forty years Cayne had devoted to Bear Stearns, since he was not technically then still an employee, Greenberg decided to charge him the full retail price. "If he doesn't like it, he should do his future business elsewhere," Greenberg told Landon Thomas Jr. of the *New York Times* in an inflammatory article that appeared on May 7. It was the first time that either man had spoken publicly about the events that destroyed the company with which they were so closely identified.

Greenberg went on to blame Cayne for the demise of Bear Stearns. He said Cayne had not taken his advice as the credit crunch unfolded during the summer of 2007. "Jimmy was not interested in my point of view," Greenberg said. "He was a one-man show—he didn't listen to anybody. That is when the real break took place." When Thomas asked him to elaborate on specifically what he had recommended that Cayne do to alleviate the crisis at the firm, Greenberg said only, "You can read about it in my book." He also criticized Cayne for bothering to still show up in his sixth-floor office. "I don't understand why he comes in," he said. "He is not employed here anymore." When asked how he felt upon learning that Cayne lost most of his fortune as a result of the collapse of Bear Stearns, according to the *Times*, "Mr. Greenberg's eyes turned cold. 'Oh, really. Goodness, that's a shame,' he deadpanned." As for Cayne causing the firm's ultimate troubles, Greenberg played it coy but transparent. "He is dreaming," he said of Cayne. "Why should I blame him? I don't need to—everyone can draw their own conclusions." When Thomas asked Greenberg if he still considered Cayne a friend, "he holds a long silence before responding. 'Oh, he is a dear friend.'"

In the article, which was prominently played on the front page of the business section, Thomas referred to Cayne as "a public piñata" who'd been "blamed by Bear employees [and] a presidential candidate"—a reference to an April 15, 2008, speech at Carnegie Mellon University in which Senator John McCain lumped Cayne together with Angelo Mozilo of Countrywide Financial as a former CEO who was "packed off with another forty or fifty million for the road"—for the firm's collapse. The article noted that Cayne's "ties with Bear will be formally severed in June. Although he still holds the title of chairman, he spends his days in relative seclusion, seeing few outside of the tight circle of his family, his two assistants and his lawyers. He personally lost about $900 million when Bear Stearns's stock price collapsed."

Cayne did not speak with Thomas for the article, at least not on the record, but his fingerprints are in and around it. For instance, Thomas described an incident between the two men in late 2007 when "Mr. Greenberg threatened to leave Bear, claiming he was not getting the respect he deserved. The departure would have represented another public relations blow for the reeling firm, and Mr. Cayne was told by his board to do what he could to appease him. Sitting down in Mr. Greenberg's office, Mr. Cayne made his appeal, mentioning in particular a recent speech he had given at a Bear dinner in which he saluted Mr. Greenberg's accomplishments and legacy. 'Alan,' Mr. Cayne said before walking out, 'this is the opposite of disrespect, so don't tell me you are disrespected.'" Pretty much Cayne alone referred to Greenberg by his given name, Alan, rather than by his nickname, Ace; in fact, Cayne charged people $100 if they said "Ace" in his presence.

But Cayne was confused and incensed by Greenberg's public humiliation of him. He said his former mentor's accusations were lies and distorted the true picture of what happened to the firm. "The anger that Greenberg has is unnatural," he said in one of a series of lengthy interviews. "It's like vindictively unnatural. Why? What happened? Well, that I'm trying to explain the best I can. I'm not a shrink, but I am close to a shrink because I hear so many stories and so many different angles of how to think about it. But talk to Sam [Molinaro]. Talk to Alan Schwartz, too. Ask them. Talk to [Warren] Spector. When did Greenberg ever say sell anything on the mortgage side? Ever? Ever? So that's like a guy going front and center with a boldfaced fucking fictional lie. And that's his calling card, telling Landon Thomas, 'Well, you'll read about it in my book.' Read about what? What's there to read about? There was never a whimper."

Cayne had not appreciated McCain's comparison of him to Mozilo back in April, either, especially since he had sold very little of his Bear Stearns stock over the years—unlike Mozilo—and because he had received no severance or payment of any kind when he retired from the firm in January. McCain had also been the recipient of Cayne's largesse to the tune of $1,000 in the 2000 presidential election, and he'd spoken to Bear's top executives back in February at Cayne's invitation. Cayne wrote McCain on April 23, "I lost 90% of my net worth, alongside many other longstanding shareholders of Bear Stearns. To indicate otherwise is categorically false. You have taken your issues with Wall Street to Main Street using my name and have treated me unfairly in the process."

At first, Cayne considered taking out full-page ads in the *New York Times* and the *Wall Street Journal* to publicize his letter to McCain. In the end, he decided to write a private letter expressing his outrage. "Quite frankly," he continued, "I am surprised that a person of your stature would stoop to populist one-liners much less take these sorts of pot-shots without checking to see if they were factually accurate. You are vilifying me in public and have done so with a lack of facts, causing irreparable harm to me and my family. When this point in history is remembered, your statements cast me as one of the leading actors and again, you have done so incorrectly and unjustly." Cayne reminded McCain how well he had been treated during his February visit to the firm. "I had hoped to be treated with the same type of respect instead of having my character and situation exploited based on misinformation and innuendo," he concluded. "As a man of honor, I would hope you would take appropriate steps to publicly set the record straight."

Cayne took elaborate steps to have the letter hand-delivered to the senator, asking Donald Tang, a Bear Stearns vice chairman, to give the letter to a friend of his, a rear admiral, who also happened to be one of McCain's friends. McCain never responded to Cayne's letter, either in writing or by calling him on the phone, which offended Cayne further.

The only public support Cayne received after the McCain speech came from the *New York Sun,* where Cayne had been the bridge columnist for a few years. The *Sun* editorialized, "There has been no evidence of any intentional wrongdoing on his part. To single this 74-year-old out for opprobrium to score political points in the middle of a presidential campaign is just inappropriate—like Attorney General [Eliot] Spitzer taking shots at Maurice Greenberg or John Whitehead. What would Mr. McCain like to see done to Mr. Cayne: have the last 6% of his wealth, accumulated in a long career according to board- and shareholder-approved contracts, punitively confiscated by the government?"

ABOUT THE ONLY unscripted moment in the maudlin—but mercifully brief—final Bear Stearns shareholders meeting on May 29 came when Cayne spoke from what appeared to be the heart about the final hand fate had dealt him. Pulling the microphone closer on the sparse dais in front of about four hundred shareholders, the nattily dressed former CEO (and still chairman of the board for another day) made his first public comments since March. The $10-a-share stock deal that shareholders were in the process of rubber-stamping at that very moment had cost Cayne nearly everything he had built in the previous forty years at the company, including both his billion-dollar fortune and his powerful throne. "It's a sad day," he said, "but we'll all get through it and hopefully be better off for it."

To that point, Cayne's words had more or less echoed those of his partner Alan Schwartz, the media banker turned beleaguered CEO, whose own impromptu remarks had focused on his ongoing gratitude to the Bear Stearns employees. As Cayne continued speaking, however, his voice became increasingly shaky and his thoughts more personal. "This is my fortieth year with the company," he continued. "And when I retired"—on January 4, after Schwartz told him it was time to go—"that was a sad moment. This is equally sad. That which doesn't kill you makes you stronger. And at this point, we all look like Hercules. Life goes on. This company achieved lofty heights for sure. But we ran into a hurricane." With some anger, he then launched into his view that nothing less than a "conspiracy" was responsible for the firm's downfall after eighty-five years and that he hoped that the authorities would "nail the guys who did it." In the end, though, he concluded, "I have no anger, only regret. Fourteen thousand families were affected. I personally apologize. I feel an enormous amount of pain and management feels an enormous amount of pain. I am sorry it happened the way it happened. Words can't describe how bad I feel."

Seconds later, the meeting concluded without questions or protest from the audience. The *fait*, as they say, was *accompli*. Ten minutes, start to finish. While other shareholders and employees, all of whom had lost fortunes, milled about the second-floor auditorium bemoaning their fates, Cayne returned quickly to his ebony lair on the sixth floor—nobody stopped him to talk—and ensconced himself back behind his curved desk. When Bear first moved into its gleaming forty-five-story headquarters in 2001, Cayne also had a palatial office on the forty-second floor, with a sumptuous and panoramic southwestern view of lower Manhattan. But after September 11, he quickly moved down to the lower floor. (The office on the high floor became a conference room with a fully stocked bar.) The undistinguished view from his sixth-floor corner office is toward the northeast and, ironically, faces the adjacent JPMorgan Chase building.

In his office, Cayne made a few phone calls and received an intermittent stream of loyalists. In contrast to his somber public performance downstairs, he now had a twinkle in his eye and his spirits seemed high. By his side he kept his trusty mini blowtorch, used to light and relight his mammoth private-label cigars. (He alone authorized himself to smoke inside the building.) David Glaser, a longtime Bear investment banker who most recently had the title of co-head of investment banking, came by to pay his final respects. Glaser was heading off to a senior position at Bank of America. Then Teddy Serure, a Bear broker, came by. Once upon a time, Cayne had spent "eleven months and twenty-three days" wooing Serure away from Merrill Lynch. "Jimmy promised me just one thing when I came," Serure said, "that this would be a fun place to work." So it was, he was happy to confirm. Even to the end.

Another big Cayne fan, Vinny Dicks, a senior executive in the brokerage business, came in and said an emotional goodbye. Cayne thanked him for the "extraordinary" letter he had written Cayne's seven grandchildren about their grandfather. And Cayne told Dicks, "You know who to come to if you need help" in the future. After a quick lunch of cold chicken salad, sent down from the dining room, one of the several executive assistants in the bullpen outside of Cayne's office came in crying and thanked him for all the wonderful memories and all the good times. They hugged.

But when the phone rang a few moments later and Cayne learned it was Jamie Dimon—the new owner of his firm—calling from his vacation refuge in Positano, on the western coast of Italy, Cayne quickly switched emotional gears. In the minute-long conversation, Cayne congratulated Dimon on the just-concluded 84 percent positive vote for the deal—a deal Cayne had been vehemently against but eventually voted for as a board member—and explained to Dimon that the shareholders' meeting had come off without any of the hitches the lawyers had been worried about (for instance, what if someone had *actually* spoken up). There was no discussion of the fact that JPMorgan owned just shy of half the Bear shares going into the vote, making the outcome a foregone conclusion.

Despite the shotgun marriage, the third time proved to be the charm for the Dimon and Cayne mating dance. In late 1998, soon after Sandy Weill, then chairman and CEO of Citigroup and Dimon's mentor, fired him as the heir apparent of Citigroup, Cayne and Dimon had talked for three hours about many things, including the possibility of Dimon taking over the Bear Stearns Securities Corporation—the firm's clearing business—in the midst of the SEC's investigation into Bear's violations of the antifraud provisions of the federal securities laws in connection with its clearing relationship with A. R. Baron, Inc., a small (and now defunct) "bucket shop." (Bear Stearns later settled the charges with the SEC about its dealings with Baron for about $38.5 million, and Richard Harriton, who ran the clearing business, was later barred for two years from the securities industry with the right to reapply and fined $1 million.) Dimon enjoyed his discussion with Cayne but declined his offer because what he really wanted to do, Dimon told Cayne, was "have your seat" in the metaphorical sense of wanting to one day run a Wall Street firm.

The two men met again a few years later, after Dimon had become CEO of Bank One, in Chicago. Dimon came calling this time because Bank One wanted to buy Bear Stearns. But Cayne told Dimon that the acquisition wouldn't work because the market would react negatively to such a dilutive deal. "Any premium for Bear Stearns shareholders would disappear after you announced the deal," Cayne told him.

Now, with a serious helping hand from the men running the U.S. Treasury and Federal Reserve along with $29 billion of the public's money, Dimon had finally gotten his prize; whether it would become a pyrrhic victory remained to be seen. At a UBS Global Financial Services Conference on May 12, eight weeks after the signing of the initial deal, Dimon had said, "You will judge us on this deal one year from now. You cannot judge us on this deal today. We would not have done it if we didn't think it made sense, but we are bearing an awful lot of risk. . . . There's a lot of risk and we are not going to sleep easy until we're done, until we get through the closing and a couple of months after that. We're completely focused to manage through this downturn."

But on May 29, as Cayne's and Dimon's brief telephone conversation was nearing an end, Cayne allowed that it had been a "sad, quite sad" day and then wished Dimon "all the best luck in the world." He then returned to the business of saying his internal good-byes.

Most of the artifacts of Cayne's illustrious career had already been boxed up—including copies of a prized book, *Gin Rummy: A Predator's Guide* by Michael Sall—and sent off to his weekend home at the shore in Elberon, New Jersey. There was one prominent exception: the Ek-Chor motorcycle that had been a fixture in his office since he became Bear's CEO. Instead of taking it with him, Cayne had decided to make a gift of the motorcycle—from the Chinese motorcycle company that Bear took public in 1993—to Fares Noujaim, a Bear vice chairman and longtime vocal Cayne supporter. Noujaim moved the motorcycle to his new office downtown at Merrill Lynch, where he was briefly president of Merrill

Lynch Middle East and North Africa. "The motorcycle is part of Wall Street history," Noujaim said.

※

WHILE CAYNE WAS holding court in his office for the last time, Paul Friedman, resigned to the inevitable, wondered aloud how his beloved Bear Stearns, where he had spent the past twenty-seven years of his life, could have evaporated so quickly and effortlessly, just shy of its eighty-fifth birthday. He had become nothing more than a "transition employee" and wasn't sure what to do next, given that the deal was supposed to close the next day and he had not been offered a job at JPMorgan. "There's no process for leaving," he said. "There's gonna be five thousand, six thousand, seven thousand people whose last day is tomorrow, and no one knows how to leave. Nobody knows. Do you just stop coming in? Do you resign to some-body? Do I turn in my ID? What happens to my corporate credit card, my BlackBerry? Nobody knows, and we're all just going to wander off into the sunset. I have a fair amount of severance and stuff that's coming, and it's subject to having signed an agreement and release that I haven't received yet, and they say somewhere in the next few weeks you'll get that. But there's no one to discuss it with, because everybody in our HR department is leaving. The whole thing is bizarre. JPMorgan, for a firm that's supposed to be legendary in their ability to do mergers, this one has been a shit show from the beginning. The classic is they keep talking about how they've hired 40 percent of Bear Stearns's employees or plan to. That's clever, because that includes a couple of thousand people we have that are clerical workers in a call center in Dallas. It includes a whole bunch of people who were hired transitionally for the next few months. Real, live people is a couple thousand, so there's prob-ably ten thousand that won't get hired or won't get hired past three to six months, and the process is just so fucked up."

Friedman paused for a moment and stared out the window onto 47th Street. When he resumed speaking, it was with a new resolve. "But having said that, we deserve it, so it's okay," he explained. "It's funny. You heard Jimmy. His only comment that he made in the meeting was, 'We're still looking at conspiracy theories, and who did what, and we'll see if they can decide who the bad guys were, and whether they can prove it.' And we're the bad guys. We did this to ourselves. We put ourselves in a position where this could happen. It is our fault for allowing it to get this far, and for not taking any steps to do anything about it. It's a classic case of mismanagement at the top. There's just no question about it."

PART II

WHY IT HAPPENED:
EIGHTY-FIVE YEARS

CHAPTER 13

CY

The demise of Bear Stearns and the financial calamities it set off in the world cannot be explained just by the events of March 2008. The roots of the firm's problems are found deep in its unique corporate culture, which developed over decades, largely defined by the actions of three larger-than-life personalities: Cy Lewis, Ace Greenberg, and Jimmy Cayne.

Just after the start of a historic six-year bull market, Joseph Ainslie Bear, then forty-four, along with two younger partners—Robert B. Stearns, thirty-five, and Harold C. Mayer, twenty-eight—founded Bear, Stearns & Co. on May Day 1923. While the firm's business dropped off substantially after the Crash of 1929, it was carefully managed during these lean years and remained profitable. Small bonuses could still be paid and layoffs were avoided. By 1933, Bear Stearns had survived sufficiently to have grown to seventy-five employees, from the original seven, and increased its capital by 60 percent, to $800,000, from $500,000.

In 1933, with the hope of starting and building a corporate bond business, one of the firm's new partners, Teddy Low (born Theodore Lowenstein), recommended that they hire Salim L. Lewis, then all of about twenty-four years old and a former professional football player and shoe salesman, to run it. Until then, most firms traded only government bonds for the simple reason that very few corporations at the time—especially during the difficult economic years of the Depression—issued bonds. Bear Stearns's decision to hire Lewis to start this new business portended that changes were afoot. The brilliant and aggressive "Cy" Lewis, as he was known, was "a huge man with a powerful voice," according to a later description in the *Times*, standing six feet two inches tall, "weighing more than 250 pounds, with an uncommonly large head . . . and a jolting temper." In short order, Cy Lewis became the driving force behind Bear Stearns's transformation from a sleepy backwater on Wall Street to a serious and scrappy player in the growing securities industry.

He was born on October 5, 1908, in Brookline, Massachusetts, to Max Lewis and Hattie Lissner Lewis. Max Lewis, an Orthodox and somewhat religious immigrant Jew, was from "either Russia or Poland, depending on where you pick the border," according to Cy's oldest son, Sandy Lewis. Hattie Lewis was a U.S. citizen, born in Boston.

Growing up, Lewis "had asthma, and he got it so bad he used to have to crawl up the stairs to get into his house," his son said. He attended Boston University for three semesters but had to drop out because his parents did not have enough money to pay the tuition. To earn some extra money, Lewis became a professional football player in Boston—perhaps playing for the Boston Badgers, although no one alive is certain. "Professional football in those days wasn't the New York Giants and Larry Tisch," Sandy Lewis said. "It was fifty and seventy-five bucks a game per player, paid from the gate. He was very tough and needed the money. On one occasion, and I've seen the result of this, he actually broke his wrist. It was a compound fracture with the bone showing. He went to the sidelines. They didn't have a substitute. There wasn't any question of what was going to happen next. They simply taped it up and he finished the game."

With his football career not leading anywhere, in 1927 Lewis decided to move to Philadelphia. He followed a girlfriend down there and soon got a job working in a shoe store. Although he loathed it, he wasn't a half-bad salesman. "In those days, shoe stores were shoe stores, and this happened to be a shoe store which sold men's shoes," his son explained. "And in comes a woman who's clearly in mourning. She had a black veil . . . over her face. She comes into the store, and it was understood that she was going to be his customer. She walks up and he says, 'Well, now, what can we do for you?' She says, 'Well, my husband's died and I would really like to be able to buy a pair of shoes for him that look terrific because we're going to have a funeral.' My father said, 'Well, probably the best-looking pair of shoes we have in the store for this occasion would be black alligator shoes. Let me show you a pair.' He shows her a pair. She says, 'Perfect.'"

After some confusion because the wife apparently did not know the husband's shoe size, Lewis suggested that since she needed the shoes immediately to give to the undertaker, she might consider buying two pairs of the alligator shoes. "Now, it happens that the owner of the store was desperate to get rid of the alligator shoes," Sandy recalled. "They just weren't moving. The reason they weren't moving was very clear. They looked great. They didn't feel so good. Until you walked, they were fine. But after you walked, these shoes were anything but terrific. My father understood from the owner that if he were able to sell these shoes in quantity, he would make more money. So the commission on one pair might be X. The commission on two pairs wasn't 2X. It was 3X. So he said to her, 'You know, if you could just estimate, what I'll do is I'll sell you a pair that's in that range and then maybe I'll sell you one that's just a tiny bit larger so you'll be covered no matter what. I might be able to give you a little discount under the circumstances that your husband died and you are buying two pairs.'"

After a quick consultation with the owner, Lewis made the widow the offer. "Of course, that was all wonderful for the owner," he continued. "Dad gets his premium. She gets the shoes. She got a little discount. The owner moved two pairs instead of one. Everybody was happy. So he sold two pairs of shoes to a dead man. This is a great story and he told it often." The story became a parable for the questionable ethical and moral behavior that Cy Lewis encountered all too often in his highly successful Wall Street career. "The reason he told it," Sandy said, "is because as far as he was concerned, the sales in Wall Street, the whole idea is to move product. It's not a particularly interesting question whether or not it fits. Just get the product out the door."

But Lewis could not stand selling shoes. His only ambition was to get a job on Wall Street. He did that through a carefully planned encounter at the North Shore Country Club, on Long Island. "He got to Wall Street through a parking lot," his son said. "He got to Wall Street because he went to the North Shore Country Club, which was a Jewish country club on the North Shore of Long Island. Herbert Salomon [the president of Salomon Brothers, the Wall Street partnership founded in 1910] had something to do with getting him there. Cy Lewis stuck to Herbert Salomon because he was hoping to get himself a job at Salomon Brothers. He ended up getting Herbert Salomon's car for him in the parking lot of the country club, which is pretty remarkable because he didn't know how to drive. That didn't bother him any. He got the car over to him. Salomon said to my father, 'Come in on Monday morning, son. We'll have a talk.' Dad showed up bright and early on Monday morning and got himself a job as a runner."

As a runner, Lewis would carry bond certificates from one Wall Street firm to another, from one client to another, through the system of underground tunnels all around the Wall Street area that kept these messengers from having to deal with inclement weather. The brilliant and ambitious Lewis quickly graduated from his delivery boy role and joined Salomon Brothers' impressive sales and trading department.

Soon enough, though, Lewis got fired from Salomon Brothers. He then moved on to Barr, Cohen & Co. He worked for three years in the sales department but got fired again. He worked at two more firms and got fired from them, too. "Dad was the kind of guy who would have ideas and want to carry them through," his son said. "He wouldn't have done anything wrong. It would have been because he was impetuous. It would have been because he had terrific ideas and he wanted to get stuff done and he would have said, 'Well, for Christ's sake, why don't we do this and this and this?' And some old partner would say, 'I don't need this nonsense. Get him out of here.' Because at the end of the day, if you were making decent money, it was a carriage trade business. The last thing this man could live with, under any circumstances, was boredom. And you'd sit in these firms and wait until the phone rings and be told, 'Buy as agent a hundred bonds or maybe a hundred shares of stock.' You're not going to get rich on that. He didn't have any money. The only way he was going to make money—and he knew this from day one, this is something that drove the whole process—you had to make money with money and it had to be other people's money. He didn't have any. You couldn't raise it. You didn't go to the bank and borrow it and then speculate on it. You had all kinds of margin requirements and structure in these firms. These firms, with the exception of Salomon Brothers, never used their own capital, including Bear Stearns."

When he was hired at Bear Stearns, Lewis's mandate was to

slowly and profitably dip the firm's toe into the water of making money judiciously using a tiny slice of the firm's $800,000 in capital. At the time, very few—if any—Wall Street firms were making a market, as principal, in corporate bonds—acting as an agent, yes, but not as a principal. "Bear Stearns's capital would have increased with these things because he made money," his son said. "This guy knew how to make money."

Five years after he landed at the firm, on May 2, 1938, he became a partner. His capital contribution to the partnership was $20,000, and this he got from his wife, who received the money as part of her second divorce settlement. This was a very slow period on Wall Street. The Depression was arguably at its worst. Trading volume on the stock market was often fewer than a million shares a day. Bear Stearns's clients in those days were said to be "mainly rich Park Avenue German Jewish widows." "People think 1932 was bad," Sandy Lewis said. "My dad told me 1938 was the worst of it. They never thought they would ever get out of this goddamn Depression. And his knowledge of that was profound." Still, the firm made slow and steady progress. In December 1940, Bear Stearns announced that it was buying the Chicago firm Stein, Brennan Co., which had acted as Bear's correspondent in Chicago since 1932.

Ironically, Lewis's big break at Bear Stearns came after the bombing of Pearl Harbor, when the United States decided the time had come to enter World War II. Cy Lewis was the father of four children, and fathers were exempted from war service. Instead, Lewis dedicated himself to making money for Bear Stearns and for his family. "The war came and Roosevelt needed to arm the nation and deliver whatever he needed to the factories and then take the product to the ports and get it out of here," his son said. "He was trying to produce airplanes, tanks, trucks, millions of things. They had to seize the railroads and force traffic over the railroads and make sure that the railroads were working just for the government to move product. You had to make sure you got it when you needed it. This was war. They broke the railroads. They put credit controls on. You couldn't borrow money."

Lewis noticed that before Roosevelt commandeered the railroads for the war effort, railroad bonds were trading at par because interest payments were still being made. "But, all of a sudden, they can't pay the coupon," Sandy Lewis said. "So they start trading what is called 'flat.' You can buy and sell a rail bond any way you please, but the coupon's not accruing. It's dead. . . . If you buy it, you can call it a future and maybe it'll be worth something someday." With these railroad bonds no longer paying interest, they were trading as low as 5¢ on the dollar. Lewis started to think about whether to buy the bonds at these severely depressed prices. He figured either Armageddon was imminent—in which case nothing much would matter—or the United States would end up winning the war and the country would desperately need its railroads back to rebuild and to supply the victorious nation. In the latter instance, railroad bonds bought at a steep discount during the war would be worth a fortune.

To implement his idea, Lewis knew he would need someone else's money, since Joe Bear would never give him what he needed from the firm's capital. So he contacted Harrie T. Shea, a loan officer at Marine Midland Bank, which had its offices near Bear Stearns at 140 Broadway. Lewis convinced Marine Midland to lend Bear Stearns the money to buy the railroad bonds. Although the rate of interest Marine Midland could charge Bear Stearns was fixed at a low level because of the war effort—lending to Wall Street was a permitted use of capital—the interest on the loan still had to be paid while Lewis was accumulating his inventory of non-interest-paying railroad bonds. To generate the needed cash to do so, Lewis became one of the largest sellers of war bonds to individual investors.

The risk of owning railroad bonds that were paying no interest heightened the fear in the Lewis home. "We had guys coming to our house and asking my father, 'How are my accounts doing with all these rail bonds?'" Sandy recalled. "And my father would tell them, 'They're trading flat, but someday they're going to be fine.' The tension in the house rose and rose and rose, because you had to pay interest on that money. Even though the interest was capped, there still was some interest, and you had to pay that interest. There was enormous emotional pressure: many cigarettes, lots of scotch, lots of talk, and lots of anxiety. It was enough to turn everybody into a nervous wreck."

Compounding Lewis's stress over his bet on the railroad bonds was the family's decision, in 1944, to buy a huge new apartment at 778 Park Avenue for the princely sum of $20,000. The family had been renting two apartments at 1192 Park Avenue, one facing the armory to the north and the other facing Park Avenue. Lewis made the purchase at the insistence of his wife, who felt its location and size were far more appropriate for her improving status. "It's like eighteen rooms and six master bedrooms," Sandy said. "Everybody's got a bathroom. This is a hell of an apartment. But this was also a disaster. He was coming home every night so depressed about the world, about his critical decision to buy these rail bonds. You couldn't sell them. This was it. Either this strategy was going to work or they weren't going very far at all."

Lewis had to move the war bonds. "This man would be gone for two weeks at a time in every single city and every single bank to get control of their portfolios and move the bonds around," Sandy Lewis said. "He was known throughout the United States. If he could do this, he could support the rail bonds. This was all about 'I'll help you. I'll rearrange your portfolio.' He could run a yield curve in his sleep. All so that he could earn enough revenue to support this huge bet that he had made."

Bear Stearns would have been bankrupt if Lewis's bet had failed. "Gone," Sandy said. "Out of business. No question about it. They weren't an underwriting firm. They weren't a mergers firm. They didn't have any other business."

After the United States and its allies won the war, the victory party played out exactly the way Cy Lewis had hoped. "The government decided to put the railroads back on their feet," his son explained. "Things got awful good awful fast. All of a sudden, these bonds rose to par. And you got par plus accrued interest from back when. All I can say is things got different. Holy shit. We got better cars . . . golf clubs. The apartment was well furnished. All kinds of things started happening. We had parties. I could see it all over the place. There were six servants. There was a chauffeur."

By January 1945, with the Allies' victory in Europe looking more likely, Bear Stearns had started adding to its inventory of railroad bonds by buying some directly from the Reconstruction Finance

Corporation at par (100¢ on the dollar) and slightly above. By February 1946, with the Allied victory sealed, railroad bonds were fetching record high prices, with a yield only slightly higher than U.S. Treasury securities—the ultimate sign that the health of the industry had improved dramatically and Lewis's bet had paid off in spades.

Flush with the extraordinary success of his railroad bet, Lewis quickly consolidated his power at Bear Stearns. But to do that, he first had to elbow out of the way his partner Teddy Low. Low was a member of the Confrérie des Chevaliers du Tastevin, a highly select group of oenophiles that devoted themselves to the wines of Bordeaux. Low, the dapper public face of the firm, always resented Lewis's intellectual prowess. Low was also "pompous, dense, stiff, a snob, and insecure," according to Sandy Lewis.

Teddy Low believed longevity should be the key criterion for selecting the firm's managing partner. "The fact that my dad built the firm up did not enter into Low's thinking," Sandy Lewis continued. "But my dad had a different view. When Low [who had served in the naval reserve] came back from the war, he attempted to take the firm back where it was and stop all principal trading. [Founding partners] Harold C. Mayer and Joe Bear said, 'Are you crazy?' And that was the end of Teddy Low's authority in that firm."

❋

IN THE WAKE of his success betting on the railroad bonds and after he consolidated his power at the firm, Lewis needed an encore. Bear Stearns did, too. So the partners focused on other event-driven deals, such as merger arbitrage (betting on whether an announced merger would happen or not) and taking controlling equity stakes in companies. In effect, after World War II, Bear Stearns was at the starting line of what has come to be known as the private equity business. "What you're looking at," Sandy Lewis said, "is how does the firm make money with money, the firm's money?" This became his father's focus after the war. He wanted to climb the ladder of success and push his firm into the limelight. But he still had to pay occasional homage to the founding partners. "Mayer's on the floor and he has to call Mayer to get approval on everything," his son continued. "Mayer was kind of a necessary nuisance."

As wealthy as the Lewises were, Cy Lewis spent much time worrying about everything, though he communicated very little to his family. Cy Lewis's growing depression began to cast a pall over the household. "My mother got the feeling from her husband that things weren't good," Sandy said. "His personality was always, 'I'm worried.' This is a guy who's very concerned about building things. He carries all the worries of the whole place on his shoulders."

And his words and actions could have powerful effects on his partners. For instance, Sandy Lewis recalled how his father devastated his partner David Finkle, whom Cy had recruited to Bear Stearns from Salomon Brothers and admired greatly. "David Finkle would come into the office with a new tie on," Sandy recalled. "My father would look at the tie and say, 'Where the fuck did you get that tie? Ah, come on, what kind of a tie is that? For Christ's sake, would you guys look at this tie? What did he spend on *that* tie?'" Lewis's supposedly friendly razzing caused Finkle to retreat to the bathroom and burst into tears. "Finkle was a very tiny little guy. Here's this massive Cy Lewis with his great presence and great gravitas. Cy Lewis walks in the room. Everybody sits up a little straighter. David Finkle walks in the room. Nobody notices he came in." By this time, all the main players at Bear Stearns had specific roles: the WASPy affectations of Teddy Low, the showbiz demeanor of Don Lillis, the avuncular paternalism of Harold C. Mayer, the outsized intimidation of Cy Lewis. Lewis wanted to push his firm into the limelight—and climb the ladder of success himself.

CHAPTER 14

ACE

Into this small second-tier Wall Street firm in 1949 came Alan C. Greenberg, a tough-minded midwestern Jew with a gambler's instinct and a serious itch to get rich. He was born in Wichita, Kansas, in 1928. He was the grandson of Russian immigrants who supposedly arrived "on these shores with nothing but dreams of America." He had great admiration for them. "Getting from Russia to America without any money or profession or speaking the language, that took a lot of courage," he explained. "And they had it." When Greenberg was six years old, his father moved the family to the upper-middle-class neighborhood of Crown Heights in Oklahoma City, Oklahoma. Theodore Greenberg started Streets, a clothing store, on West Main Street in Oklahoma City, in 1930. The next year, the store was one of the first in the country to offer customer charge accounts. Eventually, Streets grew to thirteen stores in the state of Oklahoma, with around $30 million in revenue.

Alan Greenberg was a precocious little kid. "He was a terrific boy, never a problem at all," his mother, Esther, said in 2000, when she was ninety-three years old. (She lived to be ninety-eight.) "But he was also a challenge. It's not easy to raise a boy when he's smarter than his mother. . . . After school, we would spend hours at home building model airplanes and, once, built a motor that he attached to his bicycle to power him to school." He also saw a performance of Blackstone the Magician when he was eight years old and then became hooked on magic and card tricks. This dedication to a variety of hobbies—whether magic tricks, dog training, yo-yos, bridge, or big-game hunting in Africa using a bow and arrow—started in childhood. He always prided himself on being able to leave the office at the end of the day and not worry about it.

Eventually, at both Harding Junior High School and at Classen High, he would become a standout student who was captivated by all of his classes. He was also a star athlete, although he was only five feet ten on a good day. He had more of a pugilist's density rather than a true athlete's sleekness. But he made it work all the same. He was a blue-ribbon sprinter. He was also a star halfback on the Classen High football team that had an 11-1-1 record and defeated Tulsa Central to win the first official state high school championship.

He graduated from high school during World War II, and with so many young men in the army, his football skills were sufficiently good that he received a full scholarship to play football at the University of Oklahoma, eighteen miles from home. Freshmen were allowed to play on the varsity during World War II and Greenberg started the first two games of the 1945 season. But in the second game, against Nebraska, he ruptured a disc in his back, and his intercollegiate athletic days were over. At the end of the school year, he decided he wanted to "go East" to school. He transferred to the University of Missouri, Columbia, five hundred miles from home. He majored in business. With his cousin, Ronnie Greenberg, he joined the Zeta Beta Tau fraternity. They would also go camping, hunting, and fishing together when they could. He claimed to be only a B student who focused on sports and girls, "though not necessarily in that order." He said he majored in "getting out."

It was in pursuit of co-eds that Greenberg became known forevermore as "Ace." At Mizzou, a friend advised him that it would be difficult for him to date women given his obviously Jewish name. "You know, you're not a bad-looking guy," his friend told him, "but with a name like Alan Greenberg, you're not going to do well at the University of Missouri." His friend suggested Ace Gainsboro. "I dropped the Gainsboro, but Ace stuck at the University of Missouri and it followed me to New York," Greenberg said. He also pursued his interest in playing bridge in college. "If he was up until two o'clock, it was because he was playing bridge," his Mizzou roommate (and future Bear Stearns chief operating officer) Alvin Einbender said.

Although Greenberg used to work sweeping out the family store on Saturdays growing up, he knew early on that his ambitions were far larger than running a women's clothing chain. He had his sights set on Wall Street. "I just thought it was something I might be good at," he said in 2004. "I loved playing cards, I loved—shall we say—making bets on things. So I headed to New York. Bet making was illegal at that time, so I didn't have many options." Greenberg said he took with him some valuable lessons about life he learned from his family. "My father had a tremendous amount of common sense," he said. "During World War II, a lot of people had cash. I said to my father, 'How come all these people have cash?' He said, 'They do business away from the cash register'—because at that time we had price controls. . . . So I said, 'Why don't you?' He said, 'I never want to end up working for my bookkeeper or my secretary.' And I never forgot that." According to Mark Singer, the *New Yorker* writer who profiled Greenberg in the magazine in 1999 and in whose piece this bit of homespun wisdom first appeared, "That was it, an ostensibly revelatory anecdote that terminated in a business axiom: steal from the tax man and your underlings are liable to blackmail you."

Another lesson he learned from his father the retail merchant would become the bedrock of the Greenberg myth. "There were certain things that I heard him talk about that stuck with me through Wall Street and I think pertain in any business," he said. "For instance, he'd say if you had some merchandise that doesn't look good, sell it today because tomorrow it's going to be worse. That's certainly true of securities, I assure you."

He also owed his father his everlasting thanks for staking him to the $3,000 he used to live in New York City after college while he tried to get a job, any job, on Wall Street. He had not graduated from an Ivy League school, he was Jewish, and the competition for Wall Street jobs, then as ever, was keen. "Other than the Jewish firms, Wall Street was an inhospitable place for a Jewish boy," Einbender said. Greenberg also had in his pocket a letter of recommendation from a business friend of his uncle's—whom he had never met—and he used that letter to get interviews at six of the Jewish Wall Street firms. It was very tough going.

His money was quickly running out. He was twenty-one years old. Then, at last, Bear Stearns asked him to come work as a clerk in the loan department, making $32.50 per week at the firm's new office at 1 Wall Street.

In 1949 there was no question that it was Cy Lewis's firm. He was the managing partner and had by far the largest percentage of the profits, which made sense because he and his ideas were generating most of them. Lewis presided over the growing firm from his large leather seat at the center of a U-shaped arrangement of desks. The firm had 125 employees and $17 million in capital. The firm was referred to then as "Boys' Town" for obvious reasons. Singer, in his *New Yorker* article, elaborated: "Bear Stearns had something of a Sammy Glick profile. It was a 'trading' operation—smart, sharp-elbowed, busy in the equity markets—but not an enterprise whose partners were likely to be invited to Washington to offer the President or his Cabinet members insights into how to mind the nation's business."

At first, Greenberg's tasks as a clerk were indeed menial. He was assigned to the oil-and-gas department—he was from Oklahoma, after all. He read technical journals and placed pushpins in a wall-sized map of the United States to show the location of oil-drilling activity. "I was very well prepared for that," he said once, with some sarcasm. "I had good hand-eye coordination." One of the main aspects of his job was to move the pins around the map. He started hanging around the trading floor during his lunch hour and fell in love with the action there. Its mysterious, magical quality appealed to him. His youthful curiosity came to the attention of John Slade, the partner who was then running the arbitrage department at the firm. On old Wall Street, arbitrage was a gambler's paradise, where grown men could take calculated risks on whether and when announced mergers or acquisitions would actually occur. But since the risks of the deals that arbitrageurs invested in were often beyond their knowledge—and certainly beyond their control—the roller-coaster ride could be at once thrilling and nauseating.

Slade quickly arranged for Greenberg to work for him on the arbitrage desk. Greenberg found out immediately how gut-wrenching the work could be. By midmorning on his first day, after a "verbal lashing by Slade," Greenberg headed to the bathroom and threw up. Slade, of course, was used to such tirades from Lewis, who once berated his partner for losing $400 on one bond trade at the same time he had made $80,000 in profit on another bond trade; Slade almost quit the firm as a result, but then joined the risk arbitrage department. Firm mythology held that after Slade had taken his pound of flesh out of Greenberg, never again in his career would Greenberg reveal any nervousness.

In truth, Greenberg just wanted to make money, and the arbitrage department at Bear Stearns was doing precisely that. "It was one of the few places in 1949–50 that was making any money," Greenberg explained. During those days, the arbitrage department was said to make about 30 percent of the firm's profits in a good year and all of them in a bad year.

By 1952, Cy Lewis was becoming a major figure on both Wall

Street and in New York City. He pioneered what became known as "block trading"—the buying and selling of huge blocks of stock for institutional investors—along with Gus Levy, the head of Goldman Sachs. Also along with Levy, Lewis became a tireless fund-raiser for the Federation of Jewish Philanthropies, which served as the umbrella organization for charitable gifts to more than a hundred New York area hospitals and social services organizations. Lewis, more than anyone else at Bear Stearns, initiated the practice of charitable donations at the firm, a practice that over time both Greenberg and Cayne perfected. Bear Stearns was unique on Wall Street (for requiring the firm's senior managing directors to donate 4 percent of their annual compensation to charities of their own choosing).

In 1953, at the ripe age of twenty-five, Greenberg succeeded Slade as head of the risk arbitrage department and "was on his way toward establishing a reputation as one of the shrewdest and most self-possessed traders on Wall Street," according to *The New Yorker*. That year, he married Ann Lieberman, also a native of Oklahoma City.

In 1956, a seat opened up in the U-shaped array of desks right next to Lewis, and Slade recommended to Greenberg that it would be good for his career if he could get close to the managing partner. Without the nudge from Slade, Greenberg later claimed, he would not have taken the open chair, as otherwise there was no reason to put oneself voluntarily in a position to incur Lewis's wrath. "Being seated next to Lewis meant suffering the full force of his frequent titanic rages," Judith Ramsey Ehrlich and Barry J. Rehfeld wrote about Greenberg in their 1989 book, *The New Crowd*. "If anyone disagreed with him, it was a virtually no-win situation. Lewis had an ego as large as his physical proportions. If you were wrong, he would never let you forget it. If you were right and he was wrong, then Lewis would hold a grudge." While this, sadly, is not unusual behavior on Wall Street, what was unusual was how, despite this characteristic, the two men effectively married their skills—Lewis in block trading, Greenberg in risk arbitrage—to the firm's benefit and their own. The slowly emerging world of mergers and acquisitions provided both men with the incentive to combine their talents. "The natural marriage between block trading and arbitrage is pretty obvious [since big blocks of stock start moving when a deal is rumored or announced]," Sandy Lewis said. "At Bear Stearns, that took place between Alan Greenberg and Cy Lewis sitting on the trading desk together."

In April 1957, there was a bit of a hiccup in Greenberg's career ascent. On April 2, the New York Stock Exchange accused Greenberg of violating what is now Exchange Rule 345.17 (and was then rule 434), to wit, "No member, member firm or member corporation shall permit any person to perform regularly any of the duties customarily performed by a registered person, unless such person shall have been registered with and is acceptable to the Exchange." He was suspended from the firm for two months without compensation, a significant slap on the wrist at the time. The Exchange required then—and still does now—that most people who work on Wall Street, especially those involved with clients or with buying and selling securities, must pass a test and become "registered." The Exchange has no additional detail about what Greenberg did wrong that resulted in such a significant penalty. (Greenberg declined to be interviewed on this topic.)

But the suspension had little obvious effect on Greenberg's career trajectory. He returned to the firm in June 1957 and, with his business and political skills working in tandem, became a partner of Bear Stearns in 1958, when he was thirty. The first year-end partners' celebration he attended was as simple as could be imagined: pitchers of beer in the back room of a local steakhouse after the market had closed.

A year later, Greenberg received news that any young man would find shocking: He had been diagnosed with colon cancer and the doctors told him he had about a 25 percent chance of survival. Surgery was the only choice, since in those days there was no chemotherapy. "Well, the odds aren't too bad," he told his brother Maynard, "but the stakes are awfully high." He flew off to the Mayo Clinic, in Rochester, Minnesota, and underwent what turned out to be successful surgery to remove the cancer. The cancer was cut out completely and had not spread. "According to friends and family," goes one account, "Greenberg never seemed frightened or depressed all through the months of convalescence. He did, though, have a store of mordant jokes." He would joke that for him the future now meant next week: He would only invest in short-term securities and decided he might as well rent everything, instead of buying. But, in truth, his existential crisis quite normally focused his attention with laser precision on the things he thought were most important: making money and having fun. "I never put anything off after that," he said. "I took magic lessons and judo lessons. I went to Africa. Really, I just kind of exploded."

At 1 Wall Street, Cy Lewis took the news of Greenberg's illness hard. Greenberg had proven to be a lucrative partner for the firm, which always needed new ways to make money with its own money and didn't have many sources of recurring revenue. "Brains like that don't come along like that very often," Sandy Lewis remembered his father saying about Greenberg during his illness. "The risks to the firm were substantial. There was a huge sigh of relief when his prognosis improved."

GREENBERG'S BRUSH WITH his own mortality inspired him not only to live more for the moment but also to be somewhat more confrontational with those partners who he felt were making wrongheaded decisions with the firm's capital. Suddenly, Greenberg's father's maxim of selling slow-moving inventory as soon as possible became his mantra for the securities business. Public enemy number one on this front, Greenberg thought, was the managing partner of Bear Stearns, Cy Lewis. Whereas before his cancer diagnosis Greenberg was content just to talk to the other partners about his perception that Lewis was holding on to certain securities too long, now he was willing to be more confrontational. If Lewis would not sell the firm's losers, Greenberg decided, he would just have to be the one to get him to do it. "People don't hesitate for a minute to take a small profit," he said once. "But they don't want to take losses. Which is, of course, just the opposite of what you should do. If you're wrong, you're wrong. Sell, and buy something else."

He recalled a number of "showdowns" with Lewis, and especially one from the early 1960s: "I went to Cy one day and said, 'You ever heard of a company called Rudd-Melikian?' He said, 'What's Rudd-Melikian?' I said, 'We have a position in it. It's gone from twenty to five.' I named a few similar situations and said if it didn't stop I was going to quit." Finally, one day, he told Lewis he was quitting.

"You're what?" Lewis responded.

"I'm leaving," Greenberg said. "There's nothing to talk about." He walked out of the office.

That night, Lewis called Greenberg and invited him to come over to 778 Park for a conversation. Greenberg went reluctantly. Lewis demanded to know why he was resigning. They spoke again about Rudd-Melikian, the vending-machine manufacturer in which Bear Stearns owned 10,000 shares. "It's down ten points," Greenberg told Lewis, "and you didn't know we own it. And that's why I'm leaving—because you won't take losses. You buy these things and you won't sell them."

The next day, Lewis asked Greenberg to come to his office. "All right," Lewis told him. "I'll make a deal with you. You're right. I'm a terrible seller. I hate to admit I'm wrong, so you can sell anything you want at any time. I promise I won't interfere." Lewis was true to his word, though it cost him a chunk of his legendary power at the firm. Greenberg quickly started to sell Bear Stearns's money-losing positions, including that of Rudd-Melikian, and plowed the money into the shares of American Viscose Corporation, the publicly traded manufacturer of rayon fiber based in Marcus Hook, Pennsylvania. Greenberg was betting big—with the firm's money—that American Viscose would be a takeover target. At first, though, nothing happened, and Greenberg began to worry that his gambit with Lewis would leave him wounded politically or, worse, out of a job. But then, as fortune would have it, in 1963 FMC Corporation came along and bought the company. The U.S. government tried to block the deal on antitrust grounds, but that effort failed and the deal closed. Greenberg had bet well, and wisely. His power at the firm rose exponentially from that moment.

❧

IN ADDITION TO the difficulties Lewis had with Greenberg as the latter became increasingly powerful, Lewis's personal behavior began adding to the existing turmoil. He had a long-term and very public affair with one of his wife's best friends, Valerie Dauphinot, the wife of Clarence J. Dauphinot, the founder of Deltec International, a Latin American conglomerate of which Cy Lewis and his friend Gus Levy were appointed board members in December 1955.

By the late 1950s, Cy Lewis also had health problems; in 1960 he had his right breast removed because of breast cancer, which is exceedingly rare in men. Lewis also had become a heavy drinker and was said to drink a "pitcher of martinis" every day at lunch in the Bear Stearns dining room. On top of it all, he was a very lonely man. While Lewis was still a formidable figure, Greenberg began to exert greater and greater control over Bear Stearns. "He was the only one who could stand up to the senior partner and win," Ehrlich and Rehfeld wrote in their book.

CHAPTER 15

JIMMY

In the late 1960s, against the protests of both Lewis and Low, Greenberg wanted to expand the firm's fledgling retail brokerage business based on his perception that the growing cohort of baby boomers that was starting to move into its peak earnings years would have considerable amounts of disposable income that needed to be invested.

It was in pursuit of an expanded brokerage business that, serendipitously, in 1969, Greenberg happened to interview Jimmy Cayne, then a thirty-five-year-old municipal bond salesman and championship bridge player who had never sold a share of stock to anyone in his life. At Bear Stearns, Cayne interviewed with Harold C. Mayer Jr., the son of one of the three founders of the firm, but there appeared to be no chemistry between them. As Cayne got up to leave, Mayer suggested he say hello to Greenberg, "the man who is going to run this place." Again, there seemed to be no connection between the two men, but in an effort to make a little small talk, Greenberg asked Cayne if he had any hobbies.

When Cayne told Greenberg he played bridge, "you could see the electric light bulb," Cayne recalled. "He says, 'How well do you play?' I said, 'I play well.' He said, 'Like how well?' I said, 'I play quite well.' He says, 'You don't understand.' I said, 'Yeah, I do. I understand. Mr. Greenberg, if you study bridge the rest of your life, if you play with the best partners and you achieve your potential, you will never play bridge like I play bridge.'" Enough said. On the spot, Greenberg guaranteed Cayne $70,000 a year if he joined Bear Stearns.

By then, the raffish Cayne had proved himself to be a superb salesman—of photocopiers, of scrap iron, of adding machines, of municipal bonds, but mostly of himself. For reasons that are not readily apparent from his middle-class Chicago upbringing, Cayne had fashioned himself into a supremely confident and idiosyncratic shark who felt right at home in the rough-and-tumble confines of Bear Stearns. The only son of Maurice Cayne, an Evanston, Illinois, patent attorney, and Jean Cayne, a housewife who devoted herself to fund-raising for Jewish causes on the North Side of Chicago, Jimmy Cayne supposedly spent much of his youth just having fun. He couldn't have been more different from his intellectual father, who learned by reading document after document but never took the time to take his son to a Cubs ballgame. "I don't want to read and absorb," Cayne explained. "I hear and I absorb." What he really wanted to do was become a bookie but thought that profession might bring shame upon his family. Instead, he used his brains and his card-playing skills to get ahead.

Laurie Kaplan, who would eventually become Jimmy Cayne's boss for a few years at his family's scrap iron company on the South Side of Chicago, then his brother-in-law, and eventually his ex-brother-in-law, first met Cayne when they attended summer camp together. Laurie was twelve; Jimmy was eleven. Laurie was from the South Side of Chicago; Jimmy was from the North Side. "He was very sharp," Kaplan said. "He used to get together with the thirteen-year-olds in Cabin 13. They would get people into poker games." The stakes were small potatoes—nickels and dimes—but Kaplan suspected that Cayne had teamed up with the older boys and some-how rigged the games. "It was three against one. He was very sharp."

(For his part, Cayne said Kaplan never participated in these poker games.)

Cayne and Kaplan renewed their friendship when they both found themselves at Purdue University and in the same fraternity, Sigma Alpha Mu. Cayne enrolled in the mechanical engineering program at Purdue in 1950, since his father hoped that he, too, would become a patent attorney. But Cayne didn't like the rigor of engineering and was an indifferent student at best. After two years, he transferred to the liberal arts curriculum but spent much of his time playing bridge in his fraternity at an octagonal table. His parents had played bridge, but he hadn't taken much notice of it. In college, though, the game became a passion. "I knew immediately I was better than they were at bridge," he explained of his frat brothers, "but on a scale of 0 to 100, I was still only a 2 because I had no teacher."

"He didn't study very much," Kaplan recalled. "He just was an average student, because he would spend all of his time playing bridge at the octagon table." A group of the fraternity brothers—the ones "with some money, whose fathers were successful," Kaplan said—including Cayne and Kaplan, used to go out to dinner regularly in West Lafayette to escape the tasteless food at the Purdue dining hall. "We would supposedly split the bill," Kaplan said. "But it ended up we were always short. We figured out that [Jimmy] wasn't putting the right amount of money in. So we called him on it. He was a finagler. He was always that way. He was that way when he was ten years old, and he was that way in college. He was always angling." (Cayne said he never skimped on the check.) Kaplan, using his scrap iron connections, bought Cayne a 1930s junk car for $25 that Cayne used to tool around town. But when his father found out about it, he made Cayne sell it. He would have to earn that reward, his father insisted.

On the academic side, Cayne ran into trouble almost immediately with the new liberal arts curriculum when he realized he needed two years of a foreign language to graduate. He chose French, and he managed to get through the first year with a B average by dating the daughter of his French professor. For that B, his parents gave the goal-oriented Cayne a beat-up Ford. His senior year, though, he had a different French professor and a different girlfriend. He stopped going to classes and completely lost interest in school. "I was massively irresponsible," he said. He started hanging out in downtown Lafayette and shooting pool, playing poker at Riley's, and chasing women. There were apparently seven houses of ill repute back then that Cayne frequented. "I was like Action Jackson," he said. The best the school could do for him was to give him an incomplete in French. If he wanted to graduate, he would have to return for another year of college. "The chances of me going back for another year were zero," he said.

Cayne left Purdue one semester shy of his diploma. He figured at some point he would be drafted—the Korean War was winding down—so he made the unusual choice of solving his academic problems by volunteering for the draft. He drove home to Chicago to tell his parents the news. "They were blown away," he said. "To say they were upset was an understatement." They took his car away, and kicked him out of the house. His sister let him stay with her as long as he agreed to drive her around town as directed. He decided to drive a cab in Chicago for two weeks to fulfill his sister's condition and to make some money before he headed off to Missouri for basic training. When he got his orders to ship out to the Far East, he called his parents and cried since the Korean War was over and he believed it was unlikely he would be sent overseas. But Cayne drew easy duty as a court reporter at Camp Zama, twenty-five miles southwest of Tokyo, distilling down lengthy war trial transcripts. Camp Zama looked like a mini-Pentagon surrounded by a golf course. According to Kaplan, "He told me all he did in the army was play golf."

Back home, in 1956, Cayne chose not to return to college and get his degree. His father kicked him out of the house. At first, he again drove a cab in Chicago and lived with a fraternity brother. He also thought to call Maxine Kaplan, Laurie's younger sister, whom he had met previously when she visited her brother at Purdue; by this time she had dropped out of Sarah Lawrence College and was living at home. "He knew she was attractive," her brother said, "and he knew she had some money." Because Cayne and Maxine Kaplan loved to dance, he became known as the "mamboing cab driver."

They called each other "Twerdle." They fell in love and eloped, but eventually had a ceremony in 1956 at the Standard Club, in Chicago, one of the swankiest private clubs around. She was the daughter of Harvey Kaplan, one of the seven Kaplan brothers who owned and ran the M. S. Kaplan Company, a large Chicago scrap iron and metals broker and one of the largest in the United States.

Then, thanks to Cayne's brother-in-law, Arnold Perry, he got a job at the American Photocopier Company selling copiers in a nine-hundred-mile territory stretching from Salt Lake City to Boise. Perry was the company's national sales manager. The newlyweds first moved to California before settling in Salt Lake City, and Cayne became a road warrior to cover his large territory in the mountain states. "I averaged ninety-five miles per hour," Cayne said of his frantic driving.

During one long and onerous sales trip, he ended up at a gas station in Twin Falls, Idaho, on his way to Boise. The roads were icy but he decided to push on anyway. The next thing Cayne knew, he had smashed his Ford into a telephone pole. He was thrown from car onto the ground in the frigid night air. The impact of the crash pushed the steering wheel into the driver's seat. "If I had been wearing a seat belt," he said, "I'd be dead now." He spent a couple of days in the hospital but was largely uninjured and lucky to be alive. Adopting the respectful tone he'd learned in the army, he told the local justice of the peace that there was "no excuse, sir," for his behavior. But the judge thought he needed to be taught a lesson, and restricted his license so that he could no longer drive after dusk. "You're a danger to the world," the judge told him. His career as a traveling salesman was over. The Caynes moved back to Chicago and rented an apartment near Jackson Park. His brother-in-law Laurie recommended to his father that the Kaplans hire Cayne to be a salesman in the scrap iron business. "He had experience selling," Kaplan said. "He was personable. And he was very smart and streetwise."

He was a natural and soon enough was making $30,000 a year. "One of the reasons he did very well is that he doesn't look Jewish," Kaplan continued. "His name is not Jewish, but his mind is Jewish. Most of our customers and the people he called on—factories and foundries—were not Jewish. The scrap iron business, at that time, was a Jewish business, maybe 95 percent Jewish. So they really wanted to do business with gentiles."

In 1960, the Caynes divorced—amicably, according to both parties. "I'm crazy about him and always have been," Maxine Kaplan said. "But I was a typical housewife and I wanted a husband who would walk the kids around the neighborhood on the weekends and that wasn't Jimmy." Bridge was the primary culprit. "At this time, he was one of the best bridge players in Chicago," Laurie Kaplan said. "In fact, that's the reason for the divorce. There was no other woman or anything like that. The correspondent in their divorce was bridge. He spent all of his time playing bridge—every night. He wasn't home."

Cayne remained in Chicago, rented a new apartment at 20 East Delaware Street, and continued to work for his ex-father-in-law after the divorce. "This was a testament to my sales skills," he said. "I mean, how often do Jewish ex-sons-in-law continue working for their ex-fathers-in-law?" In addition to being a well-paid salesman, Cayne was dating a Playboy bunny and honing his bridge expertise. The game was the perfect outlet for his intelligence, aggression, and tactical skills. With his then bridge partner, Gunther Polak, Cayne won the 1961 Midwest Regional Bridge tournament, among many others during the three years they played together. "He was aggressive and he was intuitive," Polak recalled about Cayne's bridge game. "His talent was apparent almost immediately. When you play with somebody really good, your success escalates as well. And he enhanced my game." But with all the time he was devoting to playing bridge, his work at M. S. Kaplan suffered. "He played so much bridge while he was working for us that he fell asleep when he came to work," Kaplan said. "He just lost interest in the business."

In 1964, Cayne moved to New York City to try to become a professional bridge player, hoping to earn $500 a week. "I lived the life of a bachelor," he said. "I had zero community responsibility. My focus was on enjoying myself." In 1966, he won the Lebhar Trophy after he and his team won the Master Mixed Teams competition, his first national bridge tournament title.

For about a year, Cayne had been playing bridge regularly at the now-defunct Cavendish Club, on East 73rd Street. One day, George Rapee, the legendary bridge champion, invited Cayne to play as a professional in twice-weekly rubbers with wealthy businessmen. "I don't know you very well," Rapee told Cayne, "but you seem to have an extremely good talent for playing with bad players." Through these games, Cayne met the likes of Percy Uris, the Manhattan real estate magnate, and Larry Tisch, the self-made billionaire and investor. He would play with these wealthy businessmen in their homes on Fifth Avenue or Park Avenue. Rapee told Cayne the rules for these games were simple: keep your cool, no frowning, no berating your partners for dumb moves, and no soliciting the players for business.

Like Cayne, the world's best bridge players started learning and playing the game at a young age and have continued playing through adulthood, often while being high achievers in another profession. "It's extremely hard to come into the game in, let's say, your fifties after you've made your multi millions and expect to become that good," explained Phillip Alder, who has played against Cayne and writes the bridge column for the *New York Times*. "It's just not possible. You had to learn when you were young. . . . People like Jimmy Cayne kept playing through careers as well. If you really want to play at top level, you have to keep playing." Alder said he thought bridge appealed to Wall Streeters. "It's primarily a mathematical game," he said, "and it's logic, deduction, and flair. In bridge you have to be able to read your opponents, to know what your opponents can and can't do, and get a sense of what they are doing and not doing at the table."

Alder said that Cayne has the ability to read his opponents' body language, and that is one of the reasons he is easily among the best hundred bridge players in the world. "He's not absolutely top drawer," Alder said, "but he's pretty close." He continued, "Bridge is addictive. You get very intense in it. And it's impossible to play perfectly, and you just try and do the best you can. Some days you're in the zone, and some days you're less in the zone."

But Cayne soon grew tired of the life of a professional bridge player. "I loved the bridge," he said, "but I needed a different experience. My net worth was zero or its equivalent. I thought, 'I can't continue this. I'm a vegetable.'" He concluded he should return to the scrap iron business, the only business he knew well. One night at a cocktail party, by serendipity, someone he was chatting with suggested he apply for a job opening "for a nice Jewish salesman" at Lebenthal & Co., the municipal bond brokerage. He interviewed with the firm's matriarch, Sayra Fischer Lebenthal, who offered Cayne the spot. He quickly became a top salesman at the firm, even though he only worked around three hours a day. Jim Lebenthal, who took over the management of Lebenthal & Co. from his mother, remembered Cayne well as a "highly decent fellow with a pleasant, courtly style" and a "cool demeanor" who learned that municipal bonds could be a safe and reliable investment. Lebenthal, who graduated from Dalton, Andover, and Princeton, said he was not concerned in the least that Cayne was cut from a different cloth.

But a problem did arise about five years later when Cayne wanted to open an account for a customer who Sayra thought was too sleazy. "Jimmy wanted to sign up a fellow who did not have the normal name, rank and serial number," recalled Jim Lebenthal. "It was the kind of character that Mother disapproved of, and Mother put her foot down and told him he could not open the account and could not do the business." Cayne's version of the story is different. A few months into his Lebenthal stint, he met Percy Foreman, a famous Texas criminal-defense attorney who represented thousands of criminals, including James Earl Ray and Jack Ruby. Foreman became one of Cayne's best and most profitable customers. But Sayra's second husband, Arnold Ross, thought Cayne and Foreman were up to no good and, according to Cayne, accused them both of being "crooks." Cayne said this could not be further from the truth. But there would be no more trading with Foreman. Cayne quickly realized his days at Lebenthal were numbered since he had lost his biggest customer.

At a bridge tournament in October 1968 he met Patricia Denner, a speech therapist with model looks and a 1960 graduate of the University of Pennsylvania who later earned both her master's in speech pathology and a doctorate in psychology from Columbia University. "It was love at first sight," Cayne said. "I was smitten."

Cayne contacted Bill Root, Denner's bridge teacher and Cayne's friend, and discovered that she was newly divorced. He got her phone number and asked her out for dinner. After dinner at Trader Vic's and a few hours of bridge, she surprised Cayne by asking him to her apartment. "I never left," he said. "Ever."

He moved in with her immediately. After about three weeks, though, she was concerned that Cayne was nothing more than a bridge bum—he only worked three hours a day at Lebenthal and played bridge the rest of the time. Denner demanded that he go to law school or find a real job, or else find a new girlfriend. Cayne told her there was a problem with him going to law school because he hadn't finished college. So he opted for the second choice, and in 1969, at age thirty-five, he tapped into his bridge network and quickly arranged interviews at Goldman Sachs, Lehman Brothers, and Bear Stearns. He had never heard much about Bear Stearns since they rarely traded or underwrote municipal bonds. But he went ahead with the interview and got the job when Ace Greenberg discovered his prowess at bridge.

CHAPTER 16

MAY DAY

Cayne went to work at Bear Stearns as one of sixteen retail brokers at the office at 1 Wall Street. He wasn't sure what to do on his first day, but then he discovered he couldn't do much of anything, by law, until he became a registered representative, which meant working at the firm for four months and then taking a test and passing it. The idea of taking such a test—which is esoteric and difficult—brought back all of Cayne's insecurities about studying and academics. The firm got him a tutor to help him study for the examination. But the idea of doing nothing for four months made him crazy. "Every day I came in," he said. "I couldn't do any business. I couldn't do anything except sit there and watch the tape."

Cayne passed the test and started making calls. But his only contacts were the municipal bond buyers he knew from Lebenthal. "I find out very quickly not many of them have any interest in the little green animals"—a reference to stock ticker symbols that flash green when the stock is up for the day. "They're not stock people. They're municipal bond people." It dawned on him quickly that he had been playing bridge at the homes of several of the largest individual investors in the market, including one—Larry Tisch—who may well have been the single largest individual investor in the market. The problem for Cayne was that he had promised George Rapee he wouldn't solicit business from people he played bridge with. He called up Rapee. "George, I need your help," Cayne said. "I want your permission to solicit Larry Tisch. I'm a broker. He's like one of the biggest guys on the Street. I might get a reception. I may not. But I'd like to try. But I can't do it without you releasing me."

Rapee gave him permission, and Cayne's first successful call at Bear Stearns was to Tisch. He'd been often to Tisch's apartment on Fifth Avenue, but this was a different kind of call. "It's like his son called him," Cayne said. " 'Jimmy!' I said, 'You remember, I was the bridge toy.' He said, 'How you doing? Nice hearing from you. What can I do for you?' I said, 'I just became a broker at Bear Stearns.' He said, 'Great. Send me the papers. You'll handle all my accounts.' And he hangs up."

It was magic. Giddy, Cayne called Greenberg and told him what had just happened. "You're not going to believe this. The best first call of all time. He's the biggest guy on the Street. Larry Tisch. He wants to do business with me." Greenberg was completely silent. Cayne recalled: "I said, 'This is a strange reaction.' He said, 'Well, that's Cy's account.' I said, 'Cy? Who's Cy?' He said, 'Cy's the senior partner of the firm.' I said, 'Wait a second. Let me get this straight. The senior partner of the firm has got an account line to Larry Tisch. A salesman working at the firm has just been told by the guy to handle all his accounts and now you're telling me there's an issue because Cy Lewis handles the account?' He says, 'Jimmy, that's the way it is. You'll hear from him. Don't be upset. Because he's a rough, tough guy and he may be a little gruff on the phone.' " Greenberg told Cayne that he had to tell Lewis what had happened with Tisch and that Lewis was certain to call him and let loose.

A row of biblical proportions ensued when Lewis called Cayne. "Did you ever see those ads when somebody's talking on the phone and he's like this?" he asked, holding the phone receiver far from his ear. "I basically heard words I never heard before, and I grew up in Chicago and I heard a lot of words. This guy reamed me. 'How dare you call my account?' and then he hangs up." Cayne reported the conversation—such as it was—to Greenberg, who told him he had to call Tisch back. "I call him back," Cayne said. "He said, 'What can I do?' I said, 'Well, it seems that the senior partner of the firm thinks you're—' Tisch interrupted, 'Jimmy, I'll take care of that.' Click." At 1 Wall Street, Bear Stearns had two floors, the sixteenth and the seventeenth. "Sixteen is the little people and seventeen is the mucky-mucks," Cayne said. Greenberg called Cayne and essentially told him never to set foot on the seventeenth floor, Cayne recalled. "Because Larry Tisch called Cy Lewis and ripped him a new one, saying, 'If that kid doesn't handle my account, I'm leaving Bear Stearns.'"

In the end, much to Lewis's ire, Tisch chose Cayne. "He became just the biggest champion you could ever have," Cayne explained. "And that wasn't just a one-time occasion. That was an all-time occasion." Using his bridge connections and his own wiles, within a few months Cayne quickly became an immensely successful broker. He only had about a dozen accounts, four of which were very active and all of which he had obtained using his contacts from the bridge table. "People for whatever reason think, 'If you're a good bridge player, you've got a good brain, so I might as well do business with you,'" Cayne said. "I never really had an opinion. Am I going to tell Larry Tisch what to buy? Doesn't that sound absurd to you? He's one of the most successful investors of all. But I executed for him."

As another example of Cayne's chutzpah, he wanted to see if he could get Sam Stayman as his client. Stayman was a world-renowned bridge player who had won the first three world championship bridge tournaments after World War II. A bridge partner of George Rapee, Stayman won nineteen national bridge titles and innovated a number of bidding conventions, including one named for him. Professionally, after owning and selling a woolen mill in Rhode Island, he started one of the first hedge funds, Strand & Co. "I knew

Sam from the bridge world," Cayne said. "Sam at the bridge table was a dick. Tough. Rough. Not nice. Brute. Crude. Away from the bridge table, a gentleman's gentleman. Pillar of society. Charitable. Philanthropic. The works. But at the bridge table, very tough. So now I have this date. I go up to see him and his brother-in-law. Tell them I'm a broker at Bear Stearns. Gave them an idea of how I could be helpful because I know that they were new-issue-oriented. So whatever new issues Bear Stearns got, he wasn't given an allocation because he didn't do any business [with us]. So what I would do is I would take the allocations of all the people here who got stock and somewhere between the bid and the ask he'd be able to buy them, so everybody was happy. That was my idea. And I think I scored. I come back to the firm, and the next day Greenberg calls me and says, 'Sam called.' And I said, 'Yeah. When do I start?' He said, 'You're not ready yet.' I wasn't a kid. I was thirty-five years old. I'm not ready yet? Interesting. Still a dick."

A few weeks later, Stayman called Cayne. Stayman told him he and his partner were looking for another pair of players to be their partners for the Vanderbilt Knockout, which was then one of the national bridge tournaments. Cayne said Stayman told him, "I thought maybe you and Chuck"—Cayne's partner Chuck Burger, from Detroit—"would like to join us." He recounted: "I said, 'Let me get this straight. You want Chuck and me to join you and another pair and play as a team?' He said, 'Yes.' I said, 'Sam.' He said, 'Yes.' I said, 'You're not ready yet.' Click." Cayne's rebuff was especially impertinent given Stayman's bridge pedigree. In short order, though, both parties reconciled. Strand became one of Cayne's accounts—"A big one," Cayne said. "A direct-line account"—and Cayne and Burger played with Stayman in the championship (and others over the years). And Stayman paid Cayne in commissions.

EVERYTHING WAS QUICKLY coming together for Cayne at Bear Stearns. His lifelong flair for hucksterism was paying off for him as a Wall Street stockbroker. He finally had found a line of work where his risk-taking skills could be married with natural talent as a salesman and pay off for him financially. Within a year or two, he said, he was making between half a million and a million dollars a year, which in 1971—in the midst of the Vietnam War and Nixon's wage and price controls—was a substantial sum. He continued playing bridge regularly, of course, and his name often appeared in Alan Truscott's bridge columns in the *New York Times* as "Jim Cayne." In April 1971, Cayne and Denner decided to get married, and the only announcement of their nuptials came in Truscott's April 21 bridge column.

His prowess in bridge was such that Cy Lewis recommended to Cayne early on in his career that he choose between Wall Street and bridge. Lewis, a modest bridge player himself, did not think Cayne could do both without each of them suffering. Cayne ignored Lewis's advice for the simple reason, according to Cayne, that "he was wrong, just like wrong all the time. Almost his entire record was perfectly wrong. . . . He was not a good leader. He didn't have the respect of almost everybody. He was a bully. Drunk. He had a pitcher of martinis at lunch. Not well respected in the community."

Two years after arriving at Bear Stearns, Greenberg offered to make Cayne a partner. "I'm a big salesman, making a lot of money"—around $900,000 annually—"on commissions," he said. "They said, 'We're better off bringing him into the partnership.'" At that time, Bear Stearns had about thirty partners, each receiving a "draw," or salary, of $20,000 a year and then a percentage of the firm's profits. "I looked at him and said, 'What does that mean, partner?'" Cayne said. "Greenberg said, 'Well, you become a partner at a Wall Street firm.'" Cayne couldn't figure out how the math worked or how the new arrangement would be better than the current arrangement. His wife encouraged him to accept the partnership. "You've got to be a partner," she told him. "That's just how it works."

But Cayne said no, since he thought a partnership seemed uneconomical. "To me, they had one person that was worthwhile," he said. "That was Greenberg. So I passed."

Still, he was clever enough to read the handwriting on the wall. When he first started out, Cayne said, he could earn a $300,000 commission for "crossing a block of stock" for Larry Tisch, the equivalent of around 30¢ a share in commission. But the days of fixed commissions were coming to an end. A year after telling Greenberg he had no interest in becoming a partner, he decided to take the Bear Stearns partnership and tie his compensation to the commonweal rather than directly to his own production. He became a partner in May 1973. He knew that in two years, May 1, 1975, fixed commissions for brokers would end on Wall Street, a day that would become known as "May Day." This fact changed Cayne's mind about accepting a partnership at Bear Stearns. "I take a partnership because I was concerned about my ability to maintain a high level of commission income based on my clientele saying, 'We're not paying thirty cents a share, twenty-five cents a share. We're paying nothing, a nickel,'" he said.

He negotiated for himself a 2 percent share of the firm's profits. In the first few years, though, that arrangement resulted in a huge pay cut for him. "I made a horrible decision my first couple of years," he said. "I didn't make any money. The firm didn't make any money, so my capital account didn't appreciate." Cayne ranked about twentieth in the partnership hierarchy in terms of compensation. Greenberg ranked second, with a 5 percent stake, behind Lewis, who had a 7 percent stake.

Despite Greenberg's success and Cayne's growing prominence, there was no question that Bear Stearns was still Cy Lewis's province. In July 1973, just as the firm was readying to move its headquarters to 55 Water Street, which would double its office space, the *New York Times* took brief stock of Bear a couple of months after it celebrated its fiftieth anniversary. "Bear Stearns has 800 employees, but in a very real sense it is a one-man firm," the *Times* reported in its first-ever profile of Bear Stearns. "That man is Salim L. Lewis, its senior partner, known as Cy to one and all."

In its attempt to glorify Lewis, the *Times* made no mention of the accomplishments of the other Bear partners. For instance, in 1973, it turned out that the firm had leased more space at 55 Water Street than it actually needed, and Greenberg landed upon the idea of offering that space rent-free to other, much smaller brokerage firms on the condition that they agree to allow Bear Stearns to settle their trades, a business known as "clearing": for a fee, Bear Stearns would make sure cash and securities were in their proper accounts and properly accounted for. This was and is a mundane, unglamorous, but immensely profitable recurring business and became a major source of the firm's profitability—and occasional brushes with the law—for the next thirty-five years. For the small brokers, having Bear Stearns clear their trades allowed them to slip the Bear Stearns name onto their customer's brokerage statement, adding a measure of prestige and reliability to what otherwise might have had the appearance of a flimsier operation.

❀

AS FOR CAYNE, he had serious ambitions. He wanted to run the firm. When he became a partner, he was one of four in the firm's retail department. But he was the only one, apparently, who had the ability to hire new brokers. One of the firm's strategic focuses at that time was to grow the brokerage business slowly as the baby boomers hit their peak earning years and the nation's wealth increased. But unlike the other large brokerage firms, Bear Stearns refused to pay brokers an up-front bonus to come to the firm. This made hiring brokers more difficult for it. "Hiring was an incredible thing," Cayne said. "It was fun because it was (a) a challenge, (b) I didn't offer anybody anything. There was no up-front. It's just like 'Come and play with me in my sandbox.'" Little by little, Cayne was able to lure brokers to the firm and his influence grew, especially as the brokerage division delivered growing profits.

When New York City's finances collapsed in 1975, Cayne saw an opportunity to make a killing. The city was teetering on the edge of bankruptcy, and one of his clients wanted to sell some of his New York City bonds, but no one wanted to buy them. Not even the firm's municipal bond desk would bid on his client's $200,000 worth of city bonds that were maturing in two months. This struck Cayne as risk-averse in the extreme, especially since the city had not actually defaulted. He also noticed that other municipalities' bonds were trading flat, without paying interest. Cayne decided to go see Melvin Lechner, the budget director for New York City, whom Cayne knew from the bridge table.

He called Lechner and asked him to introduce him to the purchasing manager for the City of New York, a Mr. Scott. "I go to see Mr. Scott," Cayne said. "I go into a huge room. It's sort of like the justice in Twin Falls, Idaho. He's sitting at a desk in a massive office with one desk and one chair in front of it. And I walk in." At first,

Cayne tried to get Scott's agreement that Bear Stearns would be hired exclusively to implement the idea he had come to discuss. But Scott balked. Cayne shared the idea anyway. "My idea was simple," Cayne said. "I started by saying, 'What does the city do with its overnight money?' He said, 'Well, I send it out overnight.' I said, 'What do you get, 2 percent, 2.5 percent? How would you like to get like a 50 percent return, annualized?' 'Well, how do you do that?' he asked. I said, 'By buying your own notes.' 'Buying our own notes? Well, what price do you have to pay?' I said, 'I think if I paid 99, I could buy a lot of notes.'" Scott liked the idea immediately, Cayne said, and agreed to give Cayne "an open order" to "buy as many as you can."

Cayne was ecstatic. Armed with all the bad press about New York's finances, an open order to buy New York City notes from Scott, and the further insight that other municipal bond houses around New York, like Lebenthal, could no longer go to a bank to finance their inventory of municipal bonds, Cayne decided that Bear Stearns should make the market in the city's bonds and notes. These small municipal bond brokerages "weren't getting 99¢ on the dollar from Chase anymore," Cayne said. "You talk about a credit crunch, you talk about a locked market. Nobody can sell. Nobody can buy. And the city is still not in default. And there's no price."

He took the idea to Bob Tighe, head of Bear's bond department. "I tell him that I think Bear Stearns has money," Cayne said. "And that we can inventory [bonds]. 'Put out an ad saying we're buying New York City securities. There is a market after all. I will not use the sales force to sell them. I'll do it myself. And I'll do it with all the little houses, cash and carry. Like you want to buy $20,000 worth of bonds, let's say face value is $20,000 and let's say they cost 50¢ on the dollar. You give me $10,000 and I'll give you twenty bonds. No credit. Can't lose.' Tighe says, 'That's the dumbest idea I've ever heard.'" Undeterred, Cayne went to Greenberg. "Little too racy," Cayne said Greenberg told him. "Little too out there. He says no." The partners of the firm were concerned that Bear Stearns already had its share of municipal bonds in inventory that were not paying interest, and they could not imagine adding to that supply at the very moment when the city seemed on the verge of default. A very sensible argument, and in keeping with what Greenberg's father had taught him about slow-moving inventory.

But Cayne was more of a gambler than Greenberg. He saw a chance for a contrarian bet, and knew just the man who might be simpatico: Cy Lewis. "Okay, I got one stop left," Cayne said. "And that's with the guy who, remember, screamed at me about Larry Tisch. But by then, I was *his* guy. I belonged to his club"—Hollywood Country Club, in Deal, New Jersey. "He was very proud of me. Liked me a lot. I said, 'Cy, you were responsible for Bear Stearns going from here to here,' because he dealt with railroad reorganization bonds in the 1940s or 1950s. And if you want to know the truth, it looked a little like the New York City thing, where you have to have a little set of balls and you go out and do something. And I said, 'Cy, I know it's bad to say you can't lose. But you can't lose.' He had one question: 'What did Greenberg say?' I said, 'Greenberg said no.' He said, 'Do it.'"

Lewis asked Cayne what he needed. Cayne replied: "I need a calculator. I need to remove myself a little bit from being full-time sales manager of the retail department. And I need $5 million." With Lewis's endorsement, Cayne placed an ad in the *New York Times* offering to buy New York City debt with a face value greater than $50,000. The ad listed Cayne's name and phone number. "On Monday morning, I'm ready to go," Cayne said. "I've cleared my desk. I've got my calculator. I've got the equivalent of Suzette"—Suzette Fasano, his current longtime assistant—"sitting there waiting for the phone to go off the hook. Nine o'clock, I get a call. It's from a trust officer in Denver, Colorado, working at one of the banks. 'Mr. Cayne, I read your ad. It seems very interesting. I've got one of my clients who'd like to know more about it.'" Cayne confirmed the client had $300,000 of New York City bonds, due 2002, for which the fellow had paid par, but now he was very nervous about getting paid his money back because of the rampant speculation about the city's bankruptcy. Cayne figured he could sell the bonds to his network of small municipal bond brokerages for somewhere around 35¢ on the dollar. The small brokerages had no inventory of bonds but were anxious to have an attractive investment to show potential clients. To make money, he figured he could offer the Denver banker around 30¢ for the bonds—for which his client had paid 100¢.

"I haven't done a trade yet," Cayne recalled. "I haven't done anything. I said, 'Yeah, I got an interest.' He said, 'What price?' I said, 'Twenty-seven.' He said, 'Twenty-seven what?' I said, 'Twenty-seven cents on the dollar.' At which point he becomes ballistic: 'I knew about you people. I knew what you were. I shouldn't have wasted my time. Your reputation precedes you.' Hangs up." Although it was just the first call, Cayne was beginning to think that maybe there really was no market for these bonds—that the bid-ask spread was just too wide for a trade to occur.

Twenty minutes later, one of his partners on the municipal desk called Cayne and asked him if he wanted to bid on the same $300,000 of New York City bonds that he had just received the call about. The Denver banker had likely advised his client to see if he could get a better bid in the market than the 27¢ that Cayne had just suggested. "I said, 'Yeah, I'll bid 23.' So they called back about forty minutes later. 'Okay. The bonds didn't trade, but you were the only bidder.' Now I know there's no market at all, *zero*. Lo and behold, the phone rings. It's the guy from Denver. Now, I wasn't there, but he obviously told his guy, 'We were given a ridiculous price [by Cayne]. I could do better.' Goes out and finds out he not only can't do better, it isn't even 27. The rancher has said, 'Get the fuck out of New York City, just get out, they're going to default. Get rid of them.' It's sort of like an interesting call because you know his dick is hanging out, he's dead. But he's got to now make nice-nice with this person he just accused of being the highway robber. He said, 'Look, I was probably a little too rough and tough.' I said, 'Sorry, I am obviously off the market.' He said, 'Yeah, I thought it was a little low.' I said, 'No, no, not low, high. Because I bought more bonds in the last two hours than I ever even dreamed existed. And I'm the only buyer. We're full for the day, probably for the month.' He knows he's in the shithouse because the rancher said, 'Get out of New York City.' He said, 'Well, I really would like to sell them.' I said, 'Well, you know I'm not holding anything against you, but I'm no longer at 27.' He said, 'Where are they?' I said, 'Twenty-two.' There was silence, then he said, 'Can't you do like what you said, the 27?' I said, 'Look, that's ridiculous. That doesn't make sense.' He says, 'Look, I sort of made a mistake.' And I said, 'I'll tell you what, I'll take these bonds and take them to 25, but that's it.'" Cayne bought the bonds at 25¢ and turned around—in an instant, he said—and sold them for 30¢ to one of the small brokers he had previously identified in New York City who wanted the bonds.

Cayne played this hand successfully for seventeen months—improving the market's perception of Bear Stearns in the process—until Lazard partner Felix Rohatyn devised the idea of creating the Municipal Assistance Corporation to refinance the city's debt, and many of the city's bonds traded back up to par. "To his credit, Greenberg never cared that I went above him," Cayne said. Thanks to this successful bet, and just like Lewis thirty years before, Cayne found that his status and authority at the firm rose dramatically.

Cayne said he was careful not to have too big an inventory of the city's bonds, which would have required the firm to put up more capital while exposing it to more risk, but when President Ford told New York City that the federal government would not bail it out and on October 30, 1975, the *Daily News* ran its famous headline, "Ford to City: Drop Dead," the value of Cayne's inventory of bonds dropped like a stone. His partners couldn't contain themselves. "It was like a valve going off," Cayne said. "They were so excited about calling me up and basically kicking the shit out of me, saying, 'Oh, you're too big there anyway. We probably lost our ass.' Nonsense, because inside two days, the market was right back."

But resentment against Cayne from some of his partners at the firm grew. For instance, after a ruling by the New York State Supreme Court invalidating the moratorium on paying interest on the city's bonds—meaning that the interest had to be paid and the bonds would trade up to par—one holder of the bonds misread the decision and offered $500,000 of the bonds for 68¢ on the dollar. Cayne pounced on the opportunity. "We just took them," Cayne said. "I mean, like that's ridiculous. They didn't read the release right. These are 68? It's going to be 98 overnight. So we complete that trade and I am really higher than a kite. I'm ecstatic." When Cayne came back to the office the next day, the trading desk told him that one of the most senior partners at the firm, Marvin Davidson, had intercepted Cayne's moneymaking trade. When Cayne asked the desk whether Davidson had placed an order, he was told there was an order. But Cayne claimed that Davidson had not placed an order for the trade; rather, when Davidson saw Cayne's trade, he took it for himself. "Marvin Davidson was the managing partner of the partnership," Cayne said. "He envisioned himself as Greenberg's right-hand man, an influential partner in the organization. Certainly I wasn't. I was a peanut. You couldn't weigh the difference between us from the standpoint of who was more important, right? Even though one of us was doing really good stuff and it was questionable whether he was getting anything done."

He went to see Greenberg to protest Davidson's action. "I walked into Greenberg's office and I said, 'You've got to rescind that. You've got to cancel that trade. That was bullshit.' He didn't have any order." Greenberg told Cayne he would not rescind Davidson's trade. "That's an impossible conclusion only because basically what he had to do was accuse Davidson of not telling the truth. You learn one thing about Alan Greenberg—his ability to take a little guy and kick the shit out of him and be a tough guy is solid." (Davidson declined to be interviewed.)

For a time, Cayne did respect Greenberg's intellect and his business acumen, but theirs was always an odd relationship. "Greenberg had very few friends and I was one of them," he said. Cayne used to pick up Greenberg at his Fifth Avenue apartment every day in his car and drive him down the slow-moving FDR Drive to the Bear Stearns office at 55 Water Street. "It's like the Mafia where the driver becomes the number two, except I insisted he sit in the front," he said. "He couldn't sit in the back." But Greenberg rarely spoke to his younger partner during these rides. "If you understand the makeup of the man, he can't carry a conversation," Cayne said. "He has lunch with you, it lasts four minutes because there's no talking, unless you talk." But Cayne could sense the opportunity and managed to turn these awkward trips to his advantage. "Well, that's ideal," he said. "I have the boss in the car. He's captive for the twenty-five minutes. What's better than me sitting there and being able to say, 'You know, this guy's full of shit and that guy's full of shit'?"

The gregarious, outgoing, and scheming Cayne could not have been more different from the cerebral and ruthless Greenberg. "We're two different people," Cayne said. "He's the opposite of me. To him, you're a piece of meat. I'm a piece of meat to serve him, to help him to have a better life. He always would constantly tell me when [Bill] Montgoris was the CFO, what a fucking idiot he was. And when Sam [Molinaro] became the CFO, what a fucking idiot he is. I said to him, 'Do you have any idea what Sam does? Could you write down like a memorandum of what are his responsibilities?'"

During one of the plethora of tedious but politically astute downtown excursions with Greenberg, Cayne decided to broach the subject of his own promotion to the firm's powerful executive committee. He had been at the firm about seven years by this time and, as he said, had "certainly delivered." The tradition at Bear Stearns was that partnership percentages were set every two years, essentially by the senior partner of the firm after some supposed vetting by the executive committee. As part of the executive committee's consideration, each partner would write down all of his successes on a piece of paper and then ask for a specific percentage of the pretax profits. This exercise was completely in keeping with Bear Stearns's reputation for being a place "where everything had a 'bid and asked,'" according to Doug Sharon, a longtime senior managing director at the firm. "Greenberg decides who gets what, period," Cayne said. "Then you get your percentage and it's in black and white. It's never changed."

When he became a partner, Cayne had a 2 percent stake in the firm's profits. After the first two-year cycle, he submitted his "paper" to Greenberg and the other members of the executive committee, making his case for an increase based on the performance of the brokerage division and the time he spent "busting my ass traveling around the country" and signing up small brokerage firms as clients for Bear Stearns's growing clearing business. "So, the first year I was a two-point partner," Cayne said, "and two years go by and they put out the new list and I was still a two-point partner."

Eventually, though, Cayne started to get larger and larger slices of the pie. He went from being a partner who had 2 percent of the firm's pretax profits—at a time when the firm wasn't making much money and all he received in pay was his $20,000-a-year draw—to one with around 5 or 6 percent of the pretax profits in the 1970s. To get that, he enumerated all of his accomplishments—including his view that "I was responsible for 80 percent of the profits at Bear Stearns one year"—and then boldly asked for 7.5 percent of the pretax profits—an act of such chutzpah and daring that Greenberg could not quite believe it. "I thought I was being really nice for saying 7.5 percent," Cayne said. "Greenberg actually said to me—he's such an egomaniac—he says, 'I have to tell you, everybody in the community thought that I helped you write your paper, until they saw you requested 7.5 points. Then they knew I couldn't have done that because it was so dumb.' I said, 'Yeah, right, really dumb, man. They really think that you helped write my letter.'"

At first Cayne didn't want the responsibility of managing the brokers, especially the poorly performing ones. But Greenberg insisted. "That's your future here," he told Cayne.

By Cayne's account, shortly thereafter, Lewis Rabinowitz, one of the other men running the department, decided he wanted to run retail himself. "I'm driving in the car," Cayne said, "and Greenberg says, 'Well, Lew has come to me and said he wants a clear title. It seems to me it's something you guys can work out.' I said, 'Well, how do you work that out? He wants to be the head of what?' Greenberg says, 'All retail.' I say to him, 'Why don't you do this? Why don't you tell him that he can have a choice. He could be head of all the retail except New York or he could be head of New York and have nothing to do with all the branches. Give him his choice.' He looks at me and says, 'Well, what if he chooses New York? What are you going to do?'"

Cayne said Greenberg was worried about Cayne leaving New York City for the provinces both because of the success Cayne was having buying and selling New York City bonds and because Cayne had started to teach Greenberg how to improve his bridge game. Greenberg didn't want to lose either of those two perquisites. "I'm waiting for him to say, 'Okay, I'll take care of it. I'll make sure he gets the branches and you get the city,'" Cayne said. "He says, 'Well, what if he chooses New York?' I said, 'He won't. It's not as glamorous as the whole head of retail.' He said, 'Well, you're making a big bet.' I said, 'Well, yeah, you're putting me in a position by not making a decision that I have to make a bet, so I'm making a bet.'"

Just as Cayne suggested, Greenberg offered Rabinowitz his choice. A week later, just as Cayne had hoped, Rabinowitz chose to be head of all retail except for the New York City office. But it wasn't a good fit. "He finds when he goes out to the branches, they don't give a shit who he is," Cayne said. "They're not reporting to him, so he finds out he's got this empty title, and he goes to Greenberg, and he says, 'I've changed my mind. I want to be the head of New York and let Jimmy be the head of everything else.'" Greenberg told Rabinowitz that it was too late to change his mind. Rabinowitz left the firm.

Although Cayne's tactic worked, he was plenty peeved at Greenberg for forcing him to make the bet. It was in this context that Cayne played his hand about wanting to be on the executive committee. "I'm driving to work with Greenberg," Cayne recalled. "I said to him, 'You know, you have an executive committee that I should be on.' He didn't say anything. I said, 'The very fact that you are in a position to do something about that and haven't done it is some issue I've got with you.' He said, 'Well, why with me? Your buddy is Lewis. Lewis is the boss. He'll take care of it. Talk to him. Talk to your buddy Lewis.' Again, look at the history of the two of us. Because synergistically there's no question about the fact [that] the two of us created something that worked. It clearly worked. He brought something to the party from the standpoint of the Street looking at who's running Bear Stearns. Never was there any question about who was running Bear Stearns. It was Alan Greenberg."

Cayne called Lewis, who agreed to receive Cayne at his Park Avenue apartment. "He's got his slippers on," Cayne said, "and he's got the butler with his scotch, and I tell him, 'Now look, Cy. It's been a while, and I've been at the firm for close to, you know, seven, eight years. And I've certainly delivered.' He's had a few drinks but says, 'I'll take care of it.'"

A month passed, and Cayne had not heard back from Lewis. "And remember I'm picking Greenberg up every day," Cayne said. "And I bide my time. And I say to him after thirty days, 'Well, whatever happened?' He says, 'Why ask me?' He says, 'You went to Lewis.' I said, 'Well, Lewis said he'd take care of it.' He said, 'Well, I guess he didn't.' So I go back to Lewis. And I said, 'Cy . . .' And he turned to me and he said, 'I'll definitely take care of it.'"

By this time—the late 1970s—Cy Lewis was no longer the vigorous and brilliant authoritarian figure that he once had been. He had become a heavy drinker and a heavy smoker. "His nose was raw and bulbous," Ehrlich and Rehfeld wrote about him. A lifetime of smoking had left him with a myriad of physical maladies, chief among them being a severe case of Buerger's disease, acute inflammation of and clotting in the arteries and veins in the extremities. In Lewis's case, the disease severely affected his feet, causing him great pain and making it difficult for him to walk.

Lewis's personal life, always immensely complicated, had turned into a complete mess. His best friend on Wall Street, Gus Levy, the senior partner of Goldman Sachs, suffered a stroke in October 1976 and died a month later. Around the same time, Lewis's longtime mistress, Valerie Dauphinot, committed suicide by taking an overdose of pills. Lewis found her body and read the note she left. The already very lonely man fell into further despair. "He was depressed long before she killed herself," Sandy Lewis said, "but I don't think that helped any." Another contributor to Lewis's ongoing melancholia was, according to his son, his realization that Alan Greenberg was the only partner at the firm who could succeed him. "Cy Lewis hated this guy," Sandy Lewis said. "Greenberg was so cold my father used to say he pissed ice water."

All of these events conspired together to make Lewis a broken man. What happened to Lewis was all of a piece with what was happening at other predominantly Jewish Wall Street firms after World War II. A force of nature—whether it was Cy Lewis at Bear Stearns, Gus Levy at Goldman Sachs, or André Meyer at Lazard—maneuvered to the top of a firm and succeeded beyond his wildest dreams. These men had everything they could have ever wanted. But in their successful climb, they lost the ability to help others get to the top. They wanted to be King of the Hill forever. "That doesn't work in nature and that doesn't work on Wall Street," Sandy Lewis said. "So as they get weaker, they get tougher. On the way up, they gather friends, they gather momentum, and they gather power. But when they get to the top and they realize they can't go on forever, there is only one way to go, and that is down."

✺

ON APRIL 26, 1978—a few days shy of the firm's fifty-fifth anniversary—the Bear Stearns partners met at the Harmonie Club for their annual dinner to celebrate another successful year. The dinner was also slated to be a retirement party for Lewis, who at age sixty-nine had come to realize that he no longer had the mental or physical energy to run the firm. For Lewis, the Harmonie Club was fraught with negative connotations. This was where a former flame's father had rejected him as the suitor for his daughter. In addition, years earlier the club had rejected him for membership. "Actually, the party setting had more to do with convenience than with any personal tribute to Lewis, who was hardly the main issue on the partners' minds," Ehrlich and Rehfeld wrote. "For many partners, he was already part of their past—or more to the point, a tyrant whom they wished would leave quietly. . . . The close of that fiscal year had confirmed that earnings had slipped from the previous year. Reversing that trend was the primary issue for everyone at that party."

During the brief ceremony to honor Lewis, John Slade recalled how when he started at the firm, earning $15 a week, Lewis had been instrumental in his career advancement. Slade told his partners he owed "everything" to Lewis for helping to make him rich. His Park Avenue apartment was lined with works by Picasso, Miró, and Chagall. Slade then gave Lewis a gold Piaget watch specially ordered from Switzerland. "As he started unwrapping his gift, Lewis began to shake violently," according to Ehrlich and Rehfeld. He had suffered a massive stroke. An ambulance rushed him to Mount Sinai Hospital, with his partners Teddy Low and Dick Fay by his side. (Some have suggested that one of Lewis's partners took his new Piaget watch.) Cy Lewis died two days later. "Dad died from the inside out," Sandy Lewis said. "He did not want to live. The rest have died from the outside in. Few came honest. None leave honest."

CHAPTER 17

HAIMCHINKEL MALINTZ ANAYNIKAL

Ace Greenberg took over the running of Bear Stearns the day Lewis died. Greenberg's management style—very different from Lewis's—began to reveal itself in the months after Lewis's death through a series of memoranda, some decidedly tongue-in-cheek, he wrote to his partners. "Bear Stearns is moving forward at an accelerated rate and everybody is contributing," Greenberg wrote in the first memo, dated October 5, 1978. "It is absolutely essential for us to be able to talk to our partners at all times. All of us are entitled to eat lunch, play golf and go on vacation. But, you must leave word with your secretary or associates where you can be reached at all times. Decisions have to be made and your input is important! I conducted a study of the 200 firms that have disappeared from Wall Street over the last few years, and I discovered that 62.349% went out of business because the important people did not leave word where they went when they left their desk if even for 10 minutes. That idiocy will not occur here."

Six months after Lewis's death, on November 16, Teddy Low died at Lenox Hill Hospital. For Greenberg, the passing of both Lewis and Low in the same year was a seminal time in the firm's history because, as he once said, it was forced to not "do anything dumb."

To Cayne, Cy Lewis's death was little more than a reminder that Lewis had not fulfilled his promise to Cayne to put him on the firm's executive committee. Cayne blamed Greenberg for letting the matter slide. "Greenberg never had the balls to take him on," Cayne said. He was determined not to let the Grim Reaper decide when and if he became the senior partner of Bear Stearns. When a socially acceptable amount of time had passed after Lewis's death, Cayne brought Greenberg back to the topic of becoming a member of the executive committee. "I get back in the car and I said to Greenberg, 'You can't hide anymore under Lewis. It's your call. I expect to be on the executive committee.' He said, 'Well, there's a problem with that.'" Cayne had figured out that several of his fellow senior partners, among them Marvin Davidson and John Rosenwald, didn't want him to be on the executive committee. Cayne told Greenberg: "Yeah, and I know who they are, and I know if they're not here, we're better off. I know they do dick. I know that they're worthless. If they're on the executive committee and you're telling me they have the ability to stop me, I'm at the wrong firm."

"Well, what does that mean?" Greenberg replied.

"It means I'm at the wrong firm," Cayne replied. Cayne prided himself on the veiled threat. He preferred to let the implication that he might leave the firm hang in the air like the smoke swirling from one of his ubiquitous imported cigars.

He also had thought a few moves ahead. Through a bridge connection and client, Cayne arranged for an interview at Goldman Sachs with the new senior partner, John Weinberg. After the interview Cayne called the client, who told him that Weinberg thought "it was the best interview he ever had" but "you're too hot to handle."

Cayne told Greenberg that he'd had the interview with Weinberg, though he didn't let on how it had gone. "He knows that if I leave, the sales force leaves and a lot of bad things happen," Cayne said. "So now I go and say to Greenberg, 'It's D-Day.'" Greenberg told him what Cayne already suspected: that Davidson and Rosenwald were blocking his promotion and that Cayne had to win them over to get what he wanted. But, according to Cayne, Davidson knew "that I tried to shoot his ship down"—a reference to Cayne's effort to block Davidson's purchase of some New York City bonds in 1975—"and basically didn't talk to him because I knew he stole. I didn't have to talk to him. Managing partner of the firm means dick to me. I didn't take any orders from him. I had nothing to do with the guy."

Cayne went to see Rosenwald and Davidson and had a blunt conversation. "Obviously, I've been requesting to become part of the executive committee because I deserve it," he said to them. "They said, 'Well, change is good, and we're going to make an addition to the executive committee. We're going to announce inside of a week that Jerry Goldstein'"—who ran the retail branch network—"'is being added to the executive committee.' I said, 'And that's it?' They said, 'Yes.' I said, 'Okay, just so you understand how I feel. I don't really know how I'm going to react when I see that in writing. Have a good day.' And I got up to leave."

About twenty minutes later Greenberg called Cayne. "I don't know what you said to these guys," Greenberg told him. "But you're in." He had succeeded in becoming a member of the firm's powerful executive committee just nine years after arriving at Bear Stearns with nothing more than some bridge contacts and a salesman's charm. Cayne credited the success of his gambit to the subtlety of his strategy with Davidson and Rosenwald. "Because when I said, 'I didn't know how I was going to react,' I didn't threaten to quit," he said. "I said, 'I don't know how I'm going to handle that,' but there was no more conversation. I just left because they were telling me no."

In short order, Cayne's partnership points were the same as Davidson's and Rosenwald's. Then Cayne was tied with just Rosenwald. Soon Davidson left; by 1982, Cayne said, he was the number two partner at the firm.

But his ambitions were still not slaked. To get to the top, he knew he would have to continue his artful and simultaneous cultivation of Greenberg as well as the other members of the executive committee. It was a delicate operation that Cayne performed with the precision of a brain surgeon. He continued to drive Greenberg to work every day; Cayne would occasionally break the painful silence of those trips to malign his partners to the boss while promoting himself. He also began to court the other leaders of the firm, or at least those whom he hadn't already alienated.

AT THE SAME time that his professional status morphed, Greenberg had been undergoing changes in his personal life as well. In 1975, he left his wife, Ann, after twenty-two years. (She later committed suicide by jumping out a window.) While his Fifth Avenue apartment remained filled with the French furniture she bought, he began to accumulate the talismans afforded him by his wealth, newfound bachelorhood, and frenetic hobbies. On one wall was the head of an antelope he'd shot in Africa using only a bow and arrow. He had a vast collection of books about magic, which he studied relentlessly to perfect his craft. He perfomed his magic tricks at dinner parties all over the Upper East Side of Manhattan. This most eligible bachelor, who looked something like a less ghoulish Uncle Fester, was becoming the toast of the town. He dated many prominent women. "There was a certain guileless charm about him," according to Ehrlich and Rehfeld. "Although he had a dry wit and seemed highly approachable, he was neither glib nor polished."

One day, during their morning drive downtown, Greenberg told Cayne a story about his personal life that Cayne never forgot. At that time, Greenberg was between marriages—he would marry Kathryn Olson, a lawyer, in 1987—and had been dating regularly but was growing increasingly concerned about the risk of contracting AIDS. "He decides he's going to get married," Cayne says. "And he's one of the guys that's dating Barbara Walters. She's dating the *schvartze* from Massachusetts [Ed Brooke, the first black U.S. senator and later a special limited partner at Bear Stearns]. She's dating Alan Greenspan. She's dating him. He says to me, 'I've decided I'm going to marry Barbara Walters.' . . . The very next day in the papers: She's engaged to Merv Adelson. I never said a word. Now, normally, you know, if it was one of my buddies, I'd say, you know, 'Pretty good call there, pal. You're marrying her, except for that she's marrying somebody else. It's not even going to be a real marriage because that's called bigamy.' But I didn't say a word."

Along with the daily car rides—and as had been foreshadowed by their very first meeting in 1969—bridge turned out to be the skeleton key that unlocked any impediments to Cayne's rapid rise at the firm. In 1967, five years before becoming a partner at Bear Stearns, Cayne had ascended to the rank of a bridge "life master," courtesy of the American Contract Bridge League. In contrast, Greenberg was a mediocre bridge player at best, by his own admission. Nevertheless, Greenberg pushed Cayne to "teach me the game and I'll become your partner." At the time, Cayne said he thought about how having Greenberg as his bridge partner would hurt his career at Bear Stearns. Supposedly, he declined Greenberg's offer.

But not for long. Soon enough, Cayne reversed course and decided that taking Greenberg under his wing—at the bridge table, anyway—would pay dividends. By November 1977, Cayne's five-member team—including Greenberg and Jim Jacoby, a Bear Stearns broker from Dallas—won the Reisinger team championship at the American Contract Bridge League's fall championship held in Atlanta. Their margin of victory was tiny but good enough to win and to qualify the team for the 1978 International Team Trials, the first step toward potentially being the country's representative to the 1979 world team championship. Cayne refered to the victory as "a miracle" that had to do more with some of the nuances of bridge than Greenberg's skill. "It happened because you have to play bridge to understand it," he said. "An uneven partnership can be very effective if the uneven guy just doesn't get in your way." When Alan Truscott, of the *Times,* wrote about Cayne's victory, he refered to the team as "the Greenberg team," a slight that must have ticked off Cayne. (Cayne said this never bothered him.)

FOR SOME AT Bear Stearns—and as if there weren't already enough pitfalls in a Wall Street career—playing bridge became an occupational hazard, what with the two top partners at the firm playing on the same team and winning national and international tournaments together. "Playing with or against the boss can be a tricky business," Alan Truscott wrote in the *Times* in 1979. "Consider, for example, the plight of Jim Rosenbloom, a young New York expert, in the final of the Big Apple Regional Knockout Team Championship played earlier this summer." Rosenbloom had just joined Bear Stearns and found himself opposite Greenberg and Cayne. "Would you try to impress the bosses with your shrewdness?" Truscott wondered. "Or would you concern yourself with keeping them happy? The latter might seem more important in view of the fact that one of the bosses was heard to announce cheerfully, 'If Rosenbloom wins, he'll be out of a job tomorrow.'" The question for Rosenbloom quickly became moot in the Big Apple Regional because Greenberg's team "galloped to an easy victory." Soon enough, though, Rosenbloom was playing on the same team as his bosses, Greenberg and Cayne, and they were all winning.

By 1982, Truscott was reporting how "bridge experts in a favorable locale can multiply like the proverbial rabbit, although rather less rapidly." He cited Bear Stearns as an example of this phenomenon. In 1975, Truscott explained, Bear "had one bridge expert, Jim Cayne, and one enthusiast, Alan Greenberg, who wanted to be an expert and with Cayne's help soon became one." Truscott described Cayne as "an ebullient fast-talking character with a great will to win." Seven years later, Bear Stearns had ten bridge players, two who had won world titles and four who had won national titles. "So students who devote their time at college to playing bridge now have the perfect answer to their complaining parents," Truscott wrote. "They are preparing themselves for a successful career in the world of finance."

Cayne claimed that in 1983, two years after winning the gold medal at the Maccabiah Games with Greenberg as his partner, Cayne told Greenberg he had decided to give up tournament bridge. What he didn't tell Greenberg was that he had decided to quit so that he could get out of having Greenberg as his partner. The team had suffered an embarrassing loss at the Grand National Team Championship, and Truscott had written that up in the *New York Times*. "When you can't win, you lose your mojo," Cayne said. "I couldn't win. Couldn't win with him."

Cayne's ultimate solution to the problem was, he said, to stop playing tournament bridge for six years. The truth appears slightly more complicated, though. Throughout the 1980s, Cayne's name appeared regularly in Truscott's bridge column, sometimes playing with Greenberg, sometimes with Chuck Berger and others. In any event, by 1989, Cayne was back playing tournament bridge with a passion but without Greenberg on his team. Indeed, Cayne designed his vacation time around these tournament bridge events, which take place in varying locations around the country three times a year for around a week at a time. The tournaments are extremely intense, with play beginning in the afternoon and continuing until late at night. Cell phones and BlackBerry-type devices are not permitted—not that Cayne used them—and during matches, players are not to be interrupted. "I got back into tournament bridge and it became part of my life," Cayne said. "Every four months I'd go away and play for a week somewhere. That was always my vacation. Christmas, we'd go for a week and a half, two weeks, to Florida or whatever, but I never took time off during the week or anything. The summers, I would go down to the shore on Friday, usually with Lewis, until he died, and then went down myself. I'd end up going down Thursday night on a chopper so I could play Thursday night, play golf Friday morning, go back to my house in Jersey, whatever. I never had an issue with being unavailable ever."

BRIDGE ASIDE, THERE was a firm to run, and Greenberg wasted little time after Lewis's death in putting his own mark on it. He used to tell people, "Tomorrow we're going to do more of the things we did today, only better." According to a former Bear Stearns senior managing director, "That was the entire strategy of that firm. It didn't matter what financial markets did. It didn't matter what innovations took place. It didn't matter that other people's cultures changed. It didn't matter. That's what we're going to do." For close to twenty years, that proved to be effective. One of the ways Greenberg chose to reinforce his business strategy with his troops was through an incessant stream of lighthearted but nonetheless often scolding memoranda that he sent to his partners. To do the admonishing, he created an alter ego, a Charlie McCarthy for his Edgar Bergen, in the form of one Haimchinkel Malintz Anaynikal, a "famous philosopher" whose role appeared to be to remind everyone to be frugal at all times. "We had to start doing things," he said of the reason the memo writing started. "The firm hadn't made much money the few years before that, and the times of course helped, there's no question about that. But we stayed alive and we started making a lot of money." March 13, 1979, marked Haimchinkel's first public appearance. Greenberg informed his partners that the firm had just signed the papers for a $12 million long-term loan from an insurance company to replace one with the First National Bank of Chicago. "The implications and the actual dollar savings of this agreement are of tremendous importance to Bear Stearns & Co.," he wrote. He also said the financial results for February were "great." "The developments at Bear Stearns certainly seem positive and as a result we will, of course, intensify our surveillance of all positions and expenses," he continued. "You know how I feel about the dangers of overconfidence. It certainly looks like we have a dynamic future in store as long as we remember the words of the famous philosopher, Haimchinkel Malintz Anaynikal: 'thou will do well in commerce as long as thou does not believe thine own odor is perfume.'" A week later, he sent around a news article to his partners and "other potential perfume lovers" about how Dean Witter, one of Bear's competitors, had reported an $886,000 second-quarter loss.

On June 15, Greenberg informed his partners that in the first quarter of 1979, the firm had generated revenue of $51.6 million, or 2.1 percent of Wall Street's revenues, and pretax income of $11.3 million, which was nearly 5 percent of the pretax profits for the entire industry. The message was clear: The firm's tight lid on expenses had enabled Bear Stearns to be relatively more profitable than its Wall Street peers, an achievement Greenberg wanted his team to repeat. "I would also like to add that the last three weeks have been a thing of beauty," he wrote. "Every department is really boiling and some of the new people that we have taken on are starting to make real contributions. Because of this good news, I think it is time for us once again to spend some time reading the works of, and reflecting on the thoughts of, Haimchinkel Malintz Anaynikal." On January 30, 1980, Greenberg was again happy to report good news about the firm's financial results. "Some of the things that have happened to us have been due to our own efforts, but equally, some of our good fortune of late has been due to luck," he wrote. "I have been around long enough to know that shoe usually falls on your head when you least expect it." He then quoted Haimchinkel Malintz Anaynikal's observations from his March 1979 memo.

On May 28, he reported that May 1980 "appears to be the best month in the history of Bear Stearns" but that "before we get carried away, there is one thing that I do want to emphasize. We are working with more capital than ever before, so if every month is not a record-breaker, we are probably getting lazy. We have plenty of room for improvement and there are still a number of leaks in the dike. In fact, the only area that I think is running at 100% efficiency is the error account. I implore our partners who supervise salesmen to increase their suveillance of all personnel. I want all partners in the trading area to pay particular attention that our positions do not increase dramatically in size and that we continue to assiduously follow the rules of Haimchinkel Malintz Anaynikal in the area of loss-taking, freshness of positions and body perfume. . . . It is up to all of us to fight our unrelenting enemies—complacency, overconfidence and conceit." On October 17, he informed his partners that the day had been the biggest in the history of Bear Stearns, by 20 percent, in terms of "number of tickets and overall commission revenues." He then reminded everyone that the "philosophy and works" of Haimchinkel Malintz Anaynikal were must reading for everyone at the firm.

GREENBERG'S MANAGEMENT STYLE and the use of his quirky alter ego—which caused many of his partners to question his sanity—were unique on Wall Street. There was no question Wall Street was changing, and fast. The back-office crisis of the early 1970s, in which many firms failed because they were unable to process effectively the increase in trades and then bulked up their staffs to do so just in time for business to drop off a cliff—drastically altered the landscape, as did May 1, 1975, when fixed commissions evaporated. Many firms failed outright or were forcibly merged with others. Greenberg repeatedly reminded the Bear brethren how proud he was that the firm had survived those tumultuous times while also confirming to his partners how precarious a place Wall Street remained.

But the biggest change to hit the small Wall Street partnerships affected their very legal structure, changing them from shared-liability partnerships to corporate structures that spread the liability from the partners according to their capital contributions to shareholders based on their ownership. Merrill Lynch was the first to change from a partnership structure to a corporate structure, in 1968, but in early 1970 Donaldson, Lufkin & Jenrette (DLJ) was the first Wall Street partnership to take the inevitable next step and sell stock to the public in an initial public offering, or IPO. For the first time, as a result of a rash of Wall Street IPOs, firms were able to raise capital easily through public offerings of both stock and bonds, but, more important, these firms' employees—no longer technically referred to as partners—were encouraged by their bosses to use their new shareholders' capital to take vastly more risk than ever before. The men running Wall Street knew full well that any liability for their risk taking—once borne by their partners—now fell to nameless, faceless shareholders (some of whom, of course, were their former partners). The holy grail of investment banking became increasing short-term profits and short-term bonuses at the expense of the long-term health of the firm and its shareholders.

While firms all around Bear Stearns went public—among others DLJ in 1970 and Merrill Lynch in 1971 (the latter the first to be listed on the NYSE)—Bear remained a private partnership, with an intense if quirky focus on cost and risk controls. Only those business lines that had proven an ability to make money—such as clearing, the brokerage, and the fixed-income division—were given more capital, albeit parsimoniously. "A firm philosophy was to never anticipate what businesses would be good or bad," explained one longtime senior Bear executive, "but to give businesses that were profitable an opportunity to reinvest their revenues. Revenues as opposed to earnings, because sometimes they didn't have earnings that quickly, but they would have more and more business. So areas of the firm—let's say clearance—that were suddenly ramping up more customers would have access to more resources. The historical view of the management of the firm was that they don't plan. They don't have business plans. At one point they were proud the only thing that was planned was the executive dining room. Everything else was opportunistic. There was a view that it is an opportunistic culture, and what opportunistic meant to them was an opportunity, was something that demonstrated that it was profitable, not a theory. It was definitely a view that if you made money for the firm, you had the right to tell the firm where it should spend money. If you didn't make money for the firm, you could have all the thoughts you wanted and they may or may not listen." This haphazard strategy, which worked well for the longest time, is key to understanding what happened in March 2008.

The lessons his father had learned in the rag trade were not lost on Alan Greenberg. Indeed, by the early 1980s, he was an inveterate proselytizer for reducing expenses and for selling off the slow-moving inventory on the firm's balance sheet. When asked once what makes a great trader, he said, "Oh, I don't know. I think the important thing in the securities business is just taking losses. Saying you are wrong. If you own securities, and if you make a mistake, you can take a loss. If you make a mistake in real estate, you have to buy a for-sale sign. And I just think the ability to take a loss and say you are wrong is something you should do."

In truth, Greenberg had a complicated relationship with risk taking. Sometimes he encouraged his traders to take more risk and sometimes he cut them off. In the two hundred or so discretionary trading accounts that he personally managed over the years, not surprisingly, he was very careful about taking risks, choosing—like Warren Buffett—to focus on a dozen or so stocks and holding them for the long term. In 1981, in the midst of DuPont's $7.5 billion acquisition of Conoco—then one of the largest acquisitions of all time and a bruising donnybrook between DuPont, Seagram, and Mobil—Robert Steinberg, who took over running risk arbitrage from Greenberg, had devised a trading strategy he described as "can't lose." The problem was that Steinberg had reached the limit of the capital the firm had allocated to him for merger arbitrage investments. Greenberg would have to sign off on increasing that limit. Alan Schwartz, then head of the firm's small investment banking department, volunteered to speak to Greenberg on Steinberg's behalf. "I went to Ace, because it seemed as if we could do even better if we bought more," Schwartz recalled years later. "Ace said to me, 'Why do you think we have these limits? To keep people from buying too much of things they *don't* really like?'" But Steinberg said that Greenberg would also frequently tell him, "'Bobby, you haven't lost enough money lately.' The message was 'You're not taking *enough* risk. Are you doing everything to maximize [your gains] or are you just being careful?'" Barry Cohen, a longtime Bear executive who was also once head of risk arbitrage and of the firm's hedge fund business, explained Greenberg's business philosophy as being a simple one. "Losing money, never upset," Cohen said. "When he hears somebody around here doesn't return a phone call, very upset."

Greenberg also began to put his imprimatur on the firm through his philosophy of hiring people cut from cloth similar to that of his own and Cayne's: a breed of smart, tough street fighters—being from the Midwest was a plus—who did not necessarily have the pedigree, bloodlines, or education of Bear's blue-blooded, better-known competitors. On May 4, 1981, *Time* ran a cover story titled "The Money Chase: What Business Schools Are Doing to Us," a lengthy explication of the growing demand among young people for graduate business degrees and what effect that might have on society. "There has been a lot of publicity lately about firms hiring students with MBA degrees," Greenberg wrote his partners the next day. "I think it is important that we continue a policy that has helped us prosper while growing from 700 people [in 1973] to over 2,600 today. Our first desire is to promote from within. If somebody with an MBA degree applies for a job, we will certainly not hold it against them, but we are really looking for people with PSD degrees"—that is, those who were poor and smart, with a deep desire to become rich. "They built this firm and there are plenty around because our competition seems to be restricting themselves to MBA's."

The desire to hire "PSDs" was also decidedly unique on Wall Street, and Greenberg celebrated it. "There's a huge pool of bright people out there that can't get jobs and didn't even go to college because of either family problems or money problems or whatever," he said. Welcomed at Bear Stearns were people like Ray Xerri, the son of a baker from the Bensonhurst section of Brooklyn, who was in charge of making sure the firm complied with the SEC's net capital rules, and Mark Konjevod, a scholarship linebacker on the 1990 University of Colorado championship football team. "It was very much a locker room mentality at Bear Stearns," Konjevod said by way of explaining why he generally felt comfortable there.

This being Wall Street, all was not sweetness and light. Greenberg could be plenty pointed and ruthless, too. This came across in his memoranda and in his relationships with his senior partners. After September 1982—"the best month in the history of Bear Stearns" and the start of a historic bull market—Greenberg admonished them nonetheless. "I think we should be on our guard against negatives that go along with great success," he wrote. "I am speaking of complacency, sloppiness, relaxing on expenses, cockiness. And just getting careless in general. This is the time to be on our guard. If the market does go our way, I want to make every dollar and leave nothing on the table. The market may turn sour again, so do not forget for a moment what the great coach Haimchinkel Malintz Anaynikal said many years ago, 'when the going gets tough, the tough start selling.'" He also announced that the executive committee had decided that no partner could make an outside investment—other than buying publicly traded stock and bonds—unless approved by the committee, which, he said, "does not want our partners worrying or thinking about any business other than Bear Stearns. Owning an equity interest in our firm is the best investment any of us will ever see; so let us give B.S. 100% of our effort."

He also shared his thoughts about his partners' work ethic. "Every partner is entitled to a vacation," he wrote in August 1982, "and we have never been particularly fussy about how long the vacation is nor do we keep score on how much time is taken over the course of the year. I do feel that if a partner is not on vacation, he should treat Friday like any other day and show up for a full day of work. Haimchinkel Malintz Anaynikal never took off a Friday in his entire life." And neither did Greenberg. For the most part, though, a culture developed at the very top of the firm—despite Greenberg's memos—of early Friday (or late Thursday) departures for the Jersey shore, Palm Beach, the Hamptons, Greenwich, Martha's Vineyard, or Nantucket. This was by no means unusual behavior on Wall Street. Nor did the senior partners' absence from the office necessarily mean they were unreachable. Nevertheless, over the years, it was not unusual for Greenberg to be the only member of the executive committee in the office on Friday (and then he would stew over this fact).

He also shared his thoughts on his partners' occasional mistakes. "I am well aware that humans will always make errors," he wrote in January 1983. "My irritation comes from the fact that these errors are not caught immediately. In many cases, this is because the producer is too lazy to look at his run the following day; too lazy to look at the registered representative copies of the confirms and too lazy to check the monthly statements. The firm has always been very understanding when errors are made. We will not be understanding if the error is not caught because of subsequent stupidity and laziness. Please see that the people who work with you and for you understand the rules because I do not want any crying when an associate blows a year's salary." He could lecture them, too: In a January 1984 memo, he wrote how he was "more determined than ever to follow the simple rules laid down by the Dean of Business Philosophers, Haimchinkel Malintz Anaynikal: 1. Stick to thine own business. 2. Watch thy shop. 3. Limit thy losses. 4. Watch thy expenses like a hawk. 5. Stay humble, humble, humble. 6. When dealing with a new account, know thy customer and know thy customer's money is up."

He belittled his partners in other, less public ways as well. One year early in his tenure as the senior partner, after he had decided upon his partners' profit points, he met with the executive committee. "You get a grade," Cayne remembered. "We're in the room and he takes the piece of paper with the points on it, and throws it on the floor for the partners to crawl down on the floor and get it. As he did that, I basically said to myself, 'This is the biggest asshole, prick, bully ever.' Here are grown men awaiting their award. Yeah, probably deep down they're saying to themselves, 'I don't deserve shit. I don't deserve it,' except that it's a game where you get points. He throws it on the floor for them to go and grovel and get it." Yet Greenberg also admonished them for feuding. "Haimchinkel Malintz Anaynikal recently brought to my attention certain intercompany feuds that have led to the downfall of firms smarter, richer and larger than ours," he wrote in April 1984. "Watching for these signs of dissension will be a high priority of mine. Whenever you have a partnership of over 80 people, there is bound to be a person or two who is not your exact cup of yogurt. For years, the partners of this firm have gotten along remarkably well and the cooperation at this time is great. One of the things I am going to be extremely sensitive about in the future—and come down very hard on when I see or hear of it—is acrimony among partners. Honest men may differ, but when the difference becomes animosity, you can have problems. I am not going to let personal conflicts have any effect on the net income of our golden goose."

❀

IN JUNE 1983, in a lengthy Sunday piece, the *Times* tried to sum up the mysterious world of Bear Stearns and its polymath senior partner. Leslie Wayne, the *Times*'s reporter, noted from the outset the sign "Let's make nothing but money" that hung outside the firm's "cavernous" trading room, and then openly questioned the way the firm went about doing just that. "What really characterizes Bear Stearns is its willingness to commit capital where other houses might fear to tread," Wayne wrote, "whether representing dissident shareholders in proxy battles that other firms shun or investing heavily in bankrupt or financially troubled companies, or in doing underwritings for corporate clients that one partner characterized as having 'not the highest bond ratings.'"

Wayne could not quite decipher what made the firm tick. "This boldness and penchant for making money has caused some to raise questions about Bear Stearns' identity," she continued, "whether it acts as an agent for clients by providing services for a fee or whether it is simply a trading vehicle for its partners, or both. Emphasis on the latter causes some to question the firm's devotion to its clients and this is often cited as one reason why Bear Stearns lacks blue chip corporations on its client list." She noted that the firm found a way to make money by buying the distressed securities of Penn Central, Chrysler, International Harvester, Manville, and Revere Copper and Brass. Bear Stearns had bought almost two million shares of the struggling Revere Copper, the value of which had nearly tripled. Firm-wide revenue was around $650 million and its net income was $160 million. Although the partners' draw was only $74,000, their bonuses reached as high as $2 million. "You move up here by making money," said Frank Martucci, the partner in charge of corporate bond trading. "The more you make, the higher you move."

This level of financial success quite naturally raised a few eyebrows on Wall Street. "Bear, Stearns is seen as a firm of bright, sharp entrepreneurs who are more self motivated or motivated for the individual gain of people within the firm rather than building a corporate entity for the long term," observed Samuel L. Hayes at Harvard Business School. Leslie Wayne cited a number of instances where the firm appeared to have a conflict of interest—"for instance, acting as a market maker in the shares of one company at the same time it was waging a proxy battle against that company's management"—but plowed ahead anyway. She noted that the firm happily represented corporate raiders, such as Irwin Jacobs in his successful effort to snatch control of the moving company Bekins from the Belzberg family of Canada, another set of well-known raiders.

Wayne also let a competitor take a potshot at the firm. "Bear Stearns has done an intelligent job of seeking segments that most people found to be too small, specialized or even vaguely repellent," said George L. Ball, president and chief executive of Prudential-Bache Securities. "Most firms will, at times, forgo profits for reasons of perception. But Bear Stearns has the idea that a legitimate transaction is one that earns a dollar—even if it's something you don't want to bring home for dinner with mother." Greenberg apparently never forgot this slight. When Ball resigned from Prudential-Bache in 1991 after a tumultuous, loss-filled nine-year reign, Greenberg sent around a memo to the firm's partners reminding them of Ball's quotation. "As Haimchinkel Malintz Anaynikal has mentioned so often, 'what comes around goes around.' Nookie added something that was particularly poignant—'you meet the same people on the way down that you met on the way up.' We have constantly stressed that people at Bear Stearns do not denigrate our competition. Your Executive Committee wants to reemphasize that position. *If you cannot say something nice about somebody, do not say it.*"

The firm continued to perform well financially, especially as the bull market of the 1980s began to switch into a higher gear. During May 1985—the first month of the new fiscal year—Greenberg reported that the firm "did get ten runs in the first inning" and that "I frankly cannot remember any time in the past where we ever broke even in the month of May, much less made money." Though when asked the previous year if Bear Stearns had considered an initial public offering of its stock, Greenberg had told a reporter in no uncertain terms that the firm intended to remain private, the internal pressure was mounting for just such an event. The firm had been performing well, with total revenues increasing to $1.8 billion in the fiscal year ended April 1985, from $393 million at the end of April 1981. During the same five-year period, Bear Stearns's net income increased from $108 million in fiscal 1981 to $169 million in fiscal 1985. The firm's equity capital—thanks to the years of positive net income—had increased to $350 million in April 1985 from $60 million five years earlier. By any measure, Greenberg's stewardship of the company was to be lauded.

Factors cited as reasons to go public included the firm's financial performance, the positive performace of the stocks of DLJ and Merrill Lynch since they went public, and the concern of some of the younger partners that a number of the top executives were getting older—Greenberg was fifty-seven, Cayne was fifty-one, Rosenwald was fifty-five, and Einbender was fifty-six—and that if any or all were to die, the firm's policy of having to pay out their estates in five years (as had occurred with the heirs of both Lewis and Low) could leave the firm in a difficult position from a capital standpoint. The other concern about staying a private partnership was one of shared liability. As the firm's partners were taking greater and greater risks with the firm's capital, the general partners were sharing ratably in the increased risk of a financial calamity. A public offering of stock would shift the liability from the general partners to the shareholders of the corporation.

By the start of fiscal 1986 (May 1985), many of the ten members of the firm's executive committee were thinking an IPO was looking like a better and better idea. Greenberg remained steadfastly against it, but soon the executive committee met to take up the question of selling stock in Bear Stearns to the public. Greenberg was in Albany and missed the meeting. "The executive committee [meeting] takes place," Cayne said, "and they say, 'Well, we have had this discussion already. We think we should go public. We're going to vote.' The vote is nine to nothing. Greenberg isn't there. . . . Greenberg always used to say, 'It's not a one-man thing. Whatever you guys do whenever I'm not around doesn't matter.'" The committee also agreed on the executive structure, with Cayne slated to be president and John Rosenwald vice chairman.

At this time, Cayne was still driving Greenberg downtown to 55 Water Street. "The next morning I pick him up, as I usually do,"

Cayne said. "He says, 'Did anything happen last night?' I said, 'Not much, except we voted to go public.' He said, 'What? You let them do that?' I said, 'Alan, it's stupid not to, and who cares?' He said, 'Well, I'm very surprised. I really am very surprised.'" Greenberg wanted to know what the management slate would be. "You'll be the chairman," Cayne told him. "Johnny [Rosenwald] will be the vice chairman. I'll be the president." Cayne said Greenberg just sat in the car without saying anything.

Two days later, Greenberg called Cayne into his office, under the pretext of wanting to talk about something to do with a commodity trade. "He calls me into his office and he's got some goofy beef about a commodity thing," Cayne said. "I know him, this has nothing to do with commodities. He's pissed off about this slate." That Saturday night, Alfred Lerner—a Brooklyn-born billionaire and longtime Greenberg friend—called Cayne at home. Lerner had also become friendly with Cayne over the years. "He was a street guy," Cayne said. "He calls me. 'You're not going to be the president.' I said, 'Bullshit.' He said, 'Greenberg is definitely not going to let that happen.' I said, 'Well, he has no choice. He's fucked. We got the agreement of the executive committee.' He says, 'Well, Jimmy, I'm just telling you. You're not going to be the president.'"

On Monday morning, Greenberg called Cayne. "The commodity thing again, and 'By the way, Johnny never agreed to be vice chairman,'" Cayne said. "I said, 'Really? I think it's a good idea.'" Cayne found himself wondering how and why this situation could have been turned around in just four days. On Wednesday, Cayne was told he would not be getting the presidency. "I'm told I have to make up my mind by Friday whether I'm going or not," Cayne said. "I'm so angry that I can't see straight. This is not only a renege. This is the big renege. This is like my entire base has reneged."

In the end, Cayne voted for the firm to go public. He capitulated to being a co-president of the firm with Rosenwald even though he felt betrayed. He was not happy. True, he had around $8 million of capital in the firm at that point, which would be worth two or three times that much after a public offering of stock. But this wasn't about money; this was about power.

On July 23, the *Wall Street Journal* broke the story that Bear

Stearns appeared to have decided to "convert to public ownership two to three months from now." The *Journal* called Greenberg "taciturn" and described how he conducted his business from a raised desk on the firm's trading floor and how he "embodies Bear Stearns' opportunistic trading philosophy" by planning no further ahead than the next trade. "What our trading positions look like at the end of the day is long-range planning as far as I'm concerned." The article also mentioned that Greenberg had an office near the trading floor, where he kept a large oak desk given to him by Cy Lewis.

On August 5, the firm's executive committee formally voted for the IPO filing and set the wheels in motion for a first filing with the SEC in mid-September 1985. But Greenberg was careful not to appear to bask in the glow of the fact that his Bear Stearns stock would, after the offering, be worth around $50 million and that his annual compensation of a salary of $150,000 plus a bonus of around another $5 million would make him—for a time—the highest-paid CEO on Wall Street. (Cayne and Rosenwald were set to have around $35 million in Bear Stearns stock.) Instead, he made only passing mention of the coming IPO in an August 9 memo to his partners—a memo that would become famous in the annals of Wall Street for its parsimonious spirit. "I was just shown the results for our first quarter," he wrote. "They were excellent. When mortals go through a prosperous period, it seems to be human nature for expenses to balloon. We are going to be the exception. I have just informed the purchasing department that they should no longer purchase paper clips. All of us receive documents every day with paper clips on them. If we save these paper clips, not only will we have enough for our own use, but we will also, in a short time, be awash in the little critters. Periodically, we will collect excess paper clips and sell them (since the cost to us is zero, the Arbitrage Department tells me the return on capital will be above average). This action may seem a little petty, but anything we can do to make our people conscious of expenses is worthwhile." Greenberg also decided to no longer authorize the purchase of both "blue envelopes used for interoffice mail" and rubber bands. "If we can save paper clips from incoming mail, we can save rubber bands, and my hope is that we can become awash in these little stretchies also."

To some extent, these missives were tongue-in-cheek, except for the fact that Bear Stearns actually did what Greenberg outlined. It became a bit of a standing joke on Wall Street that the firm would give every new employee a small bag of rubber bands and paper clips for use on the job.

As with every company that sells stock to public investors, Bear's IPO prospectus was chock full of revelatory information about the firm, the vast majority of which had never before been public. The filing revealed that the firm was primarily a fixed-income shop—involved in the buying, selling, trading, and underwriting of debt securities issued by the U.S. Treasury, affiliated government agencies, municipalities, and corporations—but also had a retail brokerage business, a clearing business, an arbitrage business dating back "more than 25 years" that had been profitable for "each of the last 15 years," and a fledgling but profitable and growing investment banking business with 287 employees. Of the firm's $1.8 billion in revenue for the year ended April 1985, some $109 million, or 6 percent, came from investment banking, and two-thirds of that from advising on mergers and acquisitions. In two years, the advisory business had doubled to $73 million in revenues from $36 million.

The prospectus also described how Bear Stearns began its "mortgage-related securities department" in 1981 and that it "makes markets and trades" in the securities of the government mortgage agencies, known colloquially as Ginnie Mae, Fannie Mae, and Freddie Mac. Bear also traded "pools of whole mortgages"—mortgages originated by mortgage brokers that had not been securitized and that were not as easily traded as securitized mortgages. Since Bear Stearns did not originate the underlying mortgages, "a staff of mortgage underwriting specialists analyzes and performs procedures to verify the authenticity of the loans before they are bought for the Company's own account," according to the prospectus. The company also conceded that all of its "principal transactions and brokerage activities" exposed the firm to risks "because securities positions are subject to fluctuations in market value and liquidity." Management monitored the "market risks" by reviewing many different reports on a daily basis as well as through the weekly meeting of the Bear Stearns Risk Committee, headed by Greenberg.

The company further revealed that "in connection with its trading activities in United States government and agency securities, [it] also enters into repurchase and reverse repurchase agreements pursuant to which it sells securities to or purchases securities from another dealer or other party which agrees to resell or repurchase them at a specified date and price"—the very financing activity that would continue through the week of March 10, 2008, until the overnight repo lenders decided to stop funding the firm. But even twenty-three years earlier, Bear Stearns knew this kind of financing was a risky proposition. Thus a prescient warning found its way into print: "While the Company takes steps to insure that these transactions are adequately collateralized, the large dollar amounts of these transactions could subject the Company to significant losses if parties entering into such agreements with the Company fail to meet their obligations and the Company incurs losses in liquidating its positions in the open market."

⁂

BY THIS TIME Greenberg had implemented at the firm a requirement that partners donate at least 4 percent of their compensation to charity. This requirement made Bear Stearns one of the most consistently charitable firms on Wall Street year in and year out. Greenberg himself became known as "the biggest giver on Wall Street." He gave millions of dollars to the United Jewish Appeal. In November 1986, he donated $1 million to the Oklahoma Medical Research Foundation to establish the Esther Greenberg Honors Chair in Biomedical Research, in honor of his mother. Greenberg has also made sizable contributions to the Johns Hopkins Medical Center, the New York Public Library, the American Museum of Natural History, and several other institutions and charities.

But Greenberg's "narcissism," as Cayne called it, led the Bear chairman to make several large donations that seemed eccentric at best. He once donated money to renovate the bathrooms at the Israel Museum, in Jerusalem, and commemorated the gift by putting up a plaque in honor of his brother, Maynard, who lived in Oklahoma City. Some wondered whether the gift meant he hated his brother or liked him. His donations to Johns Hopkins have totaled around $3 million and helped to create the Kathryn and Alan C. Greenberg Center for Skeletal Dysplasias—focusing on the study and treatment of dwarfism—and he has been honored at the annual convention of the Little People of America. Cayne made odd donations, too. For example, in March 1989, he agreed to be a financial sponsor of Gata Kamsky, then a fourteen-year-old Soviet chess prodigy, after reading a brief article in the *New York Times* about Kamsky's defection to the United States. For five years, Cayne helped to underwrite the boy's chess career—at $40,000 a year— until Kamsky abruptly quit the game after losing to Anatoly Karpov in the championship of the World Chess Federation. (Kamsky resumed playing chess full-time in 2004 and is now one of four men in contention to become world champion in 2009.)

Greenberg's most peculiar donation was his $1 million gift, in June 1998, to pay for Viagra prescriptions for men who could not otherwise afford them. Most people couldn't resist thinking that Greenberg had donated a million dollars for homeless men to have sex. He defended the gift despite the criticism. "I own stock in Pfizer," he told the *New York Times,* referring to the drug's manufacturer. "So it's not altruistic. You can quote me on that. . . . If you ask me how long I've been interested in the subject, I guess you can say I've been interested in it since I was 13 or 14." Asked the "indelicate" question of whether he used Viagra himself, he told the paper, "I'm not answering that." Cayne was livid. "It came up at the executive committee," Cayne remembered, "and I said to him, 'How dare you do this and not tell your partners? We're the laughingstock of Wall Street. It's not because it's Viagra. It's not because it's the homeless. It's because we're on the front pages being the highest-paid management team and you make so much money you give a million dollars so that people get laid, homeless people.' I told him, 'That's a decision that you should have shared.'"

THERE WAS NO doubting the firm's performance, though. For the eleven months ended March 27, 1986, the firm had revenues of close to $2 billion and net income of $118 million, compared to $1.6 billion in revenues and $79 million in net income for the previous eleven-month period. Shortly after the end of the firm's fiscal year in May 1986, Bear Stearns's managing directors decided to take advantage of the firm's success and agreed to sell 4.6 million shares in a secondary offering of stock, priced at $35 per share. The May 1986 secondary sale was the last time the partners of the firm sold stock in an underwritten offering. On July 15, 1986, the firm authorized a three-for-two stock split, the last in its history.

In the weeks leading up to the sale, Greenberg's memo writing was positively manic and focused almost exclusively on his favorite theme, reducing expenses. He even bemoaned the firm's increasing cost of using Scotch tape on the interoffice envelopes. "From this day on," he wrote on April 18, "instruct your secretary to lick only the left side of the flap when sending the envelope. The reason for this will amaze you, and make you wonder why you didn't think of this yourself. If the envelope is gently opened by the recipient, it can be used again and sealed, without using scotch tape, by your secretary licking the right side of the flap and then sealing it. After all of us have become accustomed to accurate and precise licking, a further extension of this will be to lick only the left third, and then the middle for the next trip, and the right side for the penultimate voyage. If one has a small tongue and good coordination, an envelope could be opened and resealed ten times."

Greenberg also opaquely commented on the firm's good fortune in the wake of the widening insider-trading scandal that exploded on Wall Street with the November 1986 arrest of Ivan Boesky and the exposure of a ring that included competitors at Drexel Burnham, Goldman Sachs, Kidder Peabody, and Lazard, among others. "I have never been more optimistic about the future of Bear Stearns than I am now," he wrote the firm's senior executives in February 1987, shortly after the end of the firm's third quarter. "There is only one reason for my optimism," he continued. "It has become perfectly clear to me that several of our departments have been profitable during the past few years, despite the fact that they were not exactly competing on a 'level playing field.' Certain competitors have had big advantages over our group; recent events make it clear that this inequity is coming to an end. I congratulate those departments for the job they have done against unethical competition." In closing, he warned against all the success leading to the employees "becoming complacent" and that "every con man is or will be heading for the securities industry. Stay alert!" Indeed, Greenberg encouraged Bear employees to rat out those among them committing "fraud" or "waste." He said employees would be rewarded with cash bonuses "if a suspicion is substantiated" and added, "We will also *never* criticize anyone for calling 'wolf' too often. We *are* different from other corporations. Let us stay that way."

The firm was doing so well and growing so quickly—head count had increased to 5,700 employees worldwide, 30 percent higher than when it went public—that it had outgrown its headquarters at 55 Water Street. In March 1987, Bear announced that it was moving its headquarters to 245 Park Avenue, at 46th Street, and that half of its employees would be housed there. On July 13, Greenberg announced that the firm had a "record year" while its competitors had suffered. "We may be entitled to some degree of pride in our performance," he wrote his managing directors, "but certainly not smug self-satisfaction." He reminded everyone that head count at the firm had increased by 800 during the year and that the move to 245 Park Avenue would significantly increase the firm's expenses. "Our industry is cyclical, and we are in the midst of the longest bull market in history," he wrote. "A sharp downturn could be painful if we are not lean and mean. . . . In addition, I am newly married, and I am in no mood to take a pay cut. Regardless of what your experience has been, I am finding that two cannot live as cheaply as one."

Greenberg had married the former Kathryn A. Olson, then forty—"a strikingly attractive lawyer, with long auburn hair," the *Times* reported—in June 1987. "Friends say that the marriage has done much to temper Greenberg's blunt ways," the *Times* continued, and then quoted Cayne: "I can see her influence on him. He's softer, more willing to listen." Greenberg didn't have to worry about a pay cut in 1987: He was the highest-paid executive on Wall Street, earning $5.7 million. Indeed, the top five highest-paid executives on Wall Street in 1987 all worked at Bear Stearns, with Cayne and Rosenwald each getting paid $3.9 million and Thomas Anderson and Denis Coleman Jr. each making $3.4 million.

CHAPTER 18

THE JOY OF MORTGAGE-
BACKED SECURITIES

One of the ways Bear Stearns began to increase its return on equity was through the growth of its mortgage-backed securities department. Tommy Marano started full-time at Bear Stearns in May 1983, after graduating from Columbia College. A history major, Marano started at the firm on the equity syndicate desk, working on the basic underwriting of equity offerings for Fannie Mae, Freddie Mac, and Ginnie Mae. He liked reading and writing the boring prospectuses. Then fate intervened. "I got paid a really lousy bonus one year by the head of the syndicate at that point, and I talked to my immediate boss and he said, 'You ought to go talk to John Sites'"—who founded the mortgage department at Bear Stearns in 1981 and later became co-head of fixed income—"'and ask John Sites if he has a role for you in the mortgage area because you like to read these books and they're complicated deals.'"

Bear's mortgage-backed securities business rose from the ashes of the savings-and-loans crisis of the mid to late 1980s, when failed thrifts were desperately trying to get illiquid assets off their balance sheets. At that time, the margins on trading the bonds of Fannie Mae and Freddie Mac were huge, generally $2 to $3 on a trade and sometimes $5. In other words, the difference between what a bond was bought for and what it could be sold for could be as much as five points. (Today that spread is calculated in thirty-seconds of a point.) "There were very few types of securities trading," Marano said. "You didn't have the technology or analytics we have today." Bear Stearns followed the lead of Salomon Brothers in trying to help the thrifts solve their balance sheet problems, with all those nonperforming mortgages. "The play we made in that area was following what Salomon was trying to do with the thrifts," he continued. "That was the birth of securitization, really, and what you were trying to do was get the assets off the thrifts' balance sheets to basically get them some liquidity to keep operating. And it was Bear, through John Sites, that really got the market to change in 1987 by allowing Fannie and Freddie to issue these REMICs"—real estate mortgage investment contracts—"directly, as opposed to only issuing pass-throughs or mortgage-backed bonds. Bear Stearns and Sites were key to that, as was Lehman. I actually priced and traded the very first REMIC Fannie Maes 87-1 (for $500 million). It was a new market. It was a growing market. You had none of the technology we had today, and you had [a] very wide bid-offered spread. That's really why the firm went after it, and we spent a lot of money on risk analytics and banking. We did deals for all the failed thrifts, among them American Savings and Loan and California Federal." The business took off. "It became kind of a real race between us, Salomon Brothers, Merrill, First Boston, Lehman Brothers, and DLJ," Marano said, "with Bear Stearns and Lehman taking the lead."

While Sites, with the help of Marano and others, had been building a powerful engine in the firm's mortgage securities department, the rocket fuel for it came in November 1987 when the firm hired a well-known trader named Howie Rubin. Rubin was plenty controversial. Until 1985, he had been a mortgage trader at Salomon Brothers, working for Lew Ranieri, who is generally acknowledged to be the godfather of the mortgage-backed securities business on Wall Steet and the man who coined the word "securitization" to describe buying bundles of home mortgages, slicing and dicing them into different tranches, and selling them off to investors around the world. He realized mortgages were nothing more than "math" and hired a team of Ph.D.'s to do the structuring. Ranieri once called Rubin, a Harvard MBA and onetime professional gambler, "the most gifted trader I have ever seen." In 1985, Merrill Lynch hired Rubin away from Salomon Brothers by tripling his compensation to $1 million. A year later, Rubin supposedly "exceeded his trading limits" in his mortgage-backed securities portfolio, causing Merrill to lose $37 million. As his punishment, he was promoted to chief mortgage securities trader. On April 29, 1987, the *Wall Street Journal* reported Merrill had lost $250 million—later increased to $275 million and then $337 million, and then reduced to

$85 million—as a result of unauthorized trading in mortgage securities. Merrill blamed Rubin, then thirty-six, for the loss, which at the time was the largest on a single trade in Wall Street history. Merrill executives told the *Journal* that Rubin "had far exceeded his limits in acquiring mortgages that were packaged into a particularly risky form of securities. The package involves splitting off the interest payments on the mortgages from the principal and selling each separately."

It turned out that a few weeks earlier, Rubin had sold the stream of interest payments on $500 million of mortgage bonds to Ernie Fleischer at Franklin Savings & Loan, in Ottawa, Kansas, and kept the stream of principal payments on the same bonds. Rubin tried to sell what he still owned through Merrill's vaunted sales force, but for technical reasons the strip of principal payments was plenty risky in a rising-interest-rate environment, and no buyers could be found. Some said Merrill had overpriced the securities. In any event, with his losses mounting daily, Rubin "just put them in his drawer," an unnamed Merrill executive told the *Journal*. "We didn't know he owned them." From there, the facts of the matter get murky. Supposedly, Rubin then went on vacation and locked his desk. To get into the drawer, Merrill's maintenance staff took a chainsaw and cut open the desk and found the confirmation slips for the trade. Then Merrill fired Rubin, insisting he had misled them. Rubin's ex-buddies at Salomon, including Ranieri, defended him and said it was preposterous that Rubin could have created and sold these securities—which had to be registered with the SEC, after all—without his bosses at Merrill Lynch being aware of what he was doing. (Rubin declined repeated requests to be interviewed; in 1990 he settled SEC charges brought against him, and Merrill ended up paying him deferred compensation said to total around $1 million.)

About the time Merrill fired Rubin, executives at Bear Stearns reached out to hire him. In November 1987, Bear named him one of its fourteen mortgage securities traders at a salary reported to be $100,000 a year plus 10 percent of the profits he generated, a 90 percent reduction in his compensation. Cayne said he was involved directly in the decision to hire Rubin. Sites went to Cayne and told

him he wanted Rubin. At first, Cayne was skeptical of hiring someone who had been accused of unauthorized trading and appeared to
be in trouble with the SEC. Cayne told Sites he wanted to meet
Rubin. As Cayne recalled, "The guy looked me in the eye and said,
'You really honestly think I did this?' I said, 'No, I don't.'" Cayne said
he thought Merrill Lynch made Rubin its "fall guy." The hiring of
Rubin was a perfect example of Cayne relying on his gut instinct
when interviewing a prospective employee.

Tommy Marano believed the hiring of Rubin reflected the firm's
opportunistic streak. "It was a demonstration of the firm's propensity to be comfortable taking risks even with people who might be
colorful," he said. Marano was one of Rubin's fellow traders, and
while he was a little wary of him at first, he quickly became impressed. "Howie, first of all, has the calmest demeanor of any trader
I ever interacted with, so very few situations can freak him out,"
Marano continued. "He also has an amazing mind for math. He's
just very, very quick with math. He's very organized, very creative,
and I think his strongest feature is that he has this way of putting
customers at ease." The Bear traders used to joke that even when
Rubin was screwing a customer, the customer enjoyed every minute
of it.

Marano said that Rubin—along with Sites, Chuck Ramsey,
who was in charge of the company's small mortgage bond desk, and
others—helped to get the executive committee of the firm "plugged
into" the "revenue potential" of the mortgage securities business.
"It was Howie's risk-taking propensity," Marano said, "as well as all
the money we invested in research and technology that let us really
run the first really big position" in mortgage securities on the firm's
balance sheet. In short order, under the leadership of Sites, Ramsey, Rubin, and others, the firm became a major underwriter of
mortgage-backed securities. Bear, a "negligible force" in the market
in 1986, the *Wall Street Journal* reported, was seventh in the closely
watched league tables in 1988, and by the first half of 1989 was in
first place, having underwritten $7.1 billion in mortgage-backed se-
curities, $2 billion more than Salomon Brothers, the perennial mar-
ket leader.

THE BULL MARKET was raging into the fall of 1987, but on October 19 the Dow Jones Industrial Average suffered its largest one-day crash, in percentage terms, in history, losing 22.6 percent of its value, or some $500 billion. Around Wall Street, a near-panic ensued as fortunes were lost instantly, and nerves were more than a little frayed. Bear Stearns stock lost about a third of its value that day and was trading at around $8 a share, almost two-thirds less than it had on October 1. "I was catatonic," recalled Bobby Steinberg, the head of arbitrage. "I'd never lost so much money in my life. Ace says, 'Bobby? What action are you taking?' Action? I'm sitting there helpless. He says, 'I think now's the time to start buying.' Then he gets up—everyone on the trading floor's watching—and he starts practicing his golf swing. He says, 'I think maybe I won't come in tomorrow. I think I'll play golf.'"

The image of Greenberg swinging his golf club on the trading floor in the midst of a collective panic became one of the firm's enduring legends. "It is amazing how history keeps repeating itself," Greenberg wrote the troops during the crash. "The market in stocks and bonds has taken a precipitous drop, but I am far from depressed. Why? Because once again, we are seeing and we will be seeing great opportunities in all areas, particularly in personnel. I can assure you we are pursuing every lead at this very moment. Our move to Park Avenue will start shortly, and I truly believe that the timing is perfect. Just keep in mind it was just a few years ago that two of our competitors left the clearing business. Eleven months ago several large firms closed their Arbitrage Departments"—and here he said he wished he had forced the firm's arbitrage department to go on vacation two weeks ago, because Steinberg's positions alone cost the firm around $50 million on October 19. "We will be a *winner*."

The firm lost $100 million on October 19. That money was simply removed from the accrual that had built up during the year in the discretionary bonus pool. That meant that unless things turned around before the end of the firm's fiscal year, the managing directors were likely to get smaller bonuses that year because of the loss. But the crash did cause a Hong Kong investment firm, Jardine Matheson, to renege on a $23-a-share tender offer for 20 percent of

Bear Stearns—an offer that valued the whole firm at about $2 billion. The executive committee debated whether to sue Jardine, and the final vote was nine to one in favor of the suit, with Greenberg being the lone dissenter. Eventually, the case went to trial before a jury, and Jardine's lawyers realized they were losing and folded. Bear Stearns won a $60 million settlement from Jardine (which, ironically, is also now part of JPMorgan) for the firm's shareholders. That worked out to $3.53 per share, most of which went to the senior management of the firm, since they owned close to half of the firm. Greenberg, who had never wanted to litigate the matter, had thought the firm might get at most a $12 million settlement and probably less.

CHAPTER 19

"BULLIES ALWAYS CAVE"

With the repercussions from the crash and Jardine's withdrawn offer still fresh in the minds of the executive committee—a committee that had supported Cayne against Greenberg in deciding to file a lawsuit against Jardine—Cayne decided that his co-president arrangement with John Rosenwald had become untenable. Bear Stearns *needed* a sole president, Cayne realized. It was time for another power play. "I go to Johnny Rosenwald, who happens to be a really nice guy," Cayne said. "He's not devious at all. He's like a dwarf. He's like five foot one or something. But he tells great stories and he's a gentleman. I said to him, 'We are the laughingstock of Wall Street. We don't have a president. We're the only company in the world that doesn't have a president. Now, you're a big shareholder and I'm a big shareholder. We should together go to Greenberg and say you want to be the president. You're the president. I don't care. We have to have a president. We can't have simply a vice chairman and a president turned into co-presidents. That's just ridiculous.' He agrees."

Cayne and Rosenwald went to see Greenberg with the plan that one of the two of them would be named president of the firm. "Greenberg goes completely crazy," Cayne said. "He throws his jacket on the floor." Greenberg refused to deal with his partners' request. But Cayne would not take that for an answer. " 'This is a fill or kill,' " he told Greenberg after his tantrum. " 'This doesn't happen, I'm out of here.' No anger. I told him, 'It's your firm. I don't doubt that it's your firm. But I won't be here getting coffee in the morning and the other guys' coffee in the afternoon.' " He won from Greenberg an agreement that he would make a decision in ninety days about who would be president, even though Cayne couldn't figure out why Greenberg wanted to wait other than as a stalling tactic. "Ninety days go by," Cayne said. "I walk in his office that Monday morning and say, 'Today's D-Day.' He says, 'For what?' I said, 'Don't you remember that little thing ninety days? Well, ninety days are up.' He says, 'Jimmy, we can't do that, that's not fair to Johnny.' I said, 'Tonight is the executive committee meeting. It will be announced at the executive committee,' and I walked out. Executive [committee] meeting was at 4:15. I get there at 4:10. Rosenwald and Greenberg are standing there. 'We've got to talk to you,' they say. I walk over. 'Look, Jimmy, at the end of the year we'll make the change.' I said, 'Wait a second. We just had a ninety-day period. Now, there's another four months, five months.' 'Yeah,' they said. I said, 'It's simple. We're going to go back in that room. Either you make the announcement or I'll make the announcement that I'm leaving.' Then I just walked out of the room to go to the executive committee meeting."

Of course, ever the tactician, Cayne figured he had the executive committee in his pocket. "I've got the executive committee," he said. "I've got a six-vote preference there. I walk in and I wink at everybody. This is it. It's D-Day. I don't know what the fuck he's going to do. But as far as I'm concerned, this is it. Decision. I was pretty sure what was going to happen, but it was no cinch. Greenberg said, 'It seems that Johnny wants to do a little something different, so he's going to move into the ivory tower, which leaves only one person in the presidency, and that's Jimmy. He's the president, the only president.' That's how he addresses it. Then he turns to the guy at his right and says, 'Okay. What have you got?' Like we're having a meeting and all of a sudden he's made an announcement that's earth-shaking. Rosenwald has been at the firm for thirty years. He's just been told he's going somewhere else. He calls on somebody to continue going around the table with 'What do you got?' Rosenwald says, 'Well, wait a second. I've been here for thirty years and I deserve a little more than simply "John is moving into something else." I really don't think that I was treated right.' Greenberg says, 'Yeah, well, okay, well, so what?' And he goes on."

Even the thick-skinned Cayne found Greenberg's cavalier treatment of Rosenwald appalling. "Rosenwald was not a friend of mine," Cayne said. "He was not a compadre at all. On Monday night, I'm out to dinner with Patricia and friends and I said to them, 'You know what? I got to call this guy, because what happened was so embarrassing to him.' She said, 'Well, you don't even like him.' I said, 'I know, but it's just like there's a rawness that existed, that Greenberg was a meatpacker who was treating him like he was a piece of dirt.'" When Cayne got home that night, he called Rosenwald. "I said, 'Johnny, you've given a lot to the firm and I apologize for the way this all came down.' And he said, 'I can't tell you how much this call really means. I thank you.' Even though I may be rough and tough and grew up scrambling and clawing my way, there's a basic niceness and a basic humanity. I ran the firm with an idea. The idea was be nice to everybody. It works. Pretend you're running for mayor, over and over. Have the quote boys like you. Have the clerks like you. Have the traders like you. It's better. That's what pervaded the organization—the idea that working and playing well with others is equally rewarded with production. You get rewarded for working and playing well with others. And that becomes part of the culture. That *is* the culture."

❋

AND YET THERE were legendary stories within the firm about the viciousness with which Cayne could publicly dress down subordinates. In fact, many new senior-level employees considered getting hewed out by Cayne to be both a rite of passage and an introduction of sorts to the ways of the firm. One senior managing director d how within a month of taking over the running of an important business line, he got a call from Cayne. "He says, 'Come down to my office right now.' Not hello. 'Come down to my office right now.' I open up the door to his black-walled chamber, all done in black ebony wood. Between the door and the chair, if I hadn't had almost thirty years of experience on Wall Street, I probably would have shit in my pants. Because he barked at me the moment I set foot in that office." After a fulsome, expletive-filled discussion of the managing director's supposed error in judgment—carved out in front of Alan Schwartz and Sam Molinaro, who were there, too— "he just sort of said, 'Dismissed.'"

On May 4, 1988, Bear Stearns announced that Cayne would be the sole president and Rosenwald would become a vice chairman. The consensus seemed to be that Cayne, then fifty-four, was in position to take over running the firm from Greenberg, then sixty. "It's not a big change," Cayne told the *Times*. "People will be doing the same thing they always have. It's business as usual." Greenberg made no mention of Cayne's appointment in any of his numerous internal memoranda.

Fresh on the heels of that successful gambit, Cayne pushed Greenberg again for even more power at the firm. "I recognized at some point in the late 1980s that the 'point allocator,' that's the boss," Cayne explained, referring to the senior partner who decided what the other partners get paid. "That's the guy who runs the fucking show. I don't care what the masthead says. I don't care who's responsible. The guy who pays people is the boss. I convinced two guys on the executive committee to go to him and say, 'You can't do the points by yourself. You got to do them with the number two partner, and that was Jimmy.'" But Greenberg wasn't wild about that idea, either, especially since "one of his flock," as Cayne referred to the members of the executive committee who were loyal to Greenberg, thought Cayne would treat him unfairly when it came to compensation. At first Greenberg told Cayne no. "Greenberg said to me, 'You terrify people, you put fear into people,'" Cayne explained. "I said, 'You got it exactly upside down. I don't. You may have one guy. I got six that are terrified of you.'" But once again, Greenberg relented and agreed to allow Cayne to have a role in the allocation of the profit points to the senior managing directors.

❋

A PATTERN HAD clearly emerged in the relationship between Greenberg and Cayne where Greenberg repeatedly reversed what had appeared to be an immutable position in the face of a threat from Cayne. Each time, Cayne gobbled up more and more power. Cayne had used the same approach with Cy Lewis when Lewis asked him to continue overseeing the brokerage account of Sandy Lewis's in-laws. To Cayne, the way to handle these powerful people was simple. "You stand up to a bully, the bully collapses," he said. "That's always been my theory. The second you stand up, they fall. Bullies always cave." But any number of Cayne's partners thought he was the bully. "He was an eccentric and a bully," said one of them. "He would lecture and wouldn't listen. And he was more avaricious in his pursuit of power than anyone else at the firm."

As often seemed to happen on Wall Street during the late 1980s, when bankers became more and more like rock stars and celebrities, Greenberg and Cayne took their power struggle at the firm into the business pages of the national newspapers and national magazines.

In June 1989, the *Times* caught up with Greenberg on a Saturday afternoon in the back room of Reuben's, a New York delicatessen, where he was performing magic tricks for a group of regulars. "I don't do tricks," Greenberg told the paper. "I do miracles." What followed was a breathless account of how Greenberg, in all of his avuncular quirkiness, had steered the firm from a 1,000-person private partnership with $46 million in capital to a 6,000-employee public company with $1.4 billion in capital. The profile pointed out that Bear Stearns's profits had been growing at an annualized rate of 13 percent and had a return on equity second only to the venerable Morgan Stanley. Bear had also stuck to its trading roots, largely eschewing the M&A business and the leveraged-buyout rage (led in large part by the Bear alumni at Kohlberg Kravis Roberts). Greenberg, the paper observed, relied on "old-fashioned values more prevalent in country stores than on go-go Wall Street." But the article pointed out that he was no longer a hayseed, either. He was worth millions and, after his divorce from his first wife, he started showing up regularly in gossip columns, which mentioned he was dating Lyn Revson, the former wife of cosmetics king Charles Revson, in addition to Barbara Walters, as previously noted.

"He's become far more polished in recent years," Walters was quoted in the article as saying. "I think some of his friends pulled him aside and said, 'Alan, take off the pinky ring.'"

As Greenberg had, a few months before the article appeared, celebrated his fortieth year at the firm—the typically idiosyncratic celebration lasted fourteen minutes and included videos of Greenberg performing magic tricks, the presentation to him of a huge box of cigars, and the comment from him that he "has never wanted to get up and go to work more than I do now"—the article naturally turned to the subject of who would succeed him as the leader of the firm. "At 61, Greenberg shows no sign of stepping down, and there is no mandatory retirement age," the piece said. "But he is so completely in charge, and so essential to the functioning of the firm, that it is hard to imagine Bear Stearns without him." The *Times* made no mention of the brewing power struggle between Cayne and Greenberg and suggested that with Greenberg, Rosenwald, and Cayne so close in age, the next leader of the firm would likely be someone from below their ranks. Cayne made only a cameo appearance in the article.

Four months later, Cayne had his star turn in the *Washington Post*. It was the first substantive article that appeared about him outside of Truscott's bridge columns in the *Times*. But, of course, bridge was the article's hinge. The article revealed that Cayne had made nearly $4 million in 1988 and was worth more than $30 million in Bear stock but still managed to be "out the door before 5 P.M." on most days to play bridge, as he had most of his adult life. The paper left it to Chuck Burger, Cayne's longtime bridge partner, to explain the secret to Cayne's success. "He is tenacious," Burger said. "He gets a bad result and just swallows it and gets on to the next hand. He never gives up. It is war."

Not everyone "loves or admires Jimmy Cayne," the *Post* allowed, "and his calculating, political style and tough bottom-line orientation" rubbed many people the wrong way and caused departures from the firm. But there was no question, the paper continued, about the "excellent relationship" that Cayne had with Greenberg. The *Post* even stated flat-out that "Cayne today is viewed as a complementary, non-threatening second-in-command."

A LESS POLITICALLY useful piece of PR came out in a December 1989 profile of Cayne that appeared in the short-lived *M* magazine. He made a number of comments that were critical of women at the bridge table and on Wall Street. "[B]ridge is a man's game at the competitive level," he said. "Sixty to 70 percent of the people who play bridge are women, but all of the top players are men. I'm not being chauvinistic; it's just keeping score. . . . Take a look at Wall Street. Wall Street is stress, highly emotional, and loaded with rejection. You have to be able to survive that. That's perhaps why women haven't achieved the record that they have in other areas. You don't see many women selling securities. When a guy says on the phone to a guy, 'I don't want you to bother me again; I find you to be really stupid,' a woman taking that probably isn't going to handle it as well. She'll probably have to go to the ladies' room and dab her eyes. It's the same way in bridge. At a certain emotional level, women perform not as well as men." Cayne's comments caused much consternation around Bear Stearns, especially since, as with many other Wall Street firms, there had never been—nor ever would be—a woman among the seniormost executives running the firm. When the *M* article came out, Cayne went into damage control mode and wrote the firm's employees: "I sincerely apologize to everyone for the totally false impression given by the article and assure you I disagree with its contents." He also said the quotations in the article were "fabricated, distorted or taken out of context." But Duncan Christy, the reporter, told *Fortune* that Cayne's comments were transcribed from a tape and were "meticulously accurate."

Allegations about how Cayne treated women and the press would dog him throughout his career from then on. "To escort visitors to meetings," the *Wall Street Journal* reported in 1993, "the firm this year staffed its Park Avenue headquarters with models seductively clad in short skirts. After some women executives complained, Bear clothed the models—dubbed 'geisha girls' because senior executives hatched the idea after a trip to Asia—more conservatively." At a meeting at the end of 2007 in his office with Lesley Goldwasser, one of the very few high-ranking women at Bear, and two leading private-equity executives, he looked at Goldwasser and then said to the two clients: "And she's not too bad to look at either."

Vicky Ward, a writer for *Vanity Fair* and other publications, wrote the following about Cayne in the *London Evening Standard* two weeks after the firm collapsed: "Cayne is a man of vast appetites, an online poker addict who I found to be a self-aggrandising tyrant when I met him six years ago. At that time he lied to me baldly about a story I was working on, bragged about his poker and flirted with me, showing off Bear's sumptuous offices. When later confronted with documents that proved he'd lied, he went berserk and resorted to name-calling." But she found him to be "charming, likeable but clearly a rogue" and could not believe that he was the CEO of a major Wall Street securities firm. "He had all the time in the world for me," she said. "And he also just spent hours playing poker on his computer screen." Cayne said Ward's account of their meeting was "delusionally false."

BY THE END of 1990, Wall Street was convulsed by the credit crunch that had started after the 1987 crash and then accelerated two years later after the failure to complete the financing for the $6 billion effort to take United Airlines private in a so-called employee buyout. Firms such as Drexel Burnham, Salomon Brothers, and First Boston that had used their own balance sheets to make expensive but lucrative bridge loans to leveraged-buyout firms to finance buyouts now found themselves in a struggle for their survival. Not Bear Stearns. Bear had eschewed the whole bridge loan craze. And its 1990 financial results reflected the wisdom of that decision.

Bear Stearns, at that time, also was one of the most profitable firms on the Street. The top executives, in particular Greenberg and Cayne, were making eye-popping amounts of money. In the fiscal year ended June 1991 (Bear kept changing its fiscal year end over time), the thirteen top Bear Stearns executives received an average compensation of $2.8 million, up 25 percent from the year before. Greenberg's cash compensation for the year increased to $5.3 million, from $4.2 million the year before. During 1991, the firm's stock price had more than doubled, to around $15.50 per share, and many of the executives sold some of their shares in the market.

Greenberg sold around 18 percent of his holdings, for $9.2 million. Cayne sold no stock. "The people who sold still have an awful lot of stock, and all they're doing is diversifying," he said. "The stock, at roughly one and a half times book value, is very cheap and I think it's going to go higher."

The next fiscal year would be even better. The firm reported record earnings of $275 million in the year ended June 30. "It was a record breaker and all of us should feel proud," Greenberg wrote. "Bear Stearns has never been stronger or positioned as beautifully as we are at this moment. . . . This place is rocking and our job is to keep it rolling. Everything is going our way." He made no mention of the astronomical compensation he and Cayne were about to receive, of $15.8 million and $14.7 million, respectively, putting them on a par with the co-CEOs of Goldman Sachs and some 25 percent above the pay of Merrill Lynch CEO William Schreyer. The difference, of course, was that both Goldman and Merrill Lynch had made more than $1 billion in net income that year. Graef Crystal, an executive compensation expert, said that while he liked Greenberg personally, his 1992 pay was "way too much. When they take these monster pay packages, they're draining huge amounts of profits from the firm." But Greenberg was unapologetic, citing the firm's formula for the compensation for the senior executives. "I can't make any apologies," he told USA Today. "The deal was laid out. What do you want me to do? Take dumb pills and not make money for the firm?"

A few months later, after ongoing criticism of their pay packages, Greenberg and Cayne decided to revise the formula for paying the executive committee, effectively reducing their pay by about 15 percent if the firm's earnings continued to increase. "We felt it was the fair thing to do," Greenberg said. Cayne called the change "fine-tuning" because "it looks like the compensation might have been higher than it should be." But the change didn't matter. In 1993, Cayne and Greenberg made even more money—$15.8 million each—despite the revised formula. The reason? The firm had net income of $362.4 million, 23 percent higher than the record profits of the year before. "We lowered the bonus formula because we wanted to do the right thing," Greenberg said. "But we have a problem—we keep making money."

By the summer of 1993, Greenberg was sixty-five years old and Bear Stearns was making money hand over fist. Although the firm had no mandatory retirement age—Greenberg said once that it was "ninety-two years old"—Cayne, then fifty-nine, decided the time had come for Greenberg to relinquish the title of CEO to him. A major battle ensued between the two men. Cayne said Greenberg knew that both the board of directors and the executive committee were unanimous that the time had come for Cayne to take over. According to Cayne, "I said, 'Look, I'm supposed to go to Thailand, trying to get a deal. I'm not going until you give me your decision. If your decision is not stepping down, then, of course, we have a different deal. We have war. My suggestion is just do it.' He ended up doing it, not particularly gracefully, but he did it."

On July 13, Bear announced that Cayne would become CEO. The *Times* noted that his company biography "devotes 10 lines to his achievements at Bear Stearns [and] 13 lines to his achievements at the bridge table." But the succession plan was very unusual by Wall Street standards, since the old king, Greenberg, would still be around as a member of the executive committee, as head of the risk committee, and as chairman of the board of the company. The *Times* noted that Greenberg ruled "with a growl and a smile" and "would remain the final authority at Bear Stearns."

The first rule of thumb on Wall Street is that if you are planning a coup d'état, above all else be sure to complete the job. Like George H. W. Bush's fateful decision not to invade Baghdad and take out Saddam Hussein during the first Gulf War, Cayne's decision not to take off Greenberg's head when he had the chance would have consequences, too. Cayne chalked up the reason Greenberg remained to the "synergy" that existed between the two men—the ultimate opportunistic salesman needed the ruthless trader. "I don't take cred for what happened," he said of the years of Bear's increasing profitability. "I think synergistically the combination of him being a merchant—like a midwestern storekeeper, which he was, which his dad was—and of him having a discipline that on paper doesn't make much sense, but in reality it's pretty much a good way to go, which is take your losses. But there isn't anybody that will tell you he's an honest guy. There isn't anybody who will tell you that he's sincere. There isn't anybody that would tell you they choose him as their best man, or best friend, or one who they would have lunch with or go on a trip with, or socialize with, or whatever. They don't exist. He had one friend—me."

Cayne's promotion to CEO came and went without any of Greenberg's internal memoranda mentioning it. But Greenberg remained a ubiquitous presence at the firm, in the way that Deng Xiaoping remained powerfully behind the scenes in China following his supposed relinquishing of power in 1989. "Every time there was a monthly meeting of the senior executives of the firm, the senior managing directors, Jimmy would get up in front of everybody and talk and Ace would get up and sit next to him," explained one former Bear executive. "Just the two of them. The same way that he did when he was chairman and CEO. He wouldn't give it up. At one point, Jimmy had him not go up onstage and Ace got very upset and he insisted on going up." Someone who knew both Cayne and Greenberg well found them to be nearly perfect opposites of each other. "Ace is a very peculiar character," he said. "He's extremely good at formalities—addressing people properly, opening doors for ladies, returning calls promptly—but he's the opposite of a warm guy. He's very good at formalities in the same way that the president of the United States is very good at formalities. But people who really knew him knew that he was not a very warm guy, not even a nice guy. But it didn't matter. He was reliable in a business context. He always showed up to work at the same time. He had lunch at the same time. He returned phone calls promptly. He didn't like to listen but he'd go through some of the formalities. Jimmy was the opposite. He could be extraordinarily engaging if he tried to be and always listened and was very smart politically. Ace could be brutal. He was condescending in private and brilliant in public."

AS CAYNE MANEUVERED—a word he detests to describe his rise; he prefers "ascended"—his way to the top of the firm, he began to reshape it more and more in his image. Understandably, Cayne's appointment as CEO also thwarted the dreams—or expectations—of the younger members of the executive committee who hoped, as the *Times* had implied in its 1989 profile of Greenberg, that the firm's politburo would reach down to one of them to find a new leader for the firm, instead of choosing either Cayne or Rosenwald, who were just a few years younger than Greenberg. It was akin to the hope that many in England have that Prince William and not his father, Prince Charles, will become king upon the death of Queen Elizabeth II. Many of these men left the firm in the years leading up to Cayne's appoinment as CEO or in the years just after. Denis Coleman Jr., Bill Michaelcheck, and John Sites at one time or another ran the firm's powerful fixed-income division, where by far the bulk of the firm's revenues were generated. As a result, whoever was at the top of that division no doubt thought he had a clear shot at—or deserved—the chance to run the firm. There is little question that Cayne, a retail broker, felt threatened by these younger executives who were responsible for the bulk of the firm's revenues and profits and were making that money in a language and in a way Cayne barely understood. "It was very tightly controlled at the executive committee level," a longtime Bear executive said. "The number of people that were admitted to the inner circle of the firm were very, very small and they had to have a very similar mindset about what it took to be named a very senior member. There were people who felt that they would not advance quickly enough. A contrasting model might be a Goldman model where people's careers developed, they become senior people, and they leave the firm and they go into government or service and they make room for people. The Bear model was that when people achieved executive committee membership—with an override on 20 percent of the firm's profits—they defended that position as strongly as they could. One of the ways that they defended that position was by making it difficult for very talented, slightly less senior people to succeed." Coleman left in 1989 to become a vice chairman of a discount brokerage. Michaelcheck left in 1992 to start Mariner Capital, a multibillion-dollar hedge fund. Sites left in 1995 to "spend more time wth his family." When Michaelcheck left, Cayne appointed Sites the co-head of fixed income with a young superstar trader named Warren Spector. When Sites left, Spector became the sole head of fixed income. Whether these talented executives were pushed or jumped is not clear. Cayne said he forced none of them out.

Others have a more nuanced explanation for the evisceration of those coming up fast in the Bear hierarchy. "Jimmy and Ace's view was there was always going to be another guy," explained a former Bear executive. "There always was another guy. There was Denis Coleman, then Bill Michaelcheck, then John Sites, then Warren Spector. . . . Neither one of them ever believed that any individual person mattered or anyone who left mattered, or that they even made a mistake when someone left or when they passed on an opportunity." Added another former partner: "We all got rich. Was Ace—who I loved—greedy? Sure. He was greedy. And Jimmy. Right? And the third guy? There was never a third guy. They always got rid of the third guy."

Paul Friedman had a ringside seat for Cayne's seriatim and ruthless eviscerations of Friedman's bosses in the fixed-income division. "He forced out over the years a list of extraordinarily bright people—who could have provided big amounts of leadership—because they threatened him," said Friedman, who now works for Michaelcheck at Mariner Capital. "My first boss, Denis Coleman, who when I got there was head of fixed income, was viewed by many as the ultimate successor to what was then Ace and Jimmy, but Jimmy was already taking command. He was forced out for getting in Jimmy's way. I was young enough at this time [that] I never quite understood it, other than I worked for Denis, and he walked in one morning and said, 'I'm retiring,' and I said, 'How come?' And he said, 'I'm not talking about it,' and he left the same day. Following him was Bill Michaelcheck, forced out by Jimmy in a to-do over compensation, partnership points, hierarchy, succession, who knows? Eased out. Whoever was the head of fixed income, he always took the number two and strengthened them, and used him to push out the head. Then the number two would become the number one, and he'd find somebody else to use them to push out the one ahead. The last before the end was John Sites. He used Warren to push John out. Ultimately, John quit. Warren then became head of the place, and somehow he and Jimmy worked out a truce, because Warren must have told Jimmy he was willing to be the number two until Jimmy was ready to leave, and that they were going to work on this together. And right up until the end he did nothing other than strengthen Warren. Jimmy was a big advocate of Warren—until he wasn't."

Cayne made sure to know what was going on politically around the firm before he made his moves. "Warren was the up-and-coming wonder kid, superstar trader, head of the mortgage department, and there was a point where the two of them became effectively co-heads of fixed income and rivals, and John was more in Ace's camp and Warren was Jimmy's protégé, and the two of them didn't get along," said Friedman. "It was tense. There was a lot of tension about how all of this is going to play out. I started getting calls Friday from Jimmy's office. 'Come on down, let's chat,' Cayne said to me. Ten years ago, there's no reason I should be chatting with Jimmy Cayne. We'd talk—'How are things? What's going on on the trading floor?'—and what I realized after a time was he was looking for the inside scoop on the Warren and John thing, and it got really uncomfortable, because I like Warren, and we got along well and we were friendly. But at the time I didn't work for him. I worked for John Sites, who had been wonderful to me, and it was really, really awkward. I did a probably bad job of disentangling myself from it, but I basically stopped answering Jimmy's questions. He then one day was kind of curt, and I never got called again, so he stopped. He stopped inviting me down for cigars." (Friedman didn't smoke.)

CHAPTER 20

THE MATH WHIZ AND THE BASEBALL STAR

Cigars have been as much a part of the stage set of Wall Street as private jets and bespoke Savile Row suits. At Bear Stearns, Savile Row suits were not so much part of the PSD culture, but private jets and cigars were nothing short of ubiquitous on the executive committee. To be sure, Greenberg smoked cigars around the office—*Cigar Aficionado* ranked him seventy-first among the one hundred top cigar smokers of the twentieth century, between George Gershwin and *Seinfeld* actor Michael Richards; the "best deal" he "ever made was one that kept him supplied with cigars (courtesy of Ron Perelman) for quite a while"—but for Jimmy Cayne, a cigar was like a sixth digit. "No Wall Street CEO has smoked more cigars," Charlie Gasparino, the CNBC reporter, wrote about Cayne in *Trader Monthly*. In March 1992, Greenberg reminded everyone at the firm about the smoking policy. "No smoking anywhere at Bear Stearns except in your own office with the door closed," he wrote. "There will be no exceptions—unless you have worked at Bear Stearns more than 43 years." Despite the policy, there were numerous reports of both Cayne and Greenberg smoking cigars in the corridors and in the elevators, even going so far as to flick their ashes on the floor of the elevators on their way out. When, in 2003, New York City mayor Michael Bloomberg banned smoking in all office buildings and restaurants, Cayne alone continued to smoke cigars in his office and the surrounding environs. "He smoked, and you inhaled them in his office." Paul Friedman remembered what it was like for him to go into Cayne's office. "You'd come out, and you'd smell of them." Friedman said that "for people who smoked them, I think he was fairly generous with sharing them."

As with everything he put his mind to, Cayne had a passion for cigars. One day, as a favor to Fares Noujaim, a vice chairman of Bear Stearns, Cayne agreed to have a meeting with a high school friend of Noujaim's from Lebanon. "He knows a lot about Bear Stearns," Noujaim told Cayne. "He knows a lot about Jimmy. He'd like to meet you." After spending a "delightful" thirty minutes together, Noujaim's friend gave Cayne the most incredible gift he had ever received. It was a cigar, but one with no identifying features, such as a label. "I take one puff and I never tasted anything like this," Cayne recalled. The draw was as smooth as silk. Cayne had to know more. He became obsessed with finding where the cigar came from and—more important—getting himself a steady supply. He called Noujaim. "You and I got great history," Cayne told Noujaim. "In our lifetime, you've asked me five thousand things. I have delivered five thousand times. I'm asking you for one thing. I want the name of the cigar." With the name, Cayne figured he could get himself the cigar in Switzerland, where many aficionados buy Cuban cigars.

After two weeks, Noujaim told Cayne that the cigars had come from the private stock of the prime minister of Lebanon. "I can't find out the name of the cigar," Noujaim told him, "but I'm going to Lebanon and I might be able to make a deal to get some cigars." Now obsessed, Cayne persisted in his quest. He remembered there was an employee in the firm's commodity department who was Cuban and whose family owned a tobacco farm, so he invited the fellow up to his lair. "He takes one puff," Cayne said. "He said, 'I never smoked anything like this.' I said, 'And so is it Cuban?' He said, 'Oh, yeah, it's Cuban, but the draw, Jimmy, the draw. Where did you get this?' I said, 'It's a long story.'" Cayne asked the guy to research all the different Cuban cigar manufacturers, but the source could not be found. He remained hooked on the cigars, though, and buys a regular stash through sources in Lebanon. The cigars cost him $150 each, about four times the price of a regular high-quality Cuban cigar. "Sort of stupid," he said, "but they got a fish on the line. I don't know how many other people in the world they got like me, but I'm sure they got a few. They just get cigars from this one source. And it's like oil. Whatever the price is, the price is."

CAYNE ALWAYS PRIDED himself on divining and lassoing talent. He did it by relying on his gut. If he was interviewing someone and got a good feeling, he would offer the person the job on the spot. If he noticed an unusual capability or talent in someone who already worked at the firm, he would elevate him within the organization to a position of power and authority. This had the benefit of making such people loyal to Cayne, sometimes to a fault. He was a man who made loyalty his litmus test: Loyal partners would never sell a share of stock, loyal partners would never consider a higher-paying job at another firm, loyal partners would respect his decisions. He was not a boss who communicated through memos or by walking around. Rather, he prided himself on spending the time—usually in his office—to make a personal connection with his partners to help them solve the problems brought to his attention. This approach led to the inevitable collateral damage, of course, with longtime employees—among them Coleman, Michaelcheck, and Sites—leaving the firm in the wake of his ascension. "His biggest problem was that as he became more powerful," explained a former Bear senior managing director, "you get to be more and more in a bubble and you need to be more analytical. The information coming to you comes to you differently and you need to have a keener understanding of it and of what someone's saying. And he didn't, he just wanted to go on his gut."

Warren Spector, a cerebral and highly self-assured former national high school bridge champion, was one of the people Cayne spotted and then nurtured. Spector was a trader in the fixed-income department when Cayne marked him for future greatness. "What appealed to me is this guy's making a lot of money," Cayne said. "I got to find out what he's doing. I found out that whatever desk he was on, in the mortgage department, that desk did better than any other desk. So this guy obviously was capable. He was lucky to have somebody like me who could notice him and move him up the food chain, which I did."

Spector grew up in suburban Chevy Chase, Maryland. In high school, he was on both the math team and the bridge team, and was the president of both during his junior and senior years; he also played on the chess team and the table tennis team. After his sophomore year, Spector took a year's sabbatical to play bridge. In 1976, the American Contract Bridge League named him the Scholastic King of Bridge. That fall, after graduating from high school, he matriculated at Princeton but after one semester moved on to St. John's College in Maryland. At St. John's, Spector was enrolled in the school's famous Great Books curriculum, which he loved. He also studied Latin and Greek. He gave up playing bridge because he did not want to become a bridge teacher or a bridge professional. He wanted to have a normal life.

After getting an MBA at the University of Chicago in 1983, he took a job at Bear Stearns because of the quality of the people he met there—in particular Coleman and Michaelcheck—and because the firm would allow him to start on a trading desk immediately rather than work as an analyst. He liked Coleman and

Michaelcheck immediately because they were both smart and hands-on. He would pointedly tell people: "Bridge had nothing to do with it at all."

Spector made a wise choice and in short order, as he said often, "catapulted" up the ranks of the firm far more quickly than he would have anywhere else. Four months into his career at Bear Stearns, a serendipitous "moment arrived that would make his career," according to Bloomberg. Chuck Ramsey had just finished a big trade, and Michaelcheck and Ramsey were discussing it. As Ramsey later told Bloomberg, Michaelcheck then made "a snap decision. He looked around the room and saw Warren Spector standing nearby, and he said, 'Warren, come over here.' Warren walked over, and [Michaelcheck] says, 'You now work for Chuck.' That's how Warren Spector got on the mortgage desk." He was an instant success. He became a senior managing director at twenty-seven, four years after he joined the firm, making him somewhat of a legend on Wall Street. He was invited to join the management committee (what used to be called the compensation committee) in 1990 and then the executive committee in 1992, at age thirty-four. Spector was one of the youngest senior executives on Wall Street and one of its most glamorous, having married actress Margaret Whitton, star of *Major League* and *9½ Weeks*.

He knew Greenberg a little from the weekly risk committee meetings, but he didn't meet Cayne until 1990, when he joined the management committee. "He called me because I [had] played bridge [in high school] and he had seen my name as being a star at Bear Stearns," Spector once said. "But he didn't know [if] I was [still] a bridge player. He called me up and said, 'Are you a bridge player?' I said, 'I used to be.' So bridge was something that he, Ace, and I all shared and talked about." Said Cayne, with some pride, about first discovering Spector: "Suddenly out of nowhere there's a bridge player at Bear Stearns on the bond desk."

CAYNE ALSO DECIDED that there was something special about Alan D. Schwartz, an athletic and rangy former professional baseball pitcher who held a variety of positions at the firm before becoming head of Bear's fledgling investment banking effort and one of its highest-profile M&A bankers. Schwartz was born in Bay Ridge, Brooklyn, the son of a Jewish traveling salesman and a Presbyterian housewife from Kansas. When he was a toddler, the family moved out of New York City to Wantagh, on southwestern Long Island, near Levittown. When Schwartz was a teenager, his father inherited some money and started a finance company, but as interest rates soared during the Carter administration, that proved poor timing and the business failed. His mother would pick up odd jobs in the community, as a bookkeeper or the manager of the local bowling alley.

Schwartz was a highly touted high-school pitcher and thought about becoming a professional right out of high school. He ended up going to Duke on a baseball scholarship, and in the process passed up his first opportunity to go to the major leagues.

By his own admission, Schwartz wasn't much of a student, but he was an amazing pitcher with a phenomenal fastball. He could throw a ball more than 95 miles per hour. Unfortunately, he was also prone to injury. At one point, he tore the ligaments in his elbow and underwent rehab. Still, after his junior year at Duke, the Cincinnati Reds drafted him. The Reds were intoxicated by the prospect of his fastball, but to make sure he had major-league stuff, the team wanted its scouts to watch him pitch a complete nine-inning game before it would offer him a contract. At that moment, Schwartz's instinct for investment banking kicked in, and he started to negotiate with the Reds: He wanted to know how much his signing bonus would be so he could decide whether it would be worth his while to pitch the nine innings. They reached agreement on a signing bonus of around $15,000 (now that he was in college, his leverage had been reduced, since the Reds knew he wanted to start playing professionally), and Schwartz agreed to pitch the nine innings in a minor-league park about an hour from Durham, North Carolina.

He pitched beautifully into the ninth inning, when the batter hit a ball right back at him. He tried to field the ball but it ended up hitting him in the face, between the eyes. With blood splattering everywhere, he had to come out of the game. He was rushed first to the local hospital—which could do nothing for him—and then had to endure the hour's ride back to the Duke hospital to have the bones in his face repaired. Right after the incident he thought about somehow getting back out there and continuing to pitch, as a way of fulfilling his obligation to the Reds. But then he thought better of it, since he knew he wouldn't be pitching anymore that summer anyway. He came back to Duke for his senior year and resumed his pitching career, figuring he would have another chance for the big leagues after graduating.

But again he hurt his arm. The problem was that he could pitch a few innings and then his arm would swell up. If the swelling had gone down the next day, he could have been a dazzling late-inning reliever. But the swelling would persist for four or five days at a time, and he wasn't likely to be much use to any team with that problem. On one of the rides home from the hospital, he decided that he was not meant to have a career as a professional baseball player.

While at Duke, Schwartz occasionally sold insurance policies to individuals in his spare time to make some spending money. After graduating, he thought about selling insurance full-time, but the prospect of walking into a room and having everyone immediately wonder if he was going to try to sell them insurance was not for him. For the same reason, he decided he did not want to be a retail stockbroker. He thought he would be better off selling to institutional investors rather than to individuals. He had the itch for Wall Street.

After a series of jobs at smaller firms, Schwartz agreed to join Bear Stearns in Dallas in 1976. Schwartz had a great time in Dallas, what with the oil boom filling the pockets of people he hoped would be his clients. Then Ace called him. "I want you to come back to New York," Greenberg said. Schwartz told Greenberg that he liked Dallas. "Yeah, but I want you to come back and run research," Greenberg replied. Schwartz had noticed that his clients appreciated a well-conceived research report on a given company or industry. The problem, Schwartz realized, was that the clients were gravitating to the research provided by other firms, not Bear Stearns. "Our research sucked," a Bear partner said. Schwartz told Greenberg that the firm as a whole would not take research seriously until Greenberg took it seriously. Greenberg told Schwartz: "I said I'd get involved. I have. I've figured it out. You're the guy who knows what the clients want. Why don't you come up here and deliver that high-quality product to the clients."

Schwartz put himself in charge of writing about portfolio strategy—for instance, what investors should do when interest rates go up or down, or inflation is high or low. Then, in 1984, he hired Larry Kudlow, a former economist at the Office of Management and Budget during the first Reagan administration. Together, Schwartz and Kudlow traversed the country talking about the economy and how to profit from it. They were a big hit with clients. They were constantly in demand, especially since they provided their insights for free. One of their partners noticed and told Greenberg: "Boy, Alan and Larry are being run ragged. They're being asked to be everywhere and it's really hard." Greenberg called Schwartz and Kudlow into his office for what they thought would be his praise and sympathy. "Gee, I hear you guys are really in demand," he told them. His partners beamed. "Well, of course you are," he continued. "You're free. Start charging them for you to show up. Then you'll see who really wants you." They did what they were told. But all the travel took its toll on both men: Kudlow developed a high-profile addiction to drugs and alcohol (later, after Bear fired Kudlow for missing an important meeting with institutional investors, he admitted to his weaknesses in a weepy interview with the New York Times and then successfully overcame his addictions), and Schwartz got bored with all the travel and repeating the same ideas over and over again.

Then Schwartz got another brainstorm. A few months before the firm decided to go public in the summer of 1985, Schwartz suggested to Cayne and Greenberg that he join the investment banking department, which Rosenwald was running at the time. The two senior partners thought that was a great idea, and when another partner, Glenn Tobias, decided to retire, Cayne and Greenberg asked Schwartz to *run* the investment banking effort by himself. The firm's effort was minuscule on a relative basis, but Schwartz was determined to build it up. His first deal was to supervise the Bear Stearns IPO. Soon, though, he was captivated by the excitement of M&A deals.

Based on his experience in the research department, he believed he could study an industry and predict where future deals might happen. Schwartz knew that at other firms such as Goldman Sachs, Morgan Stanley, Lazard, and First Boston, the M&A bankers flitted from deal to deal and industry to industry using their knowledge of M&A tactics and valuation as their entrée. He decided that even though Bear Stearns was a mere blip in the M&A market and had very few clients with enough financial heft to carry off such deals, the firm could make inroads by focusing on a few industries, such as health care, media, telecom, technology, and defense, and meeting with the executives in those industries on a regular basis to present them with clever, insightful ideas about what companies they might want to think about buying and why. Schwartz was onto something long before the competition realized it. Slowly but surely, his business thrived.

Schwartz's first breakthrough came when he recognized in late 1986 that the drug company A. H. Robins, which had declared bankruptcy because of lawsuits related to a contraceptive product it manufactured, would be an excellent takeover candidate for American Home Products, another drug and consumer products company. Schwartz advised American Home Products on how a rescue of Robins might work and introduced one CEO to the other. In the end, American Home Products pulled away from the deal at the time and released Schwartz to represent a different client. Unfortunately for Schwartz, a year later American Home Products returned and bought Robins. He lost out on that deal, but he'd so impressed the management of American Home Products that it hired him to represent the company on its attempted acquisition of Sterling Drug, which ultimately was purchased by Kodak.

In 1987, just after the crash, Schwartz organized at the Ritz-Carlton Hotel in Laguna Niguel, California, the first of what became twenty-one annual media industry conferences where he would bring together the CEOs of the major and not-so-major media conglomerates. Schwartz would interview them, Charlie Rose–style, or put them on panels together and let them all talk about the state of the industry, all for the benefit of Bear's clients, bankers, and investors. This was before it was common for Wall Street to host industry research conferences for investors. Obviously, the idea for the conference grew out of his time running

Bear's research department as well as from his strategy for winning M&A mandates. The closest comparison to what Schwartz was doing with the conference was the famous Allen & Co. weeklong retreat for moguls that the firm has held every summer in Sun Valley, Idaho, since 1983. Because of the similarities between the two shindigs, Schwartz became known by the nickname of "Alan and Co." Eventually, Schwartz moved the Bear Stearns media conference to the Breakers, in Palm Beach.

At one of those Allen & Co. Sun Valley affairs, the deal that ultimately made Schwartz's career was hatched—Walt Disney Company's $19 billion blockbuster acquisition of Capital Cities/ABC in August 1995. Although the bankers involved—Bear Stearns, Allen & Co., and Wolfensohn & Co.—did little negotiating and only provided fairness opinions after the fact, the prestige of being involved in the deal was momentous. More incredible was the fact that none of the big M&A powerhouses at the time were hired as advisors on the deal.

Schwartz had made it to the big time. Soon enough he and his team found themselves with a role in some of the biggest and most important mergers of all time. He would become a key advisor to TimeWarner and Verizon. "When he started with the strategy, he couldn't get anybody to believe in it," one of Schwartz's colleagues said. "So none of the senior guys he inherited wanted to spend any time on large-cap companies, because they thought it was a waste of time. From the [perspective of the] historical Bear Stearns franchise, it was. His powers of persuasion were not great. But we started seeing that we were accepted as an M&A advisor on big transactions, because we'd been around the media industry and the health care industry and had a reputation in it." Schwartz joined the firm's executive committee in 1989.

IN NOVEMBER 1993, Michael Siconolfi wrote an anecdote-filled 2,700-word front-page article in the *Wall Street Journal* peeling back the curtain on the firm's quirky, results-oriented culture. He was one of the paper's Wall Street reporters and would later—much to Cayne's chagrin and infuriation—influence a new generation of *Journal* reporters, such as Charlie Gasparino and Kate Kelly, in their highly critical coverage of Bear Stearns. In this article, Siconolfi compared Bear Stearns's opportunistic scrappiness to that of the Oakland Raiders, the bad boys of the NFL. Front and center was Howie Rubin, who, despite having been fired from Merrill Lynch for losing what Siconolfi pegged as $377 million, had been snatched up by the firm. "Its bet paid off," Siconolfi wrote. Rubin's mortgage bond trading desk supposedly made some $150 million in profit in the fiscal year that ended in June 1993 and helped the firm make a record $362 million profit, allowing Cayne and Greenberg to take home $15.9 million each and Spector to get $11.7 million. "He's a superstar," Cayne told the paper. Siconolfi explained that making such contrarian bets was part of the firm's DNA. That explained the hirings of Rubin; of Don Mullen, a former junk-bond salesman at the defunct Drexel Burnham; of Mustafa Chike-Obi, a mortgage trader fired from Kidder Peabody because of a sexual harassment charge; and of investment bankers such as Curt Welling, from First Boston, and Dennis Bovin and Mike Urfirer, from Salomon Brothers and First Boston, respectively. Urfirer brought with him a $2 billion assignment to represent Martin Marietta on its attempted acquisition of Grumman. Bovin and Urfirer then teamed up on Raytheon's $2.3 billion acquisition of E-Systems, earning a $14 million fee. Then Martin Marietta hired the duo to advise on its $10 billion merger with Lockheed, earning a $17 million fee. William Mayer, the former CEO of First Boston, observed that Bear Stearns "has been willing to take more risk on people and not let reputation or image be as much of a factor as other firms. Bear has been doing it quite successfully, as the Raiders have done over the years."

Much was made in the article about the firm's zealous and elaborate risk management apparatus. There were the weekly Monday afternoon risk committee meetings, chaired by Greenberg, where traders were put through a "cold sweat" about how big their positions were and why they still held them on the firm's books. Greenberg received reports that showed the firm's inventory of securities that remained unsold after ninety days—a clear violation of his father's dictum about merchandise and one that Greenberg himself was supposedly adamant about not permitting. "You can come in and announce you've had the best week of your life," Spector said, "and Ace will say, 'You've got $50 million of bonds that are four months old—that's terrible. It's out of control. . . . You don't get to gloat.'" Even Rubin conceded he "felt like more of an island" at Merrill, but that at Bear, "if I take a larger position, I can grab" members of senior management to discuss it. "At no time do they not know what risks I'm taking on." Mullen, the former Drexel trader, was head of the high-yield and distressed securities business. "They gave me what I always wanted—my own business," he said. "If you make money, you can run your business any way you want to." Concluded Schwartz about the Monday risk committee meeting: "You've got to go there every Monday and have these guys look you in the eyes. This isn't other people's money."

Then there were the firm's spies, to which Greenberg had occasionally referred in his internal memoranda (such as the one from February 1987) and which Siconolfi now made public. He called them "ferrets," and they had nicknames: the "snoop" was Ken Cowin, and the "hawk" was Kenneth Edlow. The "chief ferret," Michael Winchell, was once a mortgage trader. His own children called him "the weasel" because of his responsibilities at Bear Stearns. Winchell said his team had to be "savvy" and "rely on instinct" to catch wrongdoing at the firm, or what appeared to be wrongdoing. "You can see risk on people's faces, you can see problems on people's faces," Winchell said. "If there's a problem, my guys will find it nine times out of ten." When Bill Montgoris, the firm's CFO, deposited a check from another partner into his bank account, Cowin asked for an explanation. (The man owed Montgoris some money.) The ferrets helped to catch Michael Sidoti, a Bear trader and eight-year veteran who had allegedly mismarked an option position to the tune of $200,000 and then tried to cover up the incident. "The definition of a good trader is a guy who takes losses," Greenberg said. "The definition of an ex-trader is one who tries to cover up a loss." In Sidoti's case, there was "no appeal, no nothing," he said. "You're out. O-U-T."

The bottom-line message of the article was that the firm just wanted to make money for itself, its senior executives, and its shareholders. Siconolfi summed up: "The way to rise within the firm is simple: Make money." One of the best ways to do that, Greenberg and Cayne discovered over the years, was to be vigilant about costs. Stephen Cunningham, then co-head of international investment banking, remembered once when he flew back into Kennedy Airport from Mexico with Greenberg, Cunningham arranged with his secretary to get cars to pick them up. "My secretary ordered you a car," Cunningham told Greenberg. "Why?" Greenberg replied. "Are the yellow cabs on strike?"

CHAPTER 21

"WE'RE ALL GOING TO A PICNIC AND THE TICKETS ARE $250 MILLION EACH"

As the economy began to recover dramatically toward the end of the first Clinton administration—and the amount of money Wall Street bankers, traders, and executives were making started to explode—Cayne's imprimatur on Bear Stearns slowly began to emerge. Unlike Greenberg, whose public persona of the gregarious showman was the antithesis of his ruthless, curt, and condescending private behavior, Cayne tended to be sharp-elbowed in both public and private, masked by a veneer of frat-boy camaraderie. Whereas Greenberg waited for Cy Lewis to die before taking over the firm, Cayne figured out all the political angles and pounced on Greenberg when he knew the odds were in his favor. Whereas Greenberg eschewed legal confrontations—for instance, against Jardine for backing out of the 1987 tender offer—Cayne preferred to make sure that legal threats were always a serious option if a deal or situation soured. He was not afraid of a macho confrontation. He observed that Greenberg was a bully—and he m well have been—but Cayne was every bit the bully, too. To b both men were able to wrap their worst behavior in a prett when it suited them, but both were ruthless when t called for it. And when it came to public relatio proved to be a world-class magician—right until never veered from the story line of him as the

By contrast, Cayne's cold calculation that he could manipulate and browbeat reporters into seeing the world his way fell short repeatedly, especially when he failed to censor himself or thought his charm would be a sufficient palliative.

But by far the biggest difference between the two men that would slowly but surely determine the firm's future path was that Cayne had been first—and relatively briefly—a retail broker and then, for the vast majority of his career at Bear Stearns, a manager of its people. He enjoyed having the power to figure out who got promoted when and who got paid what. And he was good at it. Unlike Greenberg, who kept his seat on the trading desk and the one as head of the risk committee and to some degree his finger on the pulse of the markets, Cayne had no more than an intuitive feel for the markets or for their growing complexity. For sure, he could decide when to buy or sell a stock, but when it came to understanding the calculus of and risks inherent in, say, a CDO-squared (that is, a collateralized debt obligation backed not by a pool of bonds and loans but by CDO tranches), well, that was a bridge too far. (In this, he was most certainly *not* alone among top Wall Street executives.) And, not surprisingly for a man who learned by listening and not by reading, he was no writer of notes of exhortation. In the Cayne regime, the quaint Greenberg memos slowly petered out. Instead, like Joe Torre in his Yankees heyday, Cayne preferred to believe he was managing a team of hand-picked superstars, and he expected them to perform. He also phased out Greenberg's practice of encouraging the "ferrets" to report the goings-on at the firm. Cayne

information the ferrets provided but, accord-
go and bring it up with the per-
ecessarily be as protected as the
l it with Ace." The consequences
ad—of their different personali-
soon become apparent.

war, truth is the first casualty,"
John Sites became the first major
me, along with the truth. Sites,
firm's mortgage-backed securities
vith a 20 percent market share on

Wall Street, abruptly resigned after fifteen years to "spend more time with his family," that famous euphemism. Sites had been paid $14.6 million in 1994 and around $8.5 million in 1995, reflecting a drop in the firm's earnings. Cayne, Greenberg, and Spector all publicly expressed their disappointment with Sites's decision. In truth, Sites left because Cayne had picked Spector to be sole head of the firm's powerful fixed-income division. "Warren is a very brilliant guy but very nervous," said one of his former partners. "Bites his nails down to the quick." In an impressive display of corporate unity, all sides stayed on the message that all this was really no big deal, including Sites. That he was leaving because of friction with Spector was "the furthest thing from the truth," he said. "I resigned because I wanted to be with my family. It's that simple." Sites said both Cayne and Greenberg were "shocked" at his resignation and asked him to reconsider. But he had made up his mind. Greenberg said that the notion of a power struggle was "absolutely untrue" and "to try to blow this up and make this into some kind of power struggle between Warren and John is totally ridiculous." There were other departures, too: Both Matthew Mancuso, who headed fixed-income sales, and R. Blaine Roberts, who was co-head of the structured transactions group, left in 1995.

THEN, IN SEPTEMBER 1995, another member of the firm's executive committee, Vincent "Vinny" J. Mattone, resigned unexpectedly to "pursue his own interests." He had been at Bear Stearns since 1979 and was in charge of the firm's sales and trading business. (He and Sites were the two largest individual Bear Stearns shareholders after Cayne and Greenberg.) "He was a very big fellow," said one of his former partners. "Both important and large. Both squared." A couple of years before he resigned, Mattone, who sported a tremendous girth, a gold chain, and a pinky ring, had wanted to join a new start-up hedge fund, Long-Term Capital Management—LTCM short—which was the brainchild of his former buddies at Brothers. John Meriwether, LTCM's founder and a famous bond trader, wanted Mattone to be the sixth partner, which was headquartered in Greenwich, Connecticut explained, Mattone came to him and said he join Meriwether. "I said, 'Vinny, are you nuts?'" Cayne remembered. "'You're on the executive committee here. You're making ten million bucks.'" (Actually, Cayne paid Mattone $9 million in 1993.) "'Are you crazy? You were a fucking clerk at Salomon. Now you're a member of the executive committee, co-head of fixed income. You're talking about making a bet. Nobody can make that bet.' He said to me, 'Okay, you're right.'"

Two years later, Cayne pushed Mattone right out the door. In 1995, he was the eighth fixed-income executive to leave the firm after the firm's earnings fell 38 percent in 1995, to $241 million, due to declines in bond prices. "Jimmy called Vinny towards the end of the year one time at his house," Paul Friedman said, "and told him he was taking his share way down, and Vinny complained, and Jimmy said, 'What are you going to do? Quit?' And Vinny said, 'I should.' And Jimmy said, 'What are you going to do, quit?' And Vinny said, 'I should.' And Jimmy went, 'So I hear you're quitting, right?' And basically goaded him into quitting. By the end of the conversation, Vinny had quit. Of all the people who left, he's the only one who ever told me how it went down. The others, you just never knew. But Vinny described it. He said he had actually come home. He was angry. He'd had a couple of drinks. He allowed Jimmy to goad him into quitting. This is my version of Vinny's version. He's dead. I don't know if it's true or not. But that was Vinny's version of the story."

※

A WEEK AFTER Cayne convinced Mattone to stay at Bear Stearns in-
⟨text obscured⟩ went to Cayne's office and told
⟨text obscured⟩ Cayne about the possibility of
⟨text obscured⟩ the billions of dollars it wanted
⟨text obscured⟩ s for the hedge fund when it
⟨text obscured⟩ ne that he would be happy to see
⟨text obscured⟩ net, and that the firm would be
⟨text obscured⟩ "To clear for Long-Term Capital
⟨text obscured⟩ ssignment that a clearance firm
⟨text obscured⟩ Meriwether, "so clearly I will do
⟨text obscured⟩ hat happen. He says, 'Well, that's
⟨text obscured⟩ consideration is we want to raise

some money.' I said, 'Okay, number one, you want to go with best in class. From the standpoint of this guy [Mattone] being your account executive at Bear Stearns, watching Long-Term Capital's account here, he's the head of fixed income or a co-head. He will treat you with kid gloves. He'll make your life pleasant, and also we'll have the best structure, best platforms, best rates, you name it, because we know you. He thinks you're family, good enough for me. The other part, the fund-raising, we don't do that. John, you're going to make the final decision. Why wouldn't you go with Merrill Lynch, who doesn't give a shit about clearing? They'd love the idea of raising money for you. And they're good at it. They've got seven billion clients, and they'll drop a few Long-Term Capital things into somebody's account and nobody'll ever know. They'll raise a couple billion dollars for you. And that wouldn't be a Herculean effort for us; that would be a nonstarter for us. So, get the best of both possible worlds.' He said, 'You got it.' Just as simple as that."

Cayne then negotiated with Meriwether what the clearance arrangement would be. Cayne told him that regardless of how much money Merrill raised for LTCM, the minute the fund's net asset value fell below $500 million, Bear Stearns would no longer clear trades for the fund. "That will be in our clearance agreement," Cayne told Meriwether. "He said, 'We can't live with that.' I say, "You got to live with that.' He said, 'We can't live with that.' I said, 'Well, then you can't have a clearance agreement. But we can have an institutional-client relationship, where I'm going to enforce the $500 million level.' He said, 'Okay, maybe we can talk you out of that over time.' They never could."

Cayne personally invested $10 million in LTCM, one of about eighty Wall Street heavyweights who were allowed to invest individually. He figured LTCM would make so much money the high fees being charged would not matter. In February 1994, the firm opened for business with $1.25 billion of investors' money. But from day one, LTCM wanted to be treated differently from other clients. They did not want to put up initial margin for their trades, which required a cash deposit equal to around 5 percent of the value of the securities being bought or sold. LTCM did not want to put down any initial margin at all. Bear's derivatives desk called Cayne and told him this news. "What?" Cayne said. "The Bank of England puts up initial margin. They don't put up initial margin?" Cayne felt he had been snookered but was willing to put up with making "razor-thin" profits from LTCM and "pulled out the red carpet" for the firm "because (a) it was a great assignment, (b) it was prestigious, and (c) whatever flow there was, you're going to be able to see the flow"—meaning that Wall Street firms could piggyback LTCM trades since they were able to see in advance the supposedly brilliant trades LTCM wanted to make and could then just copy them. "Let's not kid ourselves," Cayne said. "That's part of Wall Street." But, Cayne said, Bear Stearns did not piggyback on the LTCM trades. "We never even saw their flow," he said. "We never saw their swaps. We never saw any of it. We're just clearing. We march along in life, clearing." Bear Stearns made $30 million a year clearing trades for LTCM.

As has been well documented in Roger Lowenstein's bestseller, *When Genius Failed*, LTCM combined all of Meriwether's supposed trading expertise with the technical expertise of Nobel Prize–winning economists Robert Merton and Myron Scholes (the latter one-half of the duo that devised the widely used Black-Scholes option-pricing model)—and with the regulatory expertise of David Mullins, the vice chairman of the Federal Reserve Board, who resigned his position to join LTCM. It was a partnership designed to maximize the seduction of potential investors. Needless to say, LTCM was the envy of Wall Street—in the days before hedge funds were a dime a dozen—and firms rushed to do business with the hedge fund. LTCM's computer-driven investment strategy was to make so-called convergence trades, involving securities that were mispriced relative to one another, taking long positions on the inexpensive side of a trade and a short position on the expensive side of a trade. For the first two years, the strategy worked splendidly. Investor returns were around 40 percent during that period and the assets under management swelled to $7 billion. The original partners and investors were getting even richer.

Bear Stearns, too, was performing well as the markets improved in the mid-1990s, having recovered its balance in its fiscal year ended June 1996: Net income more than doubled, to $490.6 million, and the bonus pool for the top five executives reached a stunning $81.3 million. Cayne's pay more than doubled, to $20.4 million, as did the pay of Spector ($19.5 million) and Greenberg ($19 million). Schwartz's compensation nearly tripled, to $14.6 million. Siconolfi, writing about the management's windfall in the *Wall Street Journal*, noticed that the top five starters at Bear Stearns earned $23.3 million more in compensation than the entire twelve-man roster of the NBA champion Chicago Bulls. "Which goes to show, perhaps," he wrote, "that even in today's record-setting market, the Bears sometimes can beat the Bulls." At the firm's annual meeting for shareholders, in November, Greenberg extended Siconolfi's basketball metaphor. When asked by one shareholder whether there was any "ceiling" on management's compensation, Greenberg replied there was not. "Do you know how much Shaquille O'Neal makes?" he asked, referring to the then star center of the Los Angeles Lakers. "And the Lakers don't make any money." After the meeting, Greenberg pointed out that the two shareholders who had questioned the management compensation packages had been assuaged by his explanation of how it worked and "seemed very, very satisfied." He also noted that 91 percent of the non-employee voting shareholders approved of the pay plan. The next year, Bear's top five executives split between them even more money—$87.8 million—with Cayne once again walking off with the lion's share, $23.2 million.

BUT AS 1997 came to a close, cracks were beginning to appear in Bear's façade. First came a lengthy broadside in *Forbes,* written by Gretchen Morgenson (who would later move to the *Times*), questioning the firm's role in the demise of a small "bucket shop" brokerage by the name of A. R. Baron & Co. In the language of Wall Street a "bucket shop" was considered to be a shady brokerage firm that used aggressive telephone sales tactics to sell securities that the brokerage owned and wanted to get rid of—typically inferior investment opportunities or penny stocks—and were not particularly concerned with the consequences. Morgenson wrote how the failure of the diminutive Baron, in July 1996, had cost its customers some $22 million and, more important, had "laid bare a corner of the securities industry that is rarely seen but hugely profitable: processing trades for other firms." In delicious detail, Morgenson documented numerous nefarious allegations about the firm's clearing division, which was run by Richard Harriton, then sixty-one years old, and cleared more than a hundred thousand trades a day at that time. According to Morgenson, Harriton used to introduce himself to potential customers by saying, "I run the most profitable division of Bear Stearns and I'm the most powerful man on Wall Street in clearing." She described a number of the shady clients Bear cleared for in addition to A. R. Baron, including Rooney, Pace (closed down by regulators in 1987), D. Blech & Co. (the investment firm that went out of business in 1994, leaving investors with $200 million in losses), and Stratton Oakmont (closed by regulators in early 1997). "Right now," she wrote, "Bear Stearns is the clearing firm for at least 15 brokerages that are, if not full-fledged bucket shops, close to it."

Morgenson suggested that Bear Stearns kept Baron alive for more than a year after the firm was kaput, causing investors to lose millions on shady deals. She wrote that Harriton agreed to clear for Baron—after once kicking it out of Bear Stearns in 1992—as a favor to a Bear Stearns brokerage client with "sizable accounts" at the firm and who also had an investment in Baron. Baron's president, Andrew Bressman, used to take Harriton to New York Knicks basketball games, where they would sit together in his front-row seats next to film director Spike Lee. Morgenson also implied—using an anonymous source—that Harriton was receiving kickbacks from Baron in the form of proceeds from the sale of Baron's hot IPOs. Hannah Burns, a spokeswoman for Bear, said the firm would not comment for the story because of pending litigation. "Clearing is a very, very proprietary business for us, and we don't want the public knowing about it." Summed up Morgenson: "The whole situation stinks." A few months after the *Forbes* article appeared, on May 13, 1997, the Manhattan District Attorney's Office indicted Baron "on charges of being a criminal enterprise that used lies, unauthorized trades and theft to defraud investors of at least $75 million from 1991 to 1996," according to the *New York Times*. The DA's office arrested thirteen Baron executives, all of whom either pleaded guilty to charges or were found guilty at trial. Bear Stearns and Harriton quickly found themselves caught up in the Baron litigation and the myriad of derivative lawsuits associated with it. The DA's office, under the auspices of Assistant District Attorney John W. Moscow, also opened a two-year grand jury investigation into Harriton's behavior as head of the clearing business, and the SEC began an investigation into Bear's role in the Baron debacle. As with several other incidents over the years, the Baron litigation and the SEC's investigation would give Cayne another chance to showcase his skills of macho confrontation.

BUT IF THE Baron matter showed Cayne at his toughest and most intransigent, he was also capable of great charm, nuance, and negotiating skill in an effort to obtain a coveted prize. Nowhere were these Cayne attributes on finer display than in his two-year quest to wrest control of the square block of land at 383 Madison Avenue, between 46th and 47th Streets, in Manhattan—just down the street from Bear's headquarters at 245 Park Avenue—upon which he would erect what he thought would be a monument to the firm he was guiding to higher and higher profitability and importance on Wall Street. In the end, the building was simply a gold-plated monument to Cayne's ego.

By 1997, Bear Stearns was busting out of its headquarters at 245 Park. The firm had 8,300 employees in June 1997, up 32 percent from June 1993. Its lease was up in 2002, and its recent addition of another 100,000 square feet of space at 245 Park was merely an interim solution. The firm also had smaller offices in the area, including one at 575 Lexington Avenue. Cayne had made it known in real estate circles that he was looking to build a new headquarters building in midtown, although the other options included staying at a revamped 245 Park or finding another existing office building.

Bear had several different locations under consideration for constructing a new building. But 383 Madison, right in the heart of Manhattan and owned in a partnership by First Boston, the investment bank, and Saudi Arabia's powerful al-Babtain family, was the best site. "It's filled with homeless crackheads and whatever," Cayne said. "It's a blight. But it's perfect." At one point, the British developer Howard Ronson had had an option on the site, but his option ran out before he could find an anchor tenant, and so First Boston gave Bear Stearns a call. "I'd been spending a lot of time with Jimmy and we were sort of like comrades in arms in a way because he was becoming obsessed about this whole real estate thing now," explained Tom Flexner, a Bear vice chairman and head of its real estate group. "So maybe it was beginning to turn into his monument. I mean that respectfully. So we start negotiating with First Boston and I think we negotiated this $53 million price to buy the site." The idea was to tear down the Manhattan Savings Bank building that was there and put up a skyscraper that had been designed by Skidmore, Owings & Merrill. Cayne called up Allen Wheat, the CEO of First Boston, to negotiate a deal. "Look, I'm not in the real estate business," Cayne told Wheat. "I don't think you're in the real estate business, but I understand you have a property for sale. I understand that you have an interest in selling it at $53 million. Are you still interested?" Wheat said he was interested in selling. "So we can do this?" Cayne asked. They shook on a deal at $53 million.

Cayne then called up Flexner and told him the news.

"How much did you pay for it?" Flexner asked.

"How much did I pay for it?" Cayne replied. "You told me $53."

"Yeah, but Jimmy—" Flexner began.

Cayne interrupted. "Oh, I get your question," he said. "Could I have done it at $51.9? Could I have really scored? No. You gave me a number, I did the number. We're done."

At the end of the negotiations, First Boston had mentioned that the Saudis had a right of first refusal on the property, but assured Bear that the Saudis wouldn't exercise it because "they wanted out—they had been feeding this thing for years, and they wanted out." But the Saudis exercised their option in February 1996 and paid First Boston its share of the $53 million exercise price. That would have been the end of it, except that Cayne latched on to a clever idea. He and Flexner somehow figured out that the Saudis had not obtained the air rights over nearby Grand Central Station that would be needed for them to build a skyscraper on the site. So Bear Stearns bought an option on the air rights from billionaire Carl Lindner for around $10 million contingent on Bear Stearns getting control of the site. "This was the true mutual assured destruction kind of deal because if you buy the air rights and you can never cut a deal with the owner of the building, then you've just lost 100 percent of whatever you paid for the air rights because they're only good for that building," Flexner explained. "But they weren't that expensive and we could get an option on them for a few weeks or months or something. We could use that as leverage."

The Saudis' lawyers went ballistic. "This is manipulation," they told Flexner. "This is not right. We're going to sue you. These rights can only be conferred to our site. We control this site. This is tortious interference." At that threat, Cayne, for once, backed down. He decided to confer the air rights to the Saudis for $1 and never had to pay Lindner the $10 million. "That was viewed attractively by the Middle Eastern investors, what Jimmy did," Flexner said. With the air rights, the Saudis could build their tower but still needed an anchor tenant to occupy it. Bear Stearns was the natural first party to talk to, since everyone in Manhattan's cozy commercial real estate world knew that the firm's lease would soon be up at 245 Park. Cayne and the Saudis kept talking. At one point, Cayne sought the advice of Steve Roth, at Vornado Realty, on the best strategy for winning over the Saudis. Remembered Flexner: "Steve said, 'Just pop the guy another $20 and that'll do it.' I love how that's exactly what he said. I'll never forget it—'Pop the guy another $20.'" Cayne made an offer of around $60 million for the property, a quick $7 million profit to the Saudis. He thought progress was being made.

Then the Saudis stopped returning his calls. It turned out that Chase Manhattan Bank, headquartered just north of 383 Madison at 270 Park, had contacted the Saudis about buying the site. "Chase is much bigger, could maybe pay more, be a better credit, was global, so the Middle Eastern investors knew much more about them," Flexner said. "Jimmy thought he had this great kind of rapport going with the guy. But it looked like it was dying on the vine. Jimmy thought that he had lost the building and he was desperately afraid to tell anybody because Jimmy is like, 'Hey, this is what I'm doing. We're going to get this new building.' He's not playing his cards close to his chest. He got exuberant. Now he's thinking, 'Oh, I'm so embarrassed. This is huge.'"

The loss of the 383 Madison site meant that Bear Stearns would have to reengage with Brookfield about 245 Park. "In which case, they'll just nail us," Flexner said. Then out of the blue the Saudis called Cayne and said they wanted to talk, Flexner recounted. The two sides agreed quickly on a deal whereby Bear Stearns would get a ninety-nine-year ground lease for $90 million. What had turned the tide in Bear's favor was that the Saudis had come to 270 Park Avenue to have lunch with William Harrison, then the CEO of Chase Manhattan, and, according to Flexner, "Harrison didn't show up and sent a junior guy." That offended the Saudis, who killed the deal and came back to Bear Stearns—and also became private clients of the firm.

Cayne's outside advisor on the deal for 383 Madison was Fred Wilpon, the chairman of developer Sterling Equities and the owner of the New York Mets. Since 1993, Wilpon had been a member of the Bear Stearns board of directors. "It wouldn't occur to me to go somewhere else," Cayne said. In 1996, Bear paid a joint venture controlled by Wilpon $225,000 for consulting services related to 383 Madison. The next year, Bear paid the Wilpon joint venture a $2 million fee and agreed to pay the developers of 383 Madison—another Wilpon-controlled joint venture—a $12 million fee for developing the project plus a potential discretionary bonus of another $20 million if all went well. Wilpon's joint venture was paid $3.8 million in 1999, $4.4 million in 2000, $5.4 million in 2001, and millions more in 2002.

Part of the reason Wilpon got the Bear assignment was that he and his partner in the deal, Houston developer Gerald Hines, had built the building at 450 Lexington Avenue—the home of law firm Davis Polk & Wardwell—over the railroad tracks leading in and out of Grand Central. The Bear Stearns building would require the same engineering skills. Cayne took a keen interest in the nuts and bolts of the project. His background in the scrap iron business gave him insight into the cost of steel; he constantly monitored whether Bear was getting the best price. He also hired a man whose job it was to inspect all the invoices on the job; the inspector couldn't get along with anybody, so Cayne had to fire him. As the project was nearing completion, the top floors of the building developed a mold problem, caused, Cayne said, by lumber left exposed to the rain.

Bear rectified the problem of the mold, but Cayne was not happy. When the building was completed, according to Cayne, Wilpon made it clear to Sam Molinaro, the firm's CFO, that he still wanted the discretionary bonus.

Cayne told Molinaro to tell Wilpon to forget it. "This isn't like 'I delivered a building, I delivered it on time, I delivered it better than anybody who's ever delivered anything before,'" Cayne told his CFO. "Under those circumstances, there was probably going to be a bonus, even though he had a no-bid contract with a guy that caused us a fucking insane mold issue. I hold the general contractor responsible. That's not my job to go up there and put a tarp over wood. You go back to Wilpon and tell him if he writes us a letter that his company for the rest of its life—not his life, but the life of his company—indemnifies us against any action under the mold, then he gets the bonus." Cayne believed that the letter would be easy for Wilpon to write since the mold supposedly had been eliminated. But Wilpon never wrote the letter. "So there was no special bonus," Cayne said. "We're talking about twenty million bucks, and I wasn't fucking around." On July 1, 2003, Wilpon resigned from the Bear Stearns board. He and Cayne were no longer speaking.

When Wilpon completed 383 Madison in 2001 at a cost of around $500 million for the building itself and another $200 million for the inner technology and furnishings, it was a forty-seven-floor, 755-foot, octagonal building clad in granite panels and glass. At its top was a seventy-foot-tall glass crown that was illuminated at night. The building was named one of the best new skyscrapers of 2001. Some critics, though, panned it. "This is a building you wouldn't want to get anywhere near at a cocktail party," *New York* magazine said. "Dressed nearly head to toe in dour granite, and geometrically proper, it's stiff to the point of pass-out boredom. Out of character with SOM's [Skidmore, Owings & Merrill's] current work, the design recalls the firm's unfortunate postmodern interlude a decade ago." But Cayne loved it. To him, it was a playground and the culmination of his years of leading Bear Stearns to higher and higher profitability. It had become his monument to himself. "It's the nuts," Cayne said of the building. "It's the best site in the world. It was the best building in the world. It was a city within a city." And it was only thirteen blocks from his Manhattan apartment.

※

BY THE END of 1997, Cayne had announced the deal for 383 Madison and knew that the firm would soon break ground on its soaring new world headquarters. Closer to earth, though, Cayne found himself in the thick of a meltdown occurring at Long-Term Capital Management, his other baby. In September, even though LTCM had earned $300 million in one of its best months ever, "the firm's prospects were steadily dimming," according to Roger Lowenstein, because it was having trouble finding profitable trades in the shifting markets. On September 22, Meriwether wrote investors that the fund "had excess capital" and intended to return to investors all the profits made on the money invested in 1994 and all the money invested in the fund after that date. This amounted to a return of about half the fund's $7 billion in capital. The LTCM partners and employees kept all of their money in the fund. Investors saw this not as a lucky windfall—an idea hard to imagine today—but rather as if they were being deprived of water in Death Valley. They clamored to stay fully invested in LTCM, since the geniuses who'd founded the firm were minting money. But the firm turned them down. Of course, some exceptions were made for "big strategic investors" such as the Bank of Taiwan—and for Jimmy Cayne, the boss of LTCM's clearing broker. In 1997, LTCM earned a respectable 17 percent return for its investors, after fees. The performance was the worst of the firm's short life but hardly fatal. As promised, LTCM returned to its investors $1.82 for every dollar they'd invested, although their original investment stayed in the fund.

Meriwether's concern about the markets and LTCM's prospects proved prescient as 1998 unfolded. On August 17, Russia announced a devaluation of the ruble and a moratorium on the payment of $13.5 billion of its Treasury debt. Four days later, the full import of this decision hit world markets, and a massive flight out of risky investments, such as the debt and equity of emerging markets, into the supposedly less risky Treasury securities of the United States and Germany began immediately. "Minute by minute, Long-Term was losing millions," Lowenstein wrote. That Friday, LTCM lost $553 million in a single day, or 15 percent of its capital. At the start of the year, LTCM had had $4.67 billion in capital, but after the losses suffered on August 21, the firm's capital had been reduced to $2.9 billion. Mike Alix, who had recently joined Bear Stearns in December from Merrill Lynch and had helped to raise money from Asian investors for LTCM when he was at Merrill, was in charge of monitoring LTCM's credit at Bear. "The one name that came up in every conversation he had when he first got to the firm was Long-Term Capital," explained one of Alix's colleagues. "It wasn't that we were concerned about any risk that we knew about, but we were concerned that LTCM was gigantic, it was a big clearing client, and we didn't have any one person in the organization focused on understanding the risk that Bear Stearns bore from dealing with Long-Term Capital." Alix's first task was to put a team in place at Bear that would monitor the firm's interactions with LTCM. "We are the traffic cop in this gigantic, very busy intersection," this Bear executive continued. "We want to put some armor on." By August 1998, with the losses at LTCM mounting daily, Alix became increasingly concerned about the whole operation and called the fund's CFO, who reassured Alix that all was fine and that the securities that had declined in value were now actually a good buying opportunity. Alix was skeptical. "There was a point in August that we were having daily meetings with the executive committee looking at all of the various positions that we had with them and understanding what the cash flows were going to be and collateral flows were going to be," the executive said.

As the losses mounted through August—sometimes hundreds of millions of dollars in a single day—Meriwether called his old friend Vinny Mattone at home. By this time, Cayne had forced Mattone out of the firm.

"Where are you?" Mattone asked Meriwether, referring to the fund's capital.

"We're down by half," he replied.

"You're finished," Mattone said.

Meriwether was incredulous. "What are you talking about? We still have $2 billion. We have half." He also mentioned to Mattone that he had been speaking with potential investors, including billionaire George Soros, about investing fresh capital in LTCM. "When you're down by half, people figure you can go down all the way," Mattone replied. "They're going to push the market against you. They're not going to roll"—refinance—"your trades. You're *finished*."

Although it would take a few weeks more, Mattone was right. By mid-September word of LTCM's losses had leaked into the market, and the laws of self-fulfilling prophecies took over. Late in the day on September 10, the assets that LTCM had "in the box" at Bear Stearns fell below $500 million for the first time, triggering Cayne's low threshold. Warren Spector called Meriwether and told him Bear would send a team to LTCM's offices in Greenwich that Sunday to examine the books and make a decision about whether to stop clearing for the firm, which would put LTCM out of business.

Out of desperation, Meriwether went to see Cayne. "I asked if he had any assets at all, and he said, 'I've got a $500 million line [of credit] at Chase,'" Cayne said. "I said, 'Well, take it down.' He said, 'It expires in ten days and they know we're not going to be able to pay it back.' I said, 'I know, but you can take it down.' He said, 'How do you know that?' I said, 'I don't know that. Go talk to a lawyer. But to me, if you've got a line take it down and let them go whistle or do something, but that's salvation." LTCM took Cayne's advice after letting its banker at Chase know what was happening. Chase had little choice but to let LTCM draw down the committed money and ultimately received all but $25 million. "That precipitated Chase going to the Feds and saying, 'Fuck, we had to give them $500 million and we want a meeting,'" Cayne said.

By this time, Meriwether had been scrambling for weeks to raise additional capital. He had spoken with Soros, Warren Buffett, and Jon Corzine, at Goldman Sachs, among others. And even though his hedge fund was largely unregulated, he had let the New York Federal Reserve know what was going on, specifically William McDonough, its president, and Peter Fisher, his deputy. LTCM was in a death spiral, losing money hand over fist. The potential new investors, wary to begin with, became increasingly spooked. McDonough and Fisher, meanwhile, after examining LTCM's trading positions, became increasingly concerned about the interconnectedness of all of

LTCM's trades and the leading firms on Wall Street. Not only had Wall Street invested in LTCM, but many of the firms piggybacked on LTCM's trades, as Cayne had noted. They were also counterparties with one another. The Fed was not concerned about the potential losses that investors would suffer—they were big boys—but was worried about a failure of the system. "[I]f Long-Term failed, and if its creditors forced a hasty and disorderly liquidation, [McDonough] feared that it would harm the entire financial system, not just some of its big participants," Lowenstein wrote. "McDonough evoked a parallel fear—that losses in so many markets and to so many players would spark a vicious circle of liquidations, extreme fluctuations in interest rates, and then further losses: 'Markets would . . . probably cease to function for a period of one or more days and maybe longer.'"

The time had come to act. Based on a proposal made by Herb Allison, then president of Merrill Lynch, the sixteen banks that were LTCM's largest counterparties would contribute $250 million each—a total of $4 billion—into LTCM in exchange for the vast amount of the firm's equity that had been owned by the original partners. LTCM's investors would be wiped out, but Allison hoped his plan would allow for an orderly liquidation of the firm's positions and prevent a systemic crash. On the evening of September 22, Fisher and McDonough asked the heads of the sixteen banks to come to the New York Fed building on Liberty Street to discuss a Fed-orchestrated bailout of LTCM. Fisher permitted each bank to bring two representatives. Cayne brought Spector. Earlier in the day, Cayne had heightened Fisher's concern by telling him that LTCM would make it through Tuesday but not Wednesday, in his judgment. "So they got all these guys together on that Tuesday night," Cayne said. "Get the message. We're all going to a picnic and the tickets are $250 million each. And tomorrow morning at nine o'clock, it's 'We'll meet again.'"

When they got back in the car, Cayne told Spector he wanted to have an executive committee meeting at eight the next morning, before the Fed meeting at nine. He also said he could not imagine Bear Stearns participating in the bailout. "It ought to last about four seconds," Cayne told Spector about the executive committee the next morning. "Because we're out. Why are we even there? Why are we coming up with $250 million? To do what? We might lose it. I already saw their NAV [net asset value] go from $5 billion to $500 million. It was like a run on a bank."

The next morning, Bear's executive committee met and, as Cayne predicted, voted instantly that Bear would not participate in the bailout of LTCM. "Not one person said we should be in, not one," Cayne said. "Why would they? It's stupid." Cayne was of course right that no one on the executive committee questioned the decision. But others did—not that their views influenced the decision. "My objection was completely based on being part of the solution in the community and not on any financial risk as such," one senior Bear executive said. "I thought that if LTCM blew up, it would be very ugly, and it could be ugly for other parts of our portfolio, but not life-threatening. But I was just a lowly credit guy who happened to have a pretty good understanding of what was going on there in the sense of the financial or the systemic consequences. I was expressing an opinion and I think I was thanked for that opinion and excused."

After the vote, Cayne and Spector headed downtown to the Fed. "I figure, hmm, there's somebody I know at the Fed"—Peter Fisher—"because he's been calling me every day, asking me about their position," Cayne said. "Remember, their NAV is going down and everybody in the world knows about it. 'Jimmy, how are you?' I tell him, 'Worse than yesterday'—every day, I said worse than yesterday—'no salvation in sight.' I remember specifically Peter Fisher saying to me, 'Well, you've got to protect your shareholders.' I said, 'Thanks, Pete. Appreciate that help. I'll plan on doing that.' I remember that conversation."

In the car, Cayne and Spector called Fisher at the Fed and told him not to proceed alphabetically through the list of banks asking them to support the plan to save LTCM. By this time, the effort by Buffett, Goldman Sachs, and Hank Greenberg, at AIG, to buy out the partners of LTCM for $250 million and then inject $4 billion into the firm while making LTCM part of Goldman's proprietary trading business had been rejected. "Now we get to the meeting," Cayne said. "Herb Allison is running the meeting. He said, 'All those things fell through. The things with Buffett and with Hank Greenberg and with Goldman, they all fell through. I'd like to know where we stand with everybody. Bankers Trust, are you with us?' So now we're going alphabetically."

Cayne's suggestion to Fisher not to proceed alphabetically had obviously been ignored. Cayne recalled, "I know our name is coming up. There's Barclays, and then there's Bear Stearns. I have no idea what I'm going to say. I only know it's not going to be received particularly well. 'Bankers Trust?' 'We're in.' 'Barclays?' 'We're in.' 'Bear Stearns?' I said, 'Peter, as I told you on the phone coming down here, Bear Stearns is not in.' Now, the book says pandemonium broke loose. The exact opposite occurs. You could hear a pin drop. For like thirty seconds, nobody said anything. The guy running the meeting didn't even go to the next guy. It was just quiet. Now, it might have been thirty seconds and it might have been five seconds. It felt like ten minutes. And then somebody piped up and says, 'Well, what do you know that we don't know? You're the clearance firm.' I said, 'I don't know anything you don't know. They are in compliance. They are not behind at all. Whatever their NAV is stated as, that's the real deal. They're not in default and they are in compliance.' Peter Fisher says, 'Well, you said you would think about it, right?' I said, 'Right, definitely. We'll definitely think about it.' The next guy doesn't even go. He just says, 'In the light of Bear Stearns, I have to talk to *ze* home office.' This is a French banker. The meeting is stopped. Fisher and Bill McDonough come over to me and say, 'We have to talk to you.'"

Cayne and Spector left with Fisher and McDonough for a private room so ornate that Cayne was in awe. "The little Fed room is where the mucky-mucks have their powwows," Cayne said. "That makes the big Fed room look like chopped liver. It's like gold inlay. I mean, it's beyond." In the side room, Cayne recalled, Fisher and McDonough said to him, "'Everybody is angry. Everybody is going crazy.' I said, 'Who?' They said, 'Well, for one, [David] Komansky [the CEO of Merrill Lynch].' I said, 'Get him in here.' Komansky comes in. Very nice guy. But this all flew over his head. He said, 'What the fuck are you doing, Jimmy?' I said, 'David, number one, I didn't know we were partners, like we had to sort of do the same thing. Number two, it's very clear. I've expressed myself. We have not had any counterparty exposure to these guys. We didn't see their swaps. Everybody was invited up to Greenwich to take a look at what they are. We weren't. The bottom line is that, seriously, AT&T has as much right at being here as we do. They're a vendor. We're a vendor. We're a Wall Street vendor. They're not here. Why are we?'"

Komansky insisted that Cayne go back into the room and say something to calm everyone down. Cayne continued: "I said, 'I already did say something.' He said, 'Well, you got to say something more.' I said, 'Okay, I'll make you a deal. We'll go back in the meeting because obviously people really got upset. I will make it much clearer that they're in compliance and much clearer about their lack of jeopardy. But I'm not doing that unless you announce who I am, what's your relationship with Bear Stearns, what's your feeling about Bear Stearns, what's your feeling about me. Because I don't want to walk in and sort of be like this whipping boy who has got to like now be called out. I want to be introduced as a standup guy and standup firm.'"

When they walked back into the larger meeting, according to Cayne, "all eyes are on us. Who knows what took place? These guys are all in these fucking bonds. We walk back in. Komansky gets up. Does exactly what he said he would do. 'Known Jimmy for years, solid. Bear Stearns, solid.' I said to them, 'I said it the first time. I'll say it again. They're in compliance. Meaning that their NAV is still above zero. They have paid everything on time. We paid everything for them on time. I don't see any chink in the armor. I don't see anything at all. But I also don't see a responsibility on our part to participate in something that we had nothing to do with.' They don't take that well. 'Yeah, well, you're Wall Street.' I said, 'Hold it, guys. You all had something in common. Number one, you all gave them no initial margin requirements. Number two, you all piggybacked. Who's kidding who? . . . You're all in the same boat and you're stuck in the exit door. And that's why we're not in this $250 million that you wanted.' They literally went nuts because they were a little nervous since I'm the clearance guy and I'm telling them, 'We're not in.' Well, what does that mean? Is that like their money's down the drain if they do go in?"

Cayne also told them: "The meetings that have taken place so far where you all agreed that you're going to stand still on those positions because whoever jumps the gun has got to get a better price. So you're probably antitrusting it right away by agreeing not to sell anything, which is your business. I would probably do the same thing. I'm not in your category. Bear Stearns is not where you are. As a matter of fact, we took, as it turns out, the worst clearance deal in the history of clearance deals."

For four more hours, the group beat up Cayne, exhorting him and Bear Stearns to participate. For one thing, if Bear failed to contribute, each of the other firms would have to pony up another $50 million each, or $300 million. And then there was the matter of not presenting a unified front in the battle to stem the possible systemic damage.

In one final effort to convince Cayne to go along, Komansky threatened that Bear would lose LTCM's clearing business. That set Cayne off. "I said, 'David, I just did. You've got it. We don't want it,'" Cayne recalled. "Now, what do I know? It'll take six months to [get all the data] on disks [and] moved from one firm to another. I tripled the rates on the spot. I said, 'We're not clearing anymore. You told me that we wouldn't clear. I agree. We're not. By the way, if you want to hire us back, it's triple the rate.' It's not like I was exactly a retiring fellow. But for four hours when people are telling you, 'You're a pariah, you're going to be this, you're going to be that,' there was a certain unfairness to it."

IN THE END, Bear Stearns was the only firm not to participate in the bailout of Long-Term Capital Management, which was eventually liquidated. (Lehman Brothers contributed only $100 million, creating, some have argued, almost as much resentment against it as existed for Bear Stearns.) But the consortium of banks had put their collective finger in the dike and prevented the collapse of the financial system. (A few years later, Meriwether resurfaced with a new hedge fund, which again got hammered during the credit crisis of 2007 and 2008.) Alan Greenspan, the chairman of the Federal Reserve at the time, defended the Fed-orchestrated bailout. "Had the failure of LTCM triggered the seizing up of the markets," he told the House Banking Committee on October 1, "substantial damage could have been inflicted on many market participants and could have potentially impaired the economies of many nations, including our own." When Representative Barney Frank, of Massachusetts, criticized Greenspan for having the Fed organize the bailout that left "some of the richest people in the country better off than if you didn't intervene," Greenspan countered, "No Federal Reserve funds were put at risk, no promises were made by the Federal Reserve and no individual firms were pressured to participate."

Cayne obviously disagreed with Greenspan's definition of the word "pressured." Understandably, given what happened to Bear Stearns, Cayne is hypersensitive to the suggestion that the collapse of his firm nearly ten years later was "payback" by his fellow Wall Streeters for his intransigence on participating in the rescue of LTCM. "When they talk about payback," Cayne said, "because I had heard this now, like from these talking bubbleheads [on TV]: 'Yeah, Jimmy irritated this guy. And Paulson is getting even with him, and blah blah.' Bullshit, pure bullshit. All those people are gone. They don't exist anymore. There's no corporate memory of somebody fucking you. Paulson? This was good for Paulson. This was probably how Corzine got kicked out [of Goldman Sachs]. Paulson always wanted to be the guy. And he got to be the guy because Corzine got fired because of Long-Term." Cayne's characterization of Paulson was, "He was a sharp-elbowed guy and a ferocious competitor."

Some senior executives of Bear Stearns believe that Cayne's dramatic showdown with the Wall Street cartel over LTCM didn't do the firm or him any favors. In the summer of 1998, "the trading business for all these firms got hammered," said a former Bear Stearns trading executive. "We were wondering how we were going to pay people. We kept losing money. You've got to understand how upside down the world was. You're bleeding money every single day and you're doing everything a little bit by the seat of your pants. Because none of the models that you've had in your head or on a piece of paper or in a computer are working. Then you go to a meeting and Jimmy's talking about LTCM and what the hell's going on and how everybody's going to bail it out and Goldman's leading the charge and these guys were out of their fucking minds and who the hell wants to put money in this thing? By the way, you already got a bloody nose, cauliflower ear, and a black eye from the markets before you even go to the meeting with Jimmy. He says, 'Do you want to bail LTCM out?' You say, 'Well, we don't want anybody to hate us because we got enough of that shit already.' Who wants to argue with him? We're hanging on by a thread every day down there. That was pretty much the attitude. Like pick your battles. If he's dead wrong and the Street hates us, we'll have to figure it out later. There were so many opportunities, though, in the following ten years to make things better, both on the Street and as a firm. You could decide not to participate in the LTCM bailout and be magnanimous about it post facto instead of bragging about it for ten years. There would have been a very different perception of him. If two or three years later when he was interviewed for the eighty-second time about why he wasn't in it and if he had said, 'Listen, I was very worried about my firm at the time. We, like everyone else, think it was great that the Fed and the other Wall Street firms put money in. Obviously, we couldn't afford it at the time. And we're very thankful that everyone did.' How about that? Being a little magnanimous, a little humble, makes a difference. A big difference."

For many at Bear Stearns at that time, Cayne's machismo in the LTCM crisis was a moment that defined the remainder of the firm's existence. "I think the hubristic moment for him, the turning point from which he couldn't go back, was LTCM," explained one Bear Stearns senior executive. "It was the moment where he felt like he had outwitted all these CEOs of Wall Street. That was the no-turning-back moment where his set of virtues—in his mind—were embedded in concrete." He observed that Cayne himself had no real understanding of risk per se, or of how much risk was too much risk, since he had only ever been a broker and an executive manager. Instead, Greenberg's approach to risk heavily influenced Cayne's views on the subject. "Some of those virtues, I think, are Ace's virtues that bled into him over time," he said. "I mean, Ace wouldn't risk a nickel for anybody." The key to unlocking what happened at Bear Stearns after LTCM was gaining an understanding of the lineage that ran from Greenberg through Cayne to Warren Spector.

Added a former longtime partner of the firm: "Warren and Jimmy decided that they weren't going to share in the burden with the rest of the Street. Then those guys [on Wall Street] had a perpetual erection for them. Especially for Jimmy, because he's an arrogant son of a bitch. He's a world-class bridge player. Everything he does is like he's playing a hand of bridge."

CHAPTER 22

THE FISH ROTS FROM THE HEAD

To celebrate Greenberg's fiftieth anniversary of joining Bear Stearns, there was the requisite article in the *Journal*, by Charlie Gasparino, that briefly delineated the touchstones of his career and pointed out that in 1998, with total compensation of $18.5 million, he earned in eleven and a half minutes what it had taken him a full year to earn when he was starting out as a clerk putting pushpins in a map of oil and gas wells. The secret to his long career on Wall Street was simple: "I bring in money," he told Gasparino. Greenberg also appeared on Neil Cavuto's business show on Fox News. Among other things, Cavuto asked Greenberg why he had been so obsessed with cutting costs during his reign at the top of Wall Street. "I just think that you should set a tone on how business should be run," he said. "As Mark Twain said, I think fish stink from the head, and if people up top are watching expenses, it permeates the whole organization. And I believe in it very strongly."

Public relations aside, if Twain was right about how a fish rots, there were some strange smells starting to emanate from Bear Stearns. In August 1999, the firm's litigation involving the "bucket shop" A. R. Baron—which had begun more than two years earlier, following the publication of Gretchen Morgenson's article in *Forbes*—came to a head. For some two years, a Manhattan grand jury had been investigating whether Richard Harriton, the head of Bear's clearing business, had been engaged in criminal activity involving Baron and its CEO, Andrew Bressman. John Moscow, then the assistant district attorney on the case, had aggressively pursued Harriton, in part by pressuring his co-workers and even his ex-wife to testify against him. In the end, the grand jury did not indict Harriton. But by this time, Moscow had started cooperating with the SEC on its civil suits against both Bear Stearns and Harriton. The SEC was trying through this litigation and a parallel rule change to make Wall Street's clearing businesses accountable for the questionable behavior of its clients. One Bear executive said he occasionally urged the firm not to clear for certain unsavory customers. At one such meeting, he said of one particular client, "I think he takes an unwholesome interest in the aftermarket performance of the deals he does. I would avoid him." But that recommendation fell on deaf ears. "I was taken outside and they said, 'Look, does a hotel have responsibility for what goes on its rooms?'" he recalled. "And I said, 'If enough of it goes on, the hotel gets a reputation and people don't want to stay there. But are you asking me do they have a legal liability for what goes on? The answer is probably not. But if you're asking me are there consequences? There probably are consequences.'"

At various times during the SEC's investigation, the SEC offered to settle the litigation with Bear Stearns for amounts that ranged between $5 million and $10 million. Explained one Bear Stearns executive: "But Jimmy Cayne, the ultimate bridge player, refused to settle for anything above $1 million." On August 5, Bear Stearns decided to settle with the SEC. This time, Cayne's gamble had backfired. The cost of the settlement was an eye-popping $38.5 million, which included a fine, the establishment of restitution funds to settle customer claims, payments to the Manhattan District Attorney's office, and payments of $1 million each to New York City and New York State. The SEC found that Bear's clearance business "caused violations of the antifraud provisions of the federal securities laws in connection with its clearing relations with" A. R. Baron. Specifically, the SEC found that "although Bear Stearns was aware that Baron was engaging in unauthorized trading in customer accounts, Bear Stearns charged unauthorized trades to Baron customers instead of to Baron; Bear Stearns took money and securities from customer accounts to pay for the unauthorized trades; and

Bear Stearns refused to return the customer property it took, even after Baron admitted that certain trades were unauthorized." The SEC also found that Bear Stearns "assisted Baron in staying in business when it knew that Baron lacked required capital to operate and was engaging in an ongoing fraud. By charging to customers unauthorized trades that should have been liabilities to Baron, Bear Stearns helped Baron hide its continuing capital deficiency." Suspected a senior Bear Stearns executive about the A. R. Baron clearing arrangement: "Jimmy knew everything that was going on. There were plenty of meetings in his office about all that."

Richard Walker, the SEC's enforcement director, hammered home the SEC's view that clearing firms would be held accountable for the actions of their clients: "Bear Stearns took actions that directly facilitated Baron's widespread fraudulent activity. A firm's status as a clearing broker does not immunize it from the consequences of participating in a fraud. To the contrary, a clearing firm, or any other market participant, that engages in conduct enabling a boiler room like Baron to defraud investors of millions of dollars is fully responsible for its actions." Cayne said that at first Moscow and Robert Morgenthau, the Manhattan District Attorney, concocted "conspiracy theories that Bear Stearns and Citibank were out to fuck A. R. Baron customers" and wanted "$700 million" from Bear Stearns and Citibank. "I had a whole group of lawyers," Cayne said. "They went down to see Morgenthau and his staff. They came back and gave me a report and I said, 'Now, we have grades that we give out here for everything. You guys don't even get a grade. This result is so poor that you don't get a grade.' And I walked out." In the end, Cayne said the A. R. Baron settlement was like "arguing with the umpire. The videotape shows you slid in and that you're safe, except the umpire says you're out. That's it." The SEC gave Bear Stearns one night to consider the settlement offer. Bear signed it.

The Baron incident showed that the firm did not have proper oversight of the clearance business. The real issue with Baron, one executive said, "was more like if you lie down with dogs you get up with fleas. And these were less than wholesome people. They did not represent any significant part of the business. They represented a tremendous aspect of the liability of the business. They represented no money. I think setting some guidelines on maybe less than 1 percent of the customers would have saved the firm a fortune. But Bear didn't tend to micromanage successful producers."

At first, Greenberg encouraged Harriton, his old friend, to fight the SEC charges. There was an issue of the potential conflict of interest because of Richard Lindsey, the former SEC official hired to replace Harriton. But, in the end, some eight months later, in April 2000, Harriton settled the case with the SEC. As usual, he did not admit or deny his culpability, but the SEC's nineteen-page settlement order laid many transgressions at his doorstep. He agreed to pay a $1 million fine and to be barred from the securities industry for two years. Harriton never returned to Wall Street.

On the heels of the Baron debacle, Bear Stearns found itself part of the two major Wall Street scandals after the bursting of the Internet bubble in and around March 2000 revealed any number of systemic abuses on Wall Street. The first involved the conflict that arose between the equity research departments and the investment banking departments on Wall Street, in that investment bankers put pressure on research analysts to write favorable reports about their clients in the hope of winning future underwriting and M&A business. Since at that time research analysts were paid in part from the investment banking revenues they helped to generate, the bankers were able to lean on the analysts to write favorable reports. Obviously, this conflict did not serve investors well, since they could no longer be sure whether a report reflected the analyst's true judgment about a company or a coerced judgment.

This kind of behavior, yet another example of unrestrained greed overwhelming ethics, occurred all across Wall Street, including at Bear Stearns, and showed that as Wall Street firms became bigger and bigger they became harder to control and manage. In a typical example of how the research abuse occurred, Bear Stearns was a co-manager of the IPO and secondary offerings for the emerging telecommunications company Digital River in August and December 1998, respectively. Bear Stearns, via three successive analysts, rated the stock a "Buy" from the IPO until April 2002. On April 1, 2002, the research analyst covering Digital River wrote the

Digital River banker the following e-mail: "I have to tell you, I feel a bit compromised today. I have told every client on the phone that they should avoid or short the stock over the last few months. I have been fairly hands-off on DRIV [the Digital River stock symbol], primarily because of the banking prospect that you and [another banker] have noted. Today, clearly the stock is down a lot. The artificial Buy rating on the stock, while artificial, still makes me look bad. In the future, I'd like to have more leeway with the ratings, even for companies like Digital River, where we have a relationship on the banking side. I trust it would benefit all of us."

As part of the global $1.435 billion settlement, Bear Stearns agreed to pay $80 million. Cayne had no choice but to settle, and the firm got off relatively lightly (Salomon Smith Barney paid $400 million and Merrill Lynch paid $200 million). Cayne also felt he had little choice but to settle—for $250 million—the SEC's securities fraud charges against the firm for "facilitating unlawful late trading and deceptive market timing of mutual funds by its customers and customers of its introducing brokers" from 1999 through September 2003. "Bear Stearns provided technology, advice and deceptive devices that enabled its market timing customers and introducing brokers to late trade and to evade detection by mutual funds." By late trading, Bear and its customers were able to effectively have tomorrow's *Wall Street Journal* today, enabling them to make money by making trades even though the market had closed. "The truth is I settled a lot," Cayne said. "I settled most of the time. I very rarely fought. I pretend to fight. I'd really rather settle."

※

THE TRUTH WAS that Cayne mostly fought litigation, in keeping with his pugilistic instincts. One case that he fought for years and eventually won on appeal involved a Polish refugee from the Nazis named Henry de Kwiatkowski (or as Cayne called him, "Henry de K"), who was heavily involved in currency trading. In less than five months, beginning at the end of 1994, de Kwiatkowski, a Bear Stearns brokerage client, made and lost hundreds of millions of dollars betting on the U.S. dollar by trading in currency futures. In January 1991, he transferred 4,000 Swiss franc short contracts from a

Bank Leu account in Israel to Bear Stearns—after signing all the requisite forms acknowledging a multitude of risks—in part because, he claimed, Bear executive Albert Sabini had "extolled the capacity of Bear Stearns to provide him the full services and resources he needed for large-scale foreign currency trading." De Kwiatkowski's primary bet was that the dollar would rise in value against other currencies. "He was a bettor on the dollar," Cayne said. "He never had a trade. He just had a position. And the position was long [on] the dollar against five currencies."

In September 1992, de Kwiatkowski met with Larry Kudlow, then Bear's chief economist, and Kudlow encouraged him in this view. He then made big currency bets. When he closed his position, in January 1993, de Kwiatkowski had made $219 million of profit in four months. He made no new bets on the direction of the dollar until October 1994, when Sabini called him and told him "this is the time to buy the dollar" and that "this time the dollar will do what [Kwiatkowski] always believed it would do." As of December 21, 1994, less than two months after he resumed currency speculation at Bear, Kwiatkowski had made a profit of $228 million. Cayne said that at one point Henry de K was up $500 million. When Cayne called Henry de K and asked him to increase his margin in the account to $250 million, de Kwiatkowski responded, "No problem. I can send in $500 million if you want."

When the dollar fell a week later, de Kwiatkowski lost $112 million in a single day (December 28). When the dollar fell again, on January 9, 1995, de Kwiatkowski lost another $98 million. Ten days later, on January 19, he lost $70 million more. Still, even after absorbing these losses, de Kwiatkowski was ahead $34 million on his trades since October 28, 1994. He continued losing money through the winter. Finally, on March 5, 1996, he liquidated all of his positions, after having lost tens of millions in the preceding few days. When his spree was over, he was still up $25 million overall, although he had lost hundreds of millions of dollars from the peak. "He was always in compliance [with the terms of his margin account]," Cayne said. "We couldn't have gotten him out even if we wanted to because he was in compliance. We warned him a thousand times. I personally talked to him a thousand times." In fact, when Cayne saw the losses in the account mount and saw one day there was a $2 million shortfall, he told the Bear broker that the money would come out of the broker's hide if Henry de K didn't make good on it. But he did. "And now it's over," Cayne said. "It's like a trip. It's gone from zero to $500 million to $25 million. That was his trip."

Nevertheless, de Kwiatkowski blamed Bear Stearns and Sabini for his losses. In June 1996, he sued them both (and several other Bear entities), alleging negligence and breach of fiduciary duty. In May 2000, a jury in a federal courthouse in downtown Manhattan agreed with de Kwiatkowski that Bear Stearns had been negligent, and awarded him $111.5 million, one of the largest single awards won by a brokerage client from a Wall Street firm. After the verdict, Bear Stearns filed a series of motions with the district court arguing that de Kwiatkowski's brokerage account had been a "nondiscretionary" account that required de Kwiatkowski's approval before any actions were taken and that, as a matter of law, Bear Stearns had none of the advisory duties to de Kwiatkowski that the jury found Bear Stearns had breached. As in the A. R. Baron case, Bear was arguing against what seemed to be a new legal precedent on Wall Street that would have required firms to be held responsible for the behavior of their clients.

On December 29, 2000, the district court ruled against Bear Stearns, finding that "the unique facts and circumstances of the parties' relationship permitted the jury reasonably to find that Bear undertook to provide Kwiatkowski with services beyond those that are usual for nondiscretionary accounts, and that there was evidence sufficient to find that Bear provided those services negligently." The court then applied the *coup de grâce* by adding another $53 million to the jury's damages award for prejudgment interest dating back to March 6, 1995. Now Bear Stearns owed Henry de K $164.5 million. "When I got the initial verdict that we had lost," Cayne said, "I think I got a call like four-fifteen in the afternoon from Mark Lehman [the firm's general counsel]. I sat at my desk for two hours and didn't move, literally, like I was dumbstruck, like I was tromped on. How could you lose? How could you lose this case? This is ridiculous. The most open-and-shut case in the history of the world."

Not surprisingly, Cayne decided to appeal the district court's decision to the United States Court of Appeals for the Second Circuit. "This was another little thing that took place inside of the executive committee," Cayne said. "They said to me, 'You're going to settle it, aren't you?' And I said, 'No. No settlement.'" The executive committee, as usual, went along with Cayne's desire to appeal the case without settling.

As in the district court trial, Cayne was actively involved in the January 7, 2002, hearing before the appeals court. "Their lead lawyer turned out to be about a 300-pound fag from Long Island," Cayne said, "a really irritating guy who had cross-examined me and tried to kick the shit out of me in the lower court trial. Now when we walk into the courtroom for the appeal, they're arguing another case and we have to wait until they're finished. And I stopped this guy. I had to take a piss. I went into the bathroom to take a piss and came back and sat down. Then I see my blood enemy stand up and he's going to the bathroom. So I wait till he passes and then I follow him in and then it's just he and I in the bathroom. And I said to him, 'Today you're going to get your ass kicked, big.' He ran out of the room. He thought I might have wanted to start it right there and then."

The appeals court ruled on September 19. "I get the thing delivered to me, the final appeal thing," Cayne said. "I still have it. *And we reverse.* That was great. I was in my office. I went nuts. I just started jumping up and down. I was totally vindicated. And also the money wasn't unimportant."

BY THIS TIME, there was no longer any question who was in charge at Bear Stearns—it was Jimmy Cayne. Greenberg still showed up every day at his raised desk on the trading floor, barking out orders and trading for his clients. He also continued to chair the risk committee and was chairman of the board of directors. But there was now little doubt that Cayne and his two deputies—Warren Spector and Alan Schwartz, who also were nominated for seats on the firm's nine-member board—were in control. It was evident enough in compensation, the most important Wall Street scorecard. For the fiscal year ended June 1999, Greenberg, then seventy-two years old,

took a 30 percent pay cut, to $13 million for the year, down from
$18.5 million a year earlier. Cayne was paid $21.4 million in 1999,
up around 8 percent from $19.9 million the year earlier. Spector
was paid $20.4 million, up from $19 million, and Schwartz received
$17 million. Such was Spector's belief in the firm's prospects that
he chose to take $20.2 million of his pay in the form of Bear Stearns
stock, as permitted by the firm's so-called capital accumulation
plan, or CAP, making his stock ownership in the firm, at 2.36 percent, second only to Cayne's, at 4.2 percent. The CAP, started in
1990, was a way for rising stars at the firm to accumulate meaningful ownership stakes. Executives had the option of deferring for five
years 100 percent of their total compensation into the firm's stock,
purchased effectively at a small discount to market value.

The end of the decade and the beginning of the new millen-
nium were periods of substantial change on Wall Street, perhaps
even its Golden Age. Firms were making money hand over fist—
Bear had a net income of $709 million in 1999, Morgan Stanley
earned $5.5 billion, Merrill Lynch earned $3.3 billion, and Goldman Sachs earned $3 billion. And their stocks were trading at or
near all-time highs and at price-to-earnings multiples—nineteen
times earnings for Morgan Stanley, seventeen times for Goldman
Sachs, sixteen times for Merrill Lynch—that propelled the value of
these firms and the net worths of their senior executives skyward.
Goldman, Merrill, and Morgan Stanley each came close to being
worth $100 billion. Even though the market penalized Bear Stearns
for its lack of a diversified revenue stream, all of the men on the executive committee were becoming wealthy. Cayne's 4 percent of the
company was worth around $360 million, Spector's stake was worth
about $200 million, and Greenberg's stake was worth $90 million,
in addition to all the cash they took out every year. And assuming
Cayne and the other top executives could make progress in building
the firm's investment banking business (still relatively tiny), its presence in Europe (still negligible at best), and its asset management
business (with about $15 billion of assets under management, a
peanut compared to around $600 billion of assets under manage-
ment at Merrill Lynch), there appeared to be a fair amount of upside potential in the earning power of the firm, assuming markets

stayed favorable and the management could execute. That potential helped explain Spector's decision to convert most of his compensation into the firm's stock.

And then in early 2000—just after everyone recovered from the specter of Y2K damaging Wall Street computers—the game of consolidation on Wall Street took a quantum leap forward. At first the deals were relatively small. In September 1999, Chase Manhattan Bank bought Hambrecht & Quist, a technology investment bank in San Francisco, for $1.3 billion as a way to try to participate in the Internet underwriting boom. In January 2000, Citigroup bought Schroeder's investment banking business for $2.2 billion. Then, in April, Chase bought Robert Fleming Holdings, in Hong Kong, for $6.9 billion, and a few weeks later, PaineWebber bought regional broker J. C. Bradford for $620 million. Alliance Capital, the money manager, bought Sanford C. Bernstein & Co. for $3.5 billion in June. Then, on July 13, UBS, the giant Swiss bank, announced it was buying PaineWebber for around $12 billion.

Soon enough, speculation was rife about whether Bear Stearns would be caught up in the consolidation craze. Neither Greenberg nor Cayne had ever given any indication the firm was for sale, other than the predictable noises about having to exercise a fiduciary duty to public shareholders if a serious offer for the company came along. This was not particularly surprising given the firm's quirkiness. Yes, it had been extremely profitable for a very long time and the executives who worked there made yearly bonanzas, but the firm made so much of its money from the unglamorous businesses of trading and clearing, as opposed to investment banking, that it was not an attractive target to any foreign acquirer looking to enter the United States investment banking market nor to any domestic firm, with the possible exception of Chase Manhattan. Not many people believed that Bear Stearns and Chase Manhattan would make much of a cultural marriage, the secret sauce of most mergers.

"Bear didn't have that much of an equity franchise," explained Guy Moszkowski, then a research analyst at Salomon Smith Barney, covering the financial services industry. "They were still driven very much by fixed income." In the days after UBS announced its deal for PaineWebber, as part of his job covering the financial services industry, Moszkowski went to see Cayne in his office at 245 Park. "Him, me, and the motorcycle," he said. He had been wondering about whether Cayne had any plan for how to deal with the changing dynamics on Wall Street. "This is an environment in which the markets have started to slow down a little bit," he said to Cayne. "You're seeing some deals happen at some very high prices. Given that you don't have international and you don't have equities, wouldn't you consider merging with another player that could really use what you have and create something bigger?" (In retrospect, Moszkowski noted, "What I was leaving aside of course was all the cultural issues that people always said would impede a transaction.") Then Cayne said, "This is not our market because it's all about equities right now and it's all about M&A and we're okay with those businesses but they're not a big deal for us. But trust me, the time will come when all that stuff is less important than it has been these last eighteen months, two years, during this bubble"—which was in the process of being pricked. "Fixed income will be back. We will do better and we will use the earnings from that relative strength to invest, to build out some of the other stuff."

Cayne said he was happy to remain independent. "I don't have any pressure on me to sell," he told Moszkowski. "I may not be producing the returns on equity that Goldman Sachs is right here, 25 percent or whatever." Bear's ROE was around 15 percent at this time. "But it's what we do, it's acceptable for shareholders. It's more consistent over the cycle, and we don't see any reason to give up our independence. On the other hand, I'm not crazy. I have to represent shareholders and I have to be a fiduciary, and if someone comes along and offers the right price, something that we really think is much better than what we can produce for shareholders over the long haul, of course I'll consider it." Moszkowski couldn't help asking Cayne what his price was. "I don't know," Cayne told him. "What'd you say PaineWebber was going for?"

"Three times book," Moszkowski replied.

"Well, four," Cayne said. ("I don't think there was any science to the four," Moszkowski said later.)

"I'm going to go back and I'm going to write this meeting up," Moszkowski told Cayne. "Can I say that?"

"You can, sure," Cayne replied.

Moszkowski wrote a report, in July 2000, explaining what Cayne had told him: that for the first time Bear Stearns would consider selling the firm if Cayne could get four times book value. Cayne "had signaled something of a change of attitude," Moszkowski wrote in his report about the possibility of a sale of Bear Stearns, making "it quite clear that an acquisition is not out of the question." Then Cayne added some fuel to the brushfire he had started. "The world is changing, and we recognize that a synergistic combination might be in the interest of shareholders," he told the *Wall Street Journal*. But since at that time the firm's book value was around $30 per share, Cayne had essentially put a price of $120 per share on the firm, $19 billion in total, far above the $46 per share the stock had been trading at. The obvious dichotomy put Cayne's comment more in the vein of idle chatter, a bid mentioned in passing on the off chance that someone might hit it. If that happened, Cayne's 7.7 million shares would be worth just shy of $1 billion, and who was he to turn down such a deal if offered?

In his report, Moszkowski speculated that HSBC Holdings, AIG, BNP Paribas, Société Générale, or one of several German banks could be a suitor for Bear Stearns. "We do not believe any particular deal is on the near-term horizon, and Cayne noted that to date most talks have ended relatively quickly," he wrote. But one consequence of the report was to drive Bear's stock higher. The stock went from $40 to $70 per share, Moszkowski said, well past its all-time high of $64 per share, reached two years before.

When Moszkowski's research note appeared, Cayne was in California—"I don't think it was a bridge tournament," he said—and on a Tuesday morning he got a call telling him he needed to go down to the hotel's business center and address live on closed-circuit TV the firm's seven hundred senior managing directors, who had assembled in the firm's auditorium, to explain his comments about considering a sale of the company. "I said, 'You're fucking kidding.' I had to do it. I went down to the business center. There's this screen. And I'm sitting there looking at a screen. And you don't get any feedback. I don't know if people are laughing or they're screaming. I have no idea. I just said, 'Hey, guys and gals, let's just all go back to work. It was a nonconversation with an analyst who took from it that we were selling at $30 and wanted $120 a share. Anybody who believes that that's a real story is wasting his time and I'm wasting my time. Good-bye.'"

As it turned out, the merger wave in the banking industry would soon crest with Credit Suisse First Boston's $11.5 billion acquisition of Donaldson, Lufkin & Jenrette in August and Chase Manhattan's $33 billion all-stock acquisition of J. P. Morgan in September after J. P. Morgan failed to reach a deal with Goldman Sachs. The rash of deals prompted Cayne to go see John Mack, then the president of Morgan Stanley Dean Witter, in order to learn more about potential deals for Bear Stearns. "I told him, 'Bear Stearns is not hiring you,'" Cayne said. "'Bear Stearns is coming to you and saying, "Jimmy wants to know what's out there." I'll go anywhere you want but I'm not going to pay a fee.' In the event anything did happen, he had my word that he would get the M&A assignment."

Mack introduced Cayne to Gary Parr, then the leading financial institutions banker at Morgan Stanley. They all got together again two weeks later. "They have this little outline," Cayne said. "They've done their M&A work. There are three potential buyers: Dresdner Bank, AIG, and Warren Buffett." Cayne laughed. "I don't need them to go to Warren Buffett," his old bridge partner. "And I don't need them to go to Hank Greenberg," he said. "And Dresdner is a German bank." Cayne had no intention of selling his Jewish firm to one of the German banks that had helped to finance Auschwitz. Mack realized quickly that Morgan Stanley wouldn't be getting an M&A fee out of Cayne anytime soon.

In August 2000, *Barron's* reporter Erin Arvedlund wrote a three-thousand-word article wondering who would buy Bear Stearns since "dull businesses and scandal taint this old Wall Street firm." She noted that since Moszkowski's research note, Bear stock had "roared ahead" more than 60 percent, but $120 a share seemed much too far. "Given the merger mania that prevails on Wall Street these days, someone might come along and pay that price, but don't bet on it," she wrote. "In fact, it might be unwise to bet on Bear Stearns being acquired at all." Her point was that Bear had made little headway in the businesses—asset management and investment banking—that seemed to appeal to acquirers at the moment. "Perhaps part of the problem," she wrote, "is that Greenberg and Cayne have such passion for the kind of operations that have been stalwarts at Bear Stearns for decades: executing securities trades for wealthy clients and for its own account. Greenberg made his reputation as a canny trader, and to this day it is said that he regularly grills traders on the company's Park Avenue trading floor about why they are holding a position in this stock or that." Yet, she argued, "investors dislike firms that are overly dependent on trading because it is a difficult business in which to make steady returns. Some liken it to gambling."

Barron's also noted the increasing concern among investors about who the next generation of leaders at the firm would be, now that Cayne was sixty-six years old and Greenberg was seventy-three. The obvious candidates to lead the firm—Spector, then forty-one, and Schwartz, then forty-nine—were of course mentioned. "In the shadow of Greenberg and Cayne," Arvedlund wrote, "it's hard to get a clear picture of what kind of leaders Spector and Schwartz would be. Among the initiatives they are credited with are hiring top talent from outside the firm, making use of stock options to reward outside performers, pushing into Europe and modernizing the firm's processes in an effort to cut costs." She concluded the article by remarking on the "gleaming new office tower" being built on "a full square block just west of Grand Central Station" at a cost of what would eventually rise to around $500 million. "One investing rule of thumb is to sell the stock of any financial company building a huge new headquarters," Arvedlund concluded. "And in the short run that may be good advice, especially if it becomes apparent that no one is interested in buying Bear Stearns. Longer-term, the firm has lots of potential if it can guard against future scandals, break more forcefully into the Street's most promising businesses and move the icons aside to give the younger generation a chance to shine."

At this time, notwithstanding the avuncular charm of Greenberg's cost-cutting memos, Bear had decided to hire McKinsey &

Co. at a cost of around $50 million, even though Greenberg used to question the value of outside consultants. The firm asked Paul Friedman to work with McKinsey on "Project Excel," a chunk of time he does not recall fondly. "I view it as the lost two years of my life," he said. The focus of the McKinsey study was "to try to invigorate certain of our businesses, to invigorate their growth, and to cut costs," Molinaro explained. "So it was a two-prong strategy. Invigorate growth and cut costs." But, Friedman said, there were few recommendations to increase revenues. "They come in and all they do is cut costs," he said, "and we did almost nothing on the revenue side. They cut the IT budget by hundreds of millions of dollars, some of which was needed, because it had swelled after the whole fear over Y2K. We fired a thousand people, and at the same time we were building this beautiful building. We cut a lot of costs, which just meant that when you cut your IT investment, you're mortgaging the future, which we did. We cut hundreds of clerks. We took nothing out of the executive committee compensation pool. We did nothing to the way we run the place. We did nothing to the management structure. We did nothing to the executive compensation structure. All of which, I think, set the stage for true lack of growth at the firm because it was right after that that we stopped bragging about our ROE because we went from leading the pack to trailing the pack, and milking the businesses that we had." In March 2001, after the firm announced four hundred firings from its information technology group, Molinaro said, "This is part of a cost rationalization program that we've had going on for the past six months." But even after the 1987 crash, Bear Stearns had always boasted of "hiring instead of firing," in Greenberg's words, and so the layoffs were a momentous indicator of how the firm had changed.

Just as Cayne had predicted, after the bursting of the Internet and emerging telecom bubbles in 2000 and 2001, the businesses that were important again on Wall Street were fixed-income sales and trading and clearing—Bear's two stalwarts—rather than investment banking. While the firm's revenue from its capital markets businesses stayed flat from 1999 to 2001, its revenues from investment banking as a percentage declined dramatically from 29 percent of the capital markets revenue in 1999 to 20 percent of the capital markets revenue in 2001. "Bear went through a metamorphosis in the markets," Bear banker Jeremy Sillem said. "Suddenly instead of being the laggard, it became the darling. All these other firms' valuations came rattling down. They went from four times back to one and a half times book value. Suddenly Bear was the best-performing stock of the investment bankers on Wall Street. And what did that do? It reinforced, in the minds of these guys, that the old Bear verities were right: Strategy is stupid. People who have strategic plans are dumb. The Bear way was always right."

One thing Bear Stearns was all about by 2001 was Jimmy Cayne. And on June 26, the firm made official what was already de facto: Cayne added the title of chairman of the board of directors to that of CEO, completing—finally—the transfer of power from Greenberg that had begun some ten years earlier. Once again, though, Greenberg, seventy-three, remained at the firm as a full-time trader and chairman of the executive committee. At such a cosmetically important moment in the firm's history, it was not surprising that both Cayne and Greenberg heaped accolades upon each other and failed to mention anything about the ongoing tension between them. In an interview with *BusinessWeek,* Cayne was both truthful, saying, "It was the most seamless transition in the history of Wall Street," and somewhat deceitful: "I haven't had a contentious moment with Alan Greenberg in 32 years. We're like good friends. I'm his biggest booster." At the same time as Cayne took full control of the reins of the firm, he also announced that Spector and Schwartz would be named co-presidents and co–chief operating officers. "This is a natural transition," Cayne explained to the *Wall Street Journal* before adding that "nobody has the inside track" to succeed him when he stepped down in the distant future. When asked about the likelihood of conflict between Schwartz and Spector as one of them emerged as the new leader, Cayne dismissed that idea. Charlie Gasparino, the *Journal* reporter, speculated for the first time in print that Spector had the edge in the race to succeed Cayne because of his "all-important role as head of the firm's powerful bond group" and because he "pioneered the firm's derivatives business."

Every Wall Street succession produces its casualties. In the case of Bear Stearns, the surprise departure from the firm came in the person of Donald Mullen, then forty-two, who had been head of the firm's high-yield sales and trading operation. He left to join Goldman Sachs, where his former Bear colleague David Solomon had been since leaving Bear Stearns in 1997. Mullen and Solomon had worked together at Drexel Burnham, Salomon Brothers, and Bear Stearns, so in that sense Mullen's departure was not surprising. But it was still a major blow to the firm, and one of the very few times that Cayne expressed genuine disappointment with the departure of a senior managing director.

Observers familiar with Goldman Sachs and Bear Stearns believe the quality of the people at each is similar but that the *language* of the two firms could not be more different. "The difference between Bear people and Goldman Sachs people was one of vocabulary," explained one person who knows both firms well. "It's almost like a piece of conceptual art or symbiotics. It was like reading Umberto Eco—language begets culture. At Goldman Sachs, the language is very specifically less aggressive and less hostile. So as an example, if a salesman and trader are talking about how they did a trade with a customer and they think there's a significant business opportunity that came out of that trade, at Bear Stearns they might say, 'I just ripped that fucker's head off. I'm going to make a lot of money on this trade. That's fucking crazy.' But at Goldman Sachs a salesman and a trader would talk about, 'That's a great opportunity. That was a very attractive and commercial price you purchased those securities at and I think we'll have a very interesting economic opportunity in the near future.' They just said the same thing. But the manifestation of the culture comes out of the different use of language. One protects the reputation of the firm. One presents the firm as a far more intelligent being, puts the firm in a position to be much more sought after for its thought processes, and protects it obviously legally. The other one might not do anything wrong, but the language puts us in a position that people suspect it. Don't trust it. That issue was very pervasive at Bear Stearns. The firm was never as aggressive as its reputation. But its language, its culture, and its swagger put it more at risk than its actual actions."

Bear's swashbuckling, siloed culture also put it at risk for the occasional quirky crime. For instance, in August 2001, Anamarie Giambrone, then thirty-four and secretary to Eli Wachtel, a long-time Bear Stearns senior executive, and her husband, Salvatore, were indicted on thirteen counts of grand larceny, forgery, and other crimes in connection with their theft of $800,000 from Wachtel. Anamarie Giambrone pleaded guilty to the scheme, whereby she wrote checks requested by Wachtel in disappearing ink while Wachtel signed the checks in permanent ink. After the ink on the checks faded, Giambrone rewrote the checks out to "cash" and cashed them. During the eight months Giambrone worked for Wachtel, she stole the $800,000, which she used to take a vacation and to buy her husband a pizza parlor in Flushing, Queens. She served several years in prison.

PART III

THE END OF THE
SECOND GILDED AGE

CHAPTER 23

THE 10-IN-10 STRATEGY

When the first jet hit the World Trade Center towers on the morning of September 11, 2001, Cayne was in a compensation committee meeting in a conference room down the hall from his office at 245 Park. "The phone rings," Cayne said, "and Sam [Molinaro] gets the phone and says, 'Oh, my God, there's been an accident. A plane flew into the World Trade Center.' We had no idea it was a terrorist attack." The meeting ended quickly, and Cayne went back to his office, turned on the small television in his office, and, as so many others did, watched in disbelief as the second jet hit the south tower. The firm lost none of its employees that day, unlike other firms. Later in the day, Cayne got a call from Richard Grasso, then CEO of the New York Stock Exchange, telling him that it was important to the United States government that the exchange reopen as quickly as possible. To that end, Grasso said there would be a meeting the next morning at the stock exchange among the heads of all the Wall Street firms to discuss how best to accomplish that task.

When Cayne woke up the next morning, he saw on the news that New York City had closed off access to lower Manhattan below 15th Street, including the New York Stock Exchange. Cayne called Grasso at home and offered to host the meeting at Bear Stearns. Grasso quickly agreed to Cayne's suggestion, and the meeting was held in the seventh-floor boardroom on Wednesday at two o'clock. "Everybody in the world was there," Cayne said. "Everybody. This was heavy cake." The room was so crowded that some of the executives had to stand. Cayne asked everyone to observe a moment of silence. Two hours later, a bleak picture had emerged of damaged infrastructure, demoralized employees, and inadequate communication systems. The decision was made to commence trading in U.S. government bonds the next day and to hold off stock trading for another day. "I've never seen all these people, the heads of every major firm, sit in a room and not hate each other," Cayne said.

Within weeks of the attack, Cayne was doing all he could to return to business as usual. For instance, given that the firm's move to its new headquarters at 383 Madison Avenue was imminent, Cayne was—at least according to the *Wall Street Journal*—busy deciding whether to move his burgundy Ek-Chor motorcycle from his old office to his new office, which he did, and trying to figure out who should be allowed to use the gym in the new building. "Don't scoff," the paper wrote. "Demand is so strong that Chief Executive Jimmy Cayne has to personally approve each applicant."

Cayne also struck a more sober tone in announcing the firm's third-quarter 2001 financial results, released September 26. "We would like to continue to express our sincere condolences to all those affected by the tragic events of September 11, 2001," he said. "Our focus over the past weeks has been to help our clients, our employees and our industry cope with this tragedy. We are extremely grateful to all those who came to the aid of the City and the industry during its time of need." The results, for the three months ended August 30, revealed a firm undergoing a transformation. The performance of every one of the firm's major divisions—investment banking, clearing, asset management, and institutional equities—was down meaningfully from the third quarter of the year before, with one exception: fixed income. Net revenues for fixed income were $416.1 million, up 78.4 percent from $233.3 million in the previous year's third quarter. "Although down from last quarter's record results, fixed income revenues remained strong year-over-year, with solid performances in the mortgage-backed securities, high yield and credit derivatives areas," the firm announced. In short order, Bear Stearns's fixed-income division accounted for one-third of the firm's revenues in the first nine months of 2001, up from 18 percent in the first nine months of 2000.

On October 18, the *Wall Street Journal* reported that Bear Stearns would be joining the ranks of other Wall Street firms in cutting 830 jobs, or 7.5 percent of its workforce of 11,147 employees. The move reflected the increasingly difficult market conditions on Wall Street and followed the firm's decision six months earlier to cut four hundred back-office employees. Bear Stearns had joined the rest of the pack in cutting employees during tough times. More and more, what made Bear Stearns such an unusual firm was being lost in the inexorable march of progress. "This workforce reduction will generate approximately $120 million in annualized savings," the firm predicted in an SEC filing. Cayne agreed that the five-member executive committee would cut their 2001 bonuses in half. "This has been a challenging year for all of us," he wrote in an e-mail to the firm. "Accordingly the Executive Committee has voluntarily elected to forfeit 50 percent of the bonuses we would otherwise be entitled to receive this year. Based on current earnings levels, this election is equivalent to an approximate 70 percent reduction year over year." For Cayne, who received $31.6 million in compensation in 2000, his reduction for 2001 meant he was paid $15.2 million.

In a January 2002 interview with *Chief Executive* magazine, Cayne revisited his impolitic comments to Guy Moszkowski about his willingness to consider selling Bear Stearns for four times book value, or $120 per share. Lehman Brothers was mentioned as having had discussions with Bear Stearns in November 2000, stemming from Lehman's interest in Bear's clearing business. "That was all nonsense," he said in January 2002. "There isn't anybody I talked to who had an interest in hooking up with Bear Stearns who really looked at that as a serious comment. And I wouldn't negotiate with anyone who did." He brushed aside the question of how much longer the firm could remain independent. "Since I've been around, 95 percent of the people who've competed with this company are no longer competing with this company. That's an unusual statistic." Cayne's speech was a variation on one that Greenberg had been giving for years that pointed to a tombstone advertisement listing Bear's competitors who were no longer in business. "That's the beauty of this thing," Cayne said of Wall Street. "Nobody ever knows what's going to happen."

Not mentioned in the article was the fact that Jamie Dimon, since March 2000 the CEO of Bank One, in Chicago, had been to 383 Madison to talk with Cayne about buying Bear Stearns. Dimon had suggested an all-stock acquisition of Bear Stearns by Bank One at a significant premium to the market price of the stock, then in the mid-$60 per share range. But Cayne rebuffed Dimon's offer because he feared that any premium offered would be lost in the post-announcement trading of the stock as arbitrageurs drove down the price of Bank One's stock. "It couldn't be done," Cayne said, "and he knew it. It had nothing to do with anything. There was no ego involved. Whatever premium he would have paid would have been eaten up by the arbs in one second. All I would have done was give him the keys, which I should have done. That's the mistake I made."

In February 2002, *American Banker* wrote a brief article about the rumor that Bank One was considering buying Bear Stearns. The idea had originated with Sean Ryan, a former Bear Stearns financial services analyst who left the firm after being pressured by senior management to write reports about banks he did not want to cover. "This rumor probably is as baseless as most," Paul Muolo wrote, "but the idea may not be a bad one. Although we are highly skeptical about the wisdom of merging commercial and investment banks, a Bank One/Bear Stearns marriage may not be a bad idea."

What made the combination palatable, the newspaper thought, was that Dimon had an investment banking mentality, having been in charge of Salomon Smith Barney and Citigroup's investment banking business, as well as having been the right-hand man of wheeler-dealer Sandy Weill before Weill fired Dimon in November 1998. "Bear Stearns is a scrappy, highly profitable player that keeps its eye on costs, very much the style of Weill and presumably of Dimon," Muolo wrote. "Bear Stearns could also make an especially good fit with a commercial bank because it is well-known for its fixed-income business, and its highly lucrative clearing business." (In the end, Dimon sold Bank One to JPMorgan Chase in 2004 for $58 billion in stock; by January 2005, Dimon was the CEO of the combined firm.)

❄

ON APRIL 4, Cayne and a group of dignitaries, including New York Governor George Pataki and Senator Charles Schumer, as well as eight hundred Bear Stearns employees and clients, officially opened the new building at 383 Madison. "Bear Stearns and its impressive new headquarters are fitting symbols of the strength, permanence and grandeur of New York," Pataki said, with September 11 still reverberating. "It is successful companies like Bear Stearns that have helped to make New York the financial capital it is today." Cayne, too, sought to equate the new building with Bear Stearns's solidity. "We are confident that the Bear Stearns crown"—the seven-story structure at the top of the building that was lit up as part of the ceremony—"will serve as a reminder that our firm was established here and will always be committed to this great city." The building, billed as one of the most technologically advanced in New York City, had the largest installation of cable of any in North America and contained 18,000 tons of steel, making it one of the heaviest buildings in New York. The building also had four emergency generators, a water tank "big enough for a Sea World show," and an independent phone network, all of which served not only as a monument to Cayne but also as a bulwark against any future water, phone, and power outages.

❋

THAT SAME MONTH, shortly after announcing quarterly net income of $181 million—powered yet again by the firm's fixed-income businesses, "with [a] particularly strong performance from our industry-leading mortgage-backed securities department," Cayne emphasized in an SEC filing—Cayne decided to start writing a bridge column in the now defunct *New York Sun* with Michael Ledeen, the controversial neoconservative scholar at the American Enterprise Institute who played a role in the Iran-Contra scandal in the second Reagan administration. He was a fine bridge player in his own right, although not on a par with Cayne, and had authored *Machiavelli on Modern Leadership*, a book about the relevance of Machiavelli's philosophy to modern business leaders. Cayne loved the book, one of the few he has read. In their June 4, 2002, *New York Sun* bridge column titled "Making the Best of a Bad Situation," the men observed, "As in life, much of bridge has to do with blunders and accidents. One of the big differences between winning and losing bridge players—as in most competitive aspects of life—is that winners learn to make the best of difficult situations." The same could easily have been said about Cayne in the years following September 11 and the firm's move into Cayne's tower at 383 Madison Avenue. Suddenly, as never before, the press and the market latched on to the idea that Cayne was playing a poor hand exceedingly well.

In October 2002, *Forbes* published "The Card Player" about Cayne and immediately created the impression that somehow Bear Stearns had managed to avoid the malfeasance other firms had committed with their investment bankers and research analysts. "Here's one investment bank not on Eliot Spitzer's hit list," the article stated, ignoring completely that the firm had committed many of the same sins involving investment bankers and research analysts—albeit less grievously—as had Salomon Brothers and Merrill. "They say that a card player's skill is shown by how well he plays a bad hand," *Forbes* observed. "The bear market has dealt every Wall Street firm a bad hand, and Bear Stearns' skills are showing through." The article recounted how the firm's net income had increased 21 percent through the first nine months of 2002, compared to 2001. "Credit goes to . . . Cayne," the magazine concluded. In early March 2003, *Fortune* stunned Wall Street by declaring Bear Stearns the "most admired securities firm" of 2002, ahead of both Goldman Sachs and Morgan Stanley. Bear had placed seventh on the list of most-admired securities firms the year before.

Then, on March 28, both the *New York Times* and the *Wall Street Journal* published articles lauding Bear Stearns's ability to thrive in a difficult market. The *Journal* headlined its article "A Contrary Bear Stearns Thrives," while the *Times* ran "Distinct Culture at Bear Stearns Helps It Surmount a Grim Market." Cayne declined to speak to the *Journal,* but Spector observed that the firm's decision to cut $300 million from its expense base starting in 2000 "sent a message that we're paying attention to the bottom line. People got it." Added Sam Molinaro, "We've always been skeptical of the herd mentality. It means we may miss some business in the short run but we do better in the longer run." The *Journal* article observed that part of Bear's success was due to luck—that it never had been big in M&A or equity underwriting (two businesses that had slowed considerably by 2003) or in catering to small investors. The firm had also "failed to fully broaden its earnings away from bonds, stock-clearing and other specialities, which it sought to do in the mid-1990s." Now that singular focus seemed to be paying off. "Bear

Stearns' bond operation, overseen by Mr. Spector, picked up ground as the bond market surged," the newspaper wrote. "Bear Stearns now is the biggest player in the raging mortgage-underwriting business and the fourth largest in municipal bonds. In comparison, the firm was third in mortgages and eighth in munis three years ago." Bear underwrote $98 billion of mortgage bonds in 2002, up from $22 billion in 2000, and appeared headed to underwrite north of $100 billion in mortgage bonds in 2003. Spector predicted a bright future for the firm. "We'll underperform if we go back to the insanity of 1999 and 2000 but if equity picks up we'll do as well as anyone else because of our stock clearance and wealth-management businesses."

In the dueling laudatory articles, it was Landon Thomas Jr., at the *Times,* who had Cayne "kicking back in his swivel chair" behind his "sweeping half-moon desk" to opine that what kept him up at night was the big bets his traders were making down the hall. "I'll tell you what worries me," he told Thomas. "That we might be doing something stupid." Cayne seemed at once cautious—"We are hitting on all 99 cylinders," he said, "so you have to ask yourself, What can we do better? And I just can't decide what that might be"—and cocky. "Everyone says that when the market turns around, we will suffer," he said. "But let me tell you, we are going to surprise some people this time around. Bear Stearns is a great place to be." In keeping with past precedents, he also was unapologetic about his 2002 compensation—$18 million, including $10 million in cash—which made him the highest-paid executive on Wall Street. Schwartz and Spector made $17 million each. Cayne even defended the entire Wall Street compensation scheme, which had been transformed from one of shared liabilities back when the firms were private partnerships to one of encouraging bankers and traders to take short-term risks with other people's money in the hope of making a huge, no-strings-attached bonus. "This is not an ordinary business," Cayne told Thomas. "My father was a patent attorney, and he never made more than 75 grand in his whole life. But if I don't pay my guy $1 million, nine of my competitors are willing to pay him four times that." As to the inevitable question about who would succeed Cayne, then sixty-nine, and when, Thomas noted there was "a spring in his step that belies his age" and that Bear Stearns's executives had a "history of working into their 70s," although the only one to have done so was Greenberg. Schwartz or Spector? Thomas wanted to know. "It's the $64,000 question," Cayne replied. "But there are no cabals or coups here. These guys are not champing at the bit."

❄

LURKING THEMATICALLY THROUGH the spate of positive coverage of the firm was the question of why Cayne had not diversified the firm away from its huge concentration in fixed income and clearing. True, that decision had proved lucrative to Bear Stearns in the wake of September 11 and Fed Chairman Alan Greenspan's aggressive campaign, starting in January 2001, to lower interest rates (rates dropped thirteen times between May 2000 and June 2003, going from 6.5 percent to 1.00 percent, with eleven of those rate decreases coming in 2001 alone). "The Fed's easy-money policy put a lot of the wind at the back of some of the transactions in the housing market and elsewhere we are now suffering from," explained Glenn Hubbard in December 2008, looking back at the time when he was chairman of the White House Council of Economic Advisers. The consequences of Greenspan's monetary policy would soon be felt—with dramatic consequences—across the global financial markets. "Investors said, 'I don't want to be in equities anymore and I'm not getting any returns in my bond positions,'" explained William T. Winters, the co-head of investment banking at JPMorgan Chase and one of the developers of the derivative products so prevalent today. "Two things happened. They took [on] more and more leverage, and they reached for riskier asset classes. Give me yield, give me leverage, give me return." Bear Stearns put itself at the epicenter of those consequences because of its reliance on fixed income—specifically mortgage-backed and other asset-backed securities—for its profitability and because of its failure to diversify when it had numerous chances.

The blame for the firm's failure to diversify, as Cayne now admits, rested squarely on his shoulders. In this sense, he became a Sophoclean tragic hero, ruined by his own terrible choices. For instance, in 2001, Spector brought to Cayne's attention the opportunity to buy asset manager Neuberger Berman, which at the time was publicly traded and had around $56 billion in assets under management. Bear Stearns Asset Management had about half that amount. The marriage could have been a beautiful one, as they say in Hollywood. But Cayne did not want to pursue the deal, even though Bear Stearns could have had the business for around $1 billion less than the $2.6 billion that Lehman Brothers paid in cash and stock in July 2003. "Acquisitions weren't my forte," Cayne said. "They had forty-seven brokers. That's what it was. Lehman paid $3 billion for forty-seven brokers. Who would dream of doing that? I wouldn't pay anything for forty-seven brokers."

Bear Stearns also had several opportunities to buy Pershing, the large clearing business that at the time was part of Donaldson, Lufkin & Jenrette. The first opportunity to buy Pershing came around the time Dick Harriton left Bear Stearns. Harriton had been friendly with the head of Pershing and together they cooked up a plan to merge Pershing into Bear's clearing business and then have both Bear Stearns and DLJ go private. It was a bit of a long putt, but Harriton was convinced Bear could have had Pershing for $250 million. He took the idea to Alan Schwartz, who thought it was a great idea, but told Harriton the firm had decided to pass.

Both Spector and Schwartz were frustrated by Cayne's continuing refusal to pursue acquisitions that appeared—to the two co-presidents, anyway—to make a tremendous amount of sense. Regarding the Neuberger Berman deal, Cayne and Greenberg rejected it immediately. "They turned it down flat," one senior Bear executive said. "They told me, 'This will disrupt our organization. We will not let them run our PCS [private client services] business.' They wanted to do nothing that would upset their world." Schwartz looked at it more clinically, like the world-class M&A banker he was. "In the acquisition game," someone familiar with his view explained, "there were ten things we could do out there: Two are automatic, two look pretty good, a bunch are just okay, this one's hairy. These two—Neuberger Berman and Pershing—were automatics, and if you're not going to do the automatics, why bring in the one that's a little less good than the automatics? So acquisitions were out, he realized that. Neuberger, Jimmy admits now, we should have done, and Pershing he never understood. It doesn't matter. The point was we weren't doing any of this, period."

As ever, Cayne remained wedded to growing organically the businesses the firm was already in. "We liked our hand and we really didn't have a right to like our hand as much as we liked it," explained one of Cayne's most senior partners. In that vein, in 2003 Cayne turned his attention to improving the firm's relatively tiny asset management business. The firm did not disclose much about this business in its financial statements since it was so small, but from the little bit of public information available, it was clear the division was not performing well under Doni Fordyce, one of the few senior-level women at the firm. The firm's assets under management had declined to $21 billion by May 31, down from $24 billion in both 2002 and 2001. The business's revenues—derived mostly from management fees—declined to $154 million in 2002 from $168 million in 2001. As for the division's profitability, the firm did not disclose this information in its public filings, but the profitability for both asset management and private client services—the brokers—had declined substantially in 2002, to $11.6 million from $128 million in 2000. Clearly, Cayne had a problem in the business. So on June 24, he hired Richard A. Marin as the new chairman and CEO of Bear Stearns Asset Management, or BSAM, as it was known. The son of a career United Nations diplomat and a graduate of Cornell, Marin had spent twenty-three years at Bankers Trust, and then, following the firm's acquisition by Deutsche Bank in 1999, he headed up Deutsche Asset Management, with $325 billion in assets under management. Marin's arrival meant that Fordyce had been demoted to BSAM's president. Despite her public statement that "I'm looking forward to what will be a dynamic partnership" with Marin, Fordyce was not happy. She left four months later.

Marin found a business that had some good products and some good people but that had been starved for capital and management. Spector told Marin: "Bear Stearns succeeds at anything it puts its mind to. And since we haven't really succeeded at asset management, we haven't put our mind to it. We want to put our mind to it now. We want to have you come in. And we want you to grow this, grow it more quickly than it's grown before." Marin and Spector talked about what would be reasonable metrics on which Spector could judge Marin's performance. They spoke about how both BSAM and Goldman Sachs's asset management business had both started in the same year, 1984, but that nearly twenty years later GSAM had $400 billion of assets under management and BSAM had less than $20 billion. These assets consisted of 60 percent hedge funds and 30 percent traditional asset management, with the balance a smattering of small private equity and venture capital funds that were not related to Bear Stearns's successful merchant banking fund, run by John Howard. Why couldn't BSAM be as important to Bear Stearns, they wondered, as GSAM was to Goldman Sachs? Out of this brainstorming session came the strategy known inside Bear Stearns as "10 in 10," whereby BSAM would be 10 percent of Bear Stearns's revenues and profits by 2010. This would be the metric on which Spector would judge Marin's performance. To be sure, Marin's challenge was significant given that in 2003 BSAM was about 1 percent of the firm's revenues and a negative contributor to its profits.

The first Bear Stearns–related phone call Marin received on his first day at the firm—even before he had made it to his office—came when Barry Cohen called his cell phone. Cohen had run the merger arbitrage fund at the firm for many years and made himself and his partners a bunch of money. Cohen had also been a protégé of Bobby Steinberg, who oversaw the firm's risk function. Cohen was on the board of directors of Bear Stearns & Co., the firm's broker-dealer (as opposed to the Bear Stearns Companies, the public parent company). It was considered an honor in the firm to be a member of the board of the broker-dealer. Cohen was ostensibly in charge of the firm's hedge fund business, but since he was part of the broker-dealer and not part of BSAM, where many of the firm's hedge funds actually were, this was all a bit confusing, made all the more so because Spector had earlier tried to make Cohen a co-head of BSAM with Fordyce, who successfully opposed that appointment.

On that first morning, Cohen, who knew Marin slightly, called and told him, "This is gonna be great." A few days later, Spector called Marin and told him, "You know, I've got this guy, Barry Cohen, who the firm really likes and is really good on risk, [and who] has run his own hedge fund. You might want to take a very serious look at bringing Barry Cohen over the wall" and into asset management to run the hedge fund business, reporting to Marin. Cohen did not want to give up his board seat at the broker-dealer, but in the end he did so to join the asset management business. Soon after Marin and Spector had decided on the 10-in-10 strategy, Cohen said to him, "We've got this great guy coming off the floor. Warren had seeded this fund for him six months ago. He's done really well with it. His name's Ralph Cioffi. He's got a great strategy. I want you to meet him. This is exactly the kind of thing that we want to bring in here."

The intense and solidly built Cioffi, then forty-seven, had joined Bear Stearns in 1985 as an institutional fixed-income salesman, specializing in structured finance products, after stints at Merrill Lynch, Dean Witter Reynolds, and Institutional Direct. He grew up in South Burlington, Vermont, near Lake Champlain. From 1989 to 1991, Cioffi was the New York head of fixed-income sales and then, for the next three years, served as global product and sales manager for high-grade credit products. "He was involved in the creation of the structured credit effort at Bear Stearns and was a principal force behind Bear Stearns' position as a leading underwriter and secondary trader of structured finance securities, specifically collateralized debt obligations and esoteric asset-backed securities," according to a description of him on file with the SEC.

"We all grew up with Ralph here," explained Paul Friedman. "Ralph is one of the smartest guys I've ever met and was absolutely the best salesman I've ever met. When I was a trader, he was a salesman, a fabulous salesman. He was incredibly personable, incredibly smart, creative, and could get things done." As a salesman, Cioffi covered the Ohio Public Employees Retirement System account. "It was a wonderful account," Friedman said. "We had a great relationship, and they loved us, and they did a lot of business with us, and whoever covered that account got really rich." Cioffi was making around $4 million, year after year, as a salesman. "He was the top fixed-income salesman in a firm where fixed income was king," said one senior managing director. Then Cioffi got promoted to the job of institutional sales manager. He was a disaster. "He had adult ADD," Friedman said. "In sales and trading, you work on something, you get it done, you move on to the next thing. The day ends, you've written some tickets, and you move on. In management, you come in in the morning and you're working on what you worked on yesterday, and you're trying to hire this guy, or build this business. And you're going to work on it again tomorrow, and probably the next day. Ralph didn't do well with that stuff. He would hire salespeople, and we'd get to the end of the year and find out that he'd cut deals and forgot to write them down. He couldn't remember exactly what the guy's guarantee was. He was just not a really good manager." Cioffi then moved into Bear's structured products group, where he was a "quasi-asset-backed banker," according to Friedman. "Again, he was incredibly creative but a challenge to manage. It would be the same thing, where he'd have a conversation with the rating agency about some deal he was working on and he'd forget to tell everybody about it. So, you'd have a team working down one path and Ralph's working down the other path, and they'd get to here and find out that he'd already changed it."

Like Barry Cohen, Cioffi was on the board of directors of the broker-dealer and much loved inside the firm. Spector, Friedman, and others were trying to find a role for Cioffi that would match his skills. Cioffi volunteered his interest in being a hedge fund manager. To accommodate that desire, Spector decided, in March 2003, to stake Cioffi to $10 million of the firm's money in a hedge fund that invested in mortgage-backed securities. His fund, known on Wall Street as a "carry fund," invested in securities of various credit quality, using a sliver of equity and a whole lot of debt. The interest the securities paid less the interest on the money borrowed to buy the securities created the "carry," or returns to the equity investors. "Spector gave him a little money and it grew," Friedman said. "There was a fair number of skeptics internally who couldn't figure out how this guy—who was bright but had never managed money—was now going to be running money. He knew nothing about risk management, had never written a ticket in his life that wasn't someone else's money. But we did it. I sure as hell wouldn't have given him my money. But he starts out and he's reasonably successful."

Cioffi's initial success obviated the question internally about whether he could continue to be part of the broker-dealer or whether he should be seconded to BSAM. The compliance officers decided Cioffi needed to be transferred into BSAM and report to Marin, who in turn reported to Spector. "We put him over in BSAM, where you had a guy, Rich Marin, running an asset management division that was the traditional asset management business—long only, primarily equities with a trace of fixed income—who suddenly inherits this high-octane mortgage guy and doesn't have any idea what to make of him," Friedman explained. "Every time Marin and the risk guys in BSAM would have a question with Ralph, Ralph would get Warren involved, and they'd all have this big meeting in Warren's office, and Warren would say to the BSAM, 'You don't know what you're talking about. Leave Ralph alone. He's doing fine,' and eventually they came to largely ignore him. And that's a little harsh, but not entirely wrong, because none of them really understood what he did." Explained Marin to the *New York Times* about Cioffi: "He had come up with an approach to trading those assets"—among others, mortgage-backed securities and collateralized debt obligations—"that people who are experts in that arena thought was a sound and interesting approach."

⁂

BY 2003, HEDGE funds were the rage of global finance, much as private equity funds had been a decade or so earlier. Whereas the best and the brightest bankers on Wall Street left to become private equity dons, the best and the brightest traders on Wall Street left to become hedge fund managers. As hedge funds were making money hand over fist, a number of Wall Street firms started to take large equity stakes in hedge fund management companies as a way to reap a percentage of those profits and as a way to give their talented and ambitious traders a place to go without necessarily having them leave the fold. Firms such as JPMorgan Chase, Lehman Brothers, and Morgan Stanley took equity stakes in hedge fund management companies. Many believed that Goldman Sachs—which many of the most successful hedge fund managers had left in search of even greater fame and fortune—had become nothing more than a big hedge fund itself.

Nearly alone, Bear Stearns took a different approach. The firm had numerous chances to do so but never bought a hedge fund management company or took an equity stake in one. Instead, the firm decided to try to grow its own hedge fund managers. Internally respected professionals, such as Cioffi, who expressed an interest in being hedge fund managers were occasionally given the chance to fulfill their dreams. For Bear Stearns, taking this chance kept talented salesmen, traders, and bankers at the firm at little additional cost. The same could not be said of either investing in a hedge fund or buying one outright.

In October 2003, Barry Cohen recommended to Marin that Cioffi move over to BSAM and set up a hedge fund with money from outside investors. Under the circumstances—Marin being new to the firm and having the clear recommendation of his boss—Marin agreed to bring Cioffi into BSAM to set up the High-Grade Structured Credit Fund. "He was considered extremely expert in structured trades," one of his colleagues said. "There were certainly some people who thought, 'Hey, what's he doing trading? He's a salesman.' Warren, who knew him the best, and Barry Cohen, for that matter, all said, 'You know what? It doesn't matter. He knows the market. And he's good. That's not going to be an issue.'" Helping Cioffi run the hedge fund was Matthew Tannin, six years his junior. Tannin, born in New Jersey, was a graduate of the University of San Francisco law school. He joined Bear Stearns in 1994 and spent seven years structuring collateralized debt obligations. In 2001, he moved over to research, where he studied the trading and value of CDOs.

The High-Grade Fund opened to outside investors in October 2003. Cioffi and Tannin told investors that the fund would invest in low-risk, high-grade debt securities, such as tranches of CDOs, which the ratings agencies had rated either AAA or AA. The fund would focus on using leverage to generate returns by borrowing money in the low-cost, short-term repo markets to buy higher-yielding, long-term CDOs. The difference between the interest received and the interest paid, enhanced by the use of borrowed money, would yield the fund's profits.

For the next forty months, Cioffi's hedge fund never had a losing month. During that time the High-Grade Fund achieved a 50 percent cumulative return. "Ralph was one of the biggest customers on Wall Street," Cayne said. "He was everybody's best client. I tell you, for forty months in a row it was fine." Bloomberg reported that Cioffi earned an "eight-figure compensation." In typical hedge fund fashion, BSAM kept 20 percent of the profits generated by the fund plus a 2 percent fee on the net assets under management; fees from the High-Grade Fund alone accounted for 75 percent of BSAM's total revenues in 2004 and 2005. Bear Stearns, in turn, rewarded Cioffi with many millions in compensation. He certainly lived very well. In 2000, he and his wife, Phyllis, purchased a home for $815,000 in Tenafly, New Jersey, that in 2007 was assessed for $2.6 million. He owned a home in Naples, Florida, valued at $933,000, and a home in Ludlow, Vermont, valued at $2.2 million. He bought some land in Portsmouth, Rhode Island, that he then sold for a small profit. He owned an apartment at the Stanhope, on Fifth Avenue, in Manhattan, and a $10.7 million, 6,500-square-foot home in Southampton, Long Island, that had six bedrooms, seven baths, a pool, a tennis court, and a separate guesthouse on two and a half acres. "Ralph liked to live large," one of his friends said about him.

But Cioffi's real passion was for Ferraris. At one point, he owned two of them: a $250,000 F430 convertible Spider and a $300,000 front-engine V-12 Superamerica. One day, his Ferrari dealer in Spring Valley, New York—in Rockland County—called him up and told him he had one low-mileage Ferrari Enzo for sale. Was Cioffi interested in a trade of his two Ferraris plus some cash for the Enzo? Only 399 of the Enzos were built from 2002 to 2004, and they originally cost $650,000 each. Nowadays, if you can find one, it will cost around $1.2 million. After getting the call from the dealer, Cioffi called up Doug Sharon, a longtime Bear broker and car aficionado who ran the firm's Boston office.

"Do you think I should do the trade?" Cioffi asked Sharon. "The dealer wants me to do this trade."

"Ralph, as far as I'm concerned, it's a no-brainer," Sharon told him. "You gotta do it. Your two cars and some cash for an Enzo? Enzos are hard to find."

"It's not exactly the kind of car I'm gonna drive down to the golf club with," Cioffi responded. For Sharon, the conversation with

Cioffi about the Enzo "was probably the beginning of the end, when Ralph's thinking about buying million-dollar Ferraris." He contemplated buying a partnership stake in a Gulfstream jet and was the executive producer of the 2006 independent film *Just Like My Son*, starring Rosie Perez.

CHAPTER 24

CAYNE CAPS SPECTOR

By 2004, there was no question that the businesses at the firm that reported to Warren Spector—fixed income, institutional equities, and asset management—were driving the growth of the firm. Particularly important was the exponential growth of the fixed-income business, which was without question Spector's fiefdom. Fixed-income revenue in 2004 was $3.1 billion—nearly 45 percent of the firm's overall revenue of $6.8 billion—and had increased some 63 percent, from $1.9 billion in revenues, since 2002. "These businesses benefited from the low level of interest rates, a steep yield curve and narrowing of corporate credit spreads," the firm reported in its SEC filings. "Mortgage-backed securities revenues increased significantly as residential mortgage refinancing activity reached record levels during the year, driving record new issue activity, and demand for high-quality fixed income investments continued." The firm did not break out separately the profitability of Spector's fixed-income division, but the overall grouping of investment banking (Schwartz's bailiwick), institutional equities, and fixed income had increased its pretax income to $2 billion in 2004, from $1.3 billion in 2002, and it would be safe to say that much of the increase in the pretax income came from the growth in the fixed-income division.

Slowly but surely the market and the press began to naturally assume that Spector was Cayne's heir apparent, since he ran such a substantial portion of the firm's businesses. But Cayne was careful to leave the question of his succession plenty ambiguous. He paid both Spector and Schwartz virtually the same amount year after year. In 2004, each made $18.7 million. In 2003, they made $20.5 million each, and in 2002, each made $17.2 million. He was also careful to pay them around 95 percent of what he made in any given year as a way to head off any nascent movement for a coup d'état against him. But the impression remained, fostered in part by Spector himself, that he was the likely successor to Cayne, though Cayne denied that Spector had the position wrapped up, despite his business and bridge acumen. Besides, Cayne had no intention of going anywhere. "Spector was a major, major, major, major disappointment because he was extremely smart and capable," Cayne said. "The attitudinal issue of him being an elitist with his own people was clear. There were always reports about him being an unpleasant boss to work for. But he was a favored son in the eyes of the firm. He never was told by me he was my successor. He asked for it many times. And I never said yes, never. Not out of any malice. In fact, if I had to choose—like you're dying and you've got to choose a successor—it would not have been him. Here's a guy that was right a lot of the time. His personal faults were simply bearable. The package was worthwhile."

The Oedipal quality of their relationship was becoming increasingly obvious. Ironically, though, it was Spector's careful reading of the firm's CAP—the internal mechanism created for the sole purpose of creating sufficient long-term wealth for Bear Stearns's senior management to dissuade them from leaving the firm—that created the first of many fissures in the complicated relationship between Cayne and Spector. The way the CAP worked was that an executive could choose what percentage—up to 100 percent—of his annual compensation he wanted to invest in the company's stock through the plan. The day the election was made was the day the stock would be purchased at whatever the market price of the stock was at the time. There was no discount. But there was an opaque benefit to the plan, whereby each year the CAP participant would get an additional number of shares based on the firm's earnings and the firm's stock price. Over time, it became clear that this benefit worked out to between 7 percent and 8 percent extra a year, in some years even more. Over the five-year life of each CAP, an investment in 100 shares could be turned into 140 shares simply by compounding that 7 percent annual return. This was before any increase in the firm's stock price, which throughout this period was increasing rapidly. The chance to triple one's initial investment was not unreasonable.

Spector was one of the very few senior executives at the firm to take the time to read and fully comprehend the nuances of the CAP. He figured out how lucrative the plan could be, as long as the firm's earnings and stock price were increasing. He routinely decided to invest 100 percent of his annual compensation into the CAP. What's more, as was permitted by the terms of the CAP, Spector had elected to defer the investment, including all of its tax-deferred compounding, until he retired. Since Spector was in his mid-forties at this time, and the firm obviously had never enforced a retirement age, the size of the firm's potential liability to Spector could be enormous. As was required, disclosure of the growing payments and liabilities to the senior management of the firm started to appear in the annual proxy statements. This, in turn, caught the attention of investors and the research analysts who covered the company, which in turn made the magnitude of the problem seem all the more severe. As a result of the CAP, the firm's proxy statements started to include a column for "all other compensation," which accounted for "preferential earnings paid in the form of CAP Units pursuant to the CAP Plan that exceed cash dividends paid on the equivalent shares of Common Stock." In other words, this column represented the value of additional annual 7 percent compounding on the stock in the CAP over and above what the common stock dividend would be.

Since Spector owned more stock through the CAP than anyone else, the numbers in the proxy related to his "other compensation" were getting increasingly large and were making it appear to the outside world that Spector was making more money than Cayne. For instance, the firm's 2003 proxy statement showed that Cayne owned 4.8 million shares of common stock and another 2.4 million shares through the CAP. The amount of his "other compensation" related to the CAP for 2002 was $10.2 million, and his total compensation, including that related to the CAP, was $28.4 million.

Spector, meanwhile, owned 789,482 shares of common stock and another 3.5 million shares through the CAP. His "other compensation" in 2002 related to those CAP shares was $13.9 million, bringing his total compensation in 2002 to $31.2 million. In 2003, the gap between Spector's total compensation, $38.5 million, and Cayne's, of $33.9 million, grew wider.

✻

THE FACT THAT Spector appeared to be making more money than Cayne irked the boss. After Sam Molinaro, the firm's CFO, and Steve Begleiter, the firm's head of strategy, walked Cayne through the growing magnitude of the problem, Cayne decided to force the participants in the CAP to sell their stock. Begleiter and Molinaro tried to fashion a compromise with Cayne about how to unwind the plan, but Cayne decided just to end the plan and compel the sale of the stock in it. He was well within his rights to end the plan at his sole discretion. "In the CAP plan language was a little codicil," Cayne explained. "The codicil said that anytime the company wants to call this off—this good-till-retirement thing—it may. Sam and Steve Begleiter came to me at some point and said, 'Jimmy, you don't know it, but if the stock price does this'"—stays relatively flat—"'there's no harm, no foul. But if the stock price goes like this'"—continued its upward trend—"'then Warren does just fine to the tune of $300 to $400 million over a period of four to five years and the company gets killed.' Because we pay it. We pay him as if the stock was still up. So it became imperative from a fiduciary standpoint to call it off."

Spector was livid. He suspected, correctly, that Cayne's decision to terminate the CAP was directed at him personally. "He fought it like a tiger," Cayne said of Spector. "But it's like fighting death. If I tell you you've got terminal cancer, you can fight all you want, you're not winning. He took it all the way to every board member. All he had to do was just talk to one board member"—Cayne—"and he would have told you you're wasting your time. The company has to call it off. The company will be derelict in its responsibility if they don't call it off." Cayne made the decision in September 2003, and by November, Cayne, Greenberg, Schwartz, and Spector had sold some $263 million worth of stock at a price of around $74 per share.

Spector sold $74 million worth of stock; Schwartz sold $74.5 million worth of stock. In the years following Cayne's decision, as the price of Bear's stock continued to increase, the depth of Spector's ire at Cayne only grew.

Cayne saw this as a breaking point not only in their relationship but also in Spector's attitude toward the firm. "That blew his brain, basically," Cayne said. "He stopped digging in. He became a caretaker of the inventory of the mortgage department as opposed to a manager of the inventory. That became, I believe, the prime mover for his dissent from the standpoint of responsibility. The hedge fund thing became totally him. He put a real fence around Cioffi. He didn't let the credit people in. He didn't let the repo people in. He became a one-man show with Bear Stearns Asset Management, which was doing great. Remember, Cioffi's results for forty months were sensational. After the fact, it's very easy to say, 'Well, you didn't think there was something wrong with that?' No. I didn't think there was anything wrong with it. I saw a win every month. Why, am I smarter than them?"

As is not atypical on Wall Street as wealth swells, Spector became increasingly captivated by presidential politics. He was a supporter of Bill Clinton, whom he would occasionally see on Martha's Vineyard, where the Spectors had a large home in southwest Chilmark. The Clintons would stay regularly at the compound of Dick Friedman, a Boston developer. Friedman and Spector were friendly. Tom Flexner, Spector's partner at Bear Stearns, used to rent one of the homes on the Friedmans' property before he decided to buy a home on the island, too.

During one of the Clintons' visits to Martha's Vineyard, Flexner arranged for Spector—who was a club champion golfer—to play with Clinton and with Barry Sternlicht, one of Flexner's clients and then CEO of Starwood Hotels & Resorts. "This was a brand-new experience for both Barry and Warren," Flexner said. "They'd never played with the leader." Flexner also arranged to play with Spector another time on the Vineyard along with the CEO of a private equity firm. "Warren is very focused, whether it's business, golf, bridge—whatever he does," Flexner said. "We did a reasonable amount of business with this firm, and I briefed Warren on that.

We're on one of the greens and Warren's out—it's his putt—and the CEO has his back to Warren and whatever is going through the CEO's mind, he forgets that maybe Warren's on the verge of putting, and he says something to me out loud—not screaming—at the exact moment that Warren is making his thirty-foot putt. He missed the hole by about that much. Warren goes up to the CEO and says, 'Don't you know it's rude to talk when somebody else is putting?' and he was serious. Now, I later called him on that. Warren said, 'Oh, my God. I did that? I was that rude? I've got to call him and apologize.' He genuinely wanted to apologize. I don't think Warren is an evil, malicious, vengeful type of guy."

Following the nasty business of Cayne dissolving the CAP, Spector's next run-in with his boss came a few months later, in July 2004, following Spector's decision to participate in a July 8 conference call—along with other corporate executives—to support the Democratic presidential campaign of Senator John Kerry. On the call, according to press reports, Spector, who had given around $65,000 to Democratic Party candidates and causes, criticized the Bush administration for its "very short-term, narrow-minded policies" while also observing that Kerry's economic policies were "fiscally responsible." Cayne, an avid Republican supporter of Bush, was not happy about Spector's public comments. For twelve days, Cayne said nothing about Spector's comments about Kerry. The two men had been together in New York at the annual Spingold Knockout national championship bridge tournament from July 12 to July 18. "Cayne and his crack squadron of veteran bridgies were knocked out in the quarter-finals," the *Wall Street Letter* reported in August 2004, "while Spector guided his band of tournament rookies to the finals" on July 18. Two days later, on July 20, Cayne e-mailed a memorandum to the firm while Spector was out of town. He wrote of Spector: "His comments were made in such a way as to be viewed as being attributed to Bear Stearns as a whole. Such attributions should not have been made, his views were his own, as a private individual, and not those of the firm. If any of you were upset or offended by these press reports, please accept both his and my apology. . . . Free speech should not be confused with directly or indirectly using the company to endorse political views or agendas."

According to the *Wall Street Letter*, a "bridge source" noted that some "people have suggested this [firm-wide memo against Spector] was a little bit of sour grapes" on Cayne's part at having been surpassed by Spector's team in the Spingold Knockout.

Again, Spector's anger with Cayne knew no bounds. He even went so far as to tell one of his colleagues he wanted "Jimmy to die." This was one of their worst spats. "Jimmy and Warren had this thing where Jimmy felt he needed Warren, but he didn't particularly like Warren," explained someone who knew them both well. "So every once in a while, Jimmy just smacked him way out of proportion, and that was so out of proportion. It was so stupid."

After the public rebuke, one of Spector's colleagues found him in retreat on Martha's Vineyard. The colleague called him up and said, "Warren, I got to tell you something. Forgetting for a second anything about Jimmy or you, the only person who is suffering now from you wanting Jimmy to die is you. He's not. He's having a cocktail somewhere and he's not feeling the voodoo doll stuff. But it's eating you alive. I'm just telling you to forget it. It was an overreaction. Jimmy overreacted and now you're overreacting, but forget that for a second. Even if it's not an overreaction, what good is it doing you? For your own good you've got to get it out of you." To cool down, Spector went and played a few rounds of golf afterward with Alan Schwartz, who was nearby at his home on Nantucket.

Another senior managing director at Bear Stearns thought Cayne's public rebuke of Spector was especially egregious. "When you look back and you see patterns, sometimes you miss things that were all there right in front of you," he said. "I think to myself, 'Geez, that was such an overreaction.' Jimmy's overreaction was much more typical of Jimmy, actually—that's just the way he is—than Warren's overreaction was typical of him. It just showed me a window into Warren. But now, as I look back, did that rebuke cause Warren to lose face with the Democrats? Was he thinking, 'I'm this big guy. I'm the stick at Bear Stearns. And I just got spanked in front of everybody in the organization and I can't do anything about it. So I guess I'm not the top guy'? That's why he reacted so badly. It wasn't just the publicity. It was the publicity in front of these Democrats who were Warren's buddies. Whether he wanted to be Secretary of the Treasury or just an important guy in the Democratic Party, it was embarrassing to him."

Another Bear executive often wondered about Spector's relationship with Cayne. "It was very Shakespearean," he said. "The relationship between Ace and Jimmy was very difficult. The relationship with Jimmy and Warren was very difficult. If there's anything that I have a lot of regret about, it's that I gave a lot of credibility to the status quo. I don't mean that in a bragging kind of way at all. But I had the ability to make it look like we all got along because I got along with all of them. I knew the tension, but the way I looked at the tension at the time was to say to myself, 'We've all been together twenty something years. We're like a family.' If you ever saw it from the inside, you'd say, 'Holy shit!' But I'm sure that's what the Joint Chiefs of Staff is like and the Federal Reserve. What I think about in hindsight, though, is that it wasn't healthy because we were not a family, we were a corporation. There should have been more change. If you took ten investment banks and you froze their management team in place for the next twenty years, you'd have a lot of this shit repeated too. I used to say that continuity of management was a good thing. But privately, with my wife, I would say, 'The last several years, I have to search my soul as to whether I'm just comfortable because I have my platform. I can do what I want and represent the firm. Or am I supporting the right thing?' I never can tell whether I'm rationalizing or not, because if I came to the conclusion that I'm just supporting something that doesn't work, then I've got to go. I was never going to leave. But I thought about stepping out of management partially because I wasn't really that much *in* management. I was kind of like the rest of my clients in a way. I stayed in the room keeping these guys from killing each other a lot of times."

❄

ALTHOUGH CAYNE MAY not have been fully cognizant of it, by humiliating Spector in public and by puncturing what Spector considered to be the heart of his financial incentives at the firm, he had struck a mortal blow to Spector—and possibly the firm—at the very moment when Spector's expertise and attention were most needed. During the previous decade, under Spector's watchful eye, the firm had become the premier manufacturer and distributor of an alphabet soup of exotic securities: everything from mortgage-backed securities (MBSs) to CDOs, CDOs-squared, CMOs, CLOs, and on and on. The firm was making a ton of money, and the members of the executive committee—now reduced to five people—were becoming exceedingly wealthy, but they were also exceedingly dependent on the expertise of Warren Spector, who himself was becoming more imperious and distant. Spector was the architect of the strategy to bulk up the fixed-income division—not that he did anything without the approval of the executive committee—and he was also the person who had enabled Ralph Cioffi to build a hedge fund devoted to the exotic securities the fixed-income division was manufacturing. Cayne, the former broker, had only a vague understanding of all these exotic financial instruments that Spector's salesmen and traders were creating. Intimate familiarity with inventory was not his management style. Schwartz, while plenty smart, was an M&A banker who provided world-class service to his clients. By his own admission, he was happy to cede more and more power at the firm to Spector so that he could be left alone to do his own thing. Sam Molinaro, the CFO, had an accounting background and could hardly be expected to have a view about the firm's growing inventory of exotic securities. Besides, it seemed increasingly obvious that Bobby Steinberg, the firm's chief risk officer, was unable to get from Spector a full accounting of what was going on. As for Ace Greenberg, now in his late seventies, he still had his seat on the executive committee, the board of directors, and the risk committee, but his focus, once merger arbitrage, had shifted to investing his clients' money as well as his own. Besides, Cayne was not exactly open to his rival's views by the first decade of the twenty-first century. What was needed at Bear Stearns from 2003 on, as the bull market in credit stampeded to unprecedented levels and where the only asset consistently undervalued was risk, was a fully and completely engaged Warren Spector, and that is precisely what Cayne's two decisions had done most to undermine.

Not that anyone outside the firm—or most people inside, for that matter—had the slightest inkling that the seeds of the firm's destruction had been sown. Rather, the exact opposite seemed to be occurring. To outsiders, Bear Stearns was humming along and deserving of recognition and stature beyond anything it had ever experienced in its history. Cayne, a man of considerable ego, was more than game to play along with, and even encourage, the quickly improving opinion of his firm.

In August 2004, *Barron's* observed in a cover story that Bear's stock had doubled since the stock market peaked in March 2000, while the stocks of industry leaders Morgan Stanley and Goldman Sachs had endured losses of 42 percent and 20 percent, respectively. "Consistently performing makes believers of people," Sam Molinaro explained. While the article touched on the typical tropes about the firm's lack of breadth and depth and its "reputation as a sharp-elbowed mercenary trading house that associates with dubious characters," there was also the acknowledgment that the firm's fixed-income engine was firing on all cylinders, with revenue tripling in the past three years.

The most interesting revelation in the article was not about Bear Stearns per se but rather a quote from Spector, apparently from an interview he gave to National Public Radio, about Senator John Edwards, who had just accepted the nomination for vice president on Senator John Kerry's presidential ticket. Spector supposedly told NPR, "The Republican Party is painting him as some sort of extremist. But in my dealings with him, I found him to be very open-minded and willing to listen to all sorts of business issues, concerns about legal reform, concerns about healthcare not only from a personal point of view, but also from a business point of view." Despite Cayne's public rebuke of him, Spector had decided he was not going to be so easily stifled by his boss.

The praise for the firm continued in *Investment Dealers' Digest,* a trade publication, in a January 2005 article once again touting the firm's savvy. Bear's stock had closed out 2004 at $102.31, up 29.2 percent for the year, well ahead of all of its competitors. The secret, Cayne told the magazine, was avoiding the mistakes other firms had made. "So you miss Russia, Big Bang, the Asia Crisis," he said. "The culture of the company has saved us from doing something rash." Two months later, *Fortune* named Bear Stearns the most-admired securities firm for 2004 (after being the second-most-admired securities firm in 2003). And *On Wall Street,* a trade publication, noted in a long article about the firm's brokerage business that the company had "never missed a quarterly profit," in part due to the firm's "stability," with "top management . . . running the company for nearly three decades."

CHAPTER 25

CIOFFI'S BUBBLE

But there were storm clouds brewing on the distant horizon. In a February 2005 speech at Stanford University little noticed at the time, former Fed Chairman Paul Volcker, then seventy-seven years old, made a plea of sorts for politicians and regulators to begin to take action (though he did not specify what) to let some of the air out of the balloon. "There has been a lot of good news in the past couple of years," he said, but "I have to tell you my old central banking blood still flows. Under the placid surface, at least the way I see it, there are really disturbing trends: huge imbalances, disequilibria, risks—call them what you will. Altogether the circumstances seem to me as dangerous and intractable as any I can remember, and I can remember quite a lot. What really concerns me is that there seems to be so little willingness or capacity to do much about it." Volcker's observations came some four months after Greenspan gave a speech in Washington where he allowed that although "pockets of severe stress within the household sector . . . remain a concern," the likelihood of "housing price bubbles" appeared small.

Volcker voiced his concern about Americans' low rate of savings and acknowledged the growing danger of the inflating housing bubble, although he did not explicitly refer to it as one. "We are buying a lot of housing at rising prices, but home ownership has become a vehicle for borrowing as much as a source of financial security," he said. "I will suggest to you big adjustments will inevitably come, and they will come long before the Social Security surpluses disappear or even before we cut the federal budget in half. And as things stand, it is more likely than not that it will be financial crises rather than policy foresight that will force the change. . . . I think we are skating on increasingly thin ice." A month later, Fed Governor Bernanke proclaimed there was a "global savings glut," especially in China and other developing countries where consumption was low, helping to fuel a high global demand for the debt of the United States, keeping interest rates low. "In retrospect, we didn't have a global savings glut," explained Stephen Roach, the chairman of Morgan Stanley Asia, "we had an American consumption glut. In both of these cases, Bernanke was complicit in massive policy blunders on the part of the Fed."

Eight months later, in October 2005, Meredith Whitney, the well-regarded financial services research analyst, published a report where she claimed that "10% of the population is at risk of recession" and that "constrained liquidity on both the borrower as well as lender level will be the catalyst to spark this credit and economic downturn. . . . It is important to keep in mind that historically, rising rates have not sparked recessions, credit or otherwise. Constrained liquidity has been the catalyst for most credit busts, both corporate as well as consumer." She wanted investors to know that in the mortgage market, credit rating agencies were requiring more collateral than they had previously to maintain higher credit ratings on mortgage-backed securities—an indication of a deterioration in the credit quality of the underlying assets.

Alone on Wall Street at this time, Whitney had realized that, prior to 1994, home ownership levels in the United States were fairly static at around 64 percent of the population. "That level changed fairly dramatically after 1994," she observed, "when the standards by which an individual could qualify for a mortgage and the required down payment levels became much more liberal. Due to such changes in guidelines, 1.5 million new homeowners were created and homeownership rates rose relatively steeply to 69% where they stand today. . . . The incremental 5% of new homeowners would not have qualified for a mortgage prior to 1994." She noted that in a speech a few weeks earlier, Greenspan had said he was worried that this incremental 5 percent of homeowners had current loan-to-value ratios exceeding 90 percent and that these recent new homeowners were the most highly leveraged.

According to conservative Dennis Sewell, writing in the London journal *The Spectator*, one can look to the early years of the first Clinton administration to account for this dramatic—and ultimately quite troubling—increase in home ownership. In 1993, Roberta Achtenberg took the job as Assistant Secretary for Fair Housing and Equal Opportunity at the Department of Housing and Urban Development (HUD). She began implementing the Clinton agenda to "increase home ownership among the poor, and particularly among blacks and Hispanics." Standing in the way of her mission "were the conservative lending policies of banks, which required such inconvenient and old-fashioned things as cash deposits and regular repayments—things the poor and minorities often could not provide," Sewell wrote. "Clinton told the banks to be more creative." Achtenberg set up a series of regional offices, manned with investigators and attorneys, to seek out any discriminatory lending practices among mortgage lenders, with an eye toward prosecuting them if necessary if there was even a whiff of bad behavior. "From the mid-1990s," Sewell wrote, "they began to abandon their formerly rigorous lending criteria. Mortgages were offered with only three percent deposit requirements, and eventually with no deposit requirement at all. The mortgage banks fell over one another to provide loans to low-income households and especially minority customers."

Then there were the changes the Clinton administration made to the Community Reinvestment Act of 1977, whereby banks were rated based on how much lending they did in low-income neighborhoods. "A good CRA rating was necessary if a bank wanted to get regulators to sign off on mergers, expansion, even new branch openings," Sewell wrote. "A poor rating could be disastrous for a bank's business plan." At the same time, the Clinton administration pushed Fannie Mae and Freddie Mac to expand mortgage loans to those who might not have previously qualified for them, and it put into place new rules allowing the two companies to get involved in the securitization of subprime loans. The so-called strengthening of the CRA in 1995 caused an 80 percent increase in the number of bank loans going to low- and moderate-income families.

The first such securitization of subprime loans—for a total of $385 million—was underwritten in October 1997 by Bear Stearns and First Union Capital Markets (which became part of Wachovia, which in turn is now part of Wells Fargo). Freddie Mac and its implied AAA rating guaranteed the payments on the securities. A press release commemorating the historic event captured a moment of unbridled optimism and greed coated with idealism. "The securitization of these affordable mortgages allows us to redeploy capital back into our communities and to expand our ability to provide credit to low and moderate income individuals," explained Jane Henderson, managing director of First Union's Community Reinvestment and Fair Lending Programs. "First Union is committed to promoting home ownership in traditionally underserved markets through a comprehensive line of competitive and flexible affordable mortgage products. This transaction enables us to continue to aggressively serve those markets." Her colleague Owen Williams, on the fixed-income side of the bank, hailed the seemingly limitless investor demand for the securities. "We are extremely pleased by how well this transaction was received by investors as many of the tranches were significantly oversubscribed," he said. "This offering is further proof of investors' desire for a diverse range of collateral." Added Brian Simpson, a managing director in the structuring department, "Securitizing assets enables First Union to continue to grow its loan portfolio, while at the same time generate additional fee income"—the holy grail—"[and] we also have been very successful in providing innovative asset finance services to clients. We believe there is opportunity to expand our CRA loan securitization capabilities to other companies in the market."

Naturally, the success of the securitization of the CRA loans—the first deal and many subsequent ones were several times oversubscribed—led to an explosion of such deals. The buyers of the loans, according to Dale Westhoff in a May 1998 article in *Mortgage Banking*, "were money managers and insurance companies buying the loans strictly because of their investment appeal," offering yields in excess of 7.5 percent, which in a low-interest-rate environment looked very attractive. Sewell saw the direct linkage from HUD's political pressure to the fissure in the credit markets a decade later.

"So that's how we get from there to here," he wrote, "from crude attempts at social engineering during the early, heady days of the first Clinton administration to the turmoil on Wall Street."

Sewell did not contact Achtenberg before he wrote his diatribe. After she read it, she said in an interview that Sewell's "assertions are laughable to me" and "quite inventive and preposterous." She said that with "all humility" she was "just a bit player" in her role as assistant secretary at HUD from 1993 to 1995, nudging the unregulated mortgage lenders to voluntarily improve their "best practices" and to make sure there was no discrimination going on in mortgage lending. She said that any deterioration in underwriting standards among mortgage lenders or banks "had nothing to do" with her office and she was "not sure how they came to pass." She said the goal of increasing home ownership had been a bipartisan effort and pointed to President George W. Bush's American Dream Downpayment Initiative, passed into law in December 2003, which provided up to $200 million to encourage home ownership among low-income first-time home buyers by helping to pay closing costs and down payments. Lawrence Lindsay, Bush's first chief economics advisor, told the *New York Times,* in December 2008, that from the president on down, there was no incentive to try to limit home ownership. "No one wanted to stop that bubble," he said. "It would have conflicted with the president's own policies." But Achtenberg wishes they had. "This is a serious crisis," Achtenberg said, "and it requires serious analysis. I think it is very important to figure out what parts of the crisis are attributable to what action, including the failure to regulate and the failure of deregulation and how that played a role. To the extent that underwriting criteria changed, that is important to know. But that was not part of my purview."

Other commentators who shared Sewell's conservative political views also shared his analysis. Russell Roberts, for one, a professor of economics at George Mason University, wrote in the *Wall Street Journal* that in 1996 HUD gave Fannie Mae and Freddie Mac "an explicit target" that 42 percent of their mortgage financing had to be made to borrowers "with income below the median in their area." The targets were increased to 50 percent in 2000 and to 52 percent in 2005. He pointed out that after Bear Stearns underwrote its first

CRA deal, in October 1997, the firm issued an additional $1.9 billion of CRA mortgages backed by Fannie Mae or Freddie Mac during the next ten months. "Bear Stearns is seeking to develop interest and support for loans issued to low- and moderate-income home buyers and is actively pursuing CRA loan portfolios for future securitization, including portfolios as small as $25 million," one of the firm's press releases stated in August 1998. In a separate interview, Roberts said that the 1995 changes to the CRA revised "how it was enforced and it put a wad of power in the hands of community organizations to damage banks that they felt weren't doing enough for poor people. These community organizations became the dispensers of money for zero-down mortgages for poor people, again a lovely thing, but it didn't turn out so well."

When combined with Greenspan's low-interest-rate policies and the Taxpayer Relief Act of 1997, which increased the capital gains exclusion on the sale of a home to $500,000, the HUD policies dramatically increased the demand for housing and the price of housing, Roberts wrote. "Between 1997 and 2005, the average price of a house in the U.S. more than doubled," he explained. "It wasn't simply a speculative bubble. Much of the rise in housing prices was the result of public policies that increased the demand for housing. Without the surge in housing prices, the subprime market would never have taken off." He rightly pointed out, as had Whitney, that home ownership had increased by the millions. "This was mostly the result of loans to low-income, higher-risk borrowers," he wrote. "Both Bill Clinton and George W. Bush, abetted by Congress, trumpeted that rise as it occurred."

THEN THERE WAS the outright fraud committed by greedy mortgage lenders and brokers looking to make a quick fee by preying on unsuspecting potential borrowers. It was not uncommon for mortgage lenders and real estate brokers to fictionalize a loan application in order to make sales and get fees. Consider, as but one example among hundreds of thousands, the case of Kellie S. and Gregory C., who together wanted to buy a home at 123 North Potomac Street, in the inner city of Baltimore. At the time, Kellie was thirty-one years old and lived on monthly disability checks of $600. Gregory, who suffered from epilepsy, also lived on his monthly disability checks.

At an open house, Kellie met a real estate agent, Esmeralda J. Villareal, from the Long and Foster agency in Baltimore. Villareal offered to show Kellie a property in Baltimore, for which she represented the seller, a fact she failed to mention to Kellie. When Kellie told Villareal that she and Gregory could together afford a mortgage payment of between $900 and $1,000 per month, Villareal told Kellie, "I can get that for you. I know a place that can get that for you." Villareal then showed Kellie the house on North Potomac Street, and eventually Kellie agreed to buy the house, although there did not appear to be any evidence that a purchase price for the house had been discussed or agreed to. The house also needed repairs, which Kellie and Villareal discussed.

At the closing, the various agents and lawyers asked Kellie if she had a job, and she replied no. She asked them again whether the monthly payment for the mortgage would be between $900 and $1,000 per month, and the real estate agents responded they would check Gregory's credit to see if they could "work something out." But Gregory's income and net worth never would have qualified him to receive a mortgage where the payments would have been $1,000 per month. They then checked Kellie's credit and decided that if they lowered the purchase price of the house, her credit would be sufficient for her to get a "loan you can afford." When Kellie asked again about the monthly mortgage payment, the broker finally said, "Yes, it will be between the payments." Without reading the documents, Kellie signed them, which added to her troubles.

The documents were rife with material misstatements of the facts surrounding Kellie's life. The loan application stated she had been employed at the signing date as the office manager of Always Exquisite, in Randallstown, Maryland, even though Kellie was unemployed. The employer's phone number was a nonexistent cell phone. The application listed her monthly salary as $5,000, even though her monthly disability checks totaled $600. The application stated she had $158,000 in liquid assets (including two bank accounts at M&T Bank, $31,200 in Exxon stock or bonds, and a 2001 Ford Taurus worth $6,000), $5,039 in unpaid liabilities, and a net

worth of nearly $153,000. The loan application stated that Kellie
had agreed to a monthly mortgage payment of $1,811.94 per month
(which she said she did not agree to), had made a $75,000 down
payment on the house plus another $12,000 in closing costs (when
she had actually made only a payment of $500), and had agreed to
take a mortgage of $285,000. She had put no money down on the
house and the mortgage was grossed up to include around $13,000
in closing fees. The appraisal of the home came in at $360,000—
the purchase price—even though the previous three sales of the
home had never exceeded $150,000 and the average price of a
home on the block was $191,000. MortgageIT, Inc., wrote the orig-
inal $285,000 mortgage and then sold it to GMAC, which by then
had been purchased by Cerberus, a large New York City hedge fund
and private equity fund. GMAC then sold the loan to Wells Fargo
Home Mortgage.

As for the renovations the house needed, Kellie and Villareal
discussed the costs associated with them after the closing. Villareal
agreed to pay for all the renovations, according to a tape of their
conversation. The renovations were never completed. Within three
months, Kellie could no longer afford the mortgage payments on the
house. After five months of nonpayment, Wells Fargo sold Kellie's
mortgage to EMC Mortgage, a subsidiary of Bear Stearns that originated and serviced mortgage loans of all kinds and sold them to investors. Soon thereafter, the home was put back on the market,
again through Long and Foster, at a price of $225,000—some
$75,000 below the outstanding mortgage balance of about
$300,000. The sale was subject to an agreement by EMC to permit
what was known as a "short sale," for an amount less than the mortgage. Kellie also informed EMC that she would not be able to pay
the $75,000 balance, assuming the sale happened. "Kellie keeps a
journal of her seizures," according to a document detailing her ordeal, "which reported that she experienced an increase in seizures
throughout the mortgage process. She has also experienced feelings
of betrayal, fear, stress, humiliation, and frustration. Kellie and
Gregory have experienced a serious strain on their relationship
throughout this process. Gregory has upgraded his asthma medication due to increasing frequency and severity of asthma attacks,
which he attributes to stress."

Although it may be only part of the story, Russell Roberts, the George Mason University economist, sees this kind of deceitful behavior as the natural outgrowth of the government mandates. "It's not that much of a tragedy," he said. "People talk about it for political gain. But many of the people who've lost their homes never had them in the first place. A lot of our people bought the homes with no money down. In fact, you can find Countrywide press releases where they brag about their special 103 percent loan: 'We don't just cover your mortgage, we'll lend you your closing costs, too.' And [the borrower] walks into a house and six months later they're having trouble making the payments. Then they, quote, lose their home, unquote, but they lose no equity; they were renters before. Now, they're really renters. I don't want to diminish [foreclosure]. It's embarrassing. It's humiliating. There's probably shame and despair and you maybe thought you were going to own the house but you don't. But it's not like they were thrown out on the street after they lost their equity. They didn't have any equity in these houses to start with. It's a very strange situation."

Henry Cisneros, the former mayor of San Antonio, Texas, was Clinton's Secretary of Housing and Urban Development from 1993 to 1997. In the midst of the financial crisis, in October 2008, the *New York Times* caught up with Cisneros to ask him about his role in encouraging home ownership among a group of people who would have been better off financially if they had remained renters. He said, "I have been waiting for someone to put all the blame on my doorstep." He appeared not to be joking. In the *Times* Cisneros argued that it was "impossible to know in the beginning that the federal push to increase homeownership would end so badly" and that once the housing boom started, the regulators did not have the tools to stop it. "You think you have a finely tuned instrument," he said, "that you can use to say: 'Stop! We're at 69 percent homeownership. We should not go further. These are people who should remain renters.' But you really are just given a sledgehammer and an ax. They are blunt tools." He said that people "who should not have been homeowners" had been lured by "unscrupulous participants— bankers, brokers, secondary market people. . . . The country is paying for that, and families are hurt because we as a society did not draw a line."

This lowering of credit standards as a way of increasing home ownership had begun to come home to roost by the time Whitney wrote her research report in October 2005. "Since 1996," she wrote, "sub-prime lending has grown 489%"—from $90 billion to $530 billion—"largely through the extension of credit to first-time borrowers. We believe that at least 5% of the mortgage market is at risk due to very low equity positions in homes. Greenspan's recent statements concur with this estimate based upon what he believes to be the portion of the population which has dangerously low equity positions in their houses." Whitney described how underwriting standards had deteriorated scandalously during this bubble by allowing people with lower credit scores to get mortgages, by allowing them to finance a large percentage of the purchase price, by creating new mortgage products that delay paying off the principal, and by requiring less documentation of income and assets. The introduction of adjustable-rate mortgages merely exacerbated this disastrous trend by allowing borrowers to choose from a smorgasbord of repayment options, including an option that allowed for a small monthly payment whereby the deferred interest and principal payment were merely added to the back end of the loan balance, increasing it beyond all recognition. "When interest rates rise, the borrower's total loan balances as well as monthly payments increase even more so, thus increasing the borrower's overall financial burden and likelihood of default," she observed.

She concluded with a bombshell. "We believe low equity positions in their homes, high revolving debt balances, and high commodity prices make for the ingredients of a credit implosion, particularly at this point in the consumer cycle," she wrote. "As a result, we believe those lenders with exposure to this segment (largely sub-prime lenders) will experience loss levels of great enough enormity to not only substantially erode profitability but which could also impale capital positions. However, most important, we believe restricted liquidity caused by regulatory guidelines for greater capital ratios could begin a domino effect of corporate insolvencies similar to those witnessed post-1998." Whitney's insightful report—which in retrospect revealed only a small part of the problem—was like the proverbial tree falling in the forest with no one around to hear whether it made a sound. There was simply too much money to be made as the housing bubble continued to inflate for any of the participants—not only at Bear Stearns but also across Wall Street—to stop and take notice.

The FDIC, the government agency responsible for supervising the banking system and insuring deposits, did take notice of Whitney's report. "I was the only one who caught the attention of the FDIC with such a report," she said, "and I never saw any report that mapped out the potential hazards the way my report did." Richard A. Brown, a senior economist at the FDIC, said Whitney's report "really made an impression upon the staff here at the FDIC" and he invited her to speak about her findings at a forum held at the FDIC on January 19, 2006. She reviewed for the FDIC her report and made a new and interesting observation about Wall Street banks. "The banks need to originate some product," she said. "One of the biggest problems for the banking industry today is tremendous deposit growth and very little asset growth. So you have institutions that are liability-rich and asset-poor, and they're going to put anything on the balance sheet they can. For the past five years or so, mortgages have provided the best vehicle for asset growth."

While Bear Stearns's fixed-income revenue for the year ended November 30, 2005, declined 12 percent, to $2.3 billion, from $2.6 billion in 2004, the business was still humming along quite profitably. The firm's SEC filing stated that "mortgage-backed securities origination revenues declined from the robust levels of fiscal 2004 due to a flattening yield curve, shifting market conditions and changes in product mix. A decline in agency CMO volumes was offset by an increase in non-agency mortgage originations." Regardless of the stumble in fixed income, the firm posted a record profit of $1.5 billion in fiscal 2005, up 9 percent from the $1.3 billion of net income the year before. Since the start of 2006, Bear's stock had risen nearly 25 percent, closing at $143.50 on April 17. Cayne's compensation for 2005 was $25.1 million, and his nearly 6.8 million shares of Bear Stearns stock were worth $972 million at that moment.

※

AS PAUL FRIEDMAN knew well, Ralph Cioffi was a highly regarded salesman but short on managerial skills. In a pattern that Friedman had witnessed firsthand from Cioffi's time as a manager in the fixed-income department, in 2006 Cioffi's awkwardly named High-Grade Structured Credit Strategies Fund started getting very sloppy in its paperwork regarding trades (securities bought and sold) between the hedge fund and Bear Stearns's investment bank and broker-dealer. In its offering memoranda regarding the establishment of the hedge fund, BSAM assured its High-Grade Fund investors that when Cioffi traded with Bear Stearns, the "Fund's operating procedure required disclosure, consent, and approval before the deal could be settled," according to an administrative complaint filed by the Commonwealth of Massachusetts against BSAM. "Unbeknownst to investors, the very controls and procedures established to safeguard their interests did not survive the daily ordeals of trading and managing and leveraging. Investors who sought to take advantage of the inimitable risk management reputation of Bear Stearns found themselves in a highly complex hedge fund investment program that relied on overworked junior personnel to manage a conflict reporting process required by federal law." The problem was that Cioffi had failed to get the approval of the fund's independent, unaffiliated directors before it bought securities from its Bear Stearns affiliate. In 2003, 18 percent of Cioffi's transactions failed to be properly approved. By 2006, 79 percent of his transactions with affiliates had not received approval—a technicality, to be sure, but a violation that was against federal law and that went to the heart of proper disclosure to investors.

"There was a watershed moment during the summer of 2006," Friedman said, "when the compliance people said to Ralph, 'You're not getting the trades approved correctly.' There were two parts to it. One is 'You're not getting the preapprovals on trades with Bear Stearns,' and two, 'By the way, you shouldn't be trading with Bear Stearns anyway,' and again, what a shock. Ralph had done hundreds of trades with Bear Stearns and he forgot this little thing called getting his paperwork done. It's classic Ralph. Details were just not his best trick, and equally startling was that BSAM didn't have a process to pick up on it, because it really shouldn't have been Ralph's responsibility to oversee himself. How did BSAM miss it for a year? It was hundreds of trades. How did they miss it? I've never understood."

The problem was that Cioffi made the task of disclosing these transactions and seeking approval for them "a low-priority task for junior assistants," according to the Massachusetts complaint. From the official start of Cioffi's fund, in October 2003, Joanmarie Pusateri, who had been at Bear Stearns since June 1986, was responsible for administrative and operational tasks, including obtaining written approval for trades with affiliates that were rife with potential for conflict of interest. Pusateri knew that she had to get the approvals on a timely basis but did not know that failure to do so was a violation of federal law. Neither Cioffi nor Tannin had informed her of the section of the Investment Advisers Act of 1940 that explained that it would be unlawful to make a trade with a client "without disclosing to such client in writing before the completion of such transaction the capacity in which he is acting and obtaining the consent of the client to such transaction."

She also did not know why obtaining such approvals from the fund's independent directors was essential for trades between Cioffi's hedge fund and Bear Stearns. At one point during 2004, Pusateri met with a BSAM compliance officer who informed her that she had failed to get the requisite approval for between ten and twenty affiliated trades, and she took steps to obtain the missing consents. The fact that she didn't fully understand the reasons for obtaining these approvals "caused confusion among her delegates," one of whom was Jessica Borenkind, a sales assistant to whom Pusateri assigned the task of getting approvals. But Borenkind was no better at getting the necessary approvals than was Pusateri. Once a month BSAM compliance would send Borenkind a spreadsheet showing where she had failed to get the required approvals. Of course, by then, all the trades listed had cleared and settled, so each of her clerical failures represented a violation of the law. Borenkind left Bear Stearns by "mutual agreement" on November 20, 2006. In the fall of 2005, Cioffi hired Richard Bierbaum as a trading assistant and gave him the task of getting the trading approvals, although he had never been responsible for such a job before. As Bierbaum explained, "In sort of the daily triage of the work dynamic, at first I didn't believe it to be very important." At the end of 2005, Bierbaum was placed on "a two-month probation" because he was "overworked" and unable to get his work done on a timely basis. He left Bear Stearns voluntarily three days before his colleague Borenkind.

In early 2006, before they left Bear Stearns, Borenkind and Bierbaum met with Marisol Farley, from BSAM compliance, who informed them that the Investment Advisers Act required them to get the necessary approvals before the trades settled. During the summer of 2006, in a "scare meeting," BSAM compliance put more pressure on Cioffi's team to comply, and it was then that Borenkind learned that even one missing approval "could have serious legal repercussions." Of the 2,300 trades the hedge fund had done between the start of the fund and 2006 that required prior approvals, 47 percent were not properly approved in advance.

To minimize the ongoing failure of Cioffi's team to get the approvals in advance for related party transactions, Bear Stearns decided to place a moratorium on BSAM's ability to do transactions with the Bear Stearns broker-dealer and hired the law firm Wilmer-Hale to determine whether any client had been hurt in the process (apparently not) and whether the firm needed to report voluntarily the violations to the SEC (apparently no need for that, either). "Because no clients have been harmed," one senior BSAM executive said, "we fixed the procedures. We changed it. We shored it up. And [Cioffi] thought it would be fine."

By September 7, the moratorium was in place. Alex Reynolds, yet another person hired by Cioffi to deal with getting the consents in a timely fashion, wrote Pusateri that the BSAM administrator had given the approval for a deal with Bear Stearns but then the head of Bear Stearns compliance "squashed it . . . until further notice, no trading with Bear again." The moratorium on trading with Bear raised questions in the minds of Cioffi and Matthew Tannin about the liquidity of the High-Grade Fund, which had $1.527 billion of investors' money, including around $25 million from Bear Stearns itself and several million dollars from Cioffi and Tannin. Bear Stearns was one of the fund's largest trading partners, and now that no additional trading was possible, the liquidity of the securities in the fund was theoretically diminished. The other consequence of the moratorium was an end to the eye the Bear traders had been keeping on what Cioffi was doing, since he was a counterparty on their trades. "The trading desk that from time to time would go in to Warren, or me, or somebody else," Friedman said, "and say, 'Listen, are you aware of what Ralph just bought? You might want to look into this.' Spector had an informal understanding that the mortgage guys would keep an eye on Ralph. But now it was hands off. All the people who up until then would go in to Warren on a regular basis and say, 'Look, Ralph is too highly leveraged. Ralph is doing this. Ralph's strategy doesn't make sense,' largely got backhanded and told to go away—but not entirely, Warren's not stupid—and were told, 'Hands off. You have nothing to look at. He's not a customer. Leave him alone.' We slammed the wall down." But even as late as November 2006, Cioffi was having trouble getting the message that trading with Bear Stearns was over. "I don't like to argue with you but I was told that we are definitely not allowed any repos with Bear (PTL or not)," Pusateri e-mailed him on November 9.

❋

THE "INVESTMENT PHILOSOPHY" of the High-Grade Fund, stated clearly every month on investor return summaries, was to "generate total annual returns through 'cash and carry' transactions and capital markets arbitrage. The Fund generally invests in high quality floating rate structured finance securities. Typically, 90% of the Fund's gross assets are invested in AAA or AA structured finance assets." In 2004, the High-Grade Fund had a return (net of fees and other expenses) of 16.88 percent. In 2005, the net return was 9.46 percent. At the end of January 2006, after posting a net gain for the month of 0.86 percent, the fund had 30 percent of its collateral in "asset-backed securities," which many investors assumed were either high-quality credit card receivables or auto loan receivables, and 15.2 percent in subprime residential mortgage-backed securities. At that time, Cioffi also raised the idea of a new "leveraged" fund "to better accommodate our investors who may be looking for higher return potential while staying within the [f]und's investment parameters." He encouraged interested investors to call to "reserve capacity." The idea for the new Leveraged Fund was to make investments similar to those of the High-Grade Fund, only using more borrowed money to buy them. In a March 2006 call with po-

tential investors, Cioffi and Tannin suggested that the 9.5 percent
return achieved in the High-Grade Fund for 2005 would have been
more like 15 percent to 22 percent in the new Leveraged Fund, depending on the amount of debt piled on the assets. At one point,
during an April 2006 call with a potential investor, Tannin was
asked what the "perfect storm" would be for the Leveraged Fund.
He responded, "The important point is that a perfect storm will not
cause a liquidation of assets."

Tannin also shared his views about what he and Cioffi expected the economic environment in 2007 to look like. He spoke
of a slowing economy, interest rate "easing" by the Fed, and a
widening of interest rate spreads. He said, "We are set up for wider
spreads because we are short subprime and we are properly
hedged." He explained that people were worried about the 2006
vintage of subprime loans because of "looser underwriting standards" as a result of "no-doc loans," "high loan-to-value ratios," and
a "large dispersion" of FICO scores. He said the High-Grade Fund
"had avoided that vintage," that it was "net short" mortgages issued
in 2006, and that the "data does not support a nationwide real-
estate bubble," only "isolated pockets" of trouble. He said if 2007
was like 2006, the High-Grade Fund would return 10 percent to
11 percent and the new Enhanced Leveraged Fund would return
at least 14 percent.

At the end of July 2006, the High-Grade Fund reported a net return of 0.83 percent and showed investors that 50.5 percent of the
fund was invested in "asset-backed securities" (ABS) and 6 percent
in subprime. "Despite the significant downturn in the housing market and deterioration in sub prime credit fundamentals overall
structured credit spreads remained tight and the credit performance of the Fund assets remains strong," Cioffi wrote investors.
"And [we] have not seen any significant market price weakness in
any of our particular asset sectors." There had been a fair amount of
confusion among the fund's investors about what types of securities
were actually "asset-backed securities." This subject came up on
both the January 2007 and March 2007 investor conference calls.
For instance, in January 2007, one investor asked Cioffi what
specifically the assets were in the "ABS CDO" column on the

monthly investor reports—except that the actual reports only said "ABS" on them, not "ABS CDO," an important distinction that confused many of the fund's investors, to the point where in a meeting with one of them Tannin wrote "ABS CDO" above the column where "ABS" had been printed. The investor and Cioffi had a lengthy and sometimes confusing discussion, but there was little doubt from Cioffi's answer that there were subprime mortgages in the "ABS CDO" column. "I want to be very clear about the way in which subprime risk is embedded within the structures that we own," he said. "We're not believers in the world-is-coming-to-an-end housing bubble scenario." (According to the September 2007 congressional testimony of Kyle Bass, the managing partner of hedge fund Hayman Capital—who made a fortune betting against mortgages and some say kicked off the run on Bear Stearns in March 2008 with a request to Goldman Sachs for a novation—the "ABS CDO" category was created sometime in the late 1990s and originally comprised numerous assets ranging from "aircraft receivables to mortgages" but that "by late 2003 ABS CDOs were comprised almost entirely of subprime mortgages.")

By August 2006, "the [High-Grade] fund's performance had begun to decline," according to the June 2008 indictment of Cioffi and Tannin. "In part as a response to this performance decline, and as a consequence of threatened investor withdrawals of money from the High Grade Fund," the two men completed the launch—with the support of Warren Spector—of the second fund, known as the Enhanced Leverage Fund, which invested primarily in CDOs and "employed substantially more leverage" than the High-Grade Fund while promising higher returns but only "limited additional risk, in part because it would invest in an even higher proportion of the least risky securities. The increased profits would result from increased leverage." On August 1, the High-Grade Fund was split into two funds and 36.74 percent of the money in the High-Grade Fund, or around $560 million, was transferred into the Enhanced Leverage Fund. The *Financial Times* lauded the new fund since Cioffi "had a stellar reputation and Bear [was] a giant in the mortgage business. . . . The thinking was that if anyone could clean up on rising turmoil in the mortgage market, sparked by an increase in defaults by high-risk borrowers, it would be Bear Stearns and Mr. Cioffi."

On September 17, Tannin was still concerned that the moratorium on trading with Bear Stearns could hurt the High-Grade Fund's liquidity, and he also worried about how the new Enhanced Leverage Fund would finance its positions. The next day, he wrote Cioffi, Pusateri, and Ray McGarrigal, another senior executive at the funds, with his thoughts on "what we have to do with our repo" situation. "I think we are under a clear mandate to eliminate repo with Bear as quickly as possible," he wrote. "Changing prime brokers"—away from Bear Stearns—"is a possibility but one that is not immediate and one that comes with difficulties." Tannin's best idea was to have a "certain amount" of unencumbered assets that could be financed away from Bear Stearns. He asked his partners for their thoughts, too.

On September 19, McGarrigal replied to Tannin that not being able to trade with Bear Stearns any longer could hurt the funds' investors. "Bear is #1 in [mortgage-backed securities] and in the top 5 of CDO issuers," he wrote. Not being able to trade with the firm was "all bad for our investors. I think we should work hard to put in place all necessary compliance procedures to allow [us] to continue operating as we have to date." But that never happened, and BSAM's moratorium on Cioffi trading with Bear Stearns remained in effect.

※

As IF ALL of these machinations at Cioffi's hedge funds weren't confusing enough, he and his colleagues decided to complicate the situation further by creating a new entity—first called Rampart, and then Everquest Financial when the company filed an IPO document—to hold hundreds of millions of dollars of less liquid CDOs from the two hedge funds. By selling the illiquid securities to this new entity, Cioffi's hedge funds would be able to raise cash in a creative way from the market. The for-profit Rampart would manage the portfolio for a fee. And the hedge fund's investors would also benefit from their ownership stake in Rampart when it went public in an IPO to be underwritten by Bear Stearns. Cioffi's partner in Rampart was Stone Tower, a $7.7 billion hedge fund focusing on structured credit securities.

Rampart bought the CDOs from Cioffi's two hedge funds for $548.8 million: 16 million shares of Rampart stock, valued at $25 each, and $148.8 million in cash. But even McGarrigal and Tannin had serious questions about the efficacy of the Rampart deal and raised them with Cioffi. In a September 5 e-mail to Cioffi and Tannin, McGarrigal worried that the securities being sold to Rampart "are arguably the best things we've owned" and had "given our investors a tremendous bang for the buck." He also worried that the hedge funds were giving up a portion of their management fee on those securities to Stone Tower and that the assets would be managed differently than they had been to date.

In his response, Tannin said, "I too have concerns" about Rampart. "We are putting a lot of very big eggs in one basket, including our 'signature egg.'" Tannin also worried about Rampart's "liquidity and permanent capital. Do we know if there are any special disclosure rules we'd have to make were we to want to sell shares? I am worried that any selling by us would raise questions in the minds of other shareholders and create the potential for price volatility. I know from Newcastle"—another publicly traded real estate investment company—"that investors want to know that management has their money in the deal. This seems at odds with our hope that [Rampart] will provide greater liquidity to the hedge fund. Our hedge fund would be completely exposed to public market volatility. If we were to have a problem in just one position that affected a distribution, we face unknown price action."

In an e-mail the next day, Cioffi responded to his colleagues that they raised good questions, "and God knows I've questioned this transaction a dozen times in the past 3–6 months." But he saw more benefits than concerns. Among them were "increased liquidity to our [hedge funds] from the injection of $200M of cash and reduction in CDO equity positions." Then, he wrote, there was "significant upside from the IPO in the form of liquidity and mark to market gain." Cioffi wrote that the bankers at Bear Stearns believed the funds' stake in Rampart would immediately be worth 20 percent to 30 percent more than Cioffi had paid for it, which he figured could add four to five percentage points to the funds' returns during the next year—a significant bump. He also was sure there was "significant upside to our [hedge fund] in the form of risk free [asset management] fees" paid to the hedge funds as Rampart grew; he pegged it at $5 million a year "if the IPO raises $400M." Finally, in a jargon-filled piece of banker gobbledygook, he wrote that the Rampart deal would allow the hedge funds to create a $140 million less-risky CDO-squared from a number of riskier CDOs that were harder to finance in the repo market. "We are a structured credit fund and we marketed ourselves as a fund that would engage in capital markets arbitrage, here is one of the better arbitrages I've seen in a long time so Matt I think our investors will appreciate the transaction and will trust our judgment."

McGarrigal responded to Cioffi's message by saying that as long as Cioffi was able to cut a fair deal with Stone Tower, he would support the Rampart deal. Cioffi responded, "I'll insist on it," and then wrote, "I'm fighting hard to keep our entrepreneurial spirit and drive against the backdrop of the BSAM bureaucracy and regulations. I'm not arguing against all of that, I know it's required and it's smart but I want it both ways—conform but not compromise on what got us here."

With the plan to launch Rampart coming together rapidly, Cioffi responded to Tannin's September 17 e-mail about liquidity concerns. "As far as liquidity, we have the repo on the Rampart equity and if my numbers are correct after [R]ampart we will have over $200 [million] of liquidity," he wrote. "So unless we go into a full unwind [in] the short term, liquidity is not an issue. What we need to figure out is how to get the majority of our LPs into the enhanced [leverage] fund. That will take some time but once we do that we have an easy liquidity source and that's Barclays," which had just agreed to provide a $400 million line of credit to the new Enhanced Leverage Fund. At least one plaintiff, suing BSAM, Cioffi, and Tannin, believed Cioffi's September 2006 e-mail to Tannin was evidence that they knew then that "the High-Grade Fund's longer-term outlook was so dismal that it could be alleviated only by transferring the majority of the High-Grade Fund's investors into the new Enhanced Leverage Fund."

※

IRONICALLY, BACK IN the spring of 2006, when Tannin and Cioffi were busy enticing Barclays to provide its $400 million loan to the

Enhanced Leverage Fund, the two hedge fund managers did everything possible to convey to Barclays the safety of the structure and the investments. "We are more than happy to discuss with you credit and portfolio limits for the underlying portfolios as well," Tannin wrote Barclays on April 6. "This way if there is measurable credit deterioration we can factor this in and reduce the leverage. I don't want to sound like a broken record but the value of this transaction lies in the transparency of credit information on high underlying credit quality assets. We have a lot of it and you can have it as often as you want. We'll even chew it up for you and give you customized reports. Look at the stability of the ratings in these portfolios." On May 1, as the negotiations with Barclays were progressing, Tannin e-mailed his contacts at the bank to reassure them that the Enhanced Leverage Fund would not be investing in risky assets, in keeping with the investment guidelines that had been agreed upon. He described the "AA/AAA assets" the fund would invest in as having "very very low volatility" and wrote that the new "enhanced" structure would "continue to operate [as did the High-Grade Fund] in the best parts of the capital structure," "concentrate the ultimate exposure in the highest rated floating rate kinds of assets," and "generate a prudent return for our investors which allows our portfolio managers and structuring team to concentrate on the areas in the market where there is the greatest liquidity and greatest value."

By the end of September 2006, Cioffi was ready to consummate the Rampart deal, which he designed to accomplish three tasks: to sell the funds' "high-yielding, less-liquid positions," to create a company that could be taken public and that would trade at a premium to the private market value of the securities, and to provide "a permanent capital vehicle that will have ongoing access to the capital markets." Sixty percent of the management fees from Rampart would flow to Cioffi's funds. For a variety of reasons, including that Bear Stearns would be investing $25 million in Rampart and that Cioffi was selling assets to Rampart, the independent directors of the funds needed to approve the deal after hearing a presentation from a third party about the "reasonableness of the fair market value process." The problem for Cioffi, as of September 29, was that the funds did not then have two independent board members, a sin of omission that was all of a piece with Cioffi's cavalier approach to the legal niceties of running a hedge fund. Once informed, Cioffi found "Gilmore and Gilbert"—their only identification in a Cioffi September 29, 2006, e-mail—and urged a colleague to "get them [named] official board members by Tuesday," October 3, when the independent directors were to approve the deal. In a typical last-minute rush, the directors were certified and Cioffi's deal to create Rampart was approved. But there seemed to be little doubt that Cioffi and Tannin were already aware by the end of September 2006 that the market was drying up for the complicated mortgage-related securities they had invested in.

Not only was that quickly becoming a major problem for the performance of the funds themselves—fewer buyers than sellers inevitably meant lower valuations on the securities, which meant lower returns for the funds' investors—but the truth was that Cioffi and Tannin had advertised the funds to investors as a safe investment. "The High Grade Fund's objective was to provide a modest, safe and steady source of returns to its investors," Cioffi and Tannin claimed, adding investors "could expect annual returns of approximately 10 to 12 percent." The fund was not designed to hit "home runs"; rather, the idea was that it would be "only slightly riskier than a money market fund." And this idea was reinforced in the performance statements that were sent to investors every month.

Month after month, Cioffi repeated for his investors his investment thesis. "It's a broken-record paragraph," explained one of the investors in the funds, "that basically says, 'The fund is 90 percent invested in AA and AAA structured finance assets and the goal is to generate spread through cash and carry transactions. We're expecting an economic slow-down. We think mortgage delinquencies are going to rise. We think there will be a reduced appetite for [residential mortgage-backed securities]. We are particularly concerned about the 2006 vintage. We are dialing down the leverage in the fund.'"

In an August-September 2006 commentary, Cioffi reported that the two funds' results for those months were positive—up 0.69 percent and 0.62 percent for the High-Grade Fund and the Enhanced Leverage Fund in August, respectively, and 0.99 percent and 0.96

percent in September—and that the outlook was for continued weakness in the housing sector. "As we've discussed in prior letters and calls, this is something we've been following very carefully," Cioffi wrote. "Real estate has been driving the economy for the last few years and as the sector slows it will have a drag effect on the economy." He wrote that the funds' "surveillance system monitors" would alert them "in advance" of any increase in "delinquency rates" and was "an early warning system" allowing them to "hedge those risks." He reiterated his belief that "our risk is further mitigated in that the portfolio we own is primarily at the AAA, AA and A level. Our belief is that the riskiest mortgages are those that originated in 2006 and we have been very selective and only small buyers of that vintage." Cioffi also announced to the investors the Rampart "repackaging vehicle" and his "intention to immediately begin the SEC registration process" for Rampart "with an offering timetable of 6–9 months."

When this investor received his December 2006 statements, there was an outlook comment for 2007. "It said," the investor recalled, "'As we told you at the beginning of the year [2006], the market for residential mortgage-backed securities was going to be deteriorating. Mortgage delinquencies were going to rise. We've reduced our exposure from 55% down to 22%.' If you had eighteen months of these things in your hand, you would say to yourself, 'This is my guy. He's calling for it. He's preparing for it, and he's either not going to get hurt by it or he's going to make a lot of money when the opportunity presents itself.' It's right there in print." The December statement for the High-Grade Fund not only showed a return for the month of 1.22 percent, and for the year of 10.67 percent, but also showed investors that 67 percent of that fund's collateral was in asset-backed securities, with only 6.2 percent in subprime mortgages. The idea of trouble in the housing market was reinforced by a December 2006 *New York Times* article about an auction held in Naples, Florida, to sell quickly a number of homes. The auction results, the paper reported, "suggested that the houses at the auction had lost about 25 percent of their value since 2005." David Leonhardt, the reporter, concluded the article with the prescient observation, "Over the last few decades, the world's financial system has endured a crisis roughly once every three or four years. There was the stock market crash of 1987, the Asian and Mexican meltdowns in the 1990s, the dot-com implosion of 2000 and, most recently, the aftermath of Sept. 11, 2001. We may now be living on both borrowed money and borrowed time."

By January 2007, the statement said the High-Grade Fund had a return of 1.09 percent for the month and had 77 percent of its collateral in asset-backed securities. For February 2007, Cioffi reported to investors that the fund's net return was 1.38 percent and the collateral in asset-backed securities was an astounding 81 percent of the total, with subprime being 6.1 percent.

In his monthly commentary, Cioffi acknowledged February had been a rough month—for others. "February was a volatile month in the structured credit markets," he wrote, "particularly in any credit associated with subprime mortgages. Over the course of February there were a number of failures in subprime originators as well as historically high levels of early delinquencies in subprime securitizations originated in 2006. The mass media carried many stories about potential disasters in the subprime market. The result of this was a rapid and severe widening in the subprime credit derivatives index which in turn led to a broad based widening of mortgage-backed assets up and down the capital structure." The High-Grade Fund, though, was "well positioned for this spread widening" because of hedges "put in place over the second half of 2006."

THE PROBLEM WAS that none of it was true. Cioffi had not been avoiding residential mortgage-backed securities, as he had suggested to his investors on their monthly statements. Actually, he had done precisely the opposite and had started to load up on these toxic securities at exactly the wrong moment. Since he no longer was allowed to trade with Bear Stearns, the firm had no idea what he had been doing. "I don't think not being able to buy from us or borrow from us hurt them," Paul Friedman said. "There were plenty of people willing to kill each other for Ralph's business. Careers were made from selling to Ralph and lending him the money to buy stuff. They had $14 billion of repo on when the balloon went up and had plenty of additional capacity. What hurt them was that once they stopped being counterparties of ours, no one on the dealer side of Bear paid attention to them. Previously, the credit department evaluated them frequently and the mortgage-trading desk would wander in to see me from time to time if they thought Ralph was doing something odd. Once we stopped dealing with them, no one knew what they were up to."

CHAPTER 26

"THE ENTIRE SUBPRIME MARKET IS TOAST"

If Paul Friedman had no idea what Cioffi was up to in his hedge funds, it was a pretty good bet Jimmy Cayne had no idea, either—not that the CEO of a major Wall Street firm would be expected to know what was in the portfolio of a hedge fund in which the firm had a relatively tiny $20 million investment. Still, the firm's financial performance had been nothing short of dazzling. Through the nine months that ended August 30, 2006, Bear Stearns had earned nearly $1.5 billion, more than the $1.46 billion the firm made for *all* of 2005.

In September, the firm decided to reorganize a number of departments—among them equity derivatives, clearing, and stock trading—and have these businesses report to Spector. The reorganization made it appear that all of equities reported to Spector for the first time, effectively giving control of 90 percent of the firm's income statement to him. The rank and file wondered how Schwartz had allowed that to happen. "Some people came up to Schwartz after that meeting," a Bear senior managing director recalled, "and said, 'Whoa, Warren's taking over.' He said, 'Nothing's changing, guys. We just needed to get that in one place.'" After that announcement, the idea that Spector was Cayne's heir apparent began taking on renewed momentum. "The heir apparent and all that kind of stuff, he liked that," one Bear executive said of Spector. "If he couldn't be CEO, he wanted the world to know that Jimmy was the figurehead and he was the profit machine. He also wanted to outperform. He wanted to have a good quarter and have the stock go up so he could be even wealthier." The firm's stock had been on a tear, soaring to around $150 per share by November 2006, making Cayne a billionaire, a fact celebrated by *Forbes* in its annual list of the country's four hundred wealthiest people. In 2005, *Forbes* ranked him number 384, with $900 million, and a year later, he was number 354, with $1.1 billion. The bulk of Cayne's growing wealth was tied to his 6.8 million shares of Bear Stearns stock. In fact, by the end of 2006, Cayne was the *only* billionaire CEO among the titans of Wall Street securities firms—a fact that put an extra swagger in his step not because of what he could afford to buy that his brethren could not, but rather because of the fact that a college dropout and self-made man had bested the lot of them doing it his way. Thanks to *Forbes* and Bear Stearns, the memory of Cayne the mutineer during the Long-Term Capital Management debacle seemed a distant one.

Accordingly, it was not particularly surprising that in November 2006 *Institutional Investor* made Cayne the subject of a lengthy cover story in the magazine. Along with recounting the firm's ongoing financial successes, the article also raised the question about whether the firm's huge investment in the mortgage-backed securities business would make it vulnerable when home sales inevitably fell along with the houses' value. The article's author, Pierre Paulden, noted that after the firm's $26 million purchase of Encore Credit Corporation, a subprime mortgage originator, and the 2005 initiation of Bear Stearns Residential Mortgage Corp., which originated mortgages in twenty-nine states through a (now defunct) Web site, Beardirect.com, the firm originated 31 percent of the loans it securitized in the third quarter of 2006, almost double the amount it had originated a year earlier. Bear also owned EMC Mortgage Corporation, a loan acquisition and servicing operation. The idea of these small acquisitions was to become a fully vertically integrated mortgage factory capable of originating mortgages, servicing them, packaging them into marketable securities, and selling them off. "Until lately, Bear has been running downhill," Paulden wrote. "But now the playing field is starting to tilt upward." He noted that the housing market was cooling off, with mortgage originations in the

United States falling to $2.4 trillion in 2005 from $2.7 trillion in 2004, with a further 15 percent decline expected for 2006. "When the mortgage industry comes down, it comes down relatively hard," said Richard Bove, then an analyst at Punk, Ziegel & Co. "If housing gets as weak as I think it will, the mortgage business won't be a contributor to their earnings. It will cause some deterioration in their results." But Spector—the "fixed-income guru," Paulden called him—remained confident. "We are not afraid of a bear market," he said. "We've gained market share in these cycles."

With Bear's stock now trading in excess of the four times book value that in 2000 Cayne had told Guy Moszkowski he would sell the firm for, there was the inevitable question about whether the time had come to look for a merger partner. Paulden suggested that Bear Stearns "would be the perfect target" for JPMorgan Chase, which wanted Bear's prime brokerage and mortgage securitization businesses. "It could be a marriage made in heaven," said research analyst Brad Hintz. Bruce Sherman, the big Bear shareholder, predicted it could go either way. "It's the right size for buyers, and if they were to put up a sale sign, I'm sure they would get a nice price," he said. "But they've proven they can operate just fine in this environment."

Cayne hated the article. For what must have been sport, he had Spector write a letter to the magazine in an effort to get Paulden fired. Cayne objected to a few minor errors that Paulden had made—for instance, reporting that Cayne dropped out of Purdue after two years instead of leaving one semester shy of a degree, and reporting that he crashed his car as a traveling salesman before he got married for the first time instead of after he got married.

Regardless of Cayne's nitpicking, there was no stopping investors' love affair with the Bear Stearns juggernaut. On January 17, 2007, the stock reached its all-time intraday high of $172.69 per share. At that moment, Cayne's 7.03 million shares of Bear Stearns alone were worth $1.2 billion. When he traveled around, mostly to bridge tournaments, it was by private jet or by helicopter. He had built a shingle-style palace in Elberon, New Jersey—this was where he took the helicopter on Thursday afternoons, often having it land near the first golf tee at the Hollywood Golf Club, in Deal, New Jersey—and was looking around for a bigger apartment with a more prestigious address in Manhattan. He seemed to be genuinely revered by many inside 383 Madison and grudgingly respected outside of it for his flinty ability to preside over such an impressive creation of wealth. After all, as the cliché goes, on Wall Street, wealth was the ultimate way to keep score. The other members of the executive committee were also not shy about accumulating and displaying the touchstones of wealth. Spector, also an aficionado of private jets, had his summer estate in Martha's Vineyard and his winter estate in Palm Beach, which he bought in 2001 after falling in love with the Spanish-style five-bedroom home. For daily use, he had a duplex apartment at 40 Fifth Avenue, at the southwest corner of Fifth Avenue and West 11th Street.

Like Cayne, Spector wanted a bigger place in Manhattan. In November 2006 he signed a contract for $33.148 million to buy a 55-foot-wide, 15,000-square-foot mansion at 11 West 10th Street, around the corner from 40 Fifth Avenue. Unlike Cayne—and most other Wall Street executives—Spector was not the Upper East Side type. He had moved downtown in 1985. He'd married an actress and was devoted to the Public Theater, of which he became chairman of the board in July 2005. By his own admission, he was neither a hip guy nor one who aspired to a *Town & Country* lifestyle. Indeed, he was a serious worrier who bit his fingernails down to the quick. He was also plenty rich, having sold hundreds of millions of dollars' worth of Bear Stearns stock in 2005 and 2006 after Cayne forced the changes in the CAP. He even contemplated leaving Bear Stearns in 2006 as he came to the realization that his influence was waning and that Cayne had likely blocked his path to the corner office. "He used to joke that he didn't know who would last longer at the firm, him—who was in his forties—or Jimmy, who was in his seventies," said one of Spector's colleagues.

In short order, both Cayne and Spector would have their King Lear turn. "I really do believe that ironically one of the things that hurt the firm most was that the stock price did so well," said one former senior executive at the firm. "It emboldened Jimmy to stop listening, and that was the only thing he was really good at. He would listen. On the way up, he would always listen as he consolidated power. He always knew what was going on from a political point of view. When he got on top, he thought more about consolidating his power rather than leading. He started to rely on weaker people—for instance, Sam Molinaro, who was over his head. He was a fine controller and a good CFO, but he was also trying to be the risk manager, the business leader. Ace hated him: 'Who is this dumb fucking accountant telling us what he thinks?' I thought Molinaro was a very valuable guy if you could get him to do the things he was good at. But Ace would say, 'What the fuck does that stupid accountant know?'" For Spector, the turning point came when Cayne terminated the CAP and, in a fit of pique, Spector sold most of his stock at $100 per share, a decision made all the worse by the fact that the stock was now around $170 per share. "Now he's thinking he left money on the table, which pissed him off," one Bear Stearns executive said. "So now it was just more . . . that he could shoot for the upside without taking as much downside risk as when he had his whole net worth tied up in the stock. That should have been an obvious signal to us that something had changed in him. Because when you know a guy like Warren is totally financially motivated, you should say to yourself after he sells so much stock, 'Wow, that's a big change.' Instead, what you do sometimes is run it through another filter and say, 'Well, he's still Warren, he's still got plenty of stock.' But in a guy who's very, very methodical and mathematical about things and just intuits them like a computer, that was a big change."

JUST WEEKS AFTER Bear Stearns's stock hit its all-time high on January 17, cracks began appearing in the dam that held back the tidal wave of leverage pounding against it. On February 7, New Century Financial Corporation, a publicly traded twelve-year-old real estate investment trust that was a major mortgage lender (especially to borrowers with inferior credit ratings), announced that it had not properly accounted for home mortgages it had bought back from borrowers. As a result, its earnings for much of the previous year had been overstated and it had canceled its earnings call for the next day. The company's stock fell 37 percent, to $19.24, a fifty-two-week low. The same day HSBC Holdings, the huge European and Asian bank, announced it was increasing its provision for failed mortgage loans, and Toll Brothers, the big home builder, announced that its future economic outlook was diminishing rapidly.

Two days later, the *New York Times* wrote a flattering profile of Tim Geithner, the president of the Federal Reserve Bank of New York, titled "Calm Before and During a Storm." The substance of the piece was Geithner's increasing concern about the massive— then $26 trillion and growing—credit derivatives market. "We've seen substantial change in the financial system," Geithner said, "with the emergence of a very large universe of leveraged private funds, rapid growth in exposures to more complicated and less liquid financial instruments, all during a period of very low volatility. This means we know less about market dynamics in conditions of stress." The article ended by saying: "The real test, of course, will be when a crisis hits, whatever the crisis may be."

On February 12, Gyan Sinha, a senior managing director at Bear Stearns in charge of the firm's market research regarding asset-backed securities and collateralized debt obligations, held a conference call for some nine hundred investors where he spelled out his belief that the market had overreacted to the news about New Century and HSBC. "It's time to buy the [ABX] index," he said, adding that based on his modeling, "the market has overreacted" and predictions of rising problems in the mortgage market should be taken "with a large grain of salt." (The ABX index is a series of credit default swaps related to subprime mortgages, allowing bets to be made on the value of those mortgages.) Had Sinha been less well respected—he testified in front of Congress on April 17, 2007, about the subprime market—less attention might have been paid. "When you read the research [Bear] put out, you can think of one of two things," said Thomas Lawler, a former Fannie Mae economist, after reading Sinha's research. "One is they weren't getting it as fast as others, or two, they were really trying to talk the market back up. I don't know which."

On Valentine's Day, New Century announced that a wave of shareholder lawsuits had been filed against it and that after two weeks of tough negotiations Goldman Sachs had agreed to a three-month extension of a line of credit to the company that had been set to expire the next day. Goldman had extracted its pound of flesh by insisting on the ability to get out of the agreement "at the first hint of trouble."

That night, ironically, Steve Schwarzman, one of the two founders of the Blackstone Group, gave himself a boffo $4 million sixtieth-birthday party at the Armory on Park Avenue for 350 of Manhattan's glitterati. Martin Short emceed. Rod Stewart and Patti LaBelle sang. The menu included lobster, baked Alaska, and a 2004 Louis Jadot Chassagne-Montrachet. Cayne was there. "The festivities served as a coronation of sorts for Mr. Schwarzman, a billionaire several times over, an active Republican donor and chairman of the Kennedy Center in Washington whose influence reaches deep into the worlds of finance, politics and the arts," the *Times* reported afterward.

On February 21, the stock of NovaStar Financial, which like New Century made loans to people with weak credit, fell almost 43 percent after the company announced a surprise loss of $14.4 million for the fourth quarter and told investors that it might not make enough money to pay dividends for the next four years.

Three days later, the *Wall Street Journal* interviewed Lewis Ranieri, the godfather of the mortgage-backed security and the pioneer trader of them when he was at Salomon Brothers from the 1960s until he was pushed out of the firm in 1987. The *Journal* reported that the "rumpled 60-year-old says he is worried about the proliferation of risky mortgages and convoluted ways of financing them. Too many investors don't understand the dangers. . . . The problem, he says, is that in the past few years the business has changed so much that if the U.S. housing market takes another lurch downward, no one will know where all the bodies are buried. 'I don't know how to understand the ripple effects throughout the system today,' he said during a recent seminar." The growing problem was that 40 percent of the subprime borrowers in 2006 were not required to produce pay stubs or other proof of their net worth, according to Credit Suisse Group, and lenders were relying more and more on computer models to estimate the value of homes. "We're not really sure what the guy's income is and . . . we're not sure what the home is worth," Ranieri said. "So you can understand why some of us become a little nervous." He worried further that with so many mortgages being packaged by Wall Street into CDOs and sold in slices to investors all over the world, U.S. home mortgage risks were being spead to a "much less sophisticated community." The *Journal* made it clear that "Mr. Ranieri isn't predicting Armageddon. Some of the riskier new types of mortgages probably will perform 'horribly' in terms of defaults, leading to losses for some investors. But, he says, the 'vast majority' of mortgages outstanding are based on sounder lending principles and should be fine." On February 28, Reuters published a story about lurking dangers in the subprime market, citing the problems at New Century and HSBC. "We're looking at somewhat immature markets that are going through a growth phase," Cioffi told the news service. "There is a catharsis and a cleaning out process." The story also quoted him at a recent bond conference. "Up until now, any CDO manager, primarily new CDO managers with light staffing, very little technology and unbalanced capability, was able to get a CDO done," he said. "I don't see that going forward." Cioffi told his investors, "We're going to make money on this. . . . We don't believe what the markets are saying."

On March 2, the problems increased for New Century. First, the company announced it could not file its 2006 10-K financial report with the SEC on time "without unreasonable effort and expense"—a clear sign of brewing trouble, especially given the material misstatements already announced. Then there were the margin calls from its repo lenders. Citigroup had demanded the company refinance about $710 million of Citigroup loans and assets, and on March 2, the company announced that Morgan Stanley had refinanced Citigroup and had provided another $265 million of financing secured by the company's "loan portfolio and certain residual assets." Then came the dreaded statement: "The Company is in discussions with lenders and other third parties regarding a refinancing and other alternatives to obtain additional liquidity. No assurance can be given that any of these discussions will be successful." Also that day, New Century announced the resignation of hedge fund manager David Einhorn, president of Greenlight Capital, from its board of directors.

Einhorn's departure was plenty ironic, too, coming as it did less than a year after he had waged a high-profile proxy fight against New Century to get three seats on the company's board. On March 15, 2006, Einhorn, a bridge and poker player, agreed to stop his proxy fight and take a seat on the board. Part of Einhorn's compromise with the company allowed Greenlight Capital to increase its ownership stake in New Century to 19.6 percent. "New Century is a unique and valuable franchise," Einhorn said at that time. "I look forward to sharing my perspective as the Board oversees effective allocation of the company's capital to the most attractive risk-adjusted opportunities." Just days later, the company announced it would accept no new mortgage applications and that it was the target of investigations of wrongdoing related to trading in its stock. Then came the frozen credit lines and the demands by its repo lenders that the company buy back $8.4 billion in loans, money that it did not have. New Century had begun riding the mortgage finance wave in 1996, when it made its first loan to a borrower in Los Angeles. Ten years later, in February 2006, the company had 7,100 employees, 222 sales offices nationwide, and a compounded annual growth rate in its loan production of 64 percent per year, topping out at $56.1 billion in mortgages in 2005, up from $357 million in mortgages in 1996. On April 2, New Century filed for bankruptcy protection and was liquidated. Einhorn likely lost his entire investment—once worth $109 million—in New Century.

On March 7, *BusinessWeek* made it clear that the trouble in the subprime mortgage industry was spreading rapidly. "The canaries in the coal mine are keeling over fast," the magazine observed, noting that "at least 25 subprime lenders" had gone out of business, declared bankruptcy, put themselves up for sale, or announced significant losses. "Now there's evidence that the pain is spreading to a broad swath of hedge funds, commercial banks and investment banks that buy, sell, repackage and invest in risky subprime loans." The magazine quoted Jim Grant, the respected author and publisher of *Grant's Interest Rate Observer*, that the market was "starting to wake up to the magnitude of the problem" and had entered what Grant called "the recognition stage." Terry Wakefield, the head of a mortgage-industry consulting firm, was even more blunt:

"This is going to be a meltdown of unparalleled proportions. Billions will be lost."

※

BY THE TIME of the *BusinessWeek* article and New Century's bankruptcy filing, the problems in the mortgage market and the securities tied to mortgages had begun to show up in Cioffi's hedge funds at Bear Stearns. Of course, in terms of what the public was told, these problems might as well have been happening on Mars. In the firm's 2006 Annual Report, released in mid-February 2007, the theme was "Eighty-three years of profitability" and "Twenty years as a public company." On $9.2 billion in revenue, the firm had made $2.05 billion of net income, the first time that milestone had been reached. Profit had increased 40 percent from 2005. "In the past twenty years, we have seen Bear Stearns thrive far beyond anything the founding partners could have imagined," a beaming Cayne pronounced from the third page of the report. "This progress has been built on a firm foundation. Our balance sheet is now over $350 billion and the strong credit quality of Bear Stearns continues to be recognized by bondholders as well as ratings agencies. In 2006, Standard & Poor's upgraded Bear Stearns to A+ with a stable outlook—a rating that we believe reflects the dedication to risk evaluation and management that has given us the ability to expand carefully and conservatively." The Annual Report pointed with pride to Bear Stearns's number one positions in the United States for underwriting mortgage-backed securities, mortgage-backed residential securities, whole loans, and adjustable-rate mortgages. In 2006, *Euromoney* named the firm the best investment bank in North America and noted, "Bear's strategy may become the new investment banking business model of the near future." Even BSAM, under Marin's leadership, was performing well. Net revenues increased 47 percent to $335 million in 2006, and assets under management increased to $52.5 billion, up 25 percent. The "cornerstone" of BSAM's philosophy, the report noted, was its focus on "repackaging risk," or "developing a better understanding of risk, the investor's risk appetite and the balance between risk and return." Pictured prominently in the annual report, at the start of the discussion of BSAM's performance, was Ralph Cioffi, unsmiling but formidable-looking in his bespoke suit.

Bear Stearns was certainly not shy about trumpeting its success in various mortgage-backed securities. The firm's "mortgage franchise continues to lead the industry," the Annual Report said. "We ranked number one for the third consecutive year in US mortgage-backed securities underwriting, secured the top spot in the securitization of adjustable-rate mortgages, and ranked in the top five in the global collateralized debt obligation (CDO) market. . . . Our vertically integrated mortgage franchise allows us access to every step of the mortgage process, including origination, securitization, distribution and servicing." The firm's CDO business grew by 50 percent in 2006. "Our success across all sectors of the CDO market and in both European and US issuance reflects our 10-year presence in this business, combined with strong overall market growth," the firm trumpeted. "We are a leading underwriter of collateralized loan obligations, mezzanine asset-backed securitized debt obligations, and a range of types of CDOs, including those related to commercial mortgage-backed securities, trust preferred securities and CDOs of CDOs."

Just as Bear's public stockholders were digesting all the supposed good news about the firm found in the Annual Report, Cioffi was digesting the fact that February 2007 had been a very difficult month indeed for his two hedge funds. The High-Grade Fund had reported a gross return of 1.5 percent—respectable, to be sure—but the Enhanced Leverage Fund had lost 0.08 percent, the first time either fund had lost money since Cioffi started in 2003. But that was not the message that Tannin sent to Barclays about the February performance of the Enhanced Leverage Fund. "You will be happy to know that we are having our best month ever this February," he e-mailed the bank on February 19. "Our hedges are working beautifully. We were up 1.6% in January and are up 2% so far in February." On February 21, Tannin sent an e-mail to his team in which he sounded quite happy about all the doom and gloom over subprime mortgages in the marketplace. He cited such a report from a rival hedge fund manager, and said, "This piece is mostly unhelpful and more than a bit misleading. Scare mongering. I used to fly into a rage when I would read this stuff but now it makes me happy. We need some caution and naysayers in our market—it keeps spreads wider. So I'm glad this has been printed."

On February 27, a banker at Barclays demanded that Tannin provide the written monthly performance statements, and Tannin replied to him: "Here is the relevant information for Enhanced Leverage. As you can see, despite the sell off in the subprime mortgage market—our fund continues to do well, quite well, in fact. Here are a few points I think you should be aware of: 1. Our hedges are working just as we discussed. Our hedges are lower quality than our assets—so in this market we've experienced a significant mark to market gain so far this month. 2. Our term-financed positions are not as sensitive to this market volatility—just as we've discussed. 3. We have been in touch with all of our repo counterparties—and they are uniformly very happy with all of our positions. In short, we are very pleased with our performance—but even more important than that we are pleased that our ideas about how to structure our risk and limit our volatility are once again proving to have been prudent." The first page of the report that Tannin sent to Barclays on February 27 showed BSAM's calculation of a 5.5 percent gross return and a 4.3 percent net return through February 23. The day before Tannin sent this e-mail, Pusateri had asked Barclays for a $100 million increase to its debt investment used in the Enhanced Leverage Fund. Another $100 million request was made a few weeks later. Barclays agreed to both requests, in part because of a March 8 e-mail from Tannin. "Despite dramatic volatility in the structured finance market our Fund has been extremely stable," he wrote. By the end of March 2007, Barclays had invested its total commitment of $400 million in the debt used in the Enhanced Leverage Fund.

On February 28, Cioffi wrote the team that he was thinking of "very selectively buying at these levels" since that "in and of itself would stabilize the markets." Tannin responded that he thought it would be a good idea. "Fear + illiquidity + a CDO ready and waiting = a good trade." That same day, Ben Bernanke, now chairman of the Federal Reserve, testified on Capitol Hill that he did not believe a "housing downturn" was a "broad financial concern or a major factor in assessing the state of the economy." On March 1, Cioffi told an economist who worked for the hedge funds, "Don't talk about [the funds' February results] to anyone or I'll shoot you." He also went on to say that he thought the funds might have their first down month ever and that he was disappointed by that fact. On March 2, Cioffi met informally with Tannin and two other members of the funds' management team and spoke "about the extremely difficult month" February had been for the funds, though he claimed that the funds "had averted disaster." With his team around him, Cioffi "led a vodka toast to celebrate surviving the month." Then he "directed those present not to talk about the Funds' difficulties with others, including other members" of the team.

Cioffi was becoming increasingly concerned about the funds' exposure to the subprime market, even though the monthly statements sent to investors stated that only 6 percent of the funds' money was invested in supbrime. Cioffi was concerned because he knew that actually the funds had closer to 60 percent of their money invested in subprime mortgages. On March 3, he told Tannin that at least "we have our health and families . . . [w]e are not a 19 year old Marine in Iraq." That same day, Cioffi told Tannin, "The worry for me is that sub prime losses will be far worse than anything people have modeled." By March 11, Cioffi knew March was not going to be a good month, either. "We will be hard pressed to be up" in either fund, he concluded. On March 15, he wrote a colleague by e-mail, "I'm fearful of these markets. Matt [Tannin] said it's either a meltdown or the greatest buying opportunity ever. I'm leaning more towards the former. As we discussed it may not be a meltdown for the general economy but in our world it will be." By the end of March, Cioffi had taken to going around the office and telling his colleagues, "I'm sick to my stomach over our performance in March."

Then there were the margin calls from the funds' repo lenders, which forced Cioffi to try to sell assets at unfavorable prices. "We do need to take positions down in [the High-Grade Fund]," he told a team member on March 14. "We are getting loads of margin calls." Cioffi and Tannin even discussed merging together the High-Grade and Enhanced Leverage funds as a way to increase the liquidity of the High-Grade Fund. Despite his growing concern about the liquidity of the High-Grade Fund, Cioffi made a "false statement" to a repo lender in March that the funds "had more than enough liquidity to meet any likely eventuality."

He also kept encouraging investment in the funds even though his concerns were growing. On March 7, Cioffi told a Bear Stearns broker who had more than forty of his clients invested in the funds that "we have an awesome opportunity" with the funds. That same day, Tannin told the same broker, "I think [Cioffi] and I are in agreement that we are looking at some great possibilities for the coming months. I don't know where you are putting your money now but I would suggest we speak about adding more to the fund. That's what I'm thinking." On March 15, Tannin told an investor, "We are seeing opportunities now and are excited about what is possible. I am adding capital to the Fund. If you guys are in a position to do the same I think think [sic] this is a good opportunity," and he added that "it was a very bad time to redeem." Tannin never did invest more of his own money in the funds.

At the end of March, Tannin sent a colleague, Steven Van Solkema, an e-mail. Tannin had been walking around the office speaking to potential investors using his headset and thought his conversations might have been disturbing Van Solkema. "I hope I don't disturb you with all my ranting and raving," he wrote. "Believe it or not—I've been able to convince people to add more money—which I am doing as well. No one has redeemed as far as I've seen. Please please please tell me if you think I'm not saying anything clearly or if you think there are things to say that I'm not saying. I apologize for the fact that you have to hear all of this [and] if it takes you away from your concentration. But what would be VERY helpful is if you could continually feed me the 'market intelligence' you see and hear." At the same time, though, Cioffi remained worried about the funds' liquidity. The funds "have to be very light on the investment side and continue to raise cash [in the High-Grade Fund] and maintain cash [in the Enhanced Leverage Fund]" to meet margin calls. He also told investors, "We wouldn't have made money in February if we were long, or overexposed to subprime."

Bear Stearns, meanwhile, kept rolling along despite the cracks in the subprime market. On March 15, Cayne announced the firm had made $554 million in the first quarter of 2007, up 8 percent from the first quarter a year earlier. "We are pleased with this excellent performance," he said, making no mention about whether he was also pleased to be paid $40 million for fiscal year 2006 (putting him on a par for the year with Dick Fuld, CEO of Lehman Brothers). The firm's stock had fallen to around $145 per share since its January 17 peak, but the solid first-quarter performance announcement caused the firm's stock to rally to nearly $149 per share. "Even though Bear's bread-and-butter has historically been in fixed income, given the slowdown in the residential mortgage market— meaning lower demand for mortgage-backed securities—we were impressed that Bear's credit derivative and distressed debt products more than picked up the slack," research analyst Philip Guziec wrote. An analyst at Standard & Poor's, Matthew Albrecht, wrote that although he remained "concerned by the firm's exposure to the subprime mortgage market . . . we believe much of the recent selling on the news has been overdone and we see a number of positive catalysts for the business." His twelve-month target on Bear's stock was $157 per share.

That same day, IndyMac Bancorp, a thrift based in Pasadena, California, announced that its exposure to subprime mortgages was small and that the bank had been "inappropriately categorized by many media sources as a subprime lender." (On July 12, 2008, the federal government, through the FDIC, seized control of IndyMac, which at the time was the second-largest bank failure in U.S. history.)

On March 23, Cioffi was growing increasingly nervous about his hedge funds and initiated the process of removing $2 million of the $6 million that he personally had invested in the Enhanced Leverage Fund. He moved the money to another Bear hedge fund, Structured Risk Partners, of which Cioffi had oversight responsibility beginning April 1. For appearance purposes, hedge fund managers were expected to invest in the hedge funds they managed, and Cioffi's defenders suggest that this alone was the reason he moved the cash. "At least Structured Risk Partners keeps getting better," Cioffi told Rich Marin on March 22. Cioffi's concerns about his funds' performance in March proved well founded. The High-Grade Fund lost 3.71 percent for the month. The Enhanced Leverage Fund lost 5.41 percent. Although both funds' March 2007 investor statements showed that 86 percent of the collateral was in asset-backed securities and 6 percent in subprime mortgages, Cioffi's commentary described two reasons for the losses: "continued weakness in CDOs with exposure to subprime collateral caused additional markdowns in our long asset exposure" and "our short positions rose in price as many investors who were short the subprime default index covered their positions." He added, "Our losses in March are frustrating. The widening we've seen in these asset classes will not tighten again nearly as quickly as they have widened but this market dislocation has created many opportunities."

THESE WERE BIG losses and of major concern to the executives at BSAM as well as to Cioffi and Tannin. "In an illiquid market, like for these instruments, you have to wait until the end of the month and you get marks from your trading counterparties—the Street," explained a Bear Stearns executive. "It's usually the people that you trade with that give you the marks. We have a procedure. It's all documented. There's a valuation committee at Bear Stearns. The people on the committee do their valuations. Only if there's a problem does it get elevated. The procedures call for us to get as many independent marks as we can and then average them. Clearly as this market started to get a little bit dicier, in 2007, it was harder to get marks in shops. People didn't want to value things. They were worried about their own valuations. But we were showing valuations that went from 100 cents on the dollar down to like 98. They were going down. But they were going a little bit down." The losses, though, were magnified by the amount of leverage sitting on those assets. Warren Spector, the co-president of Bear Stearns, was one person who was unfazed by what was happening in the subprime mortgage market at that moment. "The big question is will it have a broad impact on the housing market," Spector said during a March 29 "investor day" at the firm. "I don't see it." He also told investors, "We're very proud of the way we do risk management. It's an integral part of our culture. . . . We have a strong culture of no surprises."

Both Tannin and Cioffi saw the dislocation in the mortgage markets as a buying opportunity for the hedge funds. On March 31, a Saturday, Tannin wrote Cioffi an e-mail noting that he was skeptical of the naysayers. "I simply do not believe anyone who shits all over the ratings agencies," he wrote. "I've seen it all before. Smart people being too smug." He wrote that the hedge fund team has "some important decisions to make" and his "experience is biased toward the positives of acting boldly in the face of uncertainty. We are in a unique position of having access to capital at a time when we might have h[a]d our hands tied." He then laid out for Cioffi a series of trades he believed would be profitable. He wanted to "show our investors that we are acting aggressively," he wrote. "I think they will reward us with time—which is critical at this point. My biggest fear is a flat few months while economic news continues to get worse. We face a risk that our investors will lose patience, not that they will become disappointed. . . . I think we can't afford not to be aggressive, whatever we do."

On Passover, April 4, Tannin wrote Cioffi that he continued to "believe that the variables that end up contributing to subprime defaults are numerous and not subject to 'contagion'. . . . I would suggest that EXACTLY those factors which constitute the non-bubble phenomenon of housing prices . . . sum up to a very complicated series of variables leading to defaults in AAA CDOs or mortgages. AAA CDOs will have greater ratings volatility than other AAAs but good credit selection and good funding vehicles should mitigate the damage." Twelve minutes later, Cioffi replied that he agreed with Tannin's observations. "There are good AAAs and not so good ones and that is our job to find those ones that are good." On April 13, Steven Todd, a research analyst at Wachovia Securities, wrote a report, "CDO House of Blues: How Strange the Change from Major to Minor," which "critique[d] key tenants of the doom-and-gloom argument" regarding a "housing meltdown." Todd pointed investors to the "unusual value in the market" for certain mortgage-related collateralized debt obligations. "Recent stabilization in the ABX index may signal this moment as a good entry point for bargain shoppers," Todd wrote. His research report was required reading for Cioffi, Tannin, and the other professionals at the two hedge funds, who found it to be positive reinforcement for their idea that money-making opportunities lay before them.

At the end of April, Rich Marin, the head of BSAM, attended an executive committee meeting to discuss an asset management project then getting under way in Saudi Arabia. After he finished his presentation, Greenberg asked him if there was anything else going on at BSAM that the executive committee should be aware of. He mentioned the looming departure of one asset manager, and then said, according to someone who was there, "The other problem is that we don't know yet until we get the marks for April, but I think we might be heading into our second down month in the High-Grade Fund. That's going to be potentially problematic for redemptions. We've got to watch it closely." This was hardly an earthshaking thought, but when Cayne heard Marin's words, he blew up. "What!" Cayne said. "That's kind of a harsh reaction. Isn't it?" When Marin wondered why, Cayne continued, "I've had lots of investments in hedge funds. And if I've had thirty good months and then I have two bad months, I'm not going to be redeeming and pulling my money out. Why would you be concerned about it?"

Some big investors in the hedge funds, though, were starting to get nervous. On April 18, one of the investors, who had $57 million invested, informed Cioffi that he was considering redeeming his money. Cioffi told him that the portfolio managers had $8 million of their own money invested, one-third of their liquid net worth. He did not tell the investor that he had taken $2 million of his own money out and invested it in his other hedge fund. The next day, the investor informed Cioffi and Tannin that he wanted his money out. That same day, the funds' management team produced a report showing the value of the CDOs in the funds to be worth "significantly less" than previously reported. On a call with investors on April 20, Tannin said there was "a dislocation in the market" in February and March caused "by a loss of confidence by the market in the ratings of CDOs with 2006-vintage subprime exposure" but that the funds had very little exposure to this collateral.

On April 22, Tannin wrote Cioffi an e-mail from his personal Gmail account to Cioffi's wife's personal Hotmail account with the subject line "Things to Think about—Parts I and II." He wrote at times with great emotion and about his personal feelings, which may have accounted for his decision not to write the e-mail on the Bear Stearns system. Tannin, a philosophy major, was certainly waxing philosophical in the correspondence. "In January 2003, I excitedly accepted your offer to become your partner," he wrote. "While you may have had a fully fleshed out idea of where you thought we were going back then, I did not. I knew only that I trusted and respected you and that I had come to love to work with you (a feeling shared with just about everyone). So I considered myself tremendously fortunate to have been given the opportunity you gave me. Over the past four years a lot has changed—and a lot has not. We have been very successful measured in almost any conceivable way. We have raised a lot of money, we've made a lot of money, we've hired a lot of good people—but for me most importantly—we have spent our time well—and time is the ONLY thing in this life which one can't ever get back." He said he was feeling "pretty damn good" about what was happening at the funds because he had no doubt "I've done the best possible job that I could have done. Mistakes, yep, I've made them—but they do not bother me as much as they did years ago. . . . So—fuck it—all one can do is their best—and I have done this."

He went on to wonder whether the funds should be closed or significantly restructured. "Over the last few months," Tannin wrote, he had come to believe the funds should be closed or "get very very aggressive." The argument for closing the funds was based on the market and on a complex internal April 19 CDO report, which was a new analysis that Tannin had perused for the first time in previous days. "[T]he subprime market looks pretty damn ugly," Tannin wrote. "If we believe the [new CDO report] is ANYWHERE CLOSE to accurate, I think we should close the funds now. The reason for this is that if [the CDO report] is correct, then the entire subprime market is toast. . . . If AAA bonds are systematically downgraded, then there is simply no way for us to make money— ever." He wrote that he believed "we need to GUESS about the accuracy of the [new CDO report] NOW. It would be nice if we had the luxury of waiting a bit (and maybe we do—this is another discussion point)—but I do not think we have any time luxuries here." One possibility was "the likelihood of a melt-down." He concluded that "caution would lead us to conclude [the CDO report] is right— and we're in bad bad shape."

On the other hand, he wrote, he had spoken with Andrew Lipton, a veteran residential mortgage-backed securities analyst, and "sat him down on Friday and asked how serious he thought the situation was. He calmly told me that the situation was going to be as bad as people were saying. . . . We should EXTRACT every piece of information from him because I'm not sure there is anyone who knows more than he does." But he said he had his doubts about Lipton, too. "He's just been too calm during this whole period." He also said he thought their partner, Ray McGarrigal, had "lost confidence in the structures. Not long ago Ray had confidence in the structures. Ray does not fuck around. Ray has been paying attention. I trust Ray." In closing, he wondered, "Who do we talk to about this? Marin? Spector? Outside counsel? (And here we have to be careful because our outside counsel is BSAM's counsel NOT our counsel. This is another very big issue we at least need to think about.)" That night Cioffi, Tannin, and McGarrigal met at Cioffi's house in Tenafly, New Jersey. Cioffi convinced Tannin that the new computer runs were actually "good for us," not "bad for us," and that his concerns about the potential meltdown of the subprime market were misplaced. After that night, Tannin was back on board with the strategy to use the moment as a buying opportunity. On April 23, Tannin urged Cioffi not to broadcast the funds' troubles to other employees. "I think we should be cautious of statements like 'if we sold all the assets at the mark' while we are on the desk. We have a lot to do—and we'll do it—but I think it's important to keep everyone else as focused as possible." On April 24, Cioffi and Tannin told "senior BSAM personnel" that they were "confident that the Funds were in good shape and would continue to be successful."

The next day, April 25, Cioffi and Tannin held a conference call for the funds' investors. Their performance was Oscar-worthy. Cioffi kicked the discussion off with a review of the first-quarter performance at both funds. The High-Grade Fund was down a cumulative 0.34 percent in the first quarter, with the loss coming in March after a positive January and February; the Enhanced Leverage Fund had lost 4.74 percent year to date, with much of the loss coming in March. "At this point in time, the [Enhanced] fund has significant amounts of liquidity," Cioffi said. He then reviewed the funds' financing strategy of "non-recourse term funding" in order to avoid margin calls or having repo lines "removed or terminated," according to a transcript of the call. Despite what he and Tannin had been worrying about privately, he told the investors, "The repo market has been very solid and very liquid. We've had no increase in haircuts, actually, no increase in repo rates either. We've had margin calls that we've easily met. We've not had to force-sell any assets. And the reason we focus on that is if one believes their assets are good, and they are gonna pay off at maturity, the market volatility that creates mark-to-market losses is only realized if one has to sell because they lose their financing. So we have been very careful, very cautious, very diligent on that front."

He then launched into a jargon-filled discussion of how he hoped to close, in May, a $5 billion CDO financing with Bank of America—"the largest CDO of the year so far, I believe"—that would allow the Enhanced Leverage Fund to sell $2.6 billion of assets and the High-Grade Fund to sell $1.4 billion of assets to the bank. "The transaction adds significant liquidity to both funds," he said, by putting "in excess" of $200 million of "cash and liquidity" in the Enhanced Leverage Fund and $125 million, "maybe slightly more," in the High-Grade Fund after making some $100 million more in "new assets that we're in the process of identifying now in the CDO space and structured credit space." He then predicted returns of 14 percent for the year in the Enhanced Leverage Fund and 11 percent for the year in the High-Grade Fund. The new Bank of America facility, he said, would also give the funds another $1 billion with which to buy assets while reducing the repo lines that could be called by the lenders. "With all the disarray and turmoil in the market," Cioffi said, "there is some significant trade opportunities out there for us to put on. So we'll be adding carry and we'll be doing some total rate of return relative value on short trades in that space." Tannin wrote Cioffi that successfully completing the Bank of America financing would give the funds "definite mark to market gains," adding that "this is how we show investors what we can do—a few months of good positive returns and we'll be fine."

CHAPTER 27

"IF THERE'S FRAUD, WE'RE GONNA PAY"

By early 2007, there were many factors that exacerbated the exponential deterioration of the value of securities tied to the United States housing market. In no particular order, first there was the use of newfangled automated software that allowed mortgage lenders such as New Century, Countrywide, and First Franklin to process increasingly large numbers of mortgage applications far more quickly. The new software replaced the old-fashioned, labor-intensive process of collecting and reviewing a borrower's documentation. The software, of course, was not what led to lower underwriting standards, but it allowed the processing of those applications to happen much more rapidly. Then there was the fall in housing prices, which, as Paul Friedman explained, started "to crack on a surprisingly broad basis across the country" and opened a window into "just how bad the 2006 vintage of subprime and Alt-A mortgages were and how much fraud was embedded in the loans." People also began to realize that, as Friedman described it, "one of the bedrock concepts of the whole subprime securitization model, diversification"—the theory that a broad pool of borrowers provided inherent protection from price declines and defaults—"was fundamentally flawed. In fact, when we had declines around the country it became obvious that if you had a big pool of borrowers who had identical characteristics you really didn't have any diversification at all."

This problem, too, was made worse by the behavior of the ratings agencies—Standard & Poor's, Moody's, and Fitch—that provided the desired ratings on the securities, for a fee paid by the investment banks, to allow the securities to be sold to investors around the world. "The story of the credit rating agencies is a story of colossal failure," said Congressman Henry Waxman at a hearing of his Committee on Oversight and Government Reform held in October 2008. "The credit rating agencies occupy a special place in our financial markets. Millions of investors rely on them for independent, objective assessments. The rating agencies broke this bond of trust, and federal regulators ignored the warning signs and did nothing to protect the public." As an example of this breach of trust, Waxman's committee released an internal e-mail exchange between Frank L. Raiter, head of mortgage ratings at Standard & Poor's for ten years, and Richard Gugliada, an S&P managing director. Raiter had been asked to rate a collateralized debt obligation called "Pinstripe" and requested from Gugliada highly detailed data about each individual loan, known as "loan level tapes," to assess the creditworthiness of the security.

"Any request for loan level tapes is totally unreasonable!!!" Gugliada wrote Raiter. "Most investors don't have it and can't provide it. It is your responsibility to provide those credit estimates and your responsibility to devise some method for doing so."

Raiter responded: "This is the most amazing memo I have ever received in my business career."

Then there was this instant-message conversation between two S&P analysts, Rahul Shah and Shannon Mooney, in April 2007. "By the way, that deal was ridiculous," Shah wrote to Mooney.

"I know right—[the] model def[initely] does not capture half of the risk," Mooney responded.

"We should not be rating it," Shah wrote.

"We rate every deal," wrote Mooney.

"It could be structured by cows and we would rate it," Shah responded.

"But there's a lot of risk associated with it—I personally don't feel comfy signing off as a committee member," Mooney replied.

In his September 2007 congressional testimony, Kyle Bass, the managing partner of Hayman Capital who once worked at Bear Stearns, accurately defined the problem. "Unfortunately the relationship between the bond issuers and the [ratings agencies] presents a fundamental conflict of interest because the [ratings agencies] are dependent on the issuers for their revenues," he said. "The bond issuers, as sellers of risk, have an incentive to see that the risk they are selling is priced as cheaply as possible—in the marketplace this means obtaining as high a rating as possible—because once they sell the bonds they are relieved of any risk burden. It is this incentive, and the fact that they work closely with, and provide payment to, the [ratings agencies] that places into question the objectivity of the ratings provided by the [ratings agencies]. The ultimate holders of the risk, the buyers of these bonds, have the most at stake in accurately pricing risk, but instead rely upon the ratings bought and paid for by the sellers. It would be like cattle ranchers paying the Department of Agriculture to rate the quality and safety of their beef. It would undermine the integrity of the system by casting doubt on the impartiality of the body that the ultimate buyer relies upon to keep them safe from harm. But it is becoming increasingly clear as each month passes, subprime credit has become the mad cow disease of structured finance. Nobody knows who consumed the infected product and nobody has any real faith in the [rating agencies] that gave it a clean bill of health."

Paul Friedman believed the decline in Cioffi's "buying power" in the market also led to a decline in the market's liquidity. "For products that were reasonably well constructed—not CDOs of CDOs of CDOs—there was a market that was plenty deep," he said. "For the funkier stuff, there was never a deep market. Once that demand slowed, it rippled back through all the pricing of everything that was the raw material for complex CDOs, driving prices down and freaking people out."

The final factor was the creation in January 2006 of an index—known as the ABX index—that for the first time allowed investors to bet on the performance of the subprime mortgage market. The ABX was an index of securities backed by home loans issued to borrowers with weak credit. "In previous times, if the market sold off, no one really knew how much," Friedman explained. "Now you had a published index that people could observe. More importantly, it was the only real thing they could short as a hedge. As a result, the index got driven lower and lower as people looked for a way to hedge, going far lower than the underlying bonds. Potential buyers then demanded to buy bonds at the levels that the index suggested they should trade [at] when in fact no one was willing to sell there. So you had a period of time when, for example, the index would trade at 90 but the underlying bonds traded—when they traded—at 95. Hence, there would be no trades."

As a partial explanation for what happened to his funds during March and April 2007, Cioffi blamed a rally in the ABX index, which he had been short. (He had bet that subprime mortgages would decline in value during that time, and when they increased in value—as reflected in the higher ABX index—the funds lost value.) The index rallied, he said on the April 25 conference call with investors, because there was a slight decline in mortgage delinquencies and some talk about bailouts and refinancing possibilities. "There is definitely a market rationalization" going on, he said, "deals that are managed by good managers, deals that have good collateral. Specifically, those that are more seasoned and are not heavily concentrated in the 2006 subprime vintage, which is where the majority of the problems lie." He said he thought the market was "significantly better" at the end of April than it was in either February or March. "A lot of it has to do with dealers being able to sell out of inventory," he said. He then shared with the investors that the estimated returns for April would be a −.06 percent for the High-Grade Fund and −.07 percent for the Enhanced Leverage Fund (both of those numbers were wrong; the Enhanced Leverage Fund dropped 10 percent in April) and added that the ABX index had moved down in recent days, which benefited the funds. He reiterated the 14 percent and 11 percent annual return for the Enhanced Leverage and High-Grade funds, respectively.

Cioffi then turned the call over to Tannin. "The key sort of big-picture point for us at this point is our confidence that the structured credit market, and the subprime market in particular, has not systemically broken down," he said. "The dislocation that we saw in February and March is simply one where the early high delinquency numbers in many of the subprime deals has spooked the market into a position where people are simply afraid that all of the historical data that the rating agencies and the structurers and the investors have been using to assess the relative ratings volatility of these sorts of structures, right, the people are scared that what has been will not be the case in the next few years." He then explained away the "early delinquencies" as resulting from the ability of "weaker borrowers" to refinance their mortgages in 2003, 2004, and 2005 because of rising home values. Without the rising home values during those years, these borrowers would have already been flushed from the system. "When home price appreciation stopped, those weak people were already sort of on the edge and those weak people are the ones who have gone into delinquencies on their mortgages," he said. "We believe that, overall, these portfolios are not going to be that far away from the historical numbers that we've seen over the last ten to twelve years." He observed that "there's a fear" in the market that securities that the rating agencies had rated AAA—the least risky of all—were "actually going to be single-A in quality"—far more risky than thought, and that this had led to a widening of the interest rates investors were demanding to account for the increased risk.

But he remained sanguine. "We believe that that is simply not true," he said. "That while there will be weak deals and that while attention to structure and to collateral is even more critical now than it was before, this is not a systemic breakdown in the entire structured finance market." Indeed, as Cioffi had alluded to and now Tannin said explicitly, the two hedge fund managers actually told the funds' investors there was a *buying* opportunity in the market that they intended to exploit with their newfound liquidity. He said that 2005 and 2006 "was not the time to really take on significant amounts of risk" but "now is the time to do it. So the fact that we've been so cautious in the prior periods means that we have the capital and the flexibility to take advantage of spreads that are simply irrational." As for the funds' losses to date, they would reverse and the "price appreciations will come over time" as the market rebounds. He said he and Cioffi had spent the first four years of the funds' existence planning for a "dislocation" to make sure they would never be "forced sellers." He said, "The structure of the fund has performed exactly the way it was designed to perform," and added that while "it is frustrating to have had a negative month" and "it is frustrating to be in an industry where people are writing articles daily about how the world is coming to an end, but our historical experience, having been through these sorts of things before, leads us to be comfortable in our credit models and not in the sort of headlines that appear now and then about the subprime market being completely misguided."

In closing, Cioffi echoed Tannin's optimism. "We are consciously [sic] optimistic," he said. "We have a plan in place that will get the funds back on track to generate positive returns. And most importantly, we have financing and we have significant amounts of liquidity."

The call continued with questions and answers. At one point, Tannin responded to a question by saying, "It is really a matter of whether one believes that careful credit analysis makes a difference, or whether you think that this is just one big disaster. And there's no basis for thinking this is one big disaster." During the call, Cioffi also addressed the issue of investor redemptions, but he made no mention of the request by "Major Investor #1" to pull his $57 million from the funds and with whom Cioffi had met on April 18. He said the redemptions for June 30 were only "a couple million" and made no mention of the $67 million in redemptions scheduled for April 30 and May 31. In fact, he already was aware of another $47 million in redemptions for June 30, including a portion of that from "Major Investor #1" wanting to withdraw his $57 million. He also made no mention of his own personal $2 million redemption on April 1, and Tannin did not explain why he was not putting his own money into the funds despite telling investors he would.

※

SLIPPED INNOCUOUSLY INTO the conference call was the fact that Bear Stearns had decided to invest an additional $25 million on May 1 into the hedge funds, bringing the firm's total investment in the funds to $45 million, a relatively small amount in the overall scheme of things. (This investment should not be confused with the firm's $25 million investment in Rampart.) On his own authority—which the executive committee had granted him in writing—Spector had decided to make what one of his colleagues described as "an opportunistic investment" in the fund. Spector's decision seemed to be an impulsive one in the face of the redemption requests and what Cioffi was telling him about the potential opportunities as a result of the market dislocation. On the other hand, "At that moment, it didn't look like the world was blowing up," said someone who knew his thinking, "and it shows our confidence in the fund and people thought we would make money." The matter first came up during a Wednesday breakfast that Spector was having with Sam Molinaro, the CFO, and Steve Begleiter, the head of strategy. Suddenly, Rich Marin, the head of BSAM, appeared at the door, wanting to speak with Spector urgently. Marin came in, started talking to Spector about Cioffi's hedge funds, and recommended to Spector that the firm invest $25 million into the funds. (Marin had initially asked for a much larger investment.) "There were no analytics presented to Warren right then as to why we should be confident [that this was a good investment]," explained one of the participants. "It was Rich Marin saying he thought these things were cheap after talking to Ralph." Spector told Marin to go ahead with the $25 million investment in order "to show strength to the market" in the face of redemption requests. While usually the executive committee— which Spector was on—would need to approve such an investment, one person aware of the committee's routines said, "on small amounts they never didn't approve what Warren wanted to do in asset management, or other people wanted to do in other areas." In truth, the firm had made investments totaling more than $500 million of its money in hedge funds and other seed-capital-type opportunities, many of which Spector made on his own authority as well.

Even as Spector approved the investment, there was not a consensus among those who were aware of it that it was a good idea at that moment. There were at least two reasons discussed for why the investment should not be made. "One was God forbid anybody took any comfort from the fact that we were investing, and then invested or didn't redeem and lost money; we would just worsen our liability from it because we're doing this to sort of show confidence," one Bear executive said. "We're creating a false illusion. And two, we were telling people we were doing this because we wanted to calm them down. That's all the more reason not to do it. We hadn't done sufficient analytics to prove that the values were cheap. Plus, the $25 million of our shareholders' money is going to be put at risk. And if there was a problem in the fund, $25 million wasn't going to do any good. If we actually needed to have more money put in the fund to meet margin or do whatever, there's no way $25 million is the right number. The right number is probably $525 million or $425 million, and we should figure out what the right number is before we just start ladling in little dollops." But, as Cioffi reported to his investors, Bear Stearns made the $25 million investment, effective May 1.

✽

DESPITE WHAT THEY said in the April 25 conference call, by early May both Cioffi and Tannin anticipated that the funds' April results were going to be rough. "Going into the month of May, when we were waiting for our April marks, there were no cash trades that you could look at," one Bear Stearns executive explained. "That said to us, 'Wow, this market was falling like a rock.' But when we were waiting for the April marks, [Ralph and Matt] were like, 'No, let's see where they come out. We think they're going to be down. But we don't think they're going to be down outrageously.' And sure enough, we get in all these marks. And the marks are 99, 98, 97. They're still in that same ballpark. It was enough to have a second bad month. It was like down 6 percent but not disastrous. Not good, but not disastrous." Cioffi published the NAV for the Enhanced Leverage Fund for April at –6.5 percent.

A week later, "knowing full well we've published our NAV," according to this executive, Goldman Sachs sent, by e-mail, its April marks on the securities to Cioffi. As a counterparty to trades in the funds, Goldman was obligated to report its thinking about the value of the securities in the funds on a monthly basis. "Now there's a funny little procedure that the SEC imposes on you, which is that even if you get a late mark, you have to consider it," he said. "Suddenly we get these marks. Except these marks are not marks from 98 to 97. They go from 98 to 50 and 60. Okay? You get it? They give us these 50 and 60 prices. What we got from the other counterparties is 98. The SEC rules say that when you do this, you either have to average them—but they're meant to be averaging 97s and 98s, not 50s and 98s—or you can go and ask if those are the correct marks. But you can't ask the low mark. You've got to go back and ask the high mark. Everybody knows the procedure. So we got to go ask the high mark. We ask the 98 guy—another major Wall Street firm—and you know what he says? Remember, he knows he's high now. He goes, 'You're right. We were wrong. It's 95.' In other words, he gave himself a margin of error, and he said, 'I'm going to drop it severely.' He looked at it with great intensity and said 95. Now, we got nothing we can do but take the 50 and the 95 and average them. We have to repost our NAV. And now we go from minus 6 to minus 19"—minus 18.97 to be exact—"and that is game fucking over. By the way, the firm that sent us the 50 made a shit pot full of money in 2007 shorting the fucking market."

The effect of the new marks from Goldman Sachs on Cioffi's hedge funds was immediate and devastating. "Let me see if I can make this clear for you. Minus 6 percent announced this week. Oops—19 percent announced next week," he said. "Number one, 19 percent is a pretty damn big number. So we announce minus 19 percent. So what happens? Two fundamental things. One, this thing is in freefall—19 percent down. Number two, these guys are fucking idiots—6 percent one week, 19 percent the next week. How could that be?" Harder to understand, he said, was that Goldman's marks had been at 98¢ the month before. "Ninety-eight to 50?" he asked, incredulous. "They were at 98 the month before. There were no cash trades to imply anything like that. Nothing. There was nothing. And you know what? The way the procedure works, all we could [do] was go, 'But, but, but, but, but . . .'"

With the hindsight of a few months, the Bear executive's fury at Goldman had not abated. "If everybody's getting overwhelmed by a tsunami and there's a couple of guys making a fucking fortune, that usually is grounds for at least taking a closer look to see what was going on, as to why they were making a fortune. Sometimes it's because they were smarter. Guess what? The presumption, in this case, is they were smarter. But I just told you a story that is about as relevant and about as potent as nitroglycerin, if you ask me."

Gary Cohn, the co-president of Goldman Sachs, had a few reactions to the charges made by the Bear executive. First, he was clear that Goldman did not make nearly as much money in 2007 betting against the mortgage market as people think it did. "We don't disclose segment-by-segment reporting," he said. "But the market would be really disappointed if they saw our actual mortgage results last year, because they think we made a lot of money." As for the marks themselves, Cohn said that Goldman was aggressive about marking down these kinds of securities, especially during the third quarter of 2007, much to the detriment of its own income statement and those of some of their clients who would then have to account for the new Goldman marks.

He then shared an anecdote about a conversation he'd had with Nino Fanlo, one of the founding partners of KKR Financial Holdings, a specialty finance company started by KKR, the private equity kingpin. After Goldman sent out the marks in the 50¢ to 55¢ range, Fanlo called Cohn and told him, "You're way off market. Everyone else is at 80, 85." Cohn then offered to sell Fanlo $10 billion of the paper at his 55¢ price and encouraged him to sell that in the market to all the other broker-dealers at the higher prices they claimed to be marking the paper at. In other words, Cohn was offering Fanlo a windfall: buy at 55 and sell at 80. "You can sell them to every one of those dealers," Cohn told him. "Sell 80, sell 77, sell 76, sell 75. Sell them all the way down to 60. And I'll sell them to you at my mark, at 55, because I was trying to get out. So if you can do that, you can make yourself $5 billion right now." Cohn had been trying to sell the securities at 55 for a period of time and people would just hang up on him. A few days later, Fanlo called Cohn back. "He came back and said, 'I think your mark might be right,'" Cohn said. "And that mark went down to 30."

Cohn said the market changed dramatically through the course of the year. "We respect the markets," he said, "and we marked our books where we thought we could transact because some of this stuff wasn't transacting. Or where we actually had transacted. We were not misleading ourselves or our investors. We got blamed for this, by the way. We were not misleading people that bought securities with us at 98 on the first of the month, and we didn't feel like, 'Oh, my God, we sold these to investors at 98.' How can we mark them any lower than 93? We sold stuff at 98 and marked it at 55 a month later. People didn't like that. Our clients didn't like that. They were pissed."

The question was when Goldman changed its marks on these securities. Was it in early May, looking back to April, as the Bear executive suggested? Or did the dramatic shift in the marks come on July 3, when Cohn had his conversation with Fanlo at KKR Financial? Cohn explained that Goldman had a record of every mark on every security, but that Goldman had no record of their marks changing as early as May. The moment the bid-asked spread on these securities widened to the point where there needed to be such a fulsome debate about their value was the beginning of the end. "My view of common sense is if it takes you two or three weeks to get a price, you don't have a clue what the price is," one senior Bear executive said. "Perhaps their view was that 'It took two to three weeks and we've gotten it exactly right, we know exactly what the price is.' But I think that it was that level of common sense that a shoeshine boy wouldn't have been fooled by to say, 'Yeah, if you take two weeks of computing to tell me what this thing is worth, it could be worth anything, or nothing.'"

DESPITE THE APRIL disaster, which was readily apparent to Cioffi by the second week of May, he and Michael Levitt, the founder of Stone Tower, decided to push ahead with the filing of a registration statement with the SEC for an initial public offering of stock for what had been Rampart and was now known as Everquest Financial. Given the ongoing decline in the mortgage market, the decision to move ahead with the filing of the IPO documents for Everquest—which was really nothing more than a landfill for increasingly toxic mortgage securities—was an act of colossal chutzpah. On Saturday, April 21, Cioffi wrote Levitt to update him on the S-1 filing (the IPO document) and to see if Levitt wanted to play golf the next day. "Rich Marin is only waiting for an email from D&T"—Deloitte & Touche, the auditors—"stating that the 12/31/06 Everquest financials do not have to be restated to reflect the hedges [that were transferred from Cioffi's hedge funds to Everquest]," he wrote. "D&T has unequivocally stated that the financials do not have to be restated. (That's very good news.) Once we get that email, BSAM will give the go ahead to file."

On May 8, at 1:58 A.M., Tannin sent Cioffi a spreadsheet of the positions that Everquest would take over from the funds, which required a true-up payment that "is much higher than we thought," he said. "I was surprised by this initially." He concluded with the thought, "I'm frustrated and tired." The next day, May 9, Everquest filed its registration statement. Since it was a preliminary filing, no information about value was included. But there were twenty-one pages of warnings—known as "risk factors"—about the deal, including the fact that Everquest bought most of its CDOs from Cioffi's hedge funds based on valuations established, in part, by Bear Stearns that were "not negotiated at arm's length." The filing also noted that Citigroup had provided the company with a $200 million line of credit to buy the securities and that Cioffi's hedge funds received 16 million shares of Everquest and $149 million in cash in exchange for selling its CDOs to Everquest. Although Bear Stearns was the lead underwriter on the transaction and the company was nothing more than a way station for Cioffi's most illiquid mortgage-backed securities, it was surprising that Paul Friedman, one of the most senior executives in Bear Stearns's fixed-income business, had no idea about the S-1 filing until it occurred that day. "I never heard of it until it became public," he said. "Can't say if Warren knew or if the trading desk knew, but I'm pretty sure none of us in control roles away from BSAM knew about it. I can't speak for the others or for the firm, but personally I thought the notion of packaging the most opaque and complicated securities into a complicated structure and then selling it via an IPO to the widows and orphans of the world was one of the most bizarre ideas I'd ever heard." Others agreed with Friedman. "The deal appears to be an unprecedented attempt by a Wall Street house to dump its mortgage bets," Matthew Goldstein wrote in *BusinessWeek* two days after the IPO was filed. "But Everquest's portfolio could be a time bomb. A 'substantial majority' of the CDOs are backed by mortgages to home buyers with risky credit histories. . . . Trouble is, the subprime market has imploded this year, with scores of home lenders going out of business and home foreclosures on the rise."

The unsurprising result of the poor performance of Cioffi's hedge funds in April was that the number of investors wanting out expanded considerably in May. "As soon as that comes out, obviously we're starting to get into the papers," one Bear Stearns executive explained. "I think that there was something like eleven days in a row where we were in the top column of the *Wall Street Journal*. It was just amazing by any standards. Either it was a slow news period or the beginning of a massive tsunami, or both. We started getting press around that issue because you can't send something out to all these investors that says, 'Whoops, NAV's down 19' and not expect it to hit the papers right away, and it did. Immediately we start getting a lot of redemption noise and we're girding our loins for that." As the redemption notices came in, Cioffi began to get a clear picture of the money that he would need to pay out on May 1, June 1, and July 1.

Even though between March 1 and May 3, thirteen investors, including two of the largest investors and Cioffi himself, had requested redemptions, Tannin told a repo lender "the funds anticipated no large redemptions." On May 13, Cioffi wrote to Tannin and McGarrigal: "I think . . . the [Enhanced Leverage Fund] has to be liquidated which seems to be somewhat certain given the redemption activity." Notwithstanding that view, Cioffi continued to push Bank of America to complete the CDO financing. To facilitate the closing of the transaction, scheduled for May 24, Bank of America agreed to buy, on May 22, $2.89 billion of assets from Cioffi's hedge funds that would then be securitized. From that moment on, Bank of America bore the risk of holding the assets if the deal did not close. Of course, the bank claimed to be completely unaware of Cioffi's and Tannin's concerns about the viability of the funds. Late in the afternoon of May 23—the day before the CDO deal was to close—Cioffi called a Bank of America employee and said that, as a courtesy, BSAM would be sending Bank of America a letter about the redemption requests in the Enhanced Leverage Fund. Cioffi made no mention of the redemption requests in the High-Grade Fund.

At 6:30 P.M. on May 23, Patrick Fleming, a BSAM managing director, e-mailed a letter—signed by Cioffi—to Bank of America about the redemptions. "As a result," Cioffi wrote, "we expect redemptions in the months of June and July [in the Enhanced Leverage Fund] of approximately $324 million, representing 49.92 percent of the total equity capital of the fund. While we have not determined how to satisfy such redemption requests, we are considering all available options," including asset sales, gating the fund (that is, halting redemptions), or an orderly wind-down of the fund. "We believe that the foregoing developments will not materially affect our ability to perform our obligations as collateral manager [for the CDO] and we further believe that the foregoing developments will not have a material adverse effect on our business, properties, financial condition or prospects."

The next day, with the Bank of America CDO deal scheduled to close, Cioffi met with his bankers at that firm and acknowledged "that he had known of the redemption requests for some time" but had not advised the bank because "there was a possibility that investors would withdraw their requests." He also repeated his belief that BSAM was "going to unwind or liquidate the Enhanced Leverage Fund" and said that the letter the previous day had "overstated the risks" that the Enhanced Leverage Fund would be liquidated. Cioffi also agreed in that meeting to sign a side letter—a condition of the imminent closing of the deal—giving Bank of America certain rights about selecting assets to be purchased. Cioffi never signed the side letter, but based on Cioffi's representation that he would sign the letter, Bank of America closed the deal. Approximately $290 million of the proceeds of the Bank of America deal were used to repay Bear Stearns for a one-month repo loan the firm had made—without telling anyone—to the Enhanced Leverage Fund to provide badly needed liquidity. "It was a very temporary thing with a very finite end date," Paul Friedman said. "The contract with B of A seemed bulletproof, so we viewed it that we had no risk as lender."

On May 30, Cioffi told an investor that he had convinced other investors who had put in June redemption requests "of note (other than about $5M) to pull their redemptions," but quite the opposite was true. According to a complaint filed against Cioffi and Tannin, they "lied about redemptions because they knew that the news of the redemptions would trigger further redemptions by investors as well as margin calls by repo providers, and that these events could cause the Funds to collapse."

On May 31, well after Tannin and Cioffi knew that the Enhanced Leverage Fund was down 19 percent, Tannin wrote Cioffi, "I put in a call to [another major investor]. The issue is do we give them the –6.5% April or the larger down April?"

Cioffi answered eight minutes later, "Ah that's correct[.] I think that one deserves a phone call."

Tannin replied, "I was also thinking that it might be helpful to show where the losses have come from—i.e. How many bonds are responsible for the losses we've suffered. On the one hand, it focuses attention on how bad these bonds have become—and will cast doubt on our initial strategy where we leveraged these bonds so much—but on the other hand—it might explain the large loss—that it was the result of what amounts to a single very bad decision—after we made so many good ones. And this might bolster our argument that there is a way to make money now—and that we're going to do it."

In the third week of May, "after the NAVs started crashing and the market went very sour," according to one person involved, the BSAM and Bear Stearns teams that were focused on the problems in Cioffi's hedge funds—including, among others, Rich Marin, Cioffi, Tannin, Barry Cohen, Steve Begleiter, Mike Alix, and Bobby Steinberg, the latter two being the heads of Bear Stearns's risk management department—came up with the idea that Bear Stearns should invest $500 million into the funds because "the funds were in danger of failure and needed financial support" from the firm. Goldman Sachs had done something similar with one of its errant hedge funds, and this was the template the Bear group hoped Spector would follow. Also in May, UBS, the giant Swiss bank, announced it was shutting a Dillon Read Capital Management hedge fund with a large exposure to the subprime mortgage market after the fund had lost $123 million. But having Bear Stearns inject $500 million into the funds "was rejected flat out," this person said of the meeting with Spector. "He sent us back to the showers to fix the problem ourselves. It never went to the executive committee, to my knowledge, though I imagine Warren did advise them that there was a problem brewing."

The hedge funds were spinning out of control. "When we got all these redemptions in," a Bear executive remembered, "we started to say to ourselves, 'We can meet those redemptions with the cash we have.' But if we meet those redemptions, it's a little bit like letting money out the front door when all the repo counterparties are going to say, 'Wait a minute.' It's very easy to see at this point that you could have a rout and a panic. You want to do everything you can to reassure the repo counterparties. Suddenly, what's in the best interest of investors is to make sure that the repo counterparties don't put you in the tank. The nature of the repo market is such that it's so ungoverned and unregulated that basically it's like a demand loan where they can basically do whatever the freak they want. Even if you have what's called an evergreen line, that doesn't allow them to change the haircuts, so what? They mark everything down and they say margin call. Guess what? They always have that right. Always. That is the beauty, or the weakness, depending on how you want to look at it, of the repo market. It's all about confidence."

On Saturday morning, May 26, Tannin wrote Cioffi and McGarrigal an e-mail reflective of the desperate position the three hedge fund managers found themselves in. Tannin was thinking about the "building of the plan" to potentially solve the crisis. They had been batting around the idea of having Cerberus—the large, secretive private equity and hedge fund that had bought Chrysler—either take a stake in the hedge funds or buy them entirely. "Two years ago Ralph went to see Bill Gross"—the billionaire investor and then CEO of PIMCO, the huge bond fund—"and came back with the following 'Gross' observation: when involved with a trade, look around the room and determine who the chump is and if the chump is not clear to you, assume it is YOU. Well, as I sit here thinking about the Cerberus plan that we will present to Cerberus, Warren, Rich Marin and you guys, it is easy for me to see that I am the chump. Consequently I must assume that anything I could possibly think or understand is understood better and faster by the rest of the group."

The idea of selling the funds to Cerberus never got much traction. "Warren got pretty mad at Ralph for chasing Hail Mary plays and wanted him to stop and just work the asset sale and deleveraging efforts more," explained one Bear Stearns senior managing director. "What Warren wasn't realistic about was that Ralph was doing all that the market would allow, so he started chasing franchise-salvaging opportunities even though they were long shots. Ralph was trying to salvage the business, not necessarily instead of the asset value, but in addition to it. He had a strong vested interest in doing so."

The choices for the hedge funds were becoming extremely limited. The only choice that seemed logical was not to permit the redemptions to take place, essentially sealing the funds in amber so that, in time, value could be realized and investors made whole. "Suddenly we're faced with do you meet these redemptions coming up," said a Bear executive. "If we get margin calls, how are we going to meet the rest of the cash needs? We started looking at liquidity issues. What can we sell? Where can we raise cash? What can we do? We thought that suspending redemptions was actually going to make the repo counterparties more comfortable. Because you figure, all right, you're stopping the front-door leakage for the benefit of creditors."

On June 7, Cioffi announced that redemptions from the Enhanced Leverage Fund would no longer be permitted, regardless of whether a redemption notice had already been submitted. Two days later, Cioffi reportedly said, "If I can't [turn the funds around], I've effectively washed a thirty-year career down the drain." On June 26, investors in the High-Grade Fund were told the same thing. The doors of the funds had been barred. And all hell broke loose.

❧

EVER SINCE RICH Marin and the other executives at BSAM made the decision to put a moratorium on trading between Cioffi and Bear Stearns, some of the people running Bear's fixed-income business worried about what Cioffi was doing but had no authority to do anything more than worry. "All the grown-ups who were looking at him were pushed aside," said Paul Friedman. "The guys who were managing him didn't know what the hell a hedge fund was, certainly didn't know what a mortgage was, and so it was inevitable that he would get to the point where his strategy—which was also a microcosm—of more and more leverage on more and more complicated stuff blew up. He kept saying to us, 'Don't worry. I have all my funding locked up on a ten-year term, non-recourse basis. I can never get a margin call. They can never pull it from me. It doesn't matter.' We were thinking to ourselves, 'Wow, that's a beautiful thing.' In fact, he had about $10 billion like that. But he had another $14 billion that was funded month-to-month." Cioffi had supposedly figured out a way to get some long-term funding for his hedge funds by creating an "entity" that borrowed short-term in the commercial paper market and then used the proceeds to buy his long-term mortgage securities. This scheme was called "Klio Funding." "Every time you asked him, Ralph would say, 'Yeah, I just did another Klio deal. I locked up another $2 billion with Dresdner Bank for ten years, another $4 billion with Citibank for five years. Isn't it great?' We'd go, 'Wow, wish we had that.' We were jealous."

On June 5, Spector walked into Friedman's office next door and dropped a bombshell. "'I need you to go over to BSAM,'" Spector told him. "'I think Ralph's got a liquidity problem. Could you see if you could help?' Talk about your great understatement of all time." By this time, BSAM had moved out of 383 Madison Avenue into a separate office down 46th Street, at 237 Park Avenue. Friedman said he knew that Cioffi had suspended redemptions in one of the funds, but little else. "I go over to see Ralph with the BSAM guys, and not surprisingly, the announcement that he was suspending redemptions had caused his fourteen lenders to raise their margin requirements, mark down the collateral, and start to squeeze," Friedman said. "And so I sat with Ralph and I said, 'Take me through it. You must be okay. You've got all your funding locked up, non-recourse, no margin calls for term, right?' He goes, 'Yeah, most of it,' and so we go through the balance sheet, and he's got about $14 billion of mostly high-quality stuff, but not entirely, and his average funding is about a month, and I said to him, 'How long would it take you to sell that?' He goes, 'Well, I could probably sell a third in six months.' I said, 'What are you gonna do if you get a margin call?' He goes, 'Well, I've got some more of the same stuff fully paid for in the box.' I said, 'How much?' He goes, 'A few hundred million.' I went, 'You're dead. There's no way this is going to happen.' We went round and round for a couple of days."

They decided to call Tim Coleman, the partner at Blackstone in charge of the firm's restructuring group. Coleman was a friend of Marin's and a leader in the niche business of advising companies in financial distress both before and during a bankruptcy. "We went through it with Coleman," Friedman said, "but it was pretty much hopeless." They decided to call a meeting of the fund's creditors—chiefly the repo lenders at other Wall Street firms—and make a proposal to them that they hoped would stem the tide of margin calls and allow for a more orderly liquidation of the funds. The creditors' meeting, where Marin and Cioffi would present their proposal, was scheduled for June 14.

On June 6, a day before Cioffi sent out a letter to investors suspending redemptions in the fund, *Hedge Fund Alert* broke the story that the Bear hedge funds intended to block withdrawals. "Limited partners were seeking to yank about $300 million from the vehicle at the end of June—the next available redemption date," the publication reported. "But Bear has notified investors that it is suspending withdrawals. By halting redemptions rather than limiting them, Bear is seeking to prevent a run" on the Enhanced Leverage Fund. Incredibly, just before *Hedge Fund Alert*'s accurate story came out, Joanmarie Pusateri called the repo department at Bank of America to notify them that the article would soon appear "but that the article was untrue" and "redemptions were not being suspended." Pusateri made a similar call to Barclays.

That same day, BSAM issued a "Talking Points" document for use with investors when talking about what happened in the two hedge funds. The change in April NAVs was the "result of relatively large mark downs on a relatively small number of assets and our hedges have not moved up as much as our assets have moved down. . . . The difference between the initial and revised estimates is due to dealers marking the book much lower than previously." The memo said the Enhanced Leverage Fund had $240 million in redemptions for June 30. "We could meet these redemptions by selling the most liquid securities which would leave the fund with the least liquid and poorest performing assets," it said. "This would be unfair to remaining investors and we will not do it." As a result, redemptions would be suspended in the Enhanced Leverage Fund, effective June 30. The memo stated that the High-Grade Fund had $107 million of redemptions that it planned to meet "in an orderly way." The memo also noted the *Hedge Fund Alert* article: "This is unfortunate but we can assume that more articles will be written about this topic." A conference call for investors reiterated many of these same points and noted that "dealers had mis-marked their positions" in April.

The June 7 letter to investors not only announced April's 18.97 percent decline in the Enhanced Leverage Fund—just three weeks after a May 15 letter said the loss was 6.5 percent—but also announced the news that redemptions, of some $250 million on a $642 million fund, would be suspended because the "investment manager believes the company will not have sufficient liquid assets to pay investors." On a conference call with investors the next day to discuss the fund's poor performance, Cioffi and Tannin refused to answer investors' questions. "They didn't want to say anything," one investor said. Inevitably, the increasingly angry investors in the fund put the word out about what was happening. Apparently, Cioffi was also spinning tales about the Enhanced Leverage Fund's performance in May. He told Bank of America on June 7 the fund was up "approximately 1.7 percent in May" and the next day told Barclays the fund was up "2.7%" in May. (The fund was actually *down* 38 percent in May.) Between about June 8 and June 12, representatives from Barclays spoke at least twice with Tannin, where he described the recent April performance as stemming from a "pricing anomaly" in CDO-squared securities in which the Enhanced Leverage Fund had invested. "There has not been any material deterioration in the underlying credit quality," he told the bankers. "The market is stabilizing."

❊

ON JUNE 12, buried deep in the paper, the *Wall Street Journal* reported that the Enhanced Leverage Fund had fallen 23 percent in the first four months of the year and that redemptions from the fund had been blocked. "While the fund is down significantly, it is hard to tell what the actual losses will be because a few good trades could bring it back into the clear," the *Journal* wrote. "Still, given the fund's heavy exposure to this deteriorating corner of the mortgage market, in which many people are struggling to pay down their home loans, the news isn't good." The paper suggested that while the fund's losses would be a "blow" to Cioffi and Tannin, the "paper losses will have a limited impact on Bear" because the firm only had $45 million invested in the fund—the $20 million original investment and the $25 million Spector authorized for May 1. *BusinessWeek*'s Matthew Goldstein also reported on the fund's problems on June 12. "At the end of the day, I'd like someone to be honest with me about what's going on," Goldstein quoted an investor as saying.

Also on June 12, Bear Stearns's traders offered for sale a block of 150 high-quality mortgage-backed securities, with a face value of around $3.86 billion, from Cioffi's hedge funds as a way to raise cash for margin calls and for some agreed-upon redemptions. Goldstein, at *BusinessWeek,* reported that the auction for the securities was scheduled for June 14 at 10 A.M., just as the firm announced that its earnings for the second quarter of 2007 had fallen to $486 million (excluding a one-time charge) from $539 million in the same quarter a year earlier, "in part because of the implosion in the market for subprime mortgages." The results showed definitively that the firm's fixed-income engine had slowed considerably, with revenue of $962 million, down 21 percent from the same period a year earlier. On the conference call about the second-quarter earnings, Sam Molinaro said that the problem in the hedge funds was "an issue that's getting a great deal of attention here. We're focused on trying to maximize the value of our clients' assets, and we're taking every action we can to ensure that we get a successful outcome."

That same day, around noon, Tannin had a forty-five-minute conference call with Doug Sharon, the head of Bear's Boston office, whose clients had tens of millions of dollars invested in Cioffi's hedge funds. Sharon himself had a meaningful investment in the funds, around $500,000. One of Sharon's clients had put in a redemption request some months before as a result of some tax-related matters. But after forty-five minutes of talking with Tannin, the client found Tannin's explanation for what had happened and the prospects for the future so reassuring that at the end of the call, the client said, "Based on everything I have heard here, I think what we're going to do is rescind our request to redeem. I should leave my money in this fund." After that call with Tannin and his client, Sharon had a one o'clock meeting with Spector in his office. Sharon did not know Spector all that well and had had only around six face-to-face meetings with him during his twenty-year career at the firm. "Most people think he's a little bit standoffish or that he thinks he's better than everyone else," Sharon explained. "But he's always been perfectly gracious to me, except for one situation where I had a regulatory dispute, and I just didn't like the way he handled it."

He waited outside Spector's office for his meeting. "At this point, I had no idea these funds were going to collapse and go to zero within weeks," he said. "I'm waiting to go in to see Warren, I'm outside of his office, and I hear this, 'Slam!' and then I hear, 'God damn it!' I thought, 'Wow. This is probably not a good time.' Then I see some guy who I don't recognize go scurrying out of his office. I walk over to his two assistants and I say, 'Look, this isn't a good day. This can wait. I definitely don't have to talk to him today. This is definitely not a 'gotta happen today' type of thing. She says, 'No, no, no—it's all right. We're just not having a good day today.' I sat back down, and a couple minutes later she said, 'You can go in and see him now.' I went in to see him, and he had his game face on, because I don't know what rattled him, but it certainly didn't show."

Sharon explained to Spector the magnitude of his clients. One had $4 million in the hedge fund, another $5 million in the firm's merchant banking fund, and $200 million in municipal bonds; another two of his clients were among the top fifty private corporations in America. It was important for Spector to hear this from Sharon, he thought, because BSAM reported to Spector. "The reason I'm telling you this is that these are people who if these funds are in potentially the kind of dire straits that some people are suggesting, these aren't guys that are just gonna go away and say, 'Aw, shucks!'" Sharon told him. "'These are guys that do not need to use contingency lawyers. They have armies of lawyers themselves, and they're going to be pissed because I don't know what went wrong, but if these things are going to collapse, as some people have suggested, we're going to get our asses sued off.' His response to me was, 'Look, they're big boys. It's a leveraged fund. And leverage works both ways.' I said to him, 'I understand that, but this thing was sold and marketed as a very low-volatility, low-risk strategy, and that's the way people were using it. There are public corporations that have a small amount of their corporate cash in this stuff. The portfolio manager was completely aware of it because he made the presentations to them.' He said, 'Listen, what can I tell you? What was it that Ace once said? 'Hey, you can't fly like the eagles and poop like a canary.'"

Sharon was stunned that Spector would be so dismissive of the problem. "I heard that from Warren," he said, "and I basically said to myself, 'You know something? These are people who are good friends of the firm. Sometimes we've made a lot of money for them, and sometimes we haven't. But it doesn't mean we didn't have our best intentions.' It was clear to me that he didn't get it and was taking the cavalier attitude of 'Shit happens. They're big boys, hey, it's a leverage fund, and leverage works both ways,' and then he gave me that Ace Greenberg quote. I walked out of there more frustrated than ever."

※

WHILE PAUL FRIEDMAN and executives at BSAM were working overtime to stave off the meltdown of the hedge funds, the not too surprising revelation was that gating the Enhanced Leverage Fund was not giving comfort to the repo lenders. Instead of reassuring them that the assets of the fund wouldn't be paid out to investors and would be reserved for them, the decision woke them up from whatever slumber some of them were in with regard to the fund's problems. "Suspending redemptions was like a red flag in front of a bull," said one of the BSAM professionals. All the repo lenders— "This is the entire Street, for all intents and purposes. Big and small, domestic and foreign, they're all in this game," explained one executive—began clamoring for more collateral for their short-term loans to Cioffi's funds. Seemingly overnight, the lenders wanted their money. "We would hear from them, 'We're revaluing these assets. We're going to need margin of $60 million,'" he explained. "It was a little bit like, 'I don't know how much money you have in your pocket, so that'll be five bucks today. Tomorrow it'll be ten bucks.' Okay? All of a sudden, they'll start asking, 'How much cash do you have on hand? Are you getting other margin calls?' Then all of a sudden it's 'Give me my $300. I don't care. I'll take $200. Give me the money.'" That day, a worried Barclays banker sent Cioffi an e-mail: "One of the repo counterparties dealing with your fund is apparently about to pull its line; I am sure this is just one of the rumours that spread at a time like this, but would like to confirm that this is just it, in order to avoid any sense of unease spreading."

On June 13, BSAM issued a memo about how to answer for investors the question of "I thought I was invested in a high-grade fund but it sounds now like the funds may have invested in a fair amount of assets in subprime mortgages." Here, for perhaps the first time in black and white, was the admission—varnished repeatedly with gibberish—that all had not been what it seemed in the funds. "As of May 31, 2007, over 90% of the [Enhanced Leverage Fund's] assets are invested in securities rated AAA and AA. Much of the underlying collateral supporting these AAA and AA securities consists of subprime mortgages. Hence, although over 90% of the securities in the fund are AAA and AA rated, [b]ecause these securities are backed in part by subprime collateral, the press has referred to this portfolio as a subprime fund. Based upon our managements' analysis, the percentage of underlying collateral in our investment grade structures collateralized by 'subprime' mortgages is approximately 60%," or *ten times* more collateral in subprime mortgages than had previously been disclosed to investors.

With Blackstone's help, BSAM decided to call a June 14 meeting of the repo lenders to Cioffi's hedge funds. The basic gist of Bear's strategy was to ask the creditors for forbearance—first for a year and then reduced to three months—for the market to settle down so that an orderly liquidation in a less pressured environment could commence. Blackstone's theory of the situation was that the very same banks that were repo lenders to the funds were up to their eyeballs in the very same illiquid mortgage securities that Cioffi had. Therefore, no one would have any incentive to force a sale of the securities into a frozen market and thus establish a new, lower mark that everyone would have to adopt. "It was the classic Mexican standoff, where nobody wins if everybody's dead on the floor at the end of this thing," explained one person involved with the strategy. "Our point was, 'All you guys have this problem. It doesn't help any of you to flood the market with this paper. If you pull back all your assets [from the funds] and you literally just seize assets and start to dump them in the market, that can't possibly be good for you.' But it was like any other panic. If you're out early enough, maybe it *is* good for you. Think of the burning movie theater. If you're the first guy out the door, great strategy. But if you're standing in the front of the theater and you jump up and yell 'Fire!' and you can't get out the door: Very bad strategy. That's kind of a reasonable analogy for this because everybody had this problem. And it wasn't the problem of our assets that they repoed. That was the absolute thin slice of the tip of the iceberg."

The repo counterparties' meeting took place in the second-floor auditorium at 383 Madison Avenue. About sixty people attended, representing around a dozen or so lenders. Even though Bear Stearns was the prime broker for Cioffi's hedge funds plus a derivative counterparty, the decision was made that no one from Bear Stearns's securities subsidiary should attend the meeting. Paul Friedman couldn't resist watching the show, though, and he sat in the audio-video control room in the back of the room and watched the proceedings on a TV monitor.

Greg Quental, Cioffi's titular boss at BSAM—"Ralph didn't believe he reported to him," Friedman explained—started the meeting by explaining to the bankers the funds' poor perfomance for the first four months of the year and how that performance had led to an avalanche of redemption requests totaling about half of the funds' $650 million of investments. "It was clearly a function of performance," Quental said. "At that point, we actually had enough cash to meet the June redemptions, but what would have happened is . . . we would have sold off a lot of the more liquid assets," and what remained was a fund "that looked a lot different than the one they bought into. So we made the decision at that point to suspend redemptions. We also knew that all of you would feel more comfortable if cash weren't leaving the fund to pay off those redemptions, so that was also a big factor in our decision." At this point, Friedman said sarcastically, "We did it for you," and then added seriously: "We did it because we had no choice, basically, but it's a good line."

Quental then spoke about the margin calls coming from the people sitting in the audience. "Obviously, we've taken in a heavy level of margin calls," he said. "All of you are aware of that. We've covered all those calls up until yesterday, when we asked all of you to hold off until we had this meeting. We have some pending margin calls, which Ralph will talk about in a minute. We've made every attempt to meet the margin calls that have come in over the last few weeks, but they have been quite significant. We're also experiencing high margin calls in [the] High-Grade [Fund] as well. Lastly, the portfolio team is working hard at selling assets and focusing on the things that could move relatively quickly. Then we've got some longer-term assets that we're working on moving, and Ralph's going to talk about those plans. So with that, I'll turn it over to him."

Cioffi gave the group an update on the auction of the assets the funds were at that moment trying to sell through Bear Stearns to raise the much-needed cash. "We are seeing an unprecedented level of bids as it relates to the number of bids," he said, "and the prices we're getting—I couldn't be more happy. We've gotten a lot of moral support and encouragement from the Street that people were going to be aggressive, that people were going to pay strong prices for the collateral." On page seven of the accompanying presentation, Cioffi told them what they presumably already knew: He had $14 million in cash on hand to meet $145 million of "open margin calls" in the Enhanced Leverage Fund. At the end of July, after making the $145 million of margin calls, Cioffi predicted the fund would have a cash balance of $177 million.

Friedman translated Cioffi's pitch into layman's terms. "He froze redemptions," he said, "and he's got his lenders here to try and tell them—they all have the right, if he has unmet margin calls, to blow him out—so he's telling them: 'Sit tight. I'm going to do all these sales and I'm going to have enough cash.' What you have is a roomful of people, some of who are awake and have made these margin calls, and have suddenly realized there are issues, and have marked the collateral down and made margin calls. Some of them are going, 'Holy shit! Everybody else is making margin calls and we're not.' Well, the first thing all this did, when we got done, the margin calls just flooded in." Cioffi asked them all not to make any more margin calls. But that tactic backfired completely. "This is the beginning of the end. Had he not been the first fund to go, it would have had a much lower impact as well. But since it was at a time when everybody was a little squishy and there really hadn't been any significant hedge fund issues, this came out of nowhere. It was like the pebble being tossed into the pond. It was pulling on the thread. It was any analogy you want to use. This was the beginning."

In the first meeting, Cioffi made what amounted to a modest proposal. "We're looking for thirty days of breathing room so that we can implement the plan," he said. "At the end of the day, we're almost working for all of you. I mean, our job is to in an orderly and efficient manner raise liquidity and reduce positions down either through direct sales, whether it's competitive bids or otherwise. It's a thirty-day process that we think we can unfold in a workmanlike fashion. No one's interests are served if we get into a meltdown and you have ten or twelve dealers trying to sell collateral in a market that right now is very fragile."

More than an hour into the presentation, one repo lender, John Hogan, head of risk management at JPMorgan, asked about whether Bear Stearns intended to play a role in trying to solve the problems in the hedge funds by infusing capital. Hogan said he thought BSAM was "underestimating the severity of the situation," that the funds "needed to figure out how to meet margin calls," and if that meant getting money from Bear Stearns, "we recommend you do that." As the CEO of BSAM, Marin answered this question. "First of all, those of you who have asset management units, the asset management units are walled off pretty securely from the broker-dealer side of the firm," he said. "BSAM is walled off. In fact, we're in a separate building. We don't even live in this building. So we are very separate. There are a number of issues that even prevent us, from a regulatory standpoint, in dealing with Bear Stearns as a counterparty. We've had a moratorium of trading against principal positions for over a year now, and haven't done so. We've recently lifted that ban so that we could have the trading desk, which is very skilled in these particular instruments, help us in the liquidation process. We consider that to be the greater good. But they are not a major repo counterparty to us. They have not been a major repo counterparty to us. They have not been a big trading partner with us until now, as they're helping us with this process. I don't think we should look at Bear Stearns as a lender of last resort here. This is a fund that's run and owned by BSAM, and BSAM will manage its way through this process."

That answer recalled for some participants in the meeting the jarring memory of Bear's unwillingness to participate in the rescue—

nine years earlier—of the LTCM hedge fund. Steve Black, the co-head of investment banking at JPMorgan, was apparently so peeved by Marin's response that he placed calls after the meeting to both Spector and Schwartz, his Duke fraternity brother. "Is Bear going to stand behind your asset management company?" Black asked Schwartz. When Schwartz called Black back an hour later, the *Journal* reported, he said "that on the advice of Bear's lawyers the firm wasn't going to get involved." Incredibly, as the meeting with the repo lenders was happening, a BSAM executive sent an e-mail to Barclays, with a copy to Tannin, with a spreadsheet attached that "showed gains through June 12 of almost 6%" in the Enhanced Leverage Fund and "a total NAV of more than $950,000,000."

On June 16, the *Journal* reported that Merrill Lynch had ignored Cioffi's request at the June 14 meeting for a thirty-day standstill and had seized $400 million of its collateral from the funds with the intention of auctioning the assets in the market at noon on Monday. According to the June 14 presentation, Merrill had $1.46 billion in repo loans to the two funds, making the $400 million of collateral the firm seized equal to around 25 percent of its overall exposure to the funds. (Citigroup, with $1.862 billion in repo loans, and Dresdner Bank, with $1.487 billion, were the top two lenders to Cioffi's funds. In all, sixteen Wall Street firms had lent the funds $11.1 billion in repo financing.) Without saying why, the *Journal* said that Merrill's auction of a portion of its collateral could "trigger the [Enhanced Leverage] fund's dissolution" and "spur other lenders to seize fund assets," leading to "the end of Mr. Cioffi's two funds." The fear was rampant on Wall Street that the price Merrill would get for the assets—which were considered less liquid than the assets Cioffi had sold earlier in the week—would leave firms with little choice but to mark their similar securities to the new, lower, prices.

Over the weekend, Cioffi was in a panic. He managed to convince Merrill Lynch to hold off on the asset sale until he could present a new proposal—one that was to include a new short-term lending plan—to the creditors on June 18 at one o'clock in the afternoon. He hoped that he could convince Barclays, which already had a $400 million line of credit to the Enhanced Leverage Fund, to put up another $250 million in cash that could be used as collateral for the growing number of margin calls. "We've got to go to them," Cioffi e-mailed his team over the weekend. "There's no time to wait." He spent Sunday scrambling but managed to convince Barclays to step up with the additional money.

❈

AFTER DOUG SHARON met with Spector on June 12, he went back to Boston feeling more than just a little peeved by Spector's reaction. He started thinking, "You know something? These guys don't get it. They don't know what's going on, and I don't know if Warren is telling them, because based on the way he's handling it, I think he's just hoping it will go away." Since he was an investor, he pulled together every monthly report that Cioffi had sent out and decided that he needed to go back to New York, meet with Cayne, and make sure the CEO of Bear Stearns understood just how serious the situation was becoming. Sharon and Cayne had known each other for twenty years by this time, ever since Cayne hired Sharon.

On the morning of Monday, June 18, Sharon called Cayne and told him he was at the airport and on his way to see him "about the hedge funds." Cayne, who prided himself on always being accessible to Bear's people, agreed to see Sharon at three-thirty on Monday afternoon but wanted him first to meet with Michael Solender, the firm's general counsel. Sharon agreed to see Solender at one o'clock.

When Sharon arrived for his meeting with Solender, he found Dan Taub, the firm's head of litigation, in Solender's office. "I am here as a partner at Bear Stearns to tell you about why I'm concerned," Sharon told the two men. "I am here because I think we have a very big problem, and if we don't address it head-on, it's going to spin out of control. Here's where I think we have a problem. It's not just because we have a lot of loyal, great customers that are very influential that are at risk of losing a lot of money in something they thought was a very low-risk, low-volatility investment. And by the way, guys, I am an investor in this fund also." He took the sheaf of monthly statements that he had assembled and showed the two Bear Stearns lawyers month after month of Cioffi's commentaries about his high level of concern about the riskiness of various mortgage securities in the market and how he was avoiding those securities as a result. "You've got to understand something," Sharon told Solender and Taub. "This guy has been predicting in print month after month Armageddon, telling you he's avoiding the 2006 vintage, and on and on and on and on, and as it turns out, this guy jumped into a volcano."

Sharon showed the lawyers the "collateral summary" on the back of each monthly statement that listed the breakdown of the securities in which the fund invested. "It would say," Sharon recalled, "22 percent high-yield, 12 percent high-grade—and this is the smoking gun—the March 2006 collateral summary shows 6 percent subprime mortgage exposure." Sharon even remembered one of his clients who agreed to invest $250,000 into the hedge funds in April 2007 based upon the fact that the March 2007 summary showed that only 6 percent of the funds were invested in subprime mortgages. The truth was very different. In June, as the funds were rapidly dissipating, Bear Stearns issued a document called "Talking Points" for how brokers should talk to their clients who had invested in the funds. The document posed typical questions and then answered them. One of the questions deemed likely to be asked was: "I thought the fund was diversified, and now it turns out it seems to have had a fair amount of exposure to the subprime mortgage market. What exactly was the exposure?" The answer: "60 percent." "What became clear is that this fund was 60 percent exposed to the subprime mortgage market," Sharon said.

As best he could explain it to Solender and Taub, Sharon said he informed them that Cioffi had loaded up the fund—which had been marketed as a safe, low-risk fund—with a host of risky securities. On Cioffi's monthly summaries, Sharon told the lawyers, "the asset-backed securities bucket was up to 80 percent. Now, when I grew up in the bond market, asset-backed securities were credit cards and auto loans. Turns out the asset-backed securities bucket was filled up with subprime-backed CDOs, and they were not under the subprime label because that wasn't known at the time when I was having the meeting with the lawyers. But I'm explaining to them this whole manager commentary [about] Armageddon, and they said, 'Well, but these things all say "internal use only" on them.' I said, 'The reason they say "internal use only" on them is because I had them printed off on my computer this morning. This is exactly what the clients get in the mail month after month. This is what we've been telling the clients.' Solender didn't say a whole lot. But I think Dan Taub understood the gravity of the situation."

❦

AT THE SAME time that Sharon was meeting with Solender and Taub, Cioffi, Marin, and representatives from Blackstone were meeting again with the funds' repo lenders at the 383 Madison auditorium to present a new plan designed, Cioffi hoped, to keep the lenders from doing what Merrill Lynch was threatening to do—seizing collateral and selling it into the marketplace. Cioffi's new proposal called for Bear Stearns to provide a $1.5 billion repo line of credit for both funds that would be used to reduce the exposure of the funds' existing repo lenders by about 15 percent on a pro rata basis. Also, there would be a "fresh infusion" of $500 million of unsecured capital, subordinated to the repo lenders and split between the two funds. The new capital, $200 million of which was to be provided by Barclays and the balance of $300 million by an unspecified "consortium" reportedly led by Citigroup, would be used to provide the margin requirements of the existing lenders and for working capital purposes. The third component of the plan was to "sell [fund] assets in an orderly fashion and reduce credit exposure" during the coming year. But then there was Cioffi's "standstill" request to the repo lenders: For one year, the lenders would agree not to request any incremental margin calls or an increase in interest rates for the loans. The lenders would also agree not to sell any of their collateral in the market for one year. Cioffi also wanted the lenders to agree to an interim standstill through June 20 that included all of the previous requests plus a demand that all lenders agree to "pull existing bid lists" from the market and terminate any sales in progress—a demand no doubt directed at Merrill Lynch—with the hope that the lenders would sign the interim standstill virtually immediately. From June 18 to July 2, the proposal would be reduced to legal documents and negotiated, with an expected signing before July 9. "It was insane," Paul Friedman said. "It was basically 'We're going to do some sales. We can't tell you what. We're going to terminate some deals that would bring us some cash, and basically we need you to sit still for a year.'" According to the *Wall Street Journal*, both Merrill and JP-Morgan "were taken aback" by the one-year standstill proposal but Citigroup, Barclays, and Dresdner Bank were "more amenable." Said one participant in the meeting: "People had different perceptions of what was important."

After his meeting with the Bear Stearns lawyers, Sharon went to see Cayne for his scheduled appointment. He wanted to show Cayne the monthly statements from the hedge funds. "Have you ever seen these things?" Sharon asked Cayne. "He said, 'No. What are they?' I said, 'These are the monthly statements. You should look at these things.' He said, 'I don't want to see this stuff.' I said, 'You should let me read you some of the things that Ralph has been telling people.' I started reading: 'We expect delinquencies to rise. We expect housing values to decline,' the whole thing. I explained to him the types of clients that I had that are in this thing, that these guys have armies of lawyers that are on retainer for their businesses, and that we have to do something about this. I was there with him for about forty-five minutes going over this stuff. He said, 'You know, they're all down in the auditorium right now.' I said, 'Who's in the auditorium?' He said, 'All the creditors, and we were making an offer to them right now. But I wouldn't take it if I was them.' I said, 'What's the offer?' He said, 'No margin calls for a year, and I think the firm was offering to put $1 billion up somehow.'"

While Sharon was talking to Cayne, Steve Begleiter walked into the office. Sharon asked him if he had seen Cioffi's monthly reports and then, with a yellow marker, Sharon highlighted for Begleiter the misleading collateral summary, specifically about how the funds had invested only 6 percent of their assets in subprime and how Cioffi had said he saw "this meltdown coming." They then discussed how Cioffi's summaries made it clear that he had supposedly put much of the funds' money into asset-backed securities—credit cards and auto loans—that would be considered much safer than the CDOs where Cioffi had actually invested the funds. "I had always been under the impression that when I saw the collateral summary, 'Wow! Ralph is hiding in the gold,'" Sharon told Cayne and Begleiter. After Sharon finished sharing the documents with them,

Cayne said to him, "Look, if there's fraud, we're gonna pay." Cayne also wondered why "we pay lawyers all kinds of money to write these prospectuses and explain the risks to people," and then repeated, "But if there is fraud, we're gonna pay." Then, according to Sharon, Cayne turned around and yelled to his longtime assistant, Suzette Fasano, to get Rich Marin on the phone. "You better be prepared to say something at the [senior managing directors'] meeting tonight about the status of the hedge funds," Cayne told Marin.

CHAPTER 28

A VERY STUPID DECISION

In the end, Cioffi's June 18 proposal flopped. Many of the repo lenders ignored Cioffi's plea for more time and an orderly liquidation and ran for the exits as the fire raged. Merrill Lynch reversed itself again and on June 19 decided to seize and then sell into the market $850 million of its collateral from the hedge funds, more than double its initial plan. But when buyers were few and pushed for a low price, Merrill ended up keeping most of what it had seized rather than sell it for a low price and taking the markdowns to the rest of its vast portfolio of mortgage securities. "They would have locked in a lot of losses for themselves and a large slug of their client base by jamming bonds into the market," a hedge fund manager told the *New York Post* about Merrill's decision. Merrill's decision to seize its collateral struck many on Wall Street as highly unusual. "I've never seen a dealer seize another dealer like that," an unnamed trader told *National Mortgage News*. There was also the inevitable comparison made to Long-Term Capital Management and how no one on Wall Street was there to help Bear Stearns in its hour of need. "They were all friends with Bear Stearns when they thought the spreads were huge," Anthony Sanders, a former mortgage bond research analyst at Deutsche Bank, told Bloomberg. "Now that the market has turned, Bear's standing there like the lone grizzly. They looked at these high yields, this growing market, and they forgot the basic concept of risk and return. They got caught drinking their own Kool-Aid."

Cioffi also spent Tuesday negotiating bilateral agreements with both Goldman Sachs and Bank of America. The agreements allowed these firms to be repaid $2.25 billion in an effort to "help stave off painful ripple effects in the broader market for mortgage-backed securities," the *Journal* observed. Then both Lehman Brothers, with close to $650 million in repo loans to Cioffi's funds, and Credit Suisse, with $263 million in exposure, seized their collateral, too, and sold it into the market—before Merrill Lynch—with Lehman reportedly getting 50¢ on the dollar. JPMorgan, with $558 million in repo loans to the funds, intended to seize its collateral also but decided instead to engage in a bilateral negotiation with Cioffi along the lines of what Goldman Sachs and Bank of America did. According to the *New York Times*, JPMorgan was able to sell $400 million of its collateral back to Cioffi for cash, although the price of the sale was not disclosed. One hedge fund executive who had looked at Cioffi's hedge fund positions told the *New York Post*, "They haven't collapsed in price because they are often mismarked or just don't get traded. That is going to change in a big way today at 4 P.M., when the [Merrill] auction ends."

Even by the generally chaotic standard that passes for the norm at a Wall Street investment bank, June 2007 at Bear Stearns was a particularly frenetic month. As trouble was brewing at the hedge funds, Cayne, Molinaro, and Robert Upton, Bear's treasurer, had invited a small group of executives from Moody's, the rating agency, for lunch in the executive dining room. The idea had been to try to convince Moody's to begin thinking about upgrading Bear's credit ratings. A better credit rating lowered the cost of the firm's borrowing and was, according to Upton, "a competitive weapon for derivatives issuance, in particular, but it just would be a good thing to keep going north in the ratings." It was meant to be "a love-to-love lunch with Jimmy," Upton said, "and Sam and I had some key points that we wanted to make about the business." But because of the ongoing negotiations with the repo lenders, Molinaro kept getting pulled away from the lunch by frantic calls about the hedge funds. Upton worked hard to cover for Molinaro. In the middle of his comments about the relative strength of the firm's various businesses, the Moody's team kept returning the discussion to the hedge funds. Upton said it became embarrassing. "It was almost comical because you're a CEO of one of the most successful Wall Street firms, the hedge funds are blowing up, and he wasn't terribly engaged in that discussion on the phone—all the calls were to Molinaro, and he was running in and out of the room," Upton said. "God bless Jimmy, he talked about people and stories. But at this very critical juncture in the firm's history—[with] what ultimately became the first in a series of death blows—while we were trying to deflect concern from rating agencies and ultimately convince them that not only were we healthy and okay but that we were an improving credit, the CEO and the guy who was supposed to have basically control of understanding what was going on everywhere just completely missed the boat. He didn't talk about anything other than when he had lunch with Walter Shipley from Chemical Bank. It was rather telling about what I think was going to happen over the course of the next nine months."

※

As the first margin calls came into the hedge funds during and after the creditor meetings, there was a "bit of a game of chicken" going on, according to one participant, whereby the two sides would argue about the valuation of the collateral and just how much additional margin was needed. After a few days of this macho behavior, one repo lender to the fund approached BSAM directly about negotiating to buy back its collateral, allowing the hedge funds to get the cash they needed and the lender to get its collateral back at a price it thought it could make money at whenever it chose to sell the securities in the market. On the advice of Blackstone, BSAM informed all the lenders about the opportunity for bilateral negotiations.

"Suddenly everybody wanted to do a deal, including Merrill," one Bear executive said. "All these bilateral deals start getting negotiated. The problem is the bilateral deals are being cut at levels that are below book value, so every time we do one it nips away at the book value. There are so many moving parts—derivatives, which are very complex to value, and cash instruments that are very complex in their own right, and whole portfolios that have hundreds of millions of dollars and sometimes a billion dollars. All of that coming into the thin neck of the funnel of Ralph and Matt trying to do the valuations—you can imagine what kind of a shit show this was." Another bottleneck came when Marin would not allow Cioffi to agree to any bilateral deals until both BSAM and Bear Stearns had signed off. That brought the executive committee into the mix. "Now Marin's talking to Warren all day long and Warren's talking to Ralph all day long," said one observer of this bit of corporate theater. As the demand for one-off deals from the repo lenders escalated, Spector decided that Marin and Cioffi could no longer do the work themselves and decided to get his lead trader, Tommy Marano, involved.

Marano, an extremely experienced trader and Grateful Dead lover, moved over to help manage the unwinding of the High-Grade Fund. That left a big hole in the fixed-income department but was thought to be necessary under the circumstances. Marano was going to work with Paul Friedman, whom Spector had already asked to go over to the funds. The firm put out an announcement that Marano would be seconded to the hedge funds. The firm also asked Mike Alix, the firm's chief risk officer, to oversee BSAM. The firm furthermore announced that Marin would take "a stronger role" in running the two hedge funds, although Cioffi would still remain involved.

Then there was the problem of the intense pressure on the clerks, who worked for the funds, to be able to quickly and accurately reconcile the daily cash positions with all the transactions happening so quickly. "Under normal circumstances, they're perfectly competent to do that," said a BSAM executive. "It's like an airline pilot who suddenly is in a dogfight. It's outside their range of experience. They don't know how to deal with all of the variables that come into play. Just trying to keep up with it in a twenty-four-hour day had proven to be impossible." The pressure on everyone was mounting. "This is an unusual time, the shit is flying in every direction," said one executive. "The people are trying to fend off creditors, and when you're trying to fend off creditors and everybody's trying to get a piece of you and you're trying to do this in an orderly manner, people will call up and say, 'You didn't call me back. I called you an hour ago.' Well, he doesn't know that you've had fifty phone calls in that hour and you're trying to do a reconciliation. It was a nightmare."

With everyone focused, the funds started to agree to various bilateral deals with the repo lenders. "In a free-fall market, if people are willing to do block trades, that's your best way forward," explained one Bear executive. "We get one done, then we get a second and a third one done. It was like holding a yard sale before the sheriff comes. And we're watching the NAV of the fund collapse. But at least it's definable."

Then pressure started increasing on Bear Stearns, the parent company, to step up and take out the repo lenders to the hedge funds. To that point, the firm's only exposure was its $45 million equity investment, and the rest of Wall Street was waiting for the firm to put together a serious rescue plan. Cayne decided to convene a meeting of the twenty most senior executives at the firm—a combination of the executive committee and the management and compensation committees—to get an update of what was going on with Cioffi's hedge funds and to decide whether or not the firm should agree to become the repo lender to the funds. Before going into the meeting, Cayne asked Steve Begleiter, the firm's head of strategy, how much money Bear had invested in the funds. Cayne said he thought the amount was $20 million, although there had been numerous articles in the press since the funds started blowing up suggesting the number was double that amount. Begleiter told him the firm actually had $45 million invested. "I said, 'What?' He said, 'Forty-five.' I said, 'Forty-five? I thought it was 20. Where did the 25 come from?' He said, 'I don't know.' I said, 'You don't know where the 25 comes from?' He said, 'No.' We walk in, I said, 'Before we discuss what we're going to do, does anybody know about $25 million that was put into the funds at the last minute?' Spector said, 'I did. Sorry.' No, he didn't say 'I'm sorry.' He said, 'I fucked up.' If he had said 'I'm sorry,' it would have been different. He said, 'I fucked up.' Now there's silence. People were expecting me to say, 'What are you, fucking crazy? Unauthorized, you yourself authorized $25 million into a failing enterprise.' Well, I didn't, but I also didn't say anything for like a minute. I just let everybody hear him say, 'I fucked up.'"

After shining the bright light of blame on Spector's decision to invest the extra $25 million into the funds on his own authority, Cayne asked the group what to do about the funds. 'I said, 'Okay, so what are our options? It seems to me the first option is we just bag the funds. We suffer a reputational risk, which we aren't really going to avoid anyway. And we save ourselves the heartache of that crap coming into us.' Nobody said anything. Greenberg says, 'No, we can't do that. That'll kill the firm.' Somebody else says, 'Yeah, that's really bad for the rep.' I hadn't carried the day. By blowing up the factory, which basically [happens] when you say 'Bag the funds,' you're telling all the investors, 'Go fuck yourself. We're not Goldman, which just poured $3 billion in to rescue its funds.'"

The decision about what if anything Bear Stearns should do about the funds was a complicated one. "You've got the problem that there are two funds with very different capital structures," explained a Bear executive. "In one, you got Barclays and its facility, and the other one you don't. One is more leveraged and the other one isn't. It's kind of like you've got two children and there's a freight train coming and you can't save them both. Do you save one of them, or do you try and save both and maybe they both die? I mean, what do you do? It might cost you your life, too. That's the decision they had to make."

✳

THERE WAS QUITE a row at the executive committee about what to do. "In full disclosure," Friedman said, "mea culpa. In the executive committee meetings when there was discussion of what to do—Jimmy, God bless him, he was right once—Jimmy is screaming, 'Fuck them. Let the hedge funds go under. It's not our money. We didn't lend to them. Let the banks lose. Not our problem.' It was the right answer. I was one of the ones screaming, 'We can't let this happen. There's equity here. We've got to try to do something, both because it will help the investors, and because if we tell all the banks to fuck off, we can't exist in this community having done that to all the banks. It was bad enough when we did it in 1998. They all still hate us from 1998. We can't do it again.' Ace in the end carried the day, and Ace's great line at the last executive committee meeting was, 'We can't take these two hedge funds, throw them out on the sidewalk, and walk away,' and he convinced Warren and others that we had to do something, which is how we ended up bailing out the one, which was the least we could do, but we truly believed there was a lot of equity left in that fund."

Cayne took a purely tactical and unemotional approach to the difficult facts presented. "He didn't care about our reputation," Friedman said. "His view was Merrill, Citigroup, JPMorgan, and the others, if they were stupid enough to lend to Ralph against this stuff and we were smart enough not to, 'Why should we bail them out just because they were stupid to lend to him at ridiculously low margins? It's not our problem. It's not our money in the fund, basically. It's not us lending to them. Let JP, Morgan Stanley, B of A, let all these guys blow them out. Screw 'em. Who cares?' My view— and it turned out to be wrong—was both we needed it from a franchise value, and I still believed that if you took JPMorgan and Citi and B of A, and Deutsche and Dresdner and all the big banks, and told them to all pound salt, that they would strangle us to death. They'd pull all our loan facilities. We'd already spent a decade working our way back from everybody hating us from refusing to help with Long-Term, and were working our way through that. There had been so much bank consolidation in those ten years that everybody who was lending to Ralph was everybody we were borrowing from. It just seemed suicidal to stick it to them and go, 'Too bad.' Jimmy didn't get it. He didn't care." But he would be proved right.

The executive committee met nearly twice a day for two weeks in order to determine what decision to make regarding whether or not to become the secured repo lender to the hedge funds. The committee would get feedback from Marin and Cioffi about the creditors' meeting on the second floor and then meet together in Cayne's sixth-floor conference room to figure out what to do. There was a considerable cast of characters, from Marin and Cioffi of BSAM to the leaders of the firm's fixed-income business—Craig Overlander, Jeff Mayer, Tommy Marano, and Paul Friedman. "The group dynamics were fascinating," Friedman said. "By this time, Jimmy had allowed Warren and Alan to basically run the meetings. Jimmy would sit there and smoke his cigars, and Alan and Warren would debate what to do. Jimmy, in fact, in a lot of cases, would come and go in the middle of meetings. It wasn't surprising that Jimmy wasn't dictating where we were going to go on all of this because he generally didn't. Whether he was smart enough to be working on a handoff to Alan and Warren or whether they were in the process of grabbing it from him, I don't know."

Friedman said the five members of the executive committee were like the Politburo in addition to being "caricatures of themselves, in the sense that you almost don't need to have meetings because you know what everyone is going to say in advance. You can script it, particularly recurring things. You just know where everybody's going to come out. Alan was sort of the Socratic banker, negotiator, even-tempered, 'Let's get all the things on the table and let's really work it out.' Warren was the trading genius, who got quicker to the map, got quicker to the answer, 'Here's what we're going to do.' Jimmy was always sort of losing focus because he would come in and out. We were talking about bonds and stuff, and that was not exactly his best trick. Ace was the more grander, broader, ten-thousand-foot, philosophical, talking-about-the-seventy-five-year-old-firm sort of thing. Everybody fit into those roles." In the case of what to do about the hedge funds, the dynamic was different. "Sam was, in this particular case, absolutely opposed to it," Friedman said. "He kept using the phrase, 'Why are we trying to catch a falling knife?' That was his favorite phrase through that whole episode. 'Let it go. Let the knife fall on the ground and then we'll pick up what's left.' He and Jimmy were on the same page. There was a series of reasoned discussions. But it just came down to we ran out of time. There was just no more discussion available. We got to the last day, where everybody was threatening to blow us out, and we had to decide right now: 'What do we do?' Jimmy's and Sam's approach of 'Let's just give up' was not carrying the day. The mortgage guys felt fairly strongly that we could do something. We were going round and round, trying to figure out some compromise. Everybody was looking for a compromise." Greenberg was said to believe the firm's "reputation" was paramount and that he thought there "was a good chance we'll get the money back." Spector was "reluctantly in favor" of providing the repo financing "but very, very unhappy about having to do it," said someone in the meeting.

That was when the consensus formed—against Cayne's better judgment—that the firm should agree to become the repo lender to the High-Grade Fund and let the Enhanced Leverage Fund fail. Then the problem quickly became figuring out what the securities in the High-Grade Fund were worth, since Bear was going to lend against them. To that end, according to one participant in the discussions, "The executive committee says, 'What are these funds worth?' The best and the brightest from the trading desk are sitting there . . . not one of them makes less than fifteen million bucks, a fuckload more than I made, and not one of them will step up and say what it's worth—not one. These guys work in this market all day long, just in this market. I'm talking Tommy. I'm talking Jeff Mayer. I'm talking all of them. None of them would put a value on this thing. It was very hard to do. And they're prudent guys who understand that in a free-fall market you don't reach out for the knife while it's falling."

One possible way to figure out what the collateral was worth was by examining the results of the bilateral deals. "The point is we kind of know where everybody has said they would do a deal at," this participant remembered. "We can get a value based on that." Based on quickly and collectively analyzing the bilateral deals, the consensus seemed to be that "the [Enhanced Leverage] fund will be worth this much in the end," he said, "and it was nonzero. And the [High-Grade] fund will be worth this much and it was considerably nonzero. Isn't that the closest thing we have right now to a value?" After probing into the logic of this suggestion, the executive committee authorized the SWAT team to negotiate as many of the bilateral deals as they could.

By this time, Bear Stearns had also learned that Merrill's efforts to sell its $850 million of securities in the market had not gone well. "Merrill got stuck with a lot of bonds," Friedman said. "That was an interesting but troubling data point for liquidity in this stuff, but it also was a reinforcement of the notion that you can't try to sell this stuff at an auction with twelve hours' notice. People just won't bid."

Events at the hedge funds were transpiring so quickly that the Bear Stearns executives had little time to consider carefully what to do. The redemption notices were coming fast and furious, and to avoid a total meltdown, they thought it best to take out the repo lenders and allow for what they hoped would be an orderly liquidation of the fund over time. "It was over," Cayne said of the firm's decision to make the $1.6 billion available. "Bids were coming in at 50 cents. Merrill was selling us out. There were no bids on half the items. That's when the world woke up. That could be the wake-up call. That margin call. They used the words 'blow you out,' like a blowjob." Paul Friedman said the firm had "to decide in about forty-eight hours what the stuff was worth. It realistically would have taken three or four weeks to really know what this stuff was worth. We guessed that we were lending $1.2 billion against stuff that we thought was worth at least $1.5 billion or $1.6 billion. We thought the hedge fund itself had a couple of hundred million of equity. Then it turned out it didn't. It seemed at the time like this was a pretty safe loan. The theory—which was a good theory—was if we were the only lender and if this thing actually had equity in it, then we could do an orderly liquidation and preserve the equity. Have more money to pay back the investors and reduce the lawsuits, reduce the losses, and reduce the destruction on the market. That was the theory. At that point we still believed that an AAA rating meant an AAA rating, and we all believed that these things were reasonably well structured."

When pressed—since they had not had time to study the underlying assets that the firm was about to commit to lend against—Friedman and the other fixed-income executives thought it was unlikely the firm would lose any money on the loan. "Look, we don't really know what they're worth," he told the executive committee. "We can kind of cuff it. If we're really wrong, we could lose a couple hundred million dollars. We figure we've got a $400 million cushion, eat through that, and then eat through a couple hundred million more." A loss of that magnitude seemed beyond comprehension. "That seemed like such an absurd number," he said. "We used it as a throwaway—'Hey, we could lose a couple hundred million. It's okay. It would still be a good trade if we lost a couple hundred million dollars for the franchise value, for the litigation risk that we'd be reducing.' We had the view back in June that whatever these hedge funds lost, maybe not dollar for dollar but almost dollar for dollar, was going to just work its way over into a lawyer's office. We were going to be sued by all these investors and we were going to pay out a significant portion of it anyway. So if you took a couple-hundred-million-dollar loss by taking these guys out, you would get some significant portion of it back by not paying it out in legal settlements. Never did we think in our wildest dreams we could be wrong [by] $600, $700, $800 million."

In the end, Greenberg, Spector, and Schwartz overruled Cayne and Molinaro. The fateful decision to become the repo lender to the High-Grade Fund—to the tune of up to $3.2 billion at first—had been made.

※

AT EIGHT O'CLOCK on the morning of June 21, Marin made a new proposal to the creditors that it would provide $3.2 billion of financing to the High-Grade Fund, taking out all of the repo lenders if the lenders agreed to withhold margin calls on the Enhanced Leverage Fund. This proposal got little traction, and at 3 P.M., Marin made the offer of the $3.2 billion with no conditions. That night, Warren Spector was at a private dinner in Washington with other senior Wall Street executives to meet presidential candidate Senator Barack Obama. Spector introduced himself as working for Bear Stearns, "the current scourge of Wall Street." At the same time that Spector was in Washington, Steve Schwarzman's Blackstone Group priced its highly anticipated $4.75 billion IPO at $31 per share. The offering, a huge success from Blackstone's perspective, briefly made Schwarzman worth close to $8 billion. The two lead managers of the deal, Morgan Stanley and Citigroup, hoovered up around $100 million of the $202 million in underwriting fees. (Bear Stearns was a co-manager on the deal.)

By the next afternoon, Spector was back at his office in New York spending hours on the phone with other Wall Street executives. His message to them was that Bear Stearns had finally decided to step up in a significant way to help the hedge funds. But it was not quite what the market expected. Spector told his Wall Street colleagues that Bear would become the new repo lender—up to a total of $3.2 billion—to the High-Grade Fund *only* and would do nothing for the Enhanced Leverage Fund, effectively signaling that the second fund would fail and be liquidated. "The uncertainty in the marketplace surrounding these funds has made an orderly de-leveraging difficult," Cayne said in a press release on June 22, the same day the Blackstone IPO started trading and moved up 17.5 percent. "By providing the facility, we believe we stabilize financing, reduce uncertainty in the marketplace and allow for an orderly process to de-leverage the High Grade fund." He said nothing about the decision not to support the Enhanced Leverage Fund. (When the Enhanced Leverage Fund failed and was liquidated, Barclays lost virtually all of its $400 million; a civil suit between the parties, alleging fraud and deceit, among other charges, was filed.)

The same day that Bear announced its half-baked rescue plan for the funds, the decision was quietly made—not surprisingly—to shelve the plan for Everquest's IPO, and the registration statement was withdrawn from the SEC. "The wacko Everquest deal was saved from being the dumbest idea ever in the history of the world by not being done," Paul Friedman said. "I mean, 'Let's take CDO equity and residuals and all this stuff, and let's package it up and do a deal, and sell it to Mom and Pop.' Nobody's ever come up with a stupider idea in history. Had the funds not blown up, I think there's a chance they would have actually tried to bring it to market. That's another indication that there were no grown-ups minding the shop."

Asked at the time about the happenings at the Bear Stearns hedge funds, Treasury Secretary Henry Paulson said, "I tried to make clear we will be dealing with the subprime issue for some time and that there will be losses along the way. It's a natural outgrowth of what we've seen in the housing market and certain lending practices. As mortgages continue to reset, this will take time to work its way through the system. But I continue to believe that this risk is largely contained. It doesn't pose a significant risk to the economy overall."

❊

BY JUNE 26, the High-Grade Fund had sold additional assets into the market, reducing to $1.6 billion Bear Stearns's repo facility to that fund. Nothing, though, was being provided to the Enhanced Leverage Fund. Bear Stearns's decision to take out the repo lenders to the High-Grade Fund created an interesting dynamic. Those firms, such as Merrill Lynch, that had seized their collateral from the funds earlier got badly burned with losses when they tried to sell the securities in the market. Merrill begged Bear to be taken out whole after the announcement, to no avail. Other firms, such as Cantor Fitzgerald and Dresdner Bank, that were slower to catch on to the seriousness of the situation got out whole. "It was astounding to me," Friedman said. "Cantor Fitzgerald and Dresdner Bank were each lending Ralph well north of a billion dollars, neither of whom had a mortgage desk, neither of whom had any idea what the collateral was, and got their marks to make margin calls by calling Ralph up and asking him what the stuff was worth. So the true irony of this is the firm finally agrees to step in and take out the lenders because we're concerned JPMorgan and the banks and people that we cared about would hate us, and we thought we could help the investors in the funds with an orderly liquidation. In fact, those banks had already blown us out. Cantor benefits, who cares? We bailed out Cantor Fitzgerald. We bailed out Dresdner Bank, who immediately terminated everything else they had on with us and told us to lose their phone number. We bailed out Citibank, who treated us like a leper from then on, and did everything they could to crush us, and we got saddled with a billion and a half worth of stuff."

Now the hard work of figuring out what the firm had just agreed to buy had to begin. "Between June and July, we were getting our arms around what the collateral was," Friedman said. This was no easy task. "It took two or three weeks to mark," he explained. "They had about a third of the hedge fund position marked in a week. They had the rest of it marked in another two or three weeks. It literally took a dozen people on the mortgage desk night and day, and a bunch of our research people night and day and weekends, three weeks to value this stuff, which tells you just how illiquid it was."

By the time they did figure out what most of it was worth, the firm had miscalculated badly. "The trading desk was marking it to where it really belonged, which was getting lower and lower," Friedman said. "Our beliefs that there was equity in both the position and the fund were both wrong. We thought there was $400 million-ish of cushion, and in fact, as it turned out, we missed by like $1 billion out of $1.5 billion. It was not even close. You would think you could get it to the nearest billion, and a lot of it was the market deteriorating dramatically in that five or six weeks. But it was just a guess to begin with."

❀

IT WAS AT this unfortunate moment, in the midst of the ongoing round-the-clock valuation of the High-Grade Fund's assets, that the *New York Times* revealed, on June 28, that for the previous two and a half years, Rich Marin had been writing a personal blog about his love of cross-country motorcycle trips, his family, and movies. There were also a bunch of pictures from his early June 2007 trip to the Middle East—Saudi Arabia, Jordan, and Israel—for what appeared to be a business trip to meet the local businessmen who were involved in a joint venture with BSAM. There were photos of Marin and his colleagues flying on the private jet of one of their partners— "We hitched a ride," he wrote—and a description of some leisure activities. "Late afternoon brought a much needed nap and a visit to the health club and the best Indonesian/Swedish massage of my life," he wrote. "I staggered back to my room and off we went for dinner at the home of one of our partners." On June 23, he summed up the past few weeks at the office as "trying to defend Sparta against the Persian hordes of Wall Street. Nothing like a good dogfight 24x7 for a few weeks to remind you why you chose the life you chose. The good news is that after two embattled weeks both I and my loyal staff are still standing to fight another day."

Marin warned Spector the *Times* article was imminent. The *Times* article appeared that morning, and when Marin arrived at Spector's office he was informed that he had been relieved of his duties as head of BSAM. The ill-timed publicity about Marin's personal blog served as useful cover for a decision that was all but inevitable. Spector asked him to stay on as an advisor to the firm, which he did until the end of 2007. He continued to receive his salary, but the firm did not pay him a bonus. His U-5 form indicates he was not fired for cause.

❀

THAT SAME DAY, the firm announced that Marin's replacement would be Jeffrey B. Lane, sixty-five, a longtime Wall Street executive and chairman of Neuberger Berman and then vice chairman of

Lehman Brothers after Lehman bought Neuberger. "I am proud to be joining Bear Stearns," he said, "and I look forward to working with the BSAM team. I believe in the integrity of the franchise and I am excited about the prospect of continuing to build the BSAM organization." Spector had been thinking about hiring Lane, his occasional doubles partner on the tennis court, for some time, and the hedge fund blowup brought the decision to a head. (He had also tried to hire Marc Lasry, the CEO of Avenue Capital, to run the asset management business, but that did not materialize.) Lane told the *Wall Street Journal* that turning around BSAM would be a slow process. "It's like painting the Verrazano Bridge," he said. "You start painting and you keep going." Cayne said the reason for hiring Lane was to restore "investor confidence in BSAM." Lane spent a few days debriefing Marin about what had been transpiring at the hedge funds but quickly found he had little use for him.

Then Landon Thomas Jr., at the *New York Times,* interviewed Cayne to get his reaction to the hedge fund debacle. "James E. Cayne has a bellyache," he wrote. "And it is not from the crash diet that has caused Mr. Cayne . . . to shed 20 pounds over the last year." The weight loss, Cayne told Thomas, came from cutting out "red wine, bacon and salmon for breakfast and late-night deliveries from Bobby Van's steakhouse." Cayne told Thomas the hedge fund losses were a "body blow of massive proportion." He added, "I'm angry. When you walk around with a reputation for being the most rigorous risk analyzer, assessor, controller and that is trashed, well, you have got to feel bad. This is personal." He seemed to be taking it personally, as if the chink in the firm's armor was also a chink in his self-esteem. "In the last 15 years, I have never walked into a room or been at a dinner party where I did not feel that when people looked at me they thought I was O.K., successful, agile," he said. "That might have changed. I feel like people now look at me with a question mark." Cayne did not mention that Marin had been summarily demoted and Cioffi relieved of his day-to-day management of the fund or say anything about the fate of Spector, who of course was in charge of BSAM. (Cayne had invited Spector to the interview with Thomas but Spector did not show, much to Cayne's irritation.)

Cayne also did not mention that he had by this time resumed his summer Thursday afternoon ritual of taking a seventeen-minute, $1,700 helicopter ride from the East Side of Manhattan to the Hollywood Golf Club, in Deal, New Jersey, and playing a quick round of golf. He did this on both June 14 and June 21 in the midst of the tense negotiations. Indeed, records showed that between June 9 and July 15, Cayne played about twenty rounds of golf at Hollywood. He also played Friday mornings, and spent the time after golf at his home in Elberon attending to business.

ALL THE COMMOTION in the Bear hedge funds was starting to make the market very nervous. Brad Hintz, a research analyst at Sanford Bernstein and a former Lehman Brothers CFO, said that the problem was "more than a Bear Stearns issue, it is an industry issue. How many other hedge funds are holding similar, illiquid, esoteric securities? What are their true prices? What will happen if more blow up?" That answer seemed to be provided by Bill Gross, the CEO of PIMCO. Defaults on subprime loans would "grow and grow like a weed in your backyard tomato patch," he said in a June 30 interview. "There are hundreds of billions of dollars of this toxic waste, and whether or not they're CDOs or Bear Stearns's hedge funds matters only to the extent of the timing of the unwind. Alongside death and taxes you can add this to your list of inevitabilities: the subprime crisis is not an isolated event and it won't be contained by a few days of headlines in the *New York Times*. And it will not remain confined to a neat little petri dish in some mad financial derivative scientist's laboratory." There was also the small matter that the SEC had started an investigation into the collapse of the hedge funds. Despite the firm's mounting woes and negative publicity, the stock was holding up, closing on July 2 at $143.16 a share, down around 18 percent from its all-time high.

On July 17, Cayne announced the seemingly inevitable news that the hedge funds were kaput. "During June," he wrote, "the Funds experienced significant declines in the value of their assets resulting in losses of net asset value. The Funds' reported performance, in part, reflects the unprecedented declines in the valuations of a number of highly-rated (AA and AAA) securities." He then lowered the boom. "The preliminary estimates show there is effectively no value left for the investors in the Enhanced Leveraged Fund and very little value left for the investors in the High-Grade Fund as of June 30, 2007. In light of these returns, we will seek an orderly wind-down of the Funds over time. This is a difficult development for investors in these Funds and it is certainly uncharacteristic of BSAM's overall strong record of performance." In closing his letter, he tried to be upbeat and to regain the trust of the firm's clients. "Our highest priority is to continue to earn your trust and confidence each and every day, consistent with the Firm's proud history of achievement."

CHAPTER 29

NASHVILLE

The day after Bear announced the closing of the hedge funds, both Cayne and Spector headed to Nashville, Tennessee, to play bridge in the Spingold Knockout national tournament. They were not on the same team, of course, but each of them was out of the office for the next ten days. Not only were they hard to reach at times—as previously noted, no cell phones or BlackBerry devices are permitted during the intense tournament play—but the fact that both men were away from New York and the office at such a critical time violated Cayne's dictum to Spector that both men could not be out of the office at the same time playing bridge. Since a sponsor's team for such an event is lined up months in advance, the chance that Cayne was surprised by Spector's attendance at the event seems hard to fathom.

✳

WHILE CAYNE AND Spector were in Nashville playing bridge, Doug Sharon flew down to New York from Boston for another segment on his lonely journey to convey the severity of the collapse of the hedge funds from his clients' perspective to any Bear Stearns senior executive who would listen to him. He had twenty or so clients who had invested around $65 million in the hedge funds and had another $670 million of assets managed by the firm. He also noted that these clients had as much as $2.6 billion in other investable assets not managed by Bear Stearns, a potential source of new business for the firm. His message—similar to what it had been previously to Cayne, Solender, and Spector—was that the firm needed to take care of all the clients that had invested in the hedge funds. On his July 25 trip to New York, one of those steamy days when it's unbearable to be outside as soon as the sun rises, Sharon had a nine o'clock meeting with Sam Molinaro to go over the situation with his clients. In the Starbucks on Madison Avenue near 383 Madison Avenue, he ran into John Howard, the head of Bear Stearns's successful private-equity funds. Sharon started a mini-rant about how the firm didn't seem to be doing the right thing for its clients in the hedge funds and, as a result, he was beginning to lose a little faith in how the firm was being run. He told Howard he had sold a bunch of his stock and that he wouldn't be surprised to see the stock hit $60 a share before too long, even though then the stock was around $120 per share. "I hope you're wrong," Howard told him, "because I have around 700,000 shares of stock."

After this chance encounter, Sharon called up Ace Greenberg, told him he was in town, and wanted to see if he could stop by. He told Greenberg he had a nine o'clock meeting with Molinaro. Greenberg told him to stop by fifteen minutes before. Sharon respected Greenberg. "After meeting with him," he said, "you always walked out of there and felt, 'Man, this guy is just a mensch!'" In a previous meeting with Greenberg a month or so before, he'd introduced him to one of his clients with money in the hedge fund. "Let me just tell you something," Sharon's client told Greenberg. "I have the utmost respect for you as a businessman, but I have to tell you the communication with the clients has been pathetic." Remembered Sharon: "That's the word he used, 'pathetic.' Ace told him, 'Look, the problem we have is the lawyers are telling us what to do and what not to do.' . . . [The client is] about the same age as Ace, maybe a few years younger. He said, 'I run a business. I have hundreds and hundreds of employees. We do billions of dollars' worth of transactions a year. I have lots of lawyers that give me a lot of advice.

Sometimes I listen to them. Sometimes I don't. Sometimes you have to just make the tough calls and do the right thing, and I think that you guys are just frozen here, and I think it's really hurting your credibility.'"

In July, when Sharon saw Greenberg, he asked him if he had seen the monthly statements from "Ralph's Funds," as they were known inside the firm, and how the statements implied Cioffi was investing one way when he was actually investing another. Greenberg said he had not seen the statements but wanted to know what Spector had said when Sharon told him about them and made his case for taking care of the clients. When Sharon related what Spector had told him—"What was it that Ace once said? 'Hey, you can't fly like the eagles and poop like a canary'"—Greenberg couldn't believe it. He was red hot. He called up Molinaro on the phone, right in front of Sharon, and demanded that he push his meeting with Sharon until later. "We have to have an executive committee meeting right now!" Greenberg screamed into the phone.

Sharon has no idea what the outcome of that meeting was, but at eleven o'clock he did meet with Molinaro, Solender, and Begleiter to discuss the situation with his clients. "What do you think it would take for these guys to settle?" Molinaro asked him.

"I think you've got to give these guys fifty or sixty cents on the dollar," Sharon said. "The rest will be a tax deduction and they'll feel treated fairly."

"How much business do we do with these accounts?" Molinaro asked.

"I don't know," Sharon answered. "Probably $5 million a year."

"And how much did they lose in the fund collectively, this group you're showing me?" Molinaro asked.

"About $35 million," Sharon said.

"You think they'd settle for half to two-thirds?" Molinaro said. "I don't think I would pay $20 million for a $5 million book of business."

Sharon was incredulous. "Sammy, you're missing the point," he said. "You may end up paying them $20 million anyway. These guys aren't going to go away. These guys are absolutely, positively going to sue Bear Stearns for their money. They feel like they've been misled.

I've shown you all the documentation they've received—which they're going to put in the courtroom—that shows that Ralph misled them for eighteen months. He led them in the correct direction and then invested in a different way and basically lulled them into a sense of false security."

While Cayne and Spector were in Nashville playing bridge, the rapidly deteriorating condition of the hedge funds forced the firm into having to decide whether the funds should file for bankruptcy. The decision was complicated legally, since the funds were domiciled in the Cayman Islands for tax purposes, while most of the assets, the investors, and the people who worked at the funds were in the New York area. At one point, the decision was made to convene a special executive committee meeting to discuss the bankruptcy filing of the funds. Cayne made himself available for the meeting. But Spector was not so accommodating. He called Molinaro, who had arranged for the special meeting, from Nashville. "I thought he was going to kill me," Molinaro said. "He was ripping my head off. He said, 'I can't be available. I'm not available then. What do we have to talk about?' I said, 'Warren, we have to make a decision about putting this thing in bankruptcy. There are a ton of issues. We have to discuss this.' So I got a hold of Jimmy. He's available. I told Warren, 'If you're not available, we'll try to figure out how to make it work, but you need to be on this call.' He must have been playing or something. I don't know what the hell was going on. He ultimately joined the call in progress." On July 30, the hedge funds' boards of directors authorized the funds to file petitions for liquidation under the Cayman Islands' Companies Law under the supervision of the Cayman Grand Court. Subsequently, both a U.S. bankruptcy court and a U.S. district court of appeals struck down the legitimacy of the Cayman Islands venue for the filing. As a consequence of the filing, Bear Stearns seized $1.3 billion of underlying collateral—Cioffi's panoply of illiquid mortgage-backed securities—that it had been financing for all of one month and absorbed it onto the firm's balance sheet.

One senior Bear executive put what was happening into perspective. "Jimmy being away, that was standard," he said. "That was not a big deal. Jimmy being away maybe looked bad once the outside world focused on it, but the way this company worked, that was not a major problem. Warren being away, that was a major problem because Warren was the decision maker. Not that Jimmy wasn't. But the way it worked was ultimately we'd form a point of view. We'd go to Jimmy. We'd tell him what we wanted to do. We'd discuss the pros and cons. He'd make the call. But Warren was a key lieutenant and during that period we were in the middle of a crisis here. These funds are blowing up. We've got to make a decision about putting them into bankruptcy. We had a lot of big decisions to make that week and he was gone. Candidly, what was really in my mind is, 'You're the fucking president of the company. This is your area. You need to be all over this stuff because these people work for you. Not for me. I'm in the middle of this because I have to be. You're in the middle of it because you are in the middle of it. What are you doing not being here?'"

BY THE TIME Cayne returned to his sixth-floor lair at 383 Madison on July 30, after ten days in Nashville, he was loaded for bear. Spector's presence in Nashville irked Cayne no end. Although he did not say anything to him in Nashville, he thought Spector should have been back in New York the second week of July, leading the fire drill. "If I even saw him [in Nashville], he would scurry away," Cayne said. At the end of the second week, both men returned to New York—on separate flights, Cayne now white hot and Spector quietly suspecting he had successfully needled his boss. Indeed, their mutual antipathy by this point was such that when they both got on the firm's elevator at the same moment, "they did not say a word to each other for the entire ride, each staring in the opposite direction," according to the *New York Times*.

Between Spector being in Nashville in the middle of July instead of in New York, Spector's unilateral decision to invest $25 million in the hedge funds on May 1 (which he had the written authority to do), and the growing antipathy between the two men, Cayne decided Spector had to go. He made the decision on his own and impulsively, with little forethought about what the consequences might be for firing the architect of one's home at the very moment it was crumbling. "I couldn't work with him," Cayne said.

"I didn't trust him anymore. I told Schwartz, and I told Sam, and I told Greenberg. Sam had no opinion. Sam didn't even like the guy. He treated Sam like shit. Schwartz wanted to wait thirty days, because Schwartz always loved to wait thirty days. Greenberg wasn't sure. I said, 'Look, it almost doesn't matter because I can't work with the guy. So, if you're telling me you're not on board for him to be dismissed, you're telling me I'm dismissed. That's your choice. I'm not working with him anymore.'"

The other members of the executive committee, Spector aside, viewed Cayne's decision with concern. "Jimmy just really had had it with Warren," explained a Bear executive, "and, I thought, rather impulsively said, 'Warren's got to go.' Jimmy and I spent three hours going over it because I said, 'Number one, Jimmy, now is not the right time. Number two, whether it's the right thing to do or not, I'm not even going to address it. I'm not convinced it is, nor can I sit here and look you in the eye and tell you it certainly isn't.'" Many Bear executives thought the firm's situation was precarious enough at that moment that keeping the team together was paramount.

Cayne cut his colleague off. "I can't stand seeing him," Cayne said. "I can't stand coming in every day." Both Schwartz and Molinaro tried to convince Cayne to keep Spector. "But it was like the onslaught," an executive said. Other Bear executives also thought Vince Tese, the lead independent director on the board, would be sympathetic to keeping Spector around until the acute crisis passed. "But Vince was supporting Jimmy," one of them said. "My pitch to him was, 'We're a public corporation. We've had a problem. We've hired a law firm. I don't know what they're going to say. Why don't we get to work and get this freaking thing solved? Tell the law firm we want everything out on the table. I'm not passing judgment on whether Warren should be here long-term or not. I'm not. Given what's happened, I have an open mind, but I think the right thing to do is let the investigation finish, let's get all the information, and then let's talk about all the consequences."

There was also the argument made to Cayne that Spector provided a buffer for Cayne against the approaching hordes. If he fired Spector now and something else occurred in the coming months, Cayne would be on the hot seat instead of Spector. "Who knows where this thing is going?" one of his partners told Cayne. "If you take Warren out now, we've lost the ability to use Warren as 'That's how we responded.' The minute he's out, you're the target." Toward the end of their three-hour discussion, Cayne said, "There's one thing that's getting at me here. He never once said he was sorry for the mess he made."

The executive told Cayne he was sad to hear that news. "He understood a little better the magnitude of his emotion because this was a really serious thing—what happened to us—and whether Warren was directly responsible or not, he put it in place and he put the people in place. He was in charge," he said.

The executive believed that, for Cayne, discovering that Spector had authorized investing the $25 million in the hedge funds was the final straw. "The $25 million was a rounding error," this person continued. "But Ace and Jimmy went ballistic. What it implied was, 'Hey, wait a minute. If there was trouble, forget whether you put in the $25 million or not; the fact that they thought it was important [meant that it] was something the executive committee should have known. It wasn't that you put in the $25 million; it was that you didn't even tell us there was a problem and you put in the $25 million.'" Another Bear executive agreed. "The $25 million was an excuse after the fact," he said. "Jimmy needed something to be able to tell people about why he fired Warren."

A number of Bear's senior executives are still not sure Spector understood the extent to which the hedge fund debacle hurt the firm. "The screw-up in hedge funds was a pretty big screw-up," one of them said. "He didn't seem to get that. . . . I think to this day Warren thinks, in the scheme of what we were doing, in the scheme of all his responsibilities, something like that's going to happen to anybody. Jimmy jumped on it to get rid of him. It's unbelievable, but I think that's true. He did not seem contrite. He did not feel bad that it happened. He felt like, 'What's the big deal, guys?' What he didn't get was it made us the poster child for a problem in the whole industry. It's like walking into Disney and saying, 'Someone's having sex with an underage minor on your ride. It was only one kid. What's the big deal? It was only a blowjob.'"

By Wednesday, August 1, Cayne had all his ducks in a row. He called Spector down one floor to his office, which was especially dark that day because all the shades were drawn, and told him, "I think it's in the best interests of the firm for you to resign. I have to do this. I can't work with you anymore." Spector said he was stunned and thought he had been working hard to repair the problems in BSAM and in fixed income. Every time Spector tried to engage Cayne in a discussion, Cayne just reiterated that he had "lost confidence in" Spector. Cayne was in HR overdrive.

※

As ALL THIS was being hashed out on the sixth floor of 383 Madison after Cayne and Spector returned from Nashville, Robert Upton, Bear Stearns's treasurer, was in Nantucket, taking a few days off. On the afternoon of July 31, from Nantucket, Upton started calling around to the ratings agencies in New York to tell them Bear Stearns was about to suspend redemptions from *another* hedge fund, The Bear Stearns Asset-Backed Securities Fund, with about $900 million in assets. Even though the fund supposedly had less than 1 percent of those assets invested in subprime mortgages and mostly was in credit card receivables and consumer auto loans, investors suspected the fund had lost money in July and had been concerned enough about potential future losses that they started to take their money out. That's when the firm stopped the redemptions. Upton wanted the rating agencies to know. "Of course, the other funds had just declared bankruptcy, and it was like this massive scrutiny and concern about Bear," he said. He flew back to New York City that night. He returned to the office the next morning, August 1.

On the agenda that day was a call with Standard & Poor's, the ratings agency, which was "seriously evaluating putting [Bear Stearns's senior debt rating] on negative outlook," Upton said. "Not the end of the world, but in the market environment we were in, [it] certainly sends a bad signal. Real fucking problem, especially when no one else had to face that same action yet. We were very concerned, and pushing really hard" to convince Standard & Poor's to change its mind. The discussions with the ratings agency had continued Wednesday and Thursday. "All the senior guys at the firm knew this was potentially imminent," Upton said. "We were all kind of collecting our wits about us to figure out how we would deal with it. We knew it was going to be a problem. And everyone was looking to me to answer, 'Is this going to happen tomorrow, Friday the third?'" Late Thursday afternoon, Upton spoke to Scott Sprinzen, an S&P managing director, about the potential change in Bear Stearns's ratings outlook. Sprinzen was on his way out the door for the day. "We're going to hold off on making that decision until early next week," Upton recalled Sprinzen telling him. "I said, 'Okay, that's great. We'll provide you some more information. We'll talk next week.'" Upton thought for sure the firm had dodged a bullet.

The next morning, Upton was at his desk at 6:30 A.M. Ten minutes later, Sprinzen called. "Yep," Sprinzen said, "you're going on negative outlook today." Upton was shocked—"That was a shit show," he said—and said to Sprinzen, "But you told me yesterday you were going to wait till next week."

"Yeah, well, no one was on the call," Sprinzen told him.

"What he was basically saying was, 'Yeah, that's what I told you, but there's no proof that that's what I fucking said, so you're fucked,'" Upton said. "I scramble. I call Friedman. I e-mail Molinaro. I say, 'Get ahold of me. S&P's going negative this morning.'" By 7:30, S&P had sent over a copy of the press release to Upton. An hour later, Upton said, "Schwartz and Molinaro are in my office and we're fighting with this guy Sprinzen, trying to get him to clean up the press release, telling him that when they send this out, it's going to be a bad signal to the market. The market's going to think we have a massive hole in our balance sheet and we're about to fucking blow our brains out," Upton said. "He says, 'Oh, no, no, no. I'm a weasel dick,' then sends the fucking thing out anyway."

The S&P statement on August 3 sent a shock wave through the markets by questioning publicly whether the problems in the firm's hedge funds could have longer-term implications for the financial health of the firm. After revising the outlook on the firm's credit to "negative" from "stable," S&P explained that the change, according to analyst Diane Hinton (Sprinzen's colleague), "reflects our concerns about recent developments and their potential to hurt Bear Stearns' performance for an extended period. We believe Bear Stearns' reputation has suffered from the widely publicized problems of its managed hedge funds, leaving the company a potential target of litigation from investors who have suffered substantial losses." The ratings agency also noted Bear Stearns's "material exposure" to mortgages and mortgage-backed securities—not helped by taking $1.3 billion of Cioffi's securities—as well as unsold leveraged finance loans and high-yield underwritings. "The ratings could be lowered if large losses were to be incurred over the next few quarters or if earnings failed to stabilize as a satisfactory level beyond the next few quarters, which we expect will be—at best—difficult ones for the company," Hinton wrote.

The credit ratings of any company are crucial semaphores of financial health and well-being, but are especially important to firms—such as those on Wall Street—that rely not only on borrowing from others to survive but also on their confidence. "The stock drops like a stone," Upton said. "CDS [credit default swap] spreads start blowing out again. Everyone's concerned. Our fixed-income investors and repo counterparties and banks are calling in. Molinaro comes racing down to my office at like ten-thirty and says, 'We've got to do something.'"

To their credit, Molinaro and Cayne sought to stop any potentially mushrooming concern about the firm's viability by putting out a press release announcing the firm would hold a conference call for analysts at 2 P.M. "The stock crashed," Upton said. "It was basically crashing in the morning. We put the press release out. It went to the Mendoza line"—a reference to the poor .198 batting average of former shortstop Mario Mendoza and used by other players to suggest bad performance. There were 2,200 people on the conference call, eager to understand what was going wrong at the firm. Unfortunately, the call did not work out quite the way Cayne and Sam Molinaro hoped it would. "That was a fucking disaster," Upton said.

CAYNE KICKED THINGS off, as people like to say on Wall Street, by putting into perspective the increasingly difficult market conditions the firm faced. Every financial institution, Bear Stearns included, was facing an extremely challenging market environment. "I've been involved in the securities industry for more than four decades and I have seen a broad spectrum of market dislocations," he said, "in the stock market crash in the late 1980s, fixed-income troubles in the mid-1990s, and the bursting of the Internet bubble in 2001. This is not the first time and certainly will not be the last time that Wall Street and the financial community will work through difficult conditions. I understand there is a great deal of uncertainty in the marketplace surrounding the operating environment and specifically our firm. I want to assure you that we are taking this situation seriously. We are applying all of the energies and experience we have in the markets to manage the current issues. I'd also like to add that I'm extremely pleased with the way my colleagues have been working to handle this situation." Cayne made no mention on the call that he was less than pleased by the way Spector had handled the crisis.

Molinaro then made a few comments about the expected profitability of the firm in June and July, "notwithstanding the extraordinarily difficult market conditions," with "June certainly a hell of a lot better than July." He also said August would be rough, and if markets returned to some modicum of normalcy, the firm would be profitable, albeit at the low end of expectations. He then asked Mike Alix, the chief risk officer, to talk about how the firm had hedged its exposure to the risky securities on its balance sheet. "In our mortgage businesses, we've put in place a variety of hedges to mitigate the credit risk inherent in our residential mortgage inventory," Alix said. He then turned the call over to Upton to discuss the firm's liquidity and sources of financing.

Upton used his time on the call to try to reassure the market about Bear's financial might. He said the firm had approximately $11.4 billion in cash available at the parent company and that, after a concerted effort to reduce the reliance on unsecured commercial paper financing, outstandings had been reduced to $11.5 billion, down from more than $23 billion. He said the firm also had "unused committed secured bank lines" of more than $11.2 billion and $4 billion that could be drawn on an unsecured basis. There was also another $18 billion of "unencumbered collateral" that could be pledged for additional financing. This lengthening of the terms of the firm's financing did not come without a cost—in terms of both higher interest rates and the scars on Upton's back from the internal battles. Upton concluded, all in all, that the firm's financial foot-ing was "extremely solid notwithstanding the current difficult mar-ket conditions." The firm's message was one of preparedness, confidence, and stolidity, everything a bank aspires to be.

But the very fact the firm felt the need to make such reassuring comments made people nervous. The first questioner, Douglas Sip-kin, at Wachovia Securities, wondered if Molinaro could explain what had caused the rapid decrease in liquidity in the debt markets in June and July. "There's a great deal of uncertainty in the fixed in-come markets over the level of default and loss expectations in the subprime mortgage market and . . . generally in the broader mort-gage market," Molinaro answered. In other words, the world was quickly becoming a riskier place. When would the credit markets normalize? Sipkin wondered. Molinaro said he had no idea what the "catalyst" for a change would be. "We've been in a period of gridlock for quite some time," he said. "It seems that with each new day and with each new month there's new information in the mortgage mar-ket in terms of delinquencies and defaults."

Sipkin then asked Cayne if he had given any thought to buying back the firm's stock, given its decline to that point in 2007. After a moment of silence, Molinaro said that Cayne had "stepped out of the room," and in the later reporting of this meeting, the press had a field day with the fact that Cayne had not bothered to stay in the room for the meeting. Some even speculated that the reason he had left the room was to continue the negotiations with Spector—who was not part of the call, either—about his looming firing. The truth was that even though Molinaro told the analysts Cayne had left the room, he was just covering for Bear's CEO. Cayne simply did not know how to answer Sipkin's question. "All heads in the room swiveled to Jimmy, who was still sitting in the room with Sam," Paul Friedman said, "and Jimmy went blank like a deer in the headlights. Sam jumped in to save him and said Jimmy had to leave the room. Our vaunted CEO was incapable of answering a single question. I've forgotten the ques-tion, but it was pretty much a softball question, too, like 'What do you see in the markets?' or something like that. It was a nothing ques-tion. Jimmy couldn't open his mouth, so he didn't." Added Upton: "He didn't have his arms around the business. He didn't even know what liquidity was until it started to potentially become an issue. He didn't know who I was, really, until that time frame, and then [he] called me every day. 'How we doing? How we doing?' So I didn't think very highly of Jimmy, in terms of having his hands on the business and understanding the real risk issues and being able to stand up and make tough decisions when tough decisions needed to be made. It was a lot easier to just abdicate, or make no decision, or filibuster, or talk about the P&L impact, or whatever. We were the 'House of the Legacy Filibuster'—you've got to get everything perfect, because this is the way we've always done it. We don't want to upset the apple cart, and it's going to cost us more money. What is a filibuster in the Senate? It's a way of forcing a nondecision and extending it until even the most tireless people get tired and give up. So that's all he did." (In an interview, Cayne said he was *not* in the room.)

❦

THE REAL HEADLINES Molinaro made during the call came moments later, when Mike Mayo, the outspoken analyst from Deutsche Bank, asked about Cayne's remarks in which he suggested the markets were then akin to other financial crises on Wall Street. "Do we compare what you're going through now with those other, more significant times?" Mayo asked.

"I think these times are pretty significant in the fixed-income markets," Molinaro replied. "I've been at this for twenty-two years. It's about as bad as I have seen it in the fixed-income market during that period of time. This market environment we have been seeing over the last eight weeks has been pretty extreme. And yes, we would make that comparison. I think it is a reasonable comparison."

The call, of course, went on for another twenty minutes or so after Molinaro answered Mayo's question, but the damage had been done.

"He fucking blew the market up," Upton said.

That Molinaro thought the collapse in the value of various mortgage-backed securities amounted to a crisis worse than the crash of 1987, the collapse of the Internet bubble, or the meltdown of Long-Term Capital Management—when only a tiny fraction of Wall Street had even started focusing on the problem—was either a reckless and inflammatory remark by the CFO of a large Wall Street firm or remarkable prescience. Either way, the markets reacted negatively to his comment. "You could watch while he's talking," Friedman said. "Our stock is going lower and lower by the minute." Bear's stock traded as low as $106.55, down nearly 8 percent, before closing down 6 percent, well below its January 2007 high of $172.69. The cost of protecting against a default in Bear's outstanding debt was seven times higher than it had been at the beginning of 2007. Molinaro's comments moved the Dow Jones Industrial Average down 281.42 points, to 13,181.91. The stock of Lehman Brothers, which most people considered just a bigger version of Bear Stearns in terms of its fixed-income focus, fell 8 percent that day, to $55.78. "They called it the worst fixed-income markets in twenty years, grouping it with 1987 and the bursting of the Internet bubble," Mayo later told the *Journal,* "and said they needed a better August just to get to the lower end of their historical range of returns."

The next day, Saturday, the *Journal* reported on the extraordinary conference call, focusing on Upton's efforts to raise cash and to cut the firm's reliance on short-term debt. But the paper also reported—in the second paragraph—that the "firm plans to oust Warren Spector" and the board of directors was going to meet Monday to "discuss Mr. Spector's departure." That same day, Roddy Boyd, then at the *New York Post,* reported that Spector had already been fired "as a direct result of his handling" of the collapse of the two hedge funds. "Warren never got out in front on this," a source told Boyd. "In fact, it got worse on a daily basis and eventually put the firm at risk."

※

IT TURNED OUT to be a busy weekend at 383 Madison. First, Bear's increasingly bloated and illiquid balance sheet—$525 billion of assets on a $12 billion sliver of equity, a leverage ratio of nearly forty-four times—had caught the attention of the SEC, which was coming to meet with the firm on Sunday to talk about how to get the leverage down, fast. The problem was Bear had no way to convey easily to the SEC what the firm's assets looked like and how its funding was structured. On Saturday, while Cayne shot an 88—one of his better scores—at the Hollywood Golf Club, Friedman called the entire repo desk into the office to pull together a report he could use with the SEC the next day. "The whole desk came in," he said, "and spent the whole day—which shows you how fucked up our systems are—creating a funding report." The report showed the firm's assets by asset type, what its day-to-day funding looked like, and how that funding was rolling off in the coming months. "The picture was okay," Friedman said, "but you could see stress, and I thought the SEC was going to just jump all over us." Friedman met with the SEC at one o'clock Sunday and managed to assuage its concerns.

The other fire drill that weekend—organized by Steve Begleiter, the firm's head of strategy—was to "open the kimono" to KKR, the private equity firm whose founding partners had all worked at Bear Stearns a generation earlier. Begleiter had arranged for Deryck Maughan, the former CEO of Salomon Brothers who'd joined KKR in 2005 as chairman of KKR Asia, and his team of twenty to begin a preliminary review of Bear Stearns with the idea of making a large investment in the firm. The KKR meetings were Sunday morning, at the same time the Bear board of directors was meeting to decide Spector's fate. Both Cayne and Schwartz stopped by to say hello to Maughan. The idea was for KKR to inject several billion dollars into Bear in exchange for a 20 percent stake. "They were going to put a Good Housekeeping stamp of approval on us," Friedman said. "That was the theory. We spent all day Sunday with them." Various teams from Bear Stearns met seriatim with KKR to discuss the firm's funding, its mortgage positions, and its fixed-income business. "They had twenty guys prepared to spend as long as it took," Friedman said, "so that inside a week they could get to a point where they could say yes or no. It wasn't urgent."

On the afternoon of August 5, Bear Stearns's thirteen-member board of directors ratified Spector's demotion to a simple senior managing director at the firm until such time as the firm and he reached agreement on his departure. The firm announced that Spector had "resigned" his other positions at the firm, effective immediately. Bear announced that Schwartz would become the sole president of the firm, that Molinaro would add the title of chief operating officer to that of chief financial officer, and that Jeffrey

Mayer, co-head of fixed income, would replace Spector on the executive committee. Schwartz tried to convince Spector to stay on in some capacity, as a consultant of sorts to the firm. Schwartz even asked Jeff Mayer to intercede with Spector if he could. But Spector would not even consider the request. "On the one hand, he was a great guy to sacrifice," one of Spector's colleagues said. "On the other hand, he was a terrible guy to lose."

Monday was a day for spin and damage control. First, S&P released a statement suggesting that the markets might have overreacted. "Sprinzen, the weasel dick, publicly acknowledged that the market way overreacted, and that Bear Stearns fundamentally is sound, and the stock traded back up to $113," Upton said. "It was a complete overreaction in the marketplace. But that was indicative of how sensitive equity investors and, even more so, creditors were in that time frame." Cayne called other Wall Street chieftains, such as Chuck Prince, at Citigroup, and Stan O'Neal, at Merrill Lynch, to reassure them about the firm's financial health and to find out whether there was any truth to the rumor that Wall Street CEOs were meeting together to talk about Bear Stearns. (Apparently there wasn't.) He took calls from counterparties and reassured them as well. He called the firm's institutional investors reeling from the losses in the firm's stock.

Cayne also spent two hours off-air with CNBC's Charlie Gasparino, to whom he also squelched a rumor that the Federal Reserve had called Bear Stearns to "help it deal with a pending liquidity crisis." He said the purpose of the Friday conference call had been to try to put an end to the rumors. As for why he fired Spector, Cayne told Gasparino he had "lost confidence" in him after the collapse of the hedge funds. He also said an investigation at the hedge funds by Davis Polk partner Robert Fiske Jr. had turned up "preliminary problems of risk control," and since the funds were Spector's responsibility, the "ax fell on him." (In a brief interview, Fiske said he completed his investigation and made an oral report to the Bear Stearns audit committee about the hedge funds but that its contents were privileged.)

As for those who hoped that Spector's firing would lead to his own decision to step down as CEO by the end of the year, Cayne said: "Tell the people who say I'm going that in 2018 I'll be calling it a day." He also reiterated his desire to keep the firm "independent."

Some research analysts weren't buying the spin. "Jimmy Cayne's credibility is weak," Richard Bove, at Punk Ziegel, said. "To have to boast about their liquidity is a sign of terrible weakness and doesn't jibe with the record earnings they've been reporting quarter after quarter. He can't go from earning $35 million and saying he's aware of everything going on in his company and then suddenly saying, 'It's all Warren's fault' when something like this pops up." He said Cayne should resign and investors should sell their Bear Stearns stock because no one could tell what was going on at the firm. David Weidner, at Market Watch, viewed Spector's firing as the typical act of an aging Wall Street CEO feeling his own mortality. "Ultimately, Spector may have the last laugh," he wrote. "Cast into the wilderness, away from the place he had called home for 24 years, Spector is young enough to return to the industry in a better place. He has studied at the right hand of one of the toughest leaders on the Street. The odds are not against him. Meanwhile, Bear, Cayne and his new heir apparent, Alan Schwartz, have a wounded reputation to mend. And Schwartz might want to work on his resume."

On Monday morning, Alan Schwartz, now Cayne's sole heir apparent, told the fifty top executives of the firm, who had assembled in the twelfth-floor dining room, "These are the types of markets in which Bear Stearns excels."

The assembled group, including Cayne, gave Schwartz a standing ovation. Many in the audience saw the moment as an unofficial passing of the torch to Schwartz, who, if named CEO, would be the first investment banker in the firm's history to take the top job. John Rosenwald, a longtime investment banker at the firm and a vice chairman, was ecstatic. "I don't like him, I love him," Rosenwald told the *New York Times*.

In its coverage of the August 3 conference call and the weekend firing of Spector, the *Wall Street Journal* mentioned that Wall Street was "buzzing with speculation" that Bear Stearns might seek a strategic investor to bolster its relatively small capital base. The paper made no mention of KKR's visit to 383 Madison but did suggest that the firm might seek an investment from China Citic

Group, China's largest and most powerful investment bank. The paper mentioned Bear's discussion the previous year with China Construction Bank about buying a stake in Bear, although the talks apparently fizzled because the president of the Chinese bank left in the middle of the discussions. Supposedly, Donald Tang, a Bear Stearns vice chairman and native of China, was leading the efforts with China Citic.

On August 8, within a few days of Cayne's efforts to reassure the markets that the firm's capital base and liquidity were more than adequate, CNBC reported that Cayne was in the process of arranging for a trip to China to "seek a partnership and possibly a much-needed capital infusion from a Chinese firm."

It had turned out that the Chinese executive with whom Cayne had been discussing a deal at China Construction Bank the year before, Chang Zhenming, had been transferred by the Chinese government back to Citic, where he had worked previously, as a top executive. Cayne had also played bridge with Chang back in 1993 in the Great Hall during his first visit to China. Why not rekindle the discussion, Cayne thought.

ON AUGUST 9, evidence of the international spread of America's subprime crisis showed up in Paris when BNP Paribas, France's largest bank, ceased withdrawals from three investment funds, which had about $2 billion in assets on August 7, because the bank could no longer "fairly" value them due to a "complete evaporation of liquidity in certain market segments of the U.S. securitization market." BNP's action followed an August 3 announcement by Union Investment Management, Germany's third-largest mutual fund manager, that it had stopped permitting withdrawals from one of its funds after investors pulled out 10 percent of the fund's assets. Also on August 9, the European Central Bank injected £95 billion into the overnight lending market "in an unprecedented response to a sudden demand for cash from banks roiled by the subprime crisis," Bloomberg reported.

Upton believed the events of August 9 were a watershed. "All of a sudden, interbank markets and general liquidity conditions seized up, and that condition persisted off and on, in varying degrees of intensity, from August ninth right through the time that the Fed opened the window to the investment banks, which happened to correspond to on or around the day that we went kaput," he said. "I don't think that was pure coincidence, frankly. The decision was made that someone's got to experience some pain. This firm's had some scrapes with the regulators. No one really loves it that much."

On August 17, the Federal Reserve began to take its first steps to try to stanch the bleeding. The central bank cut interest rates by 50 basis points in recognition that "financial market conditions have deteriorated, and tighter credit conditions and increased uncertainty have the potential to restrain economic growth going forward." The Fed pledged to "act as needed to mitigate the adverse effects on the economy arising from the disruptions in financial markets." The Fed also announced that banks could borrow from the discount window "for as long as 30 days, renewable by the borrower," in order for banks to have "greater assurance about the cost and availability of funding." The new plan would remain in effect "until the Federal Reserve determines that market liquidity has improved materially." The two-pronged approach of lowering interest rates and effectively substituting the Fed's balance sheet for the balance sheets of the country's financial institutions, whether troubled or not, arose from a Fed off-site in Jackson Hole, Wyoming, during the third week of August 2007. New York Fed president Geithner dubbed this new approach to the growing crisis "the Bernanke doctrine."

WHILE CAYNE WAS preparing for his trip to China and KKR was still contemplating an investment in Bear Stearns (the buyout firm shortly thereafter decided to pass), other investors were lining up to take a look at whether it made sense to put money into the firm. "I was hoping we would try to do something with them," one Bear executive said of KKR. "We sort of backed off and they backed off. Jimmy thought it would look weak. He doesn't like to do things that look weak, and when he gets it in his mind that something is weak, that's something we don't do. I thought that was unfortunate because I thought that would have helped . . . once KKR is in, they can't not stay in." In mid-August, Christopher Flowers, of the eponymous private equity firm, came to 383 Madison to kick the tires about an investment in the firm for himself and, he claimed, for AIG. He met with Molinaro, Begleiter, and Friedman. But Flowers did not seem at all serious about the investment.

The firm also spent time with the Saudis' sovereign wealth fund. "We went very far down the path with the Saudis," Paul Friedman said. "We thought that they were going to make us a $10 billion loan and take a 20 percent equity stake." But that did not happen, either. Then there were the discussions with PIMCO, where several Bear Stearns alumni worked. "PIMCO was going to make around a $10 billion investment and was going to take out some equity," Friedman said. "PIMCO had a huge exposure to Bear as it was. Their funds were big buyers of our debt. On the asset management side, they were a big counterparty to us, so they had a lot of counterparty exposure. They had a lot of friends here, so they were an early call. I don't know how far that ever went. There was a lot of speculation in the press that that was really close to happening. I don't think so. I don't quite understand how PIMCO structurally would have done it."

In late August, the financial condition of the firm was continuing to deteriorate because the firm was unable to sell any of its illiquid assets and no counterparties were willing to write the firm any repos for terms longer than overnight. "All our funding is getting shorter and shorter," Friedman said, "and the rock of illiquid assets stays pretty much intact." Somehow, at the end of August, the firm was able to raise $2.5 billion in the institutional debt market. "We did a big victory lap for what we thought at the time was the worst deal in the history of the world," Friedman said. At the same time, there were so many discussions with third parties about making an investment in the firm that Friedman and Begleiter used to joke about it. Said Friedman: "I actually had a regular conversation with Steve Begleiter, which started with 'Have we sold the firm yet?' and I think the following day I went and grabbed him again and I said, 'Now can we sell the firm? Somebody please sell this fucking firm!'"

One of the many strategic discussions involved a potential merger with Fortress Investment Group, run by Wes Edens. Fortress, part hedge fund and part private equity fund, completed its IPO in February 2007. By September, the firm's market capitalization was around $8 billion, making it about half Bear's size. Tom Flexner, the Bear vice chairman, brought Edens in to meet Cayne. "Jimmy was loving the idea because, first of all, our asset management business had blown up with the hedge funds. Fortress had $38 billion of alternatives under management," Flexner said. "They bring a principal mentality, which I think Jimmy was beginning to realize you need for your core business, too, for your balance sheet. He was loving it. But he was definitely afraid of how Alan would view it. I disagreed with him. But from Jimmy's standpoint, it was, 'Well, if we do this, Wes isn't going to want to just run a little division. He's going to want to be CEO or something, and Alan would go crazy.'"

With Cayne's blessing, Flexner broached with Schwartz the idea of a merger between Bear Stearns and Fortress. "Alan was originally not enthusiastic about it because he thought it would be too dilutive on a book value basis," Flexner said. "But I said, 'That's ridiculous. We can't run our business based on book value only in today's world. You've got to look at the earnings power as well, not just book, but earnings power.'" Schwartz got sufficiently comfortable with considering the combination between Fortress and Bear Stearns that he allowed due diligence to proceed into the fall.

IN EARLY SEPTEMBER, over Labor Day weekend, Cayne and Tang (and Cayne's wife, Patricia) took Cayne's private jet from Allaire Airport, just south of Cayne's home in Elberon, New Jersey, for a secret overnight flight to Beijing. "We visited a few shops in Beijing," Tang said, before he and Cayne headed over to the St. Regis Hotel to meet the Citic executives for their quiet dinner. "We talked about a comprehensive tie-up between Citic Securities and Bear Stearns," he said. The idea was for Citic to make an equity investment in Bear Stearns and for Bear Stearns to make an investment in Citic in the form of convertible debt. Bear would then contribute its entire Asian operations, and Citic its entire non-China international operations, into a new company to be owned jointly by each firm. The joint venture would focus on business outside of China. "Their brand power can get us a lot more mandates in terms of all the financial industry business that we were aiming to do in Asia," Tang said. "Our technical expertise and capability both in Asia and in New York would be moved to the joint venture." Tang said the dinner was momentous for both firms. "Forget about the money that we were exchanging," he said. "It was really the vision and the strategic value of transforming Bear Stearns—at the time an also-ran in the business in China and in Asia—to become a significant powerhouse with Citic, the most significant player in China's investment banking world."

After the dinner, Tang devoted nearly every waking hour to reducing the oral agreement to a legal and binding contract. Teams from Citic came to New York and to Los Angeles, Tang's home, to negotiate the terms of the deal and to put together a memorandum of understanding. Tang also flew to Beijing every week to work toward getting the deal agreed and announced. There was some healthy skepticism in New York about the Citic deal. "We spent hundreds and hundreds of hours working on this thing," Paul Friedman said. "We sent people there. They sent people here. I sat in meeting after meeting trying to explain to huge delegations of Citic people what we did for a living in fixed income. If you had five years, it probably was a pretty good trade. Somewhere down the road, the Chinese were going to become more and more sophisticated in financial transactions. The theory was if nothing happened other than that we get some of the deal flow from Citic, that would pay for itself. In the long run, a pretty good thing; in the short run, insanity. To me it seemed like sort of a shell game, even beyond the fact that they were going to give us a billion dollars and we were going to give it back to them. It was a really good concept: Here is the preeminent broker-dealer in China. We get a venture with them at no cost. They're going to take us, use us, and work with us. But the venture covers non-China Asia. So what's Citic's involvement in Japan? None. So what do they bring to the table there? Nothing. We now take our Japanese employees and make them part of a joint venture with the Chinese, and there's only about a thousand years of hatred there. I never got that part. Structurally it was going to be really weird. When the firm blew up, we still hadn't resolved whether it was going to be called BearCitic or CiticBear. The managerial structure was unresolved. There were going to be co-CEOs, one from Bear and one from Citic. But that we were going to bank the whole revival of Bear Stearns on this Citic trade was like, 'What planet are we living on?' It made no sense." But the negotiations continued anyway.

While the rumor of a tie-up with Citic had been circulating since August, Cayne hoped to keep his trip as quiet as possible and figured that by going over the Labor Day weekend, when everyone else on Wall Street was at the beach, and returning home quickly, he would be able to keep news of the trip out of the business press. He succeeded. There was not even a hint of his trip in the papers when it happened. "We flew under the radar," Cayne said.

※

THE OTHER BIT of information the firm wanted to keep quiet was the fact that after Cayne returned from his trip to Beijing, he almost died. At six o'clock on the morning of September 11, Patricia Cayne placed an emergency medical call to her husband's physician, Dr. Jay Meltzer, a clinical professor of medicine at Columbia University with a private practice on Park Avenue. She told Meltzer that her husband was very weak and had no appetite. He also was having trouble drinking fluids and was experiencing dysuria, painful or slow urination. She reported that when she'd taken his temperature the night before, he had no fever. Cayne suffered from high blood pressure and Meltzer had prescribed medication for that, which he had been taking regularly. "I knew something serious had to be going wrong because this guy does not like to be sick," Meltzer said. When Meltzer arrived at the Caynes' Park Avenue apartment at around seven from his apartment on Central Park West, he took Cayne's blood pressure. "When I got there it was 133 sitting, with a pulse of 104, but when he stood up, his blood pressure fell to 116 and the pulse went up to 112," he said. "He was breathing very rapidly and deeply, which suggests that he's blowing off carbon dioxide, which is something you see in acidosis for kidney failure. He had no tremor, no edema. He was drowsy but he was responsive. His skin was very dry." Meltzer suspected he might have sepsis, an often lethal infection of the urinary tract. He decided Cayne needed to be brought to the emergency room immediately for a full examination to determine what was wrong. "It's not clear," he said, "and there's a limit to what you can do on the physical exam." Cayne seemed calm. "If he gets nervous or scared, he doesn't show that," Meltzer said. "He was saying, 'I don't really need this.' Like a lot of tough guys like that, they deny that they're [as] sick as they are, and it took a lot of convincing to get him to go to the hospital."

Meltzer decided not to call 911 or an ambulance. "He had a driver, and I thought that we could drive him to New York Hospital quite safely and get him there in time to do what we had to do," he said. "I kept it private." As they drove up in Cayne's dark sedan, Meltzer arranged for Dr. Mark Pecker, a nephrologist and an expert in emergency medicine, to treat Cayne. "I knew that Mark would take great care of him," Meltzer said. They arrived at the emergency room at eight-thirty in the morning. "Fortunately, Mark was available and he came down to the ER," he said. "We consulted together and [Cayne] was admitted to the intensive care. It turned out that he had a fever or leukocytosis, renal insufficiency, and dehydration, and he needed antibiotics and saline." The doctors also inserted a Foley catheter "to drain his bladder and get antibiotics in to treat the prostatitis, the acute inflammation of the prostate." According to Meltzer, Cayne "had the highest acute PSA elevation I've ever seen"—43—"and it proves that the infection was in the prostate itself." (Cayne's PSA levels fell to 0.4 after the infection was tamed.) Meltzer said that once the doctors figured out which "bug" was causing the infection—it turned out to be *E. coli*—and then treated it with antibiotics intravenously, "he began to turn the corner within a couple of days."

Cayne's recollection of the experience was far more apocalyptic. He remembered coming back from China, going to sleep, and "waking up in the hospital." He said that the doctor told his wife that his chances of making it out alive were fifty-fifty. "When I first went in," Cayne said, "that's when my blood pressure was 75 and the doctor went like this"—he pointed his thumbs down—"to Patricia. She said, 'He's going to be okay, right?' And he went like this"—thumbs down again—"and first of all, that's sort of dumb. Why a doctor would say that, why the doctor wouldn't say, 'Maybe, Good Lord willing everything will be fine,' I don't know. . . . For the next seven days she's like in a state of shock."

He started to recover after three days in the ICU and then was given his own private room. He was able to watch television, and he turned on CNBC and found that Charlie Gasparino was reporting inaccurately that Cayne was on his way to China, "hat in hand." Cayne was also not happy that Gasparino had reported on July 13 that Cayne was being investigated for allegedly cheating to win a July 4 golf tournament at Hollywood Golf Club. For his part, Gasparino, whom Cayne had given the nickname "Looney Tunes," was by this time angry at Cayne for giving an interview to Landon Thomas Jr. at the *New York Times*. Cayne, meanwhile, was thinking he was lucky to be alive. "I've already gone to China. I got the order and I feel good about that. But now I wonder, 'How in the world did this happen to me?'" Cayne stayed at the hospital another week or so and was out of the office for ten days total—a fact that was kept very quiet. "That came at a really bad time," Cayne said. "It came at a time where I had to hide the fact that I was in the hospital." He even returned to the office before he had fully recovered because he feared that Gasparino was on the verge of reporting that he had been out of the office for a long spell. He took Gasparino's call at his office at 383 Madison rather than have him think he was out.

After Cayne was out of the ICU, Donald Tang recalled, "I was there at the hospital for a very substantial amount of time. For hours and hours, throughout the day and night. Every time that he woke up, he asked about the Citic transaction, he asked about the stock price, he asks about the morale at the office. He had nothing else on his mind other than Bear Stearns. I don't want to get into details about how sick he was. He was totally beside himself. He was under *excruciating* pain. But the only thing he could think about is how he could do something about it. He wasn't thinking about [that] he's dying; rather, he was totally focused on the company."

❋

WHILE CAYNE WAS fighting for his life, the self-made British billionaire recluse Joe Lewis, aka "the Boxer," started amassing a large equity stake in Bear Stearns. On September 10, the day before Cayne went into the hospital, Lewis filed a report with the SEC stating that he owned close to 8.1 million shares, or nearly 7 percent, of the company's stock, making him the largest single shareholder. Lewis started his buying spree on July 20, paying around $145 per share, and then accelerated his buying in August and September as the price of the stock fell. He purchased 1.2 million shares on September 7 for $104.93. Lewis had been a longtime client of Bear broker Kurt Butenhoff, a close confidant of Cayne's. Many in the press speculated that Cayne had encouraged Lewis to buy the Bear Stearns stock because of their connection through bridge.

Although Cayne acknowledged spending time with Lewis at his massive spread in Orlando, Florida, he denied being the person who'd convinced Lewis to invest in Bear Stearns. That responsibility seemed to belong to Butenhoff, according to CNBC. Others are not sure that Cayne was not more directly involved in helping to convince Lewis that the Bear stock had fallen sufficiently far to be worth a serious look. "I do know that Jimmy Cayne has always been willing to talk confidentially to large shareholders before earnings announcements, and I have talked to Jimmy about the law in this area," one Bear executive said. "Joe Lewis was probably one that Jimmy talked to before he invested. Kurt Butenhoff was a broker and Joe Lewis was his client. Jimmy liked Kurt a lot. Kurt got Joe in front of Jimmy. They played golf together and smoked cigars."

At first, Lewis did not look so smart. On September 20, Bear Stearns reported third-quarter earnings of $171.3 million, down 62 percent from the $438 million the firm had earned a year before. Net revenues had fallen 38 percent. The results also included approximately $200 million in losses and expenses related to the High-Grade Fund. Not surprisingly, given the markets, the firm's main problems were to be found in the fixed-income division, where revenue fell to $118 million, down 88 percent from the $945 million of revenues in that business a year earlier.

A week later, Joe Lewis looked like a genius. On September 26, the *New York Times* reported that Warren Buffett, the legendary investor, appeared close to buying a 20 percent stake in Bear Stearns and that Buffett had contacted Cayne, his old bridge friend, about the potential investment. The paper also reported that Bank of

America, Wachovia, China Construction Bank, and Citic were considering investments in Bear Stearns. Bear's stock leapt $8.76 on the news, closing at $123 per share. By October 2, the stock was back to $129. Nothing about the potential Buffett bid, of course, was certain (or even accurate, Buffett said later). "But the decline in Bear's share price and its relative value—it trades slightly above its book value—has stoked the interest of outside investors," wrote Landon Thomas Jr. "Previously, Mr. Cayne negotiated from a position of strength, always reserving the right to walk away if a deal did not meet his standards. The firm seems to have survived the worst of the summer crisis, but its continuing exposure to a moribund mortgage market and its need to expand its presence in faster-growing overseas markets have made the prospect of a capital infusion, matched with the expertise and prestige of an outside partner, more compelling."

In an interview with the *Financial Times,* Cayne reiterated Thomas's view that the worst had passed for the firm. "Most of our businesses are beginning to rebound," he said. "I'm confident that Bear Stearns will weather the storm and come out a stronger, more diversified and greater organization." He also said that many of the firm's prime brokerage clients who had pulled money out of the firm in August had since "moved all their money back." Tom Marano, the firm's global head of mortgages, told the *FT* that the market had started to rebound. "It definitely feels better," he said. "Volatility has come down and we have seen significant purchases from investors all the way down through the non-investment-grade tranches of deals." Even in the early October press about an investigation by the U.S. Attorney's Office in the Eastern District of New York into the collapse of Bear's hedge funds, Cayne found reason for optimism. He said he was "confident in our future and our business, and we see compelling value in our own stock." Indeed, such was the optimism at the firm that, as part of the firm's third-quarter earnings announcement, the board authorized an increase to $2.5 billion in the firm's stock buyback program, from $2 billion.

The optimism continued at the October 4 investor day. Schwartz, Molinaro, Marano, Jeff Mayer, and Jeff Lane spoke of the great opportunities that lay ahead for Bear Stearns. Schwartz spoke about the growth in Bear's international business and of the "dynamic growth in Europe and Asia"—where Bear Stearns had never before spent much time or money—and noted that the firm's overseas year-to-date revenues of $1.4 billion had already surpassed the 2006 annual total. Understandably, he spoke about Bear's bright spots, not its problem areas, such as fixed income (the home of its increasingly toxic assets) and asset management (the home of its problem hedge funds). In his presentation, Molinaro focused on the progress the firm had made in shifting its funding mix from short-term unsecured borrowings to longer-term secured borrowings. He compared the firm's performance in the third quarter of 2007 to the firm's quarterly performance during other market "dislocations" in 1994 and 1998. In some ways, he pointed out, the prior two hiccups had been even worse. The key issue, he mused, "was the length and severity of the market correction." As part of the investor day, Lane, Mayer, and Marano also spoke about how well positioned their businesses were for the difficult market ahead. Inside the firm, this improvement seemed real. "Actually, September and October were pretty good," Friedman said. "Right after Labor Day, things got better again."

Cayne's return to 383 Madison, in improving health, meant that the man pushing the Citic deal forward was also back in the saddle. He drove his subordinates hard to get the deal signed up and announced, even though the $1 billion in cash the firm would receive from the Chinese would go right out the door again when Bear Stearns bought $1 billion worth of convertible debt in Citic. Above all, Cayne thought the strategic importance of the deal trumped the detail about whether or not the firm would actually raise badly needed capital. "We're undersized in Asia," one senior Bear executive explained, "and the short of it was Citic was probably the best entity—not just Citic Securities but the whole Citic Group—for us to align ourselves with. They were really the mother lode. It was quite a coup for us to have this opportunity."

Citic's one requirement was that Bear Stearns agree to sell them half of its non-China Asia business so Citic could begin to grow outside of China. Citic had spoken to Lehman and Citigroup about a similar deal, but these firms had declined. The problem for Bear was that it didn't really have half of an Asian business to sell Citic. "It's not like we can say, 'Here's the income statement and balance sheet,'" this executive said. "Our revenues in Asia were booked in dozens of different legal entities. Capital comes from somewhere. Derivative trades are booked somewhere else. Different departments allocate costs and revenues amongst regions differently." To actually put together a financial statement for the business was "really hard; it doesn't exist," he said. Additionally, he observed, "It's the fastest-growing region in the world and it's going very quickly for us, so why would we want to give up half the upside? Especially since we had gone from not making money to just making a little bit of money but we had big expectations. We were selling it at the wrong time. What we thought we needed to get from it was . . . an opportunity in China. It's very hard to know how to get an opportunity in China. What I argued for was, 'Well, why don't we get a revenue share on Citic securities?' because then you can just account for one number. We can work with them to grow new businesses. Any way that they win, we know we're getting paid. If we're giving up half of our growth in non-China Asia and non-Japan Asia, we need to get something in China. The revenue share is the lowest-risk, the easiest to keep track of, and the best alignment of our interests. I eventually persuaded Jimmy and Alan to allow us to ask for that in the term sheet."

At first, Citic agreed to give Bear the revenue-sharing agreement, albeit at a lower percentage than the firm hoped. But then, after Citic spoke with "some regulator" in China, the revenue-sharing agreement was withdrawn. "This started a process of where the deal got less and less good," this executive said. "Every time the deal gets less and less good, you're entitled to say, 'I don't want to do it anymore,' or you're entitled to say, 'Even though it's less and less good, I want to do it anyway.'" But regardless of how the deal changed—usually for the worse for Bear Stearns—Cayne kept pushing it forward. "There was nothing that could change in the deal where he would not want to do it," the executive said. One day in mid-October Cayne called this executive to his office. "Congratulations," Cayne said. "The deal is done. We're announcing it Monday."

"What's done?" he said.

"Well, that term sheet," Cayne said. "They agreed to it."

"Jimmy, that's not a document," his partner said. "That's deal points. There's a lot of stuff that's missing from it."

"Well, they agreed to it and we're announcing it Monday," Cayne replied.

The deal contained the idea of a cross-investment. "Jimmy, we haven't done any due diligence on the company," he said. "Can we delay the announcement a week and go visit the company? Other than Donald [Tang], nobody's been there. I have nothing bad to say about Donald—Donald's great at what he does—but he does not like digging through the financial statements of things we put $1 billion into for a living."

The executive said that "Jimmy almost took my head off. That's one of the few times he yelled at me. He said, 'We're doing this. I don't know what you are going to learn on the diligence. We're going to do it anyway. It's a great thing for us.'"

ON OCTOBER 22, Bear Stearns announced the deal with Citic. The agreement "in principle"—meaning the deal still needed almost everything, including signed documentation and approval by both boards of directors and various government agencies in the United States and China—could be canceled at any time. The two sides had agreed to work together exclusively to bring the deal Cayne and Tang negotiated in Beijing on September 3 to fruition. If it closed, each firm would make a $1 billion investment in the other—Citic's would be in the form of equity; Bear's would be in the form of convertible debt—and a new joint venture would be created in Hong Kong comprising each side's non-China Asia businesses. Despite the fact that investment banking joint ventures have a horrendous record of actually succeeding, both Citic and Bear Stearns trumpeted the deal. Wang Dongming, Citic's chairman, said the Bear Stearns partnership was ideal because of its "client-focused culture, sophisticated analytical systems and deep capital markets expertise. . . . We look forward to working effectively with Jimmy Cayne and Bear Stearns' talented management team and employees in the years ahead." For his part, Cayne called the deal "a groundbreaking alliance" that "would give Bear Stearns a unique footprint in one of the world's fastest growing economies through a strategic partnership with a premier market leader." The $1 billion investment that each firm planned to make would translate into a roughly 6 percent stake of each firm in the other.

In an interview with the *Financial Times,* Cayne called the Citic deal "the best to cross [my] desk in 40 years" and likened the Chinese investment bank to the New York Yankees. "This could either be just good for us or it could be very good," he said. He also made crystal-clear that the firm neither needed nor wanted a capital infusion from an outside investor. "We have been very clear that we have zero interest in a capital infusion," he said, and noted that the firm had close to $20 billion in cash. But the market was underwhelmed by the deal. The stock barely budged on the news, closing around $116 per share for the day, and the research analysts were blasé. Susan Katzke, at Credit Suisse, said the deal "was not the sale some were hoping for," but thought it was a decent strategic move. Michael Hecht, at Bank of America, worried that "joint ventures look good on paper strategically and are always tough to execute, particularly with a strong culture like [Bear Stearns]." He also wondered what happened to the "capital infusion." The *New York Times* observed, "The venture does not directly address Bear Stearns' balance sheet. Some investors and analysts have suggested that the firm could require a capital infusion because of its high exposure in the moribund mortgage market. But Bear Stearns has often said such an infusion is not necessary, and its deal with Citic seems to be an expression of confidence in Bear Stearns."

Behind the scenes and after the public announcement, the real work began of trying to bring the deal together. "We eventually did go and kick tires, and learn about the company," said a senior executive who worked on the deal. "We learned some stuff we wish we knew beforehand. We got a large team of people working on getting some sort of pro forma financial together. We had dozens of people working on it. What was very clear was that there was a very opaque approval process in China. And as things started to sour, what was also clear to me was that the Citic money was never coming in if we needed it. . . . If we didn't need the money, they would put it in. If we needed the money, they weren't putting it in unless maybe somebody else put in the money and they wanted to participate. There was certainly an element in our capital-raising thinking of 'Well, we got the $1 billion coming in from Citic, and that's something.' But most people, even Jimmy probably, thought there was always some element of conditionality to that money. To the extent anybody thought that the Citic money counted, they were deluding themselves. The market gave us no credit for that. I gave us no credit for that. I think others gave us no credit for that. I don't know if Alan or Sam or Jimmy gave us credit for that. They shouldn't have."

CHAPTER 30

THE CAYNE MUTINY

The problem for Bear Stearns, as the fall rolled on, was that events were no longer happening in a vacuum. The cancer that had been revealed in Bear's two hedge funds in June had now metastasized and spread throughout the world. On September 13, Northern Rock, one of the largest retail banks in England, sought liquidity support from the Bank of England. Four days later, the Bank of England guaranteed all of the bank's deposits. (Shortly thereafter, Northern Rock was nationalized.) On September 25, Moody's warned that the subprime "infection" had spread to companies such as AMBAC and MBIA that insure bonds of other companies and that these insurers would need more capital. On September 26, Chris Flowers, Bank of America, and JPMorgan Chase announced that they were all backing out of their previously announced $25 billion deal to buy and take private Sallie Mae, the student loan company. (Much threatened litigation followed before a settlement was reached and the deal scuttled.) Then came a myriad of write-downs among financial institutions—$5.9 billion at Citigroup, billions of dollars of home equity and leveraged loans at UBS, close to $1 billion of home loans at Washington Mutual—and Merrill Lynch was placed on "credit watch" due to impending losses and "poor risk management." Both Merrill Lynch and Citigroup were suffering billions of dollars in losses from their exposure to mortgage securities, and the drumbeat had started among investors and the financial press to blame their CEOs for the massive and unprecedented losses. On October 26, Merrill Lynch CEO Stan O'Neal "retired" and the firm gave him a $161 million pay package to ease his pain. On November 2 Citigroup CEO Chuck Prince offered to resign, and his offer was accepted. He walked off with $40 million.

Firms were also raising dramatic amounts of capital to replenish the equity written off as a result of these toxic assets. Citigroup raised $7.5 billion from investors in the Middle East. Freddie Mac raised $6 billion. Fannie Mae raised $7 billion. UBS raised $11.5 billion after taking a $10 billion write-down related to subprime mortgages. Merrill Lynch raised $6.2 billion and then another $6.6 billion; Morgan Stanley raised $5 billion.

Bear Stearns did nothing. In typical fashion, Cayne and Bear Stearns continued marching to their own drummer. There was no talk about raising capital. There was no talk of a Cayne coup. In fact, after the Citic deal, Cayne seemed more emboldened than ever and determined to stay in place, despite being seventy-three years old and having Alan Schwartz as his designated successor. There was also little likelihood of a genuine capital infusion finding its way onto Bear Stearns's balance sheet—although efforts to do so were ongoing—since Cayne had nixed the idea so publicly. The reasons Cayne and Schwartz were so dead set against raising equity capital were complicated. Part of it was that raising equity capital would be both a sign of strength and a sign of weakness, with Cayne thinking that, on balance, weakness was the more likely message. There was also his belief that the stock was way too cheap, at around $115 per share, to sell a big slug of it to a third party. After all, Cayne had only sold tiny amounts of his large stock holdings, so why should the firm sell at these deflated prices? There was also the feeling—shared by both Cayne and Schwartz—that capital should not just be obtained simply to prove the firm could raise capital; rather, it should be raised to serve some greater strategic purpose, such as in the case of the Citic deal (although technically no fresh capital was raised).

Part of the reason for their ongoing reluctance—which they of course deny—was that the executive committee got compensated based on the calculation of the firm's return on equity (net income divided by the firm's book value). Any increase in equity would increase the firm's book value dollar for dollar and would reduce the firm's return on equity, especially in a declining market for Bear Stearns's products. Any equity capital raised would immediately mean a smaller bonus pool for the executive committee.

But below the executive committee, the senior executives were still pushing various strategic initiatives, even after the Citic deal. Discussions were continuing with Fortress and its CEO, Wes Edens. "They have an awful lot of very smart people at Fortress," Paul Friedman said. "There were many of us who felt that the notion of a massive infusion of talent and brainpower was very appealing." But there were numerous issues that made that deal difficult to consummate. On one hand, there was the problem of the differing compensation systems at the two firms: Bear Stearns had the typical compensation structure favored by public Wall Street firms of paying bankers and traders relatively small salaries and then, depending on the revenue they generated in a given year, huge bonuses as well. This system resulted in millions of dollars in annual compensation for a wide swath of the firm's population, without a corresponding way of holding the bankers and traders responsible financially for their actions. By contrast, Fortress's compensation system was the typical one found in hedge funds and private equity firms (Fortress had both business lines), where, generally speaking, the firm received a 2 percent annual fee of funds under management plus 20 percent of the annual upside of a fund's performance. Combining these two plans was a high hurdle.

There was also a problem of meshing the firm's two business plans and the potential conflicts that might create for Bear Stearns in the market. "What Fortress did for a living was buy illiquid assets, way more illiquid than the stuff that we had," Paul Friedman said, "and fund it on really good and aggressive terms from the Street. It was such a huge fee payer to the Street that it could use that to leverage what it needed to run its business. Can you imagine a Fortress/Bear person calling up Goldman Sachs and saying, 'Listen, we need three-year nonrecourse financing on this aircraft because we're going to pay you some fees next year'? Slam that door! I didn't see any way Fortress could get any of the things done that it did if it were affiliated with a dealer. Not just us, but any Wall Street dealer. If they had been part of Goldman Sachs and we got the same call, we'd tell them to take a hike."

But probably the biggest impediment to the deal was Edens's desire to be named the CEO of the combined firm, a slightly audacious request given that Bear Stearns had twice the market capitalization of Fortress at the time. On the other hand, there was no question that Edens, a hedge fund manager, had a better understanding of capital markets, trading, and mortgage securities than did Schwartz, an M&A advisor. "When the dust settles, Wes was going to be the CEO of Bear Stearns," Friedman said. "It was the linchpin of the whole thing and, my understanding is, one of the many reasons it fell apart. I didn't get the trade at all. I didn't understand it." Complicating the transaction further was the fact that Fortress itself started having financial problems by the end of 2007. "They were having their own issues in a big way," Friedman said. "They were having P&L issues. They were having liquidity issues. I think it just sort of withered away. I'm not sure at what point somebody pulled the plug, but I had heard that we killed it over the issue of Wes being CEO." Soon enough, there would be other serious overtures as well, including from Sumitomo Bank, in Japan; PIMCO, the huge California bond fund; and ResCap, the residential mortgage business of General Motors Acceptance Corporation, or GMAC, a portfolio company of Cerberus, the hedge fund and private equity firm. These would all be turned down as well. The firm was simply too insular and too wedded to the status quo to consider any transformative transaction. "Very few people came in from the outside into senior positions," one longtime Bear executive said, "and those that did often didn't last very long and were not ultimately accepted in the culture. The people who really did well were lifers. Jimmy was a lifer, Ace was a lifer, Warren was a lifer, Alan was a lifer. . . . They all grew up in that culture and they could speak it and they didn't really do well interacting with outsiders."

Whatever modicum of control Cayne thought he might have

had over his own and Bear Stearns's destiny—his moral authority to run the firm, his ability to be Solomonic in his decisions, and his ability to steer the firm through its most significant crisis of confidence ever—all changed after the morning of November 1, when the *Wall Street Journal* published a devastating front-page account of Jimmy Cayne and his odd behavior during the summer's crisis. While Cayne and Bear Stearns had never been known for the ability that some others on Wall Street had to manipulate the press into writing or broadcasting fawning stories, the *Journal*'s story, written by Kate Kelly, was the worst kind of publicity imaginable at precisely the wrong moment and accelerated an already unfolding series of crucial events in the firm's denouement.

Kelly reported that Cayne was playing bridge "during 10 critical days of this crisis" in Nashville "without a cell phone or email device." She reported—incorrectly—that Cayne had left the "tense" August 3 conference call "after a few opening words and listeners didn't know when he returned" (the truth, of course, was much worse). She reported that Cayne had been out of the office playing golf or bridge for "10 of the 21 workdays" during the "critical month of July." Kelly made sure to include comments that refuted the central thrust of her article. "Anyone who thinks that Jimmy Cayne isn't fired up every day and ready to get to work hasn't been living in my world," Schwartz told the *Journal*. Schwartz noted that Cayne had flown to Beijing over Labor Day weekend to agree to the Citic deal. Kelly contrasted Cayne's "actions amid the turmoil" to the "hands-on roles of peers" across Wall Street. She even noted that Lloyd Blankfein, Goldman's CEO, "cancelled plans to spend the last two weeks of August at his beach house, missing a chance to spend time with his sons before they headed to college," in order to take control of the unfolding crisis at his desk.

Kelly also reported that Cayne had rebuffed Jamie Dimon's 2002 offer to have Bank One buy Bear Stearns and would only consider it "for a significant stock price premium, a big personal payout and the use of a private jet." She wrote that Cayne hated to travel for business and refused to meet with President Bush in Washington to discuss economic issues. If Bush wanted to talk to Cayne, they could meet in New York. But of all Kelly's zingers, the most embarrassing personally and professionally was the one that accused Cayne of being a regular consumer of marijuana. "After a day of bridge at a Doubletree hotel in Memphis, in 2004, Mr. Cayne invited a fellow player and a woman to smoke pot with him, according to someone who was there, and led the two to a lobby men's room where he intended to light up," Kelly reported. "The other player declined, says the person who was there, but the woman followed Mr. Cayne inside and shared a joint, to the amusement of a passerby." She also wrote that Cayne "used pot in more private settings, according to people who say they witnessed him doing so or participated with him." In the article, Cayne "denied emphatically" the alleged pot-smoking incident at the Doubletree. "There is no chance it happened," he said. "Zero chance." He told the paper he would not answer questions about whether he smoked pot generally and would respond only "to a specific allegation."

Kelly also reported on the "summertime ritual" of Cayne's $1,700 Thursday afternoon helicopter trips from New York City to the Hollywood Golf Club, followed by the rounds of golf on Friday, Saturday, and Sunday, followed by going home for "several hours of online poker and bridge and to play with his grandchildren." Kelly and her boss, Michael Siconolfi, had had lunch with Cayne on July 12 at 383 Madison, where, Kelly reported, "Mr. Cayne seemed less interested in discussing the markets than in talking about a breakfast-cereal allergy and his stash of unlabeled Cuban cigars. On another occasion, he told a visitor he pays $140 apiece for the cigars, keeping them in a humidor under his desk." For his part, Cayne does not deny the conversation at lunch with Siconolfi and Kelly but said it "was off the record," which Kelly and Siconolfi violated. As for the August 3 analyst call, Kelly reported that there was silence after he was asked a question because Cayne had "been summoned out by a lawyer advising him on the pending departure of Mr. Spector, who by then was planning to resign. Mr. Cayne later returned, but the hundreds of listeners weren't told this, leaving them with the impression that the CEO had left the call altogether." As previously noted, of course, Cayne was there, according to people in the room, but did not know how to answer the question asked about stock buybacks. "The following day, a Saturday, Mr. Cayne scored a respectable 88 at the Hollywood golf course," Kelly reported. She concluded the article with the idea that Cayne was concerned about his legacy, and she quoted John Angelo, a former Bear professional turned hedge fund manager who was Cayne's frequent golf partner at Hollywood. "It's one thing if you're 55," Angelo said. "It's another if you're 73." Angelo added that after the summertime events at Bear Stearns it would take "periods of time to get your reputation back."

❀

CAYNE IMMEDIATELY WENT into damage control mode. He told Gasparino: "It's unbelievable, the phones are ringing off the hook, and everyone wants to play golf with me." His assistant sent out a 108-word "Dear Colleagues" e-mail to the Bear Stearns family: "*The Wall Street Journal* today published an article criticizing my leadership of Bear Stearns. I stand by the record of success the firm has had over the 14 years I have had the privilege of leading this great organization. I remain, as I have been for many years, intensely focused on our business. The article also alleges I engaged in inappropriate conduct outside the firm. As I stated in the story, this is absolutely untrue. Thank you for your continued dedication to Bear Stearns, and don't be distracted by the noise. I am certainly not. Jimmy."

Cayne was pissed. He believed Siconolfi and his "spawn," Gasparino and Kelly, were out to get him. (Despite Cayne's anger at Gasparino, he would occasionally talk to him, as Cayne thought him a useful way to get information out in the market.) But he took comfort from the support he received from the Bear Stearns family. "You can get me on the phone anytime, anywhere, anytime," he said. "There's no protocol. There's nothing. It's simple. That's how you do it. That's how you create loyalty. These people would jump off a cliff for me. That's how I feel. And whether it's true or not is almost unimportant, because the bottom line is that's what I walk around with. That's my salvation. I don't feel good about being that little piñata that gets the shit kicked out of it. But I also consider the sources. I consider Looney Tunes on the tube as being just a snake of massive proportions. But there isn't anybody that doesn't think he's a snake. The cunt at *The Wall Street Journal* whose capability is zero but spawned by Siconolfi."

Cayne also saw Warren Spector's fingerprints all over the article. "Spector got some bridge player to call up the *Journal*, with" Sitrick & Co., Spector's "strategic communications" firm, "greasing the skids," Cayne said. He called Michael Sitrick a "murderer" and a "pure assassin" who "planted the article in the *Journal*." He said the article was "interesting because they never had a source, [it was] all bullshit." Cayne said he told the firm's communications team he doubted whether the *Journal* would ever print the name of the person who accused him of smoking marijuana at the bridge tournament. At first the paper had told him it would print the name; then, he said, the paper changed its mind and called him the night before to tell him there would be no name. The firm tried to convince the *Journal* not to run the article since there was no named accuser. But the *Journal* ran the story anyway. "Then there's this story about smoking marijuana with some broad in a bathroom. What are the chances of that?" For his part, Sitrick acknowledged being hired by Spector but denied that either he or Spector had any involvement in the *Journal* story. "The first time I learned about that alleged incident was when I read about it in *The Wall Street Journal*," he said.

At the time, Cayne said, he did not recognize what the consequences of that article would be. "It was far more serious when you look at it in retrospect than it was at the time," he said. "It was just massively irritating." But Cayne was in the fight of his professional life. Aside from the titillation of the pot-smoking allegation, there was genuine concern on both Wall Street and at Bear Stearns with what the fallout at the firm would be in the fourth quarter—ended November 30—from its exposure to hard-to-value "Level 3 assets," of which Bear had $20 billion, including $2.4 billion in subprime mortgages. A write-down of even a portion of these assets could wipe out a material part of the firm's $12 billion capital account—an account that Cayne decided not to add to with outside capital, unlike most other Wall Street firms by November 2007.

Not surprisingly, Bear's board of directors was unhappy with the unflattering press coverage. "It was a particularly bad article at a bad time," Vince Tese said. "A very unfair article, I thought. I have dealt with the press a lot, being in government. I find it particularly troubling when they use unnamed sources to slander people. I told that to Kate Kelly, and she said, 'Well, you've gone off the record.' I said, 'Yeah, I've gone off the record. But never to say anything bad about anybody.' I think that if you're going to accuse somebody of something, you should do it on the record. One of the great things about America is you can confront your accusers. But they had a strong feeling—and probably they were told by a lot of people—that Jimmy did some of the things in those articles. They decided to print it. Whether it was germane or not for him being chief executive is something totally different. But the article hurt.

"Jimmy is a very smart guy," Tese continued. "He's a very no-BS guy. Appearances don't mean anything to him. The things that mean stuff to him are the facts and the actual merits of doing this or not doing that. Jimmy coming up from the bridge game [during the crisis], to Jimmy wasn't that important. Because what could he have done? He was on the phone all the time. Him being there wouldn't have changed the outcome at all. That's the way he looked at it. But, you know, it's almost like George Bush not going to New Orleans the day after the hurricane. He got roundly criticized for it. But what is George Bush going to do? Fix a levee? He can do everything he can from Washington. But he should have been there, only because people wanted him there. By coming back to New York, Jimmy would have helped his own cause. I don't think he would have helped the Bear Stearns cause. But he would have helped his own cause, probably, if he would have come right back."

Then there were the bankers and traders in fixed income who remained quite unhappy that Cayne had fired Spector unceremoniously and then brought embarrassing media attention to the firm. "Around us, firms are getting rid of the people who did things wrong," Paul Friedman said. "What did we do? We got rid of the only guy who understood how our biggest business works, and we're being run by this idiot. So there were a whole bunch of us that went to Alan, individually and jointly, and kept saying to him, 'You've got to do something about this.' He kept saying, 'Don't worry. We're working on it. Jimmy's going to retire in due time. Don't worry. Don't worry.' Weeks and weeks and weeks go by and nothing. We in fixed income were probably the most arrogant about a lot of things, but we were also the angriest about losing Warren. Even as much as we blamed Warren for a lot of stuff, we were pretty angry about losing Warren. There were three of us who were particularly vocal: Dave Schoenthal, Mike Nierenberg, and myself. . . . Nierenberg, I think, called Alan once a day and said, 'When are you getting rid of Jimmy? You've got to get rid of Jimmy.' To his credit, Alan said a couple of times, 'He's not mine to fire,' but basically he said, 'Don't worry. It's gonna happen.' We bugged Molinaro about it. We bugged Steve Begleiter about it. It was like screaming into the wilderness, 'Somebody, do something about this guy. Won't somebody rid me of this man?'"

The firm's pride had been wounded. "All of us had been there forever," he continued. "Rookies at the firm had been there fifteen years and took a lot of pride in this place. It was killing us to get laughed at publicly. Charlie Gasparino on an hourly basis making fun of Jimmy. Just on and on. In addition to feeling insecure from a business standpoint, he really wasn't doing anything. He had no impact on our business. It's not like they were going to get rid of Jimmy and bring back Warren. It wasn't going to solve any of our problems. But we were just tired of being humiliated. That seems kind of petty at this point, but we were already in a bunker, backs to each other, firing out at the enemy, and then we've got this thing. We've got this Uncle Fester guy who is running the firm."

Were these the seeds of the Cayne mutiny? "Yeah," Friedman said, "except that we didn't do it. We talked about it. . . . We could have gotten twenty guys among the most senior to go up to Alan's office. We talked about staging a sit-in: 'Let's go have a mutiny. Let's go tell them we're quitting if they don't do it. Yeah, yeah, we should do that. We should do that,' and we all went back to our day jobs. We never did it."

❋

ON NOVEMBER 14, Molinaro gave a presentation to investors at a Merrill Lynch conference, and if they squinted hard, they could have left the meeting feeling that Bear Stearns's prospects were as good as ever. He spoke about the firm's thriving energy business— Bear had just completed the acquisition of all the power assets of Williams Power Company—its booming international business and equity businesses, and its restored global clearing and prime brokerage businesses. In investment banking, the firm's revenues were expected to grow at a 12 percent annualized compounded rate. It was just the kind of upbeat presentation one would expect the CFO of a large Wall Street firm to deliver. Of course, he did share with investors a slide that updated the firm's "risk exposure" to November 9, from August 31, the end of the previous quarter. Since the end of August, Molinaro noted, the firm had "gone through an exhaustive process of revaluing [its] mortgage and CDO portfolios" and had "materially reduced" its exposure to those assets. He then dropped a bombshell. "As a result," he said, "the company will be taking a net write-down of approximately $1.2 billion on these positions and others in our mortgage inventory. . . . The vast majority of these losses are attributable to write-downs on the CDO and CDO warehouse portfolio."

Molinaro also announced that the firm's write-downs in its mortgage portfolio would "suffice" and that it had "significantly increased" its short position on subprime mortgages since August 31. Now the firm had a net negative position of $52 million from what had been a net positive position of $1.1 billion. In a statement filed with the SEC the next day, the firm announced that for the first time in its eighty-four-year history, it expected to have a quarterly loss as a result of the $1.2 billion write-down. The firm's stock closed that day at $103.45, up $2.58, after having traded as high as $111.01. That same day, Moody's, the rating agency, announced it "may cut" Bear's A1 debt rating, which would affect approximately $87.3 billion of debt. "Bear's performance through the market inflection and dislocation has been more challenged than at some competitors, and reflects not only tough markets, but certain risk and strategic decisions made by the firm," Blaine Frantz, Moody's senior vice president, said in the statement. "This includes the decision to extend financing to one of its in-house structured products hedge funds, which increased Bear's on-balance sheet exposure to these problematic assets and ultimately contributed to the write-downs."

A week after Thanksgiving, on November 29, the firm announced a third round of job cuts, some 650 people, or 4 percent of the global workforce of 15,500. The previous month Bear had cut

300 jobs. Before that, the firm had cut 600 jobs from its mortgage origination business, which obviously had slowed considerably. In a memo to all employees, the firm said the new cuts were part of "an ongoing review to best position Bear Stearns for 2008 and beyond." On the news, Bear's stock increased $4.07 per share, to close at $99.50.

By this time, Cayne had already decided unilaterally that the executive committee would not get bonuses for 2007. Cayne did not consult Greenberg about this decision. He just announced it at an executive committee meeting. "He didn't like not getting paid," Cayne said of Greenberg. "I said the executive committee isn't getting paid and didn't discuss it. Everybody agreed. But he didn't say anything. But it's about him. You're a piece of meat. I'm a piece of meat. His kid's a piece of meat. His everything is a piece of meat. His dogs are pieces of meat. I guess he couldn't imagine that that would happen. Without him being told. Or have it discussed. But it was so automatic."

Cayne did not fully appreciate how upset this decision had made Greenberg until he went to Greenberg's eightieth-birthday party dinner at the Harmonie Club in November. He went by himself because his wife was at Bible class—she is a born-again Hasidic Jew—and he went up to Kathryn Greenberg to kiss her on both cheeks. "And this ice came out of nowhere," Cayne said. "Have you ever been iced before? Really iced? I would bet against it. She was standing there by herself. I walked over and I went to kiss her, and ice."

❧

CAYNE SPENT THE last week of November and the first two days of December playing bridge in San Francisco at the Reisinger Board-a-Match Teams, the premier event of the fall North American Championships. Cayne and his team won the championship by a wide margin. When he came back to the office on December 3, Schwartz and Tese came to see him and told him that Greenberg wanted to quit Bear Stearns and work somewhere else. Schwartz and Tese asked Cayne to talk to Greenberg. "First of all, I didn't give a shit if he left or not," Cayne said. "He's eighty years old. Who cares? But I said I would attempt to talk sense into him. His leaving would have been another straw. They thought. I didn't."

Cayne went to Greenberg's office on the fifth floor. "I sit down with him," Cayne said. "He says, 'I'm not respected here. I've just decided to move.' I said, 'Well, okay, let's go through the paces. Let's start with a couple of thoughts. Number one, it wasn't any longer than three weeks ago that we had a dinner, an *Institutional Investor* all-star dinner for the analysts. We have it every year. You go to it every year. I go to it every year. There are eighty to a hundred people in the room. It's a Bear Stearns feel-good.' . . . I stand up. I said, 'Well, let's not forget who started this whole thing, Alan Greenberg.' He said, 'Yes, that was nice. I remember that.' I said, 'So the idea that you're not getting respect, I challenge, number one.'"

Cayne continued, "I said, 'Number two, I know you very well. I know why this is happening. I know why you're angry. A month ago, I went to your eightieth-birthday party. Your wife was standing in the middle of the room at the Harmonie Club. And I go back a long way with her, where I was instrumental in her getting a job. I was instrumental in a lot of things for her. I support her goofy governmental, liberal causes. I went up to your wife. I went up to do the kiss-kiss. She iced me, just walked away, purposefully walked away.' He said, 'Let's keep the wives out of this.' I said, 'Alan, they're not in it. I'm giving you a thought. The thought is this: She poisons you every single day about me, and how could you not resent me? Every article that's been written in the last four months, which is shit, talks derogatorily about me. Also, by the way, you got ousted, and the *Barron's* picture of you getting kicked in the ass and her status as the queen bee since 1993 has deteriorated to the point where you can't handle it anymore because she's on you all the time. "It's no longer your firm," she says to you, "it's his firm."'" Cayne convinced Greenberg to stay at Bear Stearns.

But between Kathryn Greenberg icing him at her husband's eightieth-birthday party and his convincing Greenberg to stay at the firm a month later, Cayne was thoroughly disgusted with the man who had hired him. "One of us is a giver," he said. "One of us is not a giver. One of us is a taker. One of us reneged forty times. One of us reneged not once, not once. One of us has got the ability to sit and have a conversation, meaningful conversation, and it isn't about him. It's not about 'What can you do for me?' That's all he thinks about. . . . He and Spector were like two fucking cocks in a barn-yard hating each other because they both knew they were both the same. One of them was a little smarter than the other. One was a lit-tle more clever than the other. They were both basically pricks, bully pricks. Couldn't care less about the other fifteen thousand people. Couldn't care less. Pieces of meat, all of them."

On December 6, Joe Lewis revealed that he had been buying more shares of Bear Stearns between October 19 and December 5, at prices ranging between $110 and $120 per share. His largest pur-chase was for 1.569 million shares, on October 19, for $118.80 per share. Lewis's SEC filing indicated he owned nearly 9.3 million Bear shares, or 8 percent of the total outstanding shares, worth just over $1 billion. The filing revealed that Lewis had made the pur-chases out of the "working capital" of his investment companies. He was the second-largest Bear Stearns shareholder, after Dallas money manager Barrow, Hanley, Mewhinney, & Strauss, which had more than tripled its stake in Bear Stearns during the previous three months. "Value managers like us buy the stocks when the news is iffy," James Barrow, the president of Barrow, Hanley, told the *Financial Times* on December 10. "It's selling at book value and expected to earn $10 a share next year. So this is a good deal if you ask me." Barrow added: "I've met Jimmy Cayne and I know how he operates. If I didn't trust in his management, I wouldn't be buying the stock." Brad Hintz, the Sanford Bernstein research analyst, said of the pur-chases by Barrow and Lewis, "You're getting the bottom-feeders buying into the company. Lewis is saying, 'I can look through this cycle.' He's not worried about the leadership because there's noth-ing wrong with the current management. Remember, you're invest-ing in them, not adopting them."

❋

AROUND THIS TIME in December, after the fourth quarter had ended but before the firm's results were announced on December 20, Cayne—by his account—decided to begin a discussion with the board of directors about the possibility he would step aside and ap-point Alan Schwartz the new CEO. Even though, whenever asked, Cayne had always insisted he would stay at the helm of Bear Stearns for years and years, in truth, by the end of 2007, Cayne no longer had the fire in the belly. He also had no idea what to do to return the firm to profitability. "There was a period of not seeing the light at the end of the tunnel," he said. "It's not knowing what to do. It's not being able to make a definitive decision one way or the other because I wasn't good enough. I wasn't good enough to tell you what was going to happen."

At the fateful December board meeting, Cayne asked Molinaro, Schwartz, and Greenberg to leave the meeting so he could speak to the board alone. "I asked for a non-executive session, which means everybody else leaves except me and the board," Cayne said. "I sit down with the board and I said, 'Look, I think we need a fresh pair of eyes. I think that we need somebody to come in and take a look at our position and tell us what we're doing wrong. That person isn't going to be an incidental person.'" Among the people Cayne was considering bringing into the position—essentially replacing Spector—were Thomas Montag, then a senior fixed-income partner at Goldman Sachs who ended up at Merrill Lynch, and Tommy Maheras, a senior fixed-income executive at Citigroup who had been fired. "I don't know who it is that's going to come in," Cayne said, "but I'm going to have to offer him a big position. It's going to be unfair to Alan Schwartz if I bring the guy in as a co-president because we just had a co-president. My motivation was simple: I wanted the board's permission to pull the trigger on making Schwartz the CEO."

At first, Cayne said, the board did not see things his way. "They debated it," he said. "They had a discussion. They finally said, 'Okay.' Now, nobody at Bear Stearns knew that. They didn't know that I went to the board and asked for permission to pull the trigger myself. I wanted to be able to say at some point, 'I'm done,' and I didn't know when it was going to be. Little did I know that it was going to be January."

There were other interpretations of what happened in December. For instance, one board member said that while Cayne did approach the board in December about choosing Schwartz as his successor and one day giving up his post, there seemed to be a different interpretation of Cayne's assessment that the board did not want him to leave anytime soon. "The 'Don't panic now, we've got to have you stay on' line was not entirely accurate," this board member said. "Jimmy, at this point, was very, very not all there. He wanted to hear that he needed to stay on."

Before the Christmas break, Schwartz called together the senior executives of fixed income, equities, and banking and, according to one of the participants, gave them a pep talk. He did not want all the bankers and traders going on vacation pissed off and worried about their bonuses. He also wanted them to stay in their chairs for another year. He preferred a direct discussion about the situation rather than rumor and innuendo. "Look, guys," Schwartz told them, "let's get through year-end, compensation pressures, all that shit. We had a really bad fourth quarter. I consider it a failure of management. We let you guys down and we've got to suck it up and get it done."

But to his surprise, after each meeting with the various business leaders, there was a recurring theme, which was: "It's nice for you to say we all have to come back, but what's going on with management? Are you taking over?"

Schwartz said, "Guys, what's the difference? That's not important. We're all here. We're all a team. We screwed up as a team. We'll fix this as a team." But the executives told him they wanted to know.

Schwartz said, "Don't make that a big issue." At each meeting, the first question was "Is Jimmy staying on?" which was quickly followed by "We're not coming back for another year of this shit. The *Wall Street Journal* says our CEO smokes pot. Who needs this shit? We're getting ridiculed by clients. We're out there on the firing line with people saying, 'Nice firm you work for! You guys look ridiculous! You guys are a laughingstock!'"

After these meetings, a small group of the firm's most senior executives approached Schwartz with a crystalline message: "If before bonuses are paid on January 20, there is not a change in management, then you're going to lose a ton of people. Just know that." Now Schwartz had a serious dilemma. If he didn't approach Cayne with this news, the fact that he did not would be known inside the firm and give its best people cover to leave Bear Stearns for other places on Wall Street. "It would give people an excuse for being disloyal," one of them said. "They don't have to say, 'I'm being disloyal'; they just say, 'I told you, I was ready to stay but you called my bluff.'" From time to time over the years, Schwartz had thought about giving up his management position at the firm and assuming the mantle of *eminence grise* in the M&A world, not unlike a Felix Rohatyn or Jack Levy, who were well-regarded senior M&A bankers without a management role. He and Cayne used to joke that when Cayne left the firm, Schwartz would be a free agent to go wherever he wanted. But over the years, as Cayne stayed on and on, Schwartz began to think that he would leave the firm before Cayne. Schwartz would tell Cayne: "You're going to stay on for fucking ever. I don't even know if I can last as long as you can."

Now Schwartz was in the uncomfortable position of having to tell Cayne the time had come. Schwartz had never planned for this moment. He had always taken the position that he would leave rather than get into a fight with Spector about the leadership of the firm. But now, with Spector gone and the firm reeling, he did not feel he could just walk out the door. Nor did he feel Cayne could any longer run the firm. He spoke with a few board members about what to do. Over Christmas break, a number of directors remembered that Schwartz had said to them: "You guys had better figure out what's going on here. You need to be aware of what's going on and make the decision."

On December 18, Gasparino, at CNBC, reported that "for the first time in years, the board of Bear Stearns is actively talking about succession for Jimmy Cayne." Gasparino could not put a timetable on Cayne's prospective departure, but he said that as the longest-serving CEO on Wall Street, Cayne "has run into a number of problems that is making the board a little anxious about his tenure going forward." As "problems," Gasparino cited Cayne's age, his health, the two investigations into what happened at the hedge funds—both by the SEC and by the U.S. Attorney in the Eastern District of New York—and the firm's prospects for the future. He said his sources told him the firm's fixed-income business, long the driver of Bear's growth and profitability, was "gone for the next year or so." Gasparino predicted Schwartz would be the next CEO of Bear Stearns, although, he said, some board members were worried he was not ready for the job and would need some seasoning, a development that might keep Cayne in his seat longer. While Gasparino was breaking this news, the firm's stock was falling to around $91.35. That same day, the *Wall Street Journal* reported that Cayne and the rest of the executive committee had decided to forgo their 2007 bonuses.

On December 21, the *New York Times* ran a story, by Landon Thomas Jr., comparing Cayne to John Mack, the CEO of Morgan Stanley. Both men had presided over firms that had suffered major losses as a result of the financial crisis—for Bear Stearns, there was the $1.9 billion write-down; for Morgan Stanley, it was an $11 billion write-down—and both had agreed to give up their year-end bonuses. The difference between the two men, though, was that people were calling for Cayne's head and not Mack's. The reasoning seemed to be the two investigations into the Bear hedge funds and Cayne's penchant for playing golf and bridge as the walls of the temple were crumbling.

❋

THE DAY BEFORE, on December 20, Bear Stearns reported its fourth-quarter results. As predicted, the firm suffered the first quarterly loss in its history. But what had been on November 15 an expected $1.2 billion write-down of its mortgage portfolio had morphed into a $1.9 billion write-down a month later. As a result, the firm posted a pretax loss of nearly $1.4 billion in the fourth quarter and a net loss for the quarter (after a tax benefit) of $859 million. For the year, the firm had net income of $233 million, down 89 percent from net income of $2 billion from the year before. The massive fourth-quarter loss stemmed from two fateful decisions: First was the mistake the firm made by becoming the repo lender to the hedge funds in June. As the assets Bear Stearns had financed continued to lose value during the fall, the firm rode them down to close to zero. Then there was the decision to continue betting against subprime mortgages by buying theoretically higher-quality Alt-A mortgages. "We told investors over and over that we were short the subprime sector, and we were," Paul Friedman said. "Our trade was to be long the Alt-A sector and short the subprime, and we did it in size all along. Conceptually, it made sense, but when the market started to look beyond subprime we found that we couldn't hedge Alt-A securities—you still can't—and no one would buy them. So we had a huge position that just kept going against us."

As was leaked in the fourth-quarter results, the executive committee decided not to receive any bonuses for the year. As a Christmas present of sorts to himself, Cayne sold 172,621 shares of stock that had vested in the CAP plan for $89.01 per share, a payday of $15.4 million. Ironically, as Cayne was selling, Lewis was buying even more Bear Stearns stock. In the month of December, Lewis had purchased another 2.2 million shares, he disclosed in an SEC filing the day after Christmas. He now owned 11.1 million shares, or 9.57 percent of the company's stock, making him again the largest shareholder and proving definitively that even some of the world's most highly regarded investors make bad investments.

On the morning of December 20, Molinaro hosted the obligatory analyst conference call. It was a sober affair. During the question period, Guy Moszkowski, at Merrill Lynch, asked Molinaro if the firm felt capital-constrained or needed to raise capital. Molinaro said the firm had sufficient capital. "We have historically had very strong capital ratios [and] significant excess capital," he said. "Obviously the [fourth-quarter losses] will reduce that somewhat, but our capital ratios, we believe, are still very strong. We don't see a particular need to address that. Of course, we do expect that the closing of the $1 billion convertible security we sold to Citic will happen during the first half of the year and that will add to the equity capital base. So with that, capital ratios should move back to levels that we had been running at."

By the time of the December 20 call, the firm had decided to hire Gary Parr, the Lazard banker, to add a patina of professionalism to the seemingly random efforts to either raise capital or sell the company. In the wake of the Citic deal, the thought occurred that perhaps there were other strategic deals out there for Bear Stearns to consider. Parr was not involved with the Citic deal or the Fortress deal or any of the previous failed attempts to raise capital. "They were thinking that perhaps there was another thing to do that would involve advancing their business strategy and capital," Parr said. "It was more around the business strategy than around capital. We knocked around ideas. We talked about how to think about it. What sorts of things might make sense? What parts of the world might be the logical places to approach?" One idea that Parr and Bear's management was kicking around was whether a Middle Eastern investor would invest in Bear's prime brokerage business. At one point, Cayne had suggested to Parr that HSBC might be interested in a deal for Bear Stearns. Cayne also talked to Joe Lewis about that possibility. "Actually, Joe Lewis went and met with [the] Hong Kong [and] Shanghai Bank," Tese said. "But they had no interest. Gary Parr canvassed around several of the banks. They didn't have an interest."

But as the fall dragged on and none of Parr's efforts materialized into something substantive, pressure kept on building and building. "Jimmy was getting pressure from some of the shareholders, particularly Bruce Sherman," Tese said. "Not so much Joe Lewis. But Bruce was calling Joe Lewis. We were also getting some pressure internally because Jimmy had been sick. Maybe we needed a change of direction. Everybody knew he was sick. At first, it didn't get out for about a week. But then when he didn't come in for a week, people were starting to say he had cancer. I said to the guys, 'You know, he's sick but he doesn't have cancer.' The illness took a lot out of him physically. A couple of months after that, he was weaker, a lot weaker. The other side of it was, there was no business. We went from being busy as hell up until the summer, and then all of a sudden the mortgage business ended, which was 40 percent of our profits. The leverage lending business was over. Trading slowed down, with the exception of customer trading. But that's not a big driver of the business. Prime brokerage business was starting to show some strength. Jimmy knew exactly what the business was doing. He got a daily sheet and a weekly sheet and a monthly sheet. So he knew business was really bad. He knew that. It wasn't just us. You'd feel okay if it was just us. If everybody else was doing okay, then you could get some of that action. But business was bad all over. Your profit and loss, to a great extent, depended upon the marks on your balance sheet, which is a scary proposition, considering that a good part of your inventory is not selling particularly well. So pressure started to mount internally and externally. It became obvious Jimmy had to move out."

❦

AFTER THE HOLIDAYS, the tide started to turn against Cayne. "Everything was sort of rolling along, except that I was getting shit," he said. When he walked back into his sixth-floor office after New Year's he was getting singed by the incessant glare of publicity focused on whether or not he would be the next CEO victim of the spreading crisis. "I think I made the papers forty days in a row," he said.

Cayne knew that Bruce Sherman, the CEO of money management firm Private Capital Management and, with 6.43 million shares, Bear's fourth-largest shareholder, had been talking to the board and the press about whether it might be time for the longtime CEO to move on. Although Sherman did not know it, Cayne was even aware of the trip that Spector—when he was still at the firm— had made from his weekend home in Palm Beach to see Sherman in Naples to try to convince Sherman to fire Cayne and make Spector the CEO. "He doesn't know that I know that Spector came to see him," Cayne explained, "and said, 'Get rid of Jimmy. I want to be the CEO.' That's pretty nifty when a guy working for you does that, right? But he doesn't know that I know." Sherman had also called Schwartz, as had Barrow, and told him: "You guys better do something because I'm hearing rumblings. You've got to take over or your good people are going to leave." Schwartz did his best to deflect the shareholders' calls. Then Cayne called Sherman when he heard about the new *Journal* and *Times* articles. Sherman had been a longtime Bear shareholder, unlike both Lewis and Barrow, and had been euphoric in his praise of Cayne when the stock was steaming toward its all-time high a year earlier. Sherman's sentiment had changed. Cayne said he had decided, on January 4, the time had come. "This seemed to me to be a very good time to make a deal with Bear Stearns," Cayne said, "where I would say to Alan, 'I'm going to give up the CEO. I will stay as non-executive chairman.'" He delivered this news to Schwartz before lunch on January 4. Cayne said he simply told Schwartz the time had come for Cayne to go. "I told him, 'This is what's happening,'" Cayne said. "I also told him that I had a meeting and I was authorized to offer him the position. This isn't just 'Let's do this and go to the board for approval.' I'd already got the board. The board has already told me and they didn't tell him. They didn't tell anybody. I had it in my pocket; I asked for permission to pull the trigger. They gave it to me. What's more clear-cut than that?"

Others offered a very different account of Cayne's stepping down. The board's initial thought was not to make a change until February 14, which happened to be Cayne's seventy-fourth birthday. Schwartz told them, "That's fine with me, but I don't think it's going to work, and it looks a little silly—you're not doing this at the end of the fiscal year or at the annual meeting, but on his birthday?" The board realized Schwartz was right. Tese volunteered to talk to Cayne and tell him the board had come to a decision. But then Schwartz told Tese that would not be right, either. Schwartz himself had to be the one to tell Cayne.

On January 4, by this account, Schwartz went to see Cayne.

"We got a problem," Schwartz told Cayne. "We've got to do something."

"What should we do?" Cayne asked.

"You've got to step down," Schwartz told him. Cayne just looked at him. He was resigned to the inevitable, and physically and mentally exhausted.

"I'll do whatever you want," Cayne said. "I'm glad it's you."

At that moment, Schwartz thought, according to someone he told, "God, I agonized over this, and this was the only right way to do it. It was one of those weird things, but once you did it you said, 'Why did I even think about it?' There was nobody who could come in and have this conversation but me. He knows it's not me saying, 'This is my seething ambition and it's time to topple you.' It was like 'This is what's going on.'"

Schwartz was determined to do what had to be done to make sure bankers and traders stayed put at the firm. Cayne suggested that he could stay on as an executive and as chairman of the board. Schwartz thought that would send the wrong message to the troops and continue to make Cayne fodder for the press that wanted his scalp. If he were still an executive and retained his salary, bonus, and perks, then the press would continue to monitor his comings and goings. Anytime he left to play golf or bridge, it would be fuel for the fire. It would be better, Schwartz told him, for Cayne to retire as CEO and become non-executive chairman of the board. That would be an easier sell internally and give the press and investors what they appeared to want. Cayne agreed to become non-executive chairman of the board and to retire from the firm.

As for Cayne's version of what happened that day between him and Schwartz, Cayne said, "The mechanics of it, who asked who—who gives a shit?" Cayne said he knew nothing about the internal revolt of the bankers and traders and their December conversations with Schwartz. But he was not surprised to hear about them. "It might be convenient for them to say that," he said. "I think it might be convenient for them to say that, knowing that I'm not hearing it directly. You don't want to be on record saying the straw boss should hit the trail. That's stupid. But if it were them saying, 'We need a better way to go. We need a new CEO,' I wouldn't be surprised at all. But it wouldn't occur to any of them that I would step down. It wouldn't even occur to them."

With the writing on the wall, Cayne cut his deal with his beloved Bear Stearns. "The deal I make with the company is: I want health care, which is what you give everybody who leaves; I want the office, for a couple years anyway; I want an assistant. No problem. They say to me, 'We'd appreciate it if you didn't sell any stock before the quarter's over.' I said, 'Okay,' and the big *E* goes on the scoreboard, but I could see that. I can't step down and then sell stock." He received no severance pay or bonus or retirement compensation, unlike Stan O'Neal and Chuck Prince, despite what John McCain claimed about him on the campaign trail.

The idea was to wait a week or so before announcing the news of the management change. On Monday, January 7, Schwartz called together the President's Advisory Council—the top executives of the firm—for an eight-thirty breakfast meeting. "Alan gives this beautiful, impassioned speech of how we're going forward and all the wonderful things Jimmy has done," Paul Friedman said. "He's sort of grasping for things that Jimmy has done and accomplished. The only thing he can come up with is to say, 'Jimmy's legacy will be this wonderful building that we're all in,' and I'm sort of looking around going, 'That's the best he can do? The guy's been here forever, he's been CEO, and he was involved in a building?' Then Jimmy gets up and speaks. He mentions his health. He mentions it's time. He said, 'I'm going to be retiring. However, I just want you to know that I'll still be coming into the office all the time. I'll still be very involved in the Citic transaction. Don't worry. I'm not leaving completely.' I don't know if everybody else felt this way, but my initial thought was, 'That's not what I want to hear. I want to hear that you're leaving now and forever, and they're taking away your ID card and you can't come into the building ever again.'"

Cayne has a different recollection of his swan song. "When I left January 4, I had three different meetings," he said. "The first was with the president's advisory group, which was about eighty people. There wasn't a dry eye. Standing ovation. I was crying. The second meeting was with the retail sales force on the Web. Standing ovation. And the third was a partners' meeting that night for me to tell them that I was stepping down. Standing ovation, of the whole auditorium."

CHAPTER 31

DESPERATE TIMES CALL FOR HARE-BRAINED SCHEMES

News of Cayne's departure was leaked to the *Wall Street Journal* the next morning. On January 8, Kate Kelly reported that Cayne was "stepping down" after developing "a reputation for being a hands-off leader last year as the current credit crisis unfolded." She reported that Cayne had started notifying directors of his decision and that Schwartz would succeed him as CEO. While the choice of Schwartz was a foregone conclusion, it also marked a radical departure for the heavily fixed-income-oriented firm to appoint an M&A banker to its helm at a time when the carnage in the mortgage side of the business was rising exponentially. In her article, Kelly quoted Meredith Whitney, the research analyst. "They have incurred so much franchise damage," Whitney said, "that what investors are concerned about most is revenue replacement. How the firm did as well as it did, with such a hands-off manager, is really impressive." There also seemed to be a consensus in the analyst community that it was a mistake for the board to keep Cayne as its chairman. "Jimmy Cayne should be out of the company," Dick Bove said. "To leave him in there as chairman is, in my view, an outrage." The day before, Bear's stock closed at $76.25, down 3.3 percent and nearly $100 per share below where it had been one year earlier.

The *Journal* story turned out to be the high point of Schwartz's day. He held a series of smaller meetings with the leaders of the firm's business units and got an earful in each one. He started by having breakfast with the heads of fixed income. There were about twenty-five people together in the twelfth-floor boardroom. "He took us through 'Now that Jimmy is gone, we got a lot of things that we want to do. I'm going to be meeting with a lot of people. We really need to work together,'" Paul Friedman remembered. "He spoke really well, as he always does. He spoke for about twenty to thirty minutes, and when he got done, he was greeted by a fair amount of hostility. The opening five questions were all about, 'What are we doing to raise capital?' He gave what became his standard speech: 'There's three ways to raise capital. You don't want to raise it the wrong way. We have no immediate need to raise capital.' We're all going, 'How about now?' He's saying, 'Well, we're not ruling it out but we're going to work on it in an orderly process.' People just pounded him again: 'Everybody else has raised capital. Why aren't we?'" (By this time, Wall Street firms had raised in excess of $200 billion in capital; by June 2008 that figure would be more than $300 billion.)

The meeting broke up and the fixed-income leadership returned to the trading floor. "The view was, 'That wasn't what I wanted to hear,'" Friedman said. "He then had a similar lunch meeting with the equity guys, and I'm told it was somewhat of a similar tone, although they have fewer rude people than we do, apparently, so they were less in his face, but he got a similar response."

Despite the exhortations, Schwartz seemed determined not to

raise new capital at the firm just for the sake of raising new capital. If there were a strategic purpose, he might consider it, but just getting cash in the door was of little interest to him. He quickly set about scuttling some of the remaining potential opportunities still being bandied about the firm. One of Schwartz's first strategic decisions was to put the final nail in the coffin of the merger with Fortress for any number of reasons. As for selling the company, he said early on and publicly, "Being acquired is not a strategy. . . . We have tremendous opportunites for growth, as much as I've ever seen." On January 9, in an eighteen-minute television interview with CNBC's David Faber, Schwartz reiterated his view that the firm was adequately capitalized and was unlikely to be part of a merger or acquisition anytime soon. "The strategy has to be to grow our business profitably," he said. "We need to earn a good return on equity. We need to grow our book value and need to do that in businesses we can grow organically." Only after that would a deal make sense, he said.

Schwartz seemed pulled in many different directions right from the start. "I'm putting down my pen," Wes Edens told Tom Flexner, the Bear vice chairman who'd introduced the Fortress merger idea. "Let's visit this in two or three months. Maybe the markets will be a little bit better. We're not doing this because it's two companies in distress. We're doing this because we think one plus one is going to equal three. Obviously, too much is going on." Flexner was disappointed and blamed Schwartz. "We just really spent a huge amount of time on the deal," he said. "At the end of the day, I actually think if we'd done that deal we'd be in business today. Alan Schwartz could not pull the trigger, and I thought that it would have made a difference to our prospects."

The next opportunity came from Sumitomo Bank, one of the largest banks in Japan. Michel Péretié, the CEO of Bear Stearns in Europe and based in London, had repeatedly suggested to the New York leaders that Sumitomo had an interest in doing "something structurally" with Bear Stearns, but the response in the late fall had been one of indifference, especially since so much time and effort was being put into making the Citic deal a reality. No one wanted to stop and try to figure out if the Citic deal would work alongside something Sumitomo might be contemplating. On January 10, at a meeting of the management and compensation committees, Péretié tried again. This time he had a proposal in hand from the Japanese. The idea was for Sumitomo to buy a stake in Bear Stearns of between 9.9 percent and 30 percent—the stock was then trading around $70 per share—and to use its sales force to help sell some of Bear's warehouse of hard-to-sell assets. In particular, the Japanese thought they could sell pieces of Bear Stearns's $5 billion slug of leftover debt from Blackstone's LBO of Hilton Hotels. "This is January and things are getting pretty edgy," Friedman said. "To the outside world things may have seemed okay. But when your stock is at $170 per share, $100 looks pretty dicey. To those of us on the inside going, 'We can't sell anything. We can't raise any new money. What's our plan?' it seemed like a pretty good thing."

At the committee meeting, the Sumitomo proposal "gets a partial hearing," Friedman said. "But the issue that we kept getting hung up with is we've got this unformed, semicoherent joint venture pending with Citic. Now, you've got this trillion-dollar bank, one of the largest and most financially solvent banks in the world, that wants to get involved with us. How would you even structure this third-party joint venture with this unformed other joint venture? Could you even do it? We made this big thing about Citic. We've put all these resources into it. There was a lot of press. This would be a loss of face." The collective wisdom at the meeting was that the Sumitomo deal was just too complicated. They decided to keep the Sumitomo fish on the line, though, just in case the Citic deal fell apart, which was still a distinct possibility because of the Chinese bureaucracy and increasing nervousness about Bear's near-term performance.

Next up was perhaps the wackiest idea of them all: a merger with Residential Capital, known as ResCap, the residential mortgage business of GMAC, both of which were owned by Cerberus, the private equity firm. "This one was truly insane," Friedman said. Dubbed "Project Reno," the idea—led by Schwartz and his colleagues Richie Metrick and Mike Offitt—was to somehow merge a cleaned-up ResCap into Bear Stearns's mortgage business, in effect tripling down on the firm's residential mortgage business at precisely the wrong moment based on a belief that there would be a financial opportunity coming in distressed mortgages. There was a huge meeting on the forty-third floor of 383 Madison to begin the process of looking at this deal. "Anybody who can spell 'mortgage' and anybody who's even remotely involved in any aspect of the mortgage business gets invited to this thing," Friedman said. To make the failing business more palatable to Bear Stearns, Cerberus first planned to restructure the company's balance sheet by "cramming down" the existing debt holders, forcing them to take equity in the business (and presumably wiping out Cerberus's equity). Additionally, Cerberus would fire five thousand employees, get rid of the mortgage origination business—who needed one of those anymore, anyway?—and then Bear Stearns would issue stock to the new equity holders of ResCap for the mortgage servicing business that remained. "My initial thought was, 'So on that day, if we ever actually could do this, we would get downgraded to a single-B on the spot,'" Friedman said. "I actually asked that question and was told, 'Just hold all those thoughts until later. We've got to work out our due diligence first.'"

Teams of Bear Stearns bankers and traders spent hundreds of hours exploring this deal—which would have raised no new capital for the firm—in due diligence meetings in Minnesota and Pennsylvania. "You had twenty people from the mortgage department and all the senior people involved in this," Friedman said. "Our treasurer's department, the accounting department, the tax department, operations accounting, technology—everybody was involved. All the best and brightest, maybe fifty to a hundred people, including Steve Begleiter from our corporate strategies group—all focused now on ResCap due diligence. We've got people flying all around the country working on this trade that was just insanity. Even if it could be done, it made no sense. Our servicing portfolio at EMC Mortgage was going to go up by 500 percent. The integration concept was crazy—of taking their technology and our technology, their operations, their people, and they owned a bank, GMAC bank, that was somehow going to be folded into our crappy little bank. Nuts. It was going to take every legal and regulatory mind we had to figure out how to do that and get the OCC, the FDIC, and the SEC and all the other C's to approve it. Insane. Weeks and weeks of work go into this. Then it just sort of stopped."

The ResCap and Sumitomo opportunities were the last two to come Bear's way until the end, in March, when the deal dynamics for the firm were very different. "As the stock price gets lower and lower," Friedman said, "it becomes less and less possible to do anything because somebody putting in a couple billion dollars now owns 40 percent of the company. That wasn't going to happen. What's the old line: 'Hope is not a strategy'? Well, hope was our strategy. That was basically where we were: 'Let's just see if we can sell some things. See if things will come down. Let's get through the quarter.' Everybody was focused on 'Let's get through the first quarter with good earnings and then see if we can get the Sumitomo trade approved. If we get good earnings, the pressure will come off. Life will go on. We can go back to business. Markets will see that we, and hopefully everybody else, will do okay, and things will get better.' Since it was kind of the only thought we had and the only plan, and since it was a good quarter, it all seemed like that made sense. Even through February."

With Spector long gone, both Cayne and Schwartz—neither of whom really knew very much about fixed income or exotic securities or how to make them or sell them—started spending more and more time on the seventh floor of 383 Madison trying to pick up the gist of what went on there. Cayne's visits were superficial and the source of great amusement to the traders. "It was clear when Warren left, Jimmy had no idea what we did for a living in fixed income," Friedman said. "Unlike Alan, who didn't get it and knew he didn't get it and tried, Jimmy had no clue. He would now come up to the fixed-income floor and wander around and try to find some common ground: 'How you doing?' or 'What's going on?' He'd have heard of some customer name—Thornburg, for example, was falling apart at that point—and he'd go, 'How's Thornburg going?' It's like, 'Fine. Nothing changed since yesterday.' He couldn't find a point of intersection. There was no way he could learn it unless he experienced it. It was sort of hopeless."

Schwartz's visits were far more regular and more substantive. He started taking up residence in Spector's office on the seventh floor two mornings a week, while maintaining his office on the forty-second floor. After all, he knew he was not Lloyd Blankfein—the CEO of Goldman Sachs and a former commodities salesman—and he was determined to get his arms around the problem if he could. "But it was like Bonds 101," Friedman said. "You're starting with, 'Prices go up, yields go down. And how do you calculate duration?' And I say that not to denigrate Alan. It's not what he did for a living, and he picked up on it faster than most humans could. But he never really got it. It wasn't what he did. It would take you fifteen years to get up to speed on the funky shit that we owned."

One trade that Schwartz, after he became CEO, asked the team to explore was to sell the firm's stockpile of Alt-A mortgages. At that time, BlackRock and PIMCO were the only two potential buyers, in size, of these assets. But Schwartz quickly realized that these trades could not be done. "They both want financing," one Bear executive said. "I've got a liquidity problem because my balance sheet is frozen, so I get out of my inventory and I finance it for five years, which means when the market thaws I'm still illiquid. So I can't finance it, number one. Won't they buy it without financing? Maybe, but that's maybe down 40 points." Compounding that problem would be the inevitable leak into the marketplace that the firm was exploring such a sale. "The next thing you would hear on the Street is, 'Holy shit! Bear Stearns tried to sell its whole Alt-A portfolio and couldn't. Those guys are screwed,'" this executive continued. "It's one thing to say, 'Just get out,' when you're out and you can announce to the Street: 'I've sold my Alt-A's. I took my beating. I raised $2 billion from a sovereign wealth fund. It's dilutive, but I'm done. And oh, by the way, my business is going under.' So that you couldn't do." Schwartz also determined the firm needed to continue its hedging strategies—even though by unwinding them there was some profit embedded in them that the firm could have benefited from—from time to time during the first three months of 2008. He decided to keep the hedges on and forgo the short-term profit. "For us to have a bad quarter in a market that is not falling apart, we can survive," a senior executive said. "For us to be unhedged in a market that is falling apart, we go out of business. One is death; one is sickness. We're going for sickness."

❀

In the weeks after he relinquished his post, and aside from his random visits to the fixed-income floor, Cayne's time at the firm when he was there, three days a week, was spent trying to bring the Citic deal to conclusion, working with the firm's lawyers on the hedge fund litigation, and settling where possible with the angry investors in the firm's hedge funds. Many of these investors had sued the firm, and many others were threatening to sue. The firm also came up with a seemingly arbitrary plan of settling with investors based upon when they invested: Those who invested in May or June 2007 got all their money back, those who invested between January 2007 and April 2007 got two-thirds of their money back, and those who invested before January 2007 received one-third of their money back. Some corporate and institutional investors got some of their money back and some did not. No employees who invested got any of their money back. "I'm talking to a lot of individuals who are selling it for 30 cents on the dollar," Cayne said.

What he was not doing after January 8 was participating in any way in the managing of the firm. "Out of nowhere, I now have zero management responsibility," he said somewhat wistfully. On January 12, the august *Economist* magazine predicted the worst was yet to come for the financial sector. "The dawning of a new year is supposed to be about hope, but fear remains the dominant emotion among bankers," it opined. "This week saw another round of bloodletting as they grappled with the effects of the credit crunch," including, "to nobody's surprise," Cayne's departure. "Mr. Cayne's durability prompted one observer to dub him the 'Harry Houdini of the boardroom.'" The magazine ticked through a litany of problems found at all the major firms: Citigroup, Merrill Lynch, Morgan Stanley, UBS, Countrywide, JPMorgan Chase, MBIA, Capital One (although, surprisingly, no mention was made about problems at Lehman Brothers). "Even Goldman Sachs, hitherto relatively unscathed, has suffered," *The Economist* observed.

The future was murky indeed. "Investment banks . . . face a slowdown in a number of businesses, from advising on mergers to equity underwriting," the magazine continued. "Some areas remain vibrant—commodities, for example, and emerging markets—but much restructuring lies ahead. . . . Bank shares may have further to fall. As Betsy Graseck of Morgan Stanley points out, they are still higher, relative to tangible book value, than their lowest level in the credit crunch of 1989–91. With futures markets predicting property-price falls of up to 30% and the pain spreading beyond mortgages, the bottom may be months away. As one American banking regulator puts it: 'There aren't many places to look now and feel happy.' Unless you are an escapologist of Mr. Cayne's caliber." As if on cue, three days later Citigroup announced it was taking a write-down of $18 billion, was cutting its dividend, and was raising $14.5 billion in new capital. That same day, Merrill raised another $6.6 billion in new capital. (Neither action would be of much help to these firms in the end.) On January 21, at six o'clock at night after the market had been closed for Martin Luther King Jr. Day, the Fed agreed to cut the federal funds rate by 75 basis points, to 3.5 percent, the largest one-day reduction ever and the first time since September 2001 the Fed had cut rates between its regular meetings. Eight days later, at a scheduled meeting, the Fed cut the rate again, to 3 percent.

On February 8, Molinaro spoke at the Credit Suisse Group Financial Services Forum. He spent time reviewing in detail with investors the steps the firm had taken since late 2006 to shore up its balance sheet and its liquidity. He pointed out that Bear's "funding mix" had "shifted dramatically" from being based on unsecured commercial paper and short-term borrowings to borrowing much more on a fully secured basis. The firm's secured funding increased to nearly $33 billion, from $5 billion, while unsecured funding fell to $10 billion, from $24 billion. Commercial paper borrowings fell to $3 billion, from $20 billion. "So a very dramatic shift in the sources of financing," he said. He also was happy to report that the firm had a $17 billion cash "liquidity pool" at the parent company, increased from $3 billion. "Essentially, it's a pool of cash, and that pool of cash is kept to protect the company from a variety of potential contingent draw-downs on liquidity or a potential need for additional margin on secured repo financing." Finally, he explained that the firm's equity capital was $12 billion, with another $1 billion coming from the Citic deal (assuming it closed and ignoring the $1 billion Bear was to invest in Citic). "We think that our total capital position is in very strong shape as we come into 2008," he concluded.

Among others, Robert Upton, the firm's treasurer, was not so sure. While Molinaro, his boss, was at the Credit Suisse conference, Upton was in Europe reassuring Bear's creditors. "Let's be honest," he said. "There was creditor angst. There was fixed-income investor and creditor concern about Bear Stearns. It was particularly bad in overseas markets, arising first from the hedge funds, second from the belief—right or wrong—that our exposure to mortgage markets that were troubled was as big if not bigger than anyone else's. We were the smallest of the big five broker-dealers, and in overseas markets the perception was we were the essence of the subprime problem. That if Bear Stearns didn't exist, subprime would have never been a problem. As ludicrous as that is, that was the perception when you got overseas. I have presentations that speak to those concerns, as ridiculous as that is, because especially in Asia, that was the general perception. People were very concerned about holding our bonds, and they certainly weren't going to do a new debt deal. Banks that provided credit to us were obviously concerned."

The message Upton delivered during his European voyage was generally an upbeat one. "I was an honest believer that everything was going to be okay," he said. He told creditors the firm was likely to have a profitable first quarter and had been improving its liquidity. "We've changed our funding posture," he told creditors. "We've changed our funding position. We've got $17 billion in cash, and that number was up to $18 billion when I went home."

But on February 13, he started to get increasingly concerned. During a well-attended meeting with Molinaro, his boss, and the heads of the global equities division, Upton made a passionate plea that the firm stop using the free credit balances—essentially cash—in its hedge fund customers' prime brokerage accounts to fund other parts of the business. While the move was perfectly legal, if the hedge fund customer ever wanted his money back and it was tied up in other parts of the business, then Bear would have to use some of the precious $18 billion of cash at the parent company to

pay back the customer what was his or otherwise be forced to liquidate a position in an untimely manner. There were limits to how
long this would work, of course, especially if many of the hedge
fund customers wanted their money back at the same time. What
they should have done, in retrospect, was keep a client's cash with
a client's collateral with a client's margin loan. "We should fund his
debit by using his collateral and lock up all the money," Upton said.
"Just put it away so that if they want it back, I can give it to them.
What we did instead was we spent a lot of time getting really cute
and used XYZ's money to fund ABC's margin loan. The problem
with that was when short positions and free credit balances and
customer cash started to fly out the door, the only way we could
meet some of that was by using holding company money."

Upton told Molinaro this practice should end immediately.
"What I told them that day was that continuing to fund the prime
brokerage business using free credits . . . [was like] they were betting the firm," he said. "They quickly threw all the papers I put down
aside and said to me, 'You're full of shit. Free credits have never left.
Debits and credits leave at the same time.'" Much to Upton's dismay, that was the end of the discussion. "But the CFO should have
had the testicles to tell them, 'Upton's right. We're going to fucking
go down this road,'" Upton said. "But he didn't. Instead, we came
up with some half-assed compromise piece-of-shit decision, which
eventually could be completely gamed by the business unit, and
only increased, not lessened, my exposure to confidence-sensitive
overnight funding in the prime brokerage business."

The next day, Valentine's Day, UBS announced that it was writing off $2 billion of Alt-A mortgages, the first time that a major Wall
Street firm had fessed up to the fact a significant chunk of its supposedly higher-credit-quality mortgages—as opposed to the lower-
quality subprime mortgages—were now toxic waste. UBS's Alt-A
write-down caused firms across Wall Street—and other companies
that do business with them—great consternation and forced them
to mark down their own Alt-A mortgages. Thornburg Mortgage, for
one, had used the Alt-A mortgages on its books as collateral for its
overnight repo financing. After UBS's February 14 surprise, Thornburg's repo lenders were demanding more collateral for their

overnight loans to Thornburg, depleting the firm's cash reserves to meet the margin calls. As a direct consequence of the UBS write-down and the margin calls at Thornburg, the exact thing that Upton had worried about the day before had come to pass. Nervous hedge funds started asking Bear Stearns for the return of their cash balances, as they had the previous August, forcing Bear Stearns to dip into its $18 billion of cash reserves to meet their requests. The dominoes had started falling.

※

COINCIDENTALLY, VALENTINE'S DAY was Jimmy Cayne's seventy-fourth birthday. He celebrated by agreeing to spend $28.24 million to buy two adjacent fourteenth-floor apartments at the recently transformed and reopened Plaza Hotel, at the corner of 59th Street and Fifth Avenue. The combined apartments, with 6,000 square feet of space plus maid service and room service, were around the corner from his longtime apartment at 510 Park Avenue. Although the new digs at the Plaza would require another year and millions of dollars more in cost before the Caynes could move in, it did have a spectacular view of Central Park.

EPILOGUE

THE DELUGE

When Sandy Lewis, at home on his 1,500-acre farm on the western shore of Lake Champlain in upstate New York, began to clue in to the unraveling of his father's firm during the summer of 2007, he called Mike Minikes, the former longtime Bear treasurer who was then running the firm's prime brokerage business, and asked him to locate the bronze bust of his father that at one time was a prominent feature of the executive hallway at the firm. The bust had been the work of Dr. Maurice Hexter, the executive vice president of the Federation of Jewish Philanthropies, in New York, who late in life became a highly regarded sculptor. Hexter had given the sculpture to Cy Lewis years before his death.

"Maurice and the Federation wished to thank Dad for years of volunteering, and his strong likeness was placed in his office at Bear Stearns," Sandy Lewis explained. "Mother would not have it around, she said." When his father died, he asked for the bust back from the firm. "Alan Greenberg kept it," he said. "Said it was Bear Stearns property."

After Lewis's summertime 2007 call, Minikes found the Cy Lewis bust in storage. In March 2008, as the end was fast approaching for Bear Stearns, Sandy Lewis insisted that Minikes send him the heirloom. Bear Stearns shipped it to Essex, New York, on Wednesday, March 12. "Dad came to the farm that Thursday, delivered to a barn on a hill with a view," Lewis said. "He shares that barn with Bruno Bettelheim. They will have lots to talk about. Clearly, Dad has not lost his timing. Wonder what he thinks of all this. Dad was a smart man. I have not asked him, and do not hope to anytime soon."

❉

ON TUESDAY NIGHT, March 11, 2008, Richard Fuld, the chairman and CEO of Lehman Brothers, was at a dinner when he began to hear the rumors about Bear Stearns's financial health. "I'm hearing that some people are not accepting their counterparty exposure," he told a colleague at the dinner. "I don't understand why." The colleague recalled: "He was deeply troubled by it. That was on a Tuesday, and on Thursday Bear was gone." The weekend that JPMorgan Chase, the Treasury, and the Fed negotiated Bear's sale, Fuld was in India. But upon hearing about the crisis, he flew back immediately to New York and participated in the Sunday night call with Paulson, Geithner, and other Wall Street CEOs to hear about the deal and about the Fed's decision to open the discount window to investment banks for the first time since the 1930s. "There's a lot of hubris in our business," Erin Callan, then Lehman's CFO, said in a May 2008 interview. "I've found this just talking to my peers. No one ever thinks it'll happen to them, right? We're the only ones around who think it'll happen to us because it happened to us" in 1998, when the firm almost went under as a result of rumors and innuendo related to its role in Long-Term Capital Management.

On Monday, March 17, Lehman's stock plummeted to around

$20 per share—another "near-death experience," a Lehman banker said—as investors feared that the firm would be the next to fall, since it was just a bigger version of Bear Stearns and packed to the gills with hard-to-value and hard-to-sell mortgage and commercial real estate securities. "I don't think we're going bust this afternoon," Fuld told Lehman's senior executives. "But I can't be 100% sure about that. A lot of strange things are happening." But the market settled down after both Lehman and Goldman reported profitable first quarters that same day. Immediately afterward, Fuld set about trying to build a fortress. At the Fed's insistence, he brought down the firm's considerable leverage and raised more capital.

For instance, on April 1, Lehman sold $4 billion of preferred stock to the market. Callan boasted that the sale "demonstrates the confidence that investors have in Lehman Brothers" and was "reflective of the strength of the business model, the capital base and liquidity profile" of the firm. Two days later, Alan Schwartz and Jamie Dimon, along with Tim Geithner; Christopher Cox, the chairman of the SEC; and Robert Steele, an undersecretary of the Treasury, testified in front of the Senate Banking Committee looking into what had transpired at Bear Stearns two weeks earlier, and why. At this historic hearing, Schwartz had memorably testified that although he took responsibility for what happened, he could not think of a single thing he could have done differently that would have saved his firm from its collapse. "The buck stops here," he said. "And we and our shareholders paid a price." As for what he might have done to change the outcome, he said, "I can guarantee you it's a subject I've thought about a lot, looking backwards and with hindsight, saying, 'If I'd have known exactly the forces that were coming, what actions could we have taken beforehand to have avoided this situation?' And I just simply have not been able to come up with anything, even with the benefit of hindsight, that would have made a difference to the situation that we faced." For his part, Alan Greenberg seemed particularly cavalier about the firm's denouement. "These things happen," he told Forbes in September 2008. "We had a great run. The firm grew, and we were highly profitable. And then things happened that maybe shouldn't have, but they did."

On Friday night, April 11, Fuld had dinner with Paulson and

later that night—2:52 A.M.—wrote Tom Russo, the general counsel, a list of six "takeaways." Among them were that "we have huge brand with treasury," that Paulson "loved our capital raise," that "they want to kill the bad H[edge] F[u]nds + heavily regulate the rest," and that Paulson "has a worried view of ML"—Merrill Lynch. "All in all worthwhile," he wrote. Fuld was said to be regularly in touch with Paulson throughout the credit crisis, according to Congressman Dennis Kucinich, who has referred publicly to voluminous "call logs" between the two men.

❋

FULD'S FIRST SERIOUS strategic initiative to shore up the firm's equity capital came during the week of May 26 as Jesse Bhattal, the head of Lehman in Asia and a member of the executive committee, had been teeing up the idea of Lehman forging a strategic relationship with the Korean Development Bank. "Korea situation sounds promising," David Goldfarb, Lehman's chief administrative officer, wrote Fuld and Joe Gregory, Lehman's president, on May 26. "They really are looking to restructure and open up financial services and seem to want [an] anchor event to initiate the effort, which could be us." Goldfarb wrote that he preferred a strategic deal with either AIG or GE to one with the Koreans, but "this could become real. If we did raise $5 billion, I like the idea of aggressively going into market and spending 2 of the 5 in buying back lots of stock (and hurting Einhorn bad!!)." (David Einhorn was the founder of the hedge fund Greenlight Capital and had been aggressively and publicly questioning Lehman's accounting while shorting its stock.) Goldfarb said that while it "sounds like the Koreans are serious . . . we know these things often don't go further than the rhetoric!!!" Fuld responded, "I agree with all of it," and that he wanted the Koreans to "buy 10 com real estate," a reference to wanting them to buy $10 billion of the firm's troubled commercial real estate assets.

On May 31, a team led by Tom Russo flew overnight on one of the firm's Gulfstream jets to Seoul, South Korea, to meet with representatives of the Korean Development Bank (KDB) to discuss the possibility of the $5 billion strategic investment. The Koreans had indicated an interest in buying as much as 49.9 percent of Lehman, but the purpose of this trip was to see how far they could get on the

$5 billion. When the Lehman team arrived, they were disappointed to discover that the Koreans had not hired a U.S. lawyer or advisor and seemed more focused on discussing an investment banking joint venture. "It was kind of a joke," one of the Lehman participants said. "We ended up wasting several days there and decided to come back."

The idea had been to be able to announce the Korean investment as part of the release of the firm's poor second-quarter results on June 9. Being able to talk about a large, deep-pocketed strategic investor would have mitigated some of the sting from the write-downs of the increasingly toxic assets on Lehman's books. Instead, at the same time the firm announced a second-quarter loss of $2.8 billion, it also raised $6 billion of new capital—virtually overnight— in the form of $4 billion of common stock, at $28 per share, and $2 billion of convertible preferred stock. Among the buyers of the common stock were the New Jersey Division of Investment, which manages $82 billion in state pension funds, and Hank Greenberg, the former CEO of AIG and the current CEO of C. V. Starr, an investment company that was AIG's largest shareholder.

At the end of the day on June 9, Benoit d'Angelin, the former co-head of investment banking at Lehman in Europe who had left the firm fifteen months earlier to join Centaurus Capital, in London, wrote Skip McGee, Lehman's head of investment banking, that "many, many bankers have been calling me in the last few days" because "the mood has become truly awful . . . and for the first time I am really worried that all the hard work we have put in over the last 6/7 years could unravel very quickly." He recommended that "two things need to happen very quickly": "Some senior managers have to be much less arrogant and internally admit that some major mistakes have been made. Can't continue to say 'we are great and the market doesn't understand'" and "Some changes at the senior management level need to happen very soon. People are not and WILL not understand that nobody pays for that mess and that it is 'business as usual.'" He concluded: "Sorry to be so blunt but a serious [s]hock is needed to allow the firm to rebound quickly and aggressively." McGee passed the e-mail on to Fuld. Three days later, Fuld announced that both Joe Gregory, the firm's president, and

Erin Callan, its CFO, had been demoted. Fuld called the sacking of Gregory "one of the most difficult decisions either of us has ever had to make."

On June 19, after a six-month investigation, U.S. Attorney Benton J. Campbell, of the Eastern District of New York, announced that a federal grand jury had indicted both Ralph Cioffi and Matthew Tannin on charges of conspiracy, securities fraud, and wire fraud in conjunction with their management of the two Bear Stearns hedge funds from their inception in 2003 to their bankruptcy filing in July 2007. Cioffi was also indicted on charges of insider trading related to his decision to move $2 million of his own money out of the Enhanced Leverage Fund—without telling investors—into another hedge fund he managed that had, to that point, superior returns. The indictment also revealed that both Cioffi's notebook and Tannin's tablet computer had disappeared after federal authorities had asked for them to be produced. The indictment alleged that by March 2007, both Cioffi and Tannin "believed that the [f]unds were in grave condition and at risk of collapse. However, rather than alerting the Funds' investors and creditors to the bleak prospects of the [funds] and facilitating an orderly wind-down, the defendants made misrepresentations to stave off withdrawal of investor funds and increased margin calls from creditors in the ultimately futile hope that the [f]unds' prospects would improve and that the defendants' incomes and reputations would remain intact." The funds' investors and creditors have lost more than $1 billion since the funds collapsed. The same day, the SEC filed civil charges against both men. In November 2009, a jury of eight women and four men in Brooklyn, New York, found the two men not guilty of the government's charges. Had they been convicted of securities fraud, they faced maximum sentences of twenty years of imprisonment. Had they been convicted of conspiracy, they each faced a maximum sentence of five years.

A few weeks after the government unsealed its indictment against the Bear Stearns hedge fund managers, Skip McGee, at Lehman, called a group of bankers and let them know that there would be an all-hands meeting with Fuld and most of the executive committee on July 11 to discuss any and all strategic alternatives the firm might consider. "The stock was getting hit again, the shorts were all over us, Einhorn had kind of killed us off pretty well, and Erin Callan was gone and others, so we ceased talking to the media," one participant in the weekend meetings said. "Because it was feeling like the beginning of another crisis of confidence around us."

No possible solution was off the table, including radically shrinking the firm by ten thousand people in order to get out of businesses that required capital, instead becoming more like the businesses that Barclays ultimately bought out of Lehman: the investment management division and the commercial real estate assets. The group also decided to seriously pursue strategic or financial investors. "That weekend to me was pivotal," one Lehman banker said, "because it really set the stage for finally getting very serious and realizing that we needed to get off our tails." In addition to starting the process of spinning off the real estate assets and selling the investment management division, calls were made all around the globe looking for capital. HSBC, Royal Bank of Canada, Abu Dhabi Investment Authority, Sumitomo Bank, Citic, Bank of America, the Carlyle Group, KKR, Silver Lake Partners, and Met Life all took a quick peek before passing.

There was also the growing sense among Lehman loyalists that the hedge fund community—to say nothing of Goldman Sachs—was out to get the firm. On July 23, Lehman's new president, Bart McDade, sent Fuld a copy of an e-mail about a visit to the firm by Jarett Wait, a former Lehman senior banker who had recently joined the hedge fund Fortress Investments. "Jarett stopped by yesterday [and] commented that in just a few weeks on the 'buy' side . . . 'it is very clear that GS is driving the bus with the hedge fund kabal [and] greatly influencing downside momentum, LEH [and] others!'"

Fuld responded to McDade: "Should we be too surprised[?] Remember this though—I will."

The market's response to potentially investing in Lehman was tepid at best. Still, through the late summer, the Koreans would occasionally rekindle their interest. In early August, Fuld, McDade, and McGee, among others, headed off to Hong Kong for a meeting with the Koreans. By this time, KDB had hired Perella Weinberg, for financial advice, and Cleary Gottlieb, for legal advice, and appeared to be getting more serious. Remembered one senior banker: "But they came back again frustrated and rolling their eyes. 'Yeah, we're going to continue conversations.' But again, it was like pushing on a rope."

The Koreans resurfaced again at the beginning of September. "They thought they were getting close to a deal," explained one Lehman banker, "and the champagne was on ice." KDB had decided to invest in what was then being called "CleanCo," everything in Lehman but the commercial real estate assets. But Fuld was pushing them instead to invest in "DirtyCo," the real estate assets to be spun off. "Dick overplayed his hand," this banker continued. "He alienated them and they sort of disappeared. The conversations kept going, but they were on a respirator from that point on."

On September 8, the U.S. government announced it was taking control of Fannie Mae and Freddie Mac, the two mortgage giants. At a news conference in Washington, Treasury Secretary Paulson described the plan to put the companies into a conservatorship run by the government. The CEOs of the two companies were replaced. The plan called for the Treasury to make capital injections into the companies over time, of up to $100 billion each, and in return the government received 80 percent of the equity ownership of the companies. On September 9, Jun Kwang-woo, the chairman of Korea's Financial Services Commission, announced that the discussions between KDB and Lehman were definitively over. "There will be other opportunities," he said. Lehman's stock fell 37 percent on the news, to $7.79 per share.

After the KDB deal fell apart once and for all, hard-to-fathom rumors started circulating throughout Wall Street that Lehman would soon be filing for bankruptcy and that an announcement to that effect would be made after the market closed on September 9. Instead, Lehman said it would make an announcement early the next morning of its third-quarter earnings as well as of several "strategic initiatives."

As promised, at 7:30 A.M., Lehman announced a third-quarter loss of $3.9 billion along with its intention to sell 55 percent of its investment management division and to spin off $25 billion to $30 billion of its commercial real estate assets into a separate publicly traded company by the first quarter of 2009. All of the financing for the spinoff—including around $8 billion in equity—was to be provided by Lehman itself, but Lehman would not need to raise new equity to do it. Fuld also announced he would cut the firm's dividend to 5¢ a share, from 68¢ per share, in order to save $450 million annually. "This firm has a history of facing adversity and delivering," he said. "We have a long track record of pulling together when times are tough and then taking advantage of global opportunities."

The spinoff of the real estate assets was a tough sell in the market, made all the more difficult by the fact that Lehman had to finance the whole company, raising questions about whether it was really a sale at all. "We looked under every rock to try to do something," one Lehman banker said. "It didn't work, candidly, and then when people realized we were still seller-financing the SpinCo and that if you ate through $8 billion of equity on a $40-odd-billion portfolio then you'd be eating into the debt. The market came away not really believing we'd separated the real estate, and that, to my judgment, was really the beginning of the end."

Soon after the market had voted on the proposed Lehman restructuring, Henry Paulson began to orchestrate his private market solution for Lehman. He called Bart McDade and told him that Bank of America was interested in taking a look at Lehman Brothers. A SWAT team from Bank of America in Charlotte—which one Lehman executive referred to as akin to the Wehrmacht—parachuted into the New York offices of Sullivan & Cromwell in midtown to review Lehman's books and records. Lehman then contacted Bob Diamond, the president of Barclays, the large UK bank, to see if he wanted to take a look. Yes, at those levels he would potentially like to take a look, Diamond told the Lehman bankers. Then, of course, in a replay of the Bear Stearns meltdown scenario, Lehman's counterparties and overnight repo financing sources "started to go wiggy on us," a Lehman executive said, "and once people won't take your good collateral it was only a matter of days before we were in Bear mode." By the time Friday night rolled around and Paulson and Geithner had called Wall Street down to the Fed, JPMorgan—like others of Lehman's counterparties—had already pulled its $17 billion of cash collateral from the firm at the request of some of its clients and to protect itself. The fuse had been lit.

※

WHEN THE MOST powerful men in American capitalism convened at the New York Federal Reserve Bank's Italianate palazzo in lower Manhattan on Friday evening, September 12, to try to save Lehman Brothers from certain death, what confronted them was the knowledge that whatever actions they did or did not take that weekend could push the financial system into the abyss.

"We went into the weekend knowing it was very dark," explained Tim Geithner, then the president of the New York Fed and now the Secretary of the Treasury. "There was nobody that was part of this process that did not believe the world was exceptionally fragile and that Lehman was systemic and that the consequences of its default would be traumatic. There was nobody in that room—from the Treasury, the Fed, or from the Federal Reserve Board or from the private sector—that could have told you exactly what would happen or what the consequences would be. I made it clear over and over again in that room that if we didn't solve this, everything else would be harder to deal with. Solving this was not going to make all the other problems go away, but we did not feel we had the ability to insulate the markets from the broader consequences of default."

Henry Paulson and Christopher Cox flew up from Washington on Friday for a six o'clock meeting with Geithner to discuss what the plan for the weekend would be. Meanwhile, Ben Bernanke, the chairman of the Federal Reserve, stayed in Washington to coordinate a response with the leaders of other central banks around the globe. With Geithner at his side, at 6:15 Paulson stood before the assembled Wall Street CEOs and their top lieutenants and "pulled the fire alarm," one of them said, along with delivering a harsh message. "There will be no bailout for Lehman," Paulson said, according to someone who was there. "The only possible way out is a private sector solution." At that moment, Ian Lowitt, Lehman's CFO since June 2008, knew it was over for his firm. That night "government officials . . . indicated that emergency federal funding would not be forthcoming to stabilize Lehman Brothers and provide the liquidity needed for its operations," he wrote in an affidavit accompanying the firm's September 15 bankruptcy filing. "While the Company continued to explore a number of strategic alternatives, after the September 12 meeting no viable alternative was available."

Unlike what the government did for Bear Stearns in March or Fannie Mae and Freddie Mac in early September, or what it would soon do for AIG, there would be no taxpayer money made available to support a Lehman bailout. "There was a lot of rhetoric going into the weekend both from the Congress and from people around the Treasury about how this shouldn't be public money," Geithner said. Whether that was a clever negotiating tactic or the line in the sand that would not be crossed, the Treasury secretary had set the definitive tone for the weekend: The future of Lehman Brothers, a 158-year-old firm with origins as a dry-goods store and cotton trader in Montgomery, Alabama, rested solely with men sitting around the table in the Fed's ornate board room at 33 Liberty Street. They had to come up with a plan in forty-eight hours to save the firm from insolvency or suffer the consequences of a catastrophic unwind of the Gordian knot of Wall Street's complex and internecine financial relationships.

For better or worse, Paulson and Geithner had conceived three possible scenarios for Wall Street to consider during the weekend. First was to investigate whether there could be a "private sector liquidation consortium" that would somehow finance a gradual sale of Lehman's assets outside of bankruptcy. Second was a potential acquisition of parts of Lehman by either Bank of America or Barclays, the only two firms that had expressed even a remote interest in Lehman's assets. And third, how could the free world "contain the damage in the event there was no solution possible"? The first idea quickly became untenable, and at the outset nobody had the slightest interest in considering seriously the third scenario.

The focus of the meetings quickly became how to finance the Lehman assets that either Bank of America or Barclays did not want. (Representatives of Bank of America, Barclays, and Lehman were in and around the Fed that weekend but were not included in the meetings of the wider group for obvious reasons.) But things began to go awry by the time the teams had reconvened at the Fed on Saturday morning. Bank of America had proposed a plan that would leave "a huge chunk of stuff" behind, one participant said, and reportedly wanted the Fed to provide it with $65 billion to cover exposure to Lehman's "bad assets," more than twice the $29 billion secured loan the Fed had made to JPMorgan to facilitate its acquisition of Bear Stearns. Not only was the Bank of America proposal of a magnitude beyond what the Fed or Treasury could realistically consider, but also the request quickly became moot, as Bank of America turned its attention to what quickly became the blockbuster $50 billion acquisition that same weekend of Merrill Lynch. "I think they always preferred Merrill, and I don't think this thing was really that viable," Geithner said. "It certainly wasn't attractive in an economic sense to anybody."

That left a somewhat more attractive proposal by Barclays, whereby the British bank would take all of Lehman except for the firm's commercial real estate asset book, with a face value of $40 billion (before write-downs). These real estate assets had formed the core of the spinoff proposal that Fuld and Lowitt had announced three days before, when Lehman's stock was trading around $7.80 per share. Fuld and Lowitt, who had been vetting the spinoff proposal with the Fed and the SEC for months before its September 13 announcement, had hoped—perhaps naively—that the market would react favorably. "It was like a lead balloon," one of the participants said of the spinoff idea. "The market didn't like it. And by the weekend"—with Lehman's stock having closed at $3.65 a share on Friday—"Fuld was increasingly nervous, although he was already at a high level of anxiety. The feeling inside Lehman from friends that I have that worked there was one of increasing desperation, tinged with an increasing sense of having been betrayed, misled, and let down by Fuld and by senior management."

The assembled bankers spent much of Saturday, Saturday night, and Sunday morning poring over Lehman's commercial real estate books to see if they felt comfortable putting together financing to facilitate Barclays's acquisition of the rest of Lehman, including its global fixed-income, equities, investment banking, and asset management businesses, which totaled some $600 billion of assets.

Fuld and Lowitt had announced on Wednesday that the commercial real estate assets would be marked down to $33 billion—from $40 billion—before being contributed to "SpinCo." But on Saturday, as the bankers from Goldman Sachs, Credit Suisse, Citigroup, and Deutsche Bank—the subgroup assigned to work on the project of putting together financing for Barclays—analyzed Lehman's loan and securities portfolio, they quickly realized, according to one participant, "the effective marks on the assets should probably be $12 billion lower," or $21 billion, rather than $40 billion, almost a 50 percent discount to their marked value (notwithstanding the Wednesday revision). "There wasn't a disagreement among the group about what the write-down should be," he said. "The reaction was one of considerable surprise but also tinged with the sort of skepticism that you would expect given the way in which the company shares had been trading. . . . The fact is the market clearly didn't believe their valuations, and when the team got in there to look at it they realized why."

But there was some disagreement about the $21 billion valuation depending on whether some institutions would have to mark them to market. As a compromise, the four banks instead recommended to the other banks in the consortium that Lehman's real-estate portfolio be valued at around $25 billion. The hole the consortium of banks had to fill was closer to $15 billion, meaning that each one would need to provide around $1 billion to finance the commercial real-estate assets left behind by Barclays in what would remain of Lehman Brothers. They knew that they would have to take a write-down on their loans as the assets were sold into the market over time. But to facilitate the Barclays deal, they were willing to do it. "There was a real concern that the demise of Lehman would lead to real problems for everybody else," one banker said.

WHILE MOST OF Wall Street was hunkered down at the New York Federal Reserve to review Lehman's books, Greg Fleming, the president of Merrill Lynch and a former financial institutions banker, had been urging his boss, John Thain, Merrill's CEO, to call Ken Lewis to talk about a deal between the two firms. Fleming had grown concerned during the week as Merrill's stock fell to $17.05

per share, from $28.50 per share. Fleming also knew that Lewis had long coveted Merrill Lynch and that Fleming's previous boss, Stan O'Neal, had no interest in such a deal.

"It's an iconic name," Lewis told *Fortune* about Merrill Lynch and the "one company" he wanted "to round out" his strategic vision for Bank of America. He said owning Merrill Lynch "would give us a major presence in investment banking as well as wealth management."

Thain, who had been at the Fed on Friday night, knew by Saturday morning that Bank of America was out of the hunt for Lehman, and he had also decided that Lehman was not going to be saved. If Lehman declared bankruptcy, he figured Merrill would be the next domino to fall. He had watched the group of bankers "pummel" Bart McDade, Lehman's president, with questions about Lehman's assets "and decided he did not want to be next," according to a banker there. "It became clear to me that it would make sense to explore options for us," Thain said in the press conference after announcing the deal.

Thain got Lewis's cell phone number from Fleming, stepped out of the meeting and called the Bank of America CEO. "We began to talk about the opportunity over the phone," Lewis said. "Then a few hours later, we were talking about it in person." Rumors began circulating at the New York Fed that Thain and Lewis were talking about a deal. In the interim, Lewis flew up by private jet from Charlotte to New York. They agreed to meet secretly in a Bank of America corporate-owned apartment at the TimeWarner Center, at Columbus Circle. "It didn't take but about two seconds to see the strategic implications or [the] positive implications" of the deal, Lewis said. "It was obviously a fairly short period of time, very intense and we saw a lot of each other." Following his call to Lewis, Thain said the two men "quickly" realized "the strategic combination made a huge amount of sense, and the opportunity to put this transaction together really was [so] unique that we both decided we wanted to take the opportunity." The code name for the deal was "Project Alpha."

At his side as an advisor Lewis had J. Christopher Flowers, the head of his own private-equity firm that specialized in financial services. Flowers, an ex-Goldman partner, seemed to have examined the books of nearly every Wall Street firm by September 2008, including Bear Stearns and Merrill Lynch. "[Flowers] had done quite an amount of due diligence on Merrill Lynch fairly recently," Lewis said. "It was very, very extensive. They had looked at the marks very comprehensively. This allowed us to have him and his team as an advisor, and just update the information they already had. That was one of the key ingredients to being able to do this as quickly as we did." Flowers was very complimentary of what Thain and his team had done in terms of shedding assets, including Merrill's 25 percent stake in Bloomberg and a $30.6 billion portfolio of troubled, mortgage-backed securities for 22 cents on the dollar.

Lewis determined he had to move quickly to win Merrill. Not only had he wanted to own the firm for years, he also was aware that Goldman Sachs and Morgan Stanley were in the mix. Merrill had reached out to Morgan Stanley about a deal. Morgan Stanley passed quickly—reportedly because the firm decided there simply was not enough time.

Separately, on Saturday morning at the Fed, representatives of Goldman Sachs reached out to former Goldman partner Peter Krause, Merrill's newly recruited head of strategy, to see whether Merrill would consider allowing Goldman to make a 9.9 percent minority investment in Merrill. This set off a heated debate—according to someone who witnessed it—between Krause and Fleming about whether Merrill should pursue the Goldman deal or the Bank of America deal.

For Goldman, the idea was to save a rival and to keep the fury of the looming storm at bay. "I think about it in terms of the Great Barrier Reef," one Goldman executive said. "If you think of Bear as being an outlying piece of coral at the far eastern extremity of the reef, then Lehman is a bit closer in and then Merrill is a bit closer. Then Morgan Stanley and Goldman Sachs are on the beach but still pretty close to the water. When you have a tsunami coming in, it's getting to be pretty uncomfortable."

Merrill and Bank of America executives were closing in on an all-stock deal, in which Merrill shareholders would receive $29 per share in Bank of America stock, which valued Merrill at $50 billion, a 70 percent premium to where Merrill's stock had closed the previous Friday.

＊

MEANWHILE, BACK AT the Fed, tempers started to flare. The assembled bankers were still wrestling with how to value the Lehman real-estate assets that Barclays wanted to leave behind. "It was a question of how much equity we needed to put up," one banker said, "to make the Barclays deal fly." This led to increasing tensions on all sides. At one point, late Saturday night, Gary Shedlin, a M&A banker at Citigroup, faced off against his old boss, Michael Klein, who was there representing Barclays and his client, Archibald Cox Jr., who was appointed chairman of Barclays Americas in April 2008.

"How much equity do you need to raise to do the deal?" Shedlin asked Klein.

"Why is that important?" Klein shot back. "Why do you need to know that?"

"You're making an offer for this company and we've got to know how you're going to finance it," Shedlin countered.

"We will not have to raise any incremental capital as part of this transaction," Klein said definitively. The two men glowered at each other before turning to less confrontational matters.

Bankers worked most of the night to put together a term sheet for how they would all agree to support Barclays's acquisition of most of Lehman Brothers. Some banks—such as BNP-Paribas and Bank of New York—were not so sure they wanted to participate, causing Jamie Dimon, the CEO of JPMorgan Chase, to admonish them. "You're either in the club or you're not," he said, according to one banker. "And if you're not, you'd better be prepared to tell the secretary why not." Still, a deal seemed close.

On Sunday morning, the executive group reassembled at the Fed at nine o'clock. "Everything was ready to go on Sunday morning," one participant said. "People were happy with the term sheet, so there was a doable deal on the table." Steve Shafran, a senior advisor to Paulson and a former Goldman Sachs partner, told a group of Lehman Brothers executives at the Fed that morning, "It looks like we may have the outlines of a deal around the financing." After which, the Lehman bankers thought they had saved their firm.

The Barclays deal required the blessing of the Financial Services Authority, in London—the UK equivalent of the SEC. So Paulson spoke with his UK counterpart, Alistair Darling, the Chancellor of the Exchequer, and to the FSA. He then summoned McDade, Lehman's president, to the New York Fed and told him at around 9:45 A.M., "Deal's off. The FSA has turned it down." At roughly 10 o'clock, Paulson and Geithner briefed the bankers at the Fed. The FSA would not comment on its decision, but a number of the participants at the Fed on Sunday morning said the reasons given to them by Paulson for the FSA's rejection ranged from "the overall size of the potential exposure that Barclays was taking on and whether Barclays was in good enough shape to do it" to the fact that the "FSA was looking for some kind of a cap to avoid U.K. contagion, and the Fed had just said, 'No assistance for Lehman.' The FSA then concluded based on the amount of diligence, the risk profile, and the lack of any assistance from the U.S. that they were not going to let it proceed."

There was also the suggestion made that Barclays "wasn't really that serious about getting FSA approval" going into the weekend knowing that there might be an opportunity to buy what it wanted from Lehman later at a lower price. (Barclays did not make its senior officials involved with the Lehman deal available for comment.)

THE LEHMAN TEAM was devastated by the news. "We thought we had a trade and felt good about it and thought we were in the right place," explained one Lehman banker, "and then to have the rug pulled out from under us after we were led to believe that the Street was there on the financing, it was just horrifying from our perspective." The stunned Lehman team returned to 745 Seventh Avenue to plot its next moves. Paulson then told the remaining bankers, according to one, "Let's start talking about what the world will look like if Lehman goes under. Let's focus on a solution for stabilizing the markets." Among the people still present for Paulson's Sunday morning speech was John Thain. After Paulson and Geithner left the executives to contemplate what they could do as a consortium to keep the world's markets from collapsing completely, the assembled alpha males began talking about Merrill Lynch in front of Thain, as if he weren't there.

"Merrill could be the next to go," one banker said. "And Thain wasn't saying anything," a participant said. "If Thain hadn't been there that morning, the rumors really would have been flying," one banker said. A few minutes later, Thain got up and left the room "and he never comes back," one participant said. Thain and his team were focused on negotiating a deal with Bank of America. Merrill had planned to meet with Goldman on Sunday morning, but by this time Merrill had stopped returning calls to Goldman Sachs.

After Thain, Paulson, and Geithner had left the New York Fed Sunday morning, the following exchange ensued, according to several sources who were there. John Mack, the CEO of Morgan Stanley, spoke up. "Maybe we should let Merrill go down, too," he said.

Aghast, JPMorgan Chase's Dimon pointed out how shortsighted that was of Mack because Morgan Stanley might be the next firm that counterparties lost faith in. "John, if we do that, how many hours do you think it would be before Fidelity would call you up and tell you it was no longer willing to roll your paper?" Dimon's comment quieted Mack. "We thought Mack said that because he might be buying Merrill," someone who heard Mack's statement said, and wanted to buy the firm on the cheap. (Mack denied he made the comment through a spokesman. A spokesman for Dimon said Dimon did not remember having the conversation with Mack.)

The group quickly began refocusing on putting together what became an agreement that every firm in the room would continue to do business with every other firm in the room and would underwrite a multibillion-dollar credit facility for the firms to use in an emergency in the wake of the presumed Lehman bankruptcy. "We figured all hell would break out the next day," one banker said. "And everyone else thought so, too. Everyone was then focused on netting out their derivatives positions starting right then."

Back uptown at Lehman, Fuld and McDade were making frantic calls to whoever would listen to their pleas for help, including Paulson, Cox, and Geithner. "But it crystallized in the course of the afternoon it didn't look like they were going to do anything for us," a senior Lehman official said, despite Fuld's belief after having dinner with Paulson in April that "we have huge brand with [T]reasury." Calls also went out to Lehman's internal restructuring group, to

Harvey Miller, the lead bankruptcy counsel at the New York law firm Weil Gotshal, and to Barry Ridings, a vice chairman of Lazard and a restructuring expert, that the end was near and the bankruptcy papers—most likely for Chapter 7 liquidation—needed to be prepared.

There was no other choice, since there was no buyer and no deal to do, but for Lehman to file for bankruptcy. "We walked into that weekend," Fuld told Congress on October 6, "[and] I firmly believed we were going to do a transaction. I don't know this for a fact, but I think that Lehman and Merrill Lynch were in the same position on Friday night and they did a transaction with Bank of America. We went down the road with Barclays. That transaction, although I believe we were very close, never got consummated."

For his part, Geithner regretted that the FSA decision did not come sooner. A similar decision rendered on Friday would have given everyone assembled at the Fed that weekend more time to possibly fashion another solution. But by Sunday, there was "no buy-time solution," he said. "Lots of things might have been possible if Barclays was able to deliver. We could have had the consortium finance that. We could have looked at some way where we did part of it and they did part of it. Lots of things were possible. But when Barclays was unable to come through, then we're left with those banks and they weren't going to buy Lehman or finance them because they looked at this liquidation consortium idea and said there's just no fucking way they could have done that. That would have had them underwriting and guaranteeing a firm that was bleeding away at an accelerating rate. There was just no way. We had no legal authority to solve that problem."

He said the Fed "would have had the legal authority" to do a deal similar to the one that facilitated JPMorgan's acquisition of Bear Stearns by lending $29 billion against a pool of Bear Stearns's assets "whose value was likely to get us repaid over time." However, he said, with Lehman Brothers, there was nothing like that on the table. That was one very big difference with the Bear Stearns situation, where JPMorgan wanted to—or was urged strongly to—buy the company. There was no buyer for Lehman. When Barclays pulled out, "that left us with doing the whole thing," he said. "There was no way we could have done the whole thing. That would be like lending into cotton candy or to dry ice. The franchise value of the firm would have evaporated really quickly." The market had rendered the judgment during the preceding six months that Lehman was essentially insolvent. "To make it simple, central banks do liquidity," he said. "They don't do insolvency. No central bank I'm aware of has the authority in the law to put capital into financial institutions. That's what governments exist to do." It was that responsibility, he said, that led Bernanke and Paulson to go together to Congress to seek approval for what became the $700 billion bailout bill. "With Bear Stearns, with all the others, there was a point when someone said, 'Mr. Chairman, are we going to do this deal or not?'" Bernanke told *The New Yorker*. "With Lehman, we were never anywhere near that point. There wasn't a decision to be made."

McDade and Lowitt, on Lehman's behalf, made one last-ditch effort to convince Paulson that taxpayers should bail out Lehman. They went back down to the Fed and walked the Treasury secretary through a presentation that Lehman had put together about the likely global consequences in various markets—foreign exchange, swaps, and derivatives, among others—if Lehman was allowed to fail. After McDade finished, Paulson told him, "You're talking your own book. We've thought this over." Another senior Lehman banker who heard about this conversation was dumbfounded. "He's an arrogant son of a bitch," this person said. "You've got to be kidding me! How could any sensible human being say to McDade, 'You're talking your own book, we've thought it all through'?"

✿

PAULSON NOT ONLY told McDade and Lowitt that Lehman had no choice but to file for bankruptcy, he also apparently told them the firm had to file for Chapter 7 liquidation by 7 P.M. Sunday. That would mean a court-appointed trustee would take over the firm, the firm's doors would be locked, and its assets sold as rapidly as possible. By the time McDade and Lowitt returned to the thirty-first floor of 745 Seventh Avenue, the Lehman board of directors had assembled to vote on the bankruptcy filing. But the directors had decided to hold off until McDade and Lowitt had returned from the Fed with their report. Since McDade had taken over as president of the firm in June, he had displaced Fuld as the firm's day-to-day leader.

"The words," remembered one participant in the meeting, "that Bart used when he came into the board meeting were that 'We were mandated to file. We were mandated to file.' He was very, very, very clear on that." Some shocked board members wanted to know what that meant. What if the board decided to defy Paulson and not file for bankruptcy protection?

Because the Fed controlled Lehman's access to the money it needed to open for business the next day, the point was moot. But then lawyer Harvey Miller had an idea. "They can tell us to do it," he told his client. "But they can't tell us when. And they can't tell us what form." The Weil Gotshal team began preparing for a Chapter 11 filing—a reorganization plan, not a liquidation plan—for the Lehman Brothers parent company that would allow the operating subsidiaries, such as the broker-dealer and the asset management business, to continue operating outside of bankruptcy. In the scheme of things, it was a technicality, but it allowed Lehman a modicum of leverage and the chance to tweak Paulson.

The Lehman board of directors, with Fuld at the helm, met on Sunday night to authorize the bankruptcy filing. As it was coming to grips with the inevitable, Christopher Cox, the SEC chairman, phoned in to the meeting from Washington, and was placed on speakerphone. Cox had kept a surprisingly low profile throughout the financial crisis but had been told by Paulson to call to reinforce the idea that Lehman should file for bankruptcy. Cox told the board, according to someone there, that regardless of what it decided to do, the board needed to take *some* action. The board members then pressed Cox about Paulson's directive that the firm must file for bankruptcy. "Paulson wanted Cox to call in to the board to make it clear," this person said. "Cox, rather than saying you have to file, was very clear that you don't have to. You could do it or not do it, but whatever you did you ought to do something." The board considered Cox's ambiguity an act of defiance of sorts, although without much substance at that particular moment. "He made the call," this person continued, "but he did not say, 'You have no choice.' In the context that would have been a very difficult thing to say to a board in

the middle of a board meeting." Without the prospect of any funding from the U.S. government, the board authorized the Chapter 11
filing.

But Lehman's ordeal that Sunday night was far from over. First
came word that the Federal Reserve Board agreed to expand the collateral that investment banks could pledge to the Fed as part of both
the Primary Dealer Credit Facility—the name given to the historic
facility that allowed investment banks to borrow directly from the
Fed window after the demise of Bear Stearns on March 16—and
the Term Securities Lending Facility. "These changes represent a
significant broadening in the collateral accepted under both pro-
grams and should enhance the effectiveness of these facilities in
supporting the liquidity of primary dealers," the Fed stated in its
press release. Then, to complement the Fed's action, a consortium
of ten global commercial and investment banks agreed to establish
a $70 billion "collateralized borrowing facility" to enhance liquidity
in the marketplace.

When the Lehman executives started to hear on Sunday afternoon that these changes were in the offing, they called the New
York Fed to see if it was true. If the Fed allowed Lehman to pledge
its squirrelly collateral to the discount window, "we might get a
reprieve," one Lehman banker said. But the Fed told Lehman,
according to this Lehman banker, "'Yeah, we're doing that for
everybody else but you. We're going to let you guys go.' I can tell you,
I've tried to be very restrained about this, but if indeed those are the
facts as represented, then Paulson fucked us, excuse my expression." In less colorful language, H. Rodgin Cohen, the senior partner of Sullivan & Cromwell who first advised Lehman Brothers
before the bankruptcy filing and then, with Lehman's permission,
Barclays after it, agreed with this assessment. "Had there been government assistance, you could have done either Bank of America or
Barclays," he said. "No question about that."

As the Lehman and Weil, Gotshal teams began to get comfortable with the idea of filing Chapter 11 for the holding company and
keeping the operating companies out of bankruptcy, around eleven-
thirty Sunday evening, Mark Shafir, Lehman's global head of M&A,
and Mark Shapiro, Lehman's restructuring ace, went to see Fuld in

his thirty-first-floor office. They told Fuld there was a way Barclays could buy Lehman's U.S. securities business out of bankruptcy, which would get Barclays what it really wanted and save ten thousand jobs. The three men called Bob Diamond, Barclays's president and chief negotiator on the Lehman deal, on his cell phone. Diamond expressed to them his disappointment that Barclays had failed to get a deal done earlier in the day, but when the men suggested to him he could buy Lehman's U.S. securities business "clean," he expressed great interest but needed to talk to his lawyers at Cleary, Gottlieb. When Diamond called back twenty minutes later, he told them, "I can't talk to you tonight. Call me at seven in the morning."

By that time—at 1:45 A.M., to be precise—Lehman Brothers Holdings, Inc., had filed for Chapter 11 to, Lowitt wrote, "preserve its assets and maximize value for the benefit of all stakeholders." At seven o'clock Monday morning, as the calamitous effect of Lehman's bankruptcy began spreading virally to financial capitals all over the globe, Diamond and Michael Klein, his financial advisor and the former Citigroup senior executive, got on the phone with Fuld, McDade, Shafir, Shapiro, and Tom Russo to discuss the possibility of Barclays buying Lehman's U.S. investment banking business. Klein liked the idea, and Diamond authorized him to negotiate with Lehman to get a deal done. The Lehman team told Klein and Diamond, "We absolutely have to get this done before the open on Tuesday because we're out of money."

With that, Fuld handed the keys to Shafir, the M&A head, and told him, "Go finish it." For the next twenty-four hours, swarms of lawyers and bankers took over the thirty-second floor of the Lehman building. The terms of the deal had to be negotiated, which required a fast-track appraisal of 745 Seventh Avenue and two data centers in New Jersey that Barclays wanted to buy. Barclays wanted all of Lehman's U.S. investment banking, fixed income, equity sales and trading, research, and certain support functions. Barclays did not want the investment management division or any of the commercial real estate assets. At one point, Shafir and Klein got into "some great kabuki theater where Shafir told Klein to screw himself at the top of his lungs," one observer said.

The plan had been to announce the deal before the market opened Tuesday morning and Lehman's broker-dealer subsidiary ran out of cash to operate. But the deal could not get finalized that quickly. "The funding sources were killing us, and we knew we were hours away from a Chapter 7 liquidation proceeding," one key participant said. "But the issue was just one of waiting and trying to get the agreement signed." Barclays could not seek the FSA's approval until an agreement was close to being finalized. Finally, just as the market was opening, the terms of the deal were agreed upon: Barclays would buy the Lehman businesses it wanted for $250 million and pay another $1.45 billion for 745 Seventh Avenue and the two data centers (later reduced to $1.29 billion) plus assume some of Lehman's trading obligations. Barclays also agreed to provide a $500 million debtor-in-possession facility to the bankrupt holding company and also to refinance the $40 billion or so that Lehman's U.S. broker-dealer had borrowed from the Fed after the filing to keep operating.

With that in hand, Barclays asked the FSA for its blessing. According to a Lehman executive, "It took four hours to get out of the FSA, and we thought, 'Here we go again. They're going to turn it down and we're going to be facing a Chapter 7 liquidation anyway.'" At around 1 P.M. Tuesday, the FSA signed off and Barclays announced it had bought much of Lehman's business in the United States, subject to bankruptcy court approval, which was granted— on an extremely expedited basis—on Friday, September 19. "Lehman Brothers became a victim," Judge James Peck said in approving the deal. "In effect, the only true icon to fall in the tsunami that has befallen the credit markets. And it saddens me."

With that approval, the Lehman bankers and traders in the United States were euphoric. "We saved the U.S. businesses and ten thousand jobs," explained one senior Lehman executive. "When I walked down to my office and I smiled, the assistants and the people around started clapping and cheering, because everybody was on pins and needles to see if we could pull it off and get an agreement. There was a tremendous sense of relief, at least in the U.S., that people had jobs. Because the prospect of losing all of your equity, that's horrific. But to lose all your equity and then to find you're unemployed when there's very little prospect—unless you're one of the most senior bankers or a very highly regarded person—of getting a job in an environment where the Street is retrenching at an exponential rate is not very pleasant."

❋

THE LEHMAN BANKRUPTCY filing unleashed a global deluge of economic misery—which, in fairness, might have happened anyway— the likes of which have not been seen in the United States since the Great Depression. Lehman's fall quickly had massive financial repercussions: the $125 billion bailout of AIG, the huge insurer; the sale of Merrill Lynch to Bank of America before it could fail; the failure of Washington Mutual; the near-failure of Wachovia; the near-failure of National City Bank; the failure of at least nineteen other financial institutions nationwide; the conversion of Goldman Sachs, Morgan Stanley, and American Express into bank holding companies to stave off their demise; and the virtual incapacitation of Citigroup, once the world's biggest, most valuable, and most powerful global financial services firm. "The financial system essentially seized up and we had a system-wide crisis," Treasury Secretary Hank Paulson said in a speech at the Reagan Library on November 20. "Credit markets froze and banks substantially reduced interbank lending. Confidence was seriously compromised throughout our financial system. Our system was on the verge of collapse, a collapse that would have significantly worsened and prolonged the economic downturn that was already under way."

To combat the near-collapse of capitalism as we have known it, the federal government used nearly every device it could think of, from further lowering interest rates to continuously revising the types of securities accepted by the Federal Reserve as collateral to the historic passage—on the second try—of the $700 billion Troubled Asset Relief Program (TARP), the brainchild of Paulson and Ben Bernanke, the Federal Reserve chairman. Such a massive bailout package would have been inconceivable without the bankruptcy of Lehman Brothers and the federal rescue of AIG.

Their idea was to use the money to buy the toxic assets that nobody else would buy from the balance sheets of the banks and securities firms that had bought or manufactured them in the first place. But before that strategy could be implemented, Paulson reversed course and decided to use $125 billion to buy equity stakes in the nation's eight largest banks. The government then used another $40 billion for AIG and another $47 billion to buy stakes in other, smaller banks around the country. Finally, on November 12, Paulson announced that he had abandoned the idea of trying to buy the toxic assets. He also said he would let President-elect Barack Obama's administration figure out how to allocate the balance of the money left in the TARP.

When Bernanke and Paulson have discussed their decision to let Lehman fail, neither one has any doubts about the wisdom of their decision. "A public-sector solution for Lehman proved infeasible," Bernanke said at the Economic Club of New York on October 15, "as the firm could not post sufficient collateral to provide reasonable assurance that a loan from the Federal Reserve would be repaid, and the Treasury did not have the authority to absorb billions of dollars of expected losses to facilitate Lehman's acquisition by another firm. Consequently, little could be done except to attempt to ameliorate the effects of Lehman's failure on the financial system."

On Monday morning, September 15, as the Lehman volcano was spewing molten financial lava to every corner of the globe, a pale and tired-looking Paulson—whose brother worked for Lehman, in Chicago—said at a White House press conference that he "never once considered that it was appropriate putting taxpayer money on the line in resolving Lehman Brothers." He added, "Moral hazard is not something I take lightly."

⁂

SOME SIX WEEKS after Lehman's implosion, a relaxed Alan Schwartz reflected on the year that forever changed Wall Street. In the previous seven months, he had brushed aside numerous attractive employment opportunities in favor of setting up shop in modest office space that Rothschild made available to him at 1251 Avenue of the Americas. There he spoke to his media clients, such as Jeff Bewkes, the CEO of Time Warner, among others, and tried to keep a low profile while figuring out whether Microsoft would ever step up to take America Online off Time Warner's hands. He put his stocking feet up on his desk and started talking.

"Would Bear Stearns have survived, no matter what we did?" Schwartz wondered, according to several people who heard his soliloquy. "I don't see it. By staying solvent, might we have picked up a merger with Barclays, or something, once they realized our books were clean? Maybe. But to compete [after] the repeal of the Glass-Steagall Act [in 1999], the model became wholesale banks using collateral to finance themselves instead of using deposits. It didn't work when the collateral that was invading the world"—such as mortgage-backed securities—"became non-transparent. That's not to say that we did a good job running the firm. To me, it was a whole bunch of events that interrelated and swamped the banks, too. It's just that the infrastructure of the world to support banks as opposed to investment banks—the regulatory authorities—was very well established. They still don't know if they can save Citibank, right? So this tsunami was so big that wholesale banks of every stripe could not be fixed."

He scoffed at the idea—as many Wall Street insiders have—that the SEC's change to the net capital rules in June 2004—which allowed securities firms to increase the amount of leverage they could use on their balance sheets to forty times equity while traditional banks, by statute, had to keep the leverage closer to ten times equity—doomed them to inevitable failure. "The reality is if you take the scorecard of the banks and you take the scorecard of the investment banks, they're about the same," he continued. "A bunch of banks didn't have enough capital and had to raise more, and some investment banks didn't have enough capital and had to raise more. Some did and some didn't. So the thirty and ten times issue would have meant Goldman was gone long before Citi or UBS or anybody had to dip into the capital pool." Many people also blame what happened in 2008 on the SEC's decision in 2007 to eliminate the "uptick rule," which required that every short sale be transacted at a price higher than the price of the previous trade. By eliminating the rule, the death spiral of a stock can be accelerated. The intent of the rule was to buy time for the stock as it free-falls and force short sellers to pause before transacting. Without the uptick rule, stocks are susceptible to "bear raids," where short sellers can overwhelm a stock in huge surges of selling that intimidate buyers from stepping in. This creates a panic that can spiral ever downward. For banks and securities firms, where the confidence of counterparties is essential, the death spiral can indeed be irreversible.

To Schwartz, the near-collapse of the global financial system was caused by many factors, from Hyman Minsky's financial instability hypothesis—which suggests that whenever the economy is stable for a long period, the financial markets create their own instability—to the dramatic and unprecedented surge of global wealth. "If you go back to the period from 1970 to 1974," he told his friends, "there was a doubling of commodity prices. Commodity producers got rich, the rest of the world got poor. When they doubled again, the world got poorer. Then commodity prices fell. Commodity guys got less rich, the rest of the world got more rich. From 2002 to 2006 commodity prices doubled again, and commodity producers got rich. But this time, China, India, and Brazil took those commodities and used cheap labor and made finished goods and got rich, and the developed world's profit margins went to all-time highs. If you had said ahead of time that commodity prices are going to double, finished goods prices are going to be flat, and asked what's going to happen to profit margins, you wouldn't think they were going to record highs.

"But the way the world came together right then was the tsunami of liquidity," he continued. "At exactly the same time that that liquidity was being built, the Fed is saying, 'Hmm, we just had a collapse in *our* economy, we're missing what's going on over here.' Remember Greenspan's conundrum? 'We had better flood the world with liquidity to avoid deflation.' That's what we learned from Japan. While global wealth was building up like crazy, artificial liquidity was pushing interest rates down to unbelievably low levels and, at the very same time, in the developed economies people are moving from being long-term savers to being short-term savers for retirement, saying, 'I need a fixed-income return, but I can't take 1 percent.' You have this huge pool of money looking for return and what it was looking for was debt-backed-up assets. So they created this debt cycle. You had the rating agencies arbitraging what was there. It looked so good to everyone that it created a bubble that made the dot-com bubble look small. But, ironically, because it was against this huge, diverse pool of assets and there were real assets, it was a much more seductive bubble, because in the dot-com bubble the world got caught up, but you also had tons of people—anybody who'd been in the business as long as we have—saying, 'Guys, this ends badly. This dot-com bullshit ends badly. IPOs going up ten times, that's not lasting.'

"But this time," he continued, "there were some naysayers, but nobody saw the kind of bubble it was because all these instruments are against hard assets that are newly diversified with lots and lots of history, and they're really safe, and that's better than just a few institutions, and it's a big market, and it's diversified and all that. What got missed in all of that was it created so much excess demand versus any historical period that it so inflated the price of the assets, and then I think the trigger was [that] the rest of the world started saying, 'Wait a minute, we're going to build out our infrastructure,' so they started building these huge infrastructure projects that started to suck up some of the liquidity just as the Fed was trying to go back. So rates come up a little bit and all of a sudden you go, 'Oops, maybe we'll call a time-out on house price appreciation for a little bit around the world.' Then you have all these things like FHA and HUD and all these people saying, 'You better lend to all these poor people.' People at first said, 'No, we won't,' and then they said, 'Oh, this is a good gig.' So greed was a factor in all this, too. But these things do occur with some regularity, and we haven't ever figured out how to stop the next one from happening. I'm sure we'll figure out how to prevent something like this from happening again. Wall Street is always good at fighting the last war. But these things happen and they're big, and when they happen everybody tries to look at what happened in the previous six months to find someone or something to blame it on. But, in truth, it was a team effort. We all fucked up. Government. Rating agencies. Wall Street. Commercial banks. Regulators. Investors. Everybody."

APRÈS MOI, LE DÉLUGE

S ometimes during a violent summer thunderstorm, when the rain is coming down in tumultuous sheets, the thunder is ear-splitting, and the lightning seems to be cracking all around, the countryside itself appears overwhelmed by upheaval and kinetic energy. When the storm passes, not only has its destructive path been laid bare—along with uprooted trees and downed limbs—but often there is also an eerie calm that descends upon the landscape that seems every bit as odd and discomfiting, in its own way, as the violence that had just ended.

The same palpable eerie calm that follows a nasty summer storm has found its way into nearly every nook and cranny of what used to be known as Wall Street. One year after the mass destruction in American capitalism that swallowed up whole Bear Stearns, Lehman Brothers, Merrill Lynch, AIG, Washington Mutual, Wachovia, Fannie Mae, Freddie Mac, and scores of other smaller, regional banks—and with predictions that as many as four hundred more may fail this year—an eerie calm has replaced the creative destruction, to borrow the famous phrase used by the Austrian economist Joseph Schumpeter.

Now that the Dow has recovered to around 10,000—not up to its high of 14,164 in 2007 but up some 50 percent from its March 2009 low—and the capital markets are functioning almost normally again, some Wall Street firms—particularly Goldman Sachs and JPMorgan Chase—have figured out ways to make historic amounts of money in the wake of the global demand for their services and an equally historic lack of suppliers to meet that demand. After all by taking out the third-, fourth- and fifth-largest securities firms as competitors in the market, it stands to reason the remaining firms will benefit. The success of Goldman Sachs, in particular—which earned $8.4 billion in the first nine months of 2009, thus enjoying the most profitable stretch in its 140-year history and deciding as a result to set aside some $16.7 billion for employee bonuses, putting those bonuses on a par with those paid during the peak of the bubble in 2007—has politicians and economists at once flummoxed about how the firm has pulled this off and hopeful that maybe the worst of the financial crisis is, in fact, over. Goldman has been able to make so much money in part by taking risks and trading—both with clients and for its own account—when other firms have been reluctant to do so.

There are other hopeful signs that the worst of the financial crisis has passed. Goldman, Morgan Stanley, Bank of America, and JPMorgan Chase have paid back their TARP funds—$10 billion each by Goldman and Morgan Stanley; $25 billion in the case of JPMorgan Chase, and $45 billion by Bank of America—and both Goldman and Morgan Stanley have paid the government millions in dividends and bought back from the government the warrants granted at the time the TARP funds were forced upon them. Goldman paid $1.1 billion for its warrants; Morgan Stanley paid $950 million. The taxpayers' returns on these nine-month investments were a respectable 23 percent for Goldman Sachs and 19 percent for Morgan Stanley. Rather than negotiate the price of its warrants with the Treasury, JPMorgan has decided to let the market decide its price. But, again, it looks as if the Treasury will benefit from these investments. To date, around $116 billion in TARP funding has been repaid, including the repurchase of outstanding warrants.

There is probably no better indicator of the extent to which the system has moved away from the edge of the abyss than the fact that two of the three key architects of the rescue tactics and strategies enacted throughout 2008—Tim Geithner and Ben Bernanke—remain in their powerful positions managing the economy, as U.S. Treasury secretary and chairman of the Federal Reserve Board, respectively. While there were moments in March as the Dow circled 6,500 when there were repeated calls for Obama to consider replacing Geithner, with the Dow now closer to 10,000 and the Treasury's coffers slowly being restocked with the repayment of the TARP funds, Geithner's job looks to be secure at the moment.

As for Bernanke, when all was said and done, President Obama decided that the Fed chairman—a Republican, who was appointed by his predecessor—had performed sufficiently well during the crisis to merit an early reappointment to a new four-year term. "The president thinks that Ben's done a great job as Fed chairman, that he has helped the economy through one of the worst experiences since the Great Depression, and that he has essentially been pulling the economy back from the brink of what would have been the second Great Depression," the White House chief of staff, Rahm Emanuel, said on August 24, 2009.

The third member of the crisis troika—Hank Paulson, the former Treasury secretary—has by definition kept a far lower profile than the other two men since he is no longer in government and has been working on his memoir, *On the Brink: Inside the Race to Stop the Collapse of the Global Financial System*, to be published in February 2010. He has declined repeated interview requests and made his only public appearance, in July 2009, in front of a Congressional hearing that was investigating what he and Bernanke did in the waning days of the Bush administration to force Bank of America to complete its acquisition of Merrill Lynch. Paulson had no choice but to appear.

Paulson had previously agreed to an unusual arrangement with Todd S. Purdum, the national editor of *Vanity Fair*. Beginning in November 2007—more than a year after he took the position of Treasury secretary, when the drama in the financial markets was starting to come into focus and become increasingly more acute—he allowed Purdum a series of regular on-the-record interviews on the condition that the content of the interviews would not be shared until well after Paulson left office. The result was Purdum's October 2009 article, "Henry Paulson's Longest Night," in the magazine. Aside from scoring a reporting coup, Purdum draws a curious and not uninteresting portrait of Paulson—including sharing with readers the fact that Paulson repeatedly threw up during a February 2008 interview—but he does not shed much new light on the decision making that led up to the demise of both Bear Stearns and Lehman Brothers. Paulson did confide to Purdum that he and Bernanke "were ahead of a lot of people in understanding how serious" the approaching economic crisis might be but that "it was always bigger and more systemic even than I had for a good while anticipated it to be, or expected it to be." He said that after a bunch of years of robust economic news during the middle of the Bush administration, it was clear to Paulson that "the next shock we had was going to really stress the modern financial system." At one point he even told Bush that "there's a dry forest, and we don't know what's going to ignite the fire or set the spark," but Paulson figured that a decline in housing values after so many years of increases could cause a serious problem.

As for the collapse of Bear Stearns in less than a week's time, Paulson told Purdum a version of Geithner's speech about how "central banks do liquidity; they don't do insolvency" and seemed to have an instinctual feel for how the events could have unfolded as they did. "When financial institutions die, it's liquidity, O.K.?" he said. "If you're an investment-banking firm, it's liquidity. And when the run starts, it happens, it's over quickly." He said there were moments during the fateful weekend when he was not sure that JPMorgan's deal for Bear Stearns would come together and that he was preparing for the firm's bankruptcy filing. The plan was to "[p]ut foam on the runway," Paulson said, and pray that there was not too much collateral damage. But "then things came together," he said. "Would it have been nice if J. P. Morgan had bought it without any government help? You bet. Were we fortunate that they were there with government help? You bet."

Purdum offered no confirmation either of the widely accepted notion that Paulson had ordered JPMorgan to pay no more than $2 a share for Bear Stearns in order to avoid "moral hazard" or of whether at one time Paulson had suggested $1 per share, as then Bear Stearns Chairman Jimmy Cayne believed.

As for his decision to not provide rescue financing to Lehman—as he did two days later for AIG—and the common view that Lehman was "mandated to fail," Paulson kept to the script with Purdum. "Lehman Brothers was something that we had been focused on and worked on and worried about for a year," he said. "And we knew, and Dick Fuld knew, and we kept telling him every way we knew how that if he announced earnings like he thought he was going to announce—right after he announced the second-quarter earnings—the company would fail. And when you've got an investment bank, no one had any powers to deal with that. I certainly didn't have any powers to deal with that." Hence, Paulson's logic went, this situation demonstrated the need to create what became the $700 billion Troubled Asset Relief Program. (Paulson also confided to James B. Stewart, writing in *The New Yorker* a year after Lehman collapsed, that he thinks *now* he would have been willing *then* to spread some foam on the runway for Lehman too. "We said, 'No public money,'" Paulson told Stewart. "We said this publicly. We repeated it when these guys came in. But to ourselves we said, 'If there's a chance to put in public money and avert a disaster, we're open to it.'")

BUT WHAT OF THE NUMEROUS, lower-profile players in this historic drama? Have they been able to reconstruct their lives in the wake of the implosion of the firms from which they derived such a significant portion of their pride, wealth, and status?

The most prominent figure in the Bear Stearns collapse, Jimmy Cayne, now seventy-five, remains retired. He is no longer speaking publicly about what happened to his firm and has maintained a surprisingly low profile in the wake of the publication of this book, which he has told people he did not like (although apparently his wife did). Cayne's fellow Bear executives used to refer to him as "Osama being in the cave" when he would hole up in his sixth-floor lair at 383 Madison Avenue and hold court. That gentle ribbing would be enough to get Cayne to walk around the firm occasionally to try to get a better sense of what was going on there.

He continues to play bridge at the national level and has attended a number of major tournaments. Phillip Alder, the *New York Times'* bridge columnist, played against Cayne at the 2009 Summer Nationals tournament in Washington, D.C. "Since retiring, he has become far more amenable, smiling a lot and seeming to enjoy life," Alder wrote in an email, "though I expect his new manner was tested after his early exit from the Spingold Knockout Teams."

Alan Schwartz, now fifty-eight, chose not to retire. For almost a year after the sale of Bear Stearns to JPMorgan Chase, Schwartz fielded one impressive job opportunity after another. KKR, the private-equity leader, wanted him to head up its nascent efforts to start an investment-banking business. JPMorgan was hoping he

would stay as a senior executive. Both Morgan Stanley and Goldman Sachs worked very hard to recruit Schwartz for their firms. He
had long been recognized as a leading M&A advisor on Wall Street,
especially in the media, telecom, and health-care industries, and
nothing he had done in Bear's final two weeks as an independent
company had damaged that reputation. If anything, his reputation
as an M&A banker—as opposed to his standing as a CEO of major
securities firm—was enhanced by the events of those two weeks, for
Schwartz skillfully herded the various cats involved in the tense
drama—lawyers, board members, bankers, private equity firms, government leaders—to as successful conclusion as was possible under
the circumstances. He shone especially brightly during the week
after JPMorgan agreed to buy Bear for $2 a share when Jamie
Dimon, the JPMorgan CEO, sought to renegotiate with Schwartz a
flawed aspect of the merger agreement. Schwartz took full advantage of that rare moment of leverage to win for Bear's shareholders
$10 a share in JPMorgan's stock, a five-fold increase achieved
within the span of a week. Considering that Cayne, the board chairman, was urging his fellow board members to seriously look at the
"nuclear option" of having Bear Stearns file for bankruptcy protection, Schwartz's ability to get the deal done was all the more impressive. "I spent twenty-five years training for those weekends," he said.

No firm was more aggressive in trying to land Schwartz than
Goldman Sachs. The firm wanted him to be part of its office of
the chairman, reporting directly to Lloyd Blankfein, the chairman
and CEO. Schwartz would have sat on the firm's thirtieth floor,
where the senior executives had offices, and would have directly
advised Blankfein as well as his longtime clients, including Time-
Warner, Verizon, and Disney. Had Schwartz accepted Goldman's
overtures, the irony would have been rich, since there were many
at Bear Stearns—but not Schwartz—who believed and still believe
that Goldman fomented the negative sentiment and trading that
doomed Bear Stearns in its final week. (The SEC has supposedly
been investigating charges that Goldman spread negative rumors
about Bear Stearns at the same time that it was shorting Bear's
stock but no information on the topic has been forthcoming from
the SEC.)

There is no question that had Schwartz resurfaced at Goldman

Sachs in a senior executive position, there would have been—on the surface anyway—a modicum of vindication for him after all that had transpired since he became CEO of Bear Stearns in January 2008. His friend and fellow Duke alumnus David Rubenstein—the co-founder of the Carlyle Group, the private-equity behemoth—told him so, urging him in their private conversations to consider seriously the Goldman offer. "I think everybody looks at you as a good guy," Rubenstein told him, "but if there's any lingering question, this is cleansing. Right? You're being anointed."

But Schwartz, always a bit of an iconoclast, was not so sure he needed vindication or cleansing. He had also been in serious discussions about taking a senior position at the New York-based Guggenheim Partners, a virtually unknown diversified investment firm with $100 billion of assets under management as well as small investment-banking and merchant-banking operations. Rubenstein's comments got him thinking about his legacy and what he wanted it to be. "If people read you're going to have a big title at Goldman Sachs, people go, 'Wow,'" Rubenstein told Schwartz. "If they read you're going to Guggenheim, they say, 'What?'" Schwartz laughed at his friend's characterization of the two opportunities. "Good," Schwartz thought, "That gives me a filter that says if I believe that my reputation is so important that I have to go prove to people certain things, then I should take the Goldman job, and the good news, is I don't really care. The people that know, the people that are inside, the people that know what happened, are the people that matter." Indeed, since the firm's denouement, Schwartz regularly received e-mails from former colleagues thanking him for his work. "That's what really matters," he said, while noting—with some surprise, it seemed—that he had not "seen myself" be "tarred and feathered or pilloried either."

In June 2009 Schwartz joined Guggenheim Partners as "executive chairman," ending months of speculation in the media about what he would do next. He was to work closely with the executive team at Guggenheim to help the firm grow and have a more significant place in the financial services industry, especially in investment banking. The job was not dissimilar to the one he was considering at Goldman as a senior advisor but without any of the apparently unwanted symbolism of Schwartz conceding he needed or wanted Goldman on his résumé. "Alan Schwartz is one of the most respected figures in our industry, and we are thrilled to welcome him to the firm," stated Mark Walter, CEO of Guggenheim Partners. "Guggenheim has grown a substantial and thriving business by staying focused on its clients. Alan's counsel, experience and leadership will be invaluable across the entire firm as we continue to build on our existing businesses and pursue new opportunities." Schwartz's first strategic move at Guggenheim came in late August when he hired Kenneth Savio, formerly co-head of global equity trading at Bear Stearns, to build an equity trading desk at Guggenheim, part of what reportedly is to be Schwartz's effort to try and build Guggenheim into "the next Bear Stearns." A few weeks later, Schwartz hired Peter Cornisar, forty-two, a recently departed Goldman partner, to work in Guggenheim's Los Angeles office and to advise consumer and retail companies.

Since Bear Stearns's implosion, Schwartz has had plenty of time to think about what happened at the firm and across Wall Street in 2007 and 2008. He remains convinced that he did all he could to try to save the firm in the nearly three months he was running it, and he has said he feels especially good about what he was able to do for creditors and shareholders, given all that occurred on Wall Street six months later. "When I look back now," he said in an interview, "I feel better than I did then, simply because my own view is . . . it felt like somebody had come and set fire to our house. And I felt terrible. But then six months later, a tsunami came through town and blew away all the other houses. And I don't see how, frankly, we would have survived that tsunami. With Lehman going under, with Merrill about to go under, and Morgan Stanley and Goldman an inch away, I don't see how Bear Stearns was a big enough franchise to survive that kind of storm. So, the reality is that going through that in March probably I would say, on balance, Bear Stearns people did better than they would have if it had survived until September." He added, "It felt terrible to be the guy that got picked on and driven out of business, but, ironically, that may have been a favor."

Schwartz has also had plenty of time to reflect on what happened to Wall Street and what might have caused the crisis. And he remains troubled, as do many others, by the continued use of credit-default swaps—a form of insurance to protect against debt defaults—that can be purchased not only by the holder of the debt in question but also by anyone who wants to speculate on whether that debt will be repaid. It would be as if not only a homeowner could get fire insurance on his own home but everyone in the neighborhood could as well. Of course, the neighbors would pay their own insurance premiums but the policies would pay off only if the home burned down. Under that perverse dynamic, it would be no surprise that the home being insured by so many people other than the homeowner suddenly found itself up in flames. Schwartz said he believes Bear Stearns was a victim of such a cabal. "It's a flaw in the system," Schwartz said.

And one he thinks will likely be corrected by whatever regulatory reforms end up being approved by Congress. "Ironically, you think you've devised a system to get around it, and what happens is you devise a system to deal with all the flaws that were in place in 1929, and by 2009 there's new flaws," he said. "And so I think derivatives is one of the things that will be looked into, and things will happen now to change the way that business works. And fifty years from now, there'll be another crisis, and it'll be about some instruments that we've never heard of. If you go back to the Bible, the Jubilee period was every fifty years they forgave debt. It just happens."

But he remains unmoved by the argument that Bear Stearns could have taken any number of steps years before—among them, diversifying the firm, becoming less reliant on the fixed-income group, or raising new capital—that would have prevented the firm's ultimate demise. "That's the thing I've thought a lot about," he said, even going so far as to imagine what he would have done had he still been head of research at Bear Stearns and was responsible for issuing a written prediction about how the credit bubble of 2004 through 2007 would likely have ended. He said it would have been very easy, as a research analyst, to predict and then to write that things would end badly since the history of recent Wall Street cycles—whether in junk bonds, Internet IPOs, emerging telecom debt, or mortgage-backed securities—is that they inevitably end badly.

The far harder challenge comes as CEO of a Wall Street firm. What do you do in that position to prepare a firm that is a public company, with quarterly reporting requirements—and, in the case of Bear Stearns, the 14,000 people who work there—for an inevitable and potentially cataclysmic downturn? Could Schwartz and Cayne have taken steps, as Goldman Sachs did in December 2006, to reduce dramatically Bear Stearns's exposure to the mortgage market? Or aware early on, in March and April 2007, that the mortgage securities in the two Bear Stearns hedge funds were rapidly losing value—thanks in part to new marks Goldman Sachs had placed on the securities—should Schwartz and Cayne have hedged Bear's bets? In retrospect, the answer obviously is "Yes," but, according to Schwartz, at the time that course of action was anything but clear. "The actions you would have had to take would have been so radical," he said, "and you would have had to have been so convinced you were right, with 14,000 employees. . . . [I]t's near impossible to take that kind of 'slam-on-the-brakes' action—stall speed is what I called it—where you go so slow that you go out of business before the thing you're worried about happens." He said Bear Stearns faced a similar problem in the late 1990s, when Wall Street was consumed with inflating what would become the Internet IPO bubble and Bear Stearns made a conscious decision not to participate in such underwritings or offer trendy remuneration packages to bankers and traders. "We were really losing people left and right because we were not chasing the dot-com bubble," he said. But he does hail David Viniar, the Goldman CFO, and Goldman generally for making the decision to pull back from the mortgage market and to lengthen out the terms of its financing. "That's the kind of decision at the margin we could have made," he said.

But beyond the marginal decisions, he remains skeptical about what might have prevented the industry's collapse. "I don't see what five CEOs could have done," he said. "Clearly, on the execution front, Goldman Sachs did much better than others. Credit Suisse did better than UBS by a zillion miles. JPMorgan did better than Citigroup by a zillion miles. But as an industry, could they have slammed on the brakes? Not really. It just doesn't happen."

And he also takes exception to the idea that Bear's reliance on short-term overnight funding using long-term assets as collateral doomed the firm to its ignominious end. For years, one of the ongoing criticisms of banks generally is that they borrow for short periods of time—for instance, with demand deposits, 60-day commercial paper, or overnight repo financing—and lend for long periods of time—for example, through 364-day revolving-credit facilities or five- to ten-year term loans. Such funding arrangements can make banks episodically susceptible to losses in investor confidence, or so the criticism goes. Schwartz does not believe it. "There is no other banking system that's ever existed," he said. "The reason we have deposit insurance is because a banking system is fundamentally about raising a bunch of assets, which are short term in nature because it's the liquidity of individuals that when aggregated becomes a pool that you can lend out. That is banking."

Schwartz said "what happened in this cycle" wasn't "that a bunch of us got short-term funded" but rather that the "cycle froze." What he means is that like every other Wall Street firm, Bear Stearns looked at the "maturity profile" of its debt obligations and then asked itself, "How much [cash] do I need if I have to start liquidating? I don't want to be forced into a liquidation overnight, but if I had to take down my positions a lot, like do I have 30 days, 60 days, 90 days, or 180 days of inventory [of securities on the balance sheet]? And when your inventory is mostly Triple-A type of stuff, government agencies and stuff like that, you think that it's pretty liquid, because it has been throughout its entire history."

But, he said, from the summer of 2007, "a whole class" of debt instruments "froze" and could not be sold in the market. And as various Bear Stearns credit lines such as those set for, say, a year or eighteen months came due, they could not be renewed for those same periods of time. This was in part because of the growing concern over Bear's creditworthiness when after the collapse of the two hedge funds—the High-Grade Structured Credit Fund and the Enhanced Leverage Fund—the markets forced Bear's debt into shorter and shorter maturities until, by March 2008, the bulk of the firm's $75 billion in financing needs were taken care of in the overnight repo markets—overnight loans that were secured by the growing inventory of increasingly illiquid assets on the firm's balance sheet.

"The magnitude of your overnight [loans] in March was a function of how many of your credit lines expired previously, and couldn't be renewed," Schwartz said. "It wasn't a conscious decision. It was a byproduct of the liquidity environment, and I'm talking about the whole industry now. The whole industry had assets that became very long-term assets"—that could not be sold easily or quickly, since the market for them was disappearing—"and the vulnerability came from the fact that once the world knew that, they could pick on your short-term funding. Bear got pushed that way sooner because of the [collapse of the] hedge funds. We were in the middle of lengthening maturities when the hedge funds hit, and then we got shut down."

Schwartz said he worries that by focusing criticism on Wall Street's ongoing funding predicament—which is nothing more in his view than the very essence of banking itself—the future consequences could be devastating. "If you convey to the world that all of this was this recklessness of the financial system that ruined the economy for everybody else, you run the risk of being forced into doing things that are the exact opposite of what's going to make it better. It's like becoming the union leader by promising things that are, long-term, going to cost you jobs."

But other equally intelligent and sober industry observers believe this apparently inviolate rule of banking is precisely what makes the financial system so fundamentally precarious and subject to very extreme swings of investor confidence—with devastating ramifications for us all.

In the end, though, and with more than a year to reflect on the events that transpired, Schwartz said the only fail-safe for Bear Stearns would have been to sell the firm. In addition to trying unsuccessfully to convince Jimmy Cayne, he was an outspoken advocate on the executive committee (as was Warren Spector) for diversifying the firm by buying Neuberger Berman, the asset-management business, as well as Pershing, the clearing business, and by expanding the investment banking business into Europe and Asia. Even though Cayne blocked these initiatives, Schwartz said, "It wouldn't have mattered. There was only one choice we could have made: Sell."

❋

As for the other central figures in the Bear Stearns drama, the past twenty months—since JPMorgan closed the acquisition—have been a decidedly mixed bag. Ironically, on the one hand, many of the fourteen thousand Bear bankers, traders, and other employees, as well as the firm itself, benefited from the death order—from the fact that Bear Stearns failed first. Not only had the full magnitude of the disaster not yet unfolded, making it possible for Bear's shareholders to end up with $10 per share in JPMorgan stock and for Bear's creditors to get paid in full—unlike at Lehman, where shareholders got wiped out and creditors nearly so—but many of the employees were able to find new jobs, with a few going to JPMorgan and the balance going to other firms across the Street.

Unlike the vast majority of his former colleagues, Ace Greenberg remains at JPMorgan. He no longer answers his own phone and is not on the firm's executive committee or anywhere near its board of directors. He is now, at eighty-two years of age and a survivor of his second bout with cancer, a high-end broker in the firm's small brokerage unit acquired from Bear Stearns. He manages his own money and that of a small group of loyal friends and customers.

He has kept a low profile. Greenberg is currently working on a book with *New Yorker* writer Mark Singer (who had written the 1999 profile of Greenberg in the magazine) about his long tenure at Bear Stearns and the firm's demise. "I want to tell the story about how the firm grew," Greenberg told a reporter. Would Greenberg be writing about his "tumultuous" relationship with Cayne? "Not really," Greenberg replied. "I will just give the facts." One former Bear executive said of the project: "Who could possibly care about a book that Ace is writing, much of which will presumably be spent telling why Jimmy is really the wacko, not Ace?" In a brief telephone interview in September 2009, Greenberg said he and Singer were still writing away but that he had nothing to say about it or about anything else related to what happened to Bear Stearns. "No thoughts, no nothing," he said. Then, with thinly veiled sarcasm, he said, "Just keep relying on Jimmy Cayne, he's a great source. He absolutely speaks with a straight tongue."

Greenberg has given only one thirty-eight-minute public interview—on the *Charlie Rose Show,* in October 2008—and it was a disaster. He refused to answer Rose's questions about what had happened to Bear Stearns seven months earlier. The conversation was so frustrating that, in the end, the two spoke lamely about Greenberg's philanthropy instead.

Of the senior Bear executives, Warren Spector, the former co-president of the firm and longtime head of the highly profitable fixed-income division, has kept the lowest profile of all. Although still young, he has not resumed working in finance, nor has he been rumored to be a serious candidate for any job, although he has been asked. He continues as chairman of the Public Theatre, near his fully renovated new mansion in Greenwich Village. In May 2009 he sold his eight-room penthouse apartment at 40 Fifth Avenue for $8 million—$1 million below the original asking price—to Scott M. Pinkus, a former partner and mortgage-backed securities expert at Goldman Sachs. Ironically, at Goldman, where he was a partner for ten years, Pinkus established and headed the Credit Derivatives Group, which was responsible for the trading, structuring, and distribution of over-the-counter credit-derivative contracts, credit-linked notes, and various types of credit-intensive securitized instruments—in other words, he created many of the very obscure and hard-to-value securities that helped to trigger the financial crisis.

Others of the former Bear executives have actually thrived since the collapse of the firm. This has been particularly true for the firm's former vice chairmen. Donald Tang, who worked tirelessly to consummate the $1 billion stock swap with Citic Securities, only to watch the deal crumble along with Bear Stearns, has since March 2009 been the CEO of a boutique investment-banking firm—Citic Securities International Partners Ltd.—focused on M&A advisory assignments and private-equity investments involving Chinese companies as well as foreign companies looking to get into China. Both Citic and Evercore, a New York boutique bank, are Tang's financial partners in the new firm. Before starting his new venture, Tang worked briefly at JPMorgan Chase.

Even before the sale of Bear Stearns to JPMorgan closed, Bear vice chairman Tom Flexner announced that he had joined Citigroup as the global head of real estate commercial and investment banking as well as being put in charge of alternative investments in real estate. Obviously, though, Citigroup's fortunes worsened dramatically during the year following Flexner's arrival, giving him the unique distinction of having experienced the near-collapse of two major global financial institutions. He worries about the longer-term political, economic, and social consequences of the credit crisis. "Is the government going to become a much large permanent factor in our economy and in shaping decisions affecting the allocation of private resources?" he wrote in a recent e-mail. "Is the American consumer, who has experienced massive wealth erosion in home equity and portfolio equity, going to alter his spending habits for a generation, becoming a true net saver? How are future generations going to deal with the multi-trillion-dollar budget deficits associated with the aftermath of the financial crisis? What could a potential loss of confidence in the US dollar mean to our country's ability to maintain its global leadership status? Are we headed for sustained high inflation or deflation? How many years will it take to regenerate the jobs lost over the past two years?" He wrote that it is "remarkable that the puncturing of the credit bubble—which had built up over many years of systemic leveraging, securitization of risk across the globe, deregulation and the easy money policies of the world's central bankers—has the potential to lead to sweeping change in the tax regime, in compensation practices, in trade restrictions, in the nature of future job creation, in economic class distinctions, even in the rule of law."

Fares Noujaim, another Bear vice chairman, joined Merrill Lynch as the president of Merrill's Middle East and North Africa operations within days of the completion of the Bear sale to JPMorgan. (Noujaim, forty-six, was born in Kuwait to Lebanese parents and moved to Brooklyn when he was eight.) Like Flexner, though, Noujaim also had a front-row seat to the challenges Merrill faced, especially during the brief nine-month tenure of John Thain as Merrill's CEO. "Because of my Bear experience I had this feeling that when you die once, you can't die again," he said. "Having lost my professional family before and my wealth, there wasn't a goddamn thing anybody . . . I mean you almost feel—invincible is the wrong word. It's more your outer shell is just that much thicker. You're impervious to a lot of things that people maybe are afraid of. I got hired here to join the management committee, to be part of a small core that was going to dig Merrill out of this thing." When Noujaim arrived, Merrill was a ship that was rapidly taking on water and starting to list.

Noujaim, who reported to Merrill president Greg Fleming, had a big role in helping Merrill raise $2 billion from the Kuwait Investment Authority, a sovereign wealth fund, in December 2007 and January 2008. Noujaim also worked closely with Fleming and Thain to help orchestrate the sale of Merrill to Bank of America in September 2008. At first, Noujaim was not sure he would stay at the merged Bank of America/Merrill Lynch, especially after Fleming, who now teaches at Yale Law School, his alma mater, left, and after Ken Lewis, then Bank of America CEO, fired Thain. In the end—although the *New York Post* reported erroneously that he had a two-year, $15 million contract that might have been persuasive—Noujaim decided to stay as a vice chairman of investment banking, a powerful symbol of continuity at the firm after the departure of a barrage of longtime senior Merrill bankers and traders. (The fourth Bear vice chairman, E. John Rosenwald, now seventy-nine, has retired.)

Other principal players in the Bear drama have also done well. Mike Alix, the firm's chief risk officer at the end, is now a senior vice president in the New York Fed's bank supervision group. Geithner had hired Alix for the role in November 2008 after working closely with Alix—and being impressed by him—on a number of Geithner's risk management initiatives. "I was actively thinking about how the dominoes might fall from a system perspective," Alix said during the summer of 2009. "The experience of late 2007 and early 2008 was all about seeing some of those worst fears unfold. The loss of liquidity, the contraction of credit, and all those things that some senior people from the industry and the official sector had collectively fretted about were far worse than we had expected."

Unlike many critics of Wall Street, Alix shares many of the views of his fellow Duke alumnus Alan Schwartz and does not blame, among other things, the greed of bankers and the reliance on short-term financing for causing the collapse of the system. "I try to encourage people to resist the temptation to say that there are things that individual institutions could have done or regulators could have done that, if applied, you can say for sure would have avoided what happened," he says. "Because in my view, the downturn is just an inevitable part of capitalism and economic activity, and you never will know exactly what the right tools are, or the right approaches are, to avoid the worst of it while you're in it. You have to sort of experience it and learn from it."

Steve Begleiter, Bear's former head of strategy—a thankless job at the firm if there ever was one—joined Flexpoint Ford, a Chicago-based $1.3 billion private-equity firm that specializes in making investments in financial services and healthcare companies (and in which I am a tiny investor.) Begleiter joined Flexpoint in October 2008 as a principal and the head of the firm's New York office. But he may be better known for the fifteen minutes of fame he amassed during July 2009, playing Texas hold' em in the World Series of Poker main event. As unlikely—and ironic—as such an outcome would be, Begleiter was one of the nine finalists vying to become the World Series of Poker champion and thus one of the world's best gamblers. "Living a dream," he wrote in a July 15 e-mail. As the final denouement gets underway, scheduled for Las Vegas on November 7, Begleiter was in decent shape in third position with nearly thirty million chips. He was guaranteed a payday of at least $1.2 million regardless of whether he won or not. "I'm dancing between raindrops in the middle of a minefield and somehow I'm still standing," he told a poker website in August 2009. "I've already won. It's insane I made the final table. I'm not quite sure how I did it. My objective is to play well—so far I've played well." In September 2009 Begleiter also found himself in third place in another prestigious poker event, the World Poker Tour's Legends of Poker event. In the end, Begleiter played valiantly in November at the final table of the World Series of Poker in Las Vegas, but was eliminated in dramatic fashion at around 1:00 a.m. when—even though he was the chip leader—he lost a big pot and, in a subsequent hand, was forced "all in." He was the favorite to win the hand, and had he won, he would have regained the chip lead. Unfortunately for him, the last card of the hand foiled him and he was wiped out. He finished in sixth place, with total winnings of $1.59 million.

As for Paul Friedman, in October 2009 he left Mariner Investment Group—a hedge fund run by William Michaelcheck, one of the former heads of fixed income at Bear Stearns—to join Alan Schwartz at Guggenheim Partners, yet another example of Schwartz's efforts to reconstruct parts of Bear Stearns at Guggenheim. Friedman is trying to keep a lower profile than he had during Bear Stearns' unraveling. He has caught some flak from his former colleagues for being so publicly outspoken about his view that Bear Stearns executives were responsible for what happened, not some amorphous once-a-century tsunami—the "We killed Bear" theory. A typical refrain, conveyed by one former senior Bear executive, was that "the running joke has been about why we didn't pay Paul Friedman for managing the firm when, from reading the book, they found out that he *had* been running the firm all those years."

Friedman also agrees with Schwartz that, at the end, the market forced Bear into its lethal overnight funding scenario rather than it being something that Bear executives chose to do voluntarily. "Having so much of the firm's inventory funding [done] overnight was not by design," he wrote in an e-mail. "Rather, it was a function of the fact that after the summer of '07 no one would enter into a new term trade with Bear. Historically the overnight funding was smaller on both a notional and percentage basis."

He also had some heartfelt and articulate views about whether blame for the crisis extended into the criminal realm and whether a 9-11 style commission (which was finally appointed in July 2009 and is to submit a report to Congress by December 2010) should have the responsibility to try to ferret it out. "Do you really think some commission will find that any of this was intentional and, as a result, criminal (in the legal sense, not in the moral sense)?" he wondered. "That the guys at the top all said, 'Let's see, can we blow ourselves up and the world along with us?' What they were was stupid. They believed they had the risk under control. They believed— at least at Bear—that the math and underlying bond technology behind the alchemy of turning funky loans into complex securities and turning complex securities into securities that were even more complex actually worked—otherwise, why would they own so much and lend against so much of it? I can't tell you how many meetings I sat through with the research guys as they explained how the laws of large numbers made it clear that a diversified pool of mortgages—even subprime mortgages—would protect senior bond holders from losses. They were wrong—catastrophically wrong—but that doesn't make them criminals."

※

ONE OF THE POSSIBLE REASONS that former Bear Stearns co-president Warren Spector has stayed out of the limelight since June 2008 was that he remained a potential witness in the October 2009 criminal trial of former Bear hedge-fund managers Ralph Cioffi and Matthew Tannin. Spector's name was on the prosecution's original sixty-three-name witness list but not among the thirty-two names on the revised list, a change that may be understandable given that the prosecution wanted to pin things on Cioffi and Tannin (since they were the men indicted). Even though Spector had not been charged with any wrongdoing—nor was he even mentioned by name in the indictment of Cioffi and Tannin—many former Bear Stearns and other Wall Street executives believe that there would be no possible way for Spector not to have been fully aware of what Cioffi and Tannin were doing at the hedge funds. And they were incredulous that he would not be asked to testify. (In the end, he did not testify at their trial.) Spector liked and admired Cioffi and gave him his $10 million grubstake to start the first hedge fund. And even though Cioffi and Tannin technically reported to Rich Marin, who was head of Bear Stearns Asset Management, Cioffi knew he could always go around Marin to get to Spector, who was Marin's boss. In fact, Cioffi often did just that, as was well known inside Bear Stearns.

Whether what the two managers did was criminal—as alleged by the U.S. government in the indictment—was fully explored during their three-week trial, which began October 13, 2009, at the federal courthouse in downtown Brooklyn, New York. Not surprisingly, the legal wrangling continued right up to the start of the trial. In one example of many, Tannin's defense attorney, Susan Brune, urged Judge Frederic Block to force the government to turn over to the defense—as required by law—more detailed notes of interviews the government had been conducting with the government's witnesses. "The issue . . . is that the government has, in essence, stopped turning over notes of its interview sessions with government witnesses, although we know those sessions are ongoing," Brune wrote to the judge on July 30.

For its part, the government also sought to improve its case before it officially got underway. In an August 18, 2009, letter to Judge Block, James McGovern, an assistant U.S. Attorney, urged the judge to allow the government to introduce at the trial Cioffi's "prior uncharged acts" as "relevant evidence" that Cioffi knowingly engaged in insider trading. One of the counts in the indictment charged Cioffi with insider trading when he "redeemed $2 million worth of his holdings in the Enhanced Fund based on material, non-public information that he acquired as the result of his relationship with BSAM, his employer." In his letter to the judge, McGovern said, "The government will prove that the defendant redeemed his investment in the Enhanced Fund so that he could re-invest the $2 million in another, more profitable fund under his control."

The government said it intended to use Cioffi's ongoing failure to comply with conflict-of-interest reporting requirements regarding trades between his funds and Bear Stearns—trades that Marin eventually stopped cold during late 2006 because of Cioffi's "poor record of compliance"—as evidence of "further conflicts of interest committed by Cioffi and his management team." As another example of Cioffi's propensity toward conflicts of interest, McGovern cited Cioffi's "attempt, in late 2006" to "pledge his investment" in the Enhanced Fund as collateral for a $4.25 million loan from Busey Bank for "La Firenza," a "luxury condominium complex" in Longboat Key, Florida, that Cioffi and his brother were building. The Busey Bank loan was necessary, the government alleged, for the project to be completed and to avert a looming default. When Cioffi informed BSAM management of his intention to pledge his interest in the hedge fund as collateral for the loan, he was denied permission to do so. "Upon learning of BSAM's decision not to allow him to use his stake in the Enhanced Fund as collateral, Cioffi became extremely upset and accused the general counsel of BSAM of being behind the decision." McGovern further wrote that because of the scrutiny he received from BSAM about the Longboat Key loan, Cioffi knowingly concealed his transfer of the $2 million from BSAM management because had he asked them for permission, it also would have been denied. "Furthermore, this evidence will refute any argument Cioffi may make . . . that there is an innocent explanation for his behavior," he wrote.

Even during the trial itself, the government worked hard to convince Judge Block to allow this evidence into the trial. Prosecutors hoped to use documents and testimony to show that Cioffi and Tannin violated a directive from a superior at Bear Stearns about the line of credit, and this act indicated that the two men's alleged criminal behavior began much earlier than previously thought. In a letter sent to Judge Block on October 25, 2009, U.S. Attorney Benton J. Campbell said the government's evidence "will demonstrate that the defendants 'went criminal' months before the conspiracy charged in the indictment, which is something the jury is entitled to know." (Just as the jury was entitled to learn that Bear Stearns paid Cioffi and Tannin $22 million and $4.4 million, respectively, for the years 2005 and 2006—a fun fact that emerged during the trial.) The facts the government wanted to introduce into the trial about the Florida real-estate deal were plenty gory, including a last-minute trip Cioffi took to Busey Bank—just days before Cioffi's trial was set to begin—in a futile effort to retrieve the original documents related to the loan. Since the government had previously subpoenaed the loan documents, they could not be turned over to Cioffi during his visit. (Whether ill-gotten or not, based on Cioffi's pledge of his interests in the hedge funds, Busey Bank gave him the loan. It has since been repaid in full.)

In the end, Judge Block did not allow this last-minute evidence to be introduced into the trial. The judge also kept out of the trial the contents of a secret diary that Tannin had started in his gmail account on November 21, 2006. In his first entry that day he admitted to being highly stressed and increasingly dependent on sleeping medication and anti-anxiety drugs—two facts never before revealed to his investors. Tannin's diary makes it clear that in the summer of 2006 he was worried about "blow up risk" for investors in the two hedge funds. "This all hit me like a ton of bricks," Tannin wrote in the diary, "and the first result—almost immediately—was for me to lose my ability to sleep. Classic anxiety. I could not sleep. I would wake up an hour or two after going to be[d] . . . My mind would be focused on all of the things that I had not done and all of the things that could have gone wrong."

Tannin headed off to London for a vacation with his family during the first week of July 2006. He was not happy especially with the "schlepping" of the "kids around from place to place." He still wasn't sleeping and beginning to feel depressed. Another family vacation at the end of the summer to Canada also did little to assuage his growing depression and sleep problems. His doctor prescribed Lorazepam to help him sleep and Wellbutrin to help combat his gloominess. "Let me try and describe my mental state," Tannin wrote in his diary. "I was incredibly stressed. It is a strange thing to be sitting here now (albeit on Wellbutrin) and reflect back about the stress. . . . Spreads are tight and credit is deteriorating. I was worried that this would all end badly and that I would have to look for work."

Tannin admitted in his diary to feeling anxious about going off the sleep medication but he felt he needed to because his internist had expressed concern about the potential for him to become addicted to it. In the diary, he describes the process for weaning himself off the medication. By Thanksgiving 2006, Tannin wrote, "My moods are pretty good" but as the funds' performance started to deteriorate rapidly in February and March 2007, Tannin's anxiety would ratchet up again. But Judge Block did not allow the diary into the trial either because he felt the government's subpoena to Google, which had produced the contents of Tannin's gmail account at the last minute after first claiming it no longer existed, was overly broad.

Instead, the trial focused on the government's contention that Cioffi and Tannin had repeatedly "lied" to investors on subjects ranging from the amount of money each man had invested personally in the hedge funds—or intended to invest in the hedge funds—to the depth and breadth of the multi-million-dollar demands investors were making to Cioffi and Tannin about redeeming their investments as the hedge funds' performance deteriorated.

The government claimed Cioffi never told investors about removing his $2 million from the Enhanced Leverage fund and investing it in a third fund he was asked to manage in the spring of 2007. (Testimony in the trial revealed that the two managers of that third hedge fund had *nothing* invested in them.) The government also claimed that Tannin told lots of people, including investors, he intended to invest more money in the hedge funds but never did. The government argued that Cioffi and Tannin were dishonest about the extent of investors' concerns about the performance of the hedge funds in the spring of 2007—and the amount of money they asked to redeem from the funds—during the April 25, 2007, conference call with investors and after that date. The prosecutors argued that the case was pretty much solely about these "lies," and as evidence it used damning snippets from various e-mails Tannin and Cioffi wrote to each other in 2006 and 2007 but for some reason failed to think through how the jury would react to the obvious ambiguity in the full e-mails, not just the snippets.

Consider the e-mail messages the prosecution placed at the center of its case. In the indictment, the prosecution quoted from a note Tannin sent in April 2007 from his personal gmail account to Cioffi's wife. The government made much of the fact that Tannin chose not to send it to Cioffi himself or from his Bear Stearns' e-mail account, suggesting he was trying to hide something. "The subprime market looks pretty damn ugly," Mr. Tannin wrote, adding that if a recent financial report was correct, "I think we should close the funds now. . . . The entire subprime market is toast."

But the jury eventually saw the entire message, in which Tannin ruminated at length about various courses of action and seemed to be striving to make the soundest financial choice. In other words, it was just what you would hope your fund manager would be worrying about in a precarious time. In the end, he concluded he was feeling "pretty damn good" about what was happening at the funds and that "I've done the best possible job that I could have done."

As for the defense, its case relied heavily on this reasonable doubt and the testimony of a few expert witnesses regarding the nature of hedge funds and the prospects for recovery from losses if things improved—including the perspective of R. Glenn Hubbard, the dean of Columbia Business School and the former chairman of President George W. Bush's Council of Economic Advisors (who was paid $100,000 for his work in the case). Their clients may have been guilty of poor judgment in assessing whether the subprime mortgage market was heading for a recovery or for a meltdown. But, the defense argued, having poor judgment was not a crime and their clients were not guilty of any. And, of course, the defense made sure the full e-mails between Tannin and Cioffi were given to the jurors in all their splendid ambiguity. Cioffi and Tannin did not take the stand in their own defense, as was their right of course. "This is a case about risk," explained Susan Brune, Tannin's lawyer, in her opening statement. "It's about taking risks and making money, lots of it, and it's about taking risks and the loss of money, lots of it. It's a case about trying to do your best." In his closing remarks to the jury, Dane Butswinkas, Cioffi's counsel, questioned the prosecution's penchant for using only selected pieces of the evidence. "When you look at the world through dirty glasses, everything looks dirty," he said.

Once in a while during the three-week trial, some of Cioffi's and Tannin's old Bear Stearns colleagues would visit the Brooklyn courtroom to say hello and to follow the live proceedings. Paul Friedman attended one day toward the end and received a warm greeting from both men, who were clearly pleased to see a familiar face. And such was Tannin's level of composure during the weekend before the jurors started deliberating upon his fate that he regularly e-mailed Friedman, who was in Las Vegas watching his former partner Steve Begleiter duke it out in the final showdown at the World Series of Poker, to find out how Begleiter was doing in his quest to become the world's best poker player. "You might have thought that he had better things to worry about but maybe he was trying to escape the real world," Friedman observed of Tannin.

On November 10, 2009, after some six hours of deliberation, the jury—uniformly described as "working class" in press reports—returned a verdict of not guilty on all counts. "There was a reasonable doubt on every charge," juror Ryan Goolsby told the *Times* afterward. "We just didn't feel that the case had been proven." Another juror, Aram Hong, said, "The entire market crashed. You can't blame that on two people." She said the e-mails showed Cioffi and Tannin worked "24/7" to try to rescue the funds. "If this was really a fraud case, they wouldn't have worked that hard," Hong told the *New York Post*. "Just because you're the captain of a ship and it gets hit doesn't mean you should be blamed." One juror said she wished she could have invested her money with Cioffi and Tannin, apparently ignoring the fact that the two men lost some $1.6 billion of their investors' money.

At press time, the SEC's civil case against Cioffi and Tannin, as well as numerous lawsuits and arbitration claims filed by aggrieved investors, were still pending. As a result, no one has yet been held accountable for the 2008 financial cataclysm.

❋

WHERE DOES ALL THIS UPHEAVAL on Wall Street leave us? The nation's banks have melted down and reformulated themselves into something we are still learning about and are rightly wary of. In addition, a number of unsolved mysteries remain about the calamitous events of 2008. What follows is a decidedly unscientific list of some of them.

Was forcing Lehman Brothers to file for bankruptcy a personal drama, a political necessity, or both? Since Lehman Brothers filed for bankruptcy in the early morning hours of Monday, September 15, 2008, there have been many conflicting accounts about the role any supposed animosity between Dick Fuld, the longtime CEO of Lehman, and Hank Paulson, then Treasury secretary, played in Lehman's demise. Long before Paulson flew up from Washington, D.C., on Friday, September 12, then walked into the offices of the New York Federal Reserve and, together with Tim Geithner, the New York Fed president at the time, announced, "There is no political will for a federal bailout" of Lehman, it was well known that Fuld and Paulson were different breeds. Considering that both men were strong-willed, fiercely driven leaders, perhaps clashes were inevitable.

Yet, despite Paulson's past at Goldman Sachs, Fuld thought the two men had a decent working relationship. A case in point: On Friday night, April 11, 2008—three weeks after Bear Stearns failed and ten days after Lehman publicly raised $4 billion in new equity— Fuld had dinner with Paulson. Later that night—2:52 A.M.—Fuld wrote Tom Russo, the Lehman general counsel, a list of six "takeaways." Among them were that "we have huge brand with treasury," that Paulson "loved our capital raise," that "they want to kill the bad H[edge] F[u]nds + heavily regulate the rest," and that Paulson "has a worried view of ML"—Merrill Lynch. "All in all worthwhile," he wrote.

Fuld was said to be regularly in touch with Paulson throughout the credit crisis, according to voluminous "call logs" between the two men that have come to light as part of the House Committee on Oversight and Government Reform's investigation of Lehman's collapse.

However, at least by the end of July 2008, Fuld certainly harbored some serious antipathy toward Paulson's old firm, Goldman Sachs. After the collapse of Bear Stearns in March, there had been much speculation about the role Goldman might have played in that firm's demise. Goldman supposedly bought puts, shorted Bear's stock, and/or encouraged hedge funds to pull money from the firm. No less a personage than Jimmy Cayne suggested publicly at the firm's final shareholder meeting, in May 2008, that Goldman might have been part of a "conspiracy" to bring down Bear Stearns. He hoped that "they nail the guys who did it." At the same time, David Einhorn, a former Goldman partner who started his own hedge fund, Greenlight Capital, had been publicly questioning Lehman's accounting and the value of the assets on its books. He also had been shorting Lehman's stock. By the summer of 2008, Lehman's executives were in an all-out war with Einhorn.

A former Lehman banker, who had just joined the hedge fund Fortress that summer, reported back to Lehman that Goldman was "driving the bus on the hedge fund cabal" against Lehman, a thought that reinforced what many Lehman executives already were thinking.

In the end, Lehman executives claim that Paulson told them the firm was "mandated to fail" and that no rescue financing would be forthcoming for it, especially once the two possible buyers for the firm—Bank of America and Barclays plc, the large British bank—pulled away from the deal, Bank of America to focus on Merrill and Barclays to focus on buying what it wanted from Lehman out of bankruptcy. The day of Lehman's bankruptcy filing, Paulson said publicly he "never once considered that it was appropriate putting taxpayer money on the line in resolving Lehman Brothers." (He had revised this view somewhat by the time he spoke to James B. Stewart.) He added, "Moral hazard is not something I take lightly."

However, Paulson had no trouble putting billions of taxpayer dollars on the line for both Bear Stearns, six months earlier, and AIG, the giant insurer, two days later. And Geithner, in post-mortem interviews, has suggested that his preference would have been to try to fashion a Bear-like solution for Lehman if only there had been more time or Lehman had been more creditworthy. A number of former Lehman bankers and some conspiracy theorists have said—although not publicly—that Paulson knew the panic would ensue in the capital markets from the failure of Lehman Brothers; indeed Bart McDade, Lehman's president, gave Paulson a presentation on Sunday afternoon, September 14, about what would happen if Lehman failed—and used that fear to strengthen his hand when he went to Capitol Hill to introduce the legislation that became the $700 billion Troubled Asset Relief Program. According to *Bloomberg,* McDade's presentation to Paulson, titled "Default Scenario: Liquidation Framework," included phrases such as "massive global wealth destruction," "impacts all financial institutions," and "retail investors/retirees assets are devastated."

The presentation also predicted a freeze in short-term financing markets. "Repos default," they wrote. "Financial institutions liquidate Lehman repo collateral. Repo defaults trigger default of a significant amount of holding company debt and cause the liquidation of hundreds of billions of dollars of securities." After Paulson dismissed McDade's analysis as "talking your own book" and reiterated that Lehman was "mandated to fail," the firm had no choice but to file for bankruptcy. "They put the entire financial system at risk, and they didn't have to," Harvey R. Miller, a partner at the New York law firm Weil Gotshal & Manges LLP who represented Lehman in the bankruptcy, told *Bloomberg.* "They were warned. I told them, 'Armageddon is coming. You don't know what the consequences will be.' Their response was, 'We have it covered.'"

We may know more about how much personality played in the Lehman collapse when Paulson's memoir is published. (Or we may not. Paulson did not share with Purdum, at *Vanity Fair,* his personal views of Fuld.) Fuld's lawyers have kept him radio-silent on the specifics too, especially with three federal grand juries still actively considering bringing charges against Fuld and his executive team, stemming from the billions in capital the firm raised during the six months between when Bear Stearns failed in March and when Lehman filed for bankruptcy in September 2008. A Reuters reporter, Clare Baldwin, caught up with Fuld in September 2009 at his tasteful wood-and-stone spread in Ketchum, Idaho. For the first time in a year, Fuld offered a brief unscripted take to Baldwin—who had dared to cross a bridge spanning the Big Wood River and trespass on his property—on what had happened to Lehman. (His October 2008 Congressional testimony was anything but unscripted, of course.) "You know Freud in his lifetime was challenged, but you know what he always said, 'You know what, my mother loves me,'" Fuld said. "And you know what, my family loves me and I've got a few close friends who understand what happened and that's all I need."

When asked about Paulson, Geithner, and Bernanke and their role in Lehman's demise, he stopped short. According to Baldwin: Fuld "turned toward me and grasped my forearm. His face tightened, he paused, and in a voice that was firm, but quick and pitched higher than normal, he said: 'I'm sorry. I'm not going to do it. I'm just not going to do it.'" He said he would not defend himself publicly— at least not yet—because he said the world was not ready to hear his side of the story and because "I promised myself I wouldn't." Baldwin noted, though, that Fuld hugged her twice and said "goodbye, sweetie" to her. "Far from what you might expect from a banker nicknamed 'gorilla' for his combative and intimidating behavior," she wrote.

In the end though, Lehman may have been a victim of its own squirrelly balance sheet. Unlike at AIG, where the Fed claimed there were valuable and unencumbered assets it felt comfortable lending against, Lehman's balance sheet was clogged with securities whose underlying assets were mortgages that were rapidly losing value. The Fed claimed it had nothing to lend against at Lehman and so could not make a rescue loan to the bank that final weekend.

Was the government's injection of $85 billion into AIG an effort to stave off a financial cataclysm or was this just a way to keep Paulson's old firm, Goldman Sachs, from failing too? This may end up being the grassy knoll of last fall's events—a question that might keep Goldman-ologists busy for the next few years, even though it shouldn't. The Goldman haters point to several "facts" as evidence of Paulson favoring Goldman. First, given its role as a major trading partner and counterparty to AIG, Goldman had as much to lose as AIG if AIG failed. Second, the fact that Lloyd Blankfein, Goldman's CEO, was the only Wall Street CEO in the room at the New York Fed with Geithner when the fate of AIG was being decided by Geithner and Paulson after Lehman failed, helped to create the impression that somehow Goldman had been favored by the rescue of AIG. Third, Blankfein had numerous conversations with Paulson during the crisis—his name appeared twenty-four times on call logs during the week in September after Lehman collapsed, making it appear as if he had a red bat-phone sitting on Paulson's desk. Finally, the coup-de-grace in the conspiracy theory is that Goldman had received $12.9 billion from AIG—the most of any firm—after the government rescue. Add it up and you can see why cynics had a field day with the idea that Paulson had decided to pump billions into AIG—as of September 2009, $180 billion and counting—solely in order to save Goldman from going the way of Bear Stearns, Lehman, and Merrill Lynch.

Not so fast. The truth, or what we know of it at the moment, is far less dramatic. First, once Blankfein realized that no other Wall Street CEO was at the AIG meeting, he left the New York Fed and went back to his thirtieth floor office at 85 Broad Street. Second, Blankfein's name on a call log is the not the same as having a call with Paulson or Geithner. Besides, Blankfein said in an interview in August 2009, "Now, that was AIG week, but it was also breaking the buck on [money-market firm] First Reserve week, and it was the week when Lehman's bankruptcy caused huge problems in the prime brokerage system in London. There were a million things that I would have been talking to Geithner or [Paulson] about." (Paulson told Purdum that Blankfein "is at a different intellect level than some of the rest of us" so of course the two men would be speaking during the crisis.)

Indeed, Blankfein remains puzzled by all the attention Goldman has been getting for its supposed role in causing the crisis when he believes it came through the mess largely intact because of a number of prudent decisions, such as raising billions in capital before other firms did and before the government required it, as well as having made markets for its clients and itself when others were reluctant to do so. Goldman also recently paid back with dividends the $10 billion in TARP money Paulson forced upon it, and it also paid an above-market amount for the Goldman warrants held by the government.

As for the infamous $12.9 billion, Goldman executives have a ready explanation for that too. They claim Goldman had no financial exposure to AIG, and given the firm's risk-management skills, this seems plausible. Goldman already had in its possession much of the $12.9 billion in the form of collateral: cash and securities. Had AIG defaulted, Goldman executives believe that the firm would simply have taken full possession of that collateral. As for the balance of its exposure to AIG—some $2 billion—Goldman's CFO David Viniar said the firm had bought insurance from third parties—in the form of credit-default swaps. Had AIG defaulted, Goldman would have collected on that insurance. So, the argument goes, Goldman just received from AIG—through the government bailout—what it would have gotten anyway, had AIG defaulted. "The government's decision to bail out AIG was about the risks to the system," Blankfein said. "It wasn't about Goldman Sachs."

For his part, Paulson told Purdum that the government believed not only that AIG had unencumbered assets that could be used as collateral for its loans but also that since AIG had foolishly agreed to insure financial risks around the globe, its failure would have led to an inability to make good on those insurance contracts, causing the insured to dramatically mark down the value of the supposedly insured assets on their balance sheets and thus generate an urgent need to raise additional equity capital. "A meltdown there would have been just catastrophic," Paulson said. And, he claimed, he was not the decision-maker about these events—that job belonged to Bernanke and Geithner at the Fed. Although this strains credulity, Paulson told Purdum, "I've been a good team player. I've given them advice. I've been willing to take the hits for things that weren't done with my authorities."

Viniar conceded that an AIG bankruptcy would have been no fun for Goldman. "If AIG would have gone bankrupt, it would have affected every institution in the world, because it would have had a big effect on the entire financial system," he said in a recent interview. He did add, though, that Goldman—being Goldman—would most likely have figured out how to make money trading in the post-Lehman and post-AIG meltdown scenario.

Why did Ken Lewis, then CEO of Bank of America, allow his shareholders to vote on the bank's proposed $50 billion stock-for-stock merger with Merrill Lynch without first disclosing Merrill's growing multi-billion-dollar losses?

During the seven weeks between signing the merger agreement on September 14, 2008, and the shareholder vote on December 5, Lewis had been learning about Merrill's deteriorating financials on an almost daily basis. From the day after the announcement of the deal, Bank of America had a team said to be 200 strong crawling all over Merrill Lynch and its books. Lewis received weekly, if not daily, reports about the rapidly declining value of the toxic assets on Merrill's books, which amount to $21 billion on a pre-tax basis in the fourth quarter of 2009.

As the CEO of Bank of America, Lewis had a legal obligation to his shareholders to disclose Merrill's worsening financial situation, even if it meant that the shareholders would vote down the deal on December 5 and his dream of owning Merrill would have to die with the vote (or at least be recast). Lewis had become enthralled with the strategic logic of the merger—marrying Bank of America's process in retail commercial banking with Merrill's world-class brokerage and investment banking businesses—at least since September 2007, when he had first broached the idea of combining the two firms with former Merrill CEO Stan O'Neal. (Even though Merrill's stock was trading in the range of $70 a share at that time, Merrill's board of directors nixed the 2007 discussions.)

By the time of the shareholder vote, which would have ratified Lewis's dream, the fact was that he had in his possession knowledge of material information that, as he must have known, fell under the Securities and Exchange Commission's rule 10b-5 prohibiting any act or omission that results in fraud or deceit in connection with the purchase or sale of any security. "By November, Bank of America knew that Merrill expected pre-tax losses for the fourth quarter of nearly $9 billion," Andrew Cuomo, the New York State Attorney General, wrote in a September 2009 letter. "Those expected losses jumped to more than $14 billion just prior to the December 5, 2008, shareholder meeting convened to vote on the merger's approval. Yet Bank of America failed to disclose those large and increasing losses to its shareholders prior to the December 5, 2008, vote."

In the end, Lewis made *no* disclosures to his shareholders before the December 5 vote. Shareholders overwhelmingly approved the Merrill deal. Bank of America's stock—now trading at around $18 a share—has fallen some 50 percent since the period just before the bank announced the Merrill deal. Lewis's lack of disclosure may have been tantamount to securities fraud, and at least eight shareholder lawsuits are currently exploring that possibility. A Bank of America spokesman dismissed the idea that Lewis did anything improper. "We believe we made the required disclosures before the December 5 shareholders meeting," he said in an email. In responding to Cuomo's letter, Bank of America's outside counsel at Cleary Gottlieb reiterated its view that the company made all the proper disclosures. He wrote that public disclosures of the projected Merrill losses before the shareholder vote "were not appropriate" especially "in light of, among other things, the extensive risk disclosures Bank of America and Merrill Lynch had already issued."

Cuomo, for one, is not so sure. In his September 2009 letter, he wrote that Joe Price, Bank of America's CFO, testified that he was so concerned in November 2008 about the growing losses at Merrill—then around $9 billion—that he sought the advice of the bank's general counsel, Tim Mayopoulos, and the firm's outside counsel about whether the losses should be disclosed publicly. According to Cuomo, Price testified that based on their legal advice not to disclose the losses, he did not do so. Cuomo said Price again sought the advice of outside counsel prior to a November 20 investor conference call about whether to disclose the losses; and then, based on that advice, again did not disclose the growing Merrill losses to Bank of America investors during the November 20 conference call. Furthermore, according to Cuomo, four days *before* the shareholder vote—on December 1—Price again sought legal advice about whether the growing Merrill losses constituted a "Material Adverse Change," or MAC, in the merger agreement, which would have allowed the bank some legal ground to stop the closing of the merger (then scheduled for January 1) without legal consequences since shareholders would have voted it down. Mayopoulos gave additional advice—what exactly it was is not public knowledge, although that information was turned over to Cuomo and to Congress in October 2009 after Bank of America waived its client-attorney privilege—to Price in early December about whether the bank could invoke the MAC clause. Price testified to Cuomo that he relied upon Mayopoulos's advice. In any event, the bank did not then invoke the MAC clause nor did it disclose any of these concerns before the shareholder vote. "This fact is of tremendous significance because it is at odds with Bank of America's position that it only became concerned with mounting losses after the shareholder vote," Cuomo wrote. On December 10—five days after the Bank of America shareholders overwhelmingly approved the Merrill deal—Bank of America fired Mayopoulos.

The House Committee on Oversight and Government Reform has also focused on the question of disclosure in the Bank of America/Merrill merger. And after three public hearings during the summer of 2009, during which Lewis, Bernanke, and Paulson were questioned, a *Rashomon*-like version of the Bank of America acquisition of Merrill has emerged. Lewis defended himself repeatedly, hiding behind the advice he had supposedly received on the issue from his lawyers. However, the fact remains that four days after the shareholder vote, a worried Joe Price reported Merrill's increasing losses to the Bank of America board of directors.

In his testimony, Lewis made clear that he believed Paulson and Bernanke had forcefully urged him not to invoke the MAC provision in the merger agreement and to complete the Merrill deal as originally planned. Lewis said Paulson and Bernanke felt so strongly about Lewis not calling the MAC that they threatened to fire him and his board of directors if he did it. In return, Paulson and Bernanke avoided presiding over the collapse of another major financial institution—Merrill Lynch—which surely would have fallen had Bank of America walked from the deal. "The amount of devastation to the financial system if Merrill blew up would have been unfathomable," explained Ken Wilson, a former Goldman Sachs partner and advisor to Paulson at the Treasury, in a recent interview. "It would have been Lehman squared. Just horrific." Lewis also won from the Treasury another $20 billion in TARP funds for completing the Merrill deal—bringing Bank of America's TARP haul to $45 billion, which was repaid in December 2009—and an agreement to ring-fence (since dropped) some $118 billion of toxic assets on the combined firm's balance sheet. In their testimony, Paulson and Bernanke denied making any quid pro quo agreement with Lewis and said they just made their views known forcefully to Lewis and let him and his Board of Directors decide what route to take.

Rep. Dennis Kucinich (D-Ohio) is so exercised about Lewis's failure to disclose the growing Merrill losses to his shareholders before the December 5 vote that on August 4, 2009, he wrote a letter to Mary Schapiro, the current chairman of the SEC, urging the SEC to take up a full-scale investigation of the matter. Kucinich found after reviewing some "10,000 pages of confidential documents" from the Fed that the "top staff" at the Federal Reserve had concluded by "as early as mid-November" that Bank of America knew about a "sudden acceleration in the losses" at Merrill Lynch and that the Fed's general counsel, Scott Alvarez, thought Bank of America could be potentially liable for violating securities laws as a result. "These conclusions raise serious questions about the legality of statements to shareholders made by Bank of America before its merger with Merrill Lynch," Kucinich wrote Schapiro. "I believe that the findings and opinions expressed by high ranking officials at the Fed about Bank of America's withholding material information from investors are well founded and merit SEC review. I hereby request that the SEC expand its investigation into possible securities law violations committed by Bank of America in connection with its merger with Merrill Lynch." As of this writing, Schapiro's response to Kucinich's letter is not known, although there has been a follow-up conversation on the matter between Congress and the SEC. On October 1, 2009, Lewis agreed to resign as CEO. Some two weeks later, Bank of America agreed to turn over to Cuomo and the SEC documents related to the legal advice the bank received about the disclosures.

One thing *is* known for sure: on the morning of December 17— twelve days after the shareholder vote—Lewis called Paulson in Washington and told him he was "seriously considering [invoking] the MAC and thought we actually had [a MAC]."

"We probably should talk," Paulson told Lewis. "Could you be here by six o'clock?" The rest, sadly, is already history. Paulson and

Bernanke convinced Lewis not to invoke the MAC clause and agreed to provide Bank of America the new $20 billion in TARP funds. Bank of America closed its acquisition of Merrill Lynch on January 1, 2009, as previously scheduled, without changing a single word of the original merger agreement.

Is anyone going to jail?

In *Candide,* the philosopher Voltaire explained how the British once executed one of their own admirals who had lost an important battle *"pour encourager les autres"*—to encourage the others not to dare repeat such a public failure. Up to the present time, there has been nothing remotely like that level of accountability for the Wall Street executives who led their firms—and nearly American capitalism—into the financial abyss. Aside from losing a large percentage of their sizable fortunes, neither Jimmy Cayne nor Dick Fuld has found himself anywhere near the stockade. In such previous scandals as those at Enron and WorldCom, top executives went to jail, but this situation is less clear-cut in part because Wall Street was just playing by the regulatory rules that it helped write.

Only two men, the aforementioned Ralph Cioffi and Matthew Tannin, have been indicted on criminal charges. Of course, in November 2009, a jury of their peers acquitted them of all the criminal charges against them.

But the case had also been seen as a possible template for further prosecutions. But will there be any? Another prime hunting ground for prosecutors is Lehman Brothers. For much of the past year, three federal grand juries—in Manhattan, Brooklyn, and Newark, New Jersey—have reportedly been investigating possible criminal wrongdoing among a group of top Lehman executives related to the firm's efforts to raise capital in the months leading up to its collapse. The U.S. attorneys involved in these probes aren't talking, but speculation focuses on former Lehman executives Dick Fuld and the firm's last two CFOs, Erin Callan and Ian Lowitt, since they were the ones who had to stoke public confidence in an embattled firm. Now, of course, they are not talking. Fuld started Matrix Advisers, a "consulting" firm with an office on Third Avenue, and is helping—free of charge—the turnaround firm that is winding down what remains of Lehman. Callan, who took a job in July 2008 as a banker covering hedge funds at Credit Suisse, is on leave from the firm. Lowitt has a new job as chief operating officer of Barclays Wealth Americas.

At the beginning of the year, various combinations of federal and state prosecutors were reported to be looking for potential defendants in such disasters as AIG, Fannie Mae, Merrill Lynch, and Washington Mutual. But so far, no new perps have been walked. If the criminal probes sputter out, which they often do without any public notice, victims may be able to find whatever consolation is available to them only in civil courts, where many lawsuits are pending against, among others, AIG, Bank of America, and Wachovia. Still and all, not much has been accomplished—yet—from a judicial perspective to encourage Wall Streeters not to engage in a repeat of this kind of behavior.

Can this happen again?

The obvious answer—yes—reflects not only our ongoing collective inability to learn from mistakes, seeing as how the world has endured financial manias at least since the Dutch bid up the price of tulip bulbs to absurd levels in February 1637, but it is also tied to Congress's waning interest in reforming the way Wall Street works. After all, with the Dow up 50 percent since March 2009 and banks once again filling the reelection coffers of congressmen—for instance, by lobbying heavily (and successfully) to pressure Congress to in turn pressure the Financial Accounting Standards Board to loosen up the rules on mark-to-market accounting, which helped Wall Street firms to report whopper first- and second-quarter earnings by writing back up the value of the toxic securities they had previously written down—President Obama may not have the political capital left to push through many of the reforms that once seemed inevitable. The problem is that banking, particularly the sub-species formerly known as investment banking, is a system in which long-term bets are covered by short-term-financing. And as long as bankers' bonuses are predicated on short-term profits rather than the long-term viability of their firms (as investment bankers once were compensated during the era of private partnerships), this is unlikely to change.

So where is the next casualty likely to turn up? The best way to find out is to look where the vultures are circling. Wilbur Ross, the vulture investor who made more than $1 billion investing in the decidedly then out-of-favor steel and coal industries a few years ago, believes the next looming crisis is in commercial real-estate mortgages. A combination of decreasing cash flow and lower capitalization rates on that cash flow has rendered the bulk of these $3.5 trillion in mortgages "quite a bit underwater," especially in the nation's regional banks. "There is a reason there are 405 banks on the FDIC's watch list," he said.

Ross also believes we have learned the hard way that "it is better to overestimate the severity of problems than to underestimate them." He thinks we also know now how vulnerable the entire banking system is to a sustained loss of investor confidence, since banks borrow short and lend long. And this fact—so fundamental to banking—has not changed in the wake of the financial crisis.

A repeat of the current crisis in some reconstituted form is inevitable before too long, he believes. When he first came to Wall Street, in the 1970s, people were focused on "risk-adjusted rates of return," he said, but in the last few years, bankers have been focused on "risk-ignored rates of return." Ross believes it "is very hard to legislate about people making mistakes." During the recent long march to the recent crisis, "undue faith," he said, was placed in quantitative analysis and "black boxes, compounded by very poor analytics on the part of the rating agencies." In the future, "you won't have that exact pairing of things but there will be some other form of financial engineering, the net effect of which is that it will create another bubble and then there will be the bursting of the bubble. That's an inevitable thing if you have markets."

In our heart of hearts, we can hope that Ross is wrong. But the truth is that, in the past, he rarely has been. There is no reason to think he'll be wrong this time, either.

William D. Cohan
November 2009

NOTES

Abbreviations

NY   *The New Yorker*
NYT   *New York Times*
SEC   Securities and Exchange
        Commission
WSJ   *Wall Street Journal*

Chapter 1: The Ultimate Roach Motel

5. Thornburg had a liquidity problem: SEC filings of Thornburg Mortgage.

6. UBS filing: SEC, February 14, 2008.

6. Thornburg . . . caught a major cold: SEC filings of Thornburg Mortgage.

7. "Financial Ebola": Yahoo message board, March 2, 2008.

7. "one or two million light": "Focus: A Day in the Life of Masters of the Universe," *Independent* (U.K.), April 25, 2004.

8. fund closed in February 2008: Ron Beller letter to investors, February 28, 2008.

9. "Our mission is to be . . .": Carlyle Capital Web site.

11. sixty-three thousand jobs had been lost: *NYT,* March 7, 2008.

11. "Godot has arrived": Ibid.

12. price of the credit default swaps: *WSJ,* March 10, 2008.

12. "were off in a world of their own": *Australian,* May 29, 2008.

Chapter 2: The Confidence Game

17. "Being denied such a loan": Roddy Boyd, "The Last Days of Bear Stearns," *Fortune,* March 31, 2008.

21. "Though Bear Stearns's overall financing": *WSJ,* May 28, 2008.

22. "We are now pretending": Michael Shedlock on Mish's Global Economic Trend Analysis blog, March 10, 2008.

22. "no comment": Interview with Dean Debuck, May 21, 2008.

29. "Bear did not get out of the way fast enough": SmartMoney.com, March 13, 2008.

29. "Even if I were the most bearish": Bloomberg.com, August 11, 2008.

30. At about the moment: Interview with New York Federal Reserve public information officer Calvin Mitchell.

31. "So that left only ten days": Steven Smith, TheStreet.com, March 14, 2008.

32. At 5:06 on the afternoon of March 11: Copies of e-mails between Stuart Smith at Hayman Capital and Goldman Sachs. Christopher Kirkpatrick, the general counsel of Hayman Capi-

tal, did not respond to numerous requests to be interviewed.

36. "The prime brokerage withdrawals": Interview with Roddy Boyd. JPMorgan Chase declined to answer any questions for this account.

Chapter 3: "Bear Stearns Is Not in Trouble!"

39. "Let's stay focused": *WSJ,* May 28, 2008.

42. "Every banker knows that": Walter Bagehot, *Lombard Street: A Description of the Money Market* (New York: BiblioBazaar, 2006), 43.

43. "Mr. Schwartz's delivery": George Anders, *WSJ,* March 19, 2008.

Chapter 4: The Run on the Bank

58. "They were the ones": *NYT,* July 13, 2008.

63. Bear Stearns had trading positions with some five thousand other firms: *WSJ,* June 23, 2008.

Chapter 5: The Armies of the Night

72. "It was widely rejected out of hand": Transcript, Senate Banking Committee hearing, Sen. Chris Dodd, chairman, April 3, 2008.

76. At 2 A.M. Geithner called: John Cassidy, "Anatomy of a Meltdown," *NY,* December 1, 2008.

77. "the further we got into it": Ibid.

Chapter 6: Feeding Frenzy

88. "the final humiliation": *Financial Times,* March 15, 2008.

90. "When Bear's liquidity crisis": *NYT,* M&A blog, June 30, 2008.

92. available liquidity: Bear Stearns & Co. proxy statement, April 28, 2008, 43.

Chapter 7: Total Panic

95. "It was just clear": *WSJ,* March 18, 2008.

Chapter 8: The Price of Moral Hazard? $2

111. "We kind of slept on it": Bryan Burrough, "Bringing Down Bear Stearns," *Vanity Fair,* August 2008.

111. "That article certainly had an impact": Ibid.

112. "Things didn't firm up": *WSJ,* March 18, 2008.

116. "I believe this is the right action": Ibid.

121. "That sounds high to me": Burrough, "Bringing Down Bear Stearns."

121. "I tell people": Jamie Dimon on *The Charlie Rose Show,* July 7, 2008.

123. "jumped up": *Washington Post,* November 11, 1999.

Chapter 9: The Fed Comes to the Rescue (After the Battle Is Over)

128. two million square feet of office space: *WSJ,* March 18, 2008.

130. "What can I say?" Burrough, "Bringing Down Bear Stearns."

134. "five-vodka event": *WSJ,* March 18, 2008.

Chapter 10: Mooning at the Wake

137. "This is like waking up": *NYT,* March 17, 2008.

142. "Once you have a run": Ibid.

143. "Basically we're all wondering": *WSJ,* March 18, 2008.

143. "The hard capitalist truth": Ibid.
143. "Make no mistake": *NYT,* March 18, 2008.
148. "Same with the team at Bear Stearns": Ibid.

Chapter 11: New Developments from Hell

157. "What do you mean, *we*": *WSJ,* May 29, 2008.
159. "send Bear back into bankruptcy": *NYT,* March 24, 2008.
159. "seething, fearful": *NYT,* March 20, 2008.

Chapter 12: "We're the Bad Guys"

172. "There has been no evidence": *New York Sun,* April 16, 2008.

Chapter 13: Cy

181. Just after the start: *NYT,* May 1, 1923.
185. "mainly rich Park Avenue": Judith Ramsey Ehrlich and Barry Rehfeld, *The New Crowd* (Boston: Little, Brown & Co., 1989), 143.

Chapter 14: Ace

190. "He was a terrific boy": *Daily Oklahoman,* October 7, 2000.
191. "I just thought it was": Alan Greenberg on *The Charlie Rose Show,* January 2, 2004.
192. "That was it": Mark Singer, "The Optimist," *NY,* April 26 and May 3, 1999.
193. "I was very well prepared": *University of Missouri Alumni Magazine,* October 2005.
195. In April 1957: New York Stock Exchange records.

195. "Well, the odds aren't too bad": *NYT,* June 11, 1989.
196. "I never put anything off": *Daily Oklahoman,* October 7, 2000.
196. "I went to Cy": Singer, "The Optimist."
198. "He was the only one": Ehrlich and Rehfeld, *The New Crowd,* 147.

Chapter 16: May Day

216. When Cayne came back to the office: Marvin Davidson declined to be interviewed for this account.

Chapter 17: Haimchinkel Malintz Anaynikal

229. "We had to start": *The Charlie Rose Show,* January 2, 2004.
229. "The implications": Alan C. Greenberg, *Memos from the Chairman* (New York: Workman Publishing, 1996), 13.
230. "I would also like to add": Ibid., 15.
230. "Some of the things": Ibid., 16.
230. "appears to be": Ibid., 17.
234. "There has been a lot of": Ibid., 19.
234. "I think we should be": Ibid., 21.
235. "Every partner": Ibid., 20.
235. "I am well aware": Ibid., 22.
236. "more determined than ever": Ibid., 27.
237. "Let's make nothing but money": *NYT,* June 12, 1983.
244. "I own stock": *NYT,* June 10, 1998.
245. "From this day on": Greenberg, *Memos,* 40.
246. "a strikingly attractive": *NYT,* June 11, 1989.

Chapter 19: "Bullies Always Cave"

257. "loves or admires Jimmy Cayne": David Vise, *Washington Post,* October 29, 1989.
258. "[B]ridge is a man's game": *M,* December 1989.
259. "Cayne is a man": *London Evening Standard,* March 31, 2008.
260. "I can't make any apologies": *USA Today,* August 4, 1992.

Chapter 20: The Math Whiz and the Baseball Star

266. "best deal": *Cigar Aficionado,* November/December 1999.
266. "No Wall Street CEO": *Trader Monthly,* June 2007.
266. "No smoking anywhere": Greenberg, *Memos,* 118.
269. "moment arrived that would make": Bloomberg, October 3, 2007.
275. "Its bet paid off": *WSJ,* November 11, 1993.

Chapter 21: "We're All Going to a Picnic and the Tickets Are $250 Million Each"

283. "bucket shop": Gretchen Morgenson, "Waiting for the Other Shoe to Drop," *Forbes,* November 3, 1997.
284. "on charges of being": *NYT,* June 6, 1997.
290. "Minute by minute": Roger Lowenstein, *When Genius Failed* (New York: Random House, 2000), 145.
291. "Where are you?": Ibid., 156.

Chapter 22: The Fish Rots from the Head

312. "dull businesses and scandal": Erin Arvedlund, "Who Will Buy Bear Stearns," *Barron's,* August 7, 2000.
317. Anamarie Giambrone: *NYT,* February 28, 2002.

Chapter 23: The 10-in-10 Strategy

321. "I've never seen all these people": *Chief Executive,* January 1, 2002.
323. "That was all nonsense": Ibid.
324. "Bear Stearns and its impressive": *Business Wire,* April 4, 2002.
326. "The Card Player": *Forbes,* October 14, 2002.
328. "The Fed's easy-money": John Cassidy, "Anatomy of a Meltdown," *NY,* December 1, 2008.
328. "Investors said, 'I don't want' ": *NYT,* November 9, 2008.
334. "He had come up with an approach": *NYT,* June 28, 2007.
336. "eight-figure compensation": Bloomberg, July 3, 2007.
336. 75 percent of BSAM's total revenues: Bank of America lawsuit, filed October 29, 2008, against Bear Stearns, Ralph Cioffi, and Matthew Tannin.
336. He certainly lived very well: Details about Cioffi's lifestyle from NorthJersey.com, June 18, 2008.

Chapter 24: Cayne CAPs Spector

342. On the call: *New York Post,* August 6, 2004.
346. "Consistently performing makes": Andrew Bary, "How Sweet It Is," *Barron's,* August 2, 2004.

Chapter 25: Cioffi's Bubble

347. "pockets of severe stress": Alan Greenspan speech at America's Community Bankers Annual Convention, Washington, D.C., October 19, 2004.

348. "global savings glut": Ben Bernanke speech at the Virginia Association of Economics, Richmond, Virginia, March 10, 2005.

348. "In retrospect": John Cassidy, NY, December 1, 2008.

349. "increase home ownership": Dennis Sewell, Spectator, October 1, 2008.

351. "an explicit target": Russell Roberts, "How Government Stoked the Mania," WSJ, October 3, 2008.

355. "I have been waiting": NYT, October 19, 2008.

Chapter 26: "The Entire Subprime Market Is Toast"

358. "Fund's operating procedure": The Commonwealth of Massachusetts in the matter of Bear Stearns Asset Management, Inc., administrative complaint, docket no. E-2007-0064, filed November 14, 2007, 3.

361. "I don't like to argue": Ibid., 28.

361. The "investment philosophy": This account of the Bear Stearns hedge funds is taken from a variety of sources, including the actual monthly statements sent to investors, the Bank of America complaint, the Commonwealth of Massachusetts complaint, the amended complaint filed by Barclays against BSAM, the June 18, 2008, U.S. grand jury indictment of Cioffi and Tannin, the offering memoranda of the High-Grade and Enhanced Leverage Funds, conversations with BSAM executives and the

funds' investors, and a review of related e-mails.

363. testimony of Kyle Bass: "The Role of Credit Rating Agencies in the Structured Finance Market," September 27, 2007, at a U.S. House of Representatives subcommittee hearing.

363. "In part as a response": United States against Ralph Cioffi and Matthew Tannin, filed June 18, 2008, in the U.S. District Court for the Eastern District of New York, CR 08-415, 6.

364. Everquest Financial: Information regarding the proposed Everquest transaction was taken primarily from the Everquest S-1 document filed with the SEC on May 9, 2007, and from various other sources referred to in the note for page 305.

366. At least one plaintiff: Bank of America complaint, filed October 29, 2008, 10.

369. "suggested that the houses": NYT, December 6, 2006.

Chapter 27: "If There's Fraud, We're Gonna Pay"

373. get Paulden fired: Interview with Pierre Paulden. He directed me to Mike Carroll, the editor of Institutional Investor. Carroll did not respond to an e-mail seeking information.

376. "It's time to buy": WSJ, July 11, 2007.

376. "When you read the research": Ibid.

378. "I don't see that going forward": Bank of America complaint, 11.

382. "broad financial concern": Ben Bernanke testimony to House budget committee, February 28, 2007.

382. "Don't talk about": Ibid., 11.

385. "inappropriately categorized": *BusinessWeek,* March 15, 2007.

386. "We're very proud": Reuters, August 6, 2007.

390. The next day, April 25: The account of the April 25, 2007, conference call with investors comes from a transcript of the call.

410. "but that the article was untrue": Bank of America complaint, 29.

415. June 14 meeting: The account of the June 14, 2007, BSAM meeting with creditors comes from a transcript of the meeting.

418. "underestimating the severity": *WSJ,* June 23, 2007.

422. meeting again with the funds' repo lenders: The account of the June 18, 2007, BSAM meeting with creditors comes from a presentation used at the meeting by BSAM executives.

423. "were taken aback": *WSJ,* June 23, 2007.

Chapter 28: A Very Stupid Decision

424. "I've never seen a dealer": *National Mortgage News,* June 25, 2007.

424. "They were all friends": Bloomberg, June 25, 2007.

434. "the current scourge of Wall Street": *WSJ,* June 23, 2007.

438. hire Marc Lasry: *Financial Times,* January 10, 2008.

438. "It's like painting the Verrazano Bridge": *WSJ,* June 30, 2007.

439. Cayne played about twenty rounds of golf: Reuters, August 6, 2007.

439. "grow and grow": *Business Limited,* June 30, 2007

Chapter 29: Nashville

444. "they did not say a word": *NYT,* August 8, 2007.

453. Cayne shot an 88: *New York Post,* August 8, 2007.

458. "the Bernanke doctrine": *NY,* December 1, 2008.

Chapter 31: Desperate Times Call for Hare-Brained Schemes

495. "Jimmy Cayne should be out": *Financial Times,* January 9, 2008.

496. "Being acquired is not a strategy": *Financial Times,* January 10, 2008.

Epilogue: The Deluge

511. The e-mail correspondence referred to regarding Lehman Brothers was made public at Richard Fuld's October 6, 2008, testimony before the House Committee on Oversight.

524. "With Bear Stearns": Cassidy, *NY,* December 1, 2008.

ACKNOWLEDGMENTS

This book would have been inconceivable—literally—without any number of dedicated professionals at Doubleday. At the very top of this list is my friend and editor Bill Thomas, who woke up one day in March 2008, saw that his 401(k) had been decimated, and decided there must be a book in what became the financial crisis of 2008. Steve Rubin, another longtime friend and the former publisher of Doubleday, was also instrumental to this book's fruition. I am immensely grateful to both of them. I am also very appreciative of Sonny Mehta's support as my new publisher.

From there, in alphabetical order, I would like to thank, at Doubleday, Melissa Ann Danaczko, David Drake, John Fontana, Chris Fortunato, Rebecca Gardner, Phyllis Grann, Suzanne Herz, Rebecca Holland, Corey Hunter, Alison Rich, Kathy Trager, and Sue Warga. I would also like to thank my British team, Helen Confort, Jenny Fry, and Pen Vogler.

There were also a number of people formerly affiliated with what used to be known as Bear Stearns & Co. who were very help-ful to me in the writing of this book. They were, especially, Paul Friedman, Robert Upton, Tom Flexner, Donald Tang, Steve Begleiter, Doug Sharon, Tom Marano, Sam Molinaro, Fares Noujaim, David Glaser, Ed Levy, Vince Tese, Fred Salerno, Tony Novelly, and Suzette Fasano. A special thanks—for his insights and generosity of spirit—goes to Jimmy Cayne, the longtime CEO and personification of Bear Stearns.

Others, not affiliated with Bear Stearns, were extremely helpful, too, including Frank E. Schramm III, Sandy and Barbara Lewis, Roger Lewis, Tim Geithner, Calvin Mitchell, Susan McLaughlin, Gary Parr, Rodgin Cohen, Steve Schwarzman, Peter Rose, Larry Summers, Alan Mnuchin, John Gutfreund, Harold C. Mayer Jr., Gary Cohn, Ken Wilson, David Solomon, Michael DuVally, Lucas Von Praag, Peter Truell, Andy Merrill, Sam Heyman, John Angelo,

Patricia Cayne, Philip Alder, Russell Roberts, Michael Ledeen, Roddy Boyd, Bennet Sedacca, Meredith Whitney, Guy Moszkowski, Laurie Kaplan, Anne Norton, Alexandra Lebenthal, Dr. Jay Meltzer, Erin Callan, Felicia Grumet, and Stephen Cohen, No surprise, there were *many* others who were essential to telling this story but who would prefer to remain anonymous. They know who they are, and I thank them.

Personally, I have been sustained throughout this eight-month sprint by my usual cast of unusual characters, who always knew when to serve up either a laugh or a dose of worthy criticism. Among them were David Supino and Linda Pohs Supino, Jamie Kempner, Don and Anne Edwards, Al Garner, Jeffrey Leeds, Jeremy Sillem, David Resnick and Cathy Klema, Alan and Pat Cantor, Gil Sewall, Andy and Courtney Savin, John Buttrick, Jerome and M. D. Buttrick, Hamilton Mehlman, David Webb, Kit White and Andrea Barnet, Mary Murfitt and Bonnie Hundt, Seth Bernstein, Marc Daniel, Freddi Wald, Adam Reed, John Brodie, Andy Serwer, Carol Loomis, Shawn Tully, Jeff Liddle, Patty Marx, Robert Douglass, Gwen Greene, Peter Davidson and Drew McGhee, John Morris and Marcia Santoni, Jeff and Kerry Strong, Mike Cannell, John and Tracy Flannery, Robert and Francine Shanfield, Andy and Lauren Weisenfeld, Alan and Amanda Goodstadt, Alexandra Penney and Dennis Ashbaugh, Stuart and Randi Epstein, John Feldman, Esther Newberg, Jay and Louisa Winthrop, Stu and Barb Jones, Michael and Fran Kates, Jim and Sue Simpson, Jay Costley, Jay Pelofsky, Eric Osserman, Charlie and Sue Bell, Rick Van Zijl, Steve and Leora Mechanic, Stuart Reid, Tim and Nina Zagat, Joan Osofsky, Bryce Birdsall and Malcolm Kirk, Tina Brown and Sir Harry Evans, John Gillespie and Susan Orlean, Tom and Amanda Lister, and Gemma Nyack. I also want to thank my in-laws and relatives, the Futters and Shutkins, in toto. My parents, Suzanne and Paul, as well as my brothers, Peter and Jamie, and their wives and families, continued to be hugely supportive of me, and I thank them, again.

My dear friend and literary agent Joy Harris saw what this book could be and, as always, became its fiercest advocate. My unending thanks and considerable love go her way.

Finally, and once again most emphatically, I have been nurtured throughout this lonely journey by my adorable and loving family, Deb Futter and Teddy and Quentin Cohan.

Needless to say, any errors in fact, of omission or commission, are my responsibility alone.

INDEX